'Alvin A. Lasko, Ph.D.
1314 Westwood Boulevard
Los Angeles 24, California

McGRAW-HILL PUBLICATIONS IN PSYCHOLOGY

CLIFFORD T. MORGAN, Consulting Editor

# PERSONALITY

*A Systematic Theoretical and Factual Study*

## McGraw-Hill Publications in Psychology

### CLIFFORD T. MORGAN

CONSULTING EDITOR

John F. Dashiell was Consulting Editor of this series from its inception in 1931 until January 1, 1950.

# PERSONALITY

*A Systematic Theoretical and Factual Study*

## By RAYMOND B. CATTELL

*Research Professor, University of Illinois*

FIRST EDITION

NEW YORK    TORONTO    LONDON

McGRAW-HILL BOOK COMPANY, INC.

1950

PERSONALITY

THE MAPLE PRESS COMPANY, YORK, PA.

# PREFACE

This book aims to treat personality study by the same scientific standards as are maintained in experimental psychology and to integrate it with research and systematic psychological concepts. It caters to the student who intends to graduate in psychology or even to follow psychology as a profession.

Although the emphasis is on precise methodology and critical evaluation of concepts, data and theories varying widely in soundness of scientific foundation must also be discussed if one is not to neglect important aspects of personality. This range extends from the excessive elaborations of psychoanalysis through the unchecked observations of cultural anthropology and clinical "experience" to the arbitrary measurements of sociology and physical anthropology and so to the firmer ground of truly controlled experiment or refined statistical analysis.

It should be unnecessary to point out, nowadays, that the student of psychology must be as ready to use mathematical devices or to handle precise conceptual issues as is the student of, say, physiology, physics, or engineering. For he is dealing with phenomena at least as complex as these fields present. Accordingly I have used, in the wholistic understanding of personality and society, such statistical devices as factor analysis. However, as the experience of many teachers shows, this subject offers no difficulty to those students who happen to have missed it in their statistics course if it is presented in its geometrical, visualizable form. It is better, even at the junior level, to deal with true concepts of measurement rather than leave the student with a mere ability to score meaningless tests or a vague notion of "types" which adds nothing to what he knows from common sense—except error and some larger words.

Since the level at which the course in Personality is given varies in different situations, some art has been used in an attempt to write for two levels of understanding. For shorter or less advanced courses the professor can omit certain sections in all but the first three chapters without upsetting sequential dependence; and indeed it may be advisable to omit whole chapters, such as those on psychosomatics or abnormal psychology, for a first course. The graduate student, on the other hand, can study all that is presented and penetrate as far as he wishes into the problems and reading given at the end of each chapter.

There remain certain innovations of treatment which require discussion from the teaching angle. The first of these—the introduction to factor analysis—makes the first three chapters a *pons asinorum*, over which many students need to be especially encouraged. The basic propositions, however, are fully intelligible to anyone who can draw a graph, and it is not necessary at a first reading to grasp any implications beyond these. The reader who wants to follow the propositions of these chapters more intensively and systematically is referred to the author's *Description and Measurement of Personality* and to some works on factor analysis itself as given in the chapter bibliographies.

A second innovation consists in replacing the vague and oversimplified notion of "drive" or "need" or "instinct" (used in many diverse fashions by writers of differing viewpoints and degrees of scientific carefulness) by the more precise and as yet unpopularized concept of an "erg." This term was introduced in 1940 to overcome the objections to McDougall's concept of "propensity," which it supplanted by a more operational definition. (It also has the advantage of being a purely technical term, free from associations of general vocabulary, and it possesses the convenience of declining easily into the adjectival and adverbial forms "ergic" and "ergically.") These pointed advantages for clear discussion and for the suggestion of experimental-statistical investigation have recommended the ergic concept to psychologists, especially to those interested in putting dynamic psychology on a firmer foundation by the investigation of ergic patterns, the measurement of the strength of ergs, and the application of these concepts to learning.

Last among the innovations requiring comment is the systematization of the analysis of adaptation-adjustment problems in terms of six *dynamic crossroads*. Observations on the development of dynamic structures in personality necessarily remain today still largely at a clinical level, but they are, in major outlines, sufficiently well established to permit us to go forward to a systematization of this kind. The framework now offered not only contributes to the rapid analysis of any given situation of conflict into its essentials but also helps to indicate fruitful areas of discussion, experiment, and measurement applied to psychodynamics.

A major problem in covering so wide a field is naturally that of condensation. This demands in the first place a proper sense of proportion in not omitting any field relevant to the central problem of personality and in not giving undue space to any field which happens to be in a state of inflation through one of those fads to which psychology is still unfortunately more prone than are the more exact sciences. To cover the essential principles in a work of this size the author has been compelled, first, to write in a somewhat condensed style, and, second, to presuppose that the teacher will provide proper familiarity with the illustrations and facts which are often mentioned only by name in the discussion of the principles.

Finally, a word is necessary regarding the goal of systematization of principles. At the present stage of psychology the only genuine hypotheses are those which have a close, meaningful, and fruitful relation to the facts and are therefore relatively restricted in range. The rank and wanton pedantry of "schools," more interested in the social pomp of an all-embracing theory than in a sober desire for truth, has destroyed the genuine interests of many students in psychology and wasted the spirit of inquiry in battles over many obsolete issues that should have been by-passed. The only truly general theory that is fruitful for psychology today is the theory of scientific method. However, though we begin, for example in factor analysis, with "intervening variables" only at the level of empirical constructs, we ought certainly, quite early in the development of the subject, to be playing with possible alternate theories at higher levels of abstraction. The real objection to "rational constructs," or reasoning by analogy, applies only to developing the upper levels of the hierarchy of abstraction before the lower levels are sufficiently firm—or in importing theories that have no necessity or no real contact whatever in regard to the empirical constructs. It is to be hoped that the recent interest of philosophers, notably of Carnap, Feigl, and Morris, in the process of theory development in psychology, and particularly in the trait and type theories regarding personality, will lead to psychologists' acquiring a better sense of what is legitimate and what is misleading in systematic frameworks. The principles set out in the last chapter are thus admittedly tentative and many hypotheses are only raw material for broader hypotheses yet to come.

For the student who can devote the attention of a full graduate course to it, the book is intended to give a research orientation, with awareness of the points of germination, particularly in regard to new methods and new concepts. If one "theory" of a completely embracing nature runs throughout the presentation it is that no law or principle in particular realms of psychology, *e.g.*, perception, reflexology, testing, learning, can be fully understood or applied in prediction without reference to the structure of the total personality. Personality study is the natural hub upon which all more specialized sectors of psychology turn.

The author would like to record his indebtedness in the preparation of this book to his wife; to various colleagues; to his graduate students, notably Cecil Gibb, Marvin Adelson, Tor Meeland, David Saunders, Glen Stice, and Henrietta Williams; and to a cottage in Stoke Gabriel, Devonshire.

RAYMOND B. CATTELL

URBANA, ILL.
*April*, 1950

# CONTENTS

# CHAPTER 1

## DESCRIBING PERSONALITY THROUGH TYPES OR SYNDROMES

### 1. THE DESCRIPTIVE PHASE IN SCIENCE

**What Is the Aim of Personality Study?**　This question raises issues about goals and methods in psychology generally.　The study of psychology is divided for convenience into such branches as physiological psychology, social psychology, child psychology, the study of learning and perception, clinical and abnormal psychology, industrial psychology, educational psychology, and so on.　These divisions represent either areas of homogeneous subject matter and technical, methodological development—as in the case of physiological, child, and social psychology—or else fields of training for particular occupations and practical applications.

It is usual to make the study of general psychology, giving foundation and perspective, a prerequisite for approaching these more specialized fields. This is an excellent design for study, but an almost equally strong claim could be made for the strategic position of the psychology of personality as a necessary basis for understanding any of these fields (1).[1]

In almost any field of practical, applied psychology it is soon evident that intelligent handling of the specialized problem requires attention to most aspects of personality.　Not only are the more fundamental principles in industrial, educational, and clinical psychology one and the same, but, what is more important, the *individual* who appears now in the school and now in the factory or clinic is also the same.　He is not a pupil, a worker, a voter, or a patient; he is a person.　If the total personality is properly studied very little elaboration is required to develop the principles peculiar to these special fields.

[1] Throughout this book numbers in parentheses in the text apply to numbered references at the end of the chapter.　Where the number refers to a reference in another chapter, chapter number also is given.

1

From the standpoint of this book, however, with its emphasis on purely scientific interests—that is, on the desire to *know*—this mandate from applied psychology is less imperative than the corresponding demand from pure psychology for founding all progress in particular fields upon a study of personality. We do not deal with a "perception" or an "emotion" or a "conditioned reflex" but with an organism perceiving or acquiring a conditioned reflex, as part of some larger pattern or purpose.

This is no doctrinaire "holistic" objection to dividing phenomena piecemeal on certain occasions. All science *concentrates*, in order to advance, because our minds and memories are small. Asserting that things can be *conceived* apart is quite different from saying that they *function* apart or can be separated. But it is an objection to taking the *wrong* segments and an assertion that in the biosocial sciences, as opposed to the physical sciences, one cannot generally make good sense out of such small fragments. It is essential to bring fine laboratory instruments to bear in experiments on behavior; but it is a mistake to suppose that laws of learning, or of perception and emotion, can be found that do not take into account the total personality. In historical fact the attempts to restrict psychology to atomistic studies in the laboratory have dismally failed to give generally valid predictions of behavior; whereas the larger experimental psychology of everyday life and the clinic, using experiments and statistics on the total personality, has been far more effective.

The study of the total personality is thus the hub from which radiate all more specialized studies and it is only by turning on this center that they make progress (1,11).

**Definitions of Personality, Contingent and Connotative.** The time-honored practice of beginning study with a definition of what is to be studied is not always so *scientifically* honorable. If we can completely define an object there is not much left to be explored and studied! At this stage of scientific research even a reasonably complete definition of personality is out of the question. The precise terms, of agreed and rich significance, in which such a summary definition would need to be made, do not yet exist.

Whatever significant definition of a connotative kind can be attained will be given at the *end* of this book. Here it is necessary only to give a denotative definition, by indicating the fields of phenomena to be studied and the kind of principle or law at which we should aim. Within the preliminary outline of the object of study presented by such a definition our inquiry can proceed.

For this purpose we may say: *Personality is that which permits a prediction of what a person will do in a given situation.* The goal of psychological research in personality is thus to establish laws about what different people will do in all kinds of social and general environmental situations.

The above definition is as precise as one could wish, *e.g.*, as precise as the definition of mass, force, or electrical potential, but our connotative definition must remain a relatively generalized statement about the fields of observation. Personality is, in the first place, concerned with *all* the behavior of the individual, both overt and under the skin. It is concerned with a range of behavior extending from the individual's political and religious views to the way he digests his food. However, at one extreme—that concerned with the behavior of *groups* of personalities—the most intensive study is left to the social psychologist and the social sciences, while at the other extreme—that concerned with neurology and physiology—the more detailed examination is left to physiological psychology and the biological sciences.

**Why Description and Measurement Come First.** The youthful psychologist is usually so eager to "explain" why a person has developed the way he has; or to give deeper interpretations of the *cause* of some piece of behavior, that he rarely pauses long enough to describe the behavior itself with any accuracy. Yet it is obvious that until we have means whereby one psychologist can describe a personality, normal or abnormal, so precisely that any other psychologist can at once recognize it, know it, and match it, all attempts to penetrate into explanation are vain. Before two psychologists can hope to agree on "What makes Willy run" they have at least to agree that Willy is running.

What is true of psychological practice is also true of psychological research. We cannot hope to discover *what influences produce given personality changes* until we can describe or measure personality so accurately that the *change* can be noticed and assessed. If I claim to discover that belonging to a nursery school makes children more sociable in later life, I must know definitely what the pattern of this "sociability" behavior is, and I must have means of assigning to any individual his own particular measurement in this trait in order to demonstrate that it is greater or less than some other person's score. Or if I say that after marriage Mrs. X's anxiety neurosis gradually changed into conversion hysteria, I must use exact concepts of the syndromes or types constituted by anxiety neurosis and conversion hysteria, which agree with other people's usage of these symbols.

For this reason scientific psychology—as distinct from popular psychological chat—has to pass, as the other sciences such as biology and chemistry have passed,[2] through a phase of concentration on description and

---

[2] This descriptive phase is more obvious in the biological sciences than physics. Galileo did not begin by, say, describing accurately the movement of waves on the Mediterranean, but by dropping simple weights from a tower. It is, as it were, an accident of nature that the abstractions of physics can be quickly reached in concrete happenings. The laws of motion do not have to be analyzed out of the complex phenomena of, say, ocean waves, but

measurement.  The dictum of a famous physical scientist, Lord Kelvin, that all scientific advance depends on exact measurement—and exact measurement connotes exact description of what is measured—has been repeated in psychology by such leaders and originators as Francis Galton, Wundt, Thorndike, Spearman, Hull, Terman, and many others.  Nevertheless many lesser minds have ignored it and many psychological theories are entertained without resort to that measurement which might have given them a firm foundation.

Although theoretically a sharp dichotomy between description and interpretation can always be made, in practice the distinction that should be drawn is often difficult and often slurred over.  It is not unusual for descriptions to imply interpretations, as when I say that a certain student shows "a mother fixation"—meaning that he shows certain kinds of dependent behavior, particularly in sexual attractions, which past experience has taught us to associate with a powerful early fixation on the mother.  This sort of scientific hash is generally to be avoided, since it frequently "begs the question" either of exact description or of interpretation.  One attempt to avoid it has been the use of the terms "phenotype" and "genotype," borrowed from the science of genetics.  The former is the behavior as seen and described and the second is the underlying, hidden structure which gives rise to the observed behavior.  However, this looser, wider use of the terms that have achieved an exact meaning in genetics is perhaps unfortunate, and especially so in that it tends to imply two levels of *description*, instead of levels of description and interpretation.  There are *many* possible levels of description of a personality at various depths below the surface level.  It is therefore best to keep the essential distinction a dichotomy between (*a*) the actual surface *description* of behavior, and (*b*) the *interpretation* of observed personality in terms of structure involving reference to dynamic, physiological, and sociological principles.

**Cross-sectional and Longitudinal Study.**  The antithesis between description and interpretation must also be related to—though it is not the same as—the antithesis between cross-sectional and longitudinal study (2).  In longitudinal study we watch a personality over a time interval, perceiving how the pattern changes in response to internal and environmental influences.  In cross-sectional study we attempt to depict the personality at a given moment, without regard to how it originated or what it is going to become in the future.  We are taking an instantaneous snapshot, arresting the flow of a developing, changing personality as if we had stopped a movie

---

can be studied in a ball running down an inclined plane.  Most sciences, and especially the sciences of organic things, do not "split open" so readily into controllable experiments, and complex problems of description have therefore to be faced before the study of laws can begin.

at a particular frame. It is by viewing a succession of cross-sectional pictures that we see how personality changes and from this we can hope to arrive at the laws and principles by which it changes. Usually cross-sectional study best *precedes* attempts at longitudinal study, because before observing that something changes we have to be sure what that something looks like. One cannot have a moving picture without the individual photographs. Thus concentration on cross-sectional research prepares the way for longitudinal inquiry just as description precedes interpretation, for longitudinal study generally drags in some elements of interpretation, *e.g.*, of causality. But both cross-sectional and longitudinal study may be primarily descriptive rather than interpretative—a search for facts rather than an immediate attempt at interpretation. Let us then first see how personality is described through these cross-sectional and longitudinal methods.

## 2. DEVICES IN PERSONALITY DESCRIPTION

**Types and Traits.** If someone asks, "What sort of a person is Jones?" I may reply that he is averagely sociable, rather lacking in conscientiousness, and unduly vain; or I may say that he is a fop. In the first case I describe him by traits and in the second by pigeonholing him in a type. Initially these alternatives correspond to adjectives and nouns. All writers employ both devices: thus Shakespeare describes Hamlet's uncle by such *traits* as "remorseless, treacherous, lecherous" and his father by *types*, "Hyperion's curls, the front of Jove himself, an eye like Mars." We have the same two alternatives in describing any object whatsoever, as when we say, "It is a disk of such and such diameter of such and such percentage of copper," or alternatively, "It is like a penny."

Convenience, such as the availability of suitable types or traits, will generally dictate which we use. In modern psychology the normal personality has more frequently been described by traits and the abnormal by types. Types, which are called "syndromes" in pathology, can be illustrated by the moron, schizophrenic, Mongolian imbecile, extravert, psychopath, etc. In describing by a type we essentially point to a model and say, "He is like that," as when we remark that so and so has a Napoleonic character. Type description has been unduly popular, ever since Hippocrates and Galen started off with the division of temperaments into melancholic, choleric, phlegmatic, and sanguine types. Its popularity is unmerited because the method actually has many difficulties and pitfalls that provoke misunderstanding. For example, if the person or ideational construct I use as the model is quite eccentric—as in the case of Napoleon—there are very few people for whom I can use it. On the other hand, if it is very common it will not help in distinguishing people.

**Continuous, Discontinuous, and Species Types.** On closer examination we find that there are three distinct senses—or two senses and a hybrid sense—in which the concept type is now being used in psychology. The first is illustrated by the old but still popular division of temperaments into introverts and extraverts, due to Jung, a psychiatrist. Recent research (3) has shown that the traits "Forward" sociability, "Gregarious" sociability, Heartiness, Adventurousness, Intrusiveness, and Interest in people are correlated, somewhat in the fashion described by Jung for his notion of extraversion.[3] Similarly, coherence exists among the polar opposites of these traits, so that we find simultaneously in the introvert: Shyness, Seclusiveness, Timidity, Lack of interest in people, Reserve, and Aloofness. More

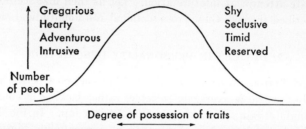

DIAGRAM 1. Traits defining "continuous types" in a normal distribution.

quantitative observations show, however, that there are few pure introverts or pure extraverts and that the distribution is rather that shown in Diagram 1 —the usual normal distribution.

Similarly, actual correlation shows that the traits Intelligent, Clear in Reasoning, Clever, Original, Good at Mathematics, Analytical and a few others, go together, constituting what we might call an "Intelligent-Analytical" type. But we know from intelligence tests that the world is not divided into intelligent and unintelligent types. The distribution is again as shown in Diagram 1. Whenever the pattern extends in this way, uniformly within a normal distribution, we shall speak of *continuous types* (2).

*Species Types.* On the other hand, when we speak of types in the sense of types of automobile, or breeds of dogs or horses, or races of men, of male and female sexes, we deal with distinct *species types* between which there are few or no intermediates. Of course, there may be overlap in any one of the characteristics that is an ingredient in the type, but *there is no overlap in the patterns.* One make of automobile may be the same color as another or have the same horsepower as a second and the same weight as a third, but the makes all differ significantly in their total patterns—*i.e.*, ratios— by which we recognize them. Similarly it would be hard to find any single

---

[3] Initial capitals are used on traits here to show that they refer to traits specifically as defined in the research on types and factors here mentioned (3).

measurement in which most pure breeds of dogs would not overlap considerably, yet we know that in total pattern they are never confused. Such overlap of single measurements with difference of total pattern is illustrated in the lower part of Diagram 2, for a three-item profile.

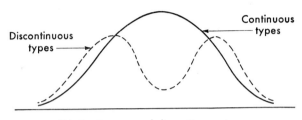

**(A) Continuous and discontinuous types**

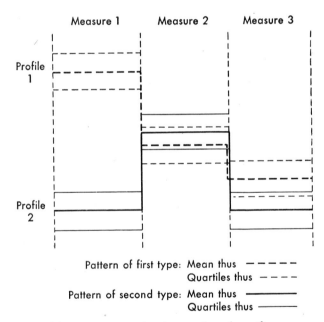

Pattern of first type: Mean thus — — — —
Quartiles thus — – – –
Pattern of second type: Mean thus ————
Quartiles thus ————

**(B) Species types, showing overlap of specific measures
(2 & 3) with no overlap of total shape**

DIAGRAM 2. Continuous, discontinuous, and species types.

Species types are rare, according to our existing knowledge, among mental characteristics, but as our methods of measurement gain in exactness we shall probably find them to be somewhat more common. At present the clearest instances are known in abnormal and in largely inherited personality formations, such as the special forms of mental defect mentioned above; in most psychoses, *e.g.*, manic-depressive personality; and in several patterns of abnormality in sensory ability, *e.g.*, color blindness, inability to taste phenyl carbamide, etc. As the results of applying attitude, sentiment, and interest measures become better organized, it is likely, however, that we shall get more definite evidence also of those species types which we now suspect to exist in acquired culture patterns of personality. For example, though the Japanese and the English populations might overlap on many single attitude measures, *e.g.*, attitude to monarchy, it is likely that the *pattern* or profile of attitudes would show *no* overlap. Even within one nation such species types might be found, such as between certain rural and urban types or between those who have long grown adjusted to different occupations.

*Discontinuous Types.* Midway in conception between continuous types and species types is the concept of *discontinuous types*, in which the pattern is not different or discontinuous but in which there is little or no overlap on single variables. This is unlikely to be of much practical importance. However, for the sake of clear thinking it is necessary to bear in mind that there are actually three type possibilities: (*a*) where, with respect both to the single measurements used in defining the type and to the pattern among the measurements (*i.e.*, the *ratio* of measurements), individuals are more or less normally distributed between two extremes; (*b*) where, although single measurements may be continuous, the patterns, gestalts, or constellations (as measured by ratios) do not overlap in their distribution; (*c*) where some parts of the type are as in (*a*) and some as in (*b*). The three basic concepts of continuous , discontinuous, and species types are illustrated in Diagram 2.

### 3. METHODS OF DISCOVERING AND MATCHING TYPES

**The Dual Task in Descriptive Methodology.** Before the psychologist can use either types or traits in describing a given personality, two facts have to be ascertained: (*a*) that the type or trait *exists*, *i.e.*, that the behavior items said to go together in the pattern really do go together. Many, many types propounded in the last century have been mere figments of armchair imagination. The discovery of types is a matter for investigation of nature, of examining existing populations of people, rather than of attempts at logical analysis; (*b*) the extent to which the individual in question resembles this pattern or possesses this trait. The methods by which this may be done, including "*Q* technique," will become evident in the statistical discussions of the next two chapters.

In the present chapter we shall concentrate on these problems as they concern the discovery and establishment of *types*, leaving the detailed investigation of *traits* to the second chapter. The correct and effective use of types in psychology actually came earlier than the technical use of traits. However, as indicated above, most of the types that are well substantiated concern the abnormal, pathological personality, which means that our whole descriptive approach to personality will first deal with the abnormal. This initial concentration on "caricatures" is no disadvantage, for in any natural study of personality the abnormal would first arrest our attention, and it is well known that the study of the exaggerated forms found in abnormality is one of the best ways to throw light on the normal.

Until practically the end of the nineteenth century (7) there was very little agreement among different countries, or even among neighboring psychiatrists and alienists, as to what types of mental disorder exist. A few patterns, such as epilepsy, general paralysis of the insane, or mania, were described in such a way that all physicians could agree, but quite different ideas existed as to how the rest of the insane should be classified. The problem of deciding on types is that of detecting *the patterns of concurrent trait endowments which are most frequent.* They must form, as it were, equilibrium points or modes in a distribution, marked by multiplication of cases at those points. One cannot make types by fiat: one has to discover them by statistical examination of the population or by the good memory that is a temporary substitute for statistics. In mental disorders, until recently, this process was carried out by the implicit statistics of clinical observation. Most of the disease entities in physical and mental disorders were in fact picked out by clinicians with sensitive perceptions and long memories, who developed, as it were, a composite photograph revealing the pattern which occurred most frequently.

**A Type As an Arbitrary Standard.** Of course, as indicated briefly above, it is *possible* to define a type arbitrarily. We may point to some real person, say Hitler, or to some portrait in a novel, say Mr. Micawber, and speak of anyone who resembles these as "Hitlerian" or "Mr. Micawber" types But unless the novelist has purposely described a very frequent pattern, as Sinclair Lewis did with Babbitt, such arbitrary types are meaningless and comparatively useless. Occasionally, however, an "ideal" type proves a useful practical measuring rod. Army authorities may define "the good officer" and officer candidates may be measured as to the extent to which they agree with this type, or the churches may concentrate on "the good Christian." Theoretically, therefore, we may speak of a fourth use of type— the "arbitrary model" type—but the three naturalistic kinds of types cover practically all uses of type in psychology.

The second problem—deciding to which type a given person belongs— has also caused many headaches in the realm of psychiatry where it was met first and frequently, in the practice of diagnosing mental disorders. Even today, when the types of disorder deemed to exist are well agreed upon, errors and doubts in diagnosis are quite common.    This weakness in practical nosology continues, partly because the matching is not yet usually done by an actually *measured* pattern and partly because a person may suffer simultaneously from some degree of two distinct types of disorder.    This matter can only be brought to a higher level of precision when we have absorbed some of the statistical concepts of Chapter 4.

**The Clinical Method.**  As indicated, the first and most time-proved method of detecting types is the method of clinical impression based on unbiased observation of cases and a good memory.    Unless otherwise stated it will be understood that in the following outline of abnormalities we deal with continuous types.    Most known abnormal conditions grade into normal. Only in some of the organic psychoses (see end of this chapter) can species types be recognized, and in general the finer observation necessary to recognize species types in normal people has not yet been made.    Naturally, clinical observation by medical men has been confined to abnormal types, but that is not the only reason for practically all types fixed by unaided observation being pathological ones.    The established types stand in this region because the abnormal is the extreme and was therefore the more noticeable in periods before exact measurement became available.

**The Statistical Method.**  Statistical analysis is a device to bring out relationships and patterns which unaided observation and memory could not perceive.    It does for the mind, struggling in an unfocused chaos of facts, what the microscope does for the unaided eye.    In a continuous type we normally have a group of, say, four to a dozen distinct traits which we believe "go together."    That is to say, the person high in one should tend to be high, relative to the average, in all others, and vice versa.    Or if, in the course of development, the person declines in one manifestation all other manifestations of this syndrome should also decline, simultaneously.

This test of unitariness we use on physical objects, too.    We recognize an object to be unitary, *e.g.*, a steamboat moving from a dock, when its parts move together, appear together, and disappear together, and when a change in one part tends to produce a change in all.    It applies also to the syndromes of physical diseases.    When a doctor pronounces a disorder to be measles he expects to find, not only a certain rise in temperature and a particular germ in the throat, but also a certain kind of skin rash, a typical duration of the fever, and so on.

Similarly, in the psychological field we speak of the moron as a type defined by lack of general mental capacity, by which we mean that he will simultaneously show poor performance in simple arithmetical problems, defective foresight in simple social situations, inability to acquire a normal vocabulary, readiness to accept silly suggestions, and so on.    The way to test whether these traits go together in a single syndrome is to take them in all possible pairs and see, by means of a correlation coefficient, if they are appreciably *positively correlated* in every case.   Thus we might take measures of arithmetical ability and of vocabulary for some 200 fourteen-year-old boys and see, by the correlation coefficient, whether their rank order in the first resembles their rank order in the second.

The student will have encountered the correlation coefficient in many situations in his general psychology course and will know that a coefficient of $+1.0$ betokens perfect agreement of the two series, $-1.0$ indicates perfect

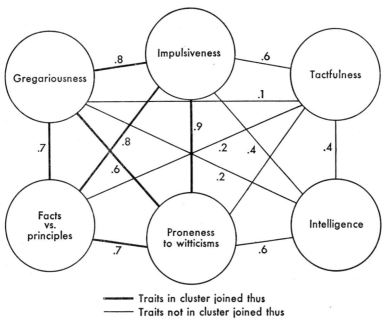

——— Traits in cluster joined thus
——— Traits not in cluster joined thus

DIAGRAM 3.   A correlation cluster among correlated variables.

inverse relationship, and 0.0 means complete absence of systematic relationship.   Most of the traits in the above syndrome of mental defect, *e.g.*, small vocabulary and inability to solve arithmetic problems, show an *r* (correlation coefficient) of about $+0.5$ in the general population.

**The Correlation Cluster.**   If now we turn to the personality characteristics of gregariousness, impulsiveness, interest in facts rather than principles, and tendency to wittiness, which have been alleged to go together in extraversion and which we now know (see Section 4, Chap. 3) to be due to the "source traits" surgency and cyclothymia, we find a set of correlations, in an adult population, as shown in Diagram 3.   All possible correlations (six) among these four traits are positive (3).   By contrast, two other traits, tactfulness and intelligence, do not truly fit into the cluster, for some of their correlations are negative or near zero.

The four traits joined by thick lines therefore form a *correlation cluster*, *i.e.*, a group of behavior items with all possible relationships among them significantly positive. *A correlation cluster is the statistical basis of a continuous type*, or rather of two opposite types—that formed by a simultaneous high endowment in the pattern of traits and that represented by a simultaneous low endowment in all the traits. The pattern itself, in pathology, is called a syndrome and, in psychology generally, as seen in the next chapter, it is most aptly generically called a *surface trait* (2).

Species types need to be established by correlating the *profiles* or patterns of numerous individuals, when the individuals forming a type will be highly positively correlated with one another. One may thus discover, by examining the correlation clusters, several distinct bunches of people, corresponding to the various species types. With species types these bunches will be very sharply distinguished, by high intracorrelations, but with continuous types there will be grading one into another. When such "correlations of individuals" (by profiles), as opposed to the usual correlations of tests, are factor analyzed the process is called $Q$ technique—a term due to Stephenson (2). The discussion of factor analysis in the next two chapters is necessary to understanding this last method.

The student interested in statistical devices should note, incidentally, that the correlation coefficient is not the best coefficient for measuring degree of similarity of profiles. It indicates perfect agreement when two individual profiles have the same *shape* even though they are actually at different *levels*. Consequently an improved *index of pattern similarity*, $r_p$, has recently been suggested for detecting species types (3a).

The surface traits or types among *normal* persons all rest nowadays on exact statistical methods, and the consideration of these is appropriately deferred to the next chapter; but the products of the method of clinical observation of the abnormal can be studied immediately.

### 4. GENERAL CLASSIFICATION OF ABNORMAL TYPES

**Amentia and Dementia.** Psychopathology, the study of the mentally abnormal, established with tolerable certainty some of the broader type divisions quite a long time ago. Let us survey these broader divisions before inspecting closely the patterns of individual types or syndromes.

One of the first broad divisions of area to emerge was that between inadequate intellect, on the one hand, and defective emotional adjustment, with disturbance of rationality, on the other. As early as the reign of Edward I in England a distinction was drawn between a "born fool" or idiot, and the lunatic who "hath had understanding, but by disease, grief, or other accident hath lost the use of his reason." One may be likened to an engine that is of too small a design to cope with requirements; the other to a sufficiently powerful engine that has become deranged.

Mental defectives, *i.e.*, individuals of insufficient intelligence to look after themselves, have therefore long been recognized as constituting a peculiar type of personality. The syndrome of mental defect includes poor ability to reason, extreme slowness in school learning, lack of foresight, inability to deal with abstractions (*e.g.*, mathematical symbols, verbal concepts), suggestibility, unintelligent handling of personal and emotional problems, etc. (10,12).

Most psychology students will be familiar already with this notion and with its subdivision into the syndromes of feeblemindedness (as in the moron), imbecility, and idiocy, in descending order of mental capacity. They will also recognize the subtypes constituted by Mongolian imbeciles, hydrocephalic idiots, cretins, and others. From the viewpoint of personality study as a whole, these uncommon forms of low intelligence are too specialized to justify further study in a book of this size.

**Psychoses and Neuroses.** The great and varied realm of psychopathology from which mental defect (amentia) has just been set aside can again be divided, into the psychoses—the true insanities—and the neuroses. The distinction is not merely that psychotics are more seriously disordered than neurotics. Some psychiatrists maintain that the difference is wholly one of kind, not one of degree, *i.e.*, that neuroses are not lesser psychoses, and that neurotics who get worse do not necessarily become psychotics. There is much truth in this and, furthermore, it is true that a person can be more incapacitated, as far as his job is concerned, by some neuroses than by certain kinds of psychoses, though the reverse generally holds.

The basic distinction is that the neurotic still retains "insight" about his condition. Only part of his mind is ill: the ego itself retains comparatively normal perspective and contact with the world as well as control of major aspects of behavior. The neurotic may suffer as much as the psychotic; indeed, being aware that he is behaving abnormally, he may suffer much more, where the psychotic would be blissfully deluded. Legally, a neurotic is usually considered responsible for his actions, whereas a psychotic is not and must accordingly be placed under restraint or supervision. A discussion of these distinctions is given in Chapter 17.

**Organic and Functional Mental Disorders.** An important cross classification, running across both amentia (mental defect) and the emotional disorders arising after infancy (dementia) is that of the mental dysfunctions which (*a*) appear due to mental causes and show no gross obvious physical origins—these are called the "functional disorders"—and (*b*) are "organic" or physical. Organic psychoses are those caused by known physical sources of disturbance, such as a blow on the head, a poisoning of the blood stream (*e.g.*, by alcohol, a disease germ, syphilis), a degeneration of the arteries, or a tumor, as in some cases of epilepsy. In "functional" psychoses, on the other hand, no immediate physical cause can be found, whereas psychological stresses often can. Furthermore, the functional psychoses are often temporary, *i.e.*, reversible to normal when the provocation ceases, whereas this is not often the case with physical brain damage. From such facts it is concluded that nothing more than the mode of operation of the nervous system is wrong in the functional psychoses, though the disorder may be quite as severe as in organic disorders (8,9).

Similarly, *neurotic* conditions can arise from physical causes, *e.g.*, gross deficiency of vitamin B in the food supply, hormone imbalance (see Chap. 8), etc., and they are then called *neuroses* (in the strict use of the term). When they are of purely psychological character and origin they are strictly called *psychoneuroses*, though in an understood context "psycho" may be dropped. These relationships are summarized in Diagram 4.

| | Psychosis | Neurosis | Amentia |
|---|---|---|---|
| Organic..... | Organic psychoses, *e.g.*, general paralysis of the insane | Neuroses, *e.g.*, pellagra | Idiocy, imbecility, feeblemindedness |
| Functional.. | Functional psychoses, *e.g.*, manic-depressive disorder | Psychoneuroses, *e.g.*, conversion hysteria | |

DIAGRAM 4. Primary classification of mental pathology.

In the following brief sampling of the most important abnormal syndromes recorded in medical taxonomy we shall confine ourselves to the functional psychoses and the psychoneuroses, which are in any case of greater interest to the psychologist.

## 5. SOME IMPORTANT PATHOLOGICAL SYNDROMES: PSYCHOSES

**The Schizophrenic Syndrome.** The most common functional psychosis, that which affects the highest percentage of people in mental hospitals, is called "schizophrenia." Schizophrenia came to replace the term "dementia praecox" when a series of classificatory improvements at the end of the last century by Kraepelin (7) and, later, Bleuler[4] recognized that most functional psychoses could be classed either as schizoid or cycloid. Cyclical or manic-depressive disorder is described below. It is an extreme disorder of emo-

---

[4] Bleuler finally settled down to the regular use of the term "schizophrenia" around 1908–1911.

tional state but without much mental derangement other than which might be ascribed to the extreme, unbalanced mood. By contrast, the four subtypes which are classified together as schizophrenia show much intellectual derangement, varied and inconsistent delusions,[5] and splitting of the individual's intentions and attitudes into incompatible purposes. The term "schizophrenia" derives from a Greek root meaning "to split," since the German psychiatrists mentioned above considered this splitting the most distinctive feature of the disorder.

The central features of the schizophrenic syndrome are withdrawal from social contacts, obstinate rigidity and inadaptability, sensitiveness, indifference alternating with hostility, and lack of emotional "rapport" with other people. In thought and speech there is lack of logical connectedness, a tendency to make bizarre associations, and to misuse words. The schizophrenic appears to live in a world of phantasy, talks to imaginary voices, shows childish emotional reactions, has many mannerisms, experiences hallucinations, and "perseverates" a good deal, *i.e.*, repeats the same words or motions meaninglessly. In extreme forms, as in what is called catatonia, the loss of contact with the world becomes seemingly complete and the patient will stand for a long time with his limbs left in whatever awkward positions they have been placed. The schizophrenic does better on an intelligence test, especially on the verbal part, than one would expect from his quixotic behavior, and only when the disease is of long standing is there reason to suspect permanent deterioration of intelligence as such (5,8,9).

The origins, course, and treatments of schizophrenia are discussed later. Here it is necessary simply to point out and define the syndrome, so that the student may know it as an abnormal personality form of considerable importance. The pattern grades into normality, and it is uncertain whether it properly should be considered a species, a discontinuous, or a continuous type.

**Manic-depressive Disorder.** This is really two distinct syndromes— mania and depression—which are known from "longitudinal" observations, *i.e.*, from the personal history of the disorder, to be phases in a single personality pattern. The two "phase" syndromes need first to be described as such.

In mania the individual shows exaltation, and usually joyous excitement. It may turn quickly to anger and destructiveness if he is thwarted. He is talkative, witty, overactive, meddlesome, and starts eagerly on an excessive number of enterprises which he has to drop unfinished. Speed may give

---

[5] A study of the content of these delusions shows 51 per cent persecutory and 4 per cent grandiose, as compared with 14 per cent and 27 per cent, respectively, among general paretics who, apart from the organically produced delusion, are more normal in their emotional balance.

the impression of illogicality of speech, but there is little cognitive disorder, hallucination, or delusion that is not, as it were, appropriate to the mood. In low degrees of mania the patient may have some insight, but soon loses it and needs to be under restraint for his own good (9).

In depression, as also in some forms of melancholia that are *not* part of the manic-depressive sequence, the patient complains of feeling terribly depressed, worthless, anxious—even desperate—and worried. His thought, speech, and movement are greatly slowed down. He may have delusions of having committed some awful sin, but he usually knows who and where he is and shows himself comparatively free from cognitive disorder, hallucinations, etc. (8).

The syndrome that links the two, because they are phases within it, has been called cyclic insanity. The type prone to cyclic insanity is called the

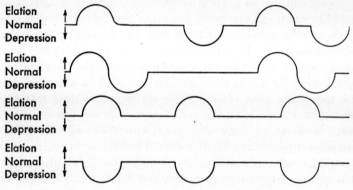

DIAGRAM 5.   Typical courses in cyclic insanity.

cycloid personality, because it is one liable to alternations of these extreme moods, generally with periods of months or years of normality of mood in between, as indicated in Diagram 5. Further characteristics are found to cluster around this liability to extreme swings of mood, principally sociability, emotional responsiveness, and qualities which in general are opposite to those of the schizophrenic person (5,8,9).

The recognition of these two opposed categories of mental disorder—schizophrenia and cyclical insanity—which together include practically all the functional psychoses, has led psychiatrists to use also the polar terms schizo*thyme* and cyclo*thyme* for those personality types which are in the direction of, but less extreme than, the abnormal schizophrenic and cycloid syndromes. The clinically perceived cyclothyme and schizothyme syndromes turn out to be well supported by statistical studies on normal groups. Both the cycloid constitution and its manic and depressive extremes merge, at least as far as overt behavior is concerned, into normality, via such intermediate states as hypomania. But genetic considerations throw doubt on the conclusion that we are dealing with a "continuous" typology; a step-like discontinuity is more probable.

**Paranoia.** A syndrome which some consider a special form of schizophrenia and others a syndrome in its own right is that in which the withdrawn, aloof behavior is also characterized by marked suspiciousness and secretiveness and an absence of the general upset of cognitive abilities shown in other schizophrenias. Paranoid schizophrenia or paranoia also differs from schizophrenia in that the delusions are systematic and well knit, while the intellect is not deteriorated or faulty, except where reasoning about the major delusion is concerned. The delusions are always centered on the self and are commonly of grandeur or of persecution. Another difficulty in defining this syndrome is that it shades off imperceptibly from cases of gross and dangerous delusions to instances of cranky people somewhat obsessed with one idea, and so to the general mass of normal people, each with his rather irrational views and obstinate prejudices on some topic or other.

The paranoid syndrome can appear in normal people temporarily, as a result of physiological deficiencies following alcoholism, or during oxygen deprivation at high altitudes, or from poisoning. But as commonly seen it is a slow, insidious development over years and rarely reverses its course.

## 6. SOME IMPORTANT PATHOLOGICAL SYNDROMES: PSYCHONEUROSES

**Obsessional-compulsive Neurosis.** The obsessional neurotic complains of a compulsion toward preoccupation with some topic or action which he recognizes as trivial or irrational. He may feel impelled to count everything, or carry out certain unimportant actions with extreme meticulousness, or he may have obsessional fears of unlikely dangers, or have persistent ideas that "run through his head" uninvited.

The type of person who is troubled by these neurotic symptoms is characteristically above average in sense of responsibility and in energy. He tends also to be obstinate, orderly, parsimonious, earnest, and aggressive (5,8).

**Anxiety Hysteria.** Here we see a pattern in which the central feature is a morbid dread, sometimes not attached to any object but sometimes irrationally fixed as a "phobia" of a certain situation, *e.g.*, closed spaces, illness, tabby cats. The sufferer knows his anxiety is unreasonable but he can do nothing to remove it. His fear, which is constantly present to some extent, but which may mount at times to the strength of a fit with partial loss of consciousness, shows its presence to the observer by real physical signs. For instance, the person may manifest an unduly rapid heartbeat, tremor, sweating of the hands and feet, and sleeplessness.

Two other syndromes, which we have no time to consider in detail here, namely anxiety neurosis and neurasthenia, have some relation to this one.

Anxiety neurosis is a pattern of physiological anxiety, lacking the mental elements, which is sometimes left over for a time when the psychological cause and condition of anxiety hysteria has been cured. Neurasthenia has most of the physical and mental symptoms of anxiety hysteria but they are overshadowed by a major symptom of fatigue, showing itself in inability to concentrate, poor memory, difficulty in making decisions, and by various bodily aches and heavinesses (5,8).

**Conversion Hysteria.**    Here we encounter one of the longest recognized and most dramatic of the psychoneuroses. In the first place, though the subject has far less mental distress than in other neuroses, he or she usually complains of a physical paralysis, contracture, blindness, loss of voice, tics, or fits for which medical examination reveals no organic cause. (Hence the title "conversion," since the patient *converts* a mental conflict into a false physical symptom.) Other symptoms which often form part of the picture are: a tendency to walking or talking in sleep, susceptibility to suggestion and hypnosis, complete forgetting of quite important incidents and remarks, and a tendency to fabricate fanciful (but generally harmless) stories about the self.

Obvious extensions of the syndrome are spread out into the total personality—the hysteric personality being described as superficially, theatrically emotional, vain, craving sympathy and attention, hypersensitive at remarks about the self, childishly and ineptly funny, and essentially undisturbed by any sense of responsibility about the neurotic symptoms (4).

A type which used to be confused with the hysteric is the psychopath (4). Here, however, the irresponsibility extends to important moral issues, and the incorrigibility is such that the syndrome is classified by some among the psychoses (4). With this glance enabling the student to recognize some half-dozen of the most important syndromes in psychopathology, we must terminate our study of types detectable by power of the naked clinical eye alone. Many type patterns among normal people have also been claimed (1,11), but with the exception of extraversion-introversion (6) and the cyclothyme-schizothyme described above, they have turned out to be imaginary and inaccurate. The few which have stood the test of time can be still more clearly demonstrated by the finer statistical methods to which we are about to turn in the next chapter.

### 7. SUMMARY

1. Both in applied and in pure psychology the study of the total personality, and of the data and laws of its operation, constitutes an essential foundation for understanding more restricted and specialized disciplines.

2. In science generally, accurate description and measurement are preconditions of further advance. In psychology the *descriptive* phase, as

exemplified in the cross-sectional and to some extent the longitudinal study of personality, has not been sufficiently developed and separated from premature *interpretation* and "explanation" of development.

3. Personality may be described and measured in terms of types or in terms of traits, the former having received more technical attention in the early days of psychology.

4. Types are of two kinds, continuous and species types, though a hybrid "discontinuous type" also exists in which there is no difference of total pattern (as in species types) but in which the separate variable is still not in a continuous, normal distribution (between polar types) as in continuous types.

5. In typology there are two tasks: (*a*) discovering what types exist in nature—since a type defined by fiat is of little practical use; and (*b*) defining to what extent a given individual belongs to the established types.

6. Types are discovered and established by (*a*) clinical forms of intensive observation aimed at noticing repeating patterns; (*b*) in the case of continuous types, by correlation, when a *correlation cluster* establishes a pair of types or syndromes; (*c*) in the case of both continuous and species types by correlation, followed by the factor-analytic method called $Q$ technique and also by the ordinary or $R$ technique.

7. Clinically established types are found largely in the abnormal field. They may be divided first into the primary and secondary amentias which are defects in cognitive functioning and into the psychoses and neuroses which are defects of emotional and general functioning.

8. The defects of emotional and dynamic functioning may be again divided into those which are of organic, physical origin and those which are "functional."

9. The syndromes of emotional and dynamic disorder may also be cross-classified into neuroses on the one hand and the psychoses on the other, the distinction depending on legal and psychological definitions. Brief descriptions are given of the neurotic syndromes: conversion hysteria, anxiety hysteria, anxiety neurosis, obsessional-compulsive neurosis, including phobias, and neurasthenia.

10. Brief essential descriptions are given of the syndromes of the schizophrenias, paranoia, mania, depression, and melancholia. The basic antithesis of cycloid and schizoid disorders is indicated.

## QUESTIONS AND EXERCISES

1. Give a contingent definition of personality.

2. Describe what is meant by cross-sectional and longitudinal study.

3. Illustrate the description of a person by (*a*) types, and (*b*) traits by taking some historical personages, *e.g.*, Henry VIII, Lincoln, Columbus.

4. What is the difference between continuous types and species types?

5. Give one or two examples of species types in the psychological realm.

6. Describe how a correlation cluster is discovered and discuss the relation of the correlation cluster to syndrome, type, and surface trait.

7. What are the chief divisions of psychopathological types?

8. Describe the syndrome of schizophrenia.

9. Describe the syndromes of mania, depression, and the cycloid personality.

10. Describe the syndrome of conversion hysteria.

## BIBLIOGRAPHY

1. ALLPORT, G. W.: *Personality*, Henry Holt and Company, New York, 1937.

2. CATTELL, R. B.: *The Description and Measurement of Personality*, World Book Company, Yonkers, New York, 1946.   Chapters 1 through 8.

3. CATTELL, R. B.: The Description of Personality: Basic Traits Resolved into Clusters, *J. abnorm. soc. Psychol.*, 38 (No. 4): 476–506, 1943.

3a. CATTELL, R. B.: $R_p$ and Other Coefficients of Pattern Similarity, *Psychometrika*, 14: 4, 1949.

4. CLECKLEY, H.: Anti-social Personalities, Chapter 12 in Pennington, L. A., and I. A. Berg: *An Introduction to Clinical Psychology*, The Ronald Press Company, New York, 1948.

5. DORCUS, R. M.: The Psychoses and the Psychoneuroses, Chapter 13 in Pennington, L. A., and I. A. Berg: *An Introduction to Clinical Psychology*, The Ronald Press Company, New York, 1948.

5a. JAENSCH, E. R.: *Eidetic Imagery*, Harcourt, Brace & Company, Inc., New York, 1930.

6. JUNG, C. G.: *Psychological Types*, Harcourt, Brace & Company, Inc., New York, 1923.

7. KRAEPELIN, E.: *Clinical Psychology*, The Macmillan Company, New York, 1907.

8. McDOUGALL, W.: *An Outline of Abnormal Psychology*, Charles Scribner's Sons, New York, 1923.

9. NOYES, A. H.: *Modern Clinical Psychiatry*, W. B. Saunders Company, Philadelphia, 1947.

10. PENROSE, L. S.: *Mental Defect*, Farrar & Rinehart, Inc., New York, 1934.

11. ROBACK, A. A.: *The Psychology of Character*, Harcourt, Brace & Company, Inc., New York, 1927.

12. SHERMAN, M.: The Mental Defective, Chapter 5 in Pennington, L. A., and I. A. Berg: *An Introduction to Clinical Psychology*, The Ronald Press Company, New York, 1948.

# CHAPTER 2

## DESCRIBING PERSONALITY THROUGH TRAITS

### 1. THE MEANING OF A UNITARY TRAIT

**How Many Traits Cover Personality?** The initial difficulty that the psychologist meets in describing personality by traits is that there are too many of them! As Allport and Odbert have shown (see (2), Chap. 3), the languages of civilized peoples typically carry from 3,000 to 5,000 words defining traits on which people can be rated. There is a chance, however, that many of these will be related, as manifestations of some larger, single underlying personality trait structures, so that by measuring the amount the individual possesses of such an underlying "source" trait we can simultaneously define, within certain limits, the extent of his possession of a great many of these lesser, dependent "trait-elements" or "trait-indicators."

The number of these lesser, narrower traits or behavior fragments, which we shall call *trait-elements* or trait-indicators, is actually not limited by the perspicuity of the dictionary. It is always possible for the experimenter to make, *ad hoc*, finer and finer divisions of behavior until he has an almost infinite number. To take a trivial example, the dictionary gives a trait of "manual dexterity"; but this could be split into "dexterity in shuffling cards," "dexterity with a screwdriver," and so on.

*Surface Traits and Source Traits.* The means by which psychology seeks larger unitary traits have already been indicated in the preceding chapter. The procedure consists in correlating trait elements until one discovers those which correlate positively in every possible internal combination. Such a collection is called a syndrome in abnormal psychology and in normal psychology a surface trait. If the surface trait is very broad we may prefer to call the extremes of it "types." A surface trait is in any case simply a collection of trait-elements, of greater or lesser width of representation, which obviously "go together" in many different individuals and circumstances.

21

*Statistical Meaning of Source Traits and Surface Traits.* At this point the student needs to cross a rather difficult methodological bridge involving statistics. For, statistically, this "going togetherness" can have two meanings. These correspond to (*a*) the notion of "surface trait" as already defined, and (*b*) the notion of "source trait," whose understanding and definition require a *general* idea of the aims and methods of *factor analysis*.

Actually the essential meaning, at least, of *source trait* can be made clear to common sense, without statistical technicalities. It is only in grasping the methods of discovering and delimiting source traits that factor analysis is necessary. Consider, for example, one of the surface traits or types already mentioned—that revealed by the three positive correlations that exist among the three measures: (*a*) size of vocabulary, (*b*) arithmetical ability, (*c*) tactfulness in social situations. If we ask how this surface trait might have come into existence, attention turns first to the influence of innate mental capacity. Other things being equal the individual of greater general mental capacity will achieve a greater size of vocabulary, will handle arithmetical problems more capably, and will also be more clever and tactful in social situations. Some of the observed positive correlations among the three variables in the surface trait will therefore have their *source* in the fact that the performances all spring in part from a single root, namely, general mental capacity. But it also happens that these three performances are about equally the objects of educational attention, so that the individual who has longer or better schooling will tend to do better at all three of them. Consequently another part (perhaps the remaining part) of the positive intercorrelation seen in the surface trait goes back to this second source—length of education. *General mental capacity* and *amount of education experienced* may therefore be considered two *source traits* accounting for the observed *surface trait.*

**The Greater Utility of Source Traits.** The correlations found in a surface trait may in general be accounted for in this way by a certain number of independent factors or source traits. As we shall see later, it is actually more useful and psychologically meaningful to assign measurements to people in terms of these source traits rather than in terms of surface traits. Two people with exactly the same amount of a particular surface trait might have different amounts of the constituent source traits. For example, in the above instance of two people who appeared much the same in level of vocabulary, social skill, and arithmetical gumption, one might be so through an exceptionally good education and moderate general ability while the other might have had only a moderate education but be possessed of exceptionally high native mental capacity.

This relation will soon be brought out more precisely and quantitatively through the following statistical approach.

## 2. GEOMETRIC REPRESENTATION OF FACTOR ANALYSIS

**Spatial Representation of a Correlation.**   The algebraic presentation of the idea of factor analysis is somewhat forbidding to students lacking college mathematics; but the equivalent geometrical picture can be grasped readily by anyone fit for so complex a study as psychology.   In the first place it is necessary to get used to the convention of representing correlation coefficients as angles, as in Diagram 6.

By this geometrical representation, if two trait indicators $A$ and $B$ are highly correlated as at (i) in the diagram they will occur close together, separated by only a small angular distance.   If they are quite uncorrelated they are set at right angles (ii) like the independent coordinates of a graph. If they are negatively correlated they are set at an obtuse angle, as at (iii).

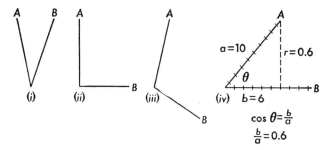

DIAGRAM 6.   Spatial representation of correlations.

The convention is that the *cosine* of the angle is made exactly equal to the given correlation coefficient, as shown at (iv).   This convention, faithfully followed through, continues to give results consonant with all that we know about the arithmetical behavior of correlation coefficients.

**Factors as Coordinates.**   If now a group of trait elements have all possible correlations among them positive, as in the surface trait illustrated numerically in Diagram 3 (see page 11), they will appear in the geometrical representation as a bunched mass, like the ribs of a half-closed umbrella or a sheaf of arrows, as shown in Diagram 7.   Now if it should happen that this surface trait, like that in the example above, is the result of only *two* general factors, these two factors can appear as the *coordinates* in Diagram 7.   To each of the trait elements—$A$, $B$, $C$, and $D$—there can now be given a *factor loading* representing the extent to which the given factor determines (for the average person) the extent of possession of that particular trait-element.   For example, the loadings of the four trait-elements—$A$, $B$, $C$, and $D$—by Factor 1 are 0.80, 0.75, 0.60, and 0.56, as shown, while the loadings in Factor 2 correspond similarly to the projections shown on the second, horizontal coordinate. In short, the factors obtained by the complex processes of factor analysis are nothing more than the coordinates—the axes—in the space created by representing the correlations between tests as angles between "test vectors."

Some idea of the meaning of the particular magnitudes of loading may be gained from the familiar case of the general intelligence factor. There it is found that ability in mathematics is loaded about 0.8 or 0.9 with the general factor, whereas ability in drawing is loaded only about 0.3 or 0.4. (The

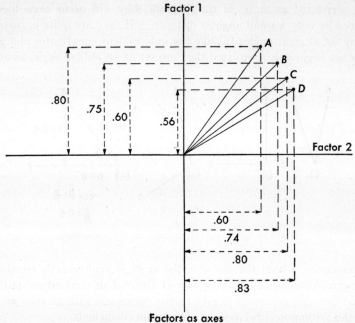

**Factors as axes**
DIAGRAM 7. Factors as coordinate axes.

reader can imagine that *A* and *D* are respectively problem arithmetic (mathematics) and drawing in the above diagram, and that intelligence is Factor 1.) This means that a large part of the variability in mathematics is due to individual differences in the source trait "intelligence." Consequently, if a class of children were selected so that all had the same intelligence (mental age) the variability in mathematical performance would fall tremendously. On the other hand a group of people all of the same intelligence would still show almost as much variance in drawing ability as a group subtending the normal variability in intelligence.

**The Meaning of Factor Loadings.** From the facts behind Diagram 7 it follows that the variability in any particular trait element can be broken down into variability in the two factors concerned, by an equation of the following form:

$$A = 0.8F_1 + 0.6F_2$$

and, as we shall see later, this can be used for any particular person, $i$, to predict or estimate his possession of $A$ from what we know about his personal endowment in the source traits $F_1$ and $F_2$, thus:

$$A_i = 0.8F_{1i} + 0.6F_{2i}$$

This means that if his personal endowment in source trait $F_1$ namely, $F_{1i}$, is high it will do more to help him in performance $A$ than a high endowment in source trait $F_2$, for the loading of $F_1$ is greater in this situation, *i.e.*, $F_1$ is more relevant to this particular performance.

**Discovering the Number of Source Traits Involved.** At this point the thoughtful student will ask, "But how did you know that there were just *two* source traits at work in the surface trait of Diagram 7? And how do you find the *number* of factors at work in any given array of trait elements?" It should be clear that *we are given in the first place only the correlation coefficients* that we have calculated among the various trait indicators (variables subtests) measured in the experiment. These correlations, represented graphically, will arrange themselves in various experiments in different ways, giving some relatively isolated "test vectors" and also a number of clusters of vectors, called surface traits. The surface traits can be seen simply from inspection of the "rays" (vectors) drawn from the central origin. *But these same correlations (this same spatial "structure") will also tell us how many factors we need.*

This fact can best be seen from an actual example. Consider the three correlations among trait elements $X$, $Y$, and $Z$ as shown in Diagram 8. The angles are already drawn in the proper convention such that their cosines are equal to the correlations found. Now if one were to cut out these angles with scissors he would find that $X$, $Y$, and $Z$ cannot be made to lie in a single plane, the plane of the diagram, as $A$, $B$, and $C$ can in Diagram 7. Instead, they force one to make a pyramid, so that the points $X$, $Y$, and $Z$ can only be represented in three-dimensional space, as shown to the right of Diagram 8. *Three coordinate axes are now required, to fix the positions of $X$, $Y$, and $Z$. This means three factors.* Consequently there will be three coordinate values for each point, *i.e.*, there will be three factor loadings for each trait element and the *specification equation* for any one test performance, $X$, will be

$$X = aF_1 + bF_2 + cF_3$$

Actually it is the rule rather than the exception for the correlations to force the model out into three-dimensional space or more (when there are many vectors). If the student will experiment cutting out paper sectors to represent the correlations among any three or four variables known to him he may find some fitting in two dimensions, many fitting into three, but still others unrepresentable in three and requiring a model of four or more dimensions—a model in "hyperspace" which only a mathematician could conceive, for it cannot be visualized or constructed.

Since most models from personality and ability correlations would require more than two- or three-dimensional space, the discovery of the number of factors required and of the projections of the test points upon them is actually found from the correlations by algebraic methods. This process begins by

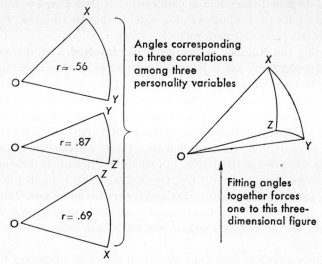

DIAGRAM 8.　Correlations demanding axes in three dimensions.

finding the average correlation of each test with every other test, but its further steps need not be studied in this general text on personality and can be left for special technical reading.

**Source Traits as Dimensions of Personality.** The process of correlating trait elements and factorizing them may therefore be regarded as a search for the dimensions of personality, *i.e.*, for the number of truly independent *directions* in which personality needs to be measured in order completely to describe it. Similarly we need, in describing any physical object, to know the number of dimensions involved, *e.g.*, that a box requires numbers for each of three dimensions, but a lawn for only two. Incidentally, the student will find that the terms factor, vector (but not "test vector"), dimension, and source trait are used interchangeably by most writers as we do here. Obviously the first great advantage of factor analysis is that it leads to a method whereby we substitute measurements on a few (about a dozen so far) factors for measurements on hundreds or even thousands of trait-elements. The second advantage is that the source traits promise to be the real structural influences underlying personality, which it is necessary for us to deal with in developmental problems, psychosomatics, and problems of dynamic integration.

The student will realize that what has been given here is only a skeleton outline of factor-analytic principles. If he is to proceed to research in personality measurement he will need to know also how to extract factor loadings from the given correlations and how to find, by algebraic, analytical methods, the number of factors, *i.e.*, the dimensions of space required. These facts can be found in one of the excellent textbooks on factor analysis in psychology now available.[1] However, it is sufficient for the essential understanding of personality measurement if the student knows that a factor is an independent direction of variation, discoverable from the examination of correlation coefficients. As such it *may* be considered an *underlying influence among* or *cause of* the observed correlations among trait-elements. For, as research is now showing, these source traits correspond to real unitary influences—physiological, temperamental factors; degrees of dynamic integration; exposure to social institutions—about which much more can be found out once they are defined. Measuring behavior in factors is thus not only more economical and fundamental, but it also presents the first step in an analytic procedure aiming to discover the structure and function of personality.

### 3. VARIETIES OF TRAITS FROM $R$, $P$, AND $Q$ TECHNIQUES OF INVESTIGATION

**Existing Syndromes Based on $R$ Technique.** Before we can examine the actual findings about personality, and before we can satisfy our curiosity about actual and particular unitary traits, it is necessary to clarify still one more point of method. So far we have dealt with the way in which correlation coefficients are analyzed in order to yield evidence of unitary traits, but have said very little about how the correlation coefficients are gathered.

As every student knows, all the important types and syndromes of the past are based on correlations of measures concerning individual differences. If we assert that extraversion is a unitary (surface) trait we mean that as we pass from individuals who are low in, say, gregariousness to individuals who are higher and higher in that trait-element we also find these individuals

---

[1] Notably Burt's *Factors of the Mind* (3); Holzinger and Harman's *Factor Analysis* (11); Thomson's *Factorial Analysis of Human Ability* (15) and Thurstone's *Multiple Factor Analysis* (16). A very valuable brief introduction is found in Guilford's *Psychometric Methods* (10), while a short but comprehensive handbook, intermediate between Guilford's chapters and the larger works, is now available in the present writer's *Factor Analysis in Science* (8a).

higher and higher in another element of the extraversion cluster, say, impulsiveness. The unitariness is revealed by *a common fate of these trait elements as we make person-to-person contrasts*. In correlation terms this means that we take any two trait-indicators or tests and measure them on *a series of persons*, obtaining a correlation coefficient between the two series thus formed. This traditional method of correlation, with the resulting extraction of clusters and factors, has been called *R* technique. The argument for general intelligence or *g*, as a single power, as well as Thurstone's discovery of seven primary abilities, such as verbal and spatial ability, rest on *R* technique (3,11,15,16).

**The Meaning of Functional Unity.** It may be argued, however, that the concept of "unitary trait" means more than that the parts "go together" in person-to-person variation. A functional unity means not only that the function behaves as a unity as we compare person with person but also that in the growth (learning or maturation) within one person the parts increase (or decline) together, and further, that when the trait is active (in one person) the parts have a simultaneous interaction.

Thus, if general ability is a unitary trait by *R* technique—the correlation of individual differences—we should expect it also to show up as a factor when we correlate increments of growth. For example, if high standing in arithmetical ability tends to go with high standing in vocabulary then, in the growth years, big increases in arithmetical ability should go with big increases in vocabulary. For organic unity should show itself in the process of growth as well as in the finished product. The pioneer work of Woodrow in studying increments (17) by precise correlation is at too early a stage to enable us to see what conclusions can be drawn here as regards personality traits. The method of clinical observation, however, uses the study of increments along with observation of individual differences, as will be obvious if one considers the syndromes such as feeblemindedness, schizophrenia, or conversion hysteria based thereon. For the *history* of a disorder—the way in which the symptoms began to appear—is taken into account in forming a diagnosis, and usually a halfway stage in the emergence of one symptom of the syndrome is associated with a halfway stage in another.

**The *P*-Technique Design.** How can we investigate, however, the third criteria of a functional unity—that the parts function as a unity in a single individual? First, it is noticeable that most human behavior characteristics *fluctuate* slightly from day to day. Some of this variation, as shown in the repeated application of intelligence tests to the same person, is due to experimental error of measurement. But it can be shown that an appreciable part is also caused by "function fluctuation," *i.e.*, by a true fluctuation of that function from day to day. On some days one's intelligence is a little clearer than on others, or one's appetite is stronger, or one's memory is a little poorer, or one's pugnacity is greater, and so on. If several trait-elements are actually manifestations of the same unitary trait then they should fluctuate together from day to day, with changes of internal, appetitive condition and of external stimulus situation.

This common fluctuation can be discovered by correlation. Thus we take a single individual and measure him on a number of trait-indicators every day for a considerable number of days, plotting their trends of fluctuation as shown in Diagram 9. Inspection alone will show that some of these go together in some degree of functional unity, whereas others fluctuate

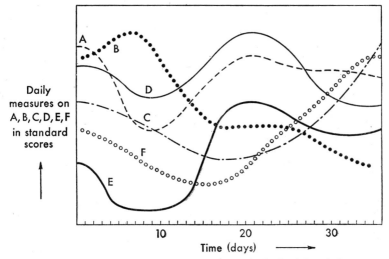

Daily measures on A, B, C, D, E, F in standard scores

Time (days)

DIAGRAM 9.   Traits in temporal covariation: the basis of *P* technique.

in quite different patterns.   Thus *A*, *D* and *E* would correlate in Diagram 9, while *C* and *F* would form a second cluster or a second factor by *P* technique.

An examination of the correlations of these tests, using the above *series of occasions* on which to base the correlation, would reveal this common fluctuation more precisely, however, than by inspection alone.   And from these correlations we can obtain either surface traits or source traits by the usual methods of analyzing correlations (Section 2).

This detection of pattern by study of the single person has been called *P* technique (6), (see also (13), Chap. 11).   Already it is clear that it substantiates some of the source traits found by *R* technique.   For example, in the next chapter are described a source trait of *cyclothymia*, covering such trait-indicators as easygoing, sociable, genial, and another source trait of *character integration*, loading such manifestations as perseverance, freedom from emotional impulsiveness, conscientiousness.   It has been shown that in a single individual these covary from day to day in the same patterns as from person to person.

**Typology and $Q$ Technique.** It has been pointed out by Burt (3) and Stephenson that there exists yet another way in which correlation can be used, namely, the correlation of persons and, to complete the trio, this has been called $Q$ technique as referred to in the last chapter. Suppose we ask Jones to rank fifty jokes in order of funniness and then ask Robinson to do the same. These two orders (or "profiles" on a series of tests) can be correlated and might in this case yield a Jones-Robinson correlation of $+0.6$. Next we might test Smith and find his $r$ with Jones to be $+0.1$ and with Robinson $-0.1$. We can conclude that Jones and Robinson have a decidedly similar sense of humor, but that Smith is unlike either of them. Later, however, we might find two other people forming a correlation cluster with Smith, independent of the Jones-Robinson cluster. $Q$ technique has for this reason been called the ideal method for discovering types.

The purest representative of a type (as revealed by such a correlation cluster of people) is the individual who shows the highest average correlation with all others in the cluster. Whereas in $R$ technique one would point to a particular trait-indicator test and say, "This is the best measure of the surface trait or factor in question," in $Q$ technique one would point to Mr. Baker and say, "This man is the most perfect expression of the type" (or he "has a 0.8 loading in it"). Individuals highly correlating in $Q$ technique and forming a type are similar with respect to their endowment in *all* factors.

If further statistical discussion were appropriate here we could show that in fact $Q$ and $R$ techniques do not lead to independent, divergent results but only to different ways of approaching or expressing the same patterns of clustering and factorization. In one case ($R$ technique), however, the pattern is identified at once by its highest tests while in the other ($Q$ technique) it is first identified by its highest persons. $Q$ technique has the advantage of being employable when there are only a few people and many tests; it lends itself better to identifying clusters (syndromes) than factors (source traits), but it cannot by some statistical magic make a study on a few people ("small sample") as accurate and generalizable as one on many. Because of the large number of tests that can be easily brought in, however, it is less likely to get into the rut of considering only some narrow aspect of personality than is $R$ technique. $P$ technique, as shown below, has the special virtue of revealing "unique" traits, *i.e.*, patterns peculiar to one individual.

**The Covariation Chart.** The search for functional unities by $R$, $Q$, and $P$ techniques begins in each with correlation coefficients worked out on a *series* peculiar to each. In $R$ technique a correlation is between two tests (or symptoms) on a series of persons; in $P$ technique it is between two tests on a series of days or occasions, and so on. While we are thinking of the general theory of manifestation and of the method of discovery of functional unities it is instructive to glance at the covariation chart shown in Diagram 10.

This is a device, discussed in greater detail elsewhere (6), reminding us that there are essentially *three* fundaments, or, rather, series of fundaments, among which the relations of correlation can be established in psychology.

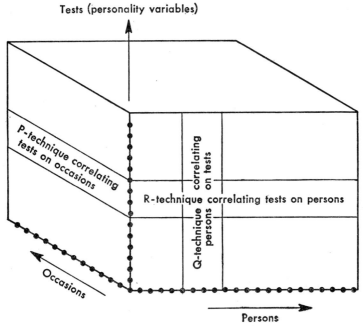

DIAGRAM 10. The covariation chart, showing exhaustively the possibilities of behavior correlation.

They are: people (or organisms); tests (or behavioral performances of any kind); and occasions (on which tests or people interact). The series in each of these constitute the three dimensions of the chart. Whenever two parallel lines are drawn on or through the parallelepiped there exist two correlatable series. Thus the band running almost horizontally to the right on Diagram 10 starts with two tests (each represented by a dot in the vertical line of test series). The length of each line is represented by a series of persons—a projection upward of the series of persons along the bottom edge. The band lies in a single vertical plane, corresponding to a single-occasion lamina (the first one) from the series of occasions represented by dots along the left lower edge. In short, it is an $R$ technique band, representing the correlation between two tests administered on one occasion to a series of people.

As the student who cares to play with this diagram will find, it directs to many untried and novel possibilities of correlation series, each capable of throwing light on functional unities in a new context. It presents approaches beyond $P$, $Q$, and $R$ techniques, such as the correlation of occasions; but the three most relevant to personality study remain the $R$, $Q$, and $P$ methods, as indicated by parallel tracks on the diagram.

### 4. THE CHIEF CATEGORIES IN TRAIT CLASSIFICATION

**Unique and Common Traits.** Since a correlation is only a statement about a general trend *in a whole group*, it follows that the pattern of elements corresponding to a correlation cluster will never be *exactly* the same in any two individuals. It is true that, as in surface trait $AA1$, below, "honesty," "self-control," and "fairmindedness-in-discussion" tend to go together, so that, in terms of standard scores, they will generally be on about the same level in any one individual. But special circumstances—say, belonging to a gang of antisocial boys—may cause a certain lad to be lower in honesty than one would expect, relative to his level in fairmindedness and self-control, and so on.

The pattern discovered in a surface trait is merely an average trend. Individual differences of heredity and upbringing will cause the pattern to be slightly different in different people. For this reason Allport has contrasted *common traits* with *unique traits* (2). The common trait is a trait which all people possess in some degree, in so far as human beings have more or less of the same fund of heredity possibilities and are subjected to more or less of much the same pattern of social pressures, *e.g.*, the pressures of family, school, and so on. On the other hand a unique trait is peculiar to the individual, in that no one else has just that pattern. Common traits may be illustrated by cyclothymia-schizothymia, general mental capacity, or degree of character integration. Unique traits, on the other hand, are probably more obvious in the field of interests and attitudes, where a man might have a powerful interest in Korean butterflies or a strong attitude in favor of reducing the tax on tricycles, which extremely few people would share to any scorable degree.

However, one must distinguish between an *intrinsically unique trait* which, like a six-fingered hand, introduces an entirely new *dimension* to be measured and a *relative unique trait* in which, as in any individual hand, there is only the usual slight deviation from the *pattern* of the average or common-trait pattern (6). Intrinsic or relative unique-trait patterns can be found by $P$ technique studies of the given individual; whereas common-trait forms are found by $R$ and $Q$ techniques. The evidence yet available suggests that unique-trait patterns do not depart much from the common-trait form, at least in the major dimensions of personality.

**General and Specific Source Traits.** Our initial presentation has sought not to complicate the picture by any introduction of the fact that factors are specific as well as general. A factor or source trait is a source of variation that covers a great number of trait-elements. In extracting these "general" factors—"general" because they spread over most trait-elements —it usually happens, however, that some part of the variability of a specific trait-element remains unaccounted for when all the general factor variances are taken out. This part has to be considered due to error or to a "specific factor." That is to say, the variations in this particular piece of behavior cannot be accounted for entirely by the action of general characteristics such as run through the whole personality, but must be partly due to something absolutely specific to the act or organ. Ability to sort colors or fear of nails might be forms of behavior in which more general factors (intelligence and timidity respectively) are less important than traits due to specific experience.

A specific factor is some narrow ability or highly particularized source of personality reaction which operates in that situation and that only, and of which all people have a certain amount, *i.e.*, it is a common trait. Specific source traits are not given further attention here because (*a*) they are too numerous and small, (*b*) in practice they are seldom used, (*c*) their exact magnitude is not really known: the tendency has been for suspected specific traits to diminish toward zero as further research succeeds in incorporating them into new general factors.

**Constitutional and Environmental-mold Traits.** Surface traits, as we have seen, are often the consequence of two or more source traits overlapping in their effects, producing steeper correlation between trait-elements than either influence would produce alone. If source traits found by factorizing are pure, independent influences, as present evidence suggests, a source trait could not be due both to heredity and environment but must spring from one or the other.

A source trait is a cause or determiner of several trait-elements showing covariation. This covariation might spring from some cause within the organism, a hormone, a neural structure, an appetitive condition, etc., which simultaneously affects several aspects of behavior. Such an origin has been suggested in the case of the factor of general mental ability, where there is a good deal of evidence that the level of general ability depends on the total number of active cells in the cortex. The source trait would then be cortical mass, a fact of neural structure, which would account for the coordination found among the many behavior manifestations loaded with this factor of "general-ability-to-perceive-relations."

Again, although the matter has not yet been treated statistically except in the case of fatigue, it is easy to see that internal conditions like alcohol, hyperthyroid states, or fatigue yield a set of covarying manifestations which factor analysis would reveal as a source trait. For example, in the case of alcohol, we should discover a pattern of increasing carelessness, talkativeness, lack of control of impulse, and so on. (Like the surgent pattern demonstrated in the next chapter.) Patterns thus springing from *internal* conditions or influences we may call *constitutional source traits* (6). The term "innate" is avoided, because all we know is that the source is physiological and *within the organism*, which will mean inborn only in a certain fraction of cases (see Chap. 5).

On the other hand, a pattern might be imprinted on the personality by something external to it. Thus it is said that one can always recognize by a pattern of disciplined habits and values the products of a certain famous school, as some detectives claim also to be able to recognize a man who has been in prison, and as we are mostly able to recognize, say, a strongly religious person from one who has not been interested in any church. The pattern of a powerful social institution, formed by the consistent rewarding of some habits and suppression of others, should thus be revealed by correlation, because the total constellation has impinged, as a whole, with different strength on different people. Thus a person who has one of the constituent trait-element habits poorly developed will tend to have others poorly developed, and another person strongly marked in one habit of the pattern will also be strongly possessed of the others. Such source traits, appearing as factors, we may call *environmental-mold* traits (6), because they spring from the molding effect of social institutions and physical realities which constitute the cultural pattern.

Source traits can be divided into constitutional and environmental-mold traits, but surface traits cannot, for these latter shapes arise from the combined action of several source traits. Thus the syndrome of schizophrenia is a surface trait, which in the extreme measure recognized as schizophrenic psychosis is fortunately uncommon. It has long been known however, (Chaps. 5 and 18) that both hereditary predisposition and environmental stress are usually needed to produce it. As we see in the next chapter, factor analysis *has* revealed two source traits in this area, one influencing a pattern of traits including obstructive, secretive, hostile, withdrawn—which may be the pattern produced by a frustrating environment—and one loading such indicators as timid, aloof, conscientious, languid, uninterested in the opposite sex—which seems to be the pattern of prepsychotic behavior found in those constitutionally prone to schizophrenia. Certainly we see here two distinct source traits which, if they are both present in sufficient endowment in the same, positive direction, will account for the surface-trait pattern of schizophrenia.

**Ability, Temperament, and Dynamic Traits.** Psychologists have long found it convenient to divide traits into three modalities, though the formal basis of this division has never been clearly set out (6). In *dynamic traits or interests* are included basic drives or ergs, on the one hand, and acquired interests, such as attitudes, sentiments, complexes, superego and ego formations, on the other. Dynamic traits are characterized by behavior arising from a stimulus situation or incentive and directed to some goal, at which the action ceases. *Abilities*, by contrast, are shown by *how well* the person makes his way to the accepted goals. Dynamic traits are thus traits in

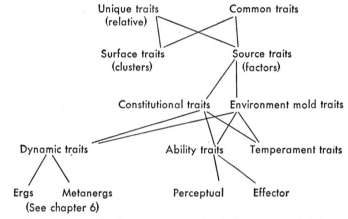

DIAGRAM 11. Classificatory scheme of trait forms and modalities.

which performance varies as the *incentive* varies; whereas abilities can be recognized as those in which performance varies in response to changes in *complexity*. *Temperament traits* are definable by exclusion as those traits which are unaffected by incentive or complexity. These are traits like highstrungness, speed, energy, and emotional reactivity, which common observation suggests are largely constitutional.

The advantage in recognizing the modality of a trait seems to be that in many practical life situations it is often possible to concern ourselves with one modality only. For example, in tests and examinations we can usually depend on dynamic traits being in equal and optimum action in all people, so that the differences in performance can be calculated from abilities alone. On the other hand, the psychoanalyst, dealing with neurotics, usually makes no test of abilities but deals with problems as if they existed wholly in the realm of dynamic traits. However, unless trait investigations are made under such conditions of constancy and exclusion one is likely to find trait unities, *i.e.*, factors which combine dynamic, temperamental, and ability manifestations.

Subclassification of abilities, temperament traits, and dynamic traits can sometimes profitably be considered (6). For example, abilities can be divided into perceptual (discriminatory) abilities and effector (motor) abilities, *e.g.*, intelligence and manual dexterity, and, by cross classification, into retentive and plastic abilities, *e.g.*, retentiveness of memory and quickness to learn new material. An introductory study cannot pursue these refinements further, and the purpose of this section will be attained if the student has a clear grasp of the possible relationships among the various major trait forms and concepts themselves. These relationships are summarized in Diagram 11.

## 5. A BRIEF CATALOGUE OF SURFACE TRAITS

**Cultural Relativity of Patterns.** It has been pointed out that the pattern of a trait in a specific individual, *i.e.*, *the unique-trait* pattern, is likely to vary a little from the pattern of the corresponding *common* trait. It is necessary further to point out that the pattern of a common trait will itself vary somewhat from country to country and population to population, just as correlations of any kind are liable to change with a change in the population in which the relation is investigated.

If a trait pattern reflects a particular social institution then the pattern may be expected to change in countries in which that social institution, with its mold of ideals, works differently. Similarly a constitutional source trait may be slightly different in different racial groups. For example, general mental capacity has a certain loading in or correlation with verbal ability, numerical ability, and spatial ability. It seems likely that in some racial groups the general ability expresses itself a little more in verbal ability and in others a little more in spatial ability. Thus, although the pattern of the general ability trait, *i.e.*, its loading of various performances, is unmistakable, it nevertheless undergoes slight changes from one population to another.

There are statistical reasons why this mutability of a common trait is greater for surface traits than source traits. For this reason, and because surface traits are very numerous and sometimes not clearly separated, it is unlikely that surface traits will ever be used so much in psychometrics, for precise personality measurement, as source traits—though surface-trait patterns are much more obvious to the eye. Consequently our survey of surface traits will not be included as an extended, systematic trait description in the following chapter, devoted to measurement and source traits, but will be dismissed with a brief immediate review in this section.

**Indexing of Surface Traits in Sectors.** Clinical observation has given very few surface traits, except abnormal syndromes, of agreed reliability; indeed extraversion-introversion and cyclothyme-schizothyme are the only clusters that have received general acceptance. Correlational research, using all the traits in the dictionary as a starting point (5) finds, however, some *fifty to sixty clusters* having four or more items and a minimum correlation among all items of around +0.5. Some of these clusters share one or two items in common and those connect in a loose network in larger "constellations" which have been called *sectors*.

As in astronomical mapping, which the correlation situation much resembles, it is convenient to index surface traits by an initial letter showing the general constellation or *sector* to which it belongs, followed by a number to indicate the specific *cluster*, *i.e.*, surface trait. The sixty tolerably well established surface traits (6) seem to be grouped in about twenty sectors. Some of these sectors, notably that which has clusters all falling in the realm of character integration or the group in the area of sociability, contain, however, a large fraction of this total of observed clusters.

The student desiring to see the complete map of surface traits should look elsewhere (5,6). Here we shall take only half a dozen of the most important from among those found each in at least four independent researches, and having a mean internal correlation, in an adult population, of +0.6. All surface traits are defined, for greater exactness, by giving both the positive and the negative poles. The trait items included carry the definition of behavior given for them in a standard dictionary. "Patent" names—as opposed to purely descriptive common terms—for these clusters are to be avoided, since they usually carry some speculative interpretation—as do even "introversion" and "extraversion." It is preferable to restrict at present to an index number and an essentially *descriptive title*.

*Surface Trait A*1, called descriptively *Integrity-Altruism vs. Dishonesty, Undependability*, has been found in at least four distinct researches. It includes:

> Honest vs. Dishonest
> Self-controlled vs. Impulsive
> Self-denying vs. Selfish
> Loyal vs. Fickle
> Fairminded vs. Partial
> Reliable vs. Undependable

This surface trait is obviously what might be called "sound character" at its positive pole, while at its negative pole it corresponds to the clinician's well-known "psychopathic-personality" syndrome (Chap. 1).

*Surface Trait AB*4. *Infantile, Demanding Self-centeredness vs. Emotional Maturity, Frustration Tolerance*

Infantile vs. Mature (emotionally)
Hypochondriacal vs. Not so
Self-pitying vs. Not so
Exhibitionist vs. Self-effacing
Unself-controlled vs. Self-controlled

Ackerson (1) notes also in behavior-problem children further characteristics on the left: Jealousy of siblings, Worrisomeness, Contrariness, Inferiority feelings, Defective conduct.

This seems to be the surface trait which in its extreme manifestations has been called the *conversion hysteria personality*.

*Surface Trait B2. Gentlemanly, Disciplined Thoughtfulness vs. Foolish, Extraverted Lack of Will*

Thoughtful vs. Unreflective
Wise vs. Foolish
Persevering vs. Quitting
Austere vs. Profligate
Polished vs. Rough

The upper pole of this surface trait is similar to the traits measured by Willoughby's test of Emotional Maturity (6). It is also similar to what Ostwald (6) described at length as the "classical temperament," though it is obviously a pattern much determined by environment.

*Surface Trait CA1. Crude Social Assertion, Exhibitionism vs. Obedience to Authority, Modesty*

Exhibitionist vs. Self-effacing
Argumentative vs. Not so
Talkative vs. Taciturn
Boastful vs. Modest
Arrogant vs. Humble

This is a pattern well established in both adults and children. It seems to be what Adler was describing as a mode of *overcompensation for inferiority*, though at the present descriptive stage we cannot pledge ourselves to any particular interpretation.

*Surface Trait CB1. Energy, Boldness, Spiritedness vs. Apathy, Timidity, Languor*

Energetic, spirited vs. Languid
Enthusiastic vs. Apathetic
Alert vs. Absent-minded
Debonair vs. Not so
Strong personality vs. Passive
Quick vs. Slow
Bold vs. Timid
Independent vs. Dependent

This is the surface trait which has been brought into popular discussion by Sheldon (14) under the name "Somatotonia." In the chapter on heredity we shall examine Sheldon's evidence for a constitutional origin; but for the present it seems best to define the trait in purely psychological terms, as $CB1$, etc. Sheldon's "Cerebrotonia," incidentally, is confirmed as Surface Trait $CB4$ (in the obverse or low side thereof), so that it is highly negatively correlated with Somatotonia, but distinct from it, *i.e.*, from its obverse.

*Surface Trait $D1$. Sociability, Adventurousness, Heartiness vs. Shyness, Timidity, Reserve*

> Sociable (forward) I vs. Shy
> Sociable (gregarious) II vs. Seclusive
> Adventurous vs. Timid
> Social interests vs. Lack of social interests
> Intrusive vs. Reserved

Whether this pattern or pattern $D4$ below corresponds to Jung's classical notion of extraversion-introversion (13) remains for library research to decide. The whole of $D$ sector includes items which Jung and many others tried to include in the notion of extraversion-introversion; but only two real clusters, $D1$ and $D4$, have claim to inherit the name. The latter is probably a better match, so that this trait is better qualified as social extraversion vs. shy introversion, for $D4$ is essentially a serious introversion, more in line with the introspectiveness stressed by Jung.

*Surface Trait $D2$. Sociability, Sentimentalism, Warmth vs. Independence, Hostility, Aloofness*

> Responsive vs. Aloof
> Affectionate vs..Cold
> Sentimental vs. Unsentimental
> Social interests vs. Lacking social interests
> Home and family interests vs. Lacking home and family interests
> Dependent vs. Independent
> Friendly vs. Hostile
> Frank vs. Secretive
> Genial vs. Coldhearted
> Even-tempered vs. Sensitive

This is the pattern which Sheldon has called "Viscerotonia" and to which he has added a number of interesting trait-elements, *e.g.*, love of comfort, food, etc., still needing confirmation.

*Surface Trait $D4$. Sociability, Personal Attractiveness, Pleasure Seeking vs. Earnestness, Asceticism, Mirthlessness*

Cheerful vs. Gloomy
Sociable vs. Seclusive
Laughterful vs. Mirthless
Attractive appearance vs. Unprepossessing
Popular vs. Not popular
Mischievous (playful) vs. Not so
Sensuous vs. Ascetic
Frivolous vs. Serious
Physical activity interests vs. Lacking physical activity interests

This is the surface trait which when first experimentally isolated by the present writer (4) was named Surgency-Desurgency. This name has now become restricted to the *source trait* (*F*) which underlies the present surface trait and others like it, but is distinct from them. Consequently, since there is no other pattern nearer to Jung's extraversion-introversion, it now seems best finally to tie down the term *extraversion-introversion* to the definite, experimentally established surface trait above. This trend of usage is indicated also by the close resemblance of the pattern to that which Jordan sketched as Active vs. Reflective types, which Jung recognized as being the embryo of his extraversion-introversion concept.

Continuing our survey we should now pass over the *E* sector, which covers varieties of emotionality, and the *F* sector's schizothyme patterns, hardly any of which are as well confirmed and defined as the above, and so come to other patterns which, though no better defined, are illustrative of less frequently discussed clusters, as follows:

*Surface Trait G1. Austerity, Thoughtfulness, Stability vs. Playfulness, Changeability, Foolishness*

Austere vs. Profligate
Thoughtful vs. Unreflective
Deliberate vs. Impulsive
Not playful vs. Mischievous (playful)
Stable emotionally vs. Changeable
Reserved vs. Intrusive
Serious vs. Frivolous
Cautious vs. Reckless

This pattern resembles most closely the antithesis which Jaensch set up between his *T* type and *B* type, Integrate and Disintegrate. This resemblance is more convincing when one includes the fuller series of trait-elements from the correlation cluster, *e.g.*, the lively self-expressiveness, which are not yet confirmed enough to list above. If this is true we have here also a surface trait presumed associated with physical, constitutional characteristics as described by Jaensch (12).

*Surface Trait H1. Thrift, Tidiness, Obstinacy vs. Lability, Curiosity, Intuition*

> Habit-bound vs. Labile
> Thrifty vs. Careless of property
> Logical vs. Intuitive
> Pedantic, tidy vs. Disorderly
> Uninquiring vs. Curious

This pattern has long been talked of in psychoanalysis as one of the character-neuroses, labeled the "obsessional" or "anal-erotic" character. Again the speculative explanation does not concern us here: the important point is the agreement of experiment and clinical impression on the pattern of a common surface trait.

Of the patterns to which the student may have heard reference in other reading probably the only ones omitted from the above are those associated with intelligence vs. dullness, emotionality vs. phlegmativeness, cyclothyme vs. schizothyme, and dominance vs. submissiveness. That is because these surface traits are also the expressions of single source traits, which will be considered as such in the next chapter.

The student should not, normally, aim to memorize these patterns. It suffices if he understands the principles of investigation and categorization, if he can recognize, with historical associations, a few of the most important surface traits, and if he knows his way to the psychological catalogues (1,5,6) where the rest may be found.

## 6. SUMMARY

1. Unitary traits, as dimensions of individual differences and functional unities, have to be established by observations of *covariation* of parts, *i.e.*, of "trait-indicator" behavior measures.

2. Covariation is explored most commonly by means of the correlation coefficient (and its derivatives) which is concerned with the covariation of two entities over a series of paired measurements. A "matrix" of correlation coefficients relating many trait indicators in all possible pairs can be analyzed for functional unities by *cluster analysis* or, more penetratingly, by *factor analysis*.

3. In cluster analysis we seek groups of elements in any one of which all the possible correlations of the elements (trait-indicators) are positive and high (above an agreed arbitrary limit). Such a correlation cluster may be called a *surface trait* (or syndrome), because it shows the actual, observed manner of "going together."

4. In factor analysis the correlations largely determine the number of independent *dimensions* required to represent the directions of variation of

all the trait-elements ("subtests"). From the process of factorization we also obtain measures of "loadings," *i.e.*, of the extent to which any given trait-indicator is involved in, and contributes to the measurement of, any given factor.

5. Factor analysis is not only an economy, in that the scores on many, many variables (some 4,000 have been used to cover personality) can be represented by some few factor scores, but is also a means of psychological analysis in that the factors are likely to be structural and functional unities in personality.

6. For this last reason factors are called *source* traits. *Source* traits and *surface* traits are interchangeable means of personality description. A single surface trait may be a result of the action of one, two, or more underlying source traits. Source traits are thus in part explanatory where surface traits are merely descriptive. The source trait, however, is an interpretation only at the level of what philosophers call an "empirical construct," though with fuller knowledge it becomes more than this.

7. The three principal designs of covariation experiment and analysis that have proved value in personality study are (*a*) *R* technique, which correlates trait indicators in terms of series of *persons* (individual differences); (*b*) *Q* technique, which correlates persons, looking for types; and (*c*) *P* technique, which correlates trait-indicators for series of occasions, within one person. The covariation chart, however, shows that, theoretically, there are other series waiting to be used for correlation research.

8. *R* technique yields *common* source traits, which may be either general, running through the whole personality, or specific to one particular kind of behavior. Actually, specific and general are extremes of a distribution, most source traits significantly affecting many, but not all, manifestations of personality. *Q* technique yields, when clusters of correlating persons are picked out, continuous and species types. *P* technique yields (relative) unique traits, the pattern of which, though peculiar to the individual, approaches that of the corresponding common trait.

9. Source traits have wider utility, stability, and meaning than surface traits. Each can either include ability, dynamic, and temperamental trait-elements in a single "wholistic" factor or be restricted, by the conditions under which the experimental data are measured, to one modality, as a "conditional" source trait. Source traits spring from influences that may be either in environmental objects and institutions—in which case they are "environmental-mold traits" or from sources within the constitution of the organism, in which case they are "constitutional traits." Surface traits may be combinations of both. Both source and surface traits are likely to vary with the culture pattern and with the range of genetic, racial constitutions in the population.

10. From as complete as possible a universe of trait indicators, constituted by the "personality sphere," some sixty or more correlation clusters or surface traits can be found of an appreciable size and significance of correlation. These include such clinically known patterns as extraversion, viscerotonia, obsessional character, etc., but also many not discernible at the clinical level of exactness. The sixty or more fall into some twenty broader groupings or "sectors."

## QUESTIONS AND EXERCISES

1. Give the simplest formula for the correlation coefficient. Guess at, and then work out, the correlation of (*a*) rated sociability and (*b*) number of recorded visits to friends per month in the following population of twenty persons (each represented by a letter):

| Persons | A | B | C | D | E | F | G | H | I | J | K | L | M | N | O | P | Q | R | S | T |
|---|---|---|---|---|---|---|---|---|---|---|---|---|---|---|---|---|---|---|---|---|
| Sociability rating | 1 | 3 | 8 | 5 | 4 | 5 | 10 | 5 | 2 | 9 | 6 | 5 | 7 | 4 | 6 | 7 | 3 | 6 | 7 | 8 |
| Recorded visits | 3 | 3 | 21 | 1 | 10 | 11 | 28 | 14 | 10 | 24 | 15 | 19 | 17 | 7 | 20 | 5 | 11 | 2 | 2 | 10 |

2. When correlation coefficients are represented graphically, as angles, what is the angle corresponding to an *r* of +1.0? of −1.0? of 0.0?

3. What is the difference between a surface trait and a source trait?

4. How do we know how many source traits are required to account for the variation in a given battery of trait-elements?

5. Refer to one well-known source trait, much used in clinical and educational measurement, and indicate its loading pattern for two or three trait-element performances.

6. Describe *P*, *Q*, and *R* techniques, indicating which has been most used, and what particular products are obtainable from each.

7. Show by a classificatory diagram the relations among unique and common, surface and source, ability, temperament, and dynamic trait forms.

8. Pick out two small correlation clusters (*i.e.*, write down the letters representing the trait-elements which belong in each), above the 0.45 level of belongingness, from the following matrix of discovered trait intercorrelations.

| | A | B | C | D | E | F | G | H | I |
|---|---|---|---|---|---|---|---|---|---|
| A | | | | | | | | | |
| B | 0.1 | | | | | | | | |
| C | 0.3 | 0.6 | | | | | | | |
| D | 0.0 | 0.1 | −0.1 | | | | | | |
| E | 0.1 | 0.6 | 0.9 | −0.3 | | | | | |
| F | 0.7 | −0.2 | −0.3 | −0.1 | 0.4 | | | | |
| G | −0.1 | −0.3 | 0.7 | 0.0 | 0.1 | −0.3 | | | |
| H | −0.8 | −0.1 | −0.3 | 0.2 | 0.0 | −0.7 | 0.3 | | |
| I | 0.5 | −0.1 | −0.3 | 0.1 | 0.4 | 0.9 | 0.1 | −0.5 | |

9. Give an example of a surface trait being due to the operation of more than one source trait, and preferably of being due to one constitutional and one environmental-mold trait.

10. Describe briefly the surface traits which have been called (*a*) Crude Social Assertion, (*b*) Somatotonia, (*c*) Social Extraversion, (*d*) Extraversion-Introversion.

## BIBLIOGRAPHY

1. ACKERSON, LUTON: *Childrens' Behavior Problems*, University of Chicago Press, Chicago, 1942.
2. ALLPORT, G. W.: *Personality* (Chapter XI), Henry Holt and Company, Incorporated, New York, 1937.
3. BURT, C.: *The Factors of the Mind*, University of London Press, Ltd., Bickley, Kent, England, 1940.
4. CATTELL, R. B.: Temperament Test I: Temperament, *Brit. J. Psychol.*, 23: 308–329, 1932.
5. CATTELL, R. B.: The Description of Personality: Basic Traits Resolved into Clusters. *J. Abnorm. Soc. Psychol.*, 38: 476–506, 1943.
6. CATTELL, R. B.: The Description and Measurement of Personality, World Book Company, Yonkers, N.Y., 1946.
7. CATTELL, R. B.: The Diagnosis of Neurotic Conditions: a Reinterpretation of Eysenck's Factors, *J. nerv. ment. Dis.*, 102: 576–589, 1945.
8. CATTELL, R. B.: The Integration of Factor Analysis with Psychology, *J. educ. Psychol.*, 39: 227–236, 1948.
8*a*. CATTELL, R. B.: *Factor Analysis in Science: An Introduction for Students and Researchers*, 1950.
9. EYSENCK, H. J.: Types of Personality: a Factorial Study of 700 Neurotics, *J. ment. Sci.*, 90: 851–861, 1944.
10. GUILFORD, J. P.: *Psychometric Methods*, (Chaps. X, XI, XII) McGraw-Hill Book Company, Inc., New York, 1936.
11. HOLZINGER, K. J., and H. H. HARMAN: *Factor Analysis: A Synthesis of Factorial Methods*, University of Chicago Press, Chicago, 1941.
12. JAENSCH, B. R.: *Eidetic Imagery*, Harcourt, Brace & Company, Inc., New York, 1930.
13. JUNG, C. G.: *Psychological Types*, Harcourt, Brace & Company., Inc., New York, 1923.
14. SHELDON, W.: *The Varieties of Temperament*, Harper & Brothers, New York, 1940.
15. THOMSON, G. H.: *The Factorial Analysis of Human Ability*, University of London Press, Ltd., Bickley, Kent, England, 1946.
16. THURSTONE, L. I.: *Multiple Factor Analysis*, University of Chicago Press, Chicago, 1947.
17. WOODROW, H.: Application of Factor Analysis to Problems of Practice. *J. gen. Psychol*, 21: 457–460, 1939.

# CHAPTER 3

## MEASURING PERSONALITY BY THE LIFE-RECORD METHOD

1. The Meaning of Measurement
2. The Observational Basis of Measurement: I. Life-record or Behavior-rating Methods
3. The Observational Basis of Measurement: II. Self-ratings and Objective-test Methods
4. Source Traits from Life-record Data
5. The Integration of Source-trait Measurements
6. Summary

### 1. THE MEANING OF MEASUREMENT

**Clarification of Source Traits by Particulars.** From the somewhat rarefied heights of generalized theory attained in the preceding chapter it may be a welcome relief to descend again to more practical and particular aspects of measurement. It is through studying particular personality source traits and the ways in which they are practically measured, moreover, that the above general propositions, if properly kept in mind, can be more thoroughly understood.

Beginning with the realization that unitary trait structure must first be sought, we have, so far, examined the covariational techniques for discovering it and seen the necessity for treating surface and source traits, common and unique traits in their proper contexts of prediction and measurement units. The relations of these trait forms in divisions and subdivisions is most readily shown[1] by Diagram 12.

We have also dealt with the way in which measurements of an individual's endowment in any source trait are (a) to be estimated from measures of particular tests or trait-indicators, and (b) to be combined in what is called a specification equation (See page 25) to predict his level in any specific performance.

Our purpose in this chapter is to deal with the means of obtaining data on trait-indicators and to see what trait-indicators are involved in some particular source traits.

---

[1] Ergs could again be subdivided in this diagram into *innate* and *displaced* ergic patterns, but these cannot be added until defined in Chapter 7.

*Philosophical Aspects of Measurement.* Before the above can be undertaken, however, it is necessary to glance around at one or two remaining general issues not falling within the systematic technical treatment of the preceding chapter. In the first place it is necessary to face the almost philosophical issues raised by those who question the very possibility of measuring so subtle an entity as personality.

These objections on grounds of sublety and tenuousness are partly rationalizations for more emotional, sentimental objections and partly truly scientific doubts. Among the emotional objections are the literary esthete's dislike of the scientific invasion of an artistic field; the moralist's fear that determinism

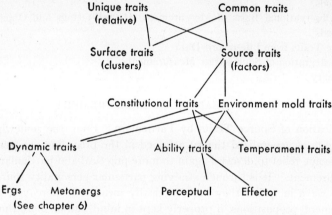

DIAGRAM 12. Review of relations of trait forms and modalities.

will remove moral obligation; the man-of-the-world's indignation at the suggestion that his own hard-won, intuitive, shrewdness is not the last word in personality estimation; and the narcistic objection by every man to the notion that his unique personality can be contained in any sort of formula. Among the scientific objections are: the possibilities of certain degrees of indeterminacy, as discussed in the last chapter of this book; the existence of such high degrees of function fluctuation that any fixed measurement is very approximate, and the fact that the variables to be taken into account are so multitudinous that the practical possibility of getting even a good sampling is remote.

The last set of objections will be discussed in due course. They concern inferences about personality structure and about further behavior from present measurements, rather than the permissibility of these measurements themselves. In regard to the latter, the philosophical objections are spurious. The psychologist here takes his stand on the position stated by Galton, Thorndike, and others, namely that mental (behavioral) phenomena, like any organic or physical phenomena, vary in amount or strength, and that therefore it is possible, at least theoretically, to measure relative magnitudes. Any expression in relative magnitudes can ultimately be reduced to some units of measurement.

**Structure and Behavior.** The remaining general and theoretical issue which might be a source of confusion concerns the use of the terms *structure* and *function*. A trait—of any variety—is a *mental structure*. That is to say, it is a relatively fixed characteristic of the individual, functioning from time to time in behavior. We *infer* the mental structure from the observed behavioral functions, just as a good engineer can infer the structure of an automobile engine, without ever seeing it, from observations of what a car can and cannot do. This does not mean that a trait is a physical, *neural* structure only. The structure we infer is an abstraction, like horsepower or the American nation. It is part of a larger inferred structure—the mind. Both the mind and any specific trait presumably have a neural structure as a substrate—the whole nervous system in the case of the former. But the mental structure, which is parallel to, or an aspect of, the neural structure is largely deduced from repeated modes of behavior.

When we say that a trait is a functional unity we mean that when the structure is in operation the resulting behavior has a functional unity. Incidentally, the degree of *efficacy* (7) of this unity may be at various levels. The fullest degree of efficacy of the unity exists when the trait indicators show covariation *in each and every situation in which we apply correlation technique*. A low degree of efficacy is that in which covariation can be found only by *R* technique, *i.e.*, the parts covary as we observe individual differences, but when the trait is in action in a single individual its parts show no functional cohesion.

Parenthetically, one should not confuse this basic notion of mental structure with "structure" as "structure of consciousness" in the sometimes historically discussed psychological school of "structuralism." Mental structure is only obliquely related to consciousness: it is, in terms of logical positivism, a "construct," and initially an "empirical construct," from observations of *behavior*.

## 2. THE OBSERVATIONAL BASIS OF MEASUREMENT: I. LIFE-RECORD OR BEHAVIOR-RATING METHODS

**Varieties of Personality Measurement.** The student doubtless has acquaintance already, even though of an unsystematic kind, with many devices used in personality measurement, *e.g.*, questionnaires, so-called "projection" tests, *i.e.*, misperception tests, miniature-situation tests, ratings, matching methods, expressive and stylistic methods like handwriting, and so on. Into what essentially different methods do these resolve themselves? Broadly the methods of gathering evidence can be divided into three, differing in the nature of the data, their reliability, and the situations for which they are suitable. These three methods, *Life-record*, *Self-rating*, and *Objective-test*, may be briefly described as follows.

**The "Life-record" or "Objective Observation of Behavior in Situ" Method.** The essential characteristics of this method are that the inferences about traits are (*a*) based on the normal behavior of the individual in characteristic everyday-life situations, and (*b*) not dependent on any self-observations by the subject.

The range of detailed methods within this category of observation of actual life behavior is wide, but essentially they consist of (*a*) *ratings*, by trained observers; (*b*) *time sampling*, in which specific behavior is observed for all subjects at specified times and places, the frequency of reactions of a certain kind being recorded; (*c*) *life-event statistics*, a kind of prolonged "sampling" in which one records the frequency of certain happenings, *e.g.*, accidents, changes of job, amount of money spent on this or that, from records of the subject's life. These three require fuller description separately.

*Behavior Rating.* (Henceforth called "*BR* data.") Throughout the following discussions of personality measuring methods it will be assumed that the student knows the meaning of two elementary test concepts: (*a*) reliability (and consistency),[2] measured by a reliability coefficient indicating how well the test agrees with itself, either as a split half or on repeated administration to the same people; (*b*) validity—the extent to which a measuring device measures the trait that it sets out to measure. This is estimated by a validity coefficient, obtained by correlating the test with a criterion supposed to be the true measure.

The validity and reliability of ratings vary so widely in different conditions that the psychologist's judgment as to the worth of the procedure depends greatly on his estimate of the conditions. As Symond's survey (13) indicates, two reasonably intelligent raters generally show an agreement of about 0.6 on a typical personality trait—which is not a very good reliability

---

[2] The split-half reliability coefficient, obtained by correlating each person's score on the odd items of the test with his score as the sum of the even ones, measures the reliability of the test, *i.e.*, its freedom from response error and experimental error. The repeat reliability coefficient, on the other hand, may be low even when test reliability is high, because of *function fluctuation*, *i.e.*, actual day-to-day changes in the strength of the trait measured. It has been suggested by the writer (7) that the split-half or immediate retest correlation be called a *reliability* coefficient, and the test-retest (after an appreciable interval) correlation, a *consistency* coefficient. The consistency coefficient thus indicates among other things the consistency or absence of fluctuation of the trait, whereas the reliability coefficient indicates the reliability of the measuring device only. From a mathematical comparison of reliability and consistency coefficients we could obtain a "constancy coefficient" showing purely the susceptibility of a trait to function fluctuation.

when compared with what we expect from tests. Rating, however, can be greatly improved by attention to the following conditions, so that consistencies of 0.9 become prevalent (9).

*The conditions of sound rating estimates.* *A*. Personality ratings should in general not be made by anyone who stands in a special emotional relation to the ratee, *e.g.*, as parent or teacher, or by one who sees him only in a special and limited situation, *e.g.*, a classroom or a factory bench. It is better to have them made by a coeval or peer before whom the subject is natural.

*B*. The judges should be trained in a very precise definition of what they are rating. The trait should finally be described in terms of actual behavior situations (the trait-elements highly loaded by the source trait in question). Thus the judges are not asked to rate "sociability" but, "How often does the person speak to a fellow worker spontaneously, without practical need?" "Does he speak to strangers first?," and so on.

It may seem superfluous to add that the judges should be intelligent! Yet it is not sufficiently realized that in dealing with such abstractions as "aspects of behavior" distinctly high intelligence is required for effective estimation. The judge need not have the perception of human nature possessed by a Shakespeare or a Freud, but it is a fact that judges of average or low intelligence show a marked falling off of skill, particularly as indicated by validity.

Symonds (13) reviews the evidence showing that some traits are constantly rated with greater reliability than others. These traits are noticeably ones issuing in more frequent overt behavior. For example, leadership, energy, originality are rated more reliably than unselfishness, adaptability, memory. The poorly rated traits are also those harder to define operationally, *i.e.*, by specific behavior occurring in one or two definite trait-elements. Moreover, in the past it must be confessed that poor rating has arisen not merely from lack of crisp definition but also from the psychologist asking for ratings on composite, *nonunitary* traits, requiring incompatible behavior to be added in the same pool!

*C*. The judge should, at one session, rate all people with regard to one trait, not all traits belonging to one person. This, together with (I) above and specific warning against total favorable and unfavorable attitudes, helps overcome the halo effect. The halo effect is the tendency to rate an approved person above average on all "desirable" traits, regardless of his actual standing.

*D*. It is better to have many judges and to average their estimates. Recent research (5) shows that the reliability of ratings goes up with increase of judges according to just the same law as that controlling the rise of reliability of a test with increase of number of pass or fail items. Obviously the

astigmatisms and random errors of the individual judge are respectively can-
celed and reduced, by overlap with his fellows.   Reliabilities for the majority
of traits have been shown, in studies by the present writer, to rise to around
0.9, *i.e.*, to the figure usual in a good objective test, when the ratings of a
group of eight or ten judges (classmates or fellow residents in a house) aver-
aged, are correlated with the pool of eight or ten others.   Of course, this still
says nothing about the *validity*, which depends more on precautions (*A*),
(*B*), and (*C*) above.

E. A limiting condition on rule (*D*) is that the circle of acquaintances
involved should not be *too* large.   Rarely do people know, or get known by,
more than twenty or thirty people—well enough to make sound personality
ratings.   The best conditions for rating are offered by a *residential* group of
about fifteen to twenty people, who are engaged together in different tasks
and situations from day to day.   The *more varied and stressful* the daily tasks
the better.   Thus the ratings obtained in platoons of soldiers or crews of
small boats during the late war tended to be higher in reliability and validity
than those obtained from pools of students of the same size.

F. Point scale ratings, *i.e.*, assigning scores on each trait from, say, 1 to 10,
are sometimes best made first as *rankings* and then converted to *rating values*.
(Most books on psychometrics carry tables for converting from percentiles
[ranks in 100 people] to standard scores—a five-point scale.)   There are two
principal reasons for preferring ranking: first, most judges cannot use a
numerical rating scale correctly and, second, ranking people forces one to
make "paired comparisons" whenever two people are adjacent.   (From
psychophysics, as well as from personality study, it is known that paired
comparisons result in a high reliability of ranking.)   Judges err in ratings by
systematically rating too high—if they are told that five is to be taken as
average on the point scale they actually tend to give out scores which average
around six or seven.   Also they cannot discriminate finely enough to use as
many as ten- to twenty-point divisions; in fact five or seven points are as
many divisions as one can profitably use with most judges.

The use of the rank procedure has the disadvantage that if one works with
small groups—and, as we see from (*E*), it is inadvisable to use large ones—the
assumptions that (*a*) every group is normally distributed, and (*b*) that all
groups have the same true average become untenable.

Defining traits in *bipolar* form has some advantages here and in other aspects
of rating.   Instead of defining sociable, or excitable, or exhibitionistic against
merely "absence" of these, one draws a dimension with sociable at one pole
and shy at the other.   Similarly, excitable and exhibitionistic are set opposite to defined phlegmatic and self-effacing behavior, respectively.   This
tends to cure the tendency to misplace the average.   It also results in much
firmer definition of the dimension being rated than if only one end of the

scale were "tied down."   In the last stage of research the true opposites have to be picked from correlation results; for logic alone gives various possible "opposites" to any quality.

**The Personality Sphere.**   Behavior ratings, on named trait-elements, have one unique advantage over other universes of trait-indicators: that a complete population of variables can be found from which any particular kind of sample can be made.   As pointed out in the preceding chapter, the languages of civilized peoples have some 3,000 to 5,000 words describing aspects of personality and human behavior.   It is probable that this number has long since reached a plateau and that, except for substitutions and peculiar minor traits, the language of Shakespeare was as adequate for describing personality as is ours 300 years later.

It is perhaps a reasonable axiom, therefore, that *any aspect of human behavior that affects the individual and his society is already represented by a symbol in the dictionary.*   Consequently it should be possible to sample the surface of personality *evenly* by taking a suitable condensation of the complete list of trait names in the language, such as that of Allport and Odbert (2).   The present writer has thus reduced the list to about two hundred, by clustering of synonyms, and then to about sixty by intercorrelating the already reduced list of traits (see (5), Chap. 2).

This representative list of traits is known as *the personality sphere* (7).   If we imagine the factors of personality as *n* dimensions this is the surface of an *n*-dimensional sphere.   It is the whole area of personal behavior.   The surface traits of the preceding chapter, and the source traits to be described in this, are based on analysis of such an evenly sampled set of variables from the personality sphere.   In the initial mapping of surface and source traits it would seem that a great advantage in comprehensiveness and certainty arises from using *BR* data, which can *alone be based on the personality sphere.* Naturally we may wish later to put the discovered factors in terms of loadings in objective tests, which are more stable, exact and universally reproducible; but the initial use of the verbal symbols of the personality sphere ensures that our factors represent the whole space.

*Time sampling.*   It goes without saying that ratings need to be based on observation over long periods of time and that the raters should observe all the ratees in similar fields of expression, *i.e.*, not one at work and another at play.   Time sampling is an attempt to put this and other features of good rating on a formal and definite footing.   The observer ignores what he knows casually about the subject (or, ideally, is chosen to have no acquaintance with him) but observes his behavior at a stated place for a stated period of time each day.   He then checks off how many times a definite kind of behavior occurs.   For example, he might observe nursery school children through a one-way screen, recording, in the fifteen-minute daily period of tool play, how many times Johnny Brown hits a playmate on the head, or, watching adults at a committee meeting, recording how many times Mr. R. smiles, or interrupts others' conversation, in the opening ten minutes.

Time-sampling studies show remarkably high reliabilities (13) even for relatively short and few samplings of behavior, so that if, say, a dozen periods are added together the coefficient approaches 0.9—that of a good objective test. This method shows what rating can be at its best. Its advantage is that it can convert comparatively careless or unintelligent raters (the majority of raters in business and applied psychology generally) into precise observers. Its disadvantage is that, like the objective test, though less completely, it has to leave out some important traits—those which flash into action only rarely—and those more subtle aspects of behavior which cannot readily be reduced to very simple, operational acts, *i.e.*, which are complex patterns rather than isolated acts. To ignore these complex patterns means that we fail to utilize the analyzing capacity of our best instrument—the human mind as it functions in our observers.

*Life-event statistics.* This is not an expression in general use and we use it, for lack of a better, to designate those real-life-situation happenings which admit of being (and frequently are) recorded. It falls in this category because it deals with behavior *in situ*, embedded in life (not in artificial laboratory or verbal estimates) and is cognate with time sampling except that here we take *all* time—all of the subject's time—for our province.

For many groups of individuals data exist on how frequently each person has been employed, how many times he has failed to attend classes, how often divorced, how often ill or in a mental hospital or in prison, what grade he received at school, how many times he has been elected to office in societies, how frequently he has spoken in public, and so on. Vital statistics and parish records offer little more than births, marriages, and deaths, events which are rare in the individual's life! But increasingly there are public and business records which permit calculating a score on a number of trait-elements, each constituted by a specific life event. If one could depend on the memory of the subject, an extremely wide and rich array of scorable events would be opened up. Some of these might be obtained from objective aspects of personal documents as suggested by Allport (1) but most personal documents and most personal memory data belong to the inferior, subjective methodology discussed in the second category below.

The disadvantage of life-event statistics lies in the paucity of available data and the tendency of the event to be too complexly determined (*e.g.*, divorce) to offer evidence on any single trait. The attraction of the method, on the other hand, lies in the expression of personality constants and predictions in terms of *events of very real practical importance*. Surprisingly little correlation for trait unities has yet been carried out on such data, though there have been studies on traits of punctuality, accident proneness, etc. Recently, however, Eysenck (6a) has established a syndrome covering frequency of unemployment, infrequency of being a member in social clubs, groups, etc., frequency of working in unskilled occupations, etc., which syndrome includes also some objective-test measures, *e.g.*, low intelligence, and suggests the form of the low-intelligence syndrome in terms of life-record data.

The student should bear in mind that the primary source traits of personality as at present defined (below) have initially been founded, deliberately, on the first of our three methods—the life-record method—though the ultimate aim of research is to translate the basic factors into factors in the other media also. This is an assurance of their pervasiveness, reality, and practical importance—an assurance which is lacking in source traits found in narrow test situations of the laboratory. Its disadvantage is that the frequently careless popular use of verbally defined traits, no matter how precisely the associated behavior has originally been defined, makes the wider use of the method, in unskilled hands, doubtful.

### 3. THE OBSERVATIONAL BASIS OF MEASUREMENT: II. SELF-RATINGS AND OBJECTIVE-TEST METHODS

**Measurement through Self-observations.** Self-ratings, and questionnaire responses on the self, of the kind that are taken at their face value, suffer from the disadvantage that their unreliability cannot be reduced by increasing the number of observers, for not even a second observer can look into the subject's consciousness or interpret his behavior from his own unique viewpoint. As for his reports on his behavior it is enough to say that in most situations, *e.g.*, competing for a job, the subject is emotionally disinclined to be honest, and that even if he wished to be, he cannot know himself objectively enough to give a true picture. As for his consciousness, *i.e.*, the consciousness indicated in such questions as "Are you subject to ups and downs of mood?" "Are you more than averagely afraid of heights?" "Do you enjoy music?" his observations are made in a *solipsistic* (see below) continuum—a world of its own—in which, even in theory, no one else's self-observations can also be scaled for comparison.

**Introspective and Objective Uses of Questionnaires.** Essentially, therefore, a questionnaire response, accepted at its overt meaning, is an introspection, subject to all the limitations of introspective psychology. However, not all tests that are *apparently* questionnaires are really so. If we treat the response simply as a piece of verbal behavior, which we prove to correlate with other personality responses and use as an indicator thereof, *regardless of verbal meaning*, it becomes an objective test. For example, I may find that people who say "yes" to the question "Do you find blue a depressing color?" are more frequently conversion hysterics than those who say "no." I then use the response, not as a proof of depression but as an indication of conversion hysteria.  However, if one plans to use verbal responses in this indirect fashion it is generally better to use responses which are not specifically liable to the above-mentioned sources of purely capricious distortion, *i.e.*, to avoid even *apparent* self-estimates, which are especially sensitive to slight changes in the social and general setting of the test.

The measurement of personality traits even by face-value questionnaire lists, however, has justification in certain specialized research situations, where the subjects are highly cooperative and motivated to honesty, and where the researcher is making a rapid preliminary exploration with such subjects before substituting for the questionnaire other and better methods, *e.g.*, observer's ratings, time sampling, or objective tests.

*Limitations of the Self-rating Questionnaire.*  The above considerations should suffice to warn the student not to regard the prevalence and popularity of simple questionnaires as any endorsement of their validity as personality measures by competent psychologists.[3]

Nevertheless, even outside exploratory studies and employment with especially reliable groups, the questionnaire still has some interest.  In the first place it is a matter of pure scientific interest to know what syndromes look like "from the inside."  One can imagine that a schizophrenic's personal view of his behavior is very different from the behavior pattern seen by the outside rater, and it is valuable to know what that view is.  By matching, through correlations, the syndromes found in questionnaires with those found in life-record or objective-test material we can finally match "behavioral exteriors" with "mental interiors."

This defining of "patterns in the consciousness of self," *i.e.*, of how certain personality exteriors "feel" from the inside, is also of *practical* value in clinical psychology in initial diagnosis, for the patient describes his symptoms in these internal terms when questioned in the consulting room.  The further

---

[3] He should be warned, for that matter, that the great company of camp followers practicing around the small nucleus of fully qualified psychologists is peculiarly liable to set afoot uncritical fashions and unsubstantial fads throughout the realm of "mental testing" and clinical personality measurement.  Against these epidemics stands at present an insufficient controlling force of scientifically well-informed and technically competent opinions.

Regarding the extent to which the above flaws invalidate the use of questionnaires, in other than the very special conditions mentioned, the recent review of psychologists' opinions by Kornhauser (11) who gathered replies by psychologists to a short questionnaire on personality inventories and the Rorschach test gives some perspective:

"None of these tests, in my opinion, has been validated."

"Moderately satisfactory for clinicians; highly unsatisfactory in industry.  For industry the subject will not 'come clean.' "

"Two years of work in the (military) service have shown no helpfulness in these tests presumed to measure 'traits' which clinicians presumed to exist."

clinical methods, such as "free association," do not belong entirely to the category of self-observation; for the psychiatrist uses the patient's introspections to draw conclusions other than those immediately stated about himself by the patient. Free association, indeed, is not primarily a method of *describing* personality, but an interpretive method of arriving at underlying (largely dynamic) connections in a personality already known as to its salient characteristics.

What has been said about the self-rating questionnaire—especially its defects—applies, of course, *a fortiori* to literal self-rating, in which the subject goes beyond assigning himself to one of two categories, as in the questionnaire, and actually attempts to rate himself quantitatively on characteristics, using, for example, a five-point scale.

**Objective-test Methods.** Since both objective tests and real-life situation records share the characteristic of being objective in the sense that they depend only on experimenters' observations of the subject's behavior in a given situation, the student may well wonder whether it is possible to draw a sharp line between them. Admitting that the life-record method observes responses in real-life situations, one may therefore ask whether an "objective personality test" is generally anything more than a prearranged real-life situation. For example, the objective "situational" test in which we send a child to fetch something from a room in which a stranger is sitting, and score him on this test according to whether he does not or does speak to the stranger, approaches very close to a life-record measure.

By an objective *test*, however, as distinct from a standardized, but natural, real-life situation as used in time sampling, we mean *a situation which is used to predict behavior in something other than the situation it presents*. A test is a convenient measuring device, having meaning in reference to a great number of other behavior situations. Further, it will normally have certain conveniences for the experimenter besides the above statistical reference to something beyond itself. It will be readily set up, transportable, accurately reproducible anywhere, objectively scorable, inexpensive, standardizable, briefer than the situations in which it attempts to predict behavior, etc. An objective test, as here defined, differs from a life-record situation as a map differs from the countryside. The practicing psychologist who has to set up a real-life situation as his "test" before he is able to predict behavior is only a little less absurd than a medical man who has no means of predicting a lethal dose of a standard drug until the patient has taken it.

Objective tests have proved far less successful in personality and dynamic traits generally than in the field of abilities, and at present are not used nearly as much as life-record and self-rating methods for personality study, which has led some psychologists to declare "no one should expect to discover how a person will behave in one situation by watching his behavior in another one."[4]  Nevertheless, as we have seen above, if a test is to have the usual characteristics of what we mean by a test, this is what it must do.  For a test may be defined as *an artificial (specially created) brief situation, easily set up anywhere, susceptible to ready reproduction and standardization, and yielding constant results with different, competent administrators."*  If it is a valid test it will, further, partially predict response in the different, more numerous, greater, *in situ* performances of everyday life.

**Comparison of Methods.**  At present, as Burt (3) has recently summed up, the life-record methods constitute the most accurate personality-measuring devices, followed by self-ratings and then by objective tests.  Of course, life-record observations of a certain kind are, in fact, the criterion against which any other measuring device has to be validated.  Among life-record methods, time sampling, and situational observations generally, such as constitute the criterion, are of greatest value, followed by behavior ratings, followed by interviews.  Actually, interviewing is better classified among objective tests than among life records, for it is an artificial situation of personality observation.  Burt observes that self-ratings (questionnaires) tie for first place in accuracy with intelligent and cooperative groups, but fall way down below every other method with ignorant and dishonest subjects—with whom psychologists have much to do!

Objective tests of personality have so far had reliabilities about two-thirds as good as those of abilities, and validities less than half as good.  But now that greater ingenuity and clinical insight are being brought to bear in test design—as in "miniature situation" tests, stylistic tests, ego defense tests (including projection), humor, aesthetic preference tests, and other tests still at the research stage—these validities are climbing so rapidly as to leave no doubt about the future of objective personality tests.  However, it must never be overlooked that the life-record methods—time sampling, trained rating of behavior, and life statistics—in one sense will always remain the most important: they provide the criteria against which all other methods have to be checked.

### 4. SOURCE TRAITS FROM LIFE-RECORD DATA

**Understanding the Loading Pattern.**  At length we are equipped, by study of factor theory and by examination of the foundation of measurement, to study with understanding the actual patterns of source traits that have so far been established.  The present section will deal with the principal source traits found in life-record (*LR*) data, largely, indeed, with factors founded on ratings of behavior in the total real-life situation (*BR*) data), while the follow-

---

[4] Another form of this view is that success can be gained only when the test very closely resembles the situation, as when Symonds ((13) p. 352) says, "If aggressiveness in selling is what is wanted, then the test situation must be one involving selling."

ing section will describe source traits found in self-rating and "opinionnaire" data.

It will be recalled that a source trait is recognized by a pattern of factor "loadings" among trait-elements or indicators. These loadings are in the form of correlation coefficients, and express *the extent to which the source trait determines the variability (for the general population) in the given trait-element behavior.* The loadings below are not listed numerically, but they mostly fall in the 0.4 to 0.7 range (which means that the source trait leaves a good deal of the trait-element behavior to be determined by other causes). One must never make the error of assuming that the source trait solely and wholly accounts for the kind of behavior listed in the trait-element. If a trait-element were loaded $+1.0$ it would be entirely *saturated* with the source trait and would be a perfect measure or test of it. This is practically the case in source trait $B$ with respect to an *intelligence test;* for $B$ seems to be the effect of intelligence in various aspects of personality and is therefore measured in essence by an intelligence test. In no other case do we yet have so good a measure of the pure source trait or factor.

**The Standard Index of Source Traits.** Although some fourteen or fifteen source traits have been found in various researches on $BR$ data, only six— $A, B, F, H, K,$ and $M$—are repeatedly confirmed and unmistakable, but twelve will be very briefly described here, omitting only $D$ and $J$ as too vague for consideration. Elsewhere (7) a "standard list" of these factors, with proper references to the numerous researches in which they occur, has been set out and the letter indexing and terminology of that list has been consistently followed in several subsequent researches and in the present book. The factor of largest variance in a typical adult population has been labeled $A$, the next $B$, and so on. At the present stage of our ignorance about the ultimate nature of these source traits it seems better to refer to them and their effects simply by standard letters, as biochemists have done with the vitamins, rather than rush into the premature attempts at interpretation indicated by other names.

However, purely descriptive or historical labels have also been used, systematically, for those who prefer verbal forms, though they must be accepted as contingent or temporary. Both the source-trait title and the constituent trait-elements below are always listed in *bipolar* fashion, corresponding to the plus and minus sign of the letter indicating the whole bipolar factor. This shows the character of the source trait at both of its poles, and reminds us that it is a "dimension" of personality. Unlike abilities, personality factors have appreciable negative loadings in many variables, *i.e.*, there are many performances for which a particular personality source trait can be a disadvantage as well as an advantage. In these lists the negative variables have always been reversed, so that the pole listed in the left column is always positive with regard to the factor.   The factors have almost identical patterns for men and women except for *C* and *E* which are different though recognizably the same.   The trait variables have their ordinary dictionary meanings, though as supplied to the raters they were further defined by specific behavior, as indicated elsewhere (7, 8, 9).

*Source Trait A.   Cyclothymia vs. Schizothymia.*   The most highly loaded trait-elements, in declining order are:

| *A+  Positively Loaded* | *A−  Negatively Loaded* |
|---|---|
| Easygoing | vs. Obstructive, cantankerous |
| Adaptable (in habits) | vs. Inflexible, "rigid" |
| Warmhearted | vs. Cool, indifferent |
| Frank, placid | vs. Close-mouthed, secretive, anxious |
| Emotionally expressive | vs. Reserved |
| Trustful, credulous | vs. Suspicious, "canny" |
| Impulsively generous | vs. Close, cautious |
| Cooperative, self-effacing | vs. Hostile, egotistical |
| Subject to personal emotional appeals | vs. Impersonal |
| Humorous | vs. Dry, impassive |

This trait is given more than a descriptive title because it is obviously related to the syndrome of "cycloid vs. schizophrenic" which Kraepelin used in classifying mental disorder[5] and to the cyclothyme-schizothyme temperament difference which Kretschmer described so skillfully on purely clinical observation.   It is probable that a certain liability to slow, prolonged ups and downs of mood, between elation and depression, also belongs on the left (positive) pole.

The student should bear in mind that the trait-element terms used above are the *extremes* of a bipolar continuum, so that they sometimes seem to indicate abnormal behavior or to imply moral judgments, *e.g.,* "obstructive" in the schizothyme pattern above.   But in most of the schizothyme individuals one meets, short of a mental hospital, this trait-element, for example, would probably be better verbally described only as "not very cooperative."   Only the extreme, very seldom reached, pole is describable as actually "obstructive."   In any case the psychologist should refrain from value judgments on temperament, for there are good and at any rate likeable aspects of both extremes, as well as special situations in which they are socially valuable. It is possible, for example, that the above rather unpleasant picture of the schizothyme arises from the traits being rated on external behavior.   Internally, as judged by the questionnaire pattern, the schizothyme "coldness" turns out to be partly shyness.

[5]The student should compare the above traits with those given in the clinical schizophrenic syndrome of Chapter 1, pp. 14–15.

The above are the mostly highly loaded indicators, but almost *all* the trait-elements in the personality sphere are affected to a lesser extent by this temperament trait. According to less-exact, general observations, this source trait ramifies very widely indeed through personality and physiology. It is associated with differences in solidity of body build (see Chap. 5), the cyclothyme being more round-bodied and heavy-limbed. Cyclothymes, *i.e.*, people with large *positive* endowment in this trait, according to Kretschmer (10), are more interested in things and people than in principles; make good organizers in business; as writers are humorous and realistic; as artists are more interested in color than form; are less able to abstract one thing alone from a percept; have a wider span of consciousness; are more disturbed, *e.g.*, in reaction time, by irrelevant stimuli; and respond more vigorously to demands of the outside world. Schizothymes, on the other hand, are more interested in abstract principles than particulars; seem to put more emphasis on moral principles than emotional appeals or temptations; do better in academic life than in business; as writers are idealistic, and sensitive lovers of nature; as artists are more interested in form than color and more frequently "classical" than "romantic"; are more tenacious ("one-track minds") in abstracting according to instructions from tachistoscopic exposures; have a faster, tenser personal tempo (see Chap. 5, page 136); have more rapid and extreme sympathetic nervous system reactions, *e.g.*, flushing, stomach upsets from psychological causes (see Chap. 5); are less able to respond to sudden demands for speed of output (6); are higher in verbal ability relative to general intelligence, especially relative to those aspects of intelligence entering into "adaptability to new situations" (7).

*Source Trait B. General Mental Capacity vs. Mental Defect.*

| B+ | B− |
|---|---|
| Intelligent | vs. Unintelligent |
| Thoughtful, cultured | vs. Unreflective, boorish |
| Persevering, conscientious | vs. Quitting, conscienceless |
| Smart, assertive | vs. Dull, submissive |

It has been shown by texts that this is the factor of general intelligence (Spearman's "G" or Thurstone's "second-order factor") as it outcrops in the realm of personality. It is perhaps a little surprising that intelligence affects so much of the personality, including the characterlike qualities of will and conscientiousness as well as those of being merely well informed and reflective, (which one might expect) but data in sections below confirms and explains these connections (see Chap. 4).

*Source Trait C. Emotionally Stable Character vs. Neurotic General Emotionality.*

|                               *C+*                               |                               *C−*                               |
| --- | --- |
| Emotionally stable            | vs. Emotional, dissatisfied                |
| Free of neurotic symptoms     | vs. Showing a variety of neurotic symptoms |
| Not hypochondriacal           | vs. Hypochondriacal, plaintive             |
| Realistic about life          | vs. Evasive, immature                      |
| Steadfast, self-controlled    | vs. Changeable                             |
| Calm, patient                 | vs. Excitable, impatient                   |
| Persevering and thorough      | vs. Quitting, careless                     |
| Loyal, dependable             | vs. Undependable morally                   |

This is one of the two most important source traits in determining character. Burt, describing its inverse as "General Emotionality," shows that it is one of the most diagnostic traits distinguishing delinquents and nondelinquents (4). There is much scattered evidence that this is the trait which is conspicuously low both in delinquents and in neurotics (and functional psychotics) (see Chaps. 16 and 17). It perhaps tends to be slightly low in artists and dramatists compared to scientists, *i.e.*, it may bring gifts even at its negative pole.

It may not be too speculative, even on the evidence yet available in the rating field, to interpret this factor as one of well-integrated will power, as opposed to a poor dynamic organization of the ego. The individual at the lower pole experiences dissatisfaction and undischarged emotionality which he is unable to keep under control.

Factor *D* is omitted, as being insufficiently confirmed by independent researches.

*Source Trait E. Dominance-Ascendance vs. Submissiveness.*

|                               *E+*                               |                               *E−*                               |
| --- | --- |
| Self-assertive, confident                            | vs. Submissive, unsure          |
| Boastful, conceited                                  | vs. Modest, retiring            |
| Aggressive, pugnacious                               | vs. Complaisant                 |
| Extrapunitive[6]                                     | vs. Impunitive, intropunitive   |
| Vigorous, forceful                                   | vs. Meek, quiet                 |
| Willful, egotistic                                   | vs. Obedient                    |
| Rather solemn                                        | vs. Light-hearted               |
| Adventurous                                          | vs. Timid, retiring             |
| Insensitive to social disapproval, unconventional    | vs. Tactful, conventional       |
| Reserved                                             | vs. Frank, expressive           |

This trait has been much investigated by those interested in leadership. Leadership is more complex than dominance, except among animals, but it seems true that highly dominant individuals like managing the affairs of

[6] Directing punishment on others, blaming others instead of self or nobody, when something goes wrong.

others and are prone to organize and use people for their own or group ends. The pattern seems to alter more than most with age.   In children "disobedience" and "antisocial behavior" are more loaded, while in adults these take less direct forms and "embittered" and "surly" come into the pattern but tough self-assertion come in both.

A similar pattern has been found in other mammals, notably chimpanzees and rats.   Here, as with humans, one finds both more sex expression and more curiosity or "enterprise" also associated with high dominance.   However, at least in humans, we have no evidence that dominance is associated with intrinsically stronger sex urge, but only with more defiance of convention or religious authority.

*Source Trait F.   Surgency vs. Desurgency (or Anxious, Agitated Melancholy).*

| *F+* | *F−* |
|---|---|
| Cheerful, joyous | vs. Depressed, pessimistic |
| Sociable, responsive | vs. Seclusive, retiring |
| Energetic | vs. Subdued, languid |
| Humorous, witty | vs. Dull, phlegmatic |
| Talkative | vs. Taciturn, introspective |
| Placid | vs. Worrying, unable to relax, obsessional |
| Resourceful, original | vs. Slow to accept the situation |
| Adaptable | vs. Bound by habit, rigid |
| Showing equanimity | vs. Unstable mood level |
| Trustful, sympathetic, open | vs. Suspicious, brooding, narrow |

As the title indicates, the extreme low endowments in this source trait apparently correspond to the clinical syndrome of anxiety hysteria and, ultimately, agitated melancholia.   The individual very low in *F* feels miserable for no reason, cannot be carefree, and becomes sensitively introspective. There is also evidence of correlation with brooding, suspicion, anger, and disgust, with extreme correctness and conventionality of behavior, with increase of nervous habits and "general neuroticism."   It is not certain, on the other hand, that extreme high *F* alone is mania—at least it is not what Moore (12) has isolated as "noneuphoric mania."

Probably people vary more from day to day in this trait than in any other; for it affects a group of trait-elements probably identifiable with those affected by the mood changes which we call elation and depression.   Nevertheless it is certain that (*a*) inter-individual differences are large compared with intra-individual differences, (*b*) that each individual tends to oscillate about a characteristic level, and (*c*) that certain physiological measures, notably alkalinity of saliva and low concentration of cholinesterase (a chemical affecting ease of nervous conduction) are correlated with surgency.   Consequently, in spite of function fluctuation, surgency-desurgency level has some tendency toward being a relatively constant individual temperament characteristic.

As the following chapter shows, surgency-desurgency is one of the most important and best defined source traits in the realm of personality, whether the medium of ratings, or questionnaire responses, or objective tests. It is one of the three largest source traits in the surface trait of extraversion-introversion. Desurgency is positively correlated with age, at least over the late adolescent range.

*Source Trait G. Positive Character vs. Dependent Character.*

| G+ | G− |
|---|---|
| Persevering, determined | vs. Quitting, fickle |
| Responsible | vs. Frivolous, immature |
| Insistently ordered | vs. Relaxed, indolent |
| Attentive to people | vs. Neglectful of social chores |
| Emotionally stable | vs. Changeable |

This factor has much resemblance to *C* on the one hand and *K* on the other, and it is sometimes difficult to separate it from either of them. However, it shows as an independent factorial dimension different from the mere emotional stability of *C* or the intellectual poise and integration of *K*, and is disinguished from both by a certain forcefulness and emotional integration of purposes. In some countries, notably Germany and to some extent in America and the British Public Schools, it corresponds to the commonly understood meaning of "Character."

*Source Trait H. Adventurous Cyclothymia vs. Withdrawn Schizothymia.*

| H+ | H− |
|---|---|
| Adventurous, likes meeting people | vs. Shy, timid, withdrawn |
| Shows strong interest in opposite sex | vs. Little interest in opposite sex |
| Gregarious, genial, responsive | vs. Aloof, cold, self-contained |
| Kindly, friendly | vs. Hard, hostile |
| Frank | vs. Secretive |
| Impulsive | vs. Inhibited, conscientious |
| Likes to "get into the swim" | vs. Recoils from life |
| Self-confident, debonnaire | vs. Lacking confidence |
| Carefree | vs. Careful, considerate |

Just as there were three related factors—*C*, *G*, and *K*—in the realm of character so there seem to be three distinct influences—*A*, *H*, and *L*—in the cyclothyme-schizothyme region, but here the differences can be seen to have possible correspondence with existing clinical or other distinctions. For example, *A*−, *H*−, and *L*− have marked resemblance respectively to catatonic schizophrenia, simple or hebephrenic schizophrenia, and paranoid schizophrenia. They also have distinct questionnaire counterparts (Chap. 4).

Alternatively *A* and *H* may turn out to be distinguished respectively as the environmental-mold pattern and the constitutional, hereditary source trait in schizothymeness. For in the extreme form of schizothyme behavior, namely, schizophrenia, it is well recognized that both hereditary and environmental factors play a part, and it is these factors which factor analysis may here have separated.

Descriptively the present factor, *H*, differs from *A* principally in carrying some adventurousness, seeking of the limelight, impulsiveness, frivolous, playful lack of conscientiousness, much positive interest in people, and strong sex interest, at the cyclothyme pole. At the same time the schizothyme pole loads *inflexibility* and hostility less and withdrawing *timidity* and shyness more. Essentially we have an adventurous, carefree warmth opposed to an aloof, withdrawing, timid mistrustfulness.

*Source Trait I. Sensitive, Infantile, Imaginative Emotionality vs. Mature, Tough Poise.*

| *I+* | *I−* |
|---|---|
| Demanding, impatient | vs. Emotionally mature |
| Dependent, immature | vs. Independent-minded |
| Aesthetically fastidious | vs. Lacking artistic feeling |
| Introspective, imaginative | vs. Unaffected by "fancies" |
| Intuitive, sensitively imaginative | vs. Practical, logical |
| Gregarious, attention-seeking | vs. Self-sufficient |
| Frivolous | vs. Responsible |

This source trait has not been foreshadowed by any type distinction in the history of psychology unless by some aspects of William James's *Tender vs. Tough-mindedness.* But it is well confirmed by independent researches. It has distinct resemblance to what is commonly called the "artistic temperament" and also to femininity and perhaps to the clinical picture of hyperthyroidism (see Chap. 7). Because of its complexity the descriptive title of the *I* factor (above) has to be rather long.

There is, about the positive *I*-factor endowment, a suggestion of infantilism, of sensitivity, and of that lability of mind which goes with far-ranging imagination. On the negative pole of this source trait we find maturity and responsibility but also a certain rigidity and smugness. The indications at present are that this is not a factor of goodness of dynamic integration or character soundness (like source traits *C* or *G*) but a factor of temperament. It is just possible, from evidence not summarizable here, that it is connected with sex-hormone balance, along the masculinity-femininity axis. For we know (see Chap. 10) that members of either sex vary along this androgen-estrogen hormone continuum.

Source trait *J* is as yet insufficiently confirmed for introductory study.

*Source Trait K. Socialized, Cultured Mind vs. Boorishness.* This has been found to load:

|  $K+$ | $K-$ |
|---|---|
| Intellectual interests, analytical | vs. Unreflective, narrow |
| Polished, poised, composed | vs. Awkward, socially clumsy |
| Independent-minded | vs. Going with the crowd |
| Conscientious, idealistic | vs. Lacking sense of any social duty |
| Aesthetic and musical tastes | vs. Lacking aesthetic interests |
| Introspective, sensitive | vs. Crude |

Among the wider ramifications indicated are, on the left: greater resistance to suggestion, large vocabulary (with less resort to slang clichés), inclination to study personalities, interest in current social problems, more interest in intellectual matters than in athletics (for their own sake), inclination to take the initiative and lead in group activities, and tendency to take an "advanced" rather than a conservative social viewpoint.

This source trait is shown by its correlations to be distinct from native intelligence ($B$ factor) with which it might otherwise be confused. Most probably it is the environmental-mold pattern arising from the influence of a more cultured home background and good education—though one must consider also (*a*) a temperamental origin and (*b*) a possible identification with the outward signs of strong superego development.

The remaining factors, of comparatively small variance will be listed only briefly.

*Source Trait L.   Trustful Cyclothymia vs. Paranoia.*

| $L+$ | $L-$ |
|---|---|
| Trustful | vs. Suspicious |
| Understanding | vs. Jealous |
| Composed | vs. Bashful |

The independence of this factor, in relation to the other two schizothyme factors, raises the question of whether the abnormal extreme of this factor—presumably paranoia—should be recognized as a distinct disease entity from the schizophrenias.

*Source Trait M.   Bohemian Unconcernedness vs. Conventional Practicality.*

| $M+$ | $M-$ |
|---|---|
| Unconventional, eccentric | vs. Conventional |
| Aesthetically fastidious | vs. Conventional |
| Sensitively imaginative | vs. Lacking artistic feeling |
| Undependable | vs. Dependable |
| Undisturbed by practical considerations, unworried | vs. Responding to practical appeals, worried |
| Fitful hysterical upsets | vs. Unemotional |

This is a somewhat subtle pattern, showing in $M+$ apparent paradoxes such as social effrontery along with emotional dependence and exhibitionism.

The term "Bohemian" is carried temporarily as best indicating to most people the total pattern. Investigation of this pattern by factorizing new specially chosen variables is needed.

*Source Trait N.  Sophistication vs. Simplicity.*

|  $N+$  |  $N-$  |
| --- | --- |
| Polished, socially skillful vs. | Clumsy, awkward |
| Exact mind vs. | Vague (sentimental) mind |
| Cool, aloof vs. | Attentive to people |
| Aesthetically fastidious vs. | Lacking definite artistic preferences |

This, one of the more restricted factors, has shown itself most clearly in groups of women, but since it has questionnaire and objective-test associations among men too, it may be regarded as a general factor of some importance in personality. It appears to reflect some tendency to "hard-headed rationalism," independence of mind, and trained "efficient" thinking (but not love of culture or spiritual qualities).

### 5. THE INTEGRATION OF SOURCE-TRAIT MEASUREMENTS

**The Relative Variance Contribution of Source Traits.** Further psychological implications of each of the above factors will become evident as we study special problems such as delinquency, neurosis, infant development, adjustment to occupation, physiological associations, and so on. Before developing further the meaning of these source traits individually, however, it is necessary to take stock of certain general problems, notably their relationships to one another and the manner of their use in measurement.

As mentioned above, the practice has been followed in the standard list of lettering the *BR* factors in alphabetical order, that with greatest contribution to individual differences *in a collection of trait elements sampled evenly from the personality sphere* being given first place. Thus factors *A*—Cyclothymia vs. Schizothymia—and *B*—General Mental Capacity vs. Mental Defect—seem to affect more of the personality than does any other factor. The order must not be accepted too rigidly: in different samples, ages, and social groups it will vary somewhat. For example, among college students, selected for intelligence to some extent, factor *B* is found to contribute much less to individual differences (variance) in personality.

That factors *A* and *B* should be found so statistically important is well in accord with the historical fact of their being the major syndromes first noticed in clinical work. Intelligence and mental defect have long been the objects of clinical and general study, while cyclothymia and schizothymia, as the major divisions of the psychoses (Chap. 1), have been the most important established dichotomy in psychiatry ever since Bleuler's searching eye saw these patterns underlying so many pathological syndromes.

By contrast to these massive influences, the source trait $I$ contributes only a moderate amount to individual differences in the personality sphere and has apparently never been clinically noted, while the factors $L$, $M$, and $N$ contribute insufficiently to justify more than the above bald listing. The remaining factors known to research ($D$, Infantile, Sthenic Emotionality; $J$, Thoughtful Neurasthenia; and $O$, Free Anxiety (worrying and suspicion)), too slight for description here, may be studied by the student elsewhere (7,8,9). Though some sixteen to twenty source traits are today detectable with more exact methods the twelve described above cover most of the variance of personality.

**Measuring a Source Trait.** To measure an individual's endowment in any source trait as pointed out dealing with the specification equation, we should first obtain measures for him on *the trait-elements which that factor loads highly*, *i.e.*, in which it is most manifested, and then compound these part scores in a way which allows greater weight to those trait-elements which have the higher loadings. But for most practical purposes it is sufficient just to throw them into a pool, *i.e.*, to average them. Thus when we measure a person's general intelligence (factor $g$ among abilities, called $B$ among personality factors) we take scores on a number of different subtests (trait-elements) such as synonyms, vocabulary, number series, classifications, spatial sense, etc., and average them (literally, we sum them only). But strictly we should take a weighted sum, the weights being derived from the relative loadings of these subtests in the factor $g$. The difference between this and an average proves too slight to justify all the trouble.

The chief *personality* source traits have so far been expressed in terms of life records, very largely in ratings by observers, *i.e.*, in $BR$ data, but the estimation of a source trait proceeds on exactly the same lines whether it is based on ratings, as here, or on questionnaires and objective tests as in the next chapter. In each case we find for that individual his *level*, in terms of standard scores, on six to a dozen of the most highly loaded trait-elements and then get a weighted or unweighted average as the individual's source-trait score.

**Expressing a Pattern of Source Traits.** The individual's personality profile may then be expressed in terms of his basic source traits, as illustrated in the upper part of Diagram 13. Such profiles or patterns have been much used in vocational guidance, in which the technique of fitting an individual to an occupation becomes in the first instance that of fitting the wards in a key to those in a lock.

If, however, we wish to keep to the mode of representation hitherto used in our factorial discussions, which represents multiple attributes by multi-dimensional space, then we shall prefer the style of representing individual endowments shown in the lower part of Diagram 13. That is to say, the person represented by a profile in the upper diagram will now be represented by a point in eight-dimensional space, with ordinates corresponding to factor endowments. Since an eight-dimensional framework cannot easily be represented in the two provided by one page, this is naturally less convenient for most practical purposes than the profile system. However, it is of theoretical

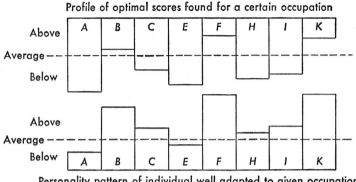

Profile of optimal scores found for a certain occupation

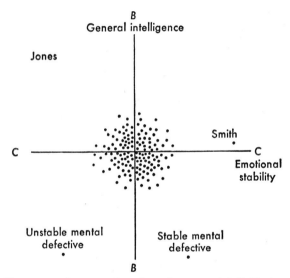

Personality pattern of individual well adapted to given occupation

DIAGRAM 13. Two ways of representing the uniqueness of individual combination of common traits.

interest and importance to follow through this multi-dimensional representation, and the principle can be sufficiently illustrated by taking two dimensions only. Let us therefore take factors *C* and *B*—*i.e.*, character integration and intelligence—as in the lower part of Diagram 13. Therein Smith, who is averagely intelligent and very emotionally stable, would be represented by the point nearly opposite the origin of the intelligence axis and high on the

*C* axis.   Jones, who is brilliant but a psychopath, impulsive, and unreliable, would fall in the upper left quadrant; and so on for the other cases represented.

This diagram reminds one that it *is not necessary to deal with unique traits in order to represent a unique personality.*   By the use of common traits— dimensions the same for all people—the uniqueness of each person is represented, as Wolfle (14) has pointed out, by a uniqueness of position, *i.e.*, of combination, and there is enough room in twelve-dimensional space for the world's population to be represented without any two points coinciding!

**Summary of the Implications of the Specification Equation.**   In the light of the above illustration and of the more concrete acquaintance with source traits gained in this chapter, it would now be advantageous to return to the specification equation introduced in the previous chapter, to bring out more clearly its nature and implications.

It has been pointed out that the common and unique traits used in that equation derive from different factorizations, respectively on *R*- and *P*-technique bases, and are introduced in different circumstances—the former when predicting individual differences, the latter when predicting time changes within one individual.

In the universe of common traits the uniqueness of the individual is therefore a uniqueness of combination of common traits, as discussed above. Thus two individuals, *h* and *i*, may be represented as to their performances *P* in a situation *j* as follows (neglecting specifics and restricting to two general source traits see page 25):

$$P_{jh} = S_{1j}T_{1h} + S_{2j}T_{2h} + \cdots$$
$$P_{ji} = S_{1j}T_{1i} + S_{2j}T_i + \cdots$$

The two personalities involved in these two equations are:

$$T_{1h} + T_{2h} + \cdots$$

and

$$T_{1i} + T_{2i} + \cdots$$

representing different patterns of endowment in the common traits $T_1 + T_2 +$, etc., and representable either as two profiles or as two points in space, as illustrated above.[7]

Now the failure to distinguish between unique traits and unique combinations, as well as the inability to imagine the consequences of the latter, sometimes leads to objections to the whole theory of common source traits, as

---

[7] The student interested in the statistics of factor analysis will notice that the above specification equation if continued would end in a term involving $T_j$—a *specific factor* peculiar to the performance $P_j$. For simplicity, and because at this stage of personality research there can be little interest in what is entirely specific, we have omitted these specific factors (of which there might be millions) from further presentation.

instanced in: "It is impossible to speak of a common trait, *e.g.*, of intelligence, because intelligence is not the same in one person as in another." This assertion of a difference of quality does not entirely lack justice: it only confuses a sound observation with an unsound inference. For a particular endowment in the source trait $T$, (in this case $B$, or intelligence) does indeed manifest itself very differently accordingly as it is combined with high or low endowment in $T_2$ (say, with high or low emotional stability with schizothyme or cyclothyme temperament and so on.) What the empathic psychologist means by differences in quality between equal "levels" of a particular source trait is essentially this difference of factor combination and context.

Similarly there are differences between equal performances of any two persons in the situation $P_j$. The situational indices $S_{1j}$, $S_{2j}$, etc., are the same for all people, but since the endowments in $T_1$ and $T_2$ are different (namely, $T_{1h}$ and $T_{1i}$, $T_{2h}$ and $T_{2i}$) the relative contributions of the two terms $S_1T_1$ and $S_2T_2$ to the total, $P_j$, are different in the two cases. For example, if $P_j$ is performance on a tennis court, and $T_1$ and $T_2$ are respectively general intelligence and general dexterity, two well-matched opponents may be equal in score because what one lacks in dexterity he makes up for by intelligent strategy. The quality or styles of $P_{ji}$ and $P_{jh}$ are different: their effects on the given specific, defined performance score are the same.

Many examples of this varying role in specific performances of the source traits already described in $BR$ data above will doubtless occur to the student as he looks for their operation in everyday life and in people known to him. A rather striking example is that revealed in the action of the cyclothyme factor $A$ and the surgent factor $F$ in contributing to the sociable talkativeness which occurs in the surface trait of "extraversion." Let $P_j$ be the situation in which two comparative strangers are thrown together and in which talkative sociability or silence constitute the extremes of a continuum of performance. Both $A$ and $F$ have considerable weights in the specification equation but it will be noticed that the talkativeness which supervenes through an individual having much $A$ is very different in quality from that of the individual who performs largely through high $F$. The cyclothyme's talkativeness is that of a warm, gentle, and sympathetic sociability, which may be cheerful or sad, whereas the talkativeness of the surgent individual is cheerful, energetic, and placidly impersonal. Conversely, the "withdrawal" of the desurgent individual is determined largely by depression and absence of energy or ideas, while the withdrawal of the schizothyme is a shy, tense silence.

Three further implications of the specification equation have been sufficiently indicated already and need only summary statements for their revision, as follows: (*a*) any source trait (other than an absolute specific) because it has some slight loading in almost any performance, may be said to enter in some degree into every act. Thus a trait is not a "piece of behavior" but a

style, a motive, or an ability which is *detectable in every "piece of behavior";*
(*b*) it follows that the total personality, in all its source-trait dimensions
(except an absolute specific), enters into any act; (*c*) the *situational indices*
(or factor loadings) which weight the dynamic, temperamental, and ability
traits entering any specification equation correspond in verbal expression of
the same psychological facts to the adjectives we should use to describe the
"meaning" of a situation. Those weighting abilities we should call "complexities" of the situation, those qualifying the dynamic terms we should call
the "incentive" values in the situations, and so on.

Finally, it is necessary to expand a little on the implication of the statement
briefly introduced earlier that the source traits, though independent in nature
and function, may themselves be somewhat correlated. In geometrical terms
this means that the coordinates instead of being orthogonal are sometimes
*oblique*. In general terms this means that a set of trait indicators $a1$, $a2$, $a3$,
etc., simultaneously covary in a source trait $A$ and another set $b1$, $b2$, $b3$,
etc., covary in a pattern constituting a second source trait $B$. But although
$A$ and $B$ are independent organizers they may themselves be correlated
because they are both subject to some larger outside influence. Thus persons in an airplane $A$ may be functionally unitary in that they all move
together, and persons in another airplane $B$ are similarly considered a unity
(the crew) in virtue of their covariation, but $A$ and $B$ may be part of the same
squadron and have some degree of common movement, so that their independence is not complete. There is evidence that source traits $B$ and $C$ are
thus appreciably correlated. So that although the trait-indicators of one
factor correlate highly, *e.g.*, as manifestations of intelligence, and another set
correlate highly as manifestations of, say, emotional maturity, the two source
traits are *themselves* slightly correlated through some common social or genetic
influence. This (see Chap. 14) creates a fair probability that the person
above average in intelligence will also be above average in emotional control.

The tendency of nature to present us with oblique factors produces changes
in the specification equation in relation to the estimation of factors which are
too complex, however, to be followed up here and the student is referred to
special detailed discussions (see 7,10,15, Chap. 2) and to the last chapter of
this book. This observation that personality traits apparently *interact*, even
sometimes to the extent of one trait appearing to act *catalytically* upon the
growth of another (as, for example, when certain kinds of mental conflict can
only begin to develop when a person has sufficient intelligence to perceive
the problem) has suggested to some psychologists that a multiplicative rather
than an additive relation should be expressed among factors in the specification equation. Mathematicians recognize, however, that summation formulae are, at least over moderate ranges, adequate approximations for
corresponding product formulae. Over no range yet has the additive for-

mula been found erroneous. If further, more exact work than the present exploratory researches reveals discrepancies it will be time enough then to experiment with modified specification equations. Meanwhile, the interaction of source traits, beyond that shown additively in predicting performance from the simple, orthogonal specification equation, is adequately taken care of by the known tendency of source traits to have some degree of obliqueness (correlation) through extraneous, second order (see (7), Chap. 12) factors.

## 6. SUMMARY

1. Mental measurement has the same philosophical basis as any other measurement—that if differences can be perceived they can be quantified in units of some kind. Organic measurements differ from inorganic measurements largely in (*a*) showing more "function fluctuation" from occasion to occasion, and (*b*) offering more difficulty to the discovery of the essential dimensions about which measurement have to be oriented.

2. The traits that are measured, of whatever kind they may be, are *mental structures*, the functioning of which is seen as actual behavior. A mental structure is an inference or construct from behavior. Structure in this sense is not to be confused with other uses, *e.g.*, as in so-called "structuralism" or in the physical sense of "neural structure."

3. The data in which personality measurement is initially obtained are of three kinds: (*a*) life-record material (including *BR* data), (*b*) self-rating, introspective, questionnaire test material, and (*c*) objective-test material.

4. Life-record (*LR*) data deal with personality *in situ* in everyday life and record the frequency or intensity of certain standard acts, generally of social or general importance. Behavior rating by observers is a rough means of estimation in this medium, but can be made as accurate and reproducible as test data if certain stringent rating conditions can be maintained.

5. Self-rating (*SR* or *Q*) questionnaire data give patterns of "mental interiors" corresponding to the behavioral exteriors of the other two methods. Self-ratings can be treated in two distinct ways: (*a*) as "face-value" assertions, which remain in the solipsistic continuum of introspection and can only be useful scientifically in very special circumstances; (*b*) as "indirect," data, of inferred meaning, in which case such questionnaires can be used, not too satisfactorily, as objective tests.

6. An objective test (*T* or *OT* data) is a defined, objectively scorable, universally reproducible situation, which is used to predict behavior in *other* situations. In the realm of personality, such tests are only just beginning to yield significant validities and to be related by understood principles to the source traits they measure.

7. About twenty common source traits are now known in the realm of life-record, *BR* data, and they account for the greater part of the total variance

in a "stratified," even sample of indicators from the whole personality sphere. They thus suffice to measure most individual differences and to "block in" a specific personality to a first approximation. They have been listed in a standard index by alphabetical symbols and descriptive titles.

8. Only ten of these factors have been confirmed by several researches. These and two others confirmed in two distinct researches are of sufficient magnitude (variance) to describe in this text. They are:

*Source Trait A*.  Cyclothymia vs. Schizothymia
*Source Trait B*.  General Mental Capacity vs. Mental Defect
*Source Trait C*.  Emotionally Stable Character vs. General Emotionality
*Source Trait E*.  Dominance vs. Submissiveness
*Source Trait F*.  Surgency vs. Desurgency
*Source Trait G*.  Positive Character vs. Dependent Character
*Source Trait H*.  Adventurous Cyclothymia vs. Withdrawn Schizothymia
*Source Trait I*.  Infantile, Imaginative Emotionality vs. Mature, Tough, Poise
*Source Trait K*.  Socialized, Cultured Mind vs. Boorishness
*Source Trait L*.  Trustful Cyclothymia vs. Paranoid Schizothymia
*Source Trait M*.  Bohemian Unconcern vs. Conventional Practicality
*Source Trait N*.  Sophistication vs. Simplicity

9. The uniqueness of personality can be represented either in unique (*P*-technique) traits or by the unique combinations of common traits. It is this uniqueness of combination of trait endowments in the specification equation which accounts for differences in "style" in otherwise equal performances by different persons, and which enters into any single act, in which all personality traits are involved.

10. Closer examination of the findings on source traits in the specification equation shows that though factors are, in a primary sense, independent, they are also to some extent correlated. The interaction of source traits in personality which occurs additively, perhaps multiplicatively, and certainly by intercorrelation from second-order factors, is worthy of increasing study.

### QUESTIONS AND EXERCISES

1. Describe the varieties of observation which come under the life-record method of measuring personality traits.

2. Describe the advantages and disadvantages of (*a*) self-ratings, (*b*) objective tests, and compare their reliabilities with those of life-record methods.

3. Compare the pattern of highly loaded trait elements in the Cyclothymia v. Schizothymia source trait, *A*, with that of the clinical syndrome of schizophrenia (Chap. 1) and discuss causes of resemblance and difference.

4. List the most important conditions for obtaining good ratings, by observers, of personality traits.

5. From the nature of the source trait *C* (emotionally stable character) in what particular real-life situations (describe at least four) would you expect its presence or absence to be important?  Give full reasons for each.

6. Write a list of twenty common situations (title only) in the life of a student in which

you would expect the reactions of a markedly surgent person to differ considerably from those of a desurgent person.

7. One can observe that the "style" with which individuals respond to the same test or real-life situation is often different even when their scores are numerically equal. How is this phenomenon clarified by our understanding of the action of source traits?

8. In a certain game, performance has been found to be largely predictable from three source traits only, as follows:

$$P = 0.7B + 0.4C + 0.6Z$$

where $B$ is the intelligence source trait, $C$ is the emotionally stable character source trait, and $Z$ is a skill specific to the game. If Smith, who has the same specific skill endowment as Jones but lesser intelligence, equals him consistently in the game, what can be deduced about other features of his personality?

9. Work out the standard score, in the above game, for Roberts and Hanson, whose standard scores in source traits $B$, $C$, and $Z$ are, respectively, 1.3, 0.2, 0.7 and 0.5, −2.3, −0.8. (The situational indexes, of course, remain unchanged.)

10. Discuss the relation of the pattern of loadings of a source trait to population sample, and particularly to changes in age, education, and variability. Illustrate by reference to the source trait of general mental capacity.

## BIBLIOGRAPHY

1. ALLPORT, G. W.: *The Use of Personal Documents in Psychological Science*, Social Science Research Council, Committee on Public Administration, Washington, D.C., 1942.
2. ALLPORT, G. W., and H. S. ODBERT: Trait-Names, a Psycholexical Study, *Psychol. Monog.*, 47: 1–171, 1936.
3. BURT, C. L.: The Assessment of Personality, *Brit. J. educ. Psychol.*, 15: 107–121, 1945.
4. BURT, C. L.: *The Young Delinquent*, University of London Press, Ltd., Bickley, Kent, England, 1948.
5. CARTER, G. C.: Student Personalities as Instructors See Them, *Purdue Univ. Stud. Higher Educ.*, 54: 46, 1945.
6. CATTELL, R. B.: An Objective Test of Character Temperament, *J. gen. Psychol.*, 25: 59–73, 1941.
6a. CATTELL, R. B.: The Diagnosis and Classification of Neurotic States: A Reinterpretation of Eysenck's Factors, *J. nerv. ment. Dis.*, 102: 576–589, 1945.
7. CATTELL, R. B.: *Description and Measurement of Personality*, World Book Company, Yonkers, New York, 1946.
8. CATTELL, R. B.: Confirmation and Clarification of Primary Personality Factors, *Psychometrika*, 12 (No. 3): 1947.
9. CATTELL, R. B.: Primary Personality Factors in Women Compared with Those in Men, *British J. Psychol.*, 5: 1948.
9a. FISKE, D.: Consistency of the Factorial Structure of Personality Ratings from Different Sources, *J. abnorm. soc. Psychol.*, 44: 329–344, 1949.
10. KRETSCHMER, E.: *The Psychology of Men of Genius*, Kegan Paul, Trench, Trubner & Co., London, 1931.
11. KORNHAUSER, A.: Replies by Psychologists to a Short Questionnaire on Personality Inventories and the Rorschach Test, *Educ. and Psych. Meas.*, 5: 317, 1945.
12. MOORE, T. V.: The Empirical Determination of Certain Syndromes underlying Praecox and Manic-depressive Psychoses, *Amer. J. Psychiat.*, 9: 719–738, 1930.
13. SYMONDS, P. M.: *Diagnosing Personality and Conduct*, D. Appleton-Century Company, Inc., New York, 1931.
14. WOLFLE, D.: Factor Analysis in the Study of Personality, *J. abnorm. soc. Psychol.*, 37: 393–397, 1942.

# CHAPTER 4

## MEASURING PERSONALITY BY SELF-RATINGS AND OBJECTIVE TESTS

1. Source Traits in Personal Inventories
2. Source Traits in Attitudes and Interests
3. Objective-test Source Traits in the Realm of Character
4. Objective-test Source Traits in the Realm of Temperament
5. Other Objective-test Traits Important in Personality
6. A Review of Objective-test Methods
7. The Matching of Personality Factors in Different Media
8. Summary

### 1. SOURCE TRAITS IN PERSONAL INVENTORIES

**The Matching of** *LR-*, *SR-*, **and** *OT*-**data Factors.** Although the source traits found in life-record observations (including *BR* data) have the satisfying quality of extending over the visible range of behavior in everyday life and of being rooted in "indicators" of practical importance, they lack a certain appeal to the psychologist possessed by the questionnaire and objective-test traits now to be studied. For the psychologist feels that he has greater control over "tests," and that they have greater utility. This is obvious in terms of practical utility, in that he can always get *measures* of a particular person when often he cannot get good rating or life-record data. It is also true in regard to theoretical advance, in that he can hope to shape tests to give purer, more saturated measures of the nature of a source trait and thus test hypotheses about its character. Moreover, he has the justifiable suspicion of the behavior-rating segment of *LR* data that, though it has wide currency and can be very accurate under proper conditions, it is frequently merely counterfeited by "ratings" on spurious foundations, made without proper care for the conditions of accuracy.

The survey to be made in this chapter of the source traits discovered in the two kinds of test media—self-rating or questionnaire tests, and objective tests—will seek constantly to relate the source traits found in the three media. It is the writer's contention that any sufficiently broad and important personality trait will show itself almost equally well in any of these media. That is to say, a factor found in life-record data should be identifiable with one found in terms of mental interiors in a questionnaire or in a loading

74

pattern in objective tests. It will not strictly be the same *factor*, for it is in a different set of measures, but the matching of any two such factors, by a very high correlation between their estimates in the two kinds of measures, will indicate that the same basic personality trait is at work in both.

In addition, however, we might expect some factors to be specific to the medium, especially in the case of test media where very similar performances can readily be multiplied in the test battery to make a special, narrow factor. For example, one might find a test factor in "dexterity with tools" or "acuity of vision" which would not appear in broad, life-record data, or one might find a *Q* factor in questionnaire or attitude material dealing with attitudes to the history of psychology, which would not show in test or life-record patterns.

The procedure here will be first to set out the principal factors found in *Q* data, then the principal factors in *T* data, reserving to the end—apart from passing references—the discussion of how these are related to one another and to *LR* data factors.

**The Varieties and Limitations of Self-rating Methods.** The advantages and disadvantages of the self-rating method have been discussed in the previous chapter, and may be summed up briefly by saying that results are easy to get, but that, *except in special conditions*, they are not scientifically acceptable as *behavioral measures* of personality, as distinct from *introspections* on mental interiors. The immense activity shown in the use of questionnaires in applied psychology is therefore likely to impress the discerning student less with the importance of the questionnaire than with the defective understanding and support of research and scientific accuracy by many workers in the applied field.

This is not, of course, a criticism of all paper-and-pencil tests in personality, which may, indeed, employ situations reaching the highest validities, and it is not a criticism of the questionnaire when the answers are validated merely as verbal behavior and not taken at face value, *i.e.*, as supposing honesty and insight. Some tests, appearing superficially as self-ratings, are actually projection or ego-defense tests; others, like the *biographical inventory*, ask merely for facts of personal history (*e.g.*, Were you ever a member of the Boy Scouts?), which questions are still subject to differences in honesty, but not in insight. The self-rating test sections of this chapter, however, deal strictly with self-rating devices, *i.e.*, with those supposing honesty and insight, the remaining techniques being considered in the further section on objective tests.

The chief fields which have so far been surveyed by what may broadly be called self-rating methods, requiring honesty and insight in the subjects, are (*a*) neurotic and general personal inventory behavior, (*b*) interests, (*c*) attitudes. This section will deal with the syndromes or source traits found in the first of these, leaving interests and attitudes to the next section.

**Personality Areas Covered by Questionnaires.** The use of the questionnaire arose most naturally in, and still best belongs to, the confessional atmosphere of the consulting room, where the neurotic, to escape from his misery, is willing to answer embarrassingly personal questions as truthfully as possible. Consequently the majority of questionnaire items experimented upon have reference to neurotic traits. Indeed it is only in the past decade, in connection with military selection and some industrial projects, that a sufficiency of questions applicable to other than neurotic aspects of personality has been tried.

Consequently, in *SR* data generally we cannot be certain that some important dimensions of personality have not been omitted; indeed in the attitude and interest tests as so far experimented upon it is certain that large areas of important attitudes and interests have not been brought into the factor space.

In behavior ratings the "personality sphere" concept—that is, the assurance of all aspects of personality being sampled, through systematic employment of all personality traits in the dictionary (5)—offers a guarantee that no major dimension of personality has been omitted. Although we cannot be certain of this in questionnaire data, and although the questions are undoubtedly concentrated more densely in the region of neurotic behavior, so many neurotic syndromes are extremes of normal patterns that it is unlikely that more than a few major normal dimensions of personality have escaped measurement.

**Item Analysis and More Refined Approaches.** Unlike objective tests or behavior ratings the questionnaire permits its score to be broken down into a number of "items," each being usually one question with a yes or no answer, and quite a number of "techniques" have grown up in psychometrics in connection with this somewhat artificial aspect of the self-rating approach. One of the earliest procedures for evaluating and improving this type of test has been given the name of "item analysis." By this technique the designer gets together a lot of questions which he considers would test the syndrome he has in mind, *e.g.*, anxiety neurosis, or general neurotic tendencies, and then throws away those questions which do not correlate either with some outside criterion or with the "pool" constituted by the sum of *all* the questions. Actually, correlation coefficients were seldom used in many early studies. Instead, the subjects given the general test were divided into a higher and a lower scoring half, according to the sum of the whole pool of questions. Then the yes and no answers on each question item were examined separately. If the high scoring half on the whole pool answered yes to a particular question more often than did the lower scoring half, that question was considered good. If not, it was thrown out.

The result of this procedure is obviously to purify the pool, *i.e.*, to make it *homogeneous*, until a single correlation cluster, syndrome, or *surface trait* of items is established. Actually, when two or more distinct surface traits are represented in the original pool this is not an efficient procedure, for several rounds of purification will take place before one of these independent traits becomes represented by a sufficient majority of items to cause the items belonging to the other to be dropped. On the other hand if one analyzes the items against an external criterion it is possible to finish with a "homogeneous test" in Loevinger's sense (24a) or a "scalable" test in Guttman's terminology in which the items are far from being factorially pure.

The student who wishes to examine these issues of item analysis in more detail should follow the literature (1a,24a,41). Our conclusion here will be that the proper role of item analysis is in preparing a test for factor analysis, as Loevinger (24a) suggests.

A test made homogeneous by internal item analysis is still, however, only a composite surface trait, in which some items contribute more to one factor and some to another. But since source traits (factors) are more widely useful and meaningful than surface traits the only satisfactory questionnaire is one in *which every item has been correlated with every other* and factorized. Such questionnaires are rare and we are indebted for the chief analyses of this kind that now exist, mainly to the Guilfords (19,20), Layman (24), Mosier (25), Reyburn and Taylor (27), Vernon (40), and the more recent studies (6) which have led to the sixteen personality factor ("16 P.F.") questionnaire (6a).

Some sixteen or more factors in questionnaires have been discovered in various researches and recorded in the standard index (5). Only the twelve that are considered sufficiently confirmed by three or more researches are briefly described below. Two of these have no clear counterparts in *BR* factors and are apparently much "larger," if not more defined, in the introspective realm than in overt behavior. All are titled by some least common donominator from the titles offered by their discoverers or, where the matching with *BR* factors is adequate, (all but two) by the letter and title of the *BR* factor involved, and in all cases have in parenthesis their number in the standard list (5) of *SR* or *OT* factors.

*Mental Interior of Source Trait A.* *Cyclothymia vs. Schizothymia.* (Called variously "Interest in Understanding Nature" (at the negative end).) Answers as shown contribute to positive pole.

1. Would you rather be an architect or chemist than a banker or office manager?
   *The latter*
2. Do you find it interesting to spend time in analyzing people's motives?  *Yes*
3. Would you rather be a personnel guidance worker or a social-science teacher than a manager in a manufacturing concern or an engineer?  *The former*
4. Do you usually tend to do your planning alone, without suggestions from and discussions with other people?  *No*
5. If the following headlines appeared in equal size in your newspaper which would you attend to more?

   (*a*) Great improvement in market conditions.

   (*b*) Protestant leaders to consult on reconciliation.        (*b*)

The actual questions in this and the other questionnaire patterns given here are more terse than those in the actual questionnaires and would probably not give *identical* results, but they suffice to show most briefly the essential nature of the reports.

This factor, which is apparently also identical with that found in the Strong Occupational Interest Blank, (see interest factors below) has been shown to correlate with *BR* factor *A* only, with which it may be identical. It is certainly easy to see that this natural interest in people and their doings, as opposed to interest in impersonal nature, would arise from the personality characteristics described by Cyclothymia-Schizothymia (page 58).

*Mental Interior of Source Trait C.   Emotionally Stable, Mature Character vs. General Emotionality.*

1. Do offenses against manners and morals by others annoy you, sometimes out of all proportion to their importance?      *No*
2. Do you often feel worried and tense with very little cause?      *No*
3. Does your mind tend to keep steadily on one track in discussion, so that you experience difficulty with people who leap from topic to topic?      *Yes*
4. Do you think the aim of the churches should be:
   (*a*) to bring out moral and charitable tendencies.
   (*b*) to convey a spiritual sense of communion with the highest.      (*b*)
5. Have you ever been a sleepwalker, or been known to do a good deal of talking in your sleep?      *No*
6. Do emotional and exciting situations upset you so that you try to avoid them?
      *No*

In this case the correlation with the *C* factor is lower than that of the corresponding *Q* factors with other *BR* factors and it is evident that the right questions remain to be invented to bring out the emotional stability factor.

*Mental Interior of Source Trait E.   Dominance Ascendance vs. Submissiveness.* (Called "Interest in Guiding People vs. Objective Interests" in *Q* factorization (6) and indexed QI. I*b* (5).)

1. Do you tend to keep in the background on social occasions?      *No*
2. Do you feel not yet well adjusted to life and that very little works out the way it should?      *No*
3. If you saw the following headlines of equal size in your newspaper which would your read?
   (*a*) Threat to constitutional government in foreign country by dictator.
   (*b*) Physicists make important discovery concerning the electron.      (*a*)
4. If something goes wrong and you feel it is not your doing, do you usually (*a*) publicly berate others or (*b*) say it *may* be your fault?      (*a*)

Like the *C* factor the *E* factor of dominance does not come out so clearly in questionnaires, by the questions yet asked, as one might expect from its definiteness as a rating factor.

*Mental Interior of Source Trait F. Surgency vs. Desurgency.* (This has been called by Guilford "Rhathymia" and is listed in the standard *Q*-factor list as QP. XI.)

1. Do you prefer the type of job that offers constant change, travel, and variety, in spite of other drawbacks? *Yes*
2. Are you well described as a happy-go-lucky, carefree, nonchalant individual? *Yes*
3. Do you enjoy being at parties and large gatherings? *Yes*
4. Are you much concerned about what others think of you? *No*
5. Would you prefer to be (*a*) an advertising man, lawyer, or waiter or (*b*) carpenter, aviator, or real-estate salesman? (*a*)

In this case it is easy to see that the mental interior looks much like the surgent exterior.

*Mental Interior of Source Trait G. Positive Character vs. Dependent Character.* (Called "Obsessionally Careful and Considerate" in *Q* factorization (6) and indexed as Q. X (5).)

1. Are you a person who is scrupulously correct in manners and social obligations and likes others to be the same? *Yes*
2. Do you think that the family should be maintained as the basis of society, since one gets more happiness from deep family ties than through many friends and acquaintances? *No*
3. Do you find it interesting to spend time analyzing people's motives? *Yes*
4. Are you cautious and considerate that you do not hurt people's feelings by unconsidered conversational remarks? *Yes*
5. Do you usually keep emotions under good control? *Yes*

The picture here gives us new insight into the *G* factor, which on ratings is not easily distinguished from *C*. We perceive that it is not so much a variable of almost physical emotionality as is *C* and that it involves certain almost obsessional will-training characteristics.

*Mental Interior of Source Trait H. Adventurous Cyclothymia vs. Withdrawn Schizothymia.* (This factor has been called by Guilford *S*, for "Shyness" and by others "Approach-Withdrawal." It is listed in the index (5) as QP. I.)

1. When coming to a new place are you painfully slow at making new friendships? *No*
2. Are you relatively free from self-conscious shyness? *Yes*
3. Are you a talkative person who enjoys any opportunity for verbal expression? *Yes*

4. Do you find it difficult to get up and address or recite before a large group? *No*
5. In conversation do you find it difficult to jump from topic to topic as some people do? *No*
6. Do you occasionally have the uncomfortable feeling that people in the street are watching you? *No*

This factor is well defined and of large variance in questionnaire material as is its behavioral expression, factor *H*, in ratings. In both the ratings and the questionnaire responses there is some tendency to overlap with factor *F*.

*Mental Interior of Source Trait I. Sensitive Imaginative Emotionality vs. Tough Poise.* (Called in *Q* factor "Emotionally Sensitive Self-sufficiency vs. Gregariousness." QP. VIII*a* in the standard list (5).)

1. Are you annoyed by the appearance of some people, *e.g.*, wearing an ill-humored expression, dressing in a slovenly way? *Yes*
2. Can you become so absorbed in creative work or an interesting job that you do not mind a lack of intimate friends? *Yes*
3. In conversation does your mind keep to one track so that you find difficulty in jumping from topic to topic? *Yes*
4. Do you like plenty of excitement in life so that you experience a real craving for it in times of monotony? *No*
5. Are you prevented from sleeping by taking coffee late at night? *Yes*
6. Would you spend a free afternoon in an art gallery or with good scenery rather than in a social meeting or game of cards? *Yes*

The responses indicate a fastidious aversion, *e.g.*, to crude people and occupations, together with interest in self-sufficient or creative activity. This agrees well with the rating picture (see page 63) as also does the evidence of emotional sensitivity (reactive to caffeine, avoiding excitement and disturbance).

*Mental Interior of Source Trait K. Cultured Mind vs. Boorishness.* (Called *Q* data "Liking thinking" and "Thinking." Indexed as QP. XVII (5).)

1. Do you find it interesting to spend time analyzing people's motives? *Yes*
2. Are you interested in serious problems of life and given to discussing them with friends? *Yes*
3. Are you more interested in athletics than in intellectual matters? *No*
4. Do you tend to be more than averagely introspective? *Yes*
5. In regard to any opposition between the scientific theory of evolution and the position of the church regarding the Old Testament which do you follow? *The former*

Thus from the questionnaire one gets a sketch of a serious minded, analytical and "progressive" person which is in good keeping with the correlated behavior rating pattern.

*Mental Interior of Factor L. Paranoid Schizothymia.* (Factor 17 in research (6).)

1. Are you well described as a happy-go-lucky person? *No*
2. When you come to a new place are you rather painfully slow at making new friendships? *Yes*
3. Do you agree that today we need more law and social authority and that the individual should learn to subordinate himself more to social regulation? *No*
4. When traveling would you rather have a friendly guide to show you everything or would you rather have the adventure of traveling alone? *The latter*
5. Are you really fond of poetry, so that you would feel deprived if prevented from reading it? *Yes*

The matching here is not too strongly supported as yet and must be regarded as tentative.

*Mental Interior of Factor M. Bohemian Unconcernedness vs. Conventional Practicality.* (Called "Hysteroid Complacency" in (6). Uncertain match with QP. VI*b* in standard index (5).)

1. Which would you rather do on a fine afternoon?
   (*a*) Enjoy the beauty of an art gallery or some fine scenery.
   (*b*) Enjoy a social meeting or a game of cards. (*a*)
2. Do you generally succeed in keeping your emotions, of whatever kind, under very good control? *No*
3. Do you tend to dislike being waited on in personal matters (*i.e.*, by personal servants)? *No*
4. Do you think that racial characters have more real influence in shaping the individual and the nation than most people believe? *No*
5. Do you ever have a fit of dread or anxiety for no ascertainable reason? *Yes*
6. Do you ever try to bluff your way past a guard or doorman? *Yes*
7. Have you ever been known to be a sleepwalker or to do a good deal of talking in your sleep? *Yes*

This factor is one of large variance in the questionnaire though it falls as far down the alphabet as *M* in the ratings; but the match is good. It suggests some resemblance to the "belle indifference" of the conversion hysteric, alternating with fits of anxiety through awkward situations created by the unrealism of the "indifference" to social requirements.

*Mental Interior of Source Trait N. Genteel Sophistication vs. Rough Simplicity.* (Q factor called "Hardheaded rationalism" and "Intellectual leadership" in (6). Indexed as QP. XVIII and QA. II.)

1. If the following headlines appeared in equal size in your newspaper which would you attend to more:
   (*a*) Great improvement in market conditions.
   (*b*) Protestant leaders to consult on reconciliation. (*a*)
2. Do you agree more with (*a*) sterilization of mental defectives and routine vaccination of nursery school children or (*b*) abolition of capital punishment and abolition of alcohol and tobacco? (*a*)

3. Would you unhesitatingly complain to a waiter or the manager if served bad food in a restaurant?                                                              *Yes*
4. Are you more interested in athletics than in intellectual matters?        *No*

These responses indicate at the pole which had been called "sophisticated" in the ratings a certain freedom from sentimentality and a tendency to cold realism and practicality.

*Mental Interior of Source Trait O.  Contingent Title: Free Anxiety.*  (Variously called "General Neurotic Maladjustment," "Depressive Tendency," "Emotionality and Self Depreciation; labeled QP. IV in the standard index (5).)

1. Do you have frequent periods of feeling lonely even when with people?     *Yes*
2. Do you often feel just miserable and in low spirits for no sufficient reason?  *Yes*
3. Do you feel not well adjusted to life and that very little works out the way it should?                                                                          *Yes*
4. Do you suffer from insomnia and take a long time to fall asleep at night?   *Yes*
5. Do you feel that on several occasions in recent years you have been found fault with more than you deserve?                                                 *Yes*
6. Are you troubled by useless stray thoughts that run through your mind uncalled for?                                                                         *Yes*

This $Q$ factor is one of the largest in variance, and in the two most recent studies it has been *the* largest.  Something of a riddle is presented, therefore, by the failure to find any $BR$ factor corresponding to it other than the very slight one, loading ratings of worrying and suspicious, mentioned above. It was at one time thought that this would correlate with the neurasthenia-like $BR$ factor $J$, but possibly $O$ is the true factor of neurasthenia, for this $Q$ factor is very close to the consulting-room picture of neurasthenic fatigue.

The student will have noticed that, as pointed out in the introduction to this chapter, the questionnaire items are a motley collection, due to the arbitrary fields in which they were first coined and the absence of any research concept corresponding to the "personality sphere" in ratings. However, they suffice to "tie down" the factors until question items of more general utility and importance can be inserted.  The fact that the same item is sometimes found among the representatives of different factors simply means, of course, that the response to that item depends on two influences.  For example, being kept sleepless by coffee seems to be partly due to the sensitiveness of the $I$ factor and partly to the emotionality of the $C$ factor.  Such mixed representation is similarly but less often found among the rating variables, and its only drawback is that if one uses the item in estimating people's endowment in two different factors a spurious correlation between the factors is likely to be produced, wherefore such items are to be avoided in scoring a person on a factor.

That the questionnaire items at present in circulation lack the even sampling of the personality sphere is shown by the finding that certain personality factors—*B*, *D*, and *J*—are totally missing from questionnaire factors while others—*C*, *E*, and *L*—have indistinct variance.   On the other hand at least four factors (labeled Radicalism or Liking Thinking (QP. XVII), Adventurous Self-sufficiency (QP. VIII*b*), Will Control (QP. IX), and Tenseness and Restlessness (except for a sex-interest rating, QP. XIII, see (6)), additional to Factor *O* above, have no well-defined equivalent in ratings.   Presumably these deal with responses too confined to the ideational and introspective fields to have anything but oblique representation in the basic, universal, behavioral manifestation of the personality sphere. This is supported by the finding that one of these *Q* factors is apparently identical with the ideational Radicalism-Conservatism factor described in attitudes below.

Naturally the items for different source traits are thoroughly intermixed in any actual questionnaire as finally presented to the subject, so that he is not tempted to a succession of yes or no responses.   Slight differences in question form, and affirmative or negative presentation, sometimes affect the absolute, and possibly the relative, scores of individuals appreciably.   Such principles of construction can be studied in the handbook to the Sixteen Personality Factor Questionnaire, now used in applied psychology and research (6*a*).

## 2. SOURCE TRAITS IN ATTITUDES AND INTERESTS

**The Meaning of Factors in This Realm.**   From everyday-life observations and from clinical data we should expect that the patterning of interests and attitudes would be a more individual and accidental matter than would the general outlines of personality as so far encountered.   But although unique traits are admittedly more prominent, and in many ways offer a more suitable scheme of analysis among dynamic traits, the fact remains that broad common traits can actually be discovered among them.

What the nature and cause of these source traits in attitudes and interests may be is not yet clear.   In Chapter 6, where an analysis of dynamic structure is attempted, it is suggested that the source traits obtained from the factorization of a host of dynamic traits will correspond to basic drives or to extensive acquired-sentiment patterns.   But since there is ample evidence (Chap. 5) that temperament is a determiner of the interests and attitudes a person acquires, it is certain that *some* source traits discovered by factorization of the latter will correspond to temperament patterns, probably identical with those already described above.

However, our present purpose is not to interpret factors but only to make the student familiar with them as dimensions for describing personality.

It may be asked why interest and attitude factors, which obviously are of great interest and importance in personality, should be described only as mental interiors, restricted to self-rating data. The answer unfortunately is that, apart from the research described in Chapter 6, all studies of attitudes and interest extensive enough for correlation have been only in terms of pencil-and-paper data in which the subject checks items in which he thinks he is interested and marks opinions which he is willing for you to believe represent his attitudes. Again the student should be reminded that a person may have stronger feelings on a subject than he imagines himself to have before he has thought it out, or before it is thrust upon him as an actual course of action. Polling results show ample evidence that in attitudes and interests an appreciable gulf may lie between the verbal reply and what a person will actually do. The factors now to be described are therefore strictly in terms of mental interiors.

**An Attitude Is a Vector Measurement.** An attitude is a dynamic trait, commonly arising from some deeper sentiment or innate drive, which it seeks to satisfy. It is a readiness to implement a certain course of action in regard to some object, and therefore characteristically has the form:

"I want so much to do this with that." For example, I may have a personal attitude that "I want very much to be introduced to Miss M," or a social attitude that "I want to work for the United Nations to achieve a true unity."

In every case, in addition to the subject who possesses the attitude and the object in connection with which the attitude is held, there is (*a*) a certain *strength* of desire or intention, and (*b*) a certain *direction* of action, *e.g.*, to support, to destroy, to know more about, to be sexually attracted to, to seek the company of, and so on.

The incorrectness of defining an attitude as "for" or "against" an object is illustrated by Diagram 14, where a variety of possible attitudes to beefsteak are considered. Each has a different direction of intention, which can be represented by measuring an attitude as a *vector* quantity, *i.e.*, as something which has both *direction* and *strength* to be defined (as with a force but not a temperature). Of course one can speak of being for or against *a course of action*, for the direction of the action then remains to be defined.

**Interests and Attitudes Related.** The *strength* of an attitude is actually a measurement of *interest*—the amount of interest in the course of action indicated. Conversely, we may speak of an attitude as showing the direction of an interest, *i.e.*, an attitude is an interest with the direction defined. A man has attitudes—of love, fear, aggression, and so on—toward all things in which he is interested, and a question in which he is not interested is one concerning which he has no attitudes. However, a man may have several attitudes about an object—for example, he may believe that beefsteak should be less expensive, that he personally likes it well cooked, that steaks are not as good as they used to be, and so on. His "total interest in beefsteak" is then some function of the interest involved in each attitude—a function the precise nature of which is best analyzed later in Chapter 6 on general dynamics. Interest measurement in all its aspects may thus amount to more than attitude measurement pure and simple. In its initial aspect, however, a measurement of interest is one study.

**Measuring Attitude Strength.** The strength of an attitude (the amount of interest in it) has so far been measured (not very satisfactorily from the

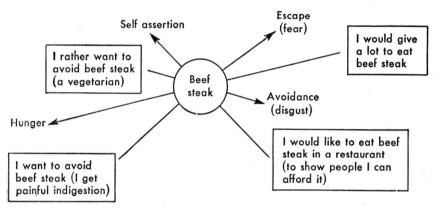

DIAGRAM 14. Attitudes as vectors varying in strength and direction.

viewpoint of objective testing, as indicated above) by means of opinions. A list of graded opinions (graded on a "cumulative" or a "differential" scale, see (24a)), representative of differing degrees of strength, is presented to the subject and he is asked to indicate that which best represents his own attitude. For example, in measuring the strength of the attitude: "I want so much to eat beefsteak," the following statements might be presented:

1. I would not give a cent for the best beefsteak in town.
2. I would give two hours' manual labor for a beefsteak.
3. I would rather have a beefsteak than any other meat.
4. I would give ten dollars for a beefsteak.

Thurstone (35) has worked out methods, depending on the frequency with which various opinions are checked in a typical population, for putting such statements in order of strength, and assigning numerical grades to them.

**Measuring Attitude Direction.** The measurement of attitude *direction* is a more complex problem, only to be fully discussed in Chapter 6, on dynamics. However, the principle can be stated simply by pointing out that the thousands of attitudes we may have are concerned with courses of action which serve a comparatively small number of biological or social goals. If the drives to these basic goals are really *unitary* traits—as is believed from general clinical experience and discussion—these traits will be revealed as dynamic source traits by the correlation and factorization of strength measures on a great number of attitudes. They will appear as factors, loading the individual attitudes which act as trait-elements.

Consequently the direction of any single attitude can be defined in terms of the goals which it serves. For example, a man's attitude to his salary may spring so much from his need to eat, so much from his self-assertive drive, and so much from the fear of social insecurity. It can thus be given numerical projections on the coordinates constituted by these three dimensions, fixing its angles from the origin. In short, the process is exactly homologous with the expression of the character of *any* trait-element, dynamic or nondynamic, as outlined in the previous chapter's discussion of source traits. But here the loadings in the equation are spoken of in terms of *directions*, because an attitude, like any other dynamic trait, is directed to one or more goals. In other words, the *situational indices* are here fixed by the *incentive* value of the situation, in terms of the extent of stimulation of specific directions of drive. However, in so far as attitude factors may also arise from temperament source traits, any representation of an attitude as a vector would include, at present, projections also on temperament coordinates. Only further research can separate the coordinates that are purely dynamic.

**Tentative Description of Source Traits among Attitudes.** Most attitude studies yet made have not only been restricted to self-rating media but also have been limited by the conceptions of sociology, polling, and applied psychology to *pro-con* dimensions. That is to say, the subject is asked whether he "likes" or "dislikes" a certain object or course of action, regardless of the quality of the liking and the ultimate goals of action to which it will lead. Such measurement actually measures only the *strength* of the attitude vector and leaves its direction *undefined*, though *fixed* to some extent by the description of the course of action which the person is for or against. (When people are asked the rather meaningless question of whether they are for or against an *object*, *e.g.*, art, however, the direction is not even fixed. Ten people may construe it in ten different ways.)

Furthermore, the social and intellectual pro-con attitudes on which measures have accumulated have been, from the standpoint of personality structure, superficial and oblique, however focal they may be socially. A very different population of attitudes—to parents and family, to self and sex, to work and play—would have been better chosen to elucidate personality factors directly. Consequently it is not surprising that only one of the attitude factors, the first listed below, has yet been definitely shown to be identical with a general personality factor.

*Attitude Factor* 1.  *Personality Q Factor* 13.  *Radicalism vs. Conservatism.* (Indexed QA. I (5).)  Those highly endowed with the positive (left) direction of this factor favor belief in evolution, in economic reform, in liberalization of divorce, in nudism, in international control of military force, in birth control, in eugenics.  The conservative factor on the other hand loads measures of orthodoxy in religion, in Sunday observance, in "one's country right or wrong," and in censorships of behavior generally (*e.g.*, prohibition). There is now evidence (6) strongly indicating that this is the same as the questionnaire factor QP. XVII, "Liking thinking."  The analytic, thoughtful individual favors newer ways and the abandonment of what he views as "obstructive superstitions."  The individual with more interest in action, in athletics, and less in "the serious problems of life," favors a more conservative set of attitudes.

*Attitude Factor* 2.  *Hardheaded Rationalism vs. Sentimental, Emotional Attitudes.*  The former is favorable to resort to war with unruly nations, capital punishment of murderers, rationalism, socialism, sterilization of hereditary disease carriers.  The negative loadings occur in attitudes of humane treatment of criminals, nonsmoking, antivaccination, abstemiousness. It is almost certainly identical with the *BR* factor of Sophistication (*N*).

*Factor QI[1].*  I and II.  *Interest in Manipulating Material vs. Interest in Sociable Activities.*  In this pattern, largely in the Strong Interest Inventory material, the positively loaded interests are the stated interests in the life of an artist, architect, aviator, chemist, carpenter, farmer, engineer, or physicist as opposed to the occupations of banker, office manager, accountant, real-estate agent, vacuum-cleaner salesman, advertising agent, lawyer, guidance worker, YMCA secretary, or insurance salesman.  In the values test there is more interest in science than in politics.

One might be tempted simply to label this Interest in people vs. things, were it not that both of the following factors also show some sort of interest in people.  However, as indicated above, this is probably personality factor *A*—the cyclothyme liking for judging, analyzing, and dealing with people as opposed to the schizothyme seeking for a more dependable (and perhaps simpler, less demanding) set of object interests.  The two following factors, on the other hand, have an interest in people, that is, in the first place, a form of altruism and, in the second, a liking for talking and showing off among them:

---

[1] The reader will recognize that letter-number references to the standard index (5) *e.g.*, QP (Questionnaire factors in personality), QA (Q factors in attitudes) and QI (Q factors in interests) are kept in regular type, whereas in general use Q, P, and factor references are in italics.

*Factor* QI. I*b*.   *Thoughtful, Idealistic Interest in Guiding People vs. Tough, Practical Interests*.   In this pattern the positive loadings are personnel-guidance worker, social-science teacher, office manager, as opposed to architect, chemist, or manager in an industrial concern.   The positive patterns also show loadings in seriousness, shyness, idealism, intellectual interests, dislike of alcohol, tobacco, and capital punishment and belief in gradualness. The interest in people is here, therefore, of an idealistic kind, suggesting that the emphasis is on guidance, as indicated.

*Factor* QI. III.   *Surgency or Rhathymia, in the Field of Interests*.   A factor found in interests, loading positively interest in occupations of an advertising man, lawyer, waiter, personnel-guidance worker, and social-science teacher, as opposed to accountant, aviator, carpenter, engineer, manager in a manufacturing concern, printer, policeman, or real-estate salesman, has been shown to be the outcropping of surgency-desurgency in interest tests.   The factor in interests as such has been variously called interest in talk, verbal persuasion, language, and people, as opposed to interest in practical control of things, especially that requiring conscientious and close attention.

**Personality as an Unstated Premise in the Syllogisms of Attitudes.**   The interests and attitudes of most people can be analyzed in terms of a chain of syllogisms or other logical propositions.   Except where "rationalization" occurs, these steps represent the necessary subsidiation connections in the satisfaction of some basic drive or the adaptation to some temperamental condition.   For example, if I have the attitude more strongly than other people that, "There should be more restaurants quite near to the campus than there are," this may spring from the logical premises (*a*) it is necessary for me to eat, and (*b*) I cannot walk far.   My stronger attitude may mean that I am more dominated by hunger than other people, or that I am less inclined to walk than others.

The above sequence, as any logician will notice, is much abridged, but in principle it remains true that any statement of an attitude can eventually be analyzed, in terms of a broadening ancestry of logical propositions, into some premise or proposition that defines the mood or temperament of the individual—as well as into many propositions dealing with purely logical, objective statements about the environment.   It has been the mistake, at least of amateur logicians, to suppose that two entirely logical people would not disagree, *i.e.*, to assume that all premises concern states of fact in the outer world.   Persons who agree on these, and found their views on logical steps, could not disagree, but these are only half of the facts to be taken into account.   The other half concerns the inner needs, moods, and temperamental conditions of the person making the statement.   The personality is in fact a "hidden premise" in each person's statement of his attitude.   If, for example, he is a person who temperamentally enjoys pain and struggle, he will arrive quite logically at a different set of attitudes about world peace than will a person of more usual temperament who follows equally logical steps.

This dependence of ultimate philosophy upon temperament was stressed by William James, as a fact of observation. The detailed analysis in terms of logical propositions, showing that a temperament premise—a straight value judgment—is found at one corner of the foundation of the logical edifice, explains why this should be so. The factor analysis of attitudes, yielding groupings related to personality, will ultimately show empirically which particular sets of attitudes stem from which particular temperamental conditions.

## 3. OBJECTIVE-TEST SOURCE TRAITS IN THE REALM OF CHARACTER

**The Meaning of Source Traits in Objective Tests.** An objective test has been defined in the previous chapter. It demands no attempt at self-evaluation by the subject and must be such as to be easily set up as a standardized situation anywhere. It may deal with verbal or nonverbal behavior and may involve laboratory apparatus or even physiological measurements.

*Any source trait found in objective tests is the criterion of validity of those tests.* That is to say, any proposed new test of such a personality factor can be validated by correlating it with *an estimate of the factor* obtained by pooling the tests already known to be highly loaded in it. This is known as "internal validation" (5). But the general *meaning* of the objective-test source trait can only be found by correlating it with source traits in life-record data, or even with individual trait-elements in life records. Thus general mental capacity ($B$ or $g$ factor) was first discovered and defined as a factor appearing in objective tests, *e.g.*, analogies, vocabulary, arithmetic problems, classification, perceptual skills, mechanical-aptitude tests, and so on. The meaning of this general ability factor, at least the meaning of the measures for practical life, was obtained by correlating such measures of it with life-record data, *e.g.*, occupational success, school success, proneness to delinquency, social class, etc. Through such "external" or "peripheral" validation (5) it is seen that the meaning of this factor corresponds to what is generally and more loosely called "intelligence."

**The Design of Objective Tests.** The first wave of research in objective measures of personality repeated somewhat mechanically the "brass instrument" measures used in psychophysics, perception, etc., and not unnaturally came to the conclusion that objective tests of personality were no good. There followed a more imaginative attempt, using experiments which presented "miniature situations" akin to the real-life situations to be measured.

The classical study here is that of Hartshorne and May (21), concerned with honesty, persistence, and other "character" traits in children. They tested children in examinations in which the extent of cheating could be accurately measured. They sent the subjects on errands and observed the honesty with which the correct change was returned. They gave them tests of persistence in wearisome tasks and measured cooperativeness in situations in which they could help their fellows. Among some twenty tests of these "character" qualities the correlations hovered around +0.3. The comparative failure of this second wave was due to errors of interpretation. The low correlations were interpreted to mean that all trait-indicators are specific, whereas factor analysis and allowance for test unreliability would have revealed patterns of extensive general traits in this material.

The later development of objective personality tests has been directed by a number of methods or hypotheses about design which are at present only loosely defined or too much in the research stage for effective summary. However, we may make the following by no means exhaustive divisions:

1. Association tests.   (Quantity and quality of memory responses.)
2. Stylistic tests.   (Assuming, as in Allport's and Vernon's work, that the same personality *style* will show in tests as in life.)
3. Misperception tests.   (Including Projection and Ego-defense tests.)
4. Psycho-physiological tests.   (Attempting measures of temperament, etc., through physiological observations.)
5. Miniature-situation tests.   (Setting up miniature situations which appear to involve the same pattern as the life situation.)
6. Formal-process tests.   (Searching by factor analysis or other means for the essential *form* of a personality process, which can then be embodied in a test.)

These designs have been used to measure both common source traits and the unique personality traits concerned with dynamic attachments to particular objects. All will receive illustration in the following descriptions of factors, but most attention will be given to the last four, which have been most rewarding. By contrast to personality tests the design of ability tests has been simple, the manifest nature of the material content or the reasoning or motor-skill processes usually being sufficient to suggest the best tests to subject to validation procedures. Occasionally the line between an ability and a personality test is not easy to draw, *e.g.*, Thurstone's $W$ factor of verbal fluency is probably the general temperamental factor of fluency $F$, in the special verbal context. But generally the ability factors are obviously "narrow" in regard to their influence on the total personality.

The greatest advance has so far been made through formal-process approaches. Herein a number of tests promising to involve whatever seems characteristic of a personality factor as seen in the rating factor are factorized. Inspection of the high-loaded tests indicates still more clearly the nature of the process, so that still more "saturated" tests can be designed and the correlation studies are repeated. Rounds of factorization thus succeed one another in a technique of "successful approximations" to the essential factor, as a chemist uses successive distillations or as the Curies used successive precipitation to arrive at radium. Thus purification of measures of the general ability factor have brought out ever more clearly that it involves "perception of complex relations" as in analogies and classifications. Similarly, in personality tests, the *BR* factor *C* showed increasingly that emotional stability and power of self-control stood at its core, and increasing saturations have been obtained with tests such as "rigidity" tests which clearly involve this power to control natural tendencies of the organism. Again, Surgency-Desurgency was indicated by ratings to deal with relaxed as opposed to tense, anxious qualities and was found to yield good loadings on tests of slowness of reversible perspective, slowness of reaction time, and carelessness in making errors.

In considering objective-test factors as in considering questionnaire factors we have to record some which have been both established as factors in objective tests and also shown to represent already known *BR* or *Q* personality factors and others which have only been established as factors in personality-test data, their wider associations and meaning still remaining obscure. As with the *Q* factors, we shall begin with the former.

*Objective-test Factor C. Emotional Stability.* This has been shown in Hull's Sway Suggestibility Test, in which one measures how far the standing subject sways in response to constant verbal suggestion that he will do so (16). It also shows itself in high *disposition rigidity* (7,13,16). Rigidity is itself a distinct factor, established by many researches and presumably enters here as a factor within the second-order *C* factor. Unfortunately the concept of rigidity has been clouded by clinicians ascribing to it many qualities which they have never proved it to have. Indeed, until recently (12) no attempt has been made to see how many distinct varieties of rigidity exist. At least two are known, that now under discussion being the older or classical "perseveration-rigidity factor" studied by a long line of experimenters from Heymans and Wiersma, through Spearman, Burri, Darroch, Stephenson, Eysenck, and others.

This factor is essentially a rigidity as resistance in breaking away from innate or old-established dynamic traits to new ones. It shows itself in high perseveration in all sorts of motor tests (10), *e.g.*, poor speed and performance on new as opposed to old ways of handwriting, pronunciation, etc.; in poor ability to restructure habitual visual perception, *e.g.*, to see "hidden" pictures in a conventional picture; and also in low speed of flicker fusion, *i.e.*, a flickering light is seen as steady (when speed is gradually increased) while other people still see it as flickering.

Measures of this $p$ factor, perseveration or disposition rigidity, have been shown to have some significant relations to general personality. It increases with fatigue and especially with general nervous fatigue and depression. Neurotics consistently have higher than average rigidity scores (10) (poor ego development), delinquents tend to fall at both the high and the low extremes, but predominantly at the high (thus accounting for the negative correlation of rigidity with character factors above). Deteriorated schizophrenics and depressives tend to have very high rigidity scores, while manics and hysterics are rather low. The term "perseveration," incidentally, was originally coined in psychiatry (by Neisser) to describe the behavior in such psychotics in which they repeat the same remark or mannerism in almost endless rigidity, as if unable to adapt by a fresh response. All these relations, particularly the oft-repeated finding of negative correlation between disposition-rigidity score and good-character integration ($G$, $C$) and dominance ($E$ factor), make the measurement of disposition rigidity of value in many fields, notably in clinical diagnosis and wherever character selection or selection for leadership is wanted. A complete survey of the associations of the classical disposition-rigidity factor is given elsewhere (10).

Several of the objective-test measures associated with $C$ factor suggest that this source trait might be equated with the psychoanalysts notion of "ego strength," *i.e.*, the ability to cope with the impulses of the organism, and the demands of the superego (see 10).

*Objective-test Factor G. Positive Character vs. Dependent Character.* A factor loading

High ratio of recall of consonant to dissonant opinions
Low ratio of color to form in sorting
Low fluctuation of attitudes

has been shown (7, 13) to correlate with this rating factor. The tests indicate, in conformity with the ratings, a certain tenacity of character.

*Objective-test Factor M. Bohemian Unconcernedness vs. Conventional Practical Concern.* Here the factor found by Thurstone in perceptual tests, expanded as shown subsequently (7) seems to be involved.

Low score in two-hand coordination test
Low ratio of dispersed to predetermined attentiveness
Excessive use of circles in C. M. S. Test (see page 112)
Embarrassment in mirror-drawing test

It is noticeable that this agrees somewhat better with the questionnaire $M$ factor than the $M$ ratings (13), for it brings out the practical incompetence, the nervous excitability, and the absent-mindedness hidden under the "other-wordly" exterior. This factor may be the obverse of what has been called "Active-will Character" (T. XIII) in the standard index (5).

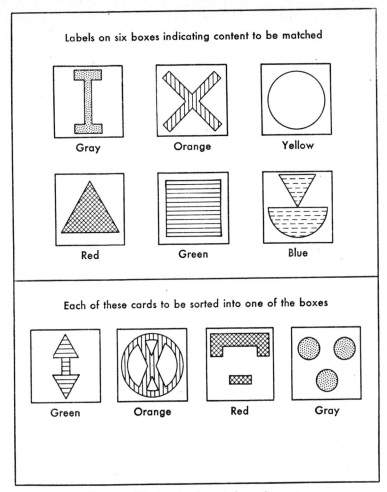

Labels on six boxes indicating content to be matched

Gray   Orange   Yellow

Red   Green   Blue

Each of these cards to be sorted into one of the boxes

Green   Orange   Red   Gray

DIAGRAM 15.   A color-form ratio sorting test.

*Objective-test Factor of Will Control and Integrity.*   Here the test factor correlates quite highly with one of the $Q$ factors mentioned above, Will Control, which has no corresponding *BR* factor.   It loads (7)

Absence of questionable preferences in reading
Large P.G.R. deflections
Maintenance of effort level on ergograph until final collapse
Low perceptual speed of closure
High aspiration level (on C.M.S. Test)

Both test and questionnaire clearly describe here a strength of will directed to high aspiration to strong inhibition of impulse (interpreting slow speed of closure as refusal to give a verdict until really certain).

This factor is probably the same as that of "Honesty and Stability" (T. XII in the standard list (5) which involves also "Good choices on a test of what a citizen should do in various moral problem situations" and tests of cooperativeness.

*Objective-test Factor of Determined Self-sufficiency and Endurance.* An objective-test factor has repeatedly been found (T. XIV) in standard index (5), as follows:

Maintaining strength of hand grip
Enduring a frightening electric shock
High self-rating on self-confidence
Radical and unconventional views
High ideomotor speed

It is possible that this is not a "character" factor, but corresponds to Dominance (*E* factor) though no proof of this disposition correlation has yet been attempted. Two other factors in the realm of "persistence and character," namely, "Masculinity" (T. XV) and "Dynamic Momentum" (T. XVI) are known as reasonably established factors and may be seen in the standard list, but have no known rating or questionnaire correlatives and will not be mentioned here.

## 4. OBJECTIVE SOURCE TRAITS IN THE REALM OF TEMPERAMENT

A separate section of "temperament factors" is begun here merely for convenience of study. No basic importance is attached at this stage to the difference between dynamic "character" factors and temperament factors. We now pass, however, also into a survey of factors which, though clear cut in terms of objective-test material, have not yet been located in terms of behavior rating or questionnaire equivalents.

*Objective-test Factor F, Surgency vs. Desurgency.* A factor has been found loading slowness of reaction time, slowness of reversible perspective, high ratio of errors to speed in the pursuit meter, cancellation, etc., low ratio of vocabulary (*V* factor) to general intelligence, alkalinity of saliva, and low concentration of cholinesterase in the blood serum. Probably the surgent individual shows also high oscillation, low and flexible aspiration level, low persistence in tests requiring effortful concentration, and a high estimation of cluster one jokes, *i.e.*, jokes of the debonaire sexuality group (11).

This picture of the surgency factor in objective tests, together with some associations pointed out in later chapters, would seem to indicate a considerable physiological determination of this pattern. The surgent individual is seen to be in a relaxed state, with little internal stress.

*Objective-test Factor I. Imaginative Emotionality vs. Tough Poise.* A factor is found in tests (7) which correlates with this rating factor and no others, as follows:

Immaturity of opinion (forming opinions which have to be modified when reminded of obvious facts)
Suggestibility to authority
Excessive use of circles in the C. M. S. Test (see below: this is a kind of panic reaction)

The nature of these objective responses agrees well with the rating picture of infantilism, imaginativeness, and nervousness in *I* factor.

*Objective-test Factor No. 3 in (7).* A very clear factor is found (7) loading:

Inability to state logical assumptions behind statements
Suggestibility to authority
Comparative slowness on "set" reaction times, *i.e.*, inability to keep mental set
Inability to suggest orderly classifications
Absence of fair-mindedness in judgments

This could be a character factor, but there are some indications of a temperamental source for this mental debility.

*Objective-test Factor No. 5 in (7).* Another clear factor not yet associated with rating or questionnaire variables is detectable in:

Freedom from oscillation (*i.e.*, steady work curve, measured at 5 second intervals)
High rate of reversible perspective fluctuation
High ideo-motor speed
Freedom from "accident proneness" in complex reaction time reactions

This is some sort of psychomotor efficiency and is apparently the same as Thurstone's (38) perceptual factor *D*. It resembles also a general speed factor found in earlier studies (T. XXI*a* in standard list) and is probably of temperamental origin.

*Factor of Fluency of Association* (T. XXVII in index (5)). Much attention has been given in clinical psychology and the experimental study of temperament not only to perseveration but also to speed, tempo, and fluency concepts. As indicated above, speed splits into several "speeds," and tempo, or "natural speed," is of different significance than "top-limit speed" under willed effort. Fluency of association has been found to be yet another distinct factor though it does affect somewhat a number of simple ideo-motor speeds (*e.g.*, speed of reading) in addition to ideational fluency.

If, instead of asking the subject to perform some definitely predesigned mental operation as in an intelligence test, we simply ask him to complete a story, or think of as many words as possible beginning with a certain letter, or "see" as many different things as he can in a series of ink blots, a very definite general factor of "fluency of association" emerges. The highly fluent person has an abundant, spontaneous "rising up" of ideas into consciousness and this general source trait shows itself in varied fields, as shown below.

DIAGRAM 16. Subtests from a standard "fluency of association" scale.

Performance in this field is always somewhat loaded with intelligence (see Thurstone's word-fluency-factor *W*), but it is more than intelligence. A distinct factor is demonstrable, loading: productivity in completing stories, thinking of words (with little or no restriction), completing drawings, or drawing as many objects as possible, speed of reading, speed of solving anagrams, tendency to continue a task when interrupted, natural tapping rate, and readiness of producing associations to ink blots.

Manics are exceptionally high on fluency and depressives are exceptionally low (33). Since the scores of these psychotics overlap to some extent with those of normal people, still better diagnostic power can be obtained by dividing the fluency score by a simple speed of writing score. For in depressives fluency drops, while sheer *willed* speed does not, whereas in normals

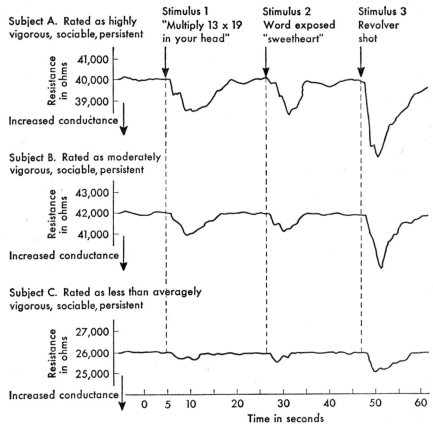

DIAGRAM 17. Individual differences in mean magnitude of psychogalvanic response.

there is commonly some correspondence. Fluency of association has been shown with children to correlate about 0.6 with surgency (*F* factor) and the surface-trait loading sociability, impulsiveness, and quickness of wit, but this fails with adults and we must be prepared to find that fluency is a factor with varying relations to personality factors according to circumstances and ranges on the factors concerned.[1]

[1] Fluency is one of those temperamental tendencies which also outcrop in abilities and are mistaken for abilities. Thus this same fluency shows itself, apparently, as Thurstone's *W*, or verbal fluency factor, sharply distinguished from *V*, or verbal ability, which is itself essentially a *knowledge* of vocabulary and correct grammatical usage.

**Temperament and Physiological Factors.** Many attempts have been made to demonstrate that temperament factors arise from, or contain in their pattern, basic physiological variables such as basal metabolic rate, endocrine concentrations, pulse rate, blood pressure, body temperature, and P.G.R. deflection magnitude. A factor involving the last has been described above. A factor (11, in this series) of *General Metabolic Activity Level* is described, more appropriately than here, in Chapter 10 on psychosomatics. Herrington (22) has shown that this general metabolic level does indeed appear strongly in general behavior also, determining general activity and "drive" boldness, energy and enthusiasm, sociability, and other qualities that would appear to be aspects of the *H* factor (Chap. 3).

This metabolic activity level will not be described again here. It loads basal metabolic rate, determined by oxygen consumption under "basal" conditions, but can also be measured from loading in pulse rate, blood pressure, and circulation volume.

### 5. OTHER OBJECTIVE-TEST TRAITS IMPORTANT IN PERSONALITY

**Personality and Abilities.** The above review has not extended to the ability source traits, which are presumably known to the student already.[2] They are important aspects of personality, especially in school and in industry, but in life adjustment as a whole can only be justly considered as less important for prediction than the major source traits of character and temperament which we have studied above. Some abilities seem, however, partly to involve orectic[3] traits. In such cases, as with "fluency" above, the source trait may *first* be discovered either as a pure ability or as a purely orectic personality trait, and later its other connections become evident, revealing what has been called (5) a "wholistic factor." In other cases the correlations among abilities and dynamic traits, though well confirmed, leave the interpretation in terms of unitary factors still obscure. For example, drawing ability has for some reason a significant positive correlation with surgency ($+F$ factor) and with cyclothymia ($+A$ factor), while high verbal ability ($V$ factor) tends to go with nervous emotionality, desurgency ($-F$ factor) and schizothymia ($-A$ factor), *i.e.*, the "introvert" has the better vocabulary and writing skill. High performance in several special abilities seems to have in common good endowment in Character Integra-

---

[2] Some ten or eleven can be regarded as well established, namely General intelligence (a second-order factor), Verbal Ability, Mechanical Ability, Spatial-Visual Ability, Manual Dexterity, General Dexterity, Numerical Ability, Reasoning Ability, Inductive or Generalizing Ability, Musical Ability (perhaps eight subfactors), Drawing Ability, and certain Retentivity factors (see (5,9,36).

[3] Orectic is a useful term, at present not much used, meaning "other than abilities," *i.e.*, temperamental, emotional dynamic traits.

tion (*G* factor) as well as in General Intelligence (*B*); for consistent application is a factor in acquiring many skills.

The only tested ability, however, which has such marked personality associates as to make it comparable in importance with the other primary personality source traits is general intelligence. General mental ability, the student will recall, was defined first as a factor in cognitive tests, loading most highly performances in the following tests.

*Objective-test Factor* 12

Analogies
Classifications
Verbal opposites and synonyms
Mathematical series
Problem solving of almost any kind

It is also the second-order factor loading Thurstone's primary abilities, such as verbal, numerical, spatial, and reasoning abilities. More recently, intelligence tests have been devised (4*a*) to measure this ability shorn of those cultural associations (especially verbal and numerical) which confuse intelligence with education, social status, etc. This involves using "perceptual" or culture-free tests (6*b*), which employ a universe of fundaments common to all people, of the series, classification, and matrix type shown in Diagram 18. This is the type of test used in establishing the personality correlations given for factor *B*, General Intelligence in Personality, in the previous chapter, for it is especially necessary to rule out here the personality effects of that education which is somewhat more likely to happen to the intelligent.

The actual loadings of the personality variables (page 59), uncorrected for attenuation, are around 0.3 to 0.5. In short there is a moderate tendency, other things being equal, for the person gifted with higher general ability, to acquire a more integrated character, somewhat more emotional stability and a more conscientious outlook. He tends to become "morally intelligent" as well as "abstractly intelligent."

*Factor* 13. *Masculinity-Femininity*. (A possible objective-test factor here has already been mentioned; TXXV in index (5).) It is scarcely surprising that one of the most frequently commented upon and readily recognized polar differences of everyday life has received a lot of experimental study. Nevertheless the sex-trait pattern is as yet better established as a surface trait than a source trait. Moreover, we may surely expect this pattern to be one which varies with cultural setting, *i.e.*, with the environmental mold of sex roles as defined by the culture pattern. Measurements of the sexes overlap appreciably, the more masculine women scoring higher on masculinity than the more feminine men, which is an agreement with clinical judgments.

Some of the objective pencil-and-paper tests in Terman and Miles' study (34) deal with reactions to the following kinds of material.

Here are some drawings a little like ink blots.   Beside each drawing four things are mentioned.   Underline the one word that tells you what the drawing makes you think of most.   (Drawings not reproduced.)

| | |
|---|---|
| dish | fish |
| ring | mirror |
| target | snow shoe |
| tire | spoon |

Here men seem more inclined to see the objects as target and snow shoe respectively and women as ring and spoon.

Another Terman test reveals differences in mental "furniture," *i.e.*, knowledge and interest, as follows.

"Marigold is a kind of fabric, flower, grain, stone," is more correctly answered by girls, while boys are more often correct on

"The earth moves round the sun in 7 days, 20 days, 180 days, 365 days." Yet another difference is found with respect to moral valuations.

Underline the degree of badness *you* think the behavior described shows.
1. Picking flowers in a public park   Wicked, decidedly bad, somewhat bad, not really bad
2. Not standing up when the Star Spangled Banner is played   Wicked, decidedly bad, somewhat bad, not really bad

Here boys are more inclined to rank the latter as more reprehensible.

The correlation cluster constituting masculinity-femininity is thus one that runs throughout objective-test responses in attitudes, in interests, and in knowledge.

**Persistence of Form and Identity in Source Traits.**   The tendency referred to in our theoretical introduction to factor analysis, for factor patterns to change somewhat with changes of sample, etc., can be best illustrated in connection with the objective-test factors now being described.

In the general ability factor (*B* in personality, or *g* among abilities), which has been more explored than any other, various changes in the factor pattern are found as one takes normal population samples at different ages.   A form board test, for example, is highly loaded in this factor among children, but very little among adults.   Evidently it is not so much a test of intelligence as of manual dexterity among adults.   This reminds us that the pattern of loadings defining any factor may change slowly as we pass to higher and higher levels, so that unless we know the intermediate patterns it may sometimes be a little difficult positively to identify a factor with some earlier pattern of itself obtained in very different circumstances.   It also reminds us that a "test variable" is not fixed by the apparatus and instructions alone, but also by definition of the population which works upon it.

The magnitude of *all* correlations or loadings in the general ability factor is smaller for older or more intelligent children than for younger or less intelligent (18). This means that with younger children it is a more important factor in determining individual differences and is more unitarily organized. On the other hand the General Control, Honesty, and Integrity factor above shows greater loadings and more definite unity with older and more intelligent children. In this case of a presumed "environmental-mold" trait the unity of character reactions is something acquired with time. At first the child is inconsistent, but the older or more intelligent child recognizes honesty-dishonesty in more aspects and situations, and succeeds in being "good" as a whole or relatively "bad" as a whole, according to his character development.

As Thurstone has shown (37), the differences that exist in otherwise equivalent populations, with respect to the extent of their "scatter" or variance in some of the things measured, will not affect the essential pattern of the factors found, but will only affect the obliqueness of the factors one to another, *i.e.*, their correlations with one another. But differences of population in other respects, *e.g.*, in cultural pattern or racial stock, will directly and sometimes powerfully affect the form of the factor expression. For example, the possession of good intelligence has been shown above to engender a pattern of greater dependability and conscientiousness. But if individuals grew up in a wholly criminal society—granted that such may be conceived—it is possible that intelligence, as a source trait, would load *immoral* qualities, since these would be what the young would be taught. However, the variations in source-trait patterns with culture and period are probably slighter than we suppose. The personalities described by Shakespeare nearly four centuries ago, or Plutarch 2,000 years ago, certainly seem to move in the same dimensions as our own. But we cannot be sure of the extent of variation of patterns till testing has been more extended, *e.g.*, to primitive as well as civilized populations.

A second general problem in dealing with personality in terms of factors, additional to the above problem of fluctuation of "shape" of pattern, concerns the interrelations of "narrow" and "broad" factors. If 200 or 300 variables are taken in a certain area instead of a dozen or so it is often found that many new, "narrow" factors appear which were not discovered in the first factorization. These factors are often quite strongly correlated, and the original "broad" factors appear as "second-order factors," organizing these smaller correlated factors, just as they were originally found organizing the correlated single variables. Thus Thurstone found nearly a dozen special-ability factors where Spearman found a single general intelligence, but the former correlate among themselves yielding a "second-order" general intelligence factor.   However, it is only when the student gets to the research level that he needs to get actively skillful in recognizing and understanding these different "levels" or "orders" of factors.

## 6. A REVIEW OF OBJECTIVE-TEST METHODS

**Tests of Generalized Source Traits and of Specific Cathexes.**   Thus far we have been principally concerned with the theory and practice of measuring common source traits or broad *dimensions* of personality.   This emphasis is warranted by the historical fact that concepts have been most confused here; but we must not overlook the equal importance to theory and practice of measuring the individual's *specific* attachments.   For example, when factor analysis has demonstrated that various behavior manifestations form part of a single dominance pattern, and shown what weighted sum of them is best taken to estimate the individual's general score on the dominance dimension, this figure still leaves unsaid much about the particular acts through which the individual expresses his dominance.

These particular attachments or expressions are more important in dynamic traits than in abilities or temperament traits.   The clinician is interested to know that the patient is of a highly aggressive disposition, but probably still more interested to know that the aggression is directed mainly against the father and an older brother.   Similarly the educational counselor needs to know how good the individual's memory and level of general information may be, but is also helped by knowing what particular fields of information are most highly developed.   These specific investments and attachments of a trait are best called *cathexes* (singular, cathexis), following the psychoanalytic definition, and they cover the area of interests and attitudes.

Now the development of tests for specific cathexes has progressed very little for the very reason that they are specific and therefore too numerous for tests to be provided for each.   Imagine anyone having standardized a test for strength of interest in insects!   But there are certain environmental presses that occur in the lives of most people, *e.g.*, the family, a sweetheart, a school, death, and taxes, which make it practicable to develop measures for such particular attachments of general source traits.   Aggression or anxiety in relation to the above are some examples.   A set of attitude measures to determine the individual's attachments to specific members of the family, for example, is illustrated in Chapter 12.   Objective devices for measuring the strength of interest in specific attitude cathexes are discussed more generally in Chapter 6.   In default of such devices the clinician depends simply on impressions from the patient's talking, and upon such aids as hypnosis or the technique of free association, but the objective methods of Chapter 6 add the psychogalvanic response, memory value, measurement of attention and information etc. to our resources for quantifying specific cathexes.

Although measures of specific attachments are something different from measures of general dynamic source traits they can to a certain extent and in a certain sense be derived from knowledge of the source-trait measurements—when the specification equation has already been discovered, by research, for that particular attachment or attitude. The specification equation shows, by situational indices, how the particular performance or attitude depends on a combination of source traits, as indicated on page 68. However, one must distinguish between $R$-technique equations, in which one deals with how much a given attitude or performance depends on a given source trait for the *general population* and the $P$-technique equation which states instead the unique weightings for a particular individual. In the former we might find that strength of attachment to one's school is *in general* a function to the extent of +0.6 of gregariousness of disposition and +0.3 of general intelligence. Any unusual strength of attachment is then due to unusual strength of the source trait of gregariousness or of the combination of gregariousness and good intelligence. On the other hand, in a $P$-technique specification equation, the weights for individual source traits in a specific cathexis are themselves unique to the individual. For example, Jones may prove to have a loading of 0.9 for the factor of dominance in the specific performance of ordering his subordinates about, whereas the loading for the average person ($R$-technique) in this cathexis may be only 0.5.

The student should not feel frustrated if the issues just raised seem complex at a first reading. Further reading about statistical ways of handling behavior measures (13a,37) will in time make the various systems of representing personality measurements sufficiently clear. Meanwhile it can be seen that the strength of the specific cathexis is partly a function of the strength of the source trait and partly something requiring specific measurement. In those fields, notably the clinical, where the specific, learned, environmental attachments are of importance for the treatment of personality the additional labor of developing special scales for measuring them, after the general source traits have been measured, is gradually beginning to be undertaken.

**Newer Methods for Exploratory and Approximate Personality Assessment.** In general, the measurement of definite, unitary source traits, or of specific cathexes or of more vaguely and confusedly defined "traits," such as are referred to in the Rorschach or the hosts of published "guidance" tests, use much the same sorts of test devices, even though they contribute to different trait concepts, and are treated by different statistical devices. Nevertheless, the condensation involved above dealing only with devices that have figured in well defined source traits has resulted in some test devices used clinically and elsewhere not being sufficiently described.

For it is unfortunately true that in the urgency of clinical work, as in most applied work, the psychometrist has not restricted his measurement only to well defined, meaningful, confirmed, functionally unitary entities. He has ventured to presume, from general clinical observation, that the functional unitariness of needs, drives, defense mechanisms, symptom formations, etc., has been demonstrated and too, has proceeded to talk about their strength (and occasionally to measure it) as if research had already caught up with the task of exploring their structure. Moreover, the clinician is often interested in *unique* rather than *common* traits, and, since he has no time for *P* technique, he must make assumptions about functional structure and try to measure, willy-nilly, such supposed traits as aggressiveness, ego strength, narcistic libido, need for punishment, etc.

The two categories of objective-test design mentioned on page 90 which have not received clear illustration in the course of the above personality factor survey are those of "association methods" and "misperception methods." These methods have their greater role in the measurement of single dynamic traits rather than in regard to temperament traits or the character traits of a general kind such as total dynamic integration or ego or superego strength. They have, however, already been extensively referred to in the chapter on the measurement of attitudes and drives and they play a part in some measures of the *E* factor of dominance.

Association tests, in which a free response to a definite stimulus is measured, can be illustrated by the Rorschach and by a variety of newer tests recently factorized (1,12*a*,16). It is comparatively difficult as yet to see principles by which the personality meaning of the associations (and the choice of suitable stimuli) can be determined beforehand, so that advance has occurred mainly by brute empiricism, *i.e.*, all possible personality predictions are tried out until one is found to stand up to correlation, *e.g.*, that more emotional people make more color associations. One of the few systematic associations found with the Rorschach is the principle revealed by Eysenck (16) that the neurotic makes more statistically *unusual* responses. This links up well with the equally systematic approach by McQuitty using responses to verbal questionnaire material. He showed (24*b*) that responses which tend to go together in the normal population do not do so with neurotics. Regardless of his *absolute* responses, the neurotic is revealed by his *eccentric association.*

**Misperception Tests.** In tests of this kind the experimenter notes the discrepancy between the subject's perception of a picture, situation, or statement and some standard (or true) interpretation. The so-called, or rather miscalled "projection" tests are of this kind.

Misperception can occur through cognitive reasons or dynamic reasons, but the personality test is concerned only with the latter. Dynamic misperceptions can occur either through the need state of the organism, as when a hungry man perceives a piece of soap as cheese or a frightened girl thinks people are threatening her, or it can arise through more permanent dynamic mechanisms, notably the ego-defense mechanisms. It is with this last fourth of the total range of possible misperception tests that personality study is mainly concerned, as summarized here and described more fully elsewhere (8).

MISPERCEPTION TESTS

| Cognitive | | Dynamic | |
|---|---|---|---|
| 1 | 2 | 3 | 4 |
| Sense or intelligence (noegenetic) defect | Experience (reproduction) defect | Mood or appetitive state | More permanent dynamisms |
| | | Disposition | Ego-defense dynamism Projection Phantasy Rationalization Repression, etc. |

It will be noted that Projection techniques constitute only one of a possible wide variety of misperception tests. The important general class of tests for personality measurement is the Ego-defense Dynamism or Ego-dynamism tests.

**Ego-dynamism Tests.** In Chapter 10, on psychoanalytic concepts, a description is presented of *ego-defense mechanisms* or *dynamisms*. Until that is read the student will have to take the theory of the present tests for granted. The chief ego-defense dynamisms are projection, rationalization, identification, repression, phantasy, and reaction formation. These processes are essentially emotional but result in shifts in intellectual viewpoints and in reasoning processes, designed to defend the individual's ego against drives which interfere with the person's self-control, with his moral views, or with his self-regard. Since these mechanisms come into action unconsciously, as far as their true purpose is concerned, they offer an admirable basis for constructing *indirect* tests (*i.e.*, those testing other than what they purport to test) of important dynamic trends in the individual.

**Projection Techniques.** In projection the subject is asked to judge the motive of a character in a story, picture, or statement, so presented that there are not really enough data to enable him to arrive at a sure, reasoned conclusion. In so far as he guesses, he will tend to project his own most frequent or powerful motives, to "judge other people by himself," or to satisfy his unconscious, unsatisfied drives by attaching them to and expressing them through the character in the story. Projection is actually a composite of some three chief mechanisms (8) and until means of separating them are found projection tests are likely to remain at the present "experimental" stage, with rather low validities.

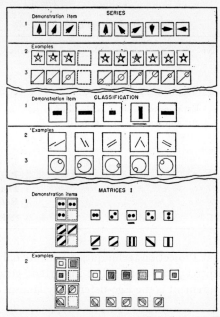

DIAGRAM 18. Series, classification, and matrices subtests from three culture-free intelligence scales. (*Courtesy of The Institute for Personality and Ability Testing, Champaign, Ill.*)

The first of the following is taken from a test for children (9) and the two last from a test in which each item contributes to a score on one source trait only, as indicated.

1. Intelligent people sometimes stay away from a circus because they are afraid that the wild animals will
(*a*) be cruelly treated.
(*b*) escape into the audience.
(*c*) hurt their trainers.

Here underlining (*a*) would indicate projection of tender protectiveness and (*b*) projection of fear. One would suspect the child who gives response (*c*) of a repressed anxiety.

2. Discussion of important topics is most frequently spoiled because too many people are

(*a*) biased, passionate, and emotional.

(*b*) stupid.

The above item is one in a series designed to measure source trait *C*. Response (*a*), indicating a person having difficulty with his own emotionality, scores toward the negative pole of *C*.

3. Most people nowadays allow themselves to become

(*a*) worried and depressed too readily.

(*b*) addicted to talking too much.

DIAGRAM 19. "Projection" items from a picture test of reaction to frustration.

Here response (*b*) scores in the positive direction of source trait *F*, *i.e.*, toward surgency, and response (*a*) toward desurgency. For in so far as projection is involved the worrying person believes that it is other people who worry. The reliability of test items of a selective answer form, designed on the above dynamic hypotheses is quite high, but discussion of their validity must be deferred a moment, because of certain complications.

The picture is an example from Rosenzweig's P-F (pictures for studying reaction to frustration) Test (28). Here the subject, who fills in the blank response for the frustrated person, presumably projects his own response to frustration.

Inventive answers as used in the above test, give a more natural situation, but do not permit the objectivity of scoring possible where selective-type answers are used, as in the earlier examples above.

**Phantasy and Free Association.** In tests utilizing phantasy, instead of giving the subject a practically complete situation, into which he is asked only to project the motive or motives, we give him merely a stimulus situation to start off with, *e.g.*, a picture, a sentence, a scene from one of his dreams, and allow his phantasy to create from there on.   That is to say, we ask him just to say whatever is strolling into his mind, or, at most, to form his daydreams into a loosely connected story, as one might any dream.

The extreme form of this procedure in which the subject is simply asked to reel off the ideas that come into his mind, regardless of their logic or appropriateness, is historically famous as the *method of free association* introduced by Freud for the exploration of the deeper aspects of personality.   The subject has to become practiced in free association, for it is not easy to drop the veil that guards our inmost wishes from public view or to dispense with the polishing that makes our nonsensical or indecent thoughts fit for communication.   Likewise, the listener has to become skilled in helping the subject over points of resistance in divining from the phantasy the underlying drives seeking expression.   In the method of free association, therefore, the quantitative estimate, concerning which of the drive attachments are strong and significant and which of them are unimportant, has the possible bias of any rating by a single observer—which normally we would not use.   However, a trained clinical psychologist, aware that waking phantasy has to be analyzed for latent content and partly by the same allowances for symbolism, condensation, dramatization, etc.—as those by which one proceeds from manifest to latent content of sleep dreams, reaches tolerable objectivity of estimation.

The best-known attempt to standardize the phantasy situation into the form of a test, and to achieve quantitative scores of drives released in phantasy, is Murray's Thematic Apperception Test.   The T.A.T. (39) is a series of provocative, dramatic pictures, around each of which the subject is given some time to elaborate a story.   It is not entirely objectively scorable because the subject's answers are inventive, not selective.[4]

Burt has achieved about the same degree of success as is normally found for the T.A.T., with "ambiguous apperception" tests, *i.e.*, tests in which several alternative objects can be made out of the same lines, according to one's interest and mood; and with "apperception of ink blots," where again what is "seen" depends upon the subject's projection or conscious desire.

In these last few tests (T.A.T. and Burt's) the responses are a mixture of phantasy (undefined stimulus situation) and projection (defined, restricted-stimulus situation) for which reason they are sometimes classified as projection tests.   The measurement even of true-phantasy responses requires more

---

[4] The student will recall that in ability tests, and test construction generally, answers are called *selective* if the subject is asked on each item to check one out of several given alternatives, and *inventive* if he is given no alternatives but supplies his own answer.   It is very difficult to get some personality tests into selective answer form; yet this alone provides a completely objective test.   In inventive tests the situation is standardized but the scoring is not, for different examiners are likely to assess the same answer differently.

research analysis than the tests have yet been subjected to; for some phantasy is a conscious but unexpressed drive and some springs from the true unconscious.

**Rationalization.**   These dynamism tests are only in an experimental stage.   They proceed on the assumption that the subject who wants to express some drive of the unconscious will most readily find a more "respectable" reason for doing the act which the drive dictates.   Thus in the following test item, designed to measure on the Dominance Continuum (source trait *E*),

> Sarcasm and ridicule are sometimes the best methods to make the lazy person "toe the line."   Agree _____ Disagree _____.

the dominant individual, addicted by nature to driving others, will be most inclined to espouse the rationalizing view that such treatment is good for people.

*Reaction Formation.*   Here we have a process which in some situations requires responses opposite to rationalization, so that the question has to be carefully chosen if the two defense reactions are not to neutralize each other. This process, as it works in the subject's mind, causes him to emphasize the moral arguments which help to keep in check his own antisocial or excessive drives.   Consider the item:

> Much more time should be given to the *social* training of young children, particularly toward overcoming shyness, even if it makes them rather overbold.   Agree _____ Disagree _____.

Here the schizothyme individual, who is naturally shy and has spent much time in overcoming his awkwardness (overcompensation), is likely to check "agree."   He will stress consciously the desirability of being bold and will see little danger in, or need to curb, social boldness.

Or again:

> Anxious, fussy, sentimental people are a worse nuisance than any other kind. They should try to acquire some poise and stability, even if they become a little hard-boiled.   Agree _____ Disagree _____.

This item is in a series designed to measure *I* factor (see description page 63).   The student will recognize for which type "Agree" is an act of overcompensation.

*Repression, through Humor.*   One of the more systematic ways in which repressed tendencies seek expression in normal people (other than by slips and forgetting, by dreams, and by other defense dynamisms) is, according to Freud and other clinical observers, through wit and humor.   Experiment has not yet reached the root of the matter, but at least it is already established that certain personalities consistently find jokes of one dynamic category more funny than others. Consider, for example, the following three jokes, from the Cattell-Luborsky Humor Test of Personality (6c, 11):

*A*. Did you hear of the kidnapping case in our block?
Heavens! No. Who was it?
Mrs. Smith missed her little boy and when she hunted for him she found the kid napping in his crib!
*B*. "How do you get your kid sister to find so many fishing worms for you?"
"Oh, it's easy" said Tommy. "Out of every ten she digs up I let her have one to eat."
*C*. "Why are you so much interested in art studies in the nude?"
"Oh, I guess it is just because I was born that way."

When the researcher finds the average laughter reactions to these jokes made by the general population he obtains an "index of funniness" for each. From this he can see how any one subject rates them relative to the population average. He then finds that people who consider (*A*) especially funny tend also to consider (*C*) funny, while they place (*B*) much lower than the general population does, *i.e.* (*A*), (*C*), and minus (*B*) constitute a cluster. Some fourteen such clusters of jokes have now been found, and it has been shown that the personality types correlating with indicated high humor response to these clusters are what one would expect on the theory that the individual enjoys best those jokes which express the drives he is most called upon to suppress in his own nature (11). Certainly it is true (11) that the dominant individual (*E*+), who presumably is never able to express his dominance enough, enjoys especially jokes of irony at the expense of the foibles and absurdities of others, and that the *H*+ person (rated high for sexual interest in the adventurous cyclothymia factor) rates sexual jokes higher than others.

Unfortunately, in spite of the vast amount of attention given to so-called projective tests, so little of it has involved skilled research attention to basic principles that even the initial question of whether the test best predicts overt, suppressed, or repressed trends is still unanswered. However, some recent work (8) indicates that ego-defense tests—whether they use projection, reaction formation, repression or other forms—show a response proportional to the amount of suppression the individual normally has to practice on the drive concerned. Since it can be shown (8) that this tends to be proportional also to the individual's constitutional eccentricity in the dynamic trait concerned, more accurate measurements are necessary before a choice between these alternative interpretations of ego-defense test measures can finally be made.

*Other Tentative Test Devices.* Ego-dynamism tests are among the more tentative, experimental devices in the whole pioneer field of objective personality tests. Few of these tests, even where a clear-cut source trait has been established, have been brought to a reliability level and degree of convenience at which sufficient data could accumulate concerning their practicality and validity in applied fields. Among other promising objective-type tests have been "level of aspiration" measures, attitude fluctuation tests, measures of disturbance through frustration, and the C.M.S. Test. In the first the subject is asked to estimate how well he will do in some trivial experimental skill, before and after he has had experience of failure. So far the reactions in different situations have not correlated well enough

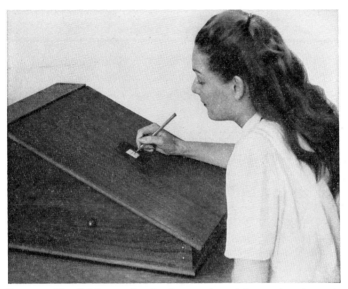

DIAGRAM 20.   Subject performing in a cursive miniature-situation test.

to justify calling "aspiration level" a single trait, but, such as it is, high aspiration level as well as rigidity of aspiration level seem quite significantly correlated with desurgency of temperament ($F-$). Thus, as Eysenck has shown, anxiety neurotics have much higher aspiration level and higher rigidity than conversion hysterics, for, among neurotics, low in $C$, conversion hysterics are surgent and anxiety hysterics desurgent.

In attitude fluctuation measurement a collection of attitude scales are administered and then readministered, from a day to a month later. Each person is given a score showing how much his attitudes have changed (the various directions of change being all added together as "change"), which is called his fluctuation score. This fluctuation, based on instability of sentiments and lack of dynamic integration, is, in certain circumstances, a good measure, as one might expect, of source trait $C$, Emotionally Stable Character (in reverse).

The C.M.S., or Cursive Miniature Situation Test, (4) assigns the subject the task of crossing out certain kinds of lines only, in a strip of paper, as it moves fairly rapidly past a small window. Situations are thus presented in a constant onslaught, which bring out the subject's degree of resourcefulness, excitability, honesty, initiative, patience, dependability, and boldness. How far do these *miniature* situations bring out the same traits as manifest themselves in real-life situations? In some cases—*e.g.*, timidity-boldness, excitability, and, to some extent, honesty—the miniature situation proves to be predictive of major situations of the same form. In others it is not.

As indicated initially, the measurement of traits by objective tests has not yet reached a satisfactory level. Though a dozen or more source traits are now clearly defined, we yet have only a limited group of their meaning and their value in the applied personality work of the clinic, the classroom, industrial personnel work, and vocational guidance. Fuller understanding of the implications of these measurements will come with their wider use in the applied field.

## 7. THE MATCHING OF PERSONALITY FACTORS IN DIFFERENT MEDIA

**Sources and Criteria of Matching.** Many studies exist showing *some degree of correlation* between a particular source trait in, say, questionnaire data, and measures of a factor in the same population couched in objective tests or ratings. Such a correlation points to a profitable area for more controlled research, but does not in itself prove that the same factor is involved in both measures; for distinct factors, *e.g.*, factor $B$ and factor $C$, *may* correlate as much as 0.4 or 0.5 with one another or some third criterion factor. If we obtain a low correlation of this kind it may simply mean what it says, *i.e.*, that we have two distinct factors that are somewhat correlated— as many source traits are. On the other hand it *may* mean that the two measures are really measures of the same factor, but that due to the unreliability of the single measurements the true correlation of 1.0 has become attenuated to 0.5.

Several studies, with such accurate knowledge of reliability of factor measures that correction for attenuation can be carried out, will be necessary before we can be sure that a given questionnaire factor is really the mental interior of a rating factor and that both are alternative expressions of a given factor in objective tests.

The first condition for satisfactory cross identification of factors is, therefore, that the same population of people be measured on *all* the major $BR$, $Q$, and $OT$ factors known. If Factor 3 in the $BR$ series then correlates *considerably* with, say, Factor 7 in the $Q$ series and 4 in the $OT$ series, and if none of these correlate appreciably with any other factors, there is a strong presumption that they are three measures of one and the same personality factor. To obtain *proof* of this it is necessary to obtain not only a considerable but a *perfect* correlation—when the reliabilities of the two measures, the selection of the population and other statistical matters are taken into consideration.

This last has not yet been obtained and indeed only one study (13) exists in which all important *BR*, *SR*, and *OT* factors have been simultaneously estimated for one population. This study, aided by evidence from a few more restricted studies, has been the basis for the matchings of factors described above in this chapter. It will be seen that only a very few source traits, namely, *C*, *F*, *G*, *M*, *I*, and possibly *H* and *L*, have their expressions in all three media mapped out and recognized. Others, namely *A*, *E*, *K*, *N*, and *O*, are recognizable both in their behavior rating and their questionnaire manifestations but have so far had no objective-test factor matched with them, though isolated tests are known to correlate, *e.g.*, with dominance (*E*). One factor, "Will Control," is known in questionnaires and tests but not in ratings. Omission from the rating area is rare, because this is the one realm in which the personality-sphere concept can guide the experimenter to a truly exhaustive sampling of possible forms of behavior.

The matching agreement demonstrated by experiment is generally intelligible from the standpoint of meaning. For example, with the *C* factor matchings the emotional instability and neuroticism shown by behavior ratings agrees well with the questionnaire picture of emotionality and dissatisfaction, which agrees again with the objective tests of fluctuation of attitudes, sway suggestibility, and uncontrollable disposition rigidity.

Wider associations and interpretations of the discovered source traits in relation to general theory may occur to the student. For example, the *C* factor has many resemblances to psychoanalysts' concept of "ego strength." If ego structures vary in strength covariation techniques should be capable of detecting the outlines of the structure, bringing its principle manifestations together as a factor. Conversely if it cannot be so demonstrated its existence and value as a concept is questionable. What we shall call for the present, descriptively, Emotional Maturity and Stability seems likely to be ultimately interpretable as ego strength.

## 8. SUMMARY

1. Self-rating (*SR*) data on personality falls largely into two realms: (*a*) Personal Inventory Questionnaire (*Q* data) material which heavily represents clinical observations and neurotic syndrome reactions, and (*b*) attitude, interest, and value self-estimates (yielding *QA* and *Q1* factors). "Mental interiors" from such methods have limited scientific value and can be used effectively only with cooperative conscientious subjects and in the preliminary stages of exploratory research.

2. Some fifteen $Q$ factors have been tolerably defined by two or more independent researches, but only seven or eight can be considered truly confirmed in adult, normal populations. Where these are related to $BR$ factors, they have been named by the same label, but otherwise by the labels of the $Q$-factor index.

3. These best established $Q$ factors are: $A$, Cyclothymia; $C$, Emotional Stability; $F$, Surgency; $G$, Positive Character; $H$, Adventurous Cyclothymia, $I$, Sensitive Emotionality; $K$, Socialized Culture; $M$, Bohemian Unconcern; $N$, Sophistication; $O$, Free Anxiety and a factor of Will Control.

4. Four factors have been found in *self-rated* attitudes and interests and the two most stable—namely Radicalism vs. Conservatism and Hard-headed Rationalism vs. Emotional Attitudes—prove to be manifestations of personality factors already known in $Q$ data, namely Guilford's $LT$ and factor $N$ above, respectively.

5. The factors analyzed from interest-attitude material might be expected to be primary drives, or environmental mold patterns or temperament qualities. These personality factors operate as "hidden premises" in the attitudes and interests to which a person reasons or at which he arrives by the logic of circumstance. Personality measurement is concerned with specific "cathexes" to particular environmental objects as well as general source traits, but scales for this purpose are yet little developed.

6. Objective-test ($OT$) factors can be drawn with well-confirmed outlines in the realm of abilities but are still tentative, in the field of general personality. However, some tolerably confirmed factors exist of which those we may roughly class as "character" factors are found to be measures of C, G, M, a set of performances which may be called Determined Self-sufficiency, two factors as yet unnamed, and the well-known factor of Disposition Rigidity (Perseveration).

7. Test factors in performances commonly considered temperamental are: $I$, $F$, Fluency of Association, Masculinity-Femininity and Autonomic Activity Level.

8. Such factors as general intelligence and mechanical aptitude also carry a pattern within dynamic, personality traits. Examination of the first reminds us that the loading pattern of source traits will vary with the average level of the given population in that trait as well as with the amount of selection, or variance remaining, in the population. Generally, these will not destroy the recognizable continuity of identity of the factor, but only the correlations *among* factors. Gross differences of culture patterns or racial composition between populations may, however, distort factor patterns.

9. Objective personality tests are at present at too exploratory a stage to permit any systematic classification of the various approaches that will ultimately be possible. But one may separate from the general mass of test

designs the principles of (*a*) associative responses, (*b*) stylistic continuity, (*c*) psycho-physiological manifestation, (*d*) miniature situation, (*e*) misperception, and (*f*) formal process. The last attempts to isolate the essential process and mode of reaction responsible for a personality factor, as manifested in the highly loaded trait indicators, and is the basis of most steady advance in the field. Another possible division is that of ego-defense dynamism tests (including projection, phantasy, humor, etc.).

10. Already it is possible to see that certain trios of *LR, SR,* and *OT* factors are the same personality source traits outcropping in the three different media. More exact factorizations, controlling population variances, reliabilities of tests, and soundness of factor estimates will be necessary before this can be proved, but matchings implied by the factor labels in this chapter are based on significant correlations and can be taken as the first reasonably confirmed indications of the role of certain personality source traits in different realms of expression. Interpretation of most of these factors has to be deferred until they are more widely applied.

## QUESTIONS AND EXERCISES

1. What are *LR, SR,* and *OT* data factors and how may their interrelations be discovered by research?

2. Discuss the validity of *SR* measures with various kinds of subjects. Describe the *SR* patterns for surgency, cyclothymia, and emotional maturity, indicating to what extent you would expect each to appear distorted relative to the *LR* factor patterns.

3. Compare and contrast the "mental interiors" of source traits *A, H,* and *L,* relating the distinctions to the corresponding *BR* and *OT* patterns.

4. Give the verbal formula which defines the essential characteristics of any attitude. Describe one source trait found among attitudes and attempt to explain it in terms of "personality as an unstated premise."

5. What objective tests have so far achieved validity as measures of *C* factor? Which of these persist into the extreme range and offer the best available measures of general neuroticism?

6. Describe the test performances which are strongly loaded in, and define, the *OT* factors: (*a*) will control and integrity, (*b*) Factor *M,* and (*c*) surgency-desurgency.

7. Discuss the extent to which psychological theory and practice are concerned respectively with (*a*) general, common, dynamic and other traits and (*b*) specific cathexes of common dynamic traits. Indicate how the latter may be handled in factor-analytic measurement.

8. What is the response measurement common to all misperception tests? Classify the chief sources of misperception and show how test or situation may be arranged to bring out each of these in comparative purity.

9. Describe the use of projection and two other defense dynamisms in what may be called Ego-defense Tests. Discuss the relative utility of selective and inventive answers in defense tests and in the vaguer realm of "protective" tests generally.

10. Discuss the utility of distinguishing ability, temperament, and dynamic traits in regard to the prediction of performance by means of source-trait measurements, and give a fundamental definition of each (see reference (5)).

## BIBLIOGRAPHY

1. BRODGEN, H. E.: A Factor Analysis of Forty Character Tests, *Psychol. Monogr.*, 52: 39, 56, 1940.

1a. BRODGEN, H. E.: Variations in Test Difficulty with Distribution of Item Difficulties and Intercorrelation, *Psychometrika*, 11: 197, 214, 1946.

2. CATTELL, R. B.: Experiments on the Psychical Correlate of the Psychogalvanic Reflex, *Brit. J. Psychol.*, 19: 357, 386, 1929.

3. CATTELL, R. B.: Fluctuation of Sentiments and Attitudes as a Measure of Character Integration and Temperament, *Amer. J. Psychol.*, 56: 195, 216, 1943.

4. CATTELL, R. B.: An Objective Test of Character Temperament: II, *J. soc. Psychol.*, 19: 99-114, 1944.

4a. CATTELL, R. B., S. N. FEINGOLD, and B. SARASON: A Culture-free Intelligence Test: II, Evaluation of Cultural Influence on Test Performance. *J. educ. Psychol.*, 32: 81-100, 1941.

5. CATTELL, R. B.: *The Description and Measurement of Personality*, Chapter 11, World Book Company, Yonkers, New York, 1946.

6. CATTELL, R. B.: The Main Personality Factors in Questionnaire, Self-estimate Material, *J. soc. Psychol.*, 1950.

6a. CATTELL, R. B.: The Sixteen Personality Factor Questionnaire, Institute for Personality and Ability Testing, Champaign, Illinois, 1950.

6b. CATTELL, R. B.: A Culture-free Test of "G." Scales II and III, Institute for Personality and Ability Testing, Champaign, Ill., 1950.

6c. CATTELL, R. B. and LUBORSKY, L. B.: The C-L Humor Test of Personality, Institute for Personality and Ability Testing, Champaign, Illinois, 1950.

7. CATTELL, R. B.: Primary Personality Factors in the Realm of Objective Tests, *Character and Pers.*, 16: 459, 487, 1948.

8. CATTELL, R. B.: Principles of Construction of Projective or "Ego-defense" Tests, Chapter 2 in Anderson, H. H.: *Projective Techniques*, Prentice-Hall, Inc., New York, 1949.

9. CATTELL, R. B.: *A Guide to Mental Testing*, University of London Press, Ltd., Bickley, Kent, England, rev. ed., 1947.

10. CATTELL, R. B.: The Riddle of Perseveration: I. Disposition Rigidity, II. Personality Structure, *J. Person. Res.*, 14: 229, 268, 1946.

11. CATTELL, R. B., and L. B. LUBORSKY: The Validation of Personality Factors in Humor, *J. Person. Res.*, 15: 283, 291, 1947.

12. CATTELL, R. B., and L. G. Tiner: The Varieties of Rigidity, *J. Person. Res.*, 17: 321, 342, 1949.

12a. CATTELL, R. B.: New Realms of Objective Tests for Primary Personality Factors, (in press).

13. CATTELL, R. B., and D. R. Saunders: The Matching of Personality Factors in Behavior Rating, Questionnaire, and Objective Test Media, *J. gen. Psychol.*, 1950.

13a. CATTELL, R. B.: *Factor Analysis in Science*, Harper & Brothers, New York. 1950.

14. CHASSELL, C. F.: *The Relation between Morality and Intellect*, Teachers College, Columbia University, New York, 1935.

15. EYSENCK, H. J.: General Social Attitudes, *J. soc. Psychol.*, 19: 207-227, 1944.

16. EYSENCK, H. J.: *Dimensions of Personality*, Kegan Paul, Trench, Trubner & Co., London, 1947.

17. FLUGEL, J. C.: Practice, Fatigue, and Oscillation, *Brit. J. Psychol. Monogr. Suppl.*, No. 13, 4: 1929.

18. GARRETT, H. E.: A Developmental Theory of Intelligence, *Amer. J. Psychol.*, 1: 372-378, 1946.

19. GUILFORD, J. P.: Personality Factors *S*, *E*, and *M* and Their Measurement, *J. Psychol.*, 2: 109–128, 1936.

20. GUILFORD, J. P., and R. B. GUILFORD: Personality Factors D, R, T and A, *J. Abnorm. soc. Psychol.*, 34: 1–30, 1939.

21. HARTSHORNE, H., M. A. MAY, and F. K. SHUTTLEWORTH: *Studies in the Organization of Character*, The Macmillan Company, New York, 1930.

22. HERRINGTON, L. P.: The Relation of Physiological and Social Indices of Activity Level, in McNemar and Merrill, *Studies in Personality*, Stanford University Press, Stanford University, Calif., 1942.

23. KRETSCHMER, E.: *Korperbau und Charakter* 7th ed., Berlin, Springer, 1929.

24. LAYMAN, E. M.: An Item Analysis of the Adjustment Questionnaire, *J. Psychol.*, 10: 87–106, 1940.

24a. LOEVINGER, J.: The Technic of Homogeneous Tests Compared with "Scale Analysis" and Factor Analysis. *Psychol. Bull.*, 45: 507, 529, 1948.

24b. McQUITTY, L. L.: Diversity of Self-endorsements as a Measure of Individual Differences in Personality, *J. Ed. and Psych. Meas.*, 9: 3, 14, 1949.

25. MOSIER, C. I.: A Factor Analysis of Certain Neurotic Symptoms, *Psychometrika*, 2: 263–286, 1937.

26. RETHLINGSHAFER, D.: The Relation of Tests of Persistence to Other Measures of Continuance of Action, *J. abnorm. soc. Psychol.*, 37: 71–82, 1942.

27. REYBURN, H. A., and J. G. TAYLOR: Some Factors of Temperament: a Reexamination, *Psychometrika*, 8: 91–104, 1943.

28. ROSENZWEIG, S.: The Picture Association Method and Its Application in a Study of Reactions to Frustration. *J. Pers. Res.*, 14: 3–23, 1945.

29. SEARS, R. R.: Survey of Objective Studies of Psychoanalytic Concepts, Social Science Research Council, Bull. 51, New York, 1943.

30. SPEARMAN, C.: *The Abilities of Man*, The Macmillan Company, New York, 1927.

31. STEPHENSON, W.: An Introduction to So-called Motor Perseveration Tests, *Brit. J. educ. Psychol.*, 41: 186–208, 1934.

32. STRONG, E. K.: *Vocational Interests of Men and Women*, Stanford University Press, Stanford University, Calif., 1943.

33. L. G. STUDMAN: Studies in Experimental Psychiatry: V. "W" and "F" Factors in Relation to Traits of Personality, *J. ment. Sci.*, 81: 107–137, 1935.

34. TERMAN, L. M., C. C. MILES, and others: *Sex and Personality*, McGraw-Hill Book Company, Inc., New York, 1936.

35. THURSTONE, L. L.: A Method of Scaling Psychological and Educational Tests, *J. educ. Psychol.* 16: 7, 1925.

36. THURSTONE, L. L.: Primary Mental Abilities, *Psychometr. Monogr.*, 1, 1938.

37. THURSTONE, L. L.: *Multiple Factor Analysis*, Chapter 19, University of Chicago Press, Chicago, 1947.

38. THURSTONE, L. L.: *A Factorial Study of Perception*, University of Chicago Press, Chicago, 1944.

39. TOMPKINS, S.: *The Thematic Apperception Test*, Grune and Stratton, Inc., New York, 1947.

40. VERNON, P. E.: The Assessment of Psychological Qualities by Verbal Methods, *Indus. Health*, Res. Council Dept. No. 83, London, H.M.S.O., 1938.

41. WHERRY, R. J., and R. H. GAYLORD: Factor Pattern of Test Items and Tests as a Function of the Correlation Coefficient: Content, Difficulty and Constant Error Factors, *Psychometrika*, 9: 237–244, 1944.

## CHAPTER 5

# INHERITED, CONSTITUTIONAL INFLUENCES IN PERSONALITY

### 1. SOME MISCONCEPTIONS CONCERNING THE INTERACTION OF HEREDITY AND ENVIRONMENT

**The Importance of a Correct Allowance for Heredity.**   Now that we have the means for describing and measuring the individual personality "in being" —for defining in just what way a given personality changes or differs from another personality—we are in a sound position to look for the *causes* of changes and differences.

Systematically and logically, the first question to be asked in longitudinal, causal inquiries is, "How much was this trait given at or by birth, before environment had anything to say in the matter?"   For until the extent of hereditary influence is known the search for environmental origins of traits may be a wild-goose chase.   Knowledge of hereditary influence helps enormously also in practical problems, clinical, educational, and social.   All intelligent attempts to influence, educate, and repair personality must take account of hereditary qualities, as a good carpenter takes account of the grain and nature of the wood, or a wise farmer adapts to the innate limitations, *e.g.*, climatic tolerance, of the plants he wants to grow.   Thus before it was realized that general mental capacity is largely inborn, many idealistic teachers became discouraged of achieving *anything* through training mental defectives—precisely because at first they had tried to do too much and to train or strain capacities that could be altered only very little by environment.   Indeed, in driving individuals of limited capacity to attempt the work of normal children, they had merely warped, with an irremediable sense of inferiority, a personality which—apart from intellect—might have been normal.

In saying that the study of personality development should begin by setting aside that part of growth or individual difference which is due to inheritance, we are not merely saying "that which is given at birth." As personality changes with age it changes partly through environmental influences and partly through inner *maturation* determined by the hereditary nature of the organism. Let us begin, therefore, by asking where heredity manifests itself and how many forms it takes. It is necessary to know what we mean by heredity and to understand the techniques by which various hereditary and environmental changes can be separately assessed, before any particular aspect of personality or personality building can be understood. For the difficulties which students sometimes find in this field arise less from intrinsic complexities than from misunderstandings and misconceptions long present in language and the cultural atmosphere.

**Inherited, Inborn, Congenital, and Constitutional Characters.** A good deal of confusion arises in the first place from incorrect use of the four terms just listed. Qualities biologically acquired from the immediate parents, or from grandparents or more remote ancestors, are called *inherited*. Not all the qualities potential in the individual germ cell at the moment of conception need be, however, inherited. It is well known that mutations are constantly occurring "spontaneously" so that the germ plasm may possess qualities not derived from any forebear, near or remote. This is forcefully illustrated in what are called "sports"—instances where a child is born with a double stomach, or a new eye form, or some change in the body chemistry. In the only animal in which genetic happenings have been closely watched—the fruit fly—these mutations have been seen to occur naturally only in a small minority of each generation. It is not known how often they occur in man, but they must be more frequent than the rare occurrence of obvious "sports" might suggest. In any case, even though they be comparatively rare, one must stress the scientific importance of the notion that, in general, what is *inborn* includes more than what is inherited. Mutations are important because they are real characters of the germ plasm—of the genes and plasmagenes—which can thenceforth be passed on by heredity.

The term *congenital* has become defined in medicine as referring to something existing at, or dating from, birth. Some constitutional characters, existing for the rest of the individual's life, are not hereditary but are acquired between conception and birth, while the embryo is growing in the womb. Mongolian imbecility and certain sensory and motor defects are among the psychological characters which are congenital but not inborn. Many congenital characters, therefore, are neither inborn nor passed on by heredity. Science lacks an accepted term for this new fraction, but "acquired-in-utero" is reasonably clear.

*Constitutional* is a very uncertain and unsatisfactory term. Writers speak of a person's "constitution" having been weakened or changed, so that it cannot be synonymous with what is congenital. On the other hand, there is no point in making it synonymous with a person's total psychological nature at a given point, with all that experience has done to his nature, for that is nothing less than his personality. Its best use seems to lie in making a relative rather than an absolute distinction, by referring to that part of the personality, at any age, which is likely to be *least* subject to change. This,

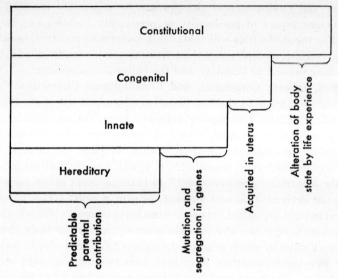

DIAGRAM 21. Definitions of contributions to personality commonly considered "non-environmental."

therefore, means largely temperament and disposition, but also some relatively fixed abilities and sentiments, as they have stabilized themselves at the time in question.

Alternatively, to give the term a more precise connotation than this relativistic one, it might prove useful to restrict it to what is physiological or somatic in the existing determination of personality. This physiological substrate would change with age, physical disease, mental stresses, and temporary drug conditions, but would constitute an abstraction from the total personality that would not be susceptible to rapid change or conscious learning. This indeed is the sense in which "constitutional" is used by many people. Whether used in this or the first sense given above, the term is wider than "congenital."

"Inheritance" itself, though a precise concept, is a term susceptible to confusion. Children of the same parents do not have the same heredity.

Siblings differ because of rearrangements of the parental genes in the process of combination. One could use three concepts here, *viz.*, *parental* inheritance, meaning the extent to which the child resembles the midparent[1]; *actual* inheritance, meaning the individual's genetic constitution other than where it is due to mutations, and *total* inheritance, the extent to which the individual resembles a weighted average of parents, grandparents, and great-grandparents.

These rather fine distinctions—summarized in Diagram 21—clarify thinking; but the more subtle of them are perhaps not highly relevant at the relatively crude stage of experimental understanding yet achieved.

## 2. THE AIMS AND METHODS OF PSYCHOLOGICAL GENETICS

**The Goals of Psychological Genetics.** What does the psychologist want to know about the interplay of genetic and environmental influences? Many matters of great practical importance depend on a correct estimate of genetic determination. The teacher wants to know how far and how fast he can get a child to acquire certain skills or certain levels of emotional control. The counselor giving vocational guidance needs to know whether the ability or temperamental trait is likely to stay pretty well at the level measured or whether a few months or years may change it completely. The psychotherapist, who happens to know that his patient's mother suffered from the same form of mental disorder as the patient, must realize how far that is likely to affect the prognosis (prediction of course of the disease) and the methods used. Finally, an understanding of the extent to which abilities, levels of attainment, emotional stability, interests, and attitudes in the whole population are dependent on heredity is of great importance in any realistic planning of the means of social progress.

**Mendelian Mechanisms.** The extent and nature of hereditary determination can be expressed in a number of different ways, resolving essentially into two. First, we can look for Mendelian hereditary units or genes—that is, for psychological traits which, apart from environmental modification, are passed on or not passed on as a whole. Under reasonably constant and normal environmental conditions these Mendelian traits will be transmitted from parent to child in an all-or-nothing fashion and according to the well-known laws governing dominance and recessiveness in genes. Since this is not a book on biology the student is referred to standard texts (19,34,56,58) to refresh his memory on the phenomena of dominant and recessive genes. A common physical example is eye color, in which blue or gray is recessive to darkness of iris. Observation of sequences and of proportions of relatives with blue or dark eyes, over several generations, has led to our understanding

---

[1] The average or total of the qualities of the two parents.

that a single gene (and its allelomorph) is involved, and to our being able to predict the sequence of eye color. For example, we know that blue-eyed parents will not have brown-eyed children, but that brown-eyed parents will have blue-eyed children in a known percentage of offspring. One must admit at the outset that the number of psychological traits yet traceable to single genes is regrettably small.

**Nature–Nurture Ratio.** The second method of expressing hereditary determination is to state what fraction of the observed scatter ("variance," to be precise[2]) of that trait in the population is due to differences (scatter or variance) of heredity and what fraction to environmental differences (61,76). If, say, 40 per cent of the variance of individual scores on a drawing-ability test is due to heredity, then, of course, 60 per cent must be due to environment (environment plus mutations if we use "hereditary" in the above precise sense of "traceable to ancestors"). Percentages for any particular trait can be discovered in either of two ways, which we will illustrate by the case of intelligence. In the first case we may discover them by controlled experiment. Here we start with the knowledge that the variance of intelligence in the adult population is about 500 (standard deviation units—points of I.Q.—squared, assuming an S.D. of 22.5) then compare this with the variance in a group of people we have selected because they all had the same environment from birth, and find it to be reduced to, say, 400. Since, by holding environment constant, we reduce the variance by 20 per cent, it suggests that 20 per cent of the normally observed variance is due to environmental variability. To check this we seek a group of people whose parents were all of the same intelligence level (and who were reared away from their parents) and find that the variance in this group is only 100 units. In other words, if we keep heredity constant the individual differences produced by environment alone are only one-fifth of those commonly encountered in our society. This confirms the finding that heredity and environment produce respectively 80 per cent and 20 per cent of the existing individual differences (variance) in intelligence.

Experimental control, in this case by selection of people for the same heredity or environment, is often extremely difficult to attain. As in a great deal of human personality investigation, we are forced to the alternative approach of dealing with the natural social situation instead of setting up an experiment. Here we must make up by ingenuity of statistical analysis for what we lack in the way of experimental control of people's lives. It

---

[2] The precise statistical concept *variance* is one of several possible quantitative indices of scatter or variability. The simplest index, the mean deviation, which equals $\Sigma d/N$, where $\Sigma d$ is the sum of the deviations of all individuals from the average and $N$ is the number in the population sample, has certain defects. A more useful index is the standard deviation $\sigma = \sqrt{\Sigma d^2/N}$. Variance is the square of the standard deviation, *i.e.*, $\Sigma d^2/N$.

happens that "variance" is a simple function of the correlation coefficient. If the intelligence of the midparent (*i.e.*, the average of the two parents) correlates 0.9 with that of the mid-offspring, then we know that $(0.9)^2$ of the (interfamilial) variance in people's intelligences is accounted for by the variance of the parents' intelligences (8,61). That is, $(0.9)^2$ or 81 per cent of the variance in intelligence in the general population would be expected to vanish if all parents were of the same intelligence and if environment remained as varied as it now is—which is approximately what we found by experiment. The relative efficacy of heredity and environment in producing individual differences in any personality trait can thus be computed from correlations with hereditary or environmental measurements. It is usual to express results obtained in this way as a *nature-nurture ratio* ($\nu$—Nu) which, in the example cited, would be 80 per cent, 20 per cent, or $\nu = 4.0$.

The above formulation of the problem is that of the simplest and commonest situation (and yet, mathematically, a special case) in which we have no reason to believe that hereditary and environmental influences on the individual are systematically correlated. In the truly general case this cannot be assumed, and the total variance in a trait is the sum of the variance due to heredity, the variance due to environment, and the variance arising from the correlation of heredity and environment, as expressed by the following formula:

$$\sigma_T^2 = \sigma_H^2 + \sigma_E^2 + 2r\sigma_H \cdot \sigma_E$$

in which $r$ is the correlation between hereditary and environmental causation and the sigmas represent the standard deviation associated with $H$, hereditary causes; $E$, environmental causes; and $T$, the observed measurements. Actually some significant degree of correlation is found in many investigated instances, and it is generally positive, for, in general, the hereditary possession of a trait puts the individual in a position to command more of the environmental conditions which favor it. Thus intelligent children of intelligent parents have a somewhat better chance of a good education, too, and emotionally unstable children of emotionally unstable parents are likely to live in or produce an environment of an emotionally traumatic kind, which may increase their instability. This fact raises complications which have so far been insuperable obstacles to the discovery of exact nature-nurture ratios, in practice, if not in theory. Greater practical and theoretical research resources than society has yet brought to bear need to be applied for proper scientific solutions—a fact which accounts for the sparseness of good data on this field.

**Common Misconceptions on Inheritance.** If it were not for the regrettable fact that the relative roles of environment and heredity have been variously exaggerated by propagandists, befouling science with politics, it might be unnecessary to emphasize that *all* traits are partly affected by environment and partly by heredity.　The nature-nurture ratio, $v$, is never zero and never infinity.　Here the student should beware of the argument that because a certain skill is wholly an acquired performance the observed individual differences in it cannot be due at all to heredity.　Reading is wholly an acquired performance.　No one is born able to read, nor does anyone grow to be able to read without practice.　Yet individual differences in speed and skill of reading are partly hereditary.　Hereditary tendencies become clothed in the cultural garb of the period, but their main outlines may still be those of heredity.

The student should also be warned against another aspect of the same error, namely, the fallacy of assuming that if a thing is not present at birth it is not inborn.　A moment's reflection should suffice to expose this deception.　One can think of drives like the sex propensity which occur relatively late in development yet without training.　One can see obviously that adult stature is to some extent inherited, yet the child does not have that stature at birth.　Whenever a trait appears after exposure to experience or training we should ask how much the level attained depends on the environment, acting through training pressures, and how much on heredity acting through (*a*) maturation, *i.e.*, inner, predetermined ripening, independent of environment, and (*b*) existing constitutional capacities to learn.

**Manifestation Rate.**　As stated at the outset, the nature-nurture ratio, $v$, is a device to express the relative roles of heredity and environment when the Mendelian mechanisms are too complicated to be at present unraveled (4,56,41).　A corresponding device for expressing relative influence exists, however, when the Mendelian mechanisms *can* be clearly followed.　If one is certain, from many kinds of evidence, that a certain trait, say a particular mental disorder, is inherited as a simple Mendelian genetic unit, he may yet notice that it fails to manifest itself in certain persons who have the genotype.　For example, a dominant which is present in both parents should manifest itself in *all* the children.　If it fails to do so in certain children we know that in these cases it is latent, but that sufficient environmental provocation has not occurred to bring it out.　The clinician expresses this fact by speaking of a *manifestation rate* which is defined as the number, out of every hundred known to inherit the *gene*, in whom the usual outward manifestation actually occurs.　Discussion of what are equivalent values in translating the figures for manifestation rate, $\mu$, into nature-nurture ratio, $v$, is too statistically involved to enter upon here; but it is obvious that they are not numerically equal.

**Methods of Investigating Roles of Nature and Nurture.**　The approaches to discovering the influence of heredity vary greatly in fineness: the coarser methods, yielding only crude indices of relationship, are appropriate to initial, reconnoitering studies. The following are the principal methods available (see (61)):

1. With "all-or-nothing" traits one may hope, especially if they are striking, to get records of their appearance in families over several generations and work out Mendelian mechanisms by a study of the genealogical tree. This has been done principally with pathological traits. It requires in addition, in most cases, studies on "Mendelian ratios" for a large number of families.

2. Proving that the mental trait in question is always associated with a physical character—*e.g.*, eye color, shape of head—which is already known to be inherited. Attempts to discover what temperamental or ability peculiarities are associated with the gene clusters we call physical races is a useful preliminary step to later analysis into separate physical features and gene associations (51,52).

3. Experimenting on animals, in which breeding is rapid and controllable, may prove—*e.g.*, by showing the possibility of segregating lines with distinctive mental characters—that certain characters are strongly hereditary. The argument from animals to humans, however, has to be by analogy, unless a common biochemical origin can be found for certain temperamental traits.

4. Comparing the resemblances of relatives, reared together and apart, with those found among unrelated people, divided into groups, reared together and apart. The resemblance is usually worked out as a correlation coefficient and the relatives taken may be parents and children, siblings, identical and fraternal twins.[3] Various comparisons give various indices and one should beware of mistaking many of the results of certain specialized comparisons for the values $\mu$ or $\nu$ described above.

An ideal comparison is that of identical twins reared apart with random members of the community (of course, reared apart). Correlations among series of the latter will be zero (save for chance error). The correlations among the former, squared, will give the percentage of existing variance in the community that is due to inborn influences. On the other hand, more readily available comparisons, such as that of the correlation between siblings reared in the family with siblings reared in different homes will yield a less useful ratio. It will give us that fraction of the general population variance which vanishes through people being born of the same *parents* (which is not the same as having the same inborn qualities[4]), and the fraction due to

[3] Twins are of two kinds (*a*) identicals, who spring from a single fertilized ovum, have identical genetic pattern, are always of the same sex; (*b*) fraternals, who resemble each other no more than ordinary siblings, arise from distinct fertilized ova and may be of different sex. If identicals (reared together) resemble each other in a certain trait decidedly more than do fraternals (reared together) it is a sure sign that the trait is affected by heredity.

[4] The difference is that between "inherited from parents" and "innate" in Diagram 21.

having the same *family* environment (which is not the same as having the same total environment). From this one cannot calculate the general $\nu$ ratio (72,76). However, for some sociological purposes these other environment-heredity ratios, notably the amounts of individual differences traceable to differences between families, are quite apt.

5. Instead of letting "general" environment produce its changes, the psychologist may bring some specific training programs or biological influences to bear on a group and compare its progress with that of an untrained group after the same lapse of time. In this way maturation can be separated from modification through experience. To obtain a nature-nurture ratio, the change produced by a given environmental influence can be compared with the magnitude of difference between two groups of the same environment but of different heredity. In this way it has been shown, for example, that treatment of diseased tonsils does not affect the I.Q., but that an attack of encephalitis lowers it, on an average, about twelve points (61). Such experiments or observations on nature's specific "experiments" are often valuable even if they concern the changes in only a single individual, exactly measured.

From the above considerations it will be evident that nature-nurture is a subject full of pitfalls and requiring careful study of its complications if one is to apply its knowledge correctly. The student need not at this stage feel that he is called upon to grasp the methods and mathematical procedures in detail. It suffices if he appreciates the kind of difficulties encountered and the necessity for qualifying statements. The rest will become clearer as we consider examples below. In leaving the field of theory one point must, however, be emphasized, namely, that both $\mu$ and $\nu$ indices are not absolute values, but ratios which alter with the degree of environmental difference and racial mixture in the population concerned. If $\mu$ for intelligence is 4 in the present population it may have been only about 3 in historical periods when gross differences of educational opportunity, nutrition, etc., caused environmental differences to account for more of the observed differences in intelligence than do the comparatively mild ones existing today. Conversely, in homogeneous communities where racial differences are slight, the role of environment will become more important and the ratio $\mu$ will decline.

With these methodological concepts in mind the student can now profitably examine evidence on the role of heredity in personality. That evidence is regrettably fragmentary and so uneven in reliability that it is very difficult as yet to construct any scientifically satisfactory over-all picture. Only one of the twelve most important personality factors, namely, general ability, has had a satisfactory variety of methods applied to it—and this is perhaps the least interesting factor from the standpoint of general personality. As in other research on general personality, the field in which data have historically been longest gathered is that of the abnormal, and this field may well be viewed first.

### 3. INHERITANCE OF ABNORMALITIES: MENTAL DISORDER AND CRIME

**Heredity in Mental Disorder and Delinquency.** The presence of a decided hereditary factor in the psychoses has long been known. On the other hand, it is generally agreed that though heredity has some role in psychoneurosis that role is far less.

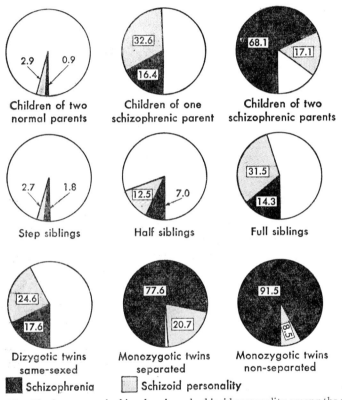

DIAGRAM 22. The frequency of schizophrenia and schizoid personality among the relatives of schizophrenics. (*After Kallmann.*)

That hereditary influence in schizophrenia is real is shown by the higher frequency of this disorder in the relatives of schizophrenics, whether or not they have had any contact with the patient (36,41,66). Cousins of schizophrenics, for instance, have a significantly higher rate than cousins of nonschizophrenics or people at random.

The extent of this greater incidence can be most readily seen from the graphical summary of results on the most extensive population yet studied (5,776 cases) by Kallmann (37). (Diagram 22.)

That schizophrenia has some tendency to be associated with a particular body build—a narrow build—we shall demonstrate in the next section. Such a physical constitution is also associated with greater tendency to tuberculosis and the tuberculosis rate, both in schizophrenics and their relatives, has been shown to be higher than average (36). Finally—though here environment cannot be ruled out—the incidence of schizophrenia in children of schizophrenics is decidedly high (nineteen times as high as in the population at random). The probability of occurrence of schizophrenia in relatives of hebephrenic and catatonic schizophrenics is about twice as high (36) as for other forms, which presents one argument for regarding the former as "nuclear" schizophrenia.

On the other hand, unlike some other mental diseases, schizophrenia may exist in both parents without any of the offspring being schizophrenics—in fact, at least 20 per cent of such marriages fail to show schizophrenic offspring. Moreover, instances are fairly numerous in which one member of a pair of hereditarily identical twins has become schizophrenic while the other has not (see white and gray sectors in Circle 8, Diagram 22). In short, while a "diathesis" or constitutional proneness to schizophrenia is inherited, the manifestation rate is low (relative to some other mental disorders) and the greater part of the decision rests in the hands of environment. Kallmann (36), Barahal (2), and others present impressive evidence for this diathesis being inherited as a Mendelian recessive.

By contrast, manic-depressive disorder is highly inheritable. Lewis's London survey (41) gives the following percentages:

|  | Manic-depressive disorder in parents | |
| --- | --- | --- |
|  | One parent affected | Both parents affected |
| Percentage of children affected (in large sample). | 33 | 67 |
| Percentage showing mood disorders of a lesser kind. | 17 | 33 |
| Percentage unaffected. | 50 | 0 |

There are indications that manic-depressive disorder has some hereditary association with more than average general ability and drive (67). The greater hereditary influence of the manic-depressive constitution is shown again by the study of Schulz (60), who found thirty families in which a schizophrenic and a manic-depressive were the parents. In twenty with early disorders, 8.4 per cent of the children were schizophrenic and 19.3 per cent manic-depressive.   In ten families where the children showed disorder late, all were manic-depressives, though of an involutional, melancholic type.

Other severe mental abnormalities with a very high heredity are mental defect—except the imbecile and idiot grades—and a degenerative palsy occurring in middle age, known as Huntington's chorea (4).   In the latter, and in a certain rare form of epilepsy (Myoclonus), the mode of inheritance has actually become clear in terms of Mendelian units, the former behaving predictably as a simple dominant and the latter as a recessive (56).

Penrose (49) has recently noticed the interesting fact, from the history of a thousand patients, that among the relatives of male patients there are more male than female abnormals, and contrariwise for female patients.   He argues that the auxiliary genes which play a part in sex determination in man are particularly liable to contain determiners of abnormality.

**Crime and Constitution.**   An Italian alienist, Lombroso, was the first seriously to claim evidence of constitutional influence in crime.   His picture of the criminal as an atavism, a biological degenerate, and an epileptic is now regarded as distorted, but Hooton (33) has shown that most of Lombroso's physical "stigmata" are indeed significantly more frequent in the criminal than the noncriminal.   The criminal tends to be smaller than the average, to have various physical defects more frequently and even to have a lower brow (33).   So popular ideas are not so false—except in confusing an average with an infallible type!

Expert opinion rejected Lombroso partly because it was so difficult to conceive of criminal tendencies *as such* being inherited, though psychiatrists had long recognized an inborn "moral imbecile" as a type incapable of moral feelings, and have recognized anew in recent years the *psychopath*, who is emotionally impulsive and incorrigible in spite of the best training.   It was the pioneer research of Lange (40) which showed that, however difficult the explanation may be for our imagination, the fact remains that a very considerable hereditary determination occurs in crime.   He covered the jails of a whole country, seeking criminals (of many convictions) who had twin brothers.   He found that when the twin was an "identical"[5] he was also, in 77 per cent of instances, a felon, whereas when he was only a "fraternal" twin, criminality of behavior was present in only 12 per cent.   This gives a very definite role to heredity, for sibling resemblance in heredity, plus similar environment, led only to 12 per cent of concordance, whereas identical heredity led to 77 per cent.   Lange's results, written up in a book called *Crime as Destiny* (40), stimulated other similar inquiries, which, as reviewed by Rosanoff along with his own study, gave results as follows:

[5] See footnote, p. 125.

PERCENTAGE OF CASES IN WHICH BOTH TWINS WERE CRIMINALS

| Investigator | No. of cases | Monozygotic twins | No. of cases | Dizygotic but of same sex |
|---|---|---|---|---|
| Lange............. | 13 | 76.9 | 17 | 11.8 |
| Legras............. | 4 | 100.0 | 5 | 0.0 |
| Rosanoff........... | 37 | 67.6 | 28 | 17.9 |
| Stumpfle........... | 18 | 72.2 | 19 | 36.8 |
| Kranz............. | 31 | 64.4 | 43 | 53.5 |
| Mean............. | .. | 69.9 | .. | 33.0 |

Stumpfle's study shows that the concordance of monozygotic twins is greater for grave criminality than for lesser offenses.

Although it may be difficult to conceive what this hereditary influence can be, especially if we insist that crime has only sociological meaning and must be sociologically determined, the undeniable fact has to be accounted for that heredity is somehow a very important determiner—in society as now organized and known to us. Our first hypothesis might be that recidivists, *i.e.*, criminals who repeatedly come up for sentence, are of low intelligence, since it is known that the mental defective is prone to get into trouble repeatedly, and we know that mental defect or low intelligence is largely inborn. But in the cases studied it was not true that the bulk of the prison population was mentally defective: we have therefore to seek some other effective, and hereditary, cause.

Of the first twelve important personality source traits only two, namely $C$ and $G$, have been considered—apart from the well-known $B$ (intelligence) trait—to have connection with delinquency. In the case of $C$ (Emotionally Stable Character vs. General Emotionality) questionnaire studies have shown decidedly more negative (emotional) scores for delinquents than nondelinquents (see (2), p. 358, Chap. 1). Further, Burt, in his classical study of the young delinquent (see Chap. 16 and (8), Chap. 16) specifically observes that the trait of general emotionality was one which most emphatically distinguished his delinquent from his control group. He also infers from his observations, that $C$ factor is largely inborn.

This cannot be considered proved—metric evidence is far too scant—but the most likely inference from the above researches seems to be that in the realm commonly considered character stability there is a temperamental factor, $C$, which has perhaps more than one-half of its variance determined genetically. Since most crime—over a large array of culture patterns—has in common a victory of impulse over restraint, it is not surprising that hereditary influence can be demonstrated.

**Neuroses, etc.** Among the neuroses and lesser mental abnormalities a noticeable apparent hereditary influence has been remarked in stuttering, enuresis, and obsessional and anxiety neuroses. Unfortunately, in none of these has the influence of family contact been sufficiently excluded. Hirsch (see Chap. 16) made a comparison of enuretics and nonenuretics among delinquents which showed 46 per cent of fathers enuretic throughout childhood in the parents of the former and only 20 per cent in the latter. (This figure from delinquents may be high for the general population.)

In fifty cases of anxiety hysteria and anxiety neurosis McInnes found that the incidence of psychosis in the parents and near relatives was no higher than in the parents and relatives of a control group free from neurosis, but the frequency of neurosis of an anxiety type was three times as great. An even more emphatic association was found with obsessional neurosis, but still one which would leave the greater part of its determination to environment. The role of heredity in neurosis generally has, in the past, been impossible to determine because of our inability to measure degree of neurosis and say when a definite degree of neurosis is present or absent. Clinicians, however, have often pointed to an hereditary element. Freud (22) speaks of an innate tendency to fixation or arrest in libido. Glover (28) concludes that the capacity to sublimate varies congenitally, while psychiatrists generally have indicated their impressions by such concepts as "neuropathic heredity." The recent extensive but as yet unpublished research of Eysenck at the Maudsley Hospital, using objective measures of general neuroticism as defined by the $C$ factor, proves a larger hereditary influence in neuroticism than had previously been admitted, at least by psychoanalysts. Eysenck found correlations of measured general neuroticism of about $+0.9$ for identical twins and only $0.5$ for fraternal twins. He has also shown a markedly greater prevalence of certain peculiarities of the microscopic appearance of the capillaries in neurotics.

With conversion hysteria the statistically excess incidence of the same neurotic syndrome in relatives appears to be smaller than for other neuroses. At the same time it is claimed that psychoses, notably mania and epilepsy, are slightly but significantly associated with the hysteric heredity. It may be that this betokens inheritance of a common basis for these in the form of the source trait either of sthenic emotionality ($D$, comprising proneness to anger, self-assertion, sociability, and self-pity) (see (5), Chap. 4,) or of surgency ($F$). Here Davenport's observation of inheritance of violent temper, apparently as a simple Mendelian dominant, ramifying through several generations, may fit in (13).

Stuttering seems definitely to be more common in twinning than in non-twinning families (3). Nelson and others (47) studied 200 twins of stutterers and found that (with one exception) none of the fraternal twins stuttered, whereas (with one exception) all the identical twins did. The hereditary determination in such minor abnormalities as stuttering and enuresis, indeed, seems to be higher than for the psychoses. The inheritance of general childhood disorders, comparing mental and physical manifestations, has been reviewed by Robb (54).

### 4. INHERITANCE OF TEMPERAMENT AND PHYSIQUE

As mentioned earlier, the expression "temperament" has had no precise meaning in psychology. It cannot be equated with all that is inherited, since many abilities are highly inheritable. It cannot be used as McDougall suggested, for "the sum total of the physiological influence upon personality," because every aspect of personality has physiological parallels. It comes nearer to being what has been defined above as "constitutional," but if so, there is no need for a second term. The usage here, following the discussion elsewhere (see (2), Chap. 1), is to use "temperamental" in a precise sense as applying to those aspects of personality that are not abilities and not specific dynamic traits (drives or interests). The properties of personality which fall in this modality or trait category show many indications of being closely related to physique. Accordingly the present section, which deals essentially with mental characteristics related to physique (*i.e.*, with anatomy but not necessarily with physiology) deals mainly with temperamental traits, though traits of other modalities may also be involved.

Preliminary hunches as to what aspects of physique are likely to have some relation to temperament can receive little guidance from human genetics, for as yet we know little about what patterns of bodily features are themselves determined by independent genes. Presumably when we do know a little more of the genetics of physique the most likely features to consider will be those which happen to be determined by the same genes as define physical development of the central nervous system, the autonomic, and the endocrines.

Meanwhile, to give us a starting point for experiment, we fall back on clinically noticed connections, mainly trends in the physique of the psychotic. Here we begin with the observation of Kretschmer (38), made at the end of the last century, to the effect that manic-depressives tend to be round-bodied, fat, and large of girth, whereas schizophrenics and schizothymes tend to be lean, narrow and angular in feature, and long or narrow in the trunk. As Sheldon (64) shows in his scholarly review of the history of speculations about body build and temperament, a general idea of this kind has cropped up again and again in medical writings. However, it was Kretschmer who first showed, by actual measurements, that significant differences exist between the average body proportions of cyclothymes and schizothymes.

Actually Kretschmer worked with a trinity of types, as some clinicians had done before, namely, the *pyknic* or round-bodied, the *athletic*, and the *asthenic*. The two last are both long-narrow or "leptosomatic" but the athletic is more muscular and heavy-boned, while the asthenic is slight in every way, as indicated in Diagram 23.

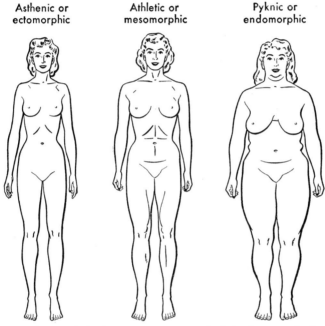

| Asthenic or ectomorphic | Athletic or mesomorphic | Pyknic or endomorphic |

DIAGRAM 23. Three principal components recognized in human physique. (*After Sheldon and Kretschmer.*)

Later, Kretschmer had doubts as to whether he could distinguish the mental traits of athletics and asthenics and tended simply to refer to a single dimension extending from broad to leptosomatic body build. But, more recently, Sheldon has returned to the trinity, renaming them Endomorph (pyknic), Mesomorph (athletic), and Ectomorph (asthenic), and adding much clinically observed detail, *e.g.*, that the athletic is more subject to frontal baldness, the ectomorph to a bald "tonsure," etc. The new nomenclature connotes a theory of the origin of each of the types in overdevelopment of one of the embryonic layers—a theory which is not yet proved. It also treats each of these components as an independent factor, so that any physique can be defined by three scores.

Before much effort is spent on relating physical features to temperament, more clinical, genetic, and factor-analytical research is needed to determine the independent components in physique itself—components which should first be shown to be independent in terms of individual differences, *i.e.*, as factors behind measurements, and, secondly, as genetically independent units. From a biological point of view it is most unlikely that some abstract mathematical index, such as that of Naccaratti (a ratio of body and limb length to weight), will coincide with a natural, organic, genetic factor.

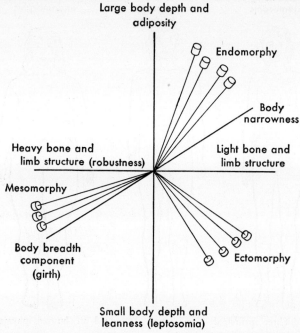

DIAGRAM 24. Probable relation of Moore and Hsü's body-build factors to Sheldon's clusters.

Some twenty factor analyses of human physique have been made by Cohen (12) and Waldrop (75), but the only one which meets the criteria of sufficient subjects, a fair range of accurate anthropological measures, and a complete multifactor-rotated analysis is that of Moore and Hsü (46a). Taken in conjunction with whatever consensus there is in earlier studies their analysis shows at least seven factors, but the three clearest (omitting the general size factor) are: (*a*) a factor of leptosomia, shown particularly in length of hands, face, nose, long bones of the limbs and, of course, stature; (*b*) a factor of girth (chest, waist, breadth of face), or pyknic, build; (*c*) a factor of robustness shown in forearm circumference, calf circumference, and thickness of neck.    There is also a suggestion in other studies of a factor of chest depth and head length as well as clear proof of factors of head size and of trunk length.    It is unfortunate that these studies have not included some of the wider variables included in Sheldon's clinical approach, such as distribution of hair, coloring, muscular development, tapering of limbs, texture of skin, and fat deposits, etc.   However, in Diagram 24 we have attempted a contingent analysis of Sheldon's clusters in terms of the above factors, putting vertically the leptosomia factor (with chest depth added) and on two horizontal axes the girth factor and the robustness factor.    Thus endomorphy, for example is a combination of low leptosomia, high girth factor and low (muscular) robustness.

On the clinical level Sheldon has related his three components to three correlation clusters (*not* independent factors) of traits which he calls viscerotonia, somatotonia, and cerebrotonia, the first two of which have been described in the review of surface traits in Chapter 2, while the third, cerebrotonia, is describable as a possibly new surface trait including the traits "inhibited," "overintense," "self-conscious," "secretive," and "neurasthenic."   Among normals, appreciable and indubitable correlations are found between physical and psychological components, but these may nevertheless not be the best components in which to express the relationship.    Fiske's study (20) indeed throws doubt on the Sheldon categories. A possible analysis of Sheldon's surface traits in terms of the basic source traits $A$, $E$, and $F$ is given in Diagram 25.

Kretschmer's correlations among the abnormal have been confirmed in Britain and America, though when corrections for the greater age and the "middle-aged spread" in the manic-depressives have been made, the relation is less emphatic.    Studies such as that of Wigant (77) have added the observation that though most schizophrenics are leptosomes (or else dysplastics, *i.e.*, individuals with a "warring heredity" of ill-adjusted physical components), not all manic-depressives are pyknics.    Moore and Hsü, (46*a*) also working with psychotics, found significance around the 1 per cent level for the following relations: nonparanoid schizophrenics were well below both the manic-depressives and the paranoids in the girth factor; they were higher in the leptosomia factor and particularly high in the ratio of leptosomia to girth and robustness.    The paranoids differed from the manic-depressives in a lower ratio of robustness factor to girth factor.    As these researchers point out, this physical finding is a clear argument for setting paranoia apart from the schizophrenic syndromes.

The general picture of the pyknic-leptosome difference is built up further by experimental observations that leptosomes react more to mental than physical stimuli on the P.G.R., show greater loss of upper tonal hearing with age, are more persevering and more suppressed, have lower perseveration

(46), less frequently suffer from diabetes, are less sensitive to color and less naively emotional, have lower serum lipoid concentration, have a higher tempo (tapping rate) and quicker reaction time (68), show more sudden onset of fatigue on ergograph, show more sudden and variable pressure in writing (39), and show poorer return of electrical skin resistance to normal after fifteen minutes of stress (see (32), Chap. 11).

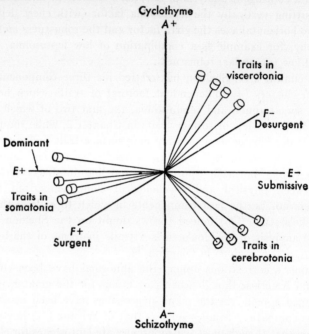

DIAGRAM 25.    Analysis of the clusters somatotonia, visceratonia, and cerebratonia in terms of primary personality factors.

The rating studies of Sahai, Burt, and others show that the factor of body breadth correlates with ratings of warmth, sociability, and sthenic emotionality, while Eysenck's results suggest also a correlation with conversion hysteria and surgent traits.    Burt's estimate of the magnitude of the correlation, when corrections for age, etc., have been made, is that it falls around 0.3.    Cohen (12) points out that the factor is connected with proneness to certain physical as well as mental disorders, the leptosome being predisposed to tuberculosis, pneumonia, dyspepsia, presbyacusia, stomach ulcers, nervous instability, and excessive excitability of the autonomic system, hyperthyroidism, physical brain disorders, and, of course, schizophrenia.    The pyknic is more prone to diabetes, nephritis, apoplexy, dropsy, circulatory disorders, gall-bladder disorder, arteriosclerosis, and cardiac diseases.

Many other minor linkages of physique and temperament, worthy of fuller exploration, are known. For example, Burks (7) observed a linkage of hair color and tooth conditions and of tooth conditions with manic-depressive disorder. Maas and Paterson (45) observed a syndrome of "persistent, unrealistic cheerfulness and grandiosity" in sufferers from an hereditary muscle dystrophy.

Jaensch (see (5a), Chap. 1), observed a constitutional connection between tetanoid features, low blood calcium, characteristics of the skin capillaries, proneness to eidetic imagery, lack of artistic interests, high emotional control, and an "independent inner life." An additional realm of study is opened up by Seltzer's (63) study of 285 cases showing that constitutional disproportions in body build, such as arise from hybridization of very different physical types, tend to be associated with instability and poorer personality integration—as if the task of integrating disparate temperamental tendencies were as difficult as integrating graceful movement with physical disproportions. It may be, therefore, that in addition to personality correlates with specific physical characters there exist correlates with the degree of over-all homogeneity of the somatic pattern.

The question ultimately arises here as in many other psychosomatic associations as to whether the physical causation is *direct* (in this field we can be sure that the physical causation is at least *primary*) or indirect, through the social reactions. Cabot (9), who studied personality traits in pyknic, asthenic, and athletic adolescents, found less evidence of correlation with the body-breadth factor than with athletic physique. The athletics tended to be better adjusted, more sociable and enthusiastic, and to show traits which Cabot was inclined to ascribe to the ready social acceptance accorded the athletic and physically impressive type. On the whole, this indirect causation is largely ruled out with regard to the breadth component, but, at least in youth, athletic build, good bodily proportions, and a handsome face may beget social reactions capable of influencing the development of personality traits.

Recently, Jost and Sontag (35) have brought interesting evidence of inheritance of autonomic reactivities, *i.e.*, of heart and respiration patterns, pulse, pressure, salivation, and skin resistance showing that the differences of siblings are less than that of random, unrelated persons and those of twins (monozygotic) less than those of siblings, are presented in the table shown on page 138. These findings on autonomic balance are fraught with great importance for the emotional life and the capacity for adaptability of the subject.

These figures are each the average of three groups (5, 5, and 6 twins; 10, 19, and 25 siblings; 361, 324, and 324 unrelated persons) as set out by Jost and Sontag in their full table (35). In that table the differences between twins and siblings approach the 5 per cent level of significance, whereas those

Mean Differences of Twins, Siblings, and Unrelated Persons in Measures of Autonomic Reactivity

|  | Twin mean | Sib mean | Unrelated mean |
|---|---|---|---|
| Vasomotor persistence (time of skin marking under pressure)........................ | 3.12 | 6.05 | 11.81 |
| Electrical skin resistance................... | 4.88 | 8.78 | 12.32 |
| Reclining pulse pressure.................... | 4.66 | 8.77 | 10.90 |

between twins and sibs on the one hand and unrelated persons on the other are frequently beyond the 1 per cent level.

**Racial Genetics.** Another rewarding approach to discovering somatic connections is through working upon the physical elements already demonstrated to be genetically independent through the studies of physical anthropologists on racial types. Unfortunately, extremely few correlations have been either sought or found under conditions of freedom from prejudice and with proper regard for technical difficulties.

The studies of Porteus (52), Porteus and Babcock (51), Fick (18), Hooton (33), and some few others stand out from a great mass of vitiated work, as indicating definite racial differences, between groups remote in physical type, in such psychological traits as intelligence, special abilities, and some temperament traits. The first are associated with differences in mean cranial volume but with no other physical traits that would be of interest or value in interindividual study. The more interesting question of temperamental and personality differences is largely unexplored beyond the above indications. Differences in racial groups in abilities and temperament undoubtedly exist, as careful and recent investigations show (15,26,65). For example, if we take Army drafts as screening groups comparable in abilities, we have the finding of Ripley and Wolf (53) that mental disorder in Negro drafts overseas was decidedly greater than in whites under the same stresses of separation from women, home, and culture, and exposure to danger. Most of the psychoses were paranoid schizophrenic. It is very rarely, however, that cultural conditions can be equated so that one can assess the relative roles of the culture patterns (as understood in Chap. 14) and of the racial, biological inheritance in determining the relative proneness to mental disorder, etc.

An instance where cultural control has been adequate is found in the association discovered (11) between high perseveration (disposition rigidity) and the Mediterranean physical race complex—dark curly hair, dark eyes, dolicocephalic skull. Prior to this, disposition rigidity was already shown to have an appreciable hereditary determination and to be connected with differences in interests and in proneness to mental disorders of a specific kind. Thus, lower disposition rigidity is associated with interests in science, mathematics, carpentry, and emotionally "dry" subjects, whereas high perseveration is associated with interests in history, languages, dramatics, religion, and subjects with immediate emotional interest. It is striking that independent approaches measuring the interests of racial groups reveal a pattern in conformity with the perseveration test findings (11).

Just what disposition rigidity means in terms of genetic units, or what the full extent of the association in this bundle of physical and mental traits is, remains to be discovered. Possibly there is only one gene at work, operating upon only a few of the physical characters that correlate to form the racial type. Possibly this temperamental trait of disposition rigidity will be traced to some difference of body chemistry, and be found to influence far more aspects of behavior than have yet been noticed. Obviously there are advantages and disadvantages in divergence from some central level of disposition rigidity—one can change ideas and way of life too rapidly or too slowly—and perhaps these racial levels indicate evolution towards adaptation to particular climatic and, especially, cultural conditions. Contingently, it seems a likely conclusion that a community of personalities of high disposition rigidity would show more conservatism in folkways than one formed of racial groups lower in this temperamental tendency.

## 5. COMPARATIVE STUDIES OF HEREDITY IN ANIMALS

**Animal Breeding and Human Inheritance.** That the physiological similarity of man and other mammals justifies our making inferences for man from experiments on apes, rats, or dogs is an axiom in medical research, as well as in learning theory and other aspects of psychology. This assumption is strengthened by such experiments as that of Tryon (74) who showed that, just as general mental capacity is one of the most heritable of human traits, so in rats it is possible by breeding to segregate strains of totally different levels of general maze-running ability.

However, the particular patterns of expressions of a given physiological tendency, *e.g.*, reactivity of the sympathetic nervous system, will necessarily be different, sometimes to the extent of making cross reference to human personality almost impossible. Consequently, animal experimentation, despite its especial appeal to geneticists by reason of the brevity of generations, cannot fulfill the purpose of a final method in psychological genetics.

Among the first experimental studies on inheritance of other than ability traits was one by Rundquist (57) who measured rats for amount of spontaneous activity in a revolving drum. The effects of selective breeding for active and inactive strains were evident, at the individual rat's first trials, by the fifth generation and at the twelfth the separation of the distribution curves of ability for the two strains was complete. The inactive strains were then found to differ also in being more sterile, in having smaller litters, in taking longer to reproduce, and in other ways. Brody (6) confirmed the results and noted further that, while inactive parents produced only inactive offspring, both sorts were produced from active parents. He concluded the effect was due to a single inhibitory gene, normally dominant, but perhaps recessive in females.

Another relatively well-defined trait investigated in animal heredity is wildness (shyness, fearful aggression). Dawson (14) showed that in mice the association of wild offspring with tame foster parents, or vice versa, had no effect. Rasmussen, however, found some temporary moderating effects from environment in rats. The tendency to wildness appears associated with physical characteristics (white rats are tame) but is genetically complex, whereas the rapid segregation of wildness which Dawson was able to obtain in mice suggested very few genes to be involved. Thorne (73) tested 178 basset hounds for shyness by an approach-withdrawal test. He found 73 per cent of offspring were shy ("fear-biters") when one parent was, and concluded that the tendency to shy, unfriendly behavior is a Mendelian dominant. In rats, as Marcuse shows (43), tameness is associated with a complex of reactivities, notably slower pulse rate and lower body weight.

Ascendant behavior is normally closely dependent on the social situation, as Mowrer, among others, has shown; so that a rat made submissive by a more dominant society takes a very long time to regain a dominant attitude with the original group. Nevertheless, a hereditary factor can also be demonstrated and has been shown to exist also among gamecocks, by Fennell (17). The fact that this is associated with an inborn tendency to greater sex activity, and that male hormone injections have repeatedly been shown to alter the individual's position in a dominance hierarchy, suggests that what is inherited here may be a hormone activity level.

"Emotionality" in the rat has long been investigated by measuring frequency of urination and defecation when placed in the "agorophobia-creating" situation of a wide open space. As common sense might suggest, and as E. E. Anderson's correlations indicate, this may not be "general emotionality" in the sense of the general factor found in human beings, but only proneness specifically to fear and anger, through sympathetic activity. Hall (30) first demonstrated, by showing the possibility of segregation in breeding, that emotion measured in this way is inheritable. As in Rundquist's study, other traits were shown by segregation to belong to the same complex. In this case there appeared a pattern of fearfulness, pugnacity, lower activity level, and more spontaneous, less stereotyped behavior, which showed itself more clearly with male sex. Later, Martin and Hall (44) bred emotional and nonemotional strains in the same manner and subjected them to the "experimental neurosis" situation of the air blast. The nonemotional strains showed not only more fits but more serious and prolonged general behavior derangements. This again seems to indicate that the "emotionality" is not to be identified with the general emotionality (*C* factor) of men, but rather with a general sympathetic system reactivity.

Perhaps the most systematic investigation of mental heredity in animals is that begun by Stockard (70). He used different breeds of dogs, made various crosses, and recorded measured behavior responses, physiological conditions, and skeletal build in each. Although the behavior was mainly investigated within a framework of reflexological concepts, much of it can be reinterpreted in dynamic terms. As indicated in Section 4, above, the most striking generalization from his work was that in dogs, as in men, an important factor of temperamental reactivity is tied up with a growth tendency towards leanness and slenderness as opposed to heavy, thickset build. The more leptosomatic animals inherited a tendency to acquire conditioned reflexes more quickly, to lose them more quickly by extinction, to become excited more readily, and to be more shy and tense.

With respect to each and all of these variables the unitary traits involved need to become more defined and fully explored in the general behavior of the animal. For, until the behavior can be referred to some unitary physiological source, in each case, we cannot be sure what patterns in man are subject to the same kind of hereditary determination. However, although the nature of the growth hormone (or whatever it may be that determines broad as opposed to leptosomatic growth) is still quite obscure, the patterns of temperamental responsiveness associated with it in man and animal are so similar that some similarity of hereditary influence is highly probable.

## 6. STUDIES OF HEREDITY IN MEASURED, NORMAL TRAITS

**Studies of Relatives in Different Environments.** As indicated in our introductory remarks, regrettably little research has been done on definitely measured personality traits of normal people, in relation to differences of heredity and environment. Only with respect to intelligence (source trait *B*, or ability trait *g*) is the research at all adequate, and there—as the student knows from his courses in general psychology and the above introductory discussion—the conclusion is that about 80 per cent of the variance is due to differences of heredity and 20 per cent to differences of environment. The present writer has evidence disagreeing with this commonly accepted view, favoring instead a determination of 90 per cent of parental heredity, and this figure Thorndike considers to be confirmed in his recent survey (72), where he finds the true sibling correlation to be $+0.70$, not $0.50$ as previously accepted.

The above applies to the normal variations of general intelligence. In definite feeblemindedness and imbecility it is well known that there are some forms that are entirely congenital, like Mongolian imbecility, and others, notably phenyl pyruvic amentia, amaurotic idiocy, and degeneration of the basal ganglia, that are entirely inborn or hereditary—in the sense that no known change of environment will affect them. The three last behave as recessives and are apparently due to the failure of some enzyme, *i.e.*, to an inherited biochemical abnormality.

Among the special abilities Brody (5) found spatial ability and mechanical aptitude to show greater resemblance in identical than in fraternal twins, while Carter (10) demonstrated the existence of familial hereditary resemblances in numerical and verbal abilities. A research by Thurstone and Albert (1) tested the members of twenty-one "complete" and thirteen incomplete families for manual dexterity, in settings where no special dexterity training differentiated the families. The agreement of level in parents and children was marked and indicated an appreciable degree of inheritance. On the other hand, Frye (25) correlated 200 siblings for mechanical-ability tests and found a positive correlation so low as to suggest little more than common environment.

All that can be said at present of special abilities is that though some hereditary influence is indicated wherever repeated researches have been pursued, the range of $v$ is great, being very high, for example, in musical ability (pitch sense) and spelling, and low in mechanical aptitude and verbal speed tests.

The initial evidence on family resemblances in personality traits other than abilities has indicated, from Pearson's early studies up to such comparatively recent studies as those of Pintner, Forlano, and Freedman (50), lower correlations than for general intelligence. The last named, for example, found intersibling correlations (378 pairs) of 0.40 for intelligence tests and only 0.15 for measures of personality adjustment. Since such results could, however, be readily explained by the comparative unreliability of personality measures, right up to the present time, it would be quite incorrect to assume that no dynamic personality traits are inherited to the same extent as general mental capacity.

Most of the interpretable evidence on inheritance of the normal range of personality traits comes either from studies comparing differences of identical with those of fraternal but like-sex twins, or from studies of identicals reared apart. The latter kind of evidence would give the ideal methodological answer if it were in quantity, but actually it trickles to us in studies of single pairs and, at most, a dozen cases. The evidence of single pairs, well observed, as in the reports of Burks (8), Gesell and Thompson (27), Gottschaldt (29), Friedman and Kasanin (23), Hoffeditz (32), Luria (42), Rosanoff (55), Schottky (59), and Seeman and Saudek (62) is, however, by no means to be despised, for it is capable of giving powerful suggestions regarding traits worthy of more exact investigation. These studies show that identical twins are likely to differ most, through different social environments, accidents of illness, etc., in such traits as (*a*) degrees of dominance, timidity, shyness, leadership, etc.; (*b*) degrees of conscientiousness, liability to sense of guilt, responsibility, and seriousness; (*c*) degrees of desire to impress, modesty, self-consciousness, (*d*) degrees of resignation or rebelliousness; and, to a slighter extent, (*e*) degrees of self-control, irritability, excitability, and neuroticism.

This consensus of clinical-type impression may be illustrated and expanded by the precise measurement study of Burks on identical girl twins (8) reared apart from nine days and studied at twelve years and again at eighteen years. Both were left-handed and turned to dextrality, were enuretic till eight or nine years, and were nail-biters. At 12.7 years their percentile ranks on questionnaires were:

| *First* | *Second* | |
|---------|----------|-------------------|
| 60 | 60 | on self-sufficiency |
| 71 | 84 | on dominance |
| 18 | 44 | on neurotic tendency |

Among twenty-six traits the eight that differed by more than one point were: generosity, humor, cheerfulness, sympathy, popularity, leadership, emotional independence, and readiness to face facts. They were very similar on physical energy, impulsiveness, competitiveness, talkativeness, lack of perseverance, and irritability. They were also observed to be very similar in expressive movement, gait, handshaking, writing tempo, style of handwriting, and "a tendency to be dissatisfied." Burks observes that the twin showing greater cheerfulness, sympathy, warmth, and skill in human relations was brought up in the home exerting less repressive discipline.

A special form of the twin-study method is where definite experimental influences are brought to bear differently on identicals. Hilgard (31) showed that an infant given special motor and memory training was overtaken later by the untrained twin, in the course of ordinary experience, though the latter still showed some difference in the form of greater "dependency, caution, or fearfulness." Thompson (71) similarly trained a 3½-year-old to be more persistent, with difficulties, etc., in play, by 45-minute training periods each day. The difference became significant, but was lost after the twins were left in the ordinary family environment for nine months.

Physiological inheritance has also been investigated by the twin method. Robb (54) gives a table of some fifty disorders that show evidence of appreciable inheritance, and mentions disorders of vision, hernia, allergy, heart lesions, hypothyroidism, and tumors as being most clear. Jost and Sontag (35) show that various autonomic reactivity indices, notably pulse rate, skin resistance, respiration, and vasomotor-persistence time are more correlated in monozygotic twins than in siblings and in siblings than in the general population. There is also a little light on the nature and specific cause of divergencies. Friedman and Kasanin (23) report a case of hypertension in only one of a pair of identical twins. This individual was more dynamic and aggressive, sociable, ambitious and tense, conscientious, and a worrier. It is suggested that for some reason he experienced a traumatic inferiority sense in early life.

Among other personality traits for which high heredity influence has been claimed is that of personal tempo, extensively studied by Frischeisen-Köhler (24). It may surprise some psychologists, though experience of the role of temperament in determining interests should mitigate the surprise, to find that the evidence for hereditary influence in such dynamic traits as interests, or the directions of free association, is as strong as for many more directly temperamental traits. Burks found marked resemblance on the Strong interest blank in the above-cited twins reared apart. Carter (10) on the same test, found a correlation of scores of 0.50 between identical twins and only 0.28 between fraternal twins. Sorensen and Carter (69) gave a word association test to 76 identical twins, 68 fraternal twins, and 144 unrelated persons, scoring each for "community of response," *i.e.*, the extent of normality of their response words. The coefficients of resemblance, corrected for attenuation, were 0.52 for identicals, 0.30 for fraternal twins, and approximately zero for unrelated persons.

In tests designed to measure temperament, such as "disposition-rigidity" measures, fluency of association, and tapping tempo (24), the agreement of identical twins is in every case greater than for fraternals. Wynn Jones found an $r$ of $+0.3$ for siblings in perseveration. Yule (78) found a correlation of $0.62 \pm 0.11$ for identicals, $0.40 \pm 0.13$ for same-sex fraternals, and $0.21 \pm 0.13$ for unlike-sex fraternals; but Cattell (11) was unable to confirm this evidence of heredity, possibly through using a different measure of perseveration. At least in fluency of association and in disposition rigidity, the variance due to environment is as great as or greater than that due to heredity, though in personal tempo the reverse may be true, as Köhler claims.

## 7. SUMMARY

1. More precise meaning can be given to the distinct concepts in the terms "parental or familial inheritance," "total inheritance," "inborn," "congenital," and "constitutional."

2. The goal of psychological genetics is (a) to isolate Mendelian units as dominant, recessive, antosomal, etc., genes; (b) to express relations, when the above is not possible, in terms of manifestation rates ($\mu$) or in a nature-

nurture ratio ($v$), showing the relative contribution of variance in heredity and environment to the total variance in the general population.

3. The methods of psychological genetics are those of human genetics generally, but five are especially useful, namely, (*a*) tracing familial incidences, (*b*) looking for associations with physical constitution, (*c*) experimental breeding with animals, (*d*) measuring individuals of various degrees of relatedness reared in different and similar environments, (*e*) measuring the effects of experimentally applied differences of environment. Certain pitfalls in reasoning from such data are indicated.

4. A decided hereditary influence exists in proneness to crime and mental disorder. Some mental disorders, *e.g.*, manic-depressive insanity, stuttering, enuresis, have much more hereditary determination than others, *e.g.*, anxiety neurosis, schizophrenia.

5. Leptosomatic body build is associated with relative predisposition to schizophrenia rather than to manic-depressive insanity and with a wide variety of psychological and physiological differences (centering on autonomic overreactivity) from the average. "Athletic" or "mesorphic" build may also have some personality associations, but an appreciable fraction of these are due to "social stimulus value."

6. Physical racial characters have been shown in the few instances adequately investigated to be related to temperamental reactivities and general and special abilities. Far more extensive research is needed, however, with better control of cultural variables and with analysis directed to detecting the particular psycho-physical genetic unities involved.

7. Breeding studies with mammals show that segregation can be brought about in relatively few generations with respect to maze-learning ability, timid emotionality, general activity level, and wildness-tameness. These prove to be genetic units, which soon manifest other qualities in the same unitary complexes, *e.g.*, fertility and autonomic reactivity along with activity level.

8. In man the highest demonstrated nature-nurture ratio is that for general mental capacity, though the lower figures for special abilities and personality traits may reflect only the poorer reliability of the measuring instruments.

9. Higher correlations for identical than for fraternal twins have been found in every psychological measure applied, but substantial hereditary determination of personality-test scores has been found principally in perseveration, general emotionality, personal tempo, fluency of association, word association tendencies, and interests.

10. From the standpoint of personality study and for better guidance of further research it may be of value to formulate the above scattered evidence in terms of nature-nurture ratios for the principal personality factors, though

this involves integrating evidence of very diverse kinds and cannot in general reach a demonstrable degree of accuracy.

Our survey suggests that the general ability factor, $B$, one of the schizothyme factors, $H$, and probably the general emotionality factor, $C$, are very largely matters of heredity. This conclusion is suggested by body-build associations, the results of tests, and the comparative studies with animals. Source traits which might be equally due to heredity and environment are dominance ($E$ factor) and character integration ($G$ factor), for though the latter might be expected to be determined wholly by upbringing, some capacity to integrate, to tolerate frustration, and to work for more remote rewards may be constitutional. The schizoid factor, $A$, the socialization factor, $K$, and surgency-desurgency, or $F$, may be more largely environmental (observe, for example, that Burks's twins, reared apart, differed in traits of the surgency and dominance pattern).

It is possible, as mentioned in Chapter 2, that further factor-analytical research will demonstrate that actual *factors* are always either *environmental-mold traits* or *constitutional traits*, because a single factor may indicate always only a single source. In that case, only correlation clusters or surface traits will be susceptible of having their variance divided into environmental and hereditary fractions. Where we now speak of a single factor it may be that there will then be discovered two, similar "cooperative factors" (see (6), Chap. 2) with slightly different emphasis. This has already happened with respect to the schizoid pattern, where $A$ and $H$ have similar loadings, and general mental proficiency, where $B$ for intelligence and $K$ for training and socialization have similar patterns.

In physical genetics it is helpful to speak of the *genotype*—the pattern of organism as given by the hereditary genes—and the *phenotype*—what environment makes out of these genes. The genotype in psychological terms is the individual endowment in *constitutional factors*, and the phenotype is the endowment in terms of *surface traits*, *i.e.*, the results of the interaction of *constitutional* and *environmental-mold* factors producing the observed clusters.

### QUESTIONS AND EXERCISES

1. Distinguish between hereditary, inborn, and congenital.

2. Give two examples of Mendelian dominants, one a physical trait, one a mental trait or syndrome.

3. If the stature of fathers and sons correlates 0.5, by what fraction would the normal variance of stature in the population be reduced if a new population were built up of sons having fathers all of the same stature?

4. Let us suppose we correlate people's endowment in a certain trait with the average of their parents and grandparents together and obtain an $r$ of 0.8. (And assume (a) no mutations, (b) separation from parents at birth.) What would be the nature-nurture ratio for this trait?

5. What index other than $\mu$ is used, especially in psychiatry, to express the relative influence of environment?

6. Name three "traits" in rats that have been shown to have a substantial hereditary determination. Can you suggest from a survey of dog breeds one or two behavior tendencies inherited by some varieties and not by others?

7. What surface trait is claimed by Sheldon to be highly correlated with endomorphic body build? Of what source trait is this the expression and what body-build factor does endomorphy represent when body measurements are factorized?

8. What is the evidence for disposition rigidity (perseveration) being highly inborn?

9. In studying heredity by comparing measurements on relatives, describe two experimental designs (other than the comparison of identical and fraternal twins) that are particularly good.

10. Name two source traits, other than general intelligence $(B)$, which are at present considered more hereditary than environmental, and three in which the level is determined more by the individual's experience through his environment.

## BIBLIOGRAPHY

1. ALBERT, R.: The Inheritance of Manual Dexterity, *Arch. gen. Psychol.*, 102: 1–63, 1938.
2. BARAHAL, H. S.: Is Dementia Praecox Hereditary? *Psychiat. Quart.*, 19: 478–502, 1945.
3. BERRY, M. F.: A Common Denominator in Twinning and Stuttering, *J. Speech Disorders*, 3: 51–57, 1938.
4. BLACKER, C. P.: *The Chances of Morbid Inheritance*, H. K. Lewis and Co. Ltd., London, 1934.
5. BRODY, D.: Twin Resemblances in Mechanical Ability, with Reference to the Effects of Practice on Performance, *Child Develpm.*, 8: 207–216, 1937.
6. BRODY, E. G.: Genetic Basis of Spontaneous Activity in the Albino Rats. *Comp. Psychol. Monogr.*, 17: No. 5, 24, 1942.
7. BURKS, B. S.: Autosomal Linkage in Man—the Recombination Ratio between Congenital Tooth Deficiency and Hair Color. *Proc. natl. Acad. Sci.*, Wash., 24: 512–519, 1938.
8. BURKS, B. S.: A Study of Identical Twins Reared Apart, Under Different Types of Family Relationships, in McNemar, Q., and M. A. Merrill, *Studies of Personality*, McGraw-Hill Book Company, Inc., New York, 1942.
9. CABOT, P. S. DE Q.: The Relationship between Characteristics of Personality and Physique in Adolescents, *Genet. Psychol. Monogr.*, 20: 3–120, 1938.
10. CARTER, H. D.: Twin Similarities in Occupational Interests, *J. educ. Psychol.*, 23: 1932.
11. CATTELL, R. B.: The Riddle of Perseveration: II. Solution in Terms of Personality Structure, *J. Person. Res.*, 14: 239–268, 1946.
12. COHEN, J. J.: Physical Types and Their Relation to Psychotic Types, *J. ment. Sci.*, 86: 602–623, 1940.
13. DAVENPORT, The Feebly-Inhibited: Violent Temper and Its Inheritance, *J. nerv. ment. Dis.*, 42: 1915.
14. DAWSON, W. M.: Inheritance of Wildness and Tameness in Mice, *Genetics*, 17: 1932.
15. DUNLAP, J. W.: Race Differences in the Organization of Numerical and Verbal Abilities, *Arch. Psychol.*, No. 124: 1931.
16. FARRIS, E. J., and E. H. YEAKEL: Emotional Behavior of Gray Norway and Wistar Albino Rats, *J. comp. Psychol.*, 38: 109–118, 1945.
17. FENNELL, R. A.: The Relation between Heredity, Sexual Activity and Training to Dominance—Subordination in Game Cocks, *Amer. Nat.*, 79: 142–151, 1945.

18. FICK, M. L.: Educability of S. A. Native, *S. A. Council for Educ. and Soc.*, No. 8: Pretoria, S.A., 1939.

19. FISHER, R. A.: *The Social Selection of Human Fertility*, Oxford University Press, New York, 1932.

20. FISKE, D. W.: A Study of Relationships to Somatype, *J. appl. Psychol.*, 28: 504–519, 1944.

21. FREEMAN, F. N.: The Resemblance of Identical and Fraternal Twins in a Variety of Traits, *Psychol. Bull.*, 26: 161–190, 1929.

22. FREUD, S.: The Predisposition to Obsessional Neurosis, *Rev. franc. Psychanal.*, 3: 437–447, 1929.

23. FRIEDMAN, M., and J. S. KASANIN: Hypertension in Only One of Identical Twins: Report of a Case, with Consideration of Psychosomatic Factors, *Arch. intern. Med.*, 72: 767–774, 1943.

24. FRISCHEISEN-KOHLER, I.: The Personal Tempo and Its Inheritance, *Character & Pers.*, 1: 1933.

25. FRYE, E. K.: The Mechanical Abilities of Siblings, *J. genet. Psychol.*, 50: 293–306, 1937.

26. GARRETT, H. E.: "Facts" and "Interpretations" Regarding Racial Differences. *Science*, 101: 404–406, 1945.

27. GESELL, A., and H. THOMPSON: Learning and Growth in Identical Infant Twins, *J. Genet. Psychol.*, 6 (No. 1): 1929.

28. GLOVER, E.: Sublimation, Substitution, and Social Anxiety, *Int. J. Psycho Anal.*, 12: 263–297, 1931.

29. GOTTSCHALDT, K.: Ueber die Vererburg von Intelligenz und Charakter, *Fortschr. Erbpath und Rassenhyg.*, 1: 1–12, 1937.

29a. CUPRA, N. S.: *Heredity in Mental Traits*, Macmillan & Co., Ltd., London, 1947.

30. HALL, C. S.: The Inheritance of Emotionality, *Sigma Xi Quart.*, 26: 17–27, 37, 1938.

31. HILGARD, J. R.: The Effect of Early and Delayed Practice on Memory and Motor Performances, Studied by the Method of Co-twin Control, *Genet. Psychol. Monogr.*, 14: 1933.

32. HOFFEDITZ, E. L.: Family Resemblance in Personality Traits, *J. soc. Psychol.*, 5: 1934.

33. HOOTON, E. A.: *Crime and the Man*, Harvard University Press, Cambridge, Mass., 1939.

34. HURST, C. C.: *Heredity and the Ascent of Man*, Cambridge University Press, London, 1935.

35. JOST, H., and L. W. SONTAG: The Genetic Factor in Autonomic Nervous System Function, *Psychosom. Med.*, 6: 308–310, 1944.

36. KALLMANN, F.: *The Genetics of Schizophrenia*, J. J. Augustin, Inc., New York, 1938.

37. KALLMANN, J. W.: The Genetic Theory of Schizophrenia, *Amer. J. Psychiat.*, 103: 309–322, 1946.

38. KRETSCHMER, E.: *Physique and Character*, Harcourt, Brace & Company, Inc., New York, 1925.

39. KRETSCHMER, E.: Tonus as a Constitutional Problem, *Z. ges. Neurol. Psychiat.*, 171: 401–407, 1941.

40. LANGE, J.: *Crime as Destiny*, George Allen & Unwin Ltd., London, 1931.

41. LEWIS, A.: Inheritance of Mental Disorders, *Eugen. Rev.*, 25: 1933.

42. LURIA, A. R.: The Development of Mental Functions in Twins, *Character & Pers.*, 5: 1936.

43. MARCUSE, F. L., and A. U. MOORE: Heart Rate in Tamed and Untamed Rats, *Amer. J. Physiol.*, 139: 261–264, 1943.

44. MARTIN, R. F., and C. S. HALL: Emotional Behavior in the Rat: V. The Incidences of

Behavior Derangements Resulting from Air-blast Stimulation in Emotional and Nonemotional Strains of Rats, *J. comp. Psychol.*, 32: 191–204, 1941.

45. MAAS, O., and A. S. PATERSON: Mental Changes in Families Affected by Dystrophia Myotonica, *Lancet*, 232: 21–23, 29, 1937.

46. MISIAK, H., and R. W. PICKFORD: Physique and Perseveration, *Nature, Lond.*, 153: 622, 1944.

46a. MOORE, T. V., and E. H. HSÜ: Factorial Analysis of Anthropological Measurements in Psychotic Patients. Hum. Biol., 18: 133–157, 1946.

47. NELSON, S. F., N. HUNTER, and M. WALTER: Stuttering in Twin Types, *J. Speech Disorders*, 10: 335–343, 1945.

48. NEWMAN, H. H., F. N. FREEMAN, and K. J. HOLZINGER: *Twins: A Study of Heredity and Environment*, University of Chicago Press, Chicago, 1937.

49. PENROSE, L. S.: Auxiliary Genes for Determining Sex as Contributory Causes of Mental Illness, *J. ment. Sci.*, 88: 308–316, 1942.

50. PINTNER, R., G. FORLANO, and H. FREEDMAN: Sibling Resemblances on Personality Traits. *Sch. & Soc.*, 49: 190–192, 1939.

51. PORTEUS, S. D., and M. E. BABCOCK: *Temperament and Race*, R. G. Badger, Boston, 1926.

52. PORTEUS, S. D.: *Primitive Intelligence and Environment*, The Macmillan Company, New York, 1937.

53. RIPLEY, H. S., and S. WOLF: Mental Illness among Negro Troops Overseas, *Amer. J. Psychiat.*, 103: 499–412, 1947.

54. ROBB, R. C.: The Relative Frequency of Fifty Commonly Inherited Disorders of Childhood, *Eugen. News*, 22: 3–6, 1937.

55. ROSANOFF, A. J., L. M. HANDY, and L. R. PLESSET: The Etiology of Manic-depressive Syndromes with Special Reference to Their Occurrence in Twins, *Amer. J. Psychiat.*, 97: 1935.

56. RUGGLES-GATES: A.: *Human Heredity*, The Macmillan Company, New York, 1946.

57. RUNDQUIST, E. E.: Inheritance of Spontaneous Activity in Rats, *J. Comp. Psychol.*, 16: 1933.

58. SCHEINFELD, A.: *You and Heredity*, Frederick A. Stokes Co., Philadelphia 1936,

59. SCHOTTKY, A.: Die Personlichkeit in Lichte der Erblehre; Leipzig, 1936.

60. SCHULZ, B.: Children of Marriages between One Schizophrenic and One Manic-depressive Partner, *Z. ges. Neurol. Psychiat.*, 170: 441–514, 1940.

61. SCHWESINGER, G. C.: *Heredity and Environment*, The Macmillan Company, New York, 1933.

62. SEEMAN, E. V., and R. SAUDEK: The Handwriting of Identical Twins Reared Apart, *Character & Pers.*, 1: 1933.

63. SELTZER, C. C.: Body Disproportions and Dominant Personality Traits, *Psychosom. Med.*, 8: 75–97, 1946.

64. SHELDON, W.: *The Varieties of Human Physique*, Harper & Brothers, New York, 1940.

65. SHUEY, A. M.: Personality Traits of Jewish and Non-Jewish Students, *Arch. Psychol.*, New York, No. 290: 1944.

66. SLATER, E.: The Inheritance of Mental Disorder, *Eugen. Rev.*, 28: 4, 1937.

67. SLATER, E.: The Inheritance of Manic-depressive Insanity and Its Relation to Mental Defect, *J. ment. Sci.*, 82: 626–633, 1936.

68. SMITH, H. C., and S. BOZORSKY: The Relation between Physique and Simple Reaction Time, *Character & Pers.*, 12: 46–53, 1943.

69. SORENSEN, M. I., and H. D. CARTER: Twin Resemblances in Community of Free Association Responses, *J. Psychol.*, 9: 237–246; 1940.

69a. STERN, C.: *Principles of Human Genetics*, W. H. Freeman, San Francisco, 1949.

70. STOCKARD, C. R.: *The Physical Basis of Personality*, W. W. Norton & Company, New York, 1931.

71. THOMPSON, H.: The Modification of Play Behavior with Special Reference to Attentional Characteristics, *J. genet. Psychol.*, 62: 165–188, 1943.

72. THORNDIKE, E. L.: The Resemblance of Siblings in Intelligence Test Scores, *J. Genet. Psychol.*, 64: 265–267, 1944.

73. THORNE, F. C.: The Inheritance of Shyness in Dogs, *J. Genet. Psychol.*, 65: 275–279, 1944.

74. TRYON, R. C.: Genetic Differences in Maze Learning Ability in Rats, *Yearb. nat. Soc. Stud. Educ.*, 39 (I): 111–119, 1940.

75. WALDROP, R. S.: A Factorial Study of the Components of Body Build, *Psychol. Bull.*, 37: 578, 1940.

76. WOODWORTH, R. S.: *Heredity and Environment*, Social Science Research Council, Committee on Public Administration, Washington, D.C., 1941.

77. WIGANT, V.: Attempts at Anthropometric Determination of the Body Types of Kretschmer, *Acta. Psychiat. neur.*, 8: 465–481, 1933.

78. YULE, E. P.: Resemblance of Twins with Regard to Perseverations, *J. Med. Sci.*, 81: 489–501, 1935.

# CHAPTER 6

# PSYCHODYNAMICS: I. THE INTRINSIC STRUCTURE OF DYNAMIC TRAITS

## 1. THE INVESTIGATION OF DYNAMIC TRAITS IN RELATION TO THE TOTAL PERSONALITY

**Dynamic Traits Most Plastic.** As explained in Chapter 4, traits are of ability, temperament, and dynamic "modalities." Any actual personality manifestation—any piece of behavior—expresses all three, but we may extract the ability aspect by asking *how well* the person is doing and the dynamic aspect by asking *why* he is doing it. By concentrating on measurements of these particular aspects of the behavior—the relation of performance to difficulty and to stimulation—we assess particular traits. For, as a review of Chapter 4 will remind us, abilities are traits whose measures alter most through changes in situational complexity, and dynamic traits are diagnosed as those which alter most in response to situational change in incentive, while temperament traits are those whose measures have least response to environmental conditions.

Though these technical criteria of modality are seldom explicitly in mind, the average psychologist has no difficulty in distinguishing abilities from drives, or either of these from temperament qualities. He knows a dynamic trait as something that has to do with reactivity to stimuli, with energizing the organism, with drive to action and striving for goals. Occasionally he may hesitate over such a trait as a motor skill, classifying it as a pure ability whereas our criterion would make it also part of a dynamic trait, which its liability to incentive changes shows it to be. But, in general, traditional practice and explicit criteria agree as to what are dynamic traits. Since we have now to deal intensively with dynamic traits it behooves us to examine more closely these characteristics by which psychologists have variously

151

defined them. The last named character of seeking for goals of satisfaction —a *telic* quality of striving for a particular end-situation—has been regarded by some as the most characteristic feature of dynamic traits. Whatever critical modification may be necessary in this approach, it certainly offers the most convenient way of *naming* particular dynamic traits—namely, by the goal each seeks and the state of satisfaction at which each line of activity ceases. Thus, if I say a man is gluttonous, I mean that much of his activity is of a kind which ceases when he has gorged himself on food, and if I say he is ambitious, I mean that eminence is the goal of much of his action. Other psychologists prefer to put the emphasis on the "drive" character, *i.e.*, the mere releasing of energy or action of an undefined sort, while there are yet other schools of psychology which emphasize the stimulus-response relation—the trigger action itself—as the characteristic of dynamic traits.

Actually, a true dynamic trait must have all of these characteristics. As in the firing of a gun there is a trigger action, the appearance of a powerful source of energy, and the direction of this energy to a specific target. Sometimes the dynamic trait is so ready to discharge that the trigger action is not noticed. For example, the clinician talks about the sex drive needing an outlet, and rarely stops to ask where it is receiving its constant stimulation. The reflexologist, on the other hand, concentrates exclusively on the stimuli, conditioned and unconditioned, which are the "cause" of, say, the salivary response, and his formulae have never taken account of how hungry the dog may be! These and other whole groups of psychologists have ignored or denied the telic, goal-seeking quality, because, forsooth, "the goal cannot reasonably be said to be the *cause* of behavior which precedes it in time!" The first task of the scientist, however, is not to ask what is reasonable but what happens in nature. Descriptively it *is* as if the end-goal determines the preceding lines of behavior. Let us admit this telic account as a rough but essential description and then try to discover the mechanical causality— the actions by causes which precede their consequences—that will explain it. For the drive to a goal will doubtless admit in the end a mechanical explanation.

Dynamic traits are our first object of study in approaching the developmental aspects of personality because they are the most plastic traits. Having assessed and set aside in the last chapter that which heredity can do, it is now possible for us to inquire how environment achieves that range of effect which the initial nature-nurture study has assigned to it. And when we examine personality as that which emerges from the impact between environment and the individual's native gifts of ability, temperamental responsiveness, and biological drives, we are bound to see at once that it is these dynamic traits which undergo most change. Temperament and the abilities—except the skills which are acquired through dynamic traits—

remain comparatively constant, in their hereditary maturation curves, but the plasticity of dynamic traits is such that the whole of a man's interests, his attitudes, his loyalties and sentiments—and even his character stability —*may* change two or three times in a lifetime. Moreover, whatever changes in temperament or ability may occur have to be understood in the framework of dynamic traits as they integrate the organism and adjust these demands to environment.

**Mapping the Dynamic Structure of the Normal Individual.** In consequence, our study of personality development will begin, and continue through the next three chapters, with an analysis of man's dynamic make-up and a search for the principles of psychodynamics. The scientific approach to this problem consists in first recognizing the dynamic structure of the typical adult and then, by contrasting it with that of an infant or an animal, attempting to infer what the culture pattern or general environment (apart from maturation) must have done to produce the observed changes. This view of the extent and manner of environmental influence may be further checked by study of the abnormal—of those personalities in which development has failed or broken down—for the clinic has been, until recently the richest cornucopia of dynamic knowledge.

Our first aim will be to observe and map dynamic *structure*. The principles which explain the rise of that structure will emerge only in the rest of the book—as far as they *can* emerge from existing research. The term "structure" is variously used in psychology, its principle alternative use to the present being to describe the structure of consciousness, with which our present behaviorist use is scarcely likely to be confused. In general, a structure is what is inferred to account for a function, *i.e.*, for a repeated pattern of behavior. A dynamic structure is thus something that accounts for the stability of dynamic functions, namely, a repeated pattern of responsiveness to a stimulus, of striving in a particular fashion, and of recurrently seeking a particular goal. An especially important aspect of structure is that which deals not only with single dynamic traits but also with the interrelation and organization of dynamic traits. It is possible, for example, that we shall find hosts of unrelated purposes, or that we shall find most minor purposive habits serving in some hierarchical fashion a few major purposes, to which they are ancillary. Again, we may find that whatever major patterns of drives exist owe their unitary character either to being inborn, biological, patterns or to being formed by cultural institutions. Let us examine these possibilities. Whatever we find it is certain that nothing is more important, in theory or practice, than to know what a man's purposes are, and in what way they are related one to another.

**Introduction to Methods of Dynamic Investigation.** It is not appropriate in this book to attempt at this point any systematic analysis of methods of investigating the form of dynamic traits, their interdependences, their connections with stimuli, responses, and incentives and the dynamic principles by which they are developed and extinguished. The detailed techniques will become known as we deal with particular problems and only in the last chapter of the book will the threads be drawn together in a series of summarizing dynamic principles.

However, one can see at the outset that the psychologist's knowledge of dynamic traits—such as it is—is drawn from very diverse sources, on such different levels of scientific objectivity that the attempt to integrate them is as difficult as mixing oil and water. In the first place, much of a fundamental nature has been gained by what we may call the *naturalistic* or common-sense approach of reasoning from observations on *human beings and animals behaving in their natural surroundings*. This naturalistic and anthropological approach works without benefit of statistics or experiment, other than the unwritten statistics of the observer's memory and the experiments provided by nature. Wielded by trained, unbiased, comprehensive minds like that of a Darwin in biology or a Freud, McDougall, or Stanley Hall in psychology, this method has yielded outlines of the major facts and principles in whole new fields, but its conclusions depend on a sort of collective common sense and are too fragile to withstand biased attacks. It is this approach which has yielded a list of the principal human propensities or drives, an initial statement of their "stimulus situation, specific emotion, and goal" structure, and the general nature of conflict and adjustment.

The second, and in sheer volume of generalizations the greatest, contributor to dynamic psychology has been the clinical, abnormal field. From methods such as free association, "projective techniques," hypnotism, and observation of the appearance and disappearance of symptoms many generalizations have been reached concerning mental conflict, maturation and regression of drives, and the phenomena of repression, sublimation, etc. The third important field, which is beginning to give more exact support for the "findings" of the first and second, is that of laboratory experiment on animals and man. This has given us such concepts as retroactive inhibition, goal gradient, extinction, and the law of effect, as well as further exact information about consequences of the conflict of drives. The fourth and last approach in the history of development of methods is the statistical one. This leads to the extraction by relatively subtle and powerful statistical methods, notably factor analysis, of more definite conclusions from the data of all three of the preceding approaches, but particularly from the "naturalistic" approach. This has brought us information about the real nature and extent of psychoanalytic mechanisms, (12) notably about ego-defense dynamisms, and has recently promised an answer to the long-insoluble question about the number and nature of the primary drives in man and other animals (see (6a), Chap. 7).

As stated above, our immediate concern is not with phenomena of conflict or with deriving ultimate dynamic laws but simply to describe the morphology of dynamic traits as they naturally appear *in situ* in the normal personality of our culture. Since we are out to study personality we shall use those data, rather than laboratory experiment, as the beginning of our quest for dynamic principles. The mapping of dynamic structure in personality begins essentially with two questions: (*a*) What dynamic traits exist? (*b*) How are they interrelated?

The first of these questions has been begged, both by laboratory and by clinical approaches. The animal experimenter states that he is experimenting with a hunger or sex drive, when in fact he has not proved (*a*) that it is a unitary drive, or (*b*) that other drives—*e.g.*, fear, pugnacity, curiosity—are not in fact operative in the given situation. He sometimes even chooses to call certain dynamic traits "secondary drives," without adequate grounds for distinguishing from common, primary drives (see the following section). The clinical psychologist, despite the advantage of dealing with very powerful dynamic traits, operating in the human wreckage thrown up in clinic and mental hospital by the turbulent currents of social life, has not made any particular contribution to defining the traits with which he deals. He is content to write of "object libido," or a "strong ego," or "parsimoniousness," implying by his semantics a unitary function, but whether in fact these are unitary traits and, therefore, quantifiable, remains an open question.

The only sure method of proving functionally unitary character, here in dynamic traits as in the general personality traits of Chapters 1 to 4, is to establish that the manifestations of the trait covary. This amounts to showing by some form of correlation, that, for example, persons higher in one manifestation tend to be higher in another (*R* technique), or that the various manifestations wax and wane together in the same person (*P* technique), or that the presence of a hormone causes the simultaneous appearance of all these behavior manifestations, and so on.

Unfortunately, except for a few isolated researches mentioned in the following chapters, we have to depend for our information about dynamic traits (and for our practice of naming them) on what is evident to the naked eye. We must contingently speak of specific attitudes, interests, sentiments, and drives as functionally unitary structures. Therefore we shall take as present illustrations those traits the unitary character of which can be most reasonably assumed and pass on to the second of the two problems above, namely the methods of establishing the interconnections of dynamic traits.

## 2. THE MEANING OF DYNAMIC SUBSIDIATION

**The Discovery of Subsidiation Sequences.** In whatever other ways dynamic traits may be interconnected, the briefest observation suffices to show that they are at least connected in some sort of "purposive" sequence.

The intractable environment continually compels a man to do one thing in order to be able to do another. In order that he may enjoy eating habits he must acquire working habits. We then say that the interests in work are subsidiated to the hunger drive. Constant repetition of such situations set up a series of response habits in which one member of the chain serves the next, and so on to some ultimate goal. Each habit of reacting—each dynamic trait—is directed to a certain interim satisfaction, but complete discharge of psychic tension comes only at the end of such a series.

The first task in mapping dynamic structure—the first task beyond that of recognizing and naming individual traits—consists, therefore, in tracing these subsidiation sequences. A good deal of psychological knowledge is based on a staggeringly simple method of doing this, namely, that of *asking* people for what end a given habit is being carried out. The student does not need to be a very shrewd psychologist to reply that this obvious approach is soon stopped, first, by people's unwillingness to admit certain motives, second, by their frank ignorance of why they do many trivial things, and third, by that opaque curtain of "repression" which we shall study below. However, let us see what happens in these relatively uncomplicated motivations where these embarrassments do not obscure the incentives. Let us, in fact, take some outspoken man who seems to know what he is about, say Macaulay's Horatius as he stands at the bridge with the gory corpse of Lars Porsena before him.

If we ask Horatius what drove him to battle so formidable a foe, he would probably reply, "I am determined to keep the Tuscan soldiers out of Rome." That is obviously not a universal human motive so we ask, "Why do you want to keep them out?" One can imagine that he would reply rather shortly, "Because I am a Roman patriot with proper sentiments about my country!" Pressed as to why the preservation of his country, its welfare, and its culture is important, he could reply, "Because I want my children to grow up in peace, security, and opportunity." But if one pressed farther and asked "Why do you love your children?" the surprise of Horatius at such a foolish question would indicate that you had come to the end of possible logical explanation. In human behavior where reason ends, instinct begins. One has come to the biological goal, a purpose which seems to the organism immediately worth while, without justification.

By rudely reiterating "Why?" to each answer, we can, therefore, in the simplest case, expose a series of *subsidiary* goals to a final goal. The person does *A* in order to do *B*, having gained the vantage point of *B* he is still unsatisfied and wants to attain *C*—and so on to the final satisfying goal at which activity ceases. This we shall call a dynamic *subsidiation* sequence (Murray (10)), and, as shown in Diagram 26, the lesser satisfactions between may be called intermediate or subsidiary goals, or means-end activities (15).

In passing along a subsidiation chain we encounter dynamic traits that we variously called "interests," "attitudes," "sentiments," and "drives" or "propensities." For example, in the above sequence Horatius may be said to have an attitude toward Lars Porsena, a sentiment toward his country and family, and a drive or propensity that urges him to come to the protection of his children. The term "interests" is best equated with "dynamic traits," unless we wish to use such a term simply for the *objects* of dynamic traits, *i.e.*, the stimulative and satisfying situations. Such interests or traits obviously include repulsions and hostilities as well as attractions—*i.e.*, it is correct to say that Horatius is interested in the Tuscan army: he wishes to destroy it.

The terms attitude, prejudice, sentiment, etc., have become stabilized in general educated vocabulary in the sense that attitudes are connected with

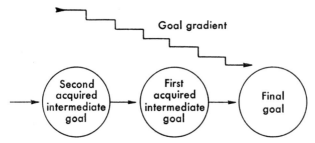

DIAGRAM 26.   Subsidiation (means-end activities) and the hypothesis of goal gradient.

minor, relatively superficial interests, whereas sentiments are stronger and deeper attitudes. Prejudices, of course, are attitudes without factual or logical support, and therefore, usually the ideals of our enemies! Further discussion below will show that we may add various more exact notions to the popular differentiation of attitude and sentiment, the first of which is that attitudes are more *remote in the subsidiation sequence from the basic goal*. The relatively strong, deep-set sentiments have the lesser attitudes and trivial interests organized around them. They are nearer, in terms of goal distance, to the basic biological needs. Last in the subsidiation stand the biological goals themselves, the drives for which have long been called in popular language "instincts." For the latter we shall now develop more exact concepts.

## 3. STRUCTURAL RELATIONS OF ATTITUDES, SENTIMENTS, AND DRIVES

**The Dynamic Lattice.** The relation of dynamic purposes proves, however, on closer examination, to be a little more complex than that of simple subsidiation. On the left of Diagram 27 are represented a set of interests and attitudes which might be those of a fairly typical citizen. One observes now that each habitual attitude or course of behavior (*a*) is normally served by more than one preceding, ancillary course of behavior and (*b*) itself serves more than one succeeding purpose. Thus a child might have to employ several courses of action (habits, traits) in order to obtain, say, the purchase of a toy pistol, and having gained the pistol he can use it to satisfy several habitual purposes, *e.g.*, to impress visitors, to frighten his brother, to give himself a sense of security in the dark.

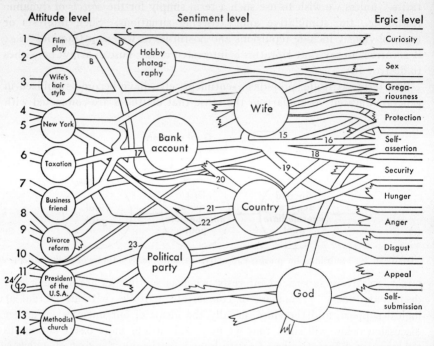

DIAGRAM 27. Fragment of a dynamic lattice, showing attitude subsidiation, sentiment structure, and ergic goals.

As the attitudes (channels in the diagram) and objects (circles in the diagram) of Diagram 27 show, an object normally has several attitudes converging upon it, *i.e.*, there are several things one wants to do with it, depending on circumstances, and each comes into its own at intervals. In other words, an object of interest usually stands in the stream of several dynamic traits, has several emotional meanings, and appeals to several interests. This amounts to saying that each of the attitudes ultimately subsidiates to several different sentiments or drive goals.

This convergence and divergence in a latticelike structure may be illustrated in Diagram 27 by the object "Bank Account." Three attitudes converge upon this object: (*a*) I want to cultivate the acquaintance of this business friend because he can show me how to increase my bank account;

(*b*) I want to see taxation reduced because it harms my bank account; (*c*) I must avoid New York because I spend too much there and damage my account. The intermediate objects (friend, taxation, New York) in these attitudes are shown in the first column of the lattice. Incidentally the bank account attitudes are not the only ones going through these objects.

The bank account, however, in turn subsidiates to other objects, in a set of *diverging* channels. For example it may subsidiate to the further attitude-objects: (*a*) that I may get my wife things she needs—15 in diagram; (*b*) that I may satisfy a need for self-assertion by making my house more impressive— 16 in diagram; (*c*) that I may increase security by more insurance—18 in diagram; (*d*) that I may buy a better camera (sentiment to hobby, not shown in diagram), and so on.

A massive sentiment object—such as one's country, one's family, or one's religion—to which many attitudes are thus tributary, will in turn subsidiate to the goals of the basic drives. For example, a sentiment to a wife may be built up on satisfactions accruing to the gregarious erg, the sex erg, the food-seeking erg, and so on. Any dynamic trait whatever is therefore like a busy crossroads, or at least a corridor, to something else. Its importance and strength depend upon the number of further satisfactions to which it can contribute. This is the essential point that is brought out by representing the personality trait structure by a *dynamic lattice* as in Diagram 27. Reluctant though the student or the lover of mathematical simplicity may be to face such a complex mode of representation, the fact remains that this is how human dynamic traits are structured, and we shall get ahead most quickly by admitting it. To the clinician, who may spend a year tracing the dynamic entanglements of a neurotic patient, the truth of the lattice concept will be immediately evident, though he may object that the present diagram is an especially simplified one, since it contains practically none of the instances in which a subsidiation chain doubles back upon or recrosses itself.

Two important conditions should be borne in mind in order properly to relate the dynamic lattice, with its appearance of constant streams or paths of energy, to the stimulus response aspect of dynamic traits.

1. In all dynamic traits the object which acts as a stimulus to action is frequently also the goal of the response. This happens more frequently in basic drives, *e.g.*, food-seeking, sex, than in derived dynamic traits. For in simpler activities the goal and the stimulus are naturally closer in time and space, while the limitations of less developed minds, *e.g.*, that connected with the limited neural equipment of lower mammals, preclude the development of stimulus meaning in anything very remote from the goal. A more careful analysis of the problems of definition of stimulus and goal, created by this tendency for slightly different aspects of the same object to represent

both environmental conditions, will be made in a later, more explicit, development of dynamic principles (Chap. 21). Here it suffices to point out that, in building the lattice around objects, we may expect the same object, in two different roles, to appear at two different points of the lattice.

2. The construction of a dynamic lattice is possible only for a person in a reasonably fixed life situation. That is to say, it presupposes the daily impinging of the same sets of stimuli in the same family, social, and business environment. Thereby certain paths of discharge become habitual and we may appropriately speak of attitudes, sentiments, and other dynamic "trait structures." The size of cross section, *i.e.*, the volume of energy discharge, in any particular channel of the lattice will depend upon (among other things) the frequency with which these environmental stimuli operate. However, the dependence of the lattice paths upon the pattern of the environment will be more immediate for attitudes than for sentiments. A man with a strong sentiment to his family, who changes his business and his town of residence, will drop one set of attitudes to business associates and clubs and acquire a new set to new specific people, but these will subsidiate still to a largely unchanged sentiment to his family. The total loss of his family might produce a more real personality change. The basic outlines of personality are thus embedded in deeper sentiments, so that changes in the peripheral attitudes of the lattice scarcely constitute change of personality.

**The Nature and Origin of Sentiment Structures.** It behooves us now to look more closely at these relatively permanent and more stable channels of discharge which have been called *sentiments*, and which so far have been only roughly defined by "depth" or subsidiation position on a series of attitudes.

The term "sentiment," introduced in this context by Shand and McDougall, has the disadvantage of having some misleading popular associations from the last century, and some psychologists may feel that the "ganglion among attitudes" which we are now discussing could better receive a new name, such as "attitude complex," "attitude focus," or "common stimulus of several attitudes." The cumbersomeness and the possibilities of misunderstanding in such terms favor continuing with "sentiment," especially since the concept is given operational definition lacking in its earlier usage. Incidentally, many psychologists, *e.g.*, Sears, at present use "secondary drive" precisely in this sense of sentiment or metanerg, but since others use it differently or far more loosely, the term *drive* seems inferior to *sentiment*, especially since "drive" connotes a generic resemblance to (primary) drives which sentiments or metanergs actually do not possess.

Initial clarification of the concept is gained by seeing it in terms of subsidiation. Let us therefore take a specific example—a man's sentiment for his home—and follow its subsidiations through the lattice, beginning at the distal end.   Such a sentiment is observed first to be a relatively permanent dynamic structure within a man's mind, in virtue of which he experiences various feelings and emotions when he sees his home, speaks of it, feels it threatened, or hopes for its future.   Home means for him, consciously or unconsciously, the partial satisfaction of such basic drives as sex, food-seeking, gregariousness, and parental protectiveness.   (For the moment we will assume these are ultimate and perhaps biological goals.)   Note the word "partial."   As a glance at Diagram 27 shows, these drives are also partially involved in other sentiments.   Indeed, it is rare for one sentiment to absorb the whole energy of a drive, or vice versa.   For the lines of dynamic subsidiation both converge and diverge with respect to sentiments, as we have seen that they do for all dynamic traits except final drives.   However, in the psychoanalytic sense, a sentiment can be described as the cathexis of an object, but not a cathexis of libido alone.   A sentiment will generally, but not always, be acquired earlier in life than the attitudes with which it is found associated.   Frequently the attitudes will have developed simply to satisfy the sentiment.

So far our discussion has dealt only with conscious sentiments, but when we come to the more difficult subject of the fragmentary and unconscious "sentiments" called complexes we shall see that attitudes can develop as mere rationalizations, or even neurotic symptoms.   The subsidiation links will then be neither logical nor consciously expressible by the person concerned.   Sentiments, because they are powerful systems of energy which offer resistance to change, both on account of normal disposition rigidity and of their being closely linked with reality, are frequently involved in mental conflict.   They may conflict with one another, as when a man's religious sentiments conflict with his patriotism, but mostly they conflict with primitive drives, which they help to keep in check, both by suppression and by "drainage" of energy into the sentiments.   These questions are more fully investigated later.

For the present it suffices to define sentiments as major acquired dynamic trait structures which cause their possessors to pay attention to certain objects or classes of objects, and to feel and react in a certain way with regard to them.

**The Functional Relationship of Attitudes and Sentiments.**   The above definition does not, however, suffice precisely to distinguish between sentiments and attitudes.   The line between sentiments and attitudes or minor interests is as hard to draw as the line between the definition of a bough and the definition of a twig, for they grade insensibly one into the other.   A sentiment is a large and complex attitude, while what we usually measure in attitude tests is a minor sentiment.   The functional relationship between them has already been indicated in the above discussion of a man's sentiment to his home. Let us pursue the relation to greater clarity with the same example. As Diagram 27 indicates, any sentiment actually has to find its behavioral expression through a host of interests, minor attitudes, and opinions. These are usually less permanent than the sentiment itself, for they alter as they adapt the sentiment to gaining its satisfaction despite changes in the person's environment. For example, a married man's sentiment to his home may express itself in interests in various kinds of insurance, in attitudes about marriage, about the education of children, in interests in gardening, and opinions about women's clubs. These are the ultimate manifestations from which the existence and magnitude of the sentiment is inferred. If minor external conditions alter—*i.e.*, conditions which do not alter the stimulation of basic drives satisfied in the sentiment—it will be a few of the attitudes rather than the total sentiment which will change appropriately. For example, if he acquires a larger bank account, though the sentiment for his family's security remains unchanged, his attitude on the question of insurance may alter. Or if he discovers that changes in income tax make it no longer possible to send his children to college, it is not his sentiment to his children and their education which alters, but his political attitudes to that government which embarrasses him with taxes.

**What Are the Chief Sentiments?** An inventory of the chief sentiments, their complex interrelations, their growth and durability has never been made. The surface has been scratched by a little attitude testing, but in the main we have to fall back again on clinical and everyday naturalistic observation methods for any complete perspective. These data will be considered in the following chapter. Murray (10) has used the term "press" to refer to each of the major objects, material or ideational, which tends to engender in the individual an emotional attitude of such strength that it becomes the object of a sentiment. Obviously the presses alter with the individual's age. At one time it is the parents, the physical home, siblings, one's body, the school, the gang; at another it is home and children, an occupation, a political party, a hobby or artistic interest, one's nation, a religion, and one's reputation. This question of particular sentiment patterns and of particular innate drives we consider in Chapter 7. Here is it necessary to persevere in clarifying the *general* nature of dynamic structure in personality.

## 4. CHARACTERISTICS OF LONG-CIRCUITED, "METANERGIC" BEHAVIOR

**The Origin of Long-circuited, Means-end Traits.** It is a truism that some forms of behavior are more satisfying than others and that certain habits of behaving which are intrinsically boring, or even repellent, are acquired because they are the only way to more-satisfying activity. Thus, children at school acquire the trait of being punctual in order that they may gain approval and avoid punishment, and, as instanced above, all over the earth men acquire industrious habits of toil in order that they may eat.

So far we have defined the basic drives only by pointing to the goal activities at which all subsidiation ends, *i.e.*, the activities which are intrinsically satisfying, leaving their number, nature and innateness for investigation in Chapter 7. Accepting these end satisfactions as thus roughly defined, we now wish to study the dynamic traits at the opposite end or level of the dynamic lattice, *i.e.*, the network of attitudes most remote from primary drive behavior. By contrasting their characteristics with those of more massive, primitive dynamic traits we can bring out important characteristics of the subsidiation path and of the dynamic lattice.

The first question that arises when one is familiar with the fact of such a subsidiation sequence as occurs in the lattice is, "Why does it arise?" In other words, why do people acquire interests in intrinsically uninteresting activities when they could go directly to the ultimate, satisfying goal activity. It is the causes and characteristics of these subsidiated activities—henceforth called *long-circuited*, or *detour means-end* activities—that we shall now study.

The answer to the last question, as we are all acutely aware in certain circumstances, is that the intrinsically attractive goal activities cannot be directly reached. *Long-circuiting invariably arises in the last resort from the blocking of the direct path to satisfaction favored by innate drives.* A hungry dog's innate tendency on seeing a luscious piece of steak is to spring upon it and eat it. His master, wishing to train him to sit up and beg, punishes him for "stealing" but rewards him when he goes through a ritual of sitting on his hind legs and submitting to a piece of meat being balanced on his nose. In this way the behavior of "begging" becomes introduced in the subsidiation sequence to the goal. The path to the goal may be even further "long-circuited" by another piece of behavior introduced before the begging. For example, the dog may be taught, when hungry, to fetch a box from another room and lay it at his master's feet before the "begging" can begin.

Just so does life, through reward and punishment, induce sometimes remarkably long-circuited behavior in human beings. Indeed it is easily seen that most of what we call civilized, cultured behavior is long-circuited instinctive behavior—*i.e.*, behavior acquired on prolonged subsidiation paths to the goals of basic drives. As we shall see later, civilization sometimes induces us even *to give up a basic goal altogether.* But in the main, since in civilization as in a state of nature we need to eat, drink, procreate, fight, and flee from danger in order that life may go on at all, in nine cases out of ten it is not the indispensable final goal that is altered but only the path to it.

Let us ask now in what ways behavior becomes different as it gets increasingly long-circuited. Since more "long-circuited" means "extending increasingly to the left of Diagram 27," this amounts to asking, "How does the behavior resulting from attitudes and minor interests differ from that springing from basic drives directly?" There are four main ways in which it is modified. It becomes intellectually more complex; emotionally more diluted; more dependent on symbols and cues rather than literal, concrete stimuli; less satisfying and more readily given up under the influence of fatigue, boredom, shock frustration, or intoxication.

**Increase in Cognitive Content.** The greater intellectual complication needs little illustration. The hunger drive normally has very little mental content—perhaps some visual and olfactory images of food. The political attitudes arising in the course of a hungry people's seeking food are full of cognitive complication—the complicated considerations of wages and dividends, costs of living, and the maneuvering of bills through the legislature. In general, any attitude test, inviting responses on a variety of complex opinion statements, involves much knowledge and ideational content. By contrast, in the instinctive behavior of animals, though we cannot be certain of the ideational content, we can see that behavior occurs with very little halt for intellectual judgment or consideration.

**Concrete Cues Become Symbolic.** This intellectual complication is related to, but not wholly identical with, the experience of substituting symbols for original instinctive situations. A male rat can be taught, by experience, that the shining of a light on a door indicates the presence of a female rat behind the door. Whereas instinctively the female herself is the stimulus for erotic activity, in the long-circuited, acquired behavior, the light becomes a symbol or cue for the stimulation of erotic action. Similarly, a human being, a woman of strong maternal feelings, may be aroused to tender solicitude regarding the plight of destitute children, not by the heart-rending spectacle of the crying children themselves, but by a number of curious black marks on paper. The newspaper account operates through symbols, in this case written symbols, the meaning of which the person has learned by experience. A rat can be taught to work a wheel in order to make food pellets fall out of a hole. Later it can be taught to carry out this first symbolic activity in order to get wooden "tokens" which it has learned can be exchanged for food by dropping them into a box. Similarly in man, money is a symbol for so many diverse instinctive satisfactions that the acquisition of this token[1] becomes the major purpose of many.

---

[1] Symbolization is sometimes used by psychologists in a dual sense. In simple symbolization, an object $A$ comes to "mean," i.e., to imply, the same satisfaction and evoke the same emotion as object $B$, for which it stands. Often, however, the symbol in addition involves generalization (abstraction, conceptualization) in that the symbol $A$ stands not simply for $B$ but for a whole class of concrete objects $X$, $Y$, $Z$. Use of "abstract" symbols of this kind is much harder to acquire, since the abstracting involves use of $g$, and most animals cannot get very far at it. Both symbol substitution and symbol generalization involve strain.

**Attentuation and Combination of Primary Emotions in Secondary, Derived Emotions.** That long-circuited behavior is "emotionally diluted or impoverished" requires fuller explanation. In one sense it is obvious, and a commonplace of everyday knowledge. We realize that the soldier performing calculations in a gun turret cannot even claim the emotional satisfaction in war felt by the savage who smites his foe with a club. We may well suspect that to conduct a love affair by an exchange of sonnets, or in the manner of Dante, would evoke less interest in most men than more direct and concrete activity. Anyone can see how a child who is listless at a "dry" grammar lesson, quickly picks up emotional zest in hunting butterflies or having a mock battle. And a speech on lynching can usually be given with more emotional emphasis and effect than one on the future of mathematics.[2]

What we might overlook, however, is that the emotional life actually becomes more complex or "rich" as well as less saturated or intense, just as the primary colors when blended lose some of their brightness but gain subtlety. Consider McDougall's example of a small boy whose playing is interrupted by a bully and who reacts first with the primary drive of pugnacity and then, being trounced by the bigger boy, with the primary drive of escape. The primary emotions of anger and of fear accompanying these respective primary drives thenceforth become fused in the response to this object, producing *a secondary or derived emotion* of hatred.

Similarly we can see how the development of a dynamic sentiment which involves the primary drives of anger and of disgust accounts for the blended emotion "loathing." When three, four, or more primary drives are involved in the same sentiment, the feeling tone accompanying the functioning of the sentiment[3] may become very subtle, and there are many shades of feeling for which we have no name.

Let us take an example of complex emotion for which a word exists—the feeling of reverence. Its composition can be analyzed as follows: First, a primary emotion of self-abasement—in face of something very great—which, together with curiosity, produces wonder. If wonder now becomes increasingly mixed with fear, the derived emotion of awe results. Awe blended with a sense of gratitude gives the feeling of reverence. A similar complexity defines the derived emotion accompanying the sentiment of love between the sexes into which there enters, in addition to simple sexual emotion or lust, the tender protectiveness excited by the childlike qualities in the other,

[2] Shakespeare has expressed the matter obliquely in Hamlet's experience that "enterprises of great pitch and moment" become "sicklied o'er with the pale cast of thought" and "lose the name of action."

[3] It is perhaps hardly necessary to remind the reader that a sentiment, like any other trait, is a mental *structure*, not a feeling in consciousness. Here the technical psychological usage differs from the popular one, in which sentiment refers both to a structure in personality *and* to a felt emotion. The term "secondary emotion" describes the emotion which is felt when a sentiment is in action.

self-assertion or pride in the lover, gregariousness or the assuaging of individual loneliness, and perhaps acquisitiveness and other drives.

The analyses made in this section are, of course, dependent primarily on the method of introspection and on naturalistic observation, such as has been carried out by psychologists, philosophers, and novelists from time immemorial. However, there is no reason why research should not advance by experimental and objective, metric methods to discover and establish the component drive satisfactions in sentiments. The analysis of the accompanying derived emotions, since it depends at present on introspection, would be harder. These newer methods are discussed in the last section of this chapter.

To say that the more complex sentiments and attitudes are emotionally impoverished relative to the primitive instinctual drives is only partly true. As the above paragraphs indicate, though there may be reduction of intensity of emotional experience there is also an increase of qualitative richness. Occasionally one can point to instances where the intensity of the derived emotion is also great. People have been known to lose their tempers while discussing the gold standard, or the correct classification of lepidoptera, while religious martyrs have faced being burned to death for opinions over an article of doctrine. But these we recognize as exceptions, due respectively to reversion in unstable people to primitive drives and to exceptional powers of experiencing emotion in long-circuited activities.

### 5. FURTHER POSSIBILITIES OF DYNAMIC-TRAIT MODIFICATION AND DERIVATION

**Functional Autonomy and Disposition Rigidity.** We have recognized so far that dynamic traits can be abstracted into two kinds[4]—certain presumed inborn drives, with inborn goals, and a far more numerous and complex patterning of derived long-circuited dynamic traits which we call sentiments or attitudes, and which differ in some four systematic ways from the inborn drives. The long-circuited activities are habits of feeling and acting which are acquired by learning, *i.e.*, by reward and punishment acting on the original drive, in ways to be considered later, but beginning essentially with blocking of the original direct behavior routes to satisfaction and accompanied by substitution of the original signals provoking action of the drive. Thus, primitive woman saw her children endangered by a wild animal and struck it with a firebrand. Now the stimulus might be some statistics on malnutrition and her aggressive response might become that of organizing a committee to fight it. To repeat: both the habits of perceiving stimuli and the habits of action become modified.

---

[4] Later, when the term erg has been defined, it will be seen that these can conveniently be referred to as ergs and metanergs.

One further comparison of the direct, preferred, innate, stimulus-response patterns and the derived, long-circuited structures that needs to be made concerns their relative permanence; a full discussion would unfortunately involve us, somewhat prematurely, in an investigation of the learning process, particularly of that aspect which has to do with forgetting, or extinction; but it is possible to postpone finer analysis of learning theory. Let us simply ask: After reward and punishment have *engendered* the long-circuited behavior, how long will it last?

There are two schools of thought here. Psychoanalysis has argued that all habits are plastic and that the moment a symptom or other mode of behavior ceases to be a road to a basic dynamic drive satisfaction, it decays. On the other hand, classical psychologists have been wont to believe, as Allport has argued (1), that a habit has a life of its own and will persist by a kind of momentum when the causes which originally created the habit no longer maintain it. This self-maintenance has been called by Allport "functional autonomy." According to this view a rat which has been taught by electric-shock punishment at the points $A$ and $B$ to approach the food box by the longer circuit $C$, will continue to do so when the shock plates are removed from $A$ and $B$. Or as Allport says, a man who has become a sailor in order to earn a living and avoid starvation, will often be found, when he has retired with a pension, still following the sea for pleasure.

As we shall see, on the learning side, mere repetition, without drive, *i.e.*, without any reward to a drive, does not produce learning, and the bulk of evidence on forgetting shows likewise that this reversed learning depends on failure of motivation or interest. This is revealed with precision in the latest animal experimentation, *e.g.*, that of Koch (6), which shows no memory value to persist when reward vanishes, and it is also the substantial conviction of all clinical psychologists. Apparent proof of Allport's contention in everyday-life observations is found principally in regard to strongly, extensively, learned habits and in old people.

Before accepting this "rigidity" explanation it is necessary to rule out the possibility of explanation by already existing principles, notably the following: (a) A habit acquired for one reason quite often happens later to satisfy also some other motive—a conspicuous case being "secondary gain" in a neurotic symptom. The removal of the primary motive may then still leave the habit in existence. (b) Many rewards—or it might be better to say many drives—are obscure and operate in traits where they are not suspected. In the aged, particularly the drive to economy of energy, *i.e.*, to rest and sleep, is stronger and it may be that the task of changing a habit—even though it would lead to ultimate gain in other drives—is avoided because of the loss to this one. (2) Learning may be slower in the aged, not because of any increased rigidity but because the strength of primary drives is less. There is less free energy to explore by trial and error the new, more rewarding, paths. It is, however, possible to maintain in learning theory that change is not only a function of drive strengths and the rewards accorded to new vs. old behavior but also of "friction" against an inherent disposition rigidity of the kind discussed in Chapter 4. It is also possible that this rigidity increases somewhat with age; but it will always be a relative, not an absolute, hindrance to change.

Our conclusion must be, on available evidence, that functional autonomy does not exist in the sense that a trait can endure when it no longer contributes to the satisfaction of any drive. Disposition rigidity, however, almost certainly *does* exist, as a general characteristic, in the form of inertia, and experimental work (see (12), Chap. 4) suggests that it is stronger in earlier than later habits and stronger in drives than in derived habits. Long-circuited behavior, in short, is likely to have less rigidity and stability than direct drive activity.

**Total Modifications Include Aim Inhibition.** So far, modification of original drives has been discussed as it affects stimulus perception (cues), the intensity and complexity of emotion, and the complication of behavior by long-circuiting, assuming that the ultimate goal remains unchanged. But in rare instances, as was observed first in clinical cases, the *goal itself* may be replaced by a substitute. This is called *aim inhibition* of drive. If the new goal is socially valuable, aim inhibition becomes *sublimation*; if it is socially disapproved, or a regression to some earlier phase of maturation, it is called *perversion*. For example, in many religions the devotees renounce the goal of ordinary, biological sexual satisfactions. They may acquire instead an intensity of spiritual life and an interest in religious goals not known in other groups. Or again, a woman who has been faced by insuperable obstacles to the direct satisfaction of maternal impulses and feelings may acquire an interest in something relatively remote—the care of flowers, the painting of pictures, the rebirth of her country. One can deduce, from an examination of energy output, that this field has inherited the energy which in most women is absorbed in direct maternal satisfaction with children. If the maternal drive expresses itself in keeping a hundred pampered cats, or the sex drive in attraction to one's own sex, we are more inclined to speak of perversion than sublimation.

Why sublimation takes place in some situations of frustration and not others cannot yet be fully explained. The process will be examined at greater length in Chapter 8. Here it needs to be examined only because it might appear that it presents an example of that functional autonomy the existence of which has just been doubted. For indeed we see therein the means to an end (the substitute "goal" in fact being often a means) acquiring such intrinsic attractiveness that the end in itself is forgotten, and there are many instances of behavior that are often brought under this heading.   The accumulation of money often becomes an end in itself.   Before such behavior is labeled functional autonomy, or even sublimation, however, other possibilities should be examined.   For example, in an elderly man collecting money the original biological goals for which it was acquired, *e.g.*, food and sex, have often declined in importance for purely biological reasons.   Meanwhile wealth has taken on *new* significance as a symbol of power and is thus still a very real means to a still valued goal—a means which, however, the person is psychologically capable of abandoning if other means present themselves, as when wealth is exchanged for political or social prestige.

The phenomenon of a means becoming an "end in itself" is probably to be explained by the same process as that underlying sublimation, *i.e.*, the acceptance of a substitute end-goal.   The activity has become the substitute goal.   Perhaps because there are certain common or similar bodily effects in the original and the substitute goal.

## 6. THE VECTORIAL MEASUREMENT OF DYNAMIC TRAITS

So far this chapter has aimed at presenting the best and most complete picture possible of normal dynamic structure and has used all available methods of investigation that might contribute to that end.   But the methods have very uneven degrees of scientific exactness and acceptability. It behooves us now to take up a more critical position and to ask on what methods and concepts the more exact psychodynamic calculus of the future should preferably be based.

As stated earlier, the main problems concern the discovery of (*a*) what traits are functionally unitary; (*b*) how subsidiation occurs among traits; to which we may also add (*c*), how is the strength of a trait to be measured? The problem of conflict and mutual suppression and repression belongs to a later stage of study.

Ideally, research on the unitariness of dynamic traits and the measurement of their strength should have preceded experimental work on their variation with physiological conditions, or their roles in learning or conflict, and much of this early experimental work may need serious revision after the factor analytic work on which they should have been based has belatedly been accomplished.   For the establishment of unitary character, the measurement of dynamic strength, and, in part, the exploration of subsidiation structure are likely to be largely the work of the factor-analytic method.

The general mode of application of factor analysis to dynamic problems has already been briefly sketched, but let us examine the method with a more detailed illustration.   A population of, say, 500 young men could be tested with respect to the strength with which each holds each of fifty attitudes. The latter would be of a general kind, as exemplified toward the left in

Diagram 27. For the moment we need not ask more about the techniques of measuring the strength of interest in each of these courses of action, except to indicate that scores might be compositely derived from such indices as the amount of time and money the individual spends on them, the magnitude of his psychogalvanic response to the proposals, and the degree of his verbal expression of interest, as shown in the usual test by Thurstone or Likert techniques of underlining opinions. If now we intercorrelate these attitudes and factor-analyze them, in the usual manner applied to a battery of ability tests, what shall we find?

If basic drives are truly functional unities we should expect to emerge with factors corresponding to each of the basic drives. For if attitudes 1, 3, 6, and 17 are all in considerable part expressions of the sex drive, the individual with a strong sex drive will tend to manifest all of them more strongly than does an individual of weak sex interest. A similar result might be anticipated if $P$ technique were substituted for $R$ technique, and here we should be able to apply experimental controls along with the factorial method. In this case the fifty attitudes would be measured in a single individual every day and in addition to being influenced by the normal oscillation of drives from day to day they could be influenced by experimentally controlled drive changes induced by special external stimulation or internal change of hormone balance. Again attitudes 1, 3, 6, and 17 could be expected to undulate together, indicating their dependence on a unitary drive, while other factor patterns in other attitudes would point to the existence of other unitary drives.

Granted that the drives are likely to appear as unitary factors, the question next arises as to whether the organization centers we have called sentiments could also be revealed and established by factor analysis—as "environmental mold" source traits. This question requires us to get down to a more precise operational definition of a sentiment than has yet been made. When many attitudes converge upon—or, rather, pass through and "use" a certain object in the dynamic lattice—there is no immediate reason to believe that they thereby come into any single dynamic organization. For example, a man may have such attitudes to his garden as, "I want to use my garden to reduce the costs of the kitchen," "I want to grow flowers whereby I win distinction at the horticultural show," and "I want a quiet retreat in which to smoke my pipe." These are obviously subsidiated to different goals and merely meet at the garden in passing. But *the continued existence of the garden is a common essential condition of all of these satisfactions* and, consequently, the extent to which the individual will *fear for the existence* of his garden (when, say, a railroad proposes to cut through it), or *fight for its existence*, is a true indication of the strength of all the attitudes that converge on it and that would be frustrated by its loss.

*The unitary character of the sentiment is thus likely to appear in a common variation of such attitudes as subsidiate to the purpose of maintaining the object in effective existence.* These particular attitudes should be proportional in strength to the man's love of the object and his hatred (fear and anger) toward whatever would destroy it. (Here "love" is used in a somewhat inexact metaphorical sense, for does a man "love" his bank account?) But there is also a second, independent source of correlation in the strength of attitudes connected with this object. The object is to some extent a stimulus for the attitudes with which it is associated. Consequently more frequent contact with the object will tend simultaneously to raise the strength of all attitudes, though they are not dynamically subsidiated. A man thrown more frequently into contact with a girl will experience an increase not only in an initial attitude of sex attraction, but also in attitudes of protectiveness, sociability, etc. Thus, for at least two reasons, covariation may be expected to exist among attitudes in a sentiment and to reveal the sentiment in factor-analytic approaches. However, one may guess that the sentiments will be less clear factors than the drives; indeed, experiment (see (6a), Chap. 7) shows that "environmental-mold" traits are usually more elusive than "constitutional" source traits.

The question of the extent and manner in which factor techniques can reveal subsidiation is too complex and speculative to pursue here; but it is clear that attitudes in the same subsidiation chain will show some correlation of strength in proportion to their proximity, just as the appearance of flood levels simultaneously in two streams and not in a third will argue some tributary connection among the first two.

In order to understand what is likely to be obtained by a factor analysis of attitudes, the student should glance back at Section 2 of Chapter 4, including Diagram 14, page 85. He should remind himself that attitudes about an object may have many different dynamic directions and that an attitude is consequently to be measured as a vector quantity. The coordinates by which the direction of a given attitude can be defined are, as we saw in Chapter 4, *the ultimate, ergic goals* of the course of action represented by the attitude. Thus a course of action may contribute so much to the ergic goal of security, so much to satisfaction of hunger, and so on. It will be shown below that the factor analysis of dynamic traits, *e.g.*, of attitudes, tends to yield primarily source traits that are basic drives. For the attitudes largely motivated by one particular drive will *covary*. For example, all the attitudes which arise from timidity will be simultaneously stronger in a man of timid disposition, *i.e.*, one in whom the fear erg is strongly active.

The vectorial, ergic theory of attitude measurement therefore permits any attitude to be analyzed by the usual factorial specification equation, in which the factors are ergs. Thus, the strength of the interest in an attitude $j$ for a given individual $i$ can be estimated as follows:

$$Iji = s_{j1}E_{1i} + s_{j2}E_{2i}$$

Where $E_1$ and $E_2$ are two factors, the ergs such as fear and gregariousness, and $s_{j1}$ and $s_{j2}$ are "situational indices" indicating the extent to which the situation of this particular attitude, $j$, is provocative, respectively, of $E_1$ and $E_2$. $I_{ji}$, the strength of the individual $i$'s interest in the course of action, represented by attitude $j$, is thus a function of the strength of his endowment in drives $E_1$ and $E_2$, for, since this attitude is a common trait, the situational pressures $s_{j1}$ and $s_{j2}$ are approximately the same for all men—at least for all in the class of men for which the factorization was carried out.

The mode of action of this formula may be illustrated by particular attitudes used in the experiment summarized in the following table. In this

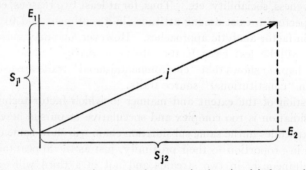

DIAGRAM 28.  Measurement of an attitude vector in situational index projections upon ergic coordinates.

experiment the strengths of each of fifty attitudes were measured for each of one hundred sixty men by objective methods—psychogalvanic reflex, preference, and information, combined as described elsewhere (4). The fifty attitude variables were intercorrelated and factorized with the result that nine dynamic-trait general factors were found (see (6a), Chap. 7). The mode of identification of these factors as ergs will be illustrated shortly, but for the moment we shall take the $E$ labels as shown at the top of the table. Only eighteen of the fifty attitudes are taken for illustration here and of these we will undertake verbal discussion of the loading for two.

Neglecting loadings of +0.10 or below we obtain a specification for Attitude 8 ("I want to attend football games and follow the fate of teams").

$$I_{8i} = 0.21E_{2i} + 0.42E_{3i} + 0.37E_{9i} + \text{specific}$$

This indicates that the motivation behind this sports interest is primarily gregarious satisfaction ($E_3$), secondly, satisfaction of the assertive erg ($E_9$) and, curiously enough, also some sexual interest ($E_2$).

Again, for Attitude 10 ("I like to see a good movie or play every week or so") we find the specification equation:

$$I_{10i} = 0.54E_{2i} + 0.38E_{9i} + \text{specific}$$

This places sex and self-assertive drives as chiefly responsible for movie attendance—an analysis which agrees well with "clinical" analysis of the themes of phantasy satisfaction most provided by movies. Similarly, by a glance at the factor loading matrix, it will be seen that Attitude 1 is largely subsidiated to the fear-drive goal; Attitude 3 to the self-sentiment, to narcism and to fear, Attitude 7 to the appeal or self-abasement erg, and so on. As the statistically trained psychologist will realize the above multipliers all operate upon standard scores. The estimation of the strength of an attitude in a given individual, $i$, will operate upon his ergic strengths ($E$ values) in standard scores and give his vector length in standard score form.

Identification of factors depends here, as elsewhere, upon contrasting the character or content of the variables (attitudes) highly loaded in the factor with those that are not loaded. In this experiment attitudes were deliberately introduced which by hypothesis would represent a certain drive and would act as statistical "markers" for it. Thus Attitudes 15 and 18 were introduced as attitudes strongly involving the parental, protective, pitying emotion of the parental, protective drive. They came out with high loadings in one factor only (Factor 1 in the table) which had the following pattern of highest loadings:

| Attitude | Loading Pattern of Parental Erg | Loading |
|---|---|---|
| 18 | I want to be able to ensure for my children the best education they could possibly have. | +0.48 |
| 43 | I want my parents never to be lacking the necessities of comfortable living. | +0.44 |
| 15 | I want to be able to do more for children who are sick, or poor, or uncared for, anywhere in the world. | +0.42 |
| 19 | I want somehow to increase my salary. | +0.42 |
| 34 | I want to get my wife the clothes she likes and to save her from the more toilsome drudgeries. | +0.38 |

It is clear that all these attitudes (with the possible exception of 19 on salary) involve the protective and succoring intention of the parental drive. (One motive for salary increase is better to be able to look after one's dependents.) Also, no attitude, anywhere among the fifty, having this goal is lacking a loading in this factor.

Similarly with the other factors it seems that ergic patterns long speculated upon have generally been picked out. The method, however, is also likely to pick out, as stated above, the major sentiment patterns, and only later

FACTOR MATRIX PROVIDING DYNAMIC SPECIFICATION OF ATTITUDES

| Attitude (Defined in basic verbal form) | Loading of attitudes in independent dynamic factors—ergs | | | | | | | | |
|---|---|---|---|---|---|---|---|---|---|
| | Pa-ren-tal | Sex | Gre-gari-ous | Ap-peal | Curi-ous | Fear | Narc-ism | Self-re-gard | As-ser-tion |
| | $E_1$ | $E_2$ | $E_3$ | $E_4$ | $E_5$ | $E_6$ | $E_7$ | $E_8$ | $E_9$ |
| 1. I want America to get more protection against the terror of the atom bomb..... | .08 | .37 | .03 | −.07 | .06 | .51 | −.09 | .19 | .07 |
| 2. I like to see fine paintings, sculpture, art exhibits.............................. | −.10 | .11 | .08 | .04 | .44 | .05 | .24 | −.04 | −.22 |
| 3. I want to avoid ever becoming an insane patient in a mental hospital............ | −.06 | −.06 | −.02 | −.02 | .09 | .37 | .16 | .29 | .10 |
| 4. I want never to do anything that would damage my self-respect................ | .01 | .03 | .08 | .23 | .07 | .12 | −.04 | .44 | .33 |
| 5. I like to enjoy the spirit of comradeship that exists among fellow students here... | .01 | .03 | .32 | .15 | .03 | −.06 | .07 | −.05 | .09 |
| 6. I want to know more science........... | .12 | −.04 | .01 | −.15 | .50 | .03 | −.08 | −.05 | .23 |
| 7. I want to see organized religion maintain or increase its influence................ | .05 | −.11 | .04 | .62 | −.07 | .14 | −.08 | .01 | −.04 |
| 8. I want to attend football games and fol-low the fate of teams.................. | −.04 | .21 | .42 | .08 | −.10 | −.07 | −.04 | −.06 | .37 |
| 9. I want to see those responsible for the present inflation—market manipulators and others—severely punished.......... | −.27 | .38 | −.09 | −.09 | .03 | .44 | −.06 | .00 | −.04 |
| 10. I like to go to a good movie or play every week or so........................... | .02 | .54 | .00 | .00 | .04 | −.05 | .05 | .00 | .38 |
| 11. I want to make love to a woman I find beautiful............................. | .02 | .41 | .08 | −.21 | −.07 | −.02 | .07 | .17 | .11 |
| 12. I want a will power that can keep all un-wise impulses under irreproachable con-trol.............................. | −.12 | −.03 | −.15 | .06 | −.08 | .04 | −.08 | .36 | .07 |
| 13. I want to feel that I am in touch with God, or some principle in the universe that gives meaning and help in my strug-gles................................. | −.05 | −.15 | −.20 | .67 | .06 | −.06 | −.01 | .18 | .06 |
| 14. I would like to spend more on really fine foods, candies, and delicacies.......... | .01 | .12 | .01 | .11 | −.17 | .20 | .47 | −.01 | −.04 |
| 15. I want to be able to do more for children who are sick, poor, or uncared for....... | .42 | .04 | −.05 | −.07 | .07 | .07 | .01 | .12 | −.19 |
| 16. I like playing indoor sociable games, such as card games...................... | −.07 | −.02 | .32 | −.04 | −.14 | −.09 | .25 | .22 | .27 |
| 17. I want to spend somewhat more on drink-ing and smoking than I am now able to do................................. | −.07 | .04 | −.19 | −.15 | .08 | .09 | .56 | .01 | −.06 |
| 18. I want to be able to ensure for my chil-dren the best education they can possibly have............................... | .48 | −.15 | −.15 | .02 | −.02 | −.03 | .05 | .07 | .01 |

genetic research can decide whether a factor is a sentiment or an erg. On inspection it seems that only one factor in the table, namely $E8$, the self-regarding sentiment, is best interpreted as a metanergic structure.

It should be borne in mind, however, that by this method of detecting ergic structures among the general dynamic traits observed in the dynamic lattice we do not actually arrive at the *innate* pattern of the erg. We obtain instead the pattern of the investment of the erg in the behaviors acquired in our culture pattern. This might well be called the *displaced erg* (displaced by the learning processes) to distinguish it from the true, innate (but seldom or never realized) ergic pattern which we discuss in the next chapter.

Whatever particular number and pattern of ergs becomes eventually established it is evidently possible in principle and practice to analyze and measure attitudes according to the vectorial ergic theory of dynamic trait measurement. The advantageousness of the ergic technique over the old fashioned pro-con treatment[5] are: (*a*) It avoids the psychological unreality of measuring all attitudes toward objects only in a pro-con dimension, and favors, instead, a definition of an attitude in keeping with the facts of the dynamic lattice. Attitudes have a far richer variety of directions than simply pro-con; in fact they share the gamut of the "derived emotions." (*b*) The ultimate goals of the attitude and the relation of the attitude to individual dynamics become defined in the attitude given as a vector quantity. (*c*) It is possible that a wider calculus may develop from the vectorial representation, both in regard to predictions of the disposition of dynamic forces in the individual and in the assessment of available energy in groups.

### 7. SUMMARY

1. Dynamic, temperament, and ability traits are defined. Since it is through the high plasticity of the first of these three that personality is chiefly modified by environment, the study of dynamic traits properly begins the investigation of environmental influence.

2. Our knowledge of dynamic psychology has arisen largely from clinical and naturalistic methods and secondarily from controlled experiment. "Findings" of the former, and even of the latter, are in process of being placed on a sounder basis by the application of more refined statistical methods. In particular, experiments and clinical conclusions need to be refounded on real conceptions as to what traits (notably drives) are really unitary, and this requires a foundation of factor-analytic research.

3. Investigation by existing methods of the adult dynamic structure in

---

[5] Our objection has been to the meaninglessness of saying pro or con an *object*. It is still appropriate to speak of being *pro or con a course of action* about an object. But it is necessary also to give the vectorial direction of this course of action.

the normal personality shows a system of attitudes organized about objects in the form of a *dynamic lattice*.

4. In the dynamic lattice attitudes tend to be subsidiated to sentiments and sentiments to basic biological drives, but all subsidiation is divergent as well as convergent and includes many instances of "retrofluxion."

5. Long-circuited metanergic behavior—that associated with the means-end paths toward the goals of basic drives, which lie before ergic goals in the dynamic lattice—always arises from blocking of more direct modes of satisfaction. It is differentiated from ergic, drive behavior by greater cognitive content (symbolization and abstraction), weaker, more blended, "derived" emotions, and greater susceptibility to fatigue, boredom, etc.

6. Functional autonomy as an absolute characteristic probably does not exist, but disposition rigidity, as a *relative* resistance to changing to more rewarded paths may be a necessary concept, distinct from (the obverse of) strength of drive.

7. Aim inhibition, or sublimation, a process descriptively distinct from long-circuiting, is also induced by culture, but less extensively. Here, in some way, the substitute goal has sufficient resemblance to the biological goal to function permanently in its stead.

8. Sentiment and drive organization within the dynamic lattice can be demonstrated by factorization of measures of a large number of attitudes. A group of attitudes largely motivated by one drive are likely to appear strongly loaded by a single factor, while sentiments may appear less definitely as factors corresponding to "environmental-mold" forms. Some eight "displaced ergic patterns" have so far been demonstrated in adults.

9. The covariation likely to reveal the cohering parts of a sentiment is not due to any dynamic interaction of the attitudes concerned but to (*a*) the fact that all the attitudes require for their satisfaction the continued existence of the object; whence the attitudes concerned with this maintenance will be correlated, and (*b*) the fact that the object is stimulus as well as goal, so that all attitudes will tend to covary with frequency of contact with the object.

10. The ergic theory of dynamic trait measurement states that all metanergic traits can be expressed as vectors with respect to ergic (drive) coordinates. The strength of an individual's interest in the course of action represented by any attitude can be represented by

$$I_{ji} = s_{j1}E_{1i} + s_{j2}E_{2i} + \cdots$$

etc., where the $s$'s are situational indices and the $E$'s basic drives (ergs) adjusted to the strength of the individual endowment. As obtained by $R$ technique these values apply only to attitudes and lattice structures that are common to everyone; but the structure of individual, unique lattices can similarly be expressed through values obtained by *P* technique.

## QUESTIONS AND EXERCISES

1. What are the three chief trait modalities? Give two source traits as examples of each.

2. Define a dynamic trait and an ability trait. Can the same ability operate in conjunction with various dynamic traits? Can the same dynamic trait employ several different abilities?

3. Define a sentiment, and indicate by what covarying elements it is likely to be discovered among attitude measurements. Give three examples of a sentiment, indicating what are the principal inborn drives operating through each.

4. What do we mean when we say two traits are dynamically subsidiated? Give an example of a four-term subsidiation sequence, from among the habits of a student.

5. Construct from your own view of your own personality a section of the total dynamic lattice that has to do with your sentiment toward the university to which you belong.

6. Name four characteristics which normally distinguish relatively long-circuited from short-circuited behavior traits.

7. Analyze into primary emotions the following secondary, derived emotions: (*a*) scorn, (*b*) awe.

8. Distinguish between long-circuiting and sublimation and discuss the extent to which disposition rigidity and functional autonomy may be necessary in explaining their persistence.

9. Explain what one might expect to obtain from intercorrelating and factorizing a widely selected population of attitudes, distinguishing between the findings of *R* technique and those of *P* technique.

10. Describe the ergic theory of attitude measurement, stating what defines the direction of a dynamic vector and writing the specification equation for strength of interest in the action defined by an attitude. What are the possible advantages of this conception over current attitude measurement practices?

## BIBLIOGRAPHY

1. ALLPORT, G. W.: *Personality*, Chapter 7, Henry Holt and Company, Incorporated, New York, 1937.

2. CATTELL, R. B.: The Description and Measurement of Personality, World Book Company, Yonkers, New York, 1946.

3. CATTELL, R. B.: The Ergic Theory of Attitude and Sentiment Measurement, *Educ. and Psych. Meas.*, 7: 221–246, 1947.

4. CATTELL, R. B., E. F. MAXWELL, B. H. LIGHT, and M. P. UNGER: The Objective Measurement of Attitudes. *Brit. J. Psychol.*, 40: 1–25, 1950.

5. FREUD, S.: *Introductory Lectures on Psychoanalysis*, Lecture 21, W. W. Norton & Company, New York, 1933.

6. KOCH, S., and W. J. DANIEL: The Effect of Satiation on the Behaviour Mediated by a Habit of Maximum Strength, *J. exp. Psychol.*, 35: 167–187, 1945.

7. LURIA, A. R.: *The Nature of Human Conflicts*, Liveright Publishing Corp., New York, 1932.

8. McDOUGALL, W.: *Outline of Psychology*, Charles Scribner's Sons, New York, 1923.

9. MOWRER, O. H., and C. KLUCKHOHN: Dynamic Theory of Personality, in *Personality and the Behavior Disorders*, Vol. I., The Ronald Press Company, New York, 1944.

10. MURRAY, H.: *Explorations in Personality*, Oxford University Press, New York, 1938.

11. PHILLIPS, H.: *The Education of the Emotions*, George Allen & Unwin, Ltd., London, 1937.

12. SEARS, R. R.: *Survey of Objective Studies of Psychoanalytic Concepts*, Social Science Research Council, Committee on Public Administration, Washington, D. C., *New York*, 1943.

13. SYMONDS, P. M.: *The Dynamics of Human Adjustment*, Appleton-Century-Crofts, Inc., New York, 1946.

14. THORNDIKE, E. L.: *The Psychology of Wants, Interests, and Attitudes*, Appleton-Century-Crofts, Inc., New York, 1935.

15. TOLMAN, E. C.: *Purposive Behavior in Men and Animals*, Appleton-Century-Crofts, Inc., New York, 1932.

16. WOODWORTH, R. E.: *Psychology*, Henry Holt and Company, Incorporated, New York, 1940.

# CHAPTER 7

# PSYCHODYNAMICS: II. THE STRUCTURE OF INNATE DRIVES

## 1. PRELIMINARY DEFINITION AND LISTING OF INNATE DRIVE PATTERNS

Before proceeding from the initial view of dynamic structure obtained in the preceding chapter to a more refined analysis, it is necessary to examine innate drives or ergs. Indeed, until the nature and degree of innateness of drives in man is settled, there can be no sure progress in human psychodynamics. Without this knowledge the teacher cannot know where education must begin, or how far it can proceed, nor can the psychiatrist decide for what ultimate motive behind behavior he needs to seek or what degree of stress is traceable to deflecting behavior from natural channels.

As the student of general psychology knows, laboratory investigation alone (small-scale study) gives clear evidence of only two kinds of innate reactivity—that due to *tropisms*, urging animals predictably in certain directions, and that due to *reflexes*, which are predictable reactions to certain stimuli and which can be modified in predictable ways by conditioning. But the former operate only with lower animals and plants, while the latter apply only to part reactions of the organism, *e.g.*, a knee jerk, an eye muscle accommodation, a gland excretion, not to the complex behavior of the total organism.

The difference between a drive and a reflex, besides the part-whole difference, is that the drive does not present a passive waiting for a stimulus. It acts as if it were a source of energy, causing the animal to go out and seek stimulation. True, this can finally be seen as a lowering of the threshold of reactivity, so that saying an animal gets active is the same as saying it can be stirred by smaller and smaller stimuli and research *might* show that this is also true of an inactive reflex. But even then the drive differs from a mere collection of reflexes, for it shows a series of nicely adjusted responses to a sequence of stimuli, and there is a "persistence with varied effort" which cannot be explained by any "penny-in-the slot" reflex concept.

**Naturalistic Evidence on Drives.**    The laboratory fails to give adequate evidence on the nature and number of drives because it operates on too small a scale to cover the whole ergic pattern.    Advance in understanding drives came from a broader basis of naturalistic observation, directed both toward analogous behavior in the lower mammals and toward an intelligent over-all analysis of human behavior.    Sometimes the method has put emphasis on trying out a rich variety of hypotheses about human drives and testing them against widespread consequences to be expected from each; but some of the best work, notably that of Darwin (8), Shand (31), and McDougall (27), has not launched into hypotheses until after a good deal of faithful observation.

For the sake of discussion it will be convenient to start with the list of drives upon which the work of most psychologists in this field, *e.g.*, McDougall (27), Murray (30), Shand (31), Hebb (19), Garnett (15), Harding (18), Yerkes (36), converges.    Neither the list nor the definition of drive reached by this first descriptive approach need be accepted as more than a preliminary foundation for work with more exact experimental and statistical methods.

*Preliminary List of Drives*

I. Organic needs:
   To seek air; to avoid physical pain, heat, cold; to seek water; to urinate and defecate.
II. Propensities which are organic, viscerogenic, appetitive:
   1. (*a*) To seek stimulation, exercise, activity when well rested.   (*b*) To play.
   2. To avoid stimulation, lie down, sleep, and rest when tired.
   3. To seek food.   This may be functionally connected with storing food, with restless wandering (as in the herbivorous animals), or with hunting readiness (as in carnivorous).
   4. To court and mate (sex drive).
   5. To feed, protect, and shelter the young.
   6. To reject and avoid noxious substances.
III. Propensities showing no clear organic rhythm, nonappetitive:
   7. To escape from violent impressions by (*a*) flight, (*b*) "freezing" to the spot.
   8. To defer, obey, abase oneself in the presence of superiority and dominance behavior in others.
   9. To appeal, cry aloud and seek help when utterly baffled.
   10. To acquire, collect, possess, and defend whatever is found useful or attractive.
   11. To explore strange places and things or manipulate and pull to pieces strange objects.

12. To remain in or seek the company of one's fellows. With this go the functionally related tendencies (*a*) to assume, by primitive passive sympathy, the feelings of the group; (*b*) to evoke emotional responses from others; and (*c*) to imitate.
13. To assert oneself, achieve, domineer, lead, display oneself.
14. To resent resistance to the expression of any propensity; to attack and destroy such resistance.
15. To laugh and destroy tension in certain tension-provoking situations.
16. (Questionable.) To construct shelter and implements.

The criteria in this "naturalistic" approach by which we can detect the above propensities in man are:

1. Does a similar behavior pattern run through the order of mammals, to which man belongs, and particularly through the primates? If we accept the fundamental principle that structure and function are closely related, it is inconceivable that man, who takes a clear place in the structural series through the mammals and the primates, could lack the basic instinctual functions which they persistently manifest. Here the studies now proceeding on chimpanzees are most valuable.

2. Is the behavior pattern universal, appearing in man despite great diversity of culture patterns? (A behavior pattern, such as driving automobiles, may be universal in one culture or one historical epoch, and yet be entirely cultural and acquired.)

3. Does it show the typical threefold pattern, as described by McDougall, of (*a*) a situation which is innately attended to, involuntarily, and "recognized" as meaningful (as shown by subsequent behavior); (*b*) an emotion of a specific quality; (*c*) the release of a course of behavior striving toward a particular goal, at which action ceases? This is equivalent to what Woodworth called "permanence of trend," *i.e.*, persistence of the essentials of an activity pattern despite modification of details by environmental learning. The notion "goal-seeking" is meant to be purely descriptive and will be examined as to its mechanisms and implications later in this chapter.

4. Is the accompanying emotion recognizable by its own peculiar, unlearned facial- and visceral-expression pattern? Darwin first showed the innateness of these expression patterns and psychologists have since studied the limits of their cultural modification.

5. Can one detect by introspection, when engaged in a certain course of behavior, an emotion characteristically accompanying such behavior? It is conceivable that behavior could be imitated, but no one could learn an emotional quality or visceral response pattern.

6. Is the behavior present at birth? This is a "one-way" proof: What the

child is born with must be innate, but what is innate is not merely what he is born with. Neglect of this elementary principle caused Watson to conclude that there are only three innate drives in man, *viz:* Fear, of falling and sudden loud sounds; anger, at obstruction of movement; and affection, stimulated by cuddling and hugging.

7. Does environmental training seem relatively powerless when it attempts to deny man the goal object and goal behavior itself?

8. Can one point to extreme forms of the behavior in the mentally disordered?

## 2. RECONCILIATION OF DISCREPANCIES BETWEEN NATURALISTIC AND CLINICAL FINDINGS

**Fragility of Naturalistic Observation Results.** In different hands the naturalistic approach, using the above criteria, has yielded a count varying from ten drives to the fourteen propensities of McDougall and to the sixteen ergs of the above list or the twenty-four or more needs of Murray. However, the real discrepancy is not as large as this would suggest, for Murray generally recognizes much the same behavior as McDougall, but gives to two parts of a propensity the status of unarticulated drives. Indeed, the agreement among psychologists using this method has been surprisingly good.

Nevertheless, the deduction of what dynamic trends are given in the biological nature of man, through the use of the naturalistic method of over-all observation of human behavior is a process requiring very wide knowledge and very balanced judgment. Since these are rare it is not surprising that in different hands the method has yielded some different results. Nor has it been impossible for some sociologists to convince limited audiences that no innate tendencies whatever exist, as an emotionally biased people denied for fifty years the theory of evolution or Freud's arguments for the predominantly sexual roots of neurosis. The evidence in all these cases is very widely dispersed, and circumstantial: it cannot be put into a single sentence or a single experiment. The application of precise but complex statistical methods—those sketched in the opening chapters—will in time transform this "naturalistic" observation approach into irrefutable evidence. However, the discrepancy of viewpoint that *has* been fruitful of new inquiry is that between the naturalistic- and the clinical-method findings.

**Clinical Evidence on Drives.** Before summarizing the best conclusion possible at the present time as to the nature and number of propensities, one more field of evidence has to be culled—that of clinical experience. The clinician has to probe deeply into dynamic causes, because he is concerned with dynamic trends that have gone wrong, becoming aberrant, antisocial, and conflicting. In his attempts to trace motives to their sources he is thrown sharply against the question of when the subsidiation sequence has truly reached its innate source. Clinical observations contribute evidence mainly under headings 2, 3, 5, 7, and 8 above.

As the student knows from his general psychology courses, Freud, studying neurotics, recognized that reiterating "Why?" would not uncover a complete subsidiation sequence because at a certain point the individual became *unconscious* of his sources of motive. This unconscious region could be approached either by hypnotism or by "free association." The method of free association consists in training the subject to ignore the inhibitions he usually places on the expression of his thoughts for reasons of propriety, discretion, logic, and self-respect. Consequently, in free association, a certain short-circuiting of long-circuited, disguising habits goes on, as well as a penetration of dissociative barriers, whereby the stream of dynamic subsidiation is more directly tracked to its source.

The conclusions of psychoanalysis, as is well known, were at first that (*a*) all neurosis arises from repression of an innate sexual drive, and (*b*) the sexual drive has infantile levels of maturation and it is these immature goals, rather than those of adult sexuality, which cause persistent conflict with social and physical realities. Later, psychoanalysts reported in their deep analyses contact also with an aggressive drive, which was not a secondary motive due to frustration of sex, but a basic, innate need for aggression. Adler, who diverged from psychoanalysis by emphasizing earlier the basic need for self-assertion, as revealed by the prevalence of the inferiority complex, similarly brought the clinical account a step nearer to McDougall's naturalistic picture. Both Adler and, by implication, Freud, recognized the existence of primary drives of hunger and of security (fear, escape); indeed, much of the conflict with sexuality comes from the ego's fears for its security.

**The Notion of Ergic Maturation.** The discrepancy between the clinical picture of three or four drives and the naturalistic, biological arguments for some fifteen or sixteen is illuminating. The teacher and the clinician who steps in where the teacher failed are both thrown most forcibly into combat with those drives which, in their innate form, fit badly into the cultural pattern. Incidentally, one of the strongest arguments for drives being innate rather than due to training is that they conflict mightily with education, so that a good part of education is concerned solely with reining them in and modifying them (evidence under 7 above). It should not surprise us, therefore, if the clinicians were quick to recognize, first, sex and aggression— the two most outlawed drives—but failed to see clear evidence of maternal (parental) propensity, of disgust-avoidance propensity, or the propensity to laughter; for these latter are expressible with approval and without conflict in civilization generally.

The discrepancy, however, illuminates more than this differential proneness to suppression. The clinical studies of neurotics indicate that during the individual's lifetime the innate propensities continually move on and change, especially with respect to the nature of their goals but also in the motor responses toward the goals. Freud accounted for part of this goal change as an inherent maturation and partly as an environmentally induced sublimation. We are concerned here only with the inherent maturation that occurs as part of the innate biological unfolding of the drive. But we must consider the *total* development in goal-character, intrinsic and environmental, because research has not yet decided whether the line between innate maturation and environmental aim inhibition is just where the psychoanalysts think it is. Let us examine instances of maturation in more detail.

## 3. THE MATURATION OF DRIVES OR ERGIC PATTERNS

**Maturation Phases in the Sex Drive.** One of the most complete accounts yet available of the maturation of a drive is that presented by psychoanalytic observations on the sex instinct. These result from innumerable records of adults, mostly neurotic, by the method of free association, and from direct observations on the behavior of children. In the former it is manifest that the sex interests of adults have linked themselves with forgotten, sensuous, childhood activities. These connections have been substantiated by observations on the growth and decline of neurotic symptoms in relation to such recall of childhood motivations.

The maturation effects, it is claimed, can be formulated in terms of two kinds of change: (*a*) changes of goal or libidinal object from the narcissistic[1] (henceforth narcistic) one of enjoyment of one's own body to the object-love direction, in which the loving and cherishing of another person is the goal. One may also distinguish a third, intermediate, goal state, in which the direction, though toward an object, is inhibited. This aim-inhibited stage occurs in the individual history before the final object expression at adolescence. Although it is partly culturally caused, it probably is also partly maturational. We shall treat it as a third phase falling historically, and to some extent logically, between the completely object-directed and the completely narcistic; (*b*) changes of means of expression in so far as bodily organs are concerned (alterations in "libidinal localization"). This occurs as a sequence of erogenous zones—bodily areas through which erotic experience is obtained. Progress according to goals and according to bodily means is to some extent independent, though tending to be correlated. Some analysts consider a third mode of maturation—that of "mode of pleasure finding"— to be almost as important as the two above. This is set out (as *B*) along

---

[1] As most students nowadays realize, this term springs from the Greek myth about the youth Narcissus, who fell in love with his own reflection in a pool, and ceased to be interested in his former love, Echo. We shall use the shorter form, "narcistic", now commonly employed.

DEVELOPMENTAL STAGES

| A. Libidinal localization | B. Aim or mode of pleasure finding | C. Libidinal object finding | | |
|---|---|---|---|---|
| Infancy period | | | | |
| Pregenital period<br>1. Oral stage | Infantile sexuality | Auto-<br>erotism | Narcism | Allo-<br>erotism |
| *a.* Early oral | Sucking, swallowing (incor-<br>porating)* | | | Oral object<br>choice |
| *b.* Late oral | Biting, devouring (destroying,<br>annihilating) | At first<br>object-<br>less | Primary<br>Narcism | Oral sadistic<br>object<br>choice |
| 2. Anal stage<br>*a.* Early anal | Expelling ⎧Looking<br>(rejecting ⎰Exhibiting<br>destroying) ⎱Handling | | | Anal and<br>anal sadis- |
| *b.* Late anal | Retaining ⎱Inflicting pain<br>(controlling ⎰Submitting to<br>possessing) ⎩ pain | | | tic object<br>choice |
| Early genital period<br>(Phallic stage) | Touching, rubbing, exhibiting<br>and looking at genitalia, in-<br>vestigating, comparing, ques-<br>tioning, phantasying (tender<br>affection) | ↓ | ↓ | Parent object<br>choice<br>Oedipus-<br>phantasies |
| Latency period | | | | |
| No new zone | Repression<br>Reaction Formation<br>Sublimation<br>Affectional trends | Further<br>decline<br>of auto-<br>erotism | Diminished<br>Narcism | Development<br>of social<br>feelings |
| Adolescent or pubertal period | | | | |
| Late Genital Period<br>Revival of zone<br>sensitivity of<br>infancy period | Reactivation of modes or aims<br>of infancy period | Revival<br>of auto-<br>erotism | Fresh<br>wave of<br>Narcism | Revival of<br>Oedipus<br>object choice<br>Homosexual<br>object choice<br>Heterosexual<br>object choice |

* Words in parenthesis refer to ego attitudes arising on basis of id impulses.

with the other two modes, on page 185, in the summary of developmental stages of libido according to Healy and Bronner (18*a*).

Only the goal change, which is more important, will be described in detail here.

*The Narcistic Phase.*   In the first year of life the libido is directed to the child's own body and does not extend beyond it.   He experiences marked sensuous satisfaction in the bodily processes of suckling, in the warmth of the mother's embrace, in urination and defecation.   Incidentally, much unnecessary misunderstanding has resulted from Freud's use of the term "sexual" in a wider sense than that in which it is commonly employed. It is objected that the term "sensual" would be more appropriate, at the narcistic stage, than sexual.   But the psychoanalyst claims that this infantile sensuality is on the direct line of ascent of sexuality, as shown by close association later with ideas of a truly sexual quality.   It is the stuff out of which adult sexual feeling is specialized.

*Objective but Aim-inhibited Oedipal and Homosexual.*   Here the libido turns outward to an object, and normally to the mother, who is the giver of affection and good things.   This is called the Oedipus attachment, again from a Greek myth in which a son, long gone from home, returns and unknowingly marries his own mother, incurring the wrath of the gods for his breaking of the incest taboo.   As the child grows older he senses the disapproval of a sensual affection for his mother.   He experiences respect, admiration, and imitativeness for his rival, the father, whom, at times, he has hated and feared as the inhibitor and maintainer of standards.   Through this cultural opposition, symbolized by the father, the first true object-directed sexuality—the Oedipus attachment—is suppressed, and driven out of consciousness.

Consequently from this age (about four to six), a relatively sexless latent period supervenes, until sexuality finally reappears in its normal adult direction at puberty.   Even in this period, however, when the child detaches himself from his mother's apron strings and develops friendships for children of his own age, some shaping of libidinal expression goes on.   The libido assumes in part a homosexual direction, expressing itself in sociability and even strong affectional attachments to persons of the same sex.   Thus the Kinsey report (see (26), Chap. 12) on sexual behavior in the normal male shows that this form of preadolescent sex play, which is decidedly more homosexual than heterosexual in expression, rises to a maximum of 38.8 per cent (see Kinsey for meaning of this complex index) at the age of twelve.   Any serious direction of libido in a homosexual direction is, however, purely temporary in normal maturation.

*Adult, Genital Sexuality.*   In the last development of the sexual drive it appears as the biologist knows it—a drive to mating with the opposite sex, with a minimum of narcistic or homosexual components.

The existence of these stages in development in the goal direction of this propensity is evidenced, according to clinical observations, also by what is seen in *regression* from adult sexuality. For reasons which are still partly obscure (see discussion in next chapter) the drive may regress from a level of maturation once attained. The individual may then fail to show a full affectional relation to a person of the opposite sex; he may become homosexual or paranoid; he may show narcistic components in the form of self-centeredness and hypochondria; or he may become completely narcistic again in schizophrenia.

Just as the sex drive develops in goal direction so it shows changes in erotic zones. In the autoerotic stage of the first year he gets most pleasure in life from the mouth region (suckling) and is said to be "oral erotic." Very soon after, as his attention becomes forced upon the control of excretions, he is said to be urethral, or anal erotic. Towards the end of infancy, say at four or five years of age, the genital organs are becoming truly the center of erotic feeling, as can be seen from the incidence of masturbation. Completely adult sexuality involves both this shift to the genital erotic zone and the shift of direction to an object outside the self. Partial regressions to earlier erotic zones can often be seen operating as widespread, ingrained cultural practices, *e.g.*, the oral erotism shown in kissing, or in sucking at cigarettes.

Environment, the psychoanalysts' observations indicate, also plays its part in transformations of the sex drive. What the naturalistic observer calls a distinct gregarious propensity—a drive to mix with others under the urge of loneliness—the clinician may consider a derivative of sexual warmth, a sociability deriving from a homosexual sublimation. Similarly, the parental propensity is considered an aim-inhibited sex derivative—the tenderness which is a component of adult sexuality without the rest of the sex drive. Even play, self-assertion and self-submission, curiosity, and acquisitiveness have been claimed, through demonstrations of association with infantile sexuality, to be aim-inhibited or transformed sexual drive. Similar but less extensive transformations have been indicated for primal aggression.

**Additional Evidence on Maturational and Other Functional Interdependencies.** Until covariation studies are made, demonstrating the presence or absence of more general factors running over several distinct drive factors, *i.e.*, tendencies among certain drives to draw upon a common fund of energy, the theory of "goal transformation by maturation" must remain an interesting probability. There is, indeed, other evidence than that of psychoanalysis supporting the notion that there develops increasing specificity of drive through maturation, but it is equally tenuous. Banham Bridges made observations on the emotional behavior patterns of infants and claimed to observe the following emergence of differentiation:

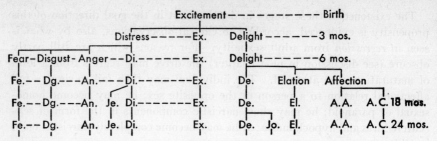

DIAGRAM 29. Approximate ages of differentiation of the various emotions during the first two years of life. Key: *A.A.*, affection for adults; *A.C.*, affection for children; *An.*, anger; *De*, delight; *Dg.*, disgust; *Di.*, distress; *El.*, elation; *Ex.*, excitement; *Fe.*, fear; *Je.*, jealousy; *Jo.*, joy.

**Adaptation Value of Maturation.** As the student knows from his general psychology, many experiments have proved the existence of late maturation, accounting for the appearance of entirely unlearned instinctive behavior in grown animals, but none has yet gone so far as to detect progressive modification (without experience) in the behavior and *goals* of some single drive. A useful approach to any hypothesis about an innate drive is to ask how biologically useful the behavior in question would be; for all innate drives show beautiful functional adaptation to ensuring survival of individual and species. Some of the Freudian "infantile forms" of what later become drives of gregariousness, self-assertion, and adult sexuality suggest, for example, a useful early adaptation to the family situation, in contrast to the later need to adapt to group life, but others, *e.g.*, the supposed sexual origin of curiosity, make no such sense. However, the naturalistic observation of chimpanzees and other primates show agreement with some clinical observations on evolution of drive specificity. For example, sexuality seems to be closely associated with, and responding to the same energies and cues as, self-assertion, self-submission, gregariousness, and parental affection. Again, naturalistic observation, *e.g.*, of chimpanzees, suggests also some functional connection among the drives of fear, self-abasement, anger, and appeal. Fright notoriously changes easily into anger. The desperate emergency situations evoking fear so frequently evoke also anger and despair that some ready functional transition may have been built up.[2]

**Maturation and the Functional Grouping of Drives.** Although neither Freud nor McDougall considered a reconciliation of their two fields of observation in terms of a maturational transition, this seems the most likely explanation of their apparently divergent formulations, from evidence

[2] In such close observation of men in primitive situations as Lawrence's *Revolt in the Desert* one finds repeatedly such sentences as "The anger of the _____ at their plight changed to fear as the day wore on and ultimately to inarticulate despair."

yet available. Obviously the discussion of many unresolved hypotheses about these connections cannot be undertaken in the space of the present outline, but it is appropriate to point out that the above-mentioned "family" groupings among drives are supported by many naturalistic observations.

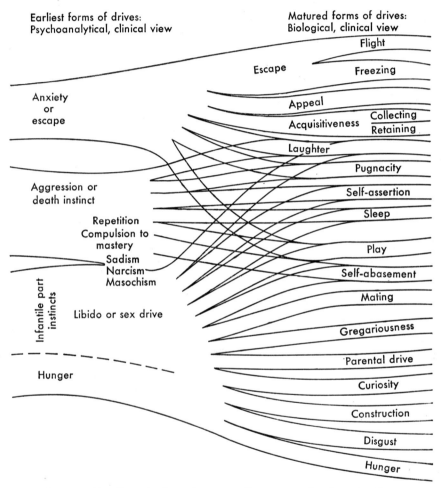

DIAGRAM 30. Tentative hypotheses regarding courses of ergic maturation.

The organic connectedness of any one family is indicated by (*a*) suggestions that they may draw upon a common source of energy (reactivity). As yet this is insufficiently established by factor-analytic studies; (*b*) similarity of or ready transformability of emotional expressions of the different drives; (*c*) a history of maturational transformation, ontogenetically and perhaps phylogenetically, between the drives and goals concerned. The diagram above is intended to state hypotheses about these connections in the condensed form possible by paths of development. An adult drive form may mature from a combination of infantile forms; for example, self-assertion may be both aggression and libidinal narcism, while acquisitiveness stems both from libido and from anxiety; but more frequently the maturational process is one of straight differentiation.

Other groupings and classifications of innate drives, *e.g.*, into approach drives and withdrawal drives (abient and adient), self-preservative and race-preservative, are logical artificialities as far as the organism is concerned, unrelated to any inherent functional characters. On the other hand the division made in the table on page 180, into appetitive (viscerogenic) and nonappetitive is likely to connote other important differences, too. In appetitive drives one can point to organic states associated with states of the drive; one sees a cyclic course of behavior from satisfaction, through tension, to satisfaction again; and usually one finds that aim inhibition of such drives is impossible. Most experimental work has, for convenience, been done on these appetitive drives, with animals, and it is questionable how far the results should be generalized; for probably unexplored differences exist between them and nonviscerogenic drives. In some writings it is erroneously assumed that drives with organic tensions are more fundamental and innate than others, but this is indefensible.[3]

## 4. THE NOTION OF STRENGTH OF DRIVE

**Measurement of Strength of Drives.** The measurement of drives has appealed to psychologists both because of its importance in understanding social issues and its relevance to the individual personality. If drives are functionally independent entities it should be possible for individuals to inherit them in distinct strengths, so that it would be reasonable to say so-and-so has an unduly strong sex drive, or an assertive disposition, or a more than averagely timid disposition. Indeed the term disposition, as

---

[3] The argument is put forward, *e.g.*, by Murphy, Klineberg, and others, that the non-viscerogenic drives are "secondary" and "derived." Typically the argument proceeds that man is not gregarious, but that, being rewarded in appetites—*e.g.* food-seeking, sex—through being in a group, the group situation thereby acquires satisfyingness as a cue to other satisfactions. Similarly, we are told, there is no maternal drive: Mothers are maternal and interested in children mainly because of the satisfaction given by social approval of good motherhood (and childhood experience has taught that social disapproval may end by being literally painful!). It is important to bear in mind that such "secondary gains" do naturally occur and complicate the dynamic subsidiation; but they can be distinguished by application of the eight criteria on pages 181–182, which show that the attempt to consider secondary gains as primary drives is fallacious.

commonly used, refers directly to *the strength of innate drives*, as McDougall pointed out (27).

The theory of drive strength measurement is still rather shaky. Obviously, it supposes in the first place that we know the unitary form of the innate pattern as well as the pattern of acquired metanergic expressions into which this potential form has been translated. Factor analysis can do much to pick out these patterns, as Anderson's experiments in the case of the rat, described below, demonstrate. When the question of selecting the right manifestations for measurement (and weighting them) is settled, we next have the question of deciding at what standard degree of deprivation—*e.g.*, of hunger—every drive should be measured. In animals or human beings, where appetitive drives are concerned (food, drink, sleep, sex, etc.) experimenters have worked with a supposed point of maximum deprivation, which is not difficult to find by trial and error; but with nonviscerogenic drives (curiosity, self-assertion, fear) a standard condition is not so easy to define.

The question which has received least attention, however, is that of the energy terms in which the manifestations shall be measured. This is examined, theoretically, in the next section. In practice, proceeding on the unanalyzed concept so far discussed, the principal manifestations used (especially in animal experiment) have been: (*a*) readiness to learn and retain, (*b*) willingness to face discomfort, (*c*) ability to overcome a supposedly standard motive (fear) in each case for the sake of the goal concerned, or (*d*) degree of manifestation of pugnacity or anxiety upon being frustrated in the drive concerned. It has not yet been established that these are always strictly proportional. For example, it is not known whether drive strength as shown by the degree of willingness to face pain would be proportional to the measure of energy available from the drive in ordinary living activities.

**Relative Strengths in Man.** In man some of the early conclusions about drive strength are not so much conclusions about the true strength of the drive as about the extent to which it happens to remain dissatisfied in the stimulation conditions and satisfaction opportunities of our particular culture. Thus sex and, next, self-assertion emerge in certain measurements as the strongest human drives, but it must not be forgotten that these measurements were made in a well-fed society, with considerable freedom from bodily danger, where curiosity can be satisfied in public libraries and thirst at the nearest drinking fountain.

Some meaning might be given to absolute strength of drive by taking the relative threshold of reaction to initially subliminal ergic stimulus situations, after a standard period of *absolute* deprivation of *all* drives, but the difference in period of various appetitive cycles makes this questionable. For the present it is more meaningful and applicable, at least in man, to set out to measure drive strengths frankly, as stated above, *under the conditions of stimulation and relative deprivation existing in our culture.*[4] This means measuring the strength of the drive for a given ratio of frequency of stimulation to frequency of satisfaction.

On whatever stimulation-satisfaction basis a drive is measured, however, it is desirable to sample the amount of activity (or other manifestation) in a score or so of common outlets of each drive. When an *R*-technique factorization is available the individual differences in total drive strength will naturally be obtained with greater accuracy by weighting the measures on each "outlet" according to the factor loading of that particular variable. For example, although both "time spent in newspaper reading" and "expenditure in travel" may be loaded with the drive of curiosity, the former, is more likely, for the average person, to be more reliably diagnostic in assessing the strength of this drive.

Available measures of disposition strength in human beings have rarely been founded on direct measures of time and money expenditures (except in certain studies by Thorndike, not analyzed into primary drives (32), but have usually been founded on indirect laboratory techniques such as: (*a*) memory for words, pictures, etc., representing various kinds of interest, (*b*) psychogalvanic response—or other measure of emotion reaction—to stimuli for different drives, and (*c*) measuring spontaneous attention to various classes of situation. A survey of some results by such methods is given in the table below:

| Erg | Colman and McRae's method | Cattell's method |
|---|---|---|
| Mating................ | 1 | 1 |
| Self-assertion........... | 6 | 2 |
| Pugnacity.............. | 5 | 3 |
| Repugnance............. | 9 | 4 |
| Appeal................ | Not included | 5 |
| Hunting............... | Not included | 6 |
| Laughter.............. | Not included | 7 |
| Self-abasement.......... | 2 | 8 |
| Construction............ | Not included | 9 |
| Flight................. | 3 | 10 |
| Curiosity.............. | 7 | 11 |
| Protection............. | 4 | 12 |
| Gregariousness.......... | 8 | 13 |
| Acquisition............. | 10 | 14 |

[4] Perhaps illustrations are hardly necessary to show that the finding above of sex and self-assertion as the strongest drives is purely a result of cultural conditions. As prison-camp, war-danger, and food-deprivation conditions show, the desire for food and safety may then far outweigh sex and self-assertion.

Colman and McRae used method (*b*), averaging the magnitudes of galvanic skin reflex to a lot of stimuli having to do with sex, fear, etc. Cattell used methods (*a*) and (*c*), *i.e.*, memory and attention for activities, words, pictures, associated, and presumably loaded, with each drive.

The measurement of ergic strengths in rats, cats, dogs, etc., examined more closely, is seen to depend principally on three methods: (*a*) the obstruction method, which places a painful electric shock between the animal and his goal, and records how often he will pass it; (*b*) the choice method, which puts the animal in a state of hunger, sexual deprivation, and/or fear before the corresponding alternative satisfactions and observes which he chooses; (*c*) the learning method, which discovers with what relative speed the animal learns a maze or some motor skill under different motivation. The agreement of different methods, with animals, is reasonably good, as Warden has shown (34) offering the following order of strength for certain ergs of the white rat.[5]

STRENGTH (RECORDED HERE BY THE
OBSTRUCTION METHOD, IN UNITS OF
"NUMBER OF CROSSINGS")

| | |
|---|---|
| Maternal erg | 22.4 |
| Thirst erg | 20.4 |
| Hunger erg | 18.2 |
| Sex erg | 13.8 |
| Exploration erg | 6.0 |
| Unknown motive | 3.5 |

## 5. THE OPERATIONAL CONCEPT OF ERG VS. REFLEXOLOGICAL AND SOCIOLOGICAL CONCEPTS

**History of the Instinct Concept.** The pioneer attempts to demonstrate that human motivation has its roots in biological drives homologous with those of the other mammals, and especially the primates, soon became involved in debates which, it must be confessed, were temporarily "solved" by dialectics rather than by new data and new methods. In fact, the unfortunate phase of American psychology which began with Watsonian reflexology kicking McDougall's dynamic psychology out of the front door and ended in the last decade with the almost surreptitious readmission of

---

[5] Further penetration into these methods will reveal, however, that they involve certain assumptions that cannot be entirely depended upon. For, example, if $A$ is stronger than $B$, and $B$ is stronger than $C$, it cannot always be assumed, in the matter of drives, that $A$ is stronger than $C$. Thus experiments show that a rat will face a greater degree of pain to satisfy sex than to satisfy hunger, yet may prefer hunger satisfaction to sex satisfaction in a choice situation. Possibly this indicates that pain is in some way involved as a stimulus, as well as an obstacle, to sex satisfaction; but it may be that more than this specific explanation is required and that the relations of dynamic intensities follow other laws than those of simple algebra.

drives by the back door is only truly to be understood by frank admission of the existence of ulterior historical influences operating on a wider stage than that of psychology itself.

The refusal to entertain drives or propensities came on the one hand from sociology, desirous of claiming the untrammeled omnipotence of the cultural pattern, and on the other from reflexologists, myopically unable to grasp sharply any concept more abstract than a neuron or a twitching leg. The latter were misled by a lack of faith that psychology would develop scientific methods of its own, and they followed the sterile path of closely imitating the methods of nineteenth-century physics. The sociological psychologists, misled by mixing political views with scientific facts, indulged in quite unnecessary wishful thinking; for belief in equality of opportunity does *not* require belief in biological equality but, rather, an acceptance of individuality. Today, as Langfeld's review of American psychology before the last International Congress[6] pointed out, a generation's overemphasis of cultural as opposed to hereditary determination of behavior is giving way to an unbiased appraisal of innate influences—in the United States if not in the U.S.S.R. With this release of psychology from the incursions of emotionally determined amnesias, and the rescue of the instinct problem from being buried alive, we may expect that facts and methods will now receive increasing attention which will lead to much more precise knowledge about the number, form, and mode of operation of innate drives.

The term "instinct" as used by Freud, Darwin, and McDougall (before modifying to "propensity") will nevertheless probably continue to be a word which "good" psychologists do not use. If so, it should not be because psychologists are unable to shake off early miseducation, but because in fact a new concept is required to distinguish the more plastic inheritances of man and the higher mammals from the largely unmodifiable instincts of lower animals and insects. And the objections of vagueness and operational uselessness brought against instinct must be recognized as applying equally to such notions as "drive," "need," "visceral tension," Lewin's "tension" (in a field or in the abstract) or the reflexologist's abortive "chain reflexes," with which psychologists in the interim have struggled to fill the gap. (For something had to be done for the robot, nondynamic man, if only to escape the outright laughter of that practical psychologist, the next-door neighbor!)

The term erg was suggested some years ago by the present writer in his *General Psychology* (5) for a working definition of inherited dynamic pattern. The ergic pattern has precise characters and investigatable assumptions, which distinguish it from "instinct," "drive," "need," or "tension." The nearest existing concept is "propensity," but this is an awkward label, not

[6] H. S. Langfeld, American Psychology To-day, 12th International Congress of Psychology, Edinburgh, 1948.

offering an easy adjective form like "ergic," an adverbial form such as "ergically," or derived terms such as "metanergic."

An *erg* is revealed in the first place as a *unitary pattern running through dynamic trait measures* as demonstrated at the end of the last chapter. In terms previously applied to patterns, it is a *source trait* or factor revealed among measures of largely dynamic modality, when analyzed either by *R* technique or *P* technique. That is to say it is a pattern of reactivity which increases or decreases *as a whole*.[7] Secondly, it must be demonstrated, *e.g.*, by studies of twins reared apart, to be *a constitutional rather than an environmental-mold* source trait.

The pattern will appear in all three aspects of behavior described for propensities, namely, (*a*) in attending to and "recognizing" a certain class of stimulus situations; (*b*) in a specific emotional reaction, and (*c*) in a predilection for (i) certain motor responses and (ii) certain particular final goals or satisfiers. In all these aspects we may expect to find not an "all-or-nothing" innate preference, but a graded series of innate preferences, so that if one is not appropriate to the environment the next will be accepted. If the individual could be experimented upon without having had previous experience, this hierarchy could be determined by finding *the relative ease with which various perceptions, motor responses, and satisfying end states are accepted and learned;* for all existing responses in the adult are acquired and the innate pattern can only be inferred.[8] But this pattern has to be determined by indirect means, such as the factor analysis and twin-study sequence described above.

The above introductory treatment of the concept of erg could be considerably expanded, notably in fuller conceptual definition, in examination

---

[7] The problem of unitariness of dynamic function may be illustrated from a recent experience of the writer as visiting examiner on a Ph.D. thesis. The researcher had set out to show that certain kinds of early experience increased the individual's anxiety level. He observed some ten or twelve areas of anxiety behavior, and added them together to get each individual's proneness to anxiety. It would have been preferable first to make a covariation study to ascertain whether these ten variables were in fact manifestations of a single anxiety disposition, or whether they represented two or more distinct varieties of anxiety.

[8] Thus children can be persuaded to express their pugnacity more readily in the artificial form of boxing than in the artificial form of criticizing one another's literary style. Similarly, the initial perceptual phase of the ergic process can be modified in some directions more easily than others: kittens may be stimulated to chase a ball of wool, but not an automobile; men seem to experience a sexual charm from soft, billowing feminine garments more readily than from braided uniforms—no matter how long women at war may wear them; and it is easier to frighten people with a cannon than with a pen, though in historical instances the latter has been more deadly. It is perhaps hardly necessary to point out that the pattern which is thus inferred is an *abstraction* from behavior, not tangible behavior itself.

of methods and operations by which a particular erg is discovered (see previous chapter), and in regard to special complications suggested by available findings; but this expansion must be brief. In conception, greater clarification is required particularly of what we may call "goal tension" and also of the distinction between "stimulus situation" and "goal." Let us examine the latter first. Mostly the ergic pattern consists of an initial "stimulus situation" which evokes early responses which bring about contact with "intermediate cue-goals." These are so described because, in bringing some degree of satisfaction as intermediate goals, they also act as cues or stimuli for the next phase of activity. Frequently, *different aspects of one and the same object constitute the initial stimulus situation, the intermediate cue-goals, and the object of the final-goal activity.* If one supposes that a certain innate

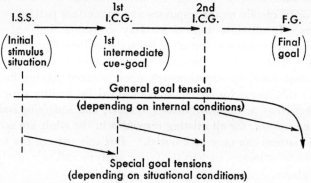

DIAGRAM 31. Goal tension in relation to final and intermediate goals.

tension determines the attention to the original stimulus situation and all that follows, it becomes necessary to suppose that this tension continually declines as the goal is approached (otherwise the organism would not approach the goal). The supposition conflicts with the observation that excitement, anger at frustration, and readiness to learn (Hull's goal gradient) all increase as the goal nears. (The first contradiction is unimportant, for excitement is merely an introspected condition, whereas the tension we are discussing is an abstract scientific concept, an abstraction from behavior.) This difficulty may be overcome, perhaps, by the concept of multiple-goal tensions. This supposes a single stimulus-to-final-goal drive, being aided by short-distance intermediate tensions, as set out in Diagram 31 and described in the last chapter of this book when summarizing psychodynamic laws.

The conceptualization may need to be expanded also, to clarify relationship to physiological events. It is already quite certain that what we have called "general goal tension" above is sometimes closely related to internal chemical conditions, notably the strength of a particular hormone, as in sex, fear, parental, sleep, and other drives.  Lashley (24) has brought cogent evidence that the chemical conditions act by sensitizing selectively certain neuron patterns, thereby lowering the threshold for certain perceptions and responses.  Similarly Richter (30a) and Young (39) have shown how the internal goal tension depends on internal homeostatic conditions.  However, it seems desirable at this stage to build up a definition of erg, in terms of behavior alone, that will stand on its own feet in any subsequent bridging of psychological and physiological findings.

In regard to examination of complications of the concept or of its investigation, an interesting example lies in the finding of such psychologists as Levy (25), Cruze (7), and the recent investigations of Lorenz (25a) in Vienna, showing that the effective appearance of an ergic pattern is sometimes critically dependent on a temporal coincidence of exercise or expression with time of maturation, and sometimes not.  The erg concept may need modification to take care of such facts as they become clearer.

Another complication has to do with the primary problem of unearthing the innate gradients of learning ease, *i.e.*, of obtaining evidence on innately preferred patterns after these patterns have been overlaid by much experience.  Possibly, when disposition rigidity has been more investigated, it will be feasible to distinguish between the rigidity due to length of establishment of a habit and that due to innate preference—or simply to discount by an appropriate allowance the degree of rigidity in responses due to length of establishment alone.

In regard to expanding the present treatment in terms of methods and operations of investigation, so little has been done on the first step of discovering the patterns themselves that it is premature to discuss in more detail the avenues that would then open up.

It is perhaps unnecessary to point out that the same criteria of ergs as are listed for the naturalistic method of approach, pages 181–182, will also apply to the factorial approach, over and above such exact methods as twin study which are applicable only to this more precise, metric method.  For example, the factor patterns due to ergs will tend to be the same in their highest loadings in all countries and cultures, whereas the environmental-mold factors of sentiments, etc., will be very different.  The previous chapter has presented a study showing evidence of ergic patterns among human attitudes.  It is appropriate in the present chapter, with its constant emphasis on linking human and mammalian study, to supplement the above with a research—the only one yet available—demonstrating the detection of ergic patterns in animals by the factor-analytic or covariational technique.

This careful and extensive study by E. E. Anderson (2,3) measured fifty-one rats with respect to some forty "traits" of a dynamic nature which could be objectively observed and measured.  The following correlation clusters (not yet expressed in factor loadings) emerged, showing clearly the functional unity of a drive existing in the region of water-seeking behavior, another in sex, and another in the behavior region we designate by curiosity. (Only three are given here for illustration, but several other ergic patterns were indicated.)

INVESTIGATION OF UNITARY ERGIC PATTERNS IN THE RAT*

Intercorrelations among behavior measures involving thirst or interest in drinking (51 rats)

|  | 2 | 3 | 4 |
|---|---|---|---|
| 1. Amount drunk (per gram body weight) | 0.07 | 0.63 | 0.19 |
| 2. Readiness to face shock for drink | .... | 1.00 | 0.09 |
| 3. Drinking time | .... | .... | 0.16 |
| 4. Readiness to jump to get water | .... | | |

Intercorrelations among measured behavior involving sex interest (51 rats)

|  | 6 | 7 |
|---|---|---|
| 5. Frequency of copulation | 0.57 | 0.44 |
| 6. Time prepared to wait at barrier to mate | .... | 0.15 |
| 7. Readiness to jump over obstruction to mate | | |

Intercorrelations among behavior measures which might be motivated by the erg of curiosity (51 rats)

|  | 9 | 10 | 11 |
|---|---|---|---|
| 8. Extent of exploration of Dashiell maze | 0.65 | 0.51 | 0.40 |
| 9. Extent of wandering over open field | .... | 0.49 | 0.65 |
| 10. Extent of exploration among pegs on a wall | .... | .... | 0.36 |
| 11. Extent of wandering when hungry | | | |

* Extracted from E. E. Anderson, The Interrelationship of Drives in the Male Albino Rat, *Comp. Psychol. Monogr.*, 19: 1–118, 1938.

The intercorrelations between the measures in the different areas (*e.g.*, 1, 2, 3, 4, with 5, 6, 7, or 5, 6, 7 with 8, 9, 10, 11) were negligible; but, as will be seen from the correlations within one area (with a few exceptions in the realm of thirst) there is evidence therein of a unitary dynamic trait— an erg, operationally defined.

It is interesting to compare the patterns of Anderson's study with those obtained by the analysis of human attitudes in the previous chapter and with the list of ergs given above from general observations. The animal study gives greater prominence to viscerogenic drives; indeed, in the well-fed human population of the attitude study there was not enough variance in the hunger drive for it to appear as a factor. The factorial study of human drives does not entirely agree with the general observation list above. It reveals ergic patterns of sex, self-assertion, fear, gregariousness, parental protectiveness, appeal or self-abasement, play and curiosity (See table, page 174). But it omits hunger (perhaps for reasons just stated), sleep, and pugnacity (also indicating special reasons), and it produces a pattern of "Narcism" not given in the above list. In the last resort the factor-analytic investigation of ergs must be the real basis of decision; but such investigation needs to be repeated before modifying the general observation list of ergs given above.

The methods of investigating ergic patterns, therefore, consist first of factor analytic studies of wide varieties of behavior, to establish source traits, and second, of genetic studies to detect which of these dynamic source traits are more constitutional. Confirmation can then be sought by learning investigations, experimental or statistical, which will rank forms of behavior or perceptual attention in order according to the readiness with which they can be acquired. The lowest points in this "gradient of difficulty of learning," *i.e.*, the ways which seem most readily learned, will indicate the innate form of the erg. The pattern is discoverable by these "paths of least resistance," even though, normally, society never allows the pattern to appear.

**The Definition of an Erg.** These considerations lead to the following final definition of an erg: *An innate psycho-physical disposition which permits its possessor to acquire reactivity (attention, recognition) to certain classes of objects more readily than others, to experience a specific emotion in regard to them, and to start on a course of action which ceases more completely at a certain specific goal activity than at any other. The pattern includes also preferred behavior subsidiation paths to the preferred goal.*

The pattern clearly has four parts: (*a*) a preferential attention to certain situations, *i.e.*, an innate *cognitive*, perceptual organization; (*b*) a specific emotional pattern, revealing itself consciously and physiologically, *i.e.*, an innate *affective* side; (*c*) a specific goal satisfaction; (*d*) an innate preference for certain ways of behaving (in reaching the goal). Parts (*c*) and (*d*) *may* be considered together as the innate, *conative* organization, reducing the aspects to three. If the student furnishes his mind with a clear recollection of what these four aspects are—the provocative situation, the emotion, the goal, the path to the goal—in each of the ergs mentioned on page 180 he will be in a position to discuss all ensuing problems of motivation with more data and more insight.

**The Stimulus Situations.** The *situations* releasing each of these ergs are reasonably clear. Escape seems to be primarily stimulated by loud sounds, large, swift-moving objects; the parental erg by distress and cries for help in small, helpless young; self-assertion by obvious superiority to other members of the group and by successful experience of influencing the feelings of the group; self-abasement by superior size, numbers, and performance in others; sex by physical attractiveness and by sex play (*e.g.*, coyness), in another; and so on. Sometimes stimulus situations are rather similar for two distinct ergs, causing liability to confusion. For example, strangeness, in mild degrees, excites curiosity; in strong measure it causes fear. The alternative conative aspects of the escape erg—flight or freezing—seem also to be partly determined by a difference in the suddenness and intensity of one and the same form of danger situation. The cues distinguishing the social situation calling for self-assertion from that requiring self-abasement are often so fine that an alternation of the two, or a kind of ergic "stutter," may ensue, which we call social embarrassment, and which is particularly marked in the adolescent exploring new social relations.

Mistakes are often made in dynamic psychology through failure to appreciate the true nature of the stimulus situation for certain ergs. Admittedly, research of a reliable, objective kind has not yet defined most of them with accurate detail, and in others the primary situation is subtle. Pugnacity, for example, at first defied formulation of the stimulus situation, until McDougall recognized it as being *frustration of any of the other drives*.

*The Ergic Affects*. The primary emotions constituting the ergic *affect* have, in almost every case, been clearly labeled from ancient times in most languages. Fear marks the erg of escape; lust accompanies the sex drive; an emotion of tender protectiveness (a component of pity) goes with the parental erg; disgust with avoidance; humility with self-abasement; loneliness and sympathetic fellowship-feeling with the two dynamic aspects of gregariousness; annoyance or rage with pugnacity; merriment with laughter; despair with appeal behavior; curiosity with the rather vaguely defined erg of exploration, and so on.[9]

Since the emotions are specific it is not unusual to name ergs by the emotion; but it is safer to define and label them by overt behavior, and, as several psychologists have pointed out (McDougall, Murphy), the classification of ergs is best ultimately based on the nature of the goal satisfactions. Consequently one speaks more accurately of ergs of escape, pugnacity and self-assertion,[10] rather than of fear, anger, and positive self-feeling.

### 6. THE NOTION OF MENTAL ENERGY

**Is Mental Energy Resolvable into Physical Energy?** The word dynamic in psychodynamic is derived from a root meaning "energy." Psychologists

---

[9] Naturally this introductory text cannot pursue discussions concerning more detailed analyses of the primary drives and emotions. However, the student proceeding further should at least be alert to the probability that some apparent modifications of the primary emotions are probably innate patterns innately tied to corresponding specialized patterns of conation and goal. Thus Hebb (19) points out three forms of anger in human beings and chimpanzees, *viz.*, rage, temper tantrums, and sulking, which are almost certainly innately maturing "modifications" of the anger response to frustration, depending on the particular form of the stimulus situation. He also points out that observation of the ergic situation indicates the necessity for adding the "desire not to be disturbed" to frustratable ergs. This is already in our ergic list as No. 3.

[10] In this ergic analysis the student may wonder how self-assertion stands in relation to the psychoanalytic concept of an "aggressive instinct" and the popular use of the term aggressiveness. The latter is an ill-defined mixture of self-assertion and pugnacity. At present the evidence overwhelmingly indicates two drives in this realm of behavior: pugnacity and self-assertion, but with some tendency for them to have special association with each other and, earlier, with sex. See the pattern of source trait *E*, page 60.

mean by dynamic traits "those concerned with motivating action," and indeed it has been a basic tenet both of Freud and McDougall that instincts or ergs are the only source of all psychic energy. To say that dynamic traits are goal directed is another way of saying the same thing. This characteristic, from an operational point of view, is easier to demonstrate and define than their energizing quality.

For despite the freedom with which clinicians and others use the concept of mental energy, it has never been precisely defined. In the first place, it is clearly not identifiable with the energy of the physicist—with $\frac{1}{2} mv^2$ and all the electrical, chemical, potential, mass and other equivalent transformations considered in the law of conservation of energy. Judged by the fatigue produced and other clinical manifestations of energy expenditure, a man may expend as much psychic energy sitting still for a couple of hours of mental calculations (say, obtaining the square root of 39,452) or in moral conflict as he would in playing a football game, though he uses up far more calories in the latter.

**Tentative Definitions.** A number of distinct approaches to definition which may be worthy of investigation can, however, be suggested.

1. *Neural Energy.* Some have suggested identifying mental energy with the theoretically measurable physical energy of the central nervous system, *i.e.*, with the oxygen consumption by nervous tissue alone. This avoids the objections which arise to the above course of measuring the organism's *total* calorie consumption, in which muscular work far outweighs and obscures purely neural activity. The objection remains that it is not a behavior measurement and that, as far as present physiological knowledge indicates, it would favor coarse, unintegrated activity relative to integrated, inhibited activities. For example, the expenditure of mental energy by a loquacious talker may be less than that of a mathematician silently wrestling with an equation, yet the neural consumption of the former may be greater. In other words, the ultimate discharge of energy by long-circuited outlets is normally as great as by direct ones, yet it probably does not involve as great a neural oxygen consumption.

2. *Energy as Total Reactivity.* An erg or any other dynamic trait is essentially a readiness to react to a stimulus situation, perhaps physiologically determined, as we see below, by the sensitization of particular nerve tracts. The more energetic person is, therefore, one who will react to more things, *i.e.*, have more interests, and at a lower threshold. It is possible, since memory is an index of interest and past attention, that a test of the total number of things *known*, *i.e.*, things to which one reacts, would be the best practicable, relative measure of the mental energy of individuals.

3. *Energy as "Goal Tension."* Physiologically, ergic activity, particularly in the appetitive ergs, can be regarded as an attempt to restore a state of equilibrium—homeostasis—which has become upset. For example, the

blood sugar level falls from the optimum level and a state of hunger arises, driving toward food seeking.  The relation of activity to internal physiological equilibrium has been systematically explored and formulated in the work of Richter, P. T. Young (38) and, less metrically, by Beach (4).  Even before physiological conditions are fully understood however, we can speak of the existence of a "goal tension" in the individual.  As we have seen, this exists strictly in the sense of an abstraction or inference from behavior which drives him to the goal of reestablishing internal equilibrium.  This links the "goal-tension" notion derived in the previous section from behavior alone with the further notion of an internal equilibrium, ultimately to be physiologically defined but at present left merely as "an internal state of the organism depending on other internal conditions."

Thus in visand viscerogenic, appetitive drives it is easy to see that there is a heightened tendency to react or discharge energy if left long unstimulated. This argues that the internal disequilibrium which we accept as the basis of the "goal tension" may be said to increase with lapse of time since the last satiation.  Physiologically, as Lashley (24) has carefully argued, this increasing goal tension may be the result of hormone or other chemical changes connected with satiation which rend certain neural tracts more sensitive as the last satisfaction recedes.  The individual's energy at a given moment would thus be the sum of the goal tensions of the various ergs.

The above three approaches could arrive at compatible aspects of a single concept.  But these further problems of the root meaning of drive, motivation, or mental energy are too profound and experimentally unexplored for further treatment in an introduction.  Nevertheless, the student should not imagine that such problems as the nature of mental energy and the determination of the actual number of ergs are matters merely for academic hair splitting.  For clinical psychology proceeds daily to practical action on the basis of such generalizations as that mental energy cannot be destroyed, but only deflected; that mental conflict locks energy in a useless investment; and that conflicts can only be solved when one knows which particular drives are failing to get satisfaction.  For practical purposes, most psychologists seem to agree upon, even though they cannot define, what is meant by mental energy or, again, on what is the range of behavior deriving from, say, the self-assertive drive; but, for greater scientific precision and theoretical insight, newer methods, involving more complex statistics, are likely to be applied to both of these problems.

### 7. SUMMARY

1. Understanding dynamic problems turns in the first place on the correctness of our conception of what is innately given.  Evidence as to the nature and number of innate drives in man rests largely on naturalistic and

clinical observation, since laboratory experiments are here applicable only to animals; but this evidence is on the threshold of being more reliably and objectively handled by statistical, covariational techniques, which yield constitutional dynamic source traits, or *ergs*, on the one hand, and the acquired *sentiments*, of especial interest to the sociologist, on the other.

2. Some eight criteria of innateness can be applied to naturalistic and clinical data, leading to the conclusion that in adults there are about sixteen appetitive and nonappetitive drives. These may be derived, by maturation, from a smaller number of somewhat differently patterned drives in young children. Even apart from being related by the fact of maturation from a common stem, drives are related in certain groups, within each of which there is some evidence of closer functional ties.

3. This "ergic maturation," with continuous shifting and evolution of the goal, can be best illustrated from clinical observation of the sex drive, though the precise line between maturation effects and environmentally produced "aim inhibition" cannot yet be drawn. Here changes have been observed both in direction (goal of activity) and in the organ activities preferred (erogenous zones).

4. The measurement of "strength of ergs" is based on observations of (a) readiness to learn and retain under the motive concerned, (b) willingness to face pain and discomfort, (c) exchange rate (preference) in regard to some standard motive, for which fear (escape) is most convenient, and (d) extent of pugnacity at frustration.

5. Strength as thus measured is always relative to a particular deprivation level—in human beings it is particularly necessary to take into account the average stimulation and degree of deprivation maintained in the culture pattern. Heeding this condition, various approaches show tolerably good agreement on the strength of ergs in man. More exact results will be possible only when factor analytic and other methods define the true boundaries of each drive and indicate the weights to be assigned to various behavior manifestations.

6. Progress in methods of exactly delineating innate drive patterns has been neglected because of dialectical sociological assertions that no innate drive patterns exist to be investigated. Neither in man nor in animals do we find behavior patterns literally inherited, in the sense that no environmental modification occurs. Indeed, in all levels of animal life dynamic roots are "ergic" rather than "instinctive." But ergic patterns may be abstracted by factor analysis and checked for innateness by the above naturalistic criteria, by twin studies and other methods of psychological genetics, and by learning experiments which show, by a "learning gradient," that some modes of perception and response are acquired more easily than others. Some eight patterns of this kind have already been demonstrated in man

and the rat and are found to correspond with ideas of drive pattern obtained from other sources.

7. An erg is defined as "an innate psychophysical disposition which permits its possessor to acquire reactivity (attention, recognition) to certain classes of objects more readily than others, to experience a specific emotion in regard to them, and to start on a course of action which ceases more completely at a certain specific goal activity than at any other. The pattern includes also preferred behavior subsidiation paths to the preferred goal."

8. Much research remains to be done on ergs, notably in clarifying (a) the nature of goal tension, (b) the existence of optimum-effectiveness periods for fixing maturation pattern by exercise, and (c) the course of maturation in terms of the perceptual, affective, and conative aspects of drives.

9. Attempts at defining mental energy in terms of (a) physical energy, (b) neural energy, (c) total reactivity, and (d) goal tensions are discussed. Though none is yet adequate, the notions of total reactivity and of goal tension may develop into more acceptably operational definitions of that concept of energy which is at present a vague but indispensable tool of clinical and dynamic psychology.

10. In contrast to the reflexological formulations summarized by $S \rightarrow R$, i.e., $R = f(S)$, the dynamic viewpoint as developed by Freud and McDougall can be formulated $S -\ominus\rightarrow R$, i.e., $R = f(O.S)$, where $O$ is the organism (see 5,6). As further developed in the ergic theory this expands to

$$R = S_1E_1 + S_2E_2 +,$$

etc., where the $S$'s are indices defining the stimulus situation and the $E$'s are the ergs. The $S$'s take account of the situational learning up to the time of measurement.

### QUESTIONS AND EXERCISES

1. By listing a few essential differences, distinguish between a reflex, a tropism, and an erg.

2. Set down eight criteria by which ergic behavior in man can be detected.

3. What innate drives have been recognized by clinical observation?

4. Describe three steps in change of goal direction during the maturation of the sex drive.

5. Name two viscerogenic and two nonviscerogenic innate drives in man, taking care to detail the three important aspects of each.

6. What are the two drives (a) in man, (b) in rats, which experiment indicates to be the strongest? Why are the results for man different from those for the rat?

7. Give some instances of behavior patterns which are (a) not present at birth, (b) expressed in terms of acquired skills, but which nevertheless depend very considerably on inheritance.

8. Define an erg, and describe some ergic patterns found by factor analysis of dynamic responses in the rat.

9. Give an example of ergic structure (a) modified in its perceptual mechanism, (b) modified by combination in its effective aspect, (c) modified in the conative (impulse to action) mechanism, and (d) modified in its goal satisfaction.

10. Give two observations, from the fields of naturalistic observation, clinical experience, experiment, or statistical analysis, which seem to indicate that man has a limited total of available ergic energy.

## BIBLIOGRAPHY

1. ADLER, A.: *Practice and Theory of Individual Psychology*, Harcourt, Brace & Company, New York, 1927.
2. ANDERSON, E. E.: Interrelationship of Drives in the Male Albino Rat: I. Intercorrelations of Measures of Drives, *J. comp. Psychol.*, 24: 73–118, 1937.
3. ANDERSON, E. E.: Interrelationship of Drives in the Male Albino Rat: II. Intercorrelations between 47 Measures of Drives and Learning, *Comp. Psychol. Monogr.*, 14 (No. 6): 119–241, 1938.
4. BEACH, F. A.: *Hormones and Behavior*, Paul B. Hoeber, Inc., New York, 1948.
5. CATTELL, R. B.: *General Psychology*, Sci-Art Publishers, Cambridge, 1941.
6. CATTELL, R. B.: The Ergic Theory of Attitude and Sentiment Measurement, *Educ. and Psych. Meas.*, 7: 221–246, 1947.
6a. CATTELL, R. B.: The Discovery of Ergic Structure in Man in Terms of Common Attitudes. *J. abnorm. soc. Psychol*, 45, 1950.
7. CRUZE, W. W.: Maturation and Learning in Chicks. *J. comp. Psychol.*, 19: 371–409, 1935.
8. DARWIN, C.: *The Expression of the Emotions in Animals and Man*, Appleton-Century-Crofts, Inc., New York, 1896.
9. DAVIS, H. V., R. R. SEARS, H. C. MILLER, and A. J. BRODBECK: Effects of Cup, Bottle and Breast Feeding on Oral Activities of Newborn Infants, *J. Pediatr.* 549-558, 1948.
10. DAVIS, W. A., and R. J. HAVIGHURST: *Father of the Man*, Houghton Mifflin Company, Boston, 1947.
11. DENNIS, W.: Infant Reactions to Restraint: An Evaluation of Watson's Theory, *Trans. N. Y. Acad. Sci.*, Series II, 2: 8, 202–218, 1940.
12. DENNIS, W.: An Experimental Test of Two Theories of Social Smiling in Infants, *J. soc. Psychol.*, 6: 214–225, 1936.
12a. EYSENCK, H. J.: A Study of Human Aversions and Satisfactions, *J. genet. Psychol.*, 62: 289–299, 1943.
13. FITE, M. D.: Aggressive Behavior in Young Children and Children's Attitudes toward Aggression, *Genet. Psychol. Monogr.*, 22 (No. 2): 1–151, 1940.
14. FREUD, S.: *Introductory Lectures to Psychoanalysis*, W. W. Norton and Company, New York, 1938.
15. GARNETT, A. C.: *Instinct and Personality*, George Allen & Unwin, Ltd., London, 1928.
16. GOODENOUGH, F. L.: *Anger in Young Children*, University of Minnesota Press, Minneapolis, 1931.
17. HALVERSON, H. M.: Infant Sucking and Tensional Behaviour, *J. genet. Psychol.*, 53: 365–430, 1938.
18. HARDING, D. C. W.: *The Impulse to Dominate*, George Allen & Unwin, Ltd., London, 1941.
18a. HEALY, W., A. F. BRONNER, and A. M. BOWERS: *The Structure and Meaning of Psychoanalysis*, 1930, New York.
19. HEBB, D. O.: On the Nature of Fear, *Psychol. Rev.*, 53: 259–263, 1946.
20. HULL, C. L.: *Principles of Behavior*, Appleton-Century-Crofts, Inc., New York, 1943.

21. ISAACS, S.: *Emotional Development in Young Children*, George Routledge and Sons, London, 1933.
22. JAMES, W.: *Principles of Psychology*, Henry Holt and Company, Incorporated, New York, 1890.
23. KOHLER, W.: *The Mentality of Apes*, Harcourt, Brace & Company, Inc., New York, 1925.
24. LASHLEY, K. S.: Experimental Analysis of Instinctive Behavior, *Psychol. Rev.*, 45: 445–472, 1938.
25. LEVY, D. M.: Experiments of the Sucking Reflex and Social Behaviour of Dogs, *Amer. J. Orthopsychiat.*, 4: 203–224, 1934.
25a. LORENZ, K.: The Companion in the Bird's World. *Auk*, 54: 245–273, 1937.
26. MASLOW, A. H.: Appetites and Hungers in Animal Motivation, *J. comp. Psychol.*, 20: 75–83, 1935.
27. McDOUGALL, W.: *The Energies of Men*, Oxford University Press, New York, 1938.
28. MEAD, M.: Anthropological Data on the Problem of Instinct, *Psychosom. Med.*, 4: 396–397, 1942.
29. MILLER, N. E., and J. DOLLARD: *Social Learning and Imitation*, Yale University Press, New Haven, 1941.
30. MURRAY, H. A.: *Explorations in Personality*, Oxford University Press, New York, 1938.
30a. RICHTER, C. P.: Biology of Drives, *J. comp. Psychol.*, 40: 129–134, 1947.
31. SHAND, A. F.: *Foundations of Character*, Macmillan & Co., Ltd., London, 1914.
32. THORNDIKE, E. L.: *The Psychology of Wants, Interests, and Attitudes*, Appleton-Century-Crofts, Inc., New York, 1935.
33. TOLMAN, E. C.: Motivation, Learning, and Adjustment, *Proc. Amer. phil. Soc.*, 84: 1941.
34. WARDEN, C. J.: *Animal Motivation*, Columbia University Press, New York, 1931.
35. WHITING, J. W. M., and I. CHILD: Fate of Basic Drives in Various Cultures. Presented to December Meeting of Society for Research in Child Development at Chicago, 1947.
36. YERKES, R. M.: Sexual Behaviour of the Chimpanzee, *Hum. Biol.*, 11: 78–111, 1939.
37. YERKES, R. M.: Social Behavior of Chimpanzees, *J. comp. Psychol.*, 30: 147–186, 1940.
38. YOUNG, P. T.: *Motivation of Behaviour*, John Wiley & Sons, Inc., New York, 1944.
39. YOUNG, P. T.: Food-seeking Drive, Affective Process and Learning, *Psychol. Rev.*, 56: 98–121, 1949.
40. ZENER, K.: Significance of Behaviour Accompanying Conditioned Salivary Secretion for Theories of the Conditioned Reflex, *Amer. J. Psychol.*, 50: 384–483, 1937.

# CHAPTER 8

## PSYCHODYNAMICS: III. THE STRUCTURES FORMED IN THE ADJUSTMENT PROCESS

1. What Is Plasticity of Dynamic Structure?
2. Basic Principles of Learning
3. Confluence and Conflict of Drives
4. Frustration and Its Sequels
5. The Fourth Dynamic Crossroads and the Eight Sequels: Suppression, Sublimation, and Repression
6. The Structures Involved in Internal Conflict and External Adjustment
7. Summary

### 1. WHAT IS PLASTICITY OF DYNAMIC STRUCTURE?

**Ergic and Metanergic Patterns.** On the one hand we have glanced at the typical structure of sentiments and attitudes developed in the civilized adult. On the other we have attempted to uncover the raw material of innate dynamic source traits or "ergs" which man shares with the higher mammals. This contrast between what we have called "ergic" and "metanergic" structure (from Greek *meta*, meaning "beyond") provokes us to understand systematically what laws govern the transformation from one to the other during the individual's lifetime. These are, in the broadest sense, the laws of learning.

Let us agree on some definite terminology here. It is obvious that all actual dynamic traits owe their structure to two influences, (*a*) the inner constraint exercised by the hereditary maturation patterns, which develop the ergs. These are revealed by correlation as constitutional source traits in the realm of dynamic manifestations; (*b*) the environmental-mold source traits resulting from cultural constraints, corresponding to institutions in the culture pattern. To such environmental-mold traits, falling in the dynamic realm, we have given the name of *metanergs*, to indicate that they constitute the patterning of dynamic traits *beyond* that due to ergs. Any given dynamic surface trait is thus neither an erg nor a metanerg: it is an actual dynamic trait structure resulting from the interaction of ergic and metanergic patterns. The latter are abstractions analyzed out of concrete behavior habits, and the observed surface traits can therefore properly be regarded as a synthesis of ergic and metanergic influences. What can at

207

present be said about ergic patterns has been told in the last chapter.   In the present chapter our object is to study the laws of metanergic modification of behavior.   Thereby we may form an idea of the principal influences which modify ergs and how they do so.

**Primary Conditions for Ergic Modification.**   From everyday-life observations, without recourse to any special psychological microscope, we can see that modification of ergs depends broadly on two conditions: (*a*) the possession by the organism of an innately adequate degree of *plasticity* (thus metanergs are readily formed in man, less readily in mammals, hardly at all in insects); (*b*) the recurrence of certain *experiences*, which "educate the emotions" as well as the motor and perceptual skills.   One can see at a first glance that the frustration and failure of innate ergic responses loom prominently in these experiences.   In sum, there must exist both the *capacity* and the *provocation* to find new ways of satisfaction.

**Three Major Factors in "Plasticity."**   On the modifiability of drive, writers such as McDougall have used the term "plasticity," but this is rather a description of the fact that a total change occurs than an analysis of a psychological capacity.   A study of any example will show that three distinct capacities make plasticity possible: (*a*) intelligence or other perceptual abilities which reveal more effective approaches to a goal (physiologically this may amount to the existence of available new neuron paths); (*b*) the actual capacity to give up one habit and acquire that perceived or found to be better (this might be called true plasticity or absence of disposition rigidity); (*c*) the capacity to remember past experience over a sufficient length of time to profit by it in anticipation, etc.

There has sometimes been a tendency to explain all phenomena observed under plasticity, *e.g.*, anticipation, learning to react to new symbols instead of waiting for those innately known, remembering the consequences of trial and error, as due wholly to intelligence.   But though intelligence may give insight into what to do, there are people, as every observer of human nature knows, who are incapable of changing their habits to do what intelligence directs.   Nor do intelligent people always show greater ability to remember lessons that have momentarily been clearly understood.

To the above formulation it may be objected that (*c*) is superfluous, a mere antonym of (*b*).   Low rigidity and high retention could logically be opposites, but the general psychological consensus at present seems to be that rigidity is something over and above retentivity.   For example, recent research (see (12), Chap. 4) has shown that two factors of rigidity exist, one of which is that "difficulty in changing to new ways" which has long been investigated under the title of "perseveration."   For the present, however, all we need to note is that the possibility of learning lies in qualities of (*a*) retentivity and (*b*) freedom from rigidity, additional to (*c*) intelligence—and that these are the preconditions underlying dynamic learning laws.

## 2. BASIC PRINCIPLES OF LEARNING

**Unimpeded Living Shows Innate Patterns.**  Granted these capacities to change, we have then to explain how environment enforces the change. If the normal cues to ergic action and the usual avenues to satisfaction existed on all sides, it seems very likely that the behavior of man would remain largely that prescribed in his innate dynamic patterns.  No one has studied such a purely "natural" man, but as we study increasingly primitive people, whose culture interferes less and less with a pre-stone-age mode of living, we can see much direct, simple, ergic behavior accounting for the daily round of activity (or inactivity!).  By extrapolation we can infer that if the "natural" man existed he would begin to hunt for food only when he felt hungry; respond to sexual attraction by a very direct process of courtship and mating; flee from danger without sense of duty or self-respect; and so on through the gamut of possible innate responses.

**The First Dynamic Crossroads.**  Let us see what happens, however, when satisfaction fails.  Here and in later study of the several problems of dynamic adjustment we shall employ systematically the concept of a series of *dynamic crossroads*, for they provide the most economical and comprehensive means for the solution of any dynamic adjustment question.  The first dynamic crossroad represents the alternative sequels at the initial attempt of a drive or need to obtain satisfaction.  As Diagram 32 shows, there are four possible endings to the provocation of a drive, as follows:

$\alpha 1$. Satisfaction as a result of the innate response being adapted to environmental conditions.

$\alpha 2$. Continued dissatisfaction through innate perceptions and responses being unadapted to novel facts of environment.

$\alpha 3$. Modification or supersession of the first drive by the stronger provocation of some other drive in the interim.

$\alpha 4$. Frustration by a barrier when the path to satisfaction is otherwise clear.

For example, a hungry kitten may see a mouse (never having seen one before) and, as experiment shows, is likely in that case to pursue it, by an innate hunting pattern, and eat it.  This is the $\alpha 1$ path.  But it may never see a mouse, or it may see a dead but edible mouse and, because the innate perception pattern requires a chase, fail to recognize it as food.  Or, perceiving a mouse in a cage, its innate motor pattern may prove unfitted to opening a cage.  In instances, covered by the $\alpha 2$ path, it persists in a state of continued deprivation and dissatisfaction.  $\alpha 3$ is illustrated by the cat suddenly encountering a fierce dog, whereupon a new drive—escape—is stimulated and takes precedence.  $\alpha 4$ is illustrated by the cat pursuing the mouse and encountering a barrier, say in the form of another cat seizing it first.  The pugnacity and subsequent responses ensuing along the $\alpha 4$ path we shall follow up later.   Here we shall begin more detailed study, systematically of all paths, beginning with α1.

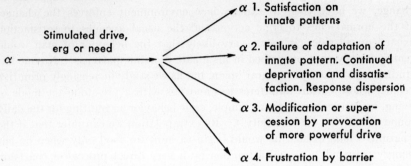

Stimulated drive,
erg or need

α

*α* 1. Satisfaction on
innate patterns

*α* 2. Failure of adaptation of
innate pattern. Continued
deprivation and dissatis-
faction. Response dispersion

*α* 3. Modification or supercession by provocation
of more powerful drive

*α* 4. Frustration by barrier

DIAGRAM 32.   The first dynamic crossroads and the α (Greek letter alpha) sequels: initial fate of a stimulated drive.

**Deprivation Contrasted with Frustration.**   The α1 path needs no discussion; it is the simple fulfillment of the ergic perception, feeling, and response pattern as described in the previous chapter.   It is the α2 path, which is principally concerned with the modifications of dynamic structure, that we are interested to study.   At this point it is necessary to distinguish between dissatisfaction or deprivation on the one hand—as in α2—and frustration or thwarting on the other—as in α4.   Dissatisfaction is characterized by restless activity which becomes increasingly random, *i.e.*, increasingly remote from the usual innate pattern, as deprivation increases in intensity. This we shall call "response dispersion" or "ergic dispersion"—an important phenomenon worthy of more study than psychology has yet given to it. (One might here compare the observation of an old saying that "in proportion to their ravenousness, appetites become indiscriminate.")   The organism cannot find the cue situations which provoke definite innate behavior patterns or, if experiencing the provocations, cannot succeed in reaching the goal by the innate behavior responses, which happen to be inapt, as in the case above of the cat seeing a mouse in a cage, or a dog pursuing an electric hare.

In frustration, on the other hand, the organism sees definitely what it wants to do (an intermediate goal even if not the final goal).   It is in the midst of a definitely indicated response (perceivable by an observer as a directed, structured piece of behavior) and is prevented by an equally definite obstacle from completing it.   The subjective feeling is rage, not dissatisfaction, and the behavior is pugnacity.   Incidentally it is best to reserve the terms *Deprivation* and *Frustration* respectively to describe these distinct dynamic *situations*, just as we use *Dissatisfaction* and *Rage* to describe the corresponding *feelings* or internal states and *Response dispersion* (or *Restlessness*) and *Pugnacity* (or *Aggression*) for the two corresponding *motor actions*. However, this clear distinction is not to deny that there exists a continuum of intermediate states. For wherever the provocative situation is clearly perceived, and the innate responses are made in vain, there is to some extent a perceived goal, and if the failure of the innate responses can be ascribed by the organism in these circumstances to some definite object, the deprivation situation passes over into a frustration situation with ensuing aggression against the object (rightly or wrongly chosen!)

This transition from restlessness to pugnacity can often be seen in human behavior, where it probably occurs more readily than in animals because (*a*) human beings generally have a comparatively long view of the goals they are working for—a view which more readily admits of obstruction; (*b*) by rationalization (see Chap. 2), as well as by intelligent generalization, human beings can more readily concentrate what is obstructing them into a single attackable object. Pugnacity is preferred to restlessness because it provides an innate channel of direct discharge—however foolish—in place of long circuited restlessness. Thus the nagging deprivations of poverty can be ascribed to capitalism or the trade unions' systematization of human laziness—according to one's preferred rationalizations. Similarly the oblique deprivations of sex expression may by some disgruntled lover be blamed on the individual woman, but by a more intelligent one, on religion or the whole cultural pattern.

**The Laws of Learning.** The above discussion systematizes the situations in which learning is forced upon the organism; it does not deal with the internal-process learning itself. Historically, the laws of learning have unfortunately been studied in much narrower contexts than the above and they need to be viewed again in these wider circumstances if certain difficulties of formulation are to be avoided.

Two main principles have been developed to account for the array of facts in learning. As every general psychology student knows, they are (*a*) the dynamic principle of rewarded responses or "the law of effect," which states that the responses bringing satisfaction (or bringing the organism nearer its goal) are learned in preference to responses which do not, and (*b*) the principles of conditioning, based on the paradigm that the repeated occurrence of a new stimulus immediately before one to which the organism innately reacts with a reflex response will lead to a conditioned reflex in which the response becomes made to the new stimulus alone.

Various attempts have been made to take the step of subsuming one under the other or both under some new single principle. Zener carried out experiments showing the dependence of classical conditioning upon dynamic conditions, while the present writer has put forward tentative explanations of conditioning in terms of dynamic laws (1) as also have Hilgard (7a) and Postman and Egan (15a).  On the other hand, Maier and Schneirla (9), as well as Skinner (17) and others brought up in reflexological rather than dynamic schools, have attempted to bring trial-and-error dynamic learning under the label of "instrumental conditioning" and allied notions.

None of these attempts is wholly successful as yet.  Some, by over-simplifying the facts to be explained or by using unfortunate terms, have probably only added to the confusion.  Thus "instrumental conditioning" describes a process fundamentally different from conditioning, while reflexo-logical, stimulus-response systematists such as Hull (8) or Skinner (17) have continued with a nomenclature which may inadvertently hide from students the fact that they are now following the dynamic principles of McDougall and Thorndike.  Hull, for example, introduced into his equations the drive state of the organism, substituting the McDougallian $S -\!\!\!O\!\!\rightarrow R$ for the reflexological $S \rightarrow R$, and used a goal distance concept in learning such as had been stated by the present writer (see (1), p. 388) and other followers of dynamic principles.

Whatever ultimate common principle may be reached it is probable that the marked difference between the conditioned-reflex phenomena and the phenomena of learning a path to a goal will require that the explanation of one of them be modified by a subprinciple.  The former deals with the sub-stitution of a new perception or stimulus situation for an old one, both leading to the same response.  If it has to explain the attachment of a new response to an old stimulus situation it has to proceed in a very roundabout fashion—by finding the new response existing as an innate response to some other stimulus—as if a man who wants a new headlight for his car should have to buy a car with such a headlight and transfer it to his own car.  On the other hand, trial-and-error learning principles formulate the attachment of a new response to an old stimulus situation or goal pursuit, and also the rise of attention to new cues.

The weakness of the dynamic, law-of-effect explanation, *i.e.*, that that item of random behavior becomes learned which most helps the organism to its goal, lies in its inadequate account of what random behavior is, and by what stimulus and response attachments any particular item is defined.  Pri-marily random, trial-and-error learning arises through that *response dispersion* which, as we have seen in Chapter 7, occurs with increasing drive deprivation. If we avoid the confusion of calling goal tension an "inner stimulus" (there *are*, of course, inner stimuli, such as images and other cognitive data) we have to admit that the "random responses" are responses (innate or acquired), reflex in nature, to cognitive stimuli to which heightened deprivation has produced sensitivity.  If now one of these responses to a particular stimulus proves successful, it is made more readily to that stimulus, *or to some con-*

*ditioned stimulus which occurred at the same time,* on a future occasion. Let us suppose that an itch in the dog's ear caused it to lower its head at the moment it was facing the latch on the box and that this movement released the dog to get food. Our hypothesis is that when next it is hungry *it will make this response more readily either to the itch or to the sight of the latch.* Since the latter is likely to be the only constant stimulus in the situation, the facilitation of the conditioned response is more important in learning than the facilitation of the existing response.

While this formulation makes conditioning a part of trial-and-error learning, the more important point is that it makes conditioning *dependent upon the reflex occurring in the field of force created by a goal tension.* Pavlov has references to conditioning of salivary reflexes being "inhibited" when hunger was displaced by interfering motivations and Zener's experiments bring out the effect of the goal tension in conditioning (an irrelevant side issue for Pavlov) more clearly and systematically.

The pure conditioning phenomenon in the above sequence has been left so far, however, without a dynamic explanation. But tentative dynamic interpretations of this substitution of perceptions can be offered. If stimulus $B$ normally releases the organism in some action toward its goal, and stimulus $A$ repeatedly and reliably precedes and acts as a signal or cue for $B$, then the organism makes a dynamic saving by reacting to $A$ instead of $B$. This saving may be either that it more quickly approaches the goal of the specific drive concerned, or that it rewards the ever-present "drive to save energy and avoid fatigue" (Drive II, see (2) Chap. 7).

One of the chief objections to any dynamic explanation of conditioning is that conditioning sometimes seems to bring more punishment than reward. A rat punished by an electric shock for pressing a lever to get food (as in Mowrer's (14) experiment) shows fear and avoidance of the lever whenever it gets hungry. The explanation offered is that the internal stimulus constituted by images of touching the lever conditions the anxiety-fear response. It is suggested that this could not be explained dynamically because this particular association is unrewarding—in fact it prevents the rat from eating. *This theoretical difficulty is typical of what happens through couching learning theory in the narrow context of a single drive.* If we consider *all* the satisfactions of the rat, the conditioning association is actually rewarding: it enables him to escape shock, which is evidently more important to him than eating. In other instances, *e.g.,* salivary conditioning not followed by food, it is objected that the conditioning occurs even when it does not result in the organism reaching its goal. Here it may be necessary to bring in the concept of a continually declining goal tension as set out in Chapter 7, which would make it rewarding to be advanced some distance toward the goal even if one does not actually reach it.

Basically, the explanation of learning here offered therefore begins with law of effect—that the response to a stimulus which brings the organism nearer to its goal will tend to be learned. But within this law it supposes (*a*) that the use of the random trial-and-error responses occurs through conditioning of reflexes, possible only in a goal-tension field, and (*b*) that this conditioning may itself be determined by dynamic gains. Thus a hungry cat, failing to find the innate cues provided by mice, suffers a lowering of reflex thresholds under deprivation. The restless behavior that now results is a hash of conditioned and unconditioned reflexes and of responses normally made in the course of drives other than hunger. For example, the cat knocks over a milk bottle (this utilization of acts of other drives straying across the main one is perhaps insufficiently stressed) and as a "grooming reflex," or out of curiosity, licks the milk. The reward favors the conditioning of these "knocking over" responses to the sight of the milk bottle and the milk.

For brevity, the above principles will in most situations simply be referred to as *the dynamic law of effect;* for the main, over-all happening is the acquisition of a response to a situation because that response brings the organism nearer to its goal; but it should be understood that this includes inner mechanisms of conditioning and leaves open the question of whether the association of conditioned and unconditioned responses is entirely to be explained dynamically or whether a distinct subprinciple is involved.

**Sentiments through the Law of Effect.** The basic method by which innate ergs are modified, therefore, is by the law of effect. Failing satisfaction through innate response adequate for a natural setting, dissatisfaction mounts, behavior becomes more varied or "dispersed" and eventually some response is made which fits the situation and leads to the goal satisfaction. This acquired manner of perceiving, and behaving, if it continues to yield satisfaction, becomes a relatively fixed habit, sentiment, or, in the most general sense, attitude.

The reader may object that with human beings other ways than blind trial and error usually operate in the building of sentiments. For example, the individual acquires patriotic sentiments toward his country because he is deliberately taught the component attitudes in school. Or he acquires an attitude of respect for automobiles through intelligent perception, without having to be knocked down several times in order to learn. While it is true that imitation, or intelligent analysis, or insight, frequently operates in this way, their intrusion does not affect the basic generalization that new ways of behaving, however adopted, must also yield satisfaction of a dissatisfied drive if they are to have any permanence as sentiments. They are alternative ways of obtaining associations, but the associations once made still require the law of effect for their consolidation.

The satisfactions used in formal learning in home and school are often different from those which will eventually have to sustain or justify the sentiment. A child may learn to be economical in order to please his parents, but thrift will later be sustained by more personal rewards. A boy may learn to like mathematics because it satisfies self-assertion through his successful competition with others in class grades, but the sentiment may grow later because it satisfies his curiosity. Gregariousness—the satisfaction from feeling and thinking the same as others—has sometimes been the motive for acquiring patriotic sentiments of a warlike nature, which, in later experience of the waste and agony of war, have proved to be unsatisfying attitudes. In short, the motivations sustaining a sentiment or producing it may shift a good deal at certain periods of its existence.

Those modifications of innate drives which we call sentiments could consequently have their modes of origin subclassified in various ways (see (1)), but basically they are all examples of the law of effect. The law of effect can give permanence to attitudes acquired by intelligent insight, or imitation, as well as trial and error; but even in human life it could almost certainly be shown that the greater part of ergic learning, of the attachment of emotions to new objects, and the acquisition of new personal attitudes, proceeds by response dispersion and blind trial and error.

### 3. CONFLUENCE AND CONFLICT OF DRIVES

**Dynamic Problems Multiergic Not Uniergic.** So far we have considered the learning process in the field of a single drive, as if it were the only drive the organism possessed. Actually, as shown by path $\alpha_3$, it generally operates in the context of other drives. The nature of the organism is such that it demands a balance in the satisfaction of all its drives, and to that end the satisfaction of any single drive may be modified in ways we have not yet studied.

Obviously, in many cases a perfectly open path to the satisfaction of a drive is forsworn either because it prevents later, greater satisfaction of that same drive or because the behavior would get in the way of the satisfaction of another drive. A boy may abstain from eating his younger brother's ice-cream cone because he remembers that his parents deprived him of ice cream for a week the last time he did so. Or he may refrain from spending his pocket money on ice cream because he wants to go to the circus, to satisfy an eager curiosity about performing elephants. If a person is very clever he may find a way of behaving which will satisfy simultaneously several drives, by *confluence*, i.e., a habit subsidiating to goals initially conflicting, but there will always remain some drives whose satisfactions are in conflict.

As a glance at the dynamic lattice (Diagram 27, page 158) shows, most of the behavior habits to which a person eventually settles down show confluence. For example, working for money satisfies a whole lot of desires, which is perhaps why it is so common! Playing football, for one who plays well, may satisfy not only gregariousness and the physical need of exercise, but also self-assertion. A sentiment for keeping animal pets may simultaneously satisfy the need to dominate something and the parental, protective impulse. Such confluence has been shown more precisely by the statistical analysis of attitudes on page 174. Confluence commonly occurs also in neurotic symptoms, as we shall see later, *e.g.*, where both conscience and an antisocial impulse are satisfied in the same symptom. In this clinical context it is usually called "overdetermination." But in many cases satisfying one drive precludes, partially or totally, the satisfaction of another, and then we have emotional conflict. Thus, a child may love roast chestnuts and be deterred from eating them as fast as he would like because he also wants to avoid burning his fingers. Or he may be given to tyrannically dominating his playmates and discover that they then refuse to play with him. To satisfy gregariousness he therefore learns to restrict to some extent his self-assertive satisfactions.

**Confluence, Conflict, and Long-circuiting.** It should now be evident that the sentiment structures discussed in Chapter 6 express and determine modes of behavior which arise from ergs as (*a*) special paths to satisfaction discovered when innate responses no longer produce satisfaction, (*b*) in some cases as "confluence structures," *i.e.*, ways of behaving modified to lead simultaneously to greatest satisfaction of two or more drives, (*c*) in some cases—extreme cases of (*b*) in which conflict of drives is permanent—as compromise structures, *i.e.*, with incomplete confluence, involving some suppression of one drive. The first of these we may call long-circuiting, because the taking of a less-direct route to a goal has come to be the only way of reaching it. The second and third may also involve long-circuiting, but tend toward one or the other extremes of a further "resolution" or modification process, which extremes may be called, respectively, confluence and conflict.

**Adjustment as Resolution of Forces.** Confluence and conflict may be considered extremes of the process of "resolution of forces." As every student of introductory physics knows, one can take extensible springs, or weights on cords over pulleys, fixed at a number of different points, and attach them to a common object. An equilibrium position for the object will normally be reached in which the forces balance. In the case of springs a point will be reached which gives the maximum over-all reduction of tension, *i.e.*, the greatest total "satisfaction." How far the calculations from physical forces can be used as more than an analogy in psychodynamics remains to be seen. But in principle the situation is the same: the education

of personality brings into a polygon of forces sensuous or selfish ergic satisfactions, along with the desire to please the parents, the fear of punishment,
the desire to stand well in the group—and allows these to reach an equilibrium.

**Reward and Punishment.** It is possible, and in some schools popular,
to speak of dynamic modification as brought about by reward and punishment of trial-and-error responses. But, as Thorndike pointed out in his
further investigations of the law of effect, it is strictly true to say only that
*new habits appear through reward* and not that *old ones disappear through
punishment.*

How is this reconcilable with the common experience that punishment
discourages a trait? The difficulty is largely a verbal one. Strictly there
is no such thing as punishment: it is only the creation of a *new drive* by pain
or deprivation stimuli. Pain and loss provoke fear—the drive to escape.
The escape drive is rewarded by the lessening of pain. To cause pain by
"punishment" is to *bring into existence* an immediately dissatisfied, deprived
need. If one remembers that fear is simply another drive among drives,
then all learning is due to *reward* of drives, *i.e.*, to satisfaction as opposed to
continued deprivation or tension, and punishment is nothing more than
continued deprivation. Punishment is an unsatisfactory term because,
as popularly used, it sometimes means deprivation of an existing drive and
sometimes physical pain, without realization that the latter amounts to the
creation of a new, unsatisfied drive. There is no objection to punishment-
reward terminology providing it is consistently used to mean deprivation-
satisfaction.

**Machinery of Interaction and Modification.** Curiosity naturally prompts
us next to ask how one drive operates in conflict to suppress another, or how
a long-circuited response can suppress a more direct one. This raises
profound issues concerning the nature of the dynamic process, which cannot
yet be answered. Psychoanalysis shows at least, however, that drives
operate by way of their *cognitive* content. They are like streams which
block one another by means of the sediment they carry. That is to say, a
drive is denied a chance to express itself by the process of keeping from
consciousness the stimuli or memories that might provoke it. In everyday
life we can avoid an undesired drive by avoiding the situations which provoke
it, as Ulysses' shipmates stopped their ears when near the sirens. This
can be continued into avoidance of images and symbols in memory. An
increasing drive tension, on the other hand, lowers the threshold for recognition of such symbols, as when a hungry man constantly sees images of
food or readily notices cooking smells. When two drives are in conflict,
therefore, we shall assume that the process operates through suppression of
cognitive associations. Since mental energy is limited, the more powerful
drive causes any attention to the provoking images and symbols of the less

powerful to disappear.　But much work remains to be done on this crucial problem before we can claim to understand it more fully.

### 4. FRUSTRATION AND ITS SEQUELS

**The Second Dynamic Crossroads.**　The process of adjustment now needs to be followed through further "dynamic crossroads" before we can understand the structures that finally arise.　As we have seen, some of the $\alpha$ paths need be followed no further: they lead to satisfaction or to situations already clarified.　The path that leads to further adjustive problems is $\alpha 4$—the reaction to frustration.

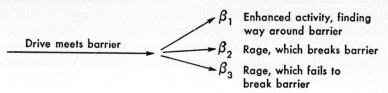

DIAGRAM 33.　The second dynamic crossroad and the $\beta$ (Greek letter beta) sequels: drive meets barrier.

Recent pedantry has tended to emphasize, without clarifying, the "frustration-aggression hypothesis"[1] included in our second dynamic crossroads. Without psychological institutes it has long been known that a man crossed tends to get angry.　The generalization that pugnacity is an innate drive or propensity, associated with the affect of rage and the behavioral goal of destroying the obstruction, was first clearly pointed out by McDougall, who recognized that the stimulus situation for this erg is *the thwarting of any other erg in process of gaining satisfaction.*

Let us suppose that a definite obstacle or barrier has been met at $\alpha 4$. What then can happen?　In the first place, if the hindrance is not too sudden and the obstacle not too definite, the organism simply heightens its efforts and becomes more varied in its trial-and-error responses—either at the physical level, which may lead to a successful blind response, or at the imaginal level, which may lead to insight.　This increase of variety of memory resources tried upon the situation is too well known to need illustration, and it suffices alone, very often, to produce an insightful or blind, subconscious solution in the form of a path around the obstacle.

If this, the first of the $\beta$ paths, fails, the second is normally an outbreak of rage, which by sheer violence may break the obstacle.　But if the situation is such that this also fails, then we have to consider a new set of paths or

---

[1] Aggression is an unfortunate term for, although precise enough in politics, it covers psychologically such distinct drives as self-assertion, pugnacity, sadism, and even "energy of temperament"!　The phrase frustration-aggression also suggests that aggression is the necessary sequel, whereas, as we shall see, there are some five different psychological sequels to being balked.　Indeed there are more if we take account of differential frustration of distinct dynamic structures within the personality (see pages 231 and 655).

sequels which have been called $\gamma$ paths because they really arise at a third crossroads, labeled response to an unbreakable barrier, as indicated in Diagram 34.

**The Third Crossroads—Irremediable Frustration.** The first reaction—$\gamma 1$—to insoluble frustration, *i.e.*, when the barrier is unavoidable and unbreakable as at $\beta 3$, is despair, with its specific emotional quality of more or less agitated depression, its arrest of gross activity, its weeping or other

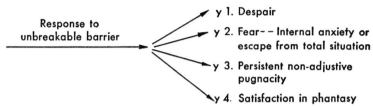

DIAGRAM 34. The third dynamic crossroad and the $\gamma$ (Greek letter gamma) sequels: irremediable frustration.

appeal behavior, and its innate goal of exciting sympathetic help. This can also appear secondarily in the second reaction—$\gamma 2$—when it does not remove the organism from the field. The second reaction is created by the fact that *many barriers, especially human or living ones—and even some inanimate ones!—themselves react violently when attacked.* Consequently in an instant the erg of pugnacity can be replaced by an erg of fear (escape) so that, at least in all frustration situations of which the organism has prior experience (the great majority), the immediate reaction to frustration *may* come to be fear. Because of the closeness of the two types of frustration situation which evoke them, the $\gamma 1$ and $\gamma 2$ reactions, namely fear and despair, may readily become fused, as we have found empirically in the factor pattern known as Desurgency (see Chap. 3) and in agitated (involutional) melancholia.

The third and last of the possible reality-accepting frustration sequels is $\gamma 3$—persistent, nonadjustive attack and hostility, oscillating in an almost appetitive cycle. As mentioned above, Hebb has pointed out very clearly that the anger pattern in chimpanzees, as in man, assumes two relatively clearly differentiated forms—violent rage and smoldering, sulking hostility. The latter, as far as analysis of the $\gamma 3$ situation permits us to judge, is the emotional accompaniment of the behavior there considered, specifically a kind of "persistent nonadjustive"[2] reaction, as indicated in $\gamma 3$. Escape into phantasy constitutes the lowest path of Diagram 34.

**Does Pugnacity Accompany All Long-circuiting?** Another of the unsolved —and frequently unposed—questions about the sequels of frustration is as follows: Does the aggression evoked by an unbreakable barrier, as in the last

[2] This useful phrase was first coined by Shaffer (16).

discussed reaction, persist (*a*) so long as the original drive remains at the same tension of frustration with regard to this path of action? (*b*) In some degree (due to disposition rigidity) after the desire which was frustrated has been satisfied in other ways, or at sublimated levels? Certainly many observations on personality suggest that satisfaction merely at highly sublimated levels leaves a permanent residue of pugnacity, which, however, may in turn express itself in sublimated fashions, to which the term aggression—as a modified pugnacity—could perhaps appropriately be given.

**The Development of Anxiety and Internal Conflict.** Normally the individual may be expected to repeat the reactions and sequences in the second and third crossroads if a solution is not found; and repetition may result in a break-through to satisfaction. But if it does not, and if the individual does not follow the second γ reaction of escaping from the whole situation, then he is compelled, as indicated in the first γ situation, to remain in the stimulating situation (in a state of despair) and to renounce the drive.

The fourth crossroads, which this sequel opens up, is therefore concerned *only with the possible ways of giving up the drive*, under the influence of the more powerful conflicting drives at length brought into action. Among the latter, of course, are not only conflicting individual ergs but also the organized drives of the ego and superego, organized for the preservation of the self and the group. The study of the situation thus created plunges us at once into the whole problem of defining that which enters into personality structure and which operates in neurosis formation. With this transition from the third to the fourth crossroads we also pass from the study of what are mainly *external* adjustments, *i.e.*, adjustments at once evident in external behavior, to *internal* adjustments, where the unseen interactions of dynamic traits have mainly to be inferred. This break is indicated in Diagram 41 representing the whole sequence of dynamic adjustment crossroads.

**Comparison of the Varieties of Inhibition.** Obviously, the principal new drive which is responsible for the renunciation or modification of the originally active drive is fear—fear aroused by the results of attacking the barrier. At this point it is necessary to glance back momentarily at the sequence of dynamic crossroads up to this level, to discuss, for theoretical clarity the difference between the ergic inhibition now about to occur and that occurring earlier. For this is not the *only* point in the dynamic history at which ergic modification is *enforced*. It *can* occur at the first crossroads, where the drive is suppressed, *i.e.*, superseded by a drive with more powerful stimulation, to give greater satisfaction to some other drive. In that case also the second drive can be "fear"—fear that some greater satisfaction may be lost if satisfaction of the first drive is attempted. But this is not the same as the primary fear of a retaliating barrier. A generic resemblance must be admitted, however, between modification by escape needs at this fourth crossroads, and modification by *any* alternative drive as at the first cross-roads. In both cases the first drive is given up under pressure of a greater one; but the specific nature of escape, differing from that of all other drives, justifies considering the situation at the fourth crossroads as something quite different from a mere circling back of the $\gamma$ paths to the situations at the first or $\alpha$ crossroads. The principal qualitative difference is that fear seems to evoke repression far more readily than does any other drive, and the principal dynamic-situational difference is that the reactions of the first, second, and third crossroads have already been tried. Incidentally, the solution through "supersession by another, more powerfully stimulated, drive," as at $\alpha 3$, could be tacked on to every one of the six dynamic crossroad diagrams, but is omitted from all but the first, for simplicity of representation.

Further, to this brief, broader review of the forms of inhibition encountered at various crossroads, one may point out that some modification of the extent or manner of goal satisfaction may occur, additional to the merely cognitive modifications, in many actual instances of circumventing the barrier by more dispersed or more intelligent responses, *i.e.*, by the $\beta 1$ path.

Here and throughout the text the term "inhibition" is used generically to cover both suppression and repression, but not the mere fading of a response through failure of drive. Thus at $\gamma_1$ or $\gamma_2$ we may say that a point is reached where inhibition, both of the original drive and of the supervening pugnacity occurs in face of the fear created by the retaliating barrier.[3]

Thus, for example, a rat can be taught to face a pellet of food without eating it, by means of a painful electric shock inflicted every time it tries to pass a barrier to pick up the food. In time the sound of a buzzer alone, which once occurred with the shock, is sufficient symbol to arouse the escape erg (the satisfaction of which means more to the organism than the satis-faction of hunger) so that this stimulus can be used to inhibit any new drive.

**Reinforcements of Inhibition in Man.** At this point in the succession of crossroads as indicated above, we enter the realm of internal, inferred con-flict, and have to begin to take account of personality structure.

In man, owing to the greater plasticity and power of integration, the metanergic structure has become much more complex, which means that among the drives opposing the "drive-to-be-suppressed" may be harnessed many other drives additional to fear, in fact all those ergs functionally knit in the ego and the superego. Suppression by a single stronger drive fre-quently occurs in man, either at the suppression point before frustration ($\alpha 3$) or at that occurring after ($\gamma 2$), but these prerepression conflicts do not constitute the major, persistent, adaptation and conflict situations which the psychologist and psychiatrist are most frequently called in to study.

[3] It may scarcely be necessary to point out that in many cases the barrier, although *apparently* quite passive, is in fact creating fear by something it has come to symbolize.

The step from crossroads 3 to crossroads 4 is especially important in that the whole problem of anxiety arises there. The relation of anxiety to fear must be clarified. Introspectively and by behavior pattern we can distinguish several varieties of fear, but the two most obvious are the *fright* or terror inspired by a sudden alarming situation and the pervasive *anxiety*, which is less intense but more prolonged and which arises sometimes from anticipation of a real danger or loss and sometimes, apparently, "for no reason at all," especially in neurotics.

**The Genesis of Anxiety.** It behooves us to clarify, in the framework of our dynamic analysis, what this "anxiety" really is. Early in the clinical study of anxiety hysteria (the neurosis in which the individual complains of a "nameless dread" or "free floating anxiety" which may attach itself to the most unlikely objects) it was found that the condition commonly associated itself with the arousal of sexual drive followed by suppression and repression. At first the explanation offered was that sexual libido had somehow become "transformed" into anxiety. Later it was realized that the anxiety arose from unconscious connections, anticipating that punishment which had previously met overt sexual expression. Moreover, the same anxiety was shown to arise also from repressed sadism or pugnacity and could no longer be considered, therefore, as specific to sex.

From this initial discovery we have progressed to the recognition of anxiety as a signal of *past punishment* of sex, pugnacity, or any drive whatever which has reached the impasse situation constituted by the first $\gamma$ path at the third crossroads. Quite frequently we shall find that the punishment of a drive is bound up also with punishment of the aggression which *may* follow the first obstruction or punishment of the drive. And in these cases the anxiety is generally more severe because, at least in authoritarian education, the punishment of pugnacity against the educator is on principle made more severe than that of the originally forbidden drive.

Psychiatrically it has now become customary to speak of anxiety as the "cause" of many clinically observed, dynamic readjustments or symptoms. For example, it is said to be the cause of repression and of other ego defenses (with which we shall soon deal) or of reactions against the superego, of symptoms, particularly obsessional and expiatory symptoms, of regression, and of psychosomatic changes. It would be more correct to say that the punishment, the symbol of the punishment, or *reactivated memories* of the punishing incident (reactivated by desire), are the cause; but to the experienced reader it is understood that the anxiety is a representative of these. One must remember, too, that anxiety may itself come to be a "conditioned" symbol of desire and so to some extent set up a vicious circle, in which anxiety stimulates (recalls) desire and desire anxiety.

To realize more fully the difference between anxiety and fear one must consider further aspects of the situations provoking anxiety. Those who recall the early reactions to psychoanalysis in the popular press will remember the surprise at Freud's purely empirical dictum that all neurosis and neurotic anxiety arise from sex. Fear, in the traumatic situations of war, it was asserted, in opposition to this view of Freud, could produce anxieties in its own right. It is true that war neuroses *could* be found, due to protracted fear of real dangers, but these cleared up at once when the soldier was given respite from strain. On the other hand, the examination of most really intractable war neuroses actually revealed a sex conflict in which the traumatic war situation was incidental. The important deduction from this and other aspects of neurosis is that fear, to produce its neurotic effects, *must rest upon an appetitive erg.* Escape itself is not appetitive: it drives only when a danger situation appears. An appetitive drive, like hunger, thirst, or sex, can be active, on the other hand, without external stimulation or with extremely little. It generates conscious or unconscious phantasies which reactivate memories of earlier punishment of the drive and thus create continuous anxiety, through an activation of the fear drive proportionate in strength and duration to the strength and duration of the appetite.

**Appetitive Drives and Anxiety.** That sex, rather than hunger, maternal feeling, thirst, fatigue, or any other appetitive, viscerogenic erg, is the prime cause of neurosis is merely an accident of our culture pattern, which assigns no disgrace to and demands no continuous suppression of other appetitive drives. Whether the *continuous* stimulation of a nonappetitive erg, *e.g.*, fear, curiosity, gregariousness, with repression of the resultant impulses, would produce neurosis, has never been experimentally verified, but the above-mentioned observations of the rarer kinds of neurosis in the recent war, in men continuously subjected to imminent danger under the urge of duty—neuroses which cleared up completely when the strain was removed—suggests that it is the nagging continuity of the appetitive-type conflict that alone differentiates it from the conflict typically arising from other drives.

**The Nature of Anxiety.** So much for the *genesis* of continual anxiety, essentially occurring through appetitive conflicts. But what of the intrinsic characteristics of anxiety? Anxiety employs the same bodily mechanisms as fear. It shows itself in tremor, jumpiness, sweating, coldness of extremities, abnormality of heartbeat and breathing, excessiveness of adrenal secretion with resulting congestion of the alimentary tract, etc. It differs in quality from fear, first because it is fear maintained at a lower intensity, and second because it arises from internal cues, often fragmentary, obscure, and secondarily reactivated by appetite, as shown above, instead of from the full-blooded, immediate, definite, external situation which provokes terror. Last, it differs because it has the quality of anticipation and uncertain imminence. That is to say, it is a long-circuited response, involving learning and memory, and occurring sometimes as a reaction to a symbol of a symbol of a reality. This uncertainty of meaning and imminence may be responsible for some of the peculiar characters differentiating anxiety from the primary fear response from which it is derived.

The role of anxiety, at the third adaptation crossroads, needs to be thoroughly understood if one is to master the prediction of general dynamic adjustment and especially of neurosis. It may be summarized by saying that anxiety is the first offspring of internal conflict and the father of all defense mechanisms and symptom formations.

### 5. THE FOURTH DYNAMIC CROSSROADS AND THE DELTA SEQUELS: SUPPRESSION, SUBLIMATION AND REPRESSION

**The Cultural Denial of Pugnacity and Escape.** Anxiety is not, however, the necessary or the only offspring of internal conflict. It does not occur at $\gamma 1$, $\gamma 3$, and $\gamma 4$, and it need not appear more than temporarily in the fourth crossroads. Individuals tolerate conflict and anxiety with very different degrees of success, depending upon the goodness of their existing personality integration (soundness of ego structure) and the manner in which they go about settling the conflict. Factors favoring anxiety development, such as "neurotic hesitation," etc., we shall look at more closely in the following chapter on the abnormal personality.

There is some uncertainty as to whether the alternatives at this crossroad ($\delta 1$, $\delta 2$, $\delta 3$, and $\delta 4$) are undertaken only at the instigation of anxiety or directly from the impact of the punishing "press" as at $\gamma 2$, or whether the despair and appeal behavior of $\gamma 1$ can also, if long continued, beget an internalized habit of denying the drive. At this stage of discussion the issue can be passed over: it is sufficient to regard the delta sequels as courses necessitated because a drive has to be denied its expression. Before proceeding, it will assist clear discussion if we illustrate the course of dynamic adjustments up to this crucial fourth crossroads by an epitome taken from an all-too-common childhood story.

A hungry child demands candy from a tired mother in a crowded bus. He is told to wait till he gets home, whereupon he has a temper tantrum and tries to tear the grocery bag to pieces. His mother smacks him in return. He attempts to escape into the crowded bus which makes his mother still more angry. On this he bursts into tears and howls and is smacked again for making a public disturbance. This distressing little sequence of need, frustration, anger, frustration of pugnacity, and appeal, as well as of the original need leading to the final necessity of obtaining control over the need, is the epitome of human experience in culture. In the child who is treated very considerately by intelligent parents the conflict is not always so overt or direct, but it has to be gone through in order to approach the same goal of impulse restriction or self-control.

Coercion to deny expression to a drive, which leads to the practice of renunciation as shown at γ2, may sometimes be followed by failure to maintain the once accepted inhibition, with regression to impulsive or criminal behavior (if the denial emanated from social restrictions). This is shown as the δ4 alternative and constitutes a return to the persistent nonadjustive behavior of the earlier crossroads at γ3, (see Diagram 34) though it will be of a slightly different quality from such behavior before the attempt at self-inhibition. On the other hand the accepted fiat of inhibition may stand firm and be followed by an act of *suppression*, *i.e.*, conscious recognition by the self that expression is undesirable, and a deliberate holding in check of the impulse by the will. This requires vigilance by the will and may create immediate, conscious phantasy as the temptation returns to con-

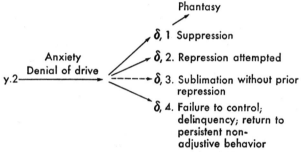

DIAGRAM 35. The fourth dynamic crossroad and the δ (Greek letter delta) sequels: anxiety and drive denial.

sciousness to be dealt with by the will. Phantasy can give a certain relief to tension which justifies calling it an "expression" of drive. In any case a certain kind and degree of phantasy is therefore accepted, as indicated by the Diagram 35, as a normal concomitant of suppression.

The third alternative, repression, cannot be understood without a preliminary acquaintance with those neurotic mechanisms otherwise relegated to discussion in the next chapter. Let us consider a case of neurosis, say that classical instance of *conversion hysteria* (Chap. 1), analyzed by Freud and perhaps familiar to the student from his general psychology course. A young woman suffered from paralyses not of physical origin, from speech disturbance, from somnambulism. Freud and Breuer, working by hypnosis and later by free association, brought the patient to recall and relive a very distressing incident which had been completely forgotten in her normal waking life, whereupon most of the symptoms vanished. The incident was connected with sexual phantasies in regard to her father. Freud put forward the theory that hysteria is due to an intensely emotional idea or memory which, because of its unpleasant character, becomes rejected by consciousness, split off, and buried in an "unconscious" region of the mind. Here it continues activity, producing disconcerting symptoms in consciousness.

**The Notions of Complex, Repression, Unconscious.** As every student of general psychology knows, this was the origin of the notions of a "complex," of the "unconscious mind," and of "repression." Clinical psychology quickly brought thousands of case histories supporting these hypotheses and extended the generalizations to all kinds of neurotic manifestations. For the sake of completeness we shall restate briefly the hypotheses that constitute the generally accepted foundation of the dynamics of the unconscious.

1. A neurosis arises when strongly emotional ideas and memories (*i.e.*, a powerful ergic drive with its accompanying associations) which conflict with the system of ideas constituting one's self-respect, become split off from consciousness and are forgotten. Such repressed memories are called *complexes*. They are not to be understood as invariably pathological in their effects, though the predominance of clinical investigation might give this impression.

2. The process of forgetting, although not consciously initiated, is nonetheless deliberate. It is the last resort of the mind in attempting to end an intolerable, chronic mental conflict. To this live burial Freud gave the name "repression."

3. Consequently, apart from the thoughts and desires of which we are conscious, *i.e.*, of which we can become conscious, there must exist for each of us a buried, unconscious mind, the existence and nature of which can only be demonstrated indirectly, by noting obscure and irrational forms of thought and behavior.

The act of repression is still insufficiently understood. It proceeds by breaking association bonds so that recollections with a certain feeling tone, which would normally subsidiate to other ideas or memories in the same drive, fail to do so. Associations also become broken in the realm of logic (as in rationalization: see next section), so that logical connections which should be made are avoided. Indeed repression and rationalization involve the same processes to an extent not yet sufficiently explored. Repression is not an irreversible process, for by hypnosis, by drugs which "knock out" the censor, by analysis of dreams, and by bringing other powerful dynamic trends to bear in a steady process of digging into the unconscious, as in the method of free association, the complexes resulting from repression can be released again.

It is now a commonplace that the unconscious is a realm not only of rejected ideas and drives but also of ergic "part instincts" which have never, from the beginning, been able to find expression in civilized life. The evidence for the unconscious is no longer taken solely from the symptom formations of neurotics but also from dreams, from errors such as slips of pen, tongue, and memory among normal people, from wit, and many other sources of observation of behavior.

**Sublimation.** The fourth possible alternative at the delta crossroads, namely δ3, is *sublimation*, a process which again owes its discovery and definition to clinical, psychoanalytic observations. In sublimation, sometimes called aim inhibition, the drive is given an expression in which the original aim of the drive is no longer retained. As illustrated in Chapter 6, there is a substitute satisfaction not merely in the *means* to the goal but *in the goal itself*. However, the new goal has some stylistic or qualitative resemblance to the original, innate goal which makes it acceptable.

The evidence is as follows: It has been observed that some of a person's repressed or suppressed drives seem to diminish in intensity at the same time that new interests grow up, almost unnoticed, in some field vaguely related to the goal of the drive. Thus a repressed sex drive may reappear as an ardent interest in art, or music, or religion. Such an interest, as pointed out earlier, is called an "aim-inhibited" drive, because the original biological goal has been forsworn. Aim-inhibited drives also include perversions. The influences that determine whether adjustment by aim inhibition shall be successful are not yet fully understood, nor is the kind of resemblance clearly demonstrated between original and sublimated activity that is necessary for easy transition.

Some drives are not as amenable to sublimation as others. For example, it is almost impossible to sublimate hunger and thirst (though some saints and martyrs have achieved it), perhaps because the organism would die almost at once if they were successfully sublimated. Mating and parental drives are slightly less rigid as to goal. At first this is surprising, for natural selection would eliminate plastic susceptibility to unbiological sex satisfactions as quickly as abnormalities of hunger or thirst, namely, in one generation. But the elimination is not as immediate in time—an individual might be sexually abnormal for a phase of his life without ultimately reducing his effective fertility, especially with the greater reduced fertility of human societies, while certain countervailing advantages for survival of individual or group are gained in other ways by capacity for sublimation. Drives such as self-assertion, curiosity, gregariousness probably represent a still greater degree of goal plasticity. Possibly extreme experimental conditions would induce slight sublimation even of hunger and thirst: shipwrecked sailors have been known to eat the leather off their oars or drink seawater, neither of which is a natural goal or biologically effective.

**Differentiation of Sublimation and Perversion.** Plasticity of goal makes possible both sublimation and perversion. The difference between these is in the first place cultural. Unwin has shown (19) that the richness of religious life in a great range of cultures, from the most backward tribes of the New Hebrides to the highest groups in cultural achievement, is inversely related to the freedom of sexual expression permitted in the social mores and customs. This offers strong statistical proof for the psychoanalytic speculation that much religious activity is a sexual sublimation. In particular clinical cases it has also been brought out that art, mathematics, zeal in social reform, and many other cultural activities arise from aim-inhibited (goal-deflected) sex. It is noteworthy, however, that these activities seem to pass over very readily into perversions, as, for example, in some primitive religious rites which have degenerated. It is also noteworthy that homosexuality is more common among highly cultured peoples, and individuals who have been brought up with rigid sexual inhibitions, than in people nearer to nature. (Note, for example, Kinsey's finding on the social class distribution in America.) Whether a goal change shall be called sublimation or perversion depends on whether the culture considers that change to be for or against the good of society. It happens, however, that perversions are also more frequently regressive than are sublimations, *i.e.*, the former are reactivations of earlier instinct fixations. This will not be clear until after the next chapter, but we must note here that the distinction is not *entirely* based on social purpose rather than on the biological quality of individual dynamics.

A query about the main adaptation processes which we must face here concerns whether sublimation (and perversion) can occur at all without prior repression. Can it occur, for example, by an act of modification of aim by the will, associated with partial suppression? Typical sublimation occurs *after* repression, *i.e.*, at the fifth crossroads, rather than the fourth, and by means not yet fully understood. It is likely, however, that some degree of sublimation can occur at the fourth, or delta crossroads, before repression is completed. Because of this uncertainty, we have indicated the sublimation path, $\delta 3$ on Diagram 35, only by a dotted line, indicating that more precise research is needed.

### 6. THE STRUCTURES INVOLVED IN INTERNAL CONFLICT AND EXTERNAL ADJUSTMENT

**What Are the Contesting Dynamic Traits?** The study of internal conflict and anxiety has shown us that one dynamic trait can suppress, or repress, or force sublimation upon another, after circumstances have finally denied the organism expression of the second trait. But in studying the general process we have not stopped to take note of the particular nature of the contestant dynamic traits. They can be any dynamic traits—ergs, sentiments or attitudes, and in Freud's early writings he dealt principally with, for example, the conflicts of and between the ego instincts and the sex instinct; but we shall now see that, at least on one side of the conflict, it is *not ergs but developed sentiment structures that are principally involved*.

Indeed, before we can study the adjustment process further, in the next chapter, it is necessary to take stock here of the nature and number of dynamic traits developed by the adjustment process so far considered. For the finer adjustments and conflicts are peculiar to particular dynamic traits. Moreover we have to take more account of the new type of dynamic trait— the "complex"—encountered in the last section and not studied in our initial chapter on the intrinsic structure of dynamic traits.

**The Ego Structure.** Reflection on everyday-life conflicts, and the various examples discussed above, shows that generally the control of undesirable drives comes from fear, or pride (self-assertion); but also from parental protective drive, and many others. However, it is obvious also that these checking forces are generally integrated in a sentiment, such as a man's sentiment for his home, his self-regard, his country etc. In the next chapter we shall study the integration of these sentiments in more detail. Here it will suffice to get the first rough picture of their grouping as found from clinical study and particularly from psychoanalysis. Psychoanalysis has found, by the pragmatic success of psychotherapy, that the participants in dynamic conflict can be treated as if they fell into only three essential structures. The uncurbed, unmodified ergic forces which are the original sources of all reactivity are classed together as the *id*. The id also contains the rejected drive fragments called complexes, defined in the last section. A considerable part of the *unconscious*, defined in the last section, consists of these chaotic drives, continually demanding satisfaction, governed by the *pleasure principle*—"I want"—unaware of the difficulties which the knowing, thinking part of the individual faces in the external world in attempting to gain satisfaction for these drives.[4]

The developing front of the mind as it gains experience, and which exercises all essential control, we popularly call the "will." It consists of the drives that are tempered by experience, by perception of external difficulties, and memories of punishment. It is called in psychoanalysis the *ego*. It is that part of the organism's strivings which are conscious, organized, and far-sighted. The ego is in contact with reality, and it tries to obtain as much satisfaction for the needs of the id as is possible without risk of destruction.

The study of neuroses, however, has shown that mental conflicts are by no means confined to those between the ego and the id. For example, some individuals, notably melancholiacs, experience painful guilt feelings though they are consciously unaware of any transgression or of any act or phantasy

---

[4] There are a number of interesting and important further differences between the principles governing the dynamic arrangements of the id and the ego. The id readily tolerates quite inconsistent drives, *e.g.*, hate and love, destruction and preservation of the same object. The ego relates and reconciles drives to some compromise behavior. The id has no sense of time—satisfaction is here and now. The ego is bound by the realities of logic, which it discovers in its hard contacts with the outer world, but the id knows only the pleasure principle, namely, that desire must be immediately satisfied.

from the id which the ego has had to suppress.   Further, it is evident from
our conscious experience that some very painful conflicts can occur, not
between the ego and our *worst* impulses but between a "reasonable," realistic
ego and our *best* impulses, *i.e.*, our consciences.

**The Superego.**   Clinical psychology therefore introduced the notion of
the *superego*, which is essentially what has always been called conscience,
but which is free of some traditional entanglements of the word "conscience"
and contains a number of scientific and detailed implications.   The superego
is partly unconscious, because the earliest prohibitions, *e.g.*, on nakedness,
careless excretion, autoerotic behavior, are imposed by our parents at an
age within the period of infantile amnesia, *i.e.*, the first two or three years of

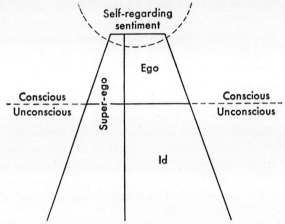

DIAGRAM 36.   The dynamic structures in personality as deduced from observations on
conflict.

life.   Most memories from this period are shut off by repression because
they contain a preponderance of infantile sexuality, in all its "polymorphous
perverse"[5] forms.   The ego may thus offend the superego without having
expected to do so.   That is to say, a person may feel ashamed of something
though consciously he believes it to be entirely justifiable and moral.   For
example, an "emancipated" woman may agree with herself that it is a good
thing to join a nudist colony, only to find that when she is uncovered she is
still covered with confusion.   Furthermore, the unconscious part of the
superego may sense directly the seething amoral phantasies of the unconscious id, causing the emergence of a guilt sense for which the ego, with
access only to the conscious superego, can find no cause, as in the pathological
cases above.

[5] "Polymorphous perverse" is discussed in the section on Ergic Regression (page 250).
It refers to the fact that the earlier, immature expressions of the sex drive manifest most of
the behavior forms which are later regarded in adults as biological and social perversions.

**The Interplay of Id, Ego, and Superego.**  The notion of dynamic structure to which this leads is that shown in Diagram 36.  The conscious ego has to deal with the "I want" of the id, by suppression, careful, modified expression, or frantic repression.  At the same time it has to accommodate to the immutable "The situation *is* thus and so," presented by the intractable external-world conditions.  Meanwhile it is caught on the flank by the rigid, aggressive "Thou shalt not" of the superego.  As we shall see in the chapter on psychopathology, it is this worse than "between-the-devil-and-the-deep-sea" situation which accounts for the ego sometimes giving up and relapsing into neurosis or psychosis.

It is perhaps hardly necessary to remind the student who passed through elementary psychology that the three divisions of Diagram 36 do not mean divisions of the brain.  One can indeed perceive *some* corresponding localization—the hypothalamus being the seat of the untutored drives and the cortex the seat of ego and superego modifications—but this is an accidental similarity; the id, ego, and superego are dynamic organizations or traits, and Diagram 36 is essentially a diagram of forces.

As to the relation of what has been described by a series of psychologists as the *self-sentiment* to these clinically observed divisions, research still has little to say.  Obviously, in a general sense, what Freud called the ego McDougall called the self-sentiment, but in later study we shall see reason to consider the self-sentiment concept as an integration of ego and conscious superego.

### 7. SUMMARY

1. New structures—dynamic traits derived from innate ergic patterns— are formed in the adjustment process in proportion to the organism's plasticity.  Plasticity is proportional in part to intelligence and in part to low disposition rigidity, power of remembering, and possibly other factors.

2. Granted plasticity, the new dynamic traits are formed by environmental experience under the influence of unsatisfied needs.  Learning occurs, in emotional as in cognitive matters, through the operation of laws of learning, operating, however, in a wider dynamic context than has previously been envisaged for these laws.

The laws of learning fall under two paradigms: (*a*) response to new stimuli, covered by the conditioned reflex, and (*b*) new responses to existing situations, covered by the dynamic law of effect.

3. Though no adequate reconciliation of these in a single principle has yet been generally accepted, it is possible to consider the conditioning of reflexes as occurring through dynamic reward in the field of a drive.  But the law of effect in return requires the inclusion of reflex conditioning to explain the learning of new responses.  These reflexes occur in ergic dispersion (or response dispersion, the tendency toward "persistence with

varied effort") under increasing deprivation and become conditioned to new environmental objects. Such responses may be either insightful or blind trial and error. Those which lead toward the goal become stabilized responses.

4. The sentiments and attitudes thus formed manifest the operation of both confluence and conflict. In confluence a single mode of behavior is discovered, which leads to satisfaction, in some degree, of two or more different drives. In conflict, behavior favoring the satisfaction of one drive frustrates that of another. In the latter situation either alternating expression may follow or one drive may more permanently suppress or repress the other, doing so by control of cognitive stimuli (attention, memory) or by enforcing motor action incompatible with the weaker drive.

5. The process of adjustment, *i.e.*, of obtaining stable, effective habits of satisfaction through confluence and the resolution of conflicts, can be most comprehensively treated by the schema of a series of *dynamic crossroads*. The first or $\alpha$ crossroads shows four possible sequels to the stimulation of a drive. The second or $\beta$ crossroads reveals three possible sequels to meeting a barrier to satisfaction. The third, $\gamma$ crossroads, shows the four possible sequels when the barrier proves unbreakable.

6. "Pugnacity" better defines the behavior at frustration than does the ambiguous term "aggression." Anger and pugnacity are not the invariable consequence of frustration. A specific type of frustration generates pugnacity; but the conditions of its persistence, etc., are not yet worked out.

7. The fourth or $\delta$ crossroads occurs where it becomes necessary to renounce the satisfaction of a drive, *i.e.*, in the presence of continued stimulation, other than by temporary "supersession" through distracting stimulation of another drive (as in $\alpha 3$) and leads to four possibilities: $\delta 1$, suppression; $\delta 2$, repression, $\delta 3$, sublimation; and $\delta 4$, failure of control. The rise of these alternatives is closely bound up with the maintenance of anxiety, generated from the fear situation to which the $\gamma$ crossroads has led.

8. Repression proceeds by breaking association bonds in cognitive material, and is generically related to rationalization, in which logical associations are broken in favor of pseudological ones. It leads to the creation of complexes and the unconscious.

9. Sublimation, the mechanism of which is not fully understood, may occur at the fourth or fifth dynamic crossroads under slightly different conditions. It is distinguished from perversion according to the ethical evaluation of the culture, as well as by the intrinsic psychological characteristics of ergic regression.

10. Most conflicts in man are not merely between drive and drive but involve one or more sentiments. A first approach to defining these sentiment structures has been made by psychoanalysis, with its definition of the *ego* and *superego* as opposed to the unmodified drives of the *id*. In this con-

nection the notion of the complex—a detached, unintegrated, and unconscious structure (contrasted to the integrated and largely conscious sentiment or attitude) is defined.

## QUESTIONS

1. Discuss the statement that the final dynamic structures resulting from learning have a pattern deducible from the factor patterns of ergic and metanergic traits.

2. Examine the distinction between reward and punishment in the light of the law of effect, and define the law of effect in such a way as to bring both into relation with the single concept of "facilitating approach to a goal."

3. Draw the diagram (from memory) of the first dynamic crossroads and describe each of the possible sequels.

4. Give three instances, from human behavior, of conflict being followed by confluence, resulting in stable sentiments.

5. Describe the second dynamic crossroads and discuss whether pugnacity or aggression is a better description of the reaction to a perceived barrier. Does pugnacity accompany all long-circuiting?

6. Draw the diagram for the third dynamic crossroads and discuss the causes for the difference between anxiety and fear.

7. Describe the mechanisms appearing at the renunciation of a drive—suppression, repression, and sublimation. Offer some hypothesis as to their mode of operation, and distinguish between sublimation and perversion.

8. Describe the psychoanalytic account of complexes and give other available evidence for the existence of the unconscious mind. Point out some of the confusing differences of meaning with which the term "unconscious" is employed in psychology.

9. Describe the ego, superego, and id, and the typical varieties of conflict that occur among them.

10. Discuss the analogy between the resolution of forces in physics and the attempt of the individual to obtain maximum satisfaction simultaneously for a number of drives. Give instances showing the limitation of solutions imposed by the individual's level of (*a*) intelligence, (*b*) capacity for tolerating long-circuited behavior.

## BIBLIOGRAPHY

1. CATTELL, R. B.: *General Psychology* (2d ed.), Chapter VIII, Sci-Art Publishers, Cambridge, 1947.

2. DOLLARD, J., and others: *Frustration and Aggression*, Yale University Press, New Haven, 1939.

3. FLUGEL, J. C.: *Men and Their Motives*, International Universities Press, Inc., New York, 1947.

4. FREUD, S.: *The Ego and the Id*, Hogarth Press, London, 1927.

5. FREUD, S.: *A General Introduction to Psychoanalysis*, Garden City Publishing Company, Inc., Garden City, New York, 1943.

6. FREUD, S.: *New Introductory Lectures on Psychoanalysis*, W. W. Norton & Company, New York, 1933.

7. HAMILTON, G. V.: *An Introduction to Objective Psychopathology*, The C. V. Mosby Company, Medical Publishers, St. Louis, 1925.

7*a*. HILGARD, E. R.: *Theories of Learning*, Appleton-Century-Crofts, Inc., New York, 1948.

8. HULL, C. L.: *Principles of Behavior*, Appleton-Century-Crofts, Inc., New York, 1943.

9. MAIER, N. R. F., and SCHNEIRLA, T. C.: Mechanisms in Conditioning. *Psychol. Rev.*, 49: 117–134, 1942.

10. MASSERMAN, J.: *Behavior and Neurosis*, University of Chicago Press, Chicago, 1943.

11. McDOUGALL, W.: *The Energies of Men*, Methuen & Co., Ltd., London, 1932.

12. MILLER, N. E.: An Experimental Investigation of Derived Drives, *Psychol. Bull.*, 38: 534–535, 1941.

13. MILLER, N. E., and J. DOLLARD: *Social Learning and Imitation*, Yale University Press, New Haven, 1941.

14. MOWRER, O. H.: A Stimulus-Response Analysis of Anxiety and Its Role as a Reinforcing Agent, *Psychol. Rev.*, 46: 553–565, 1939.

15. MOWRER, O. H.: Anxiety-reduction and Learning, *J. exp. Psychol.*, 27: 497–516, 1940.

15a. POSTMAN, L., and J. P. EGAN: *Experimental Psychology*, Harper & Brothers, New York, 1949.

16. SHAFFER, L. F.: *The Psychology of Adjustment*, Houghton Mifflin Company, Boston, 1936.

17. SKINNER, B. F.: *The Behaviour of Organisms*, Appleton-Century-Crofts, Inc., New York, 1938.

18. THORNDIKE, E. L.: *Human Learning*, Appleton-Century-Crofts, Inc., New York, 1931.

19. UNWIN, J. D.: *Sex and Culture*, Oxford University Press, New York, 1934.

20. ZENER, K.: The Significance of Behaviour Accompanying Conditioned Salivary Secretion for Theories of the Conditioned Responses, *Amer. J. Psychol.*, 50: 384–403, 1937.

# CHAPTER 9

## PSYCHODYNAMICS: IV. THE SELF—
## ITS INTEGRATION, ADAPTION, AND ADJUSTMENT

1. Normal and Abnormal Growth of the Superego
2. The Sentiments and the Structure of the Self
3. Maladjustment and the Ego Defenses
4. The Formation of Neurotic Symptoms
5. Some Modifications of Clinical Theory
6. Adaptation, Integration, and Adjustment of the Personality within Society
7. Summary

### 1. NORMAL AND ABNORMAL GROWTH OF THE SUPEREGO

**Objectives and Methods.** So far we have reviewed the main outlines of the natural history of human mental conflict and adjustment, and have defined the principal metanergic structures which ensue. The present chapter pursues these issues to more precise, refined concepts. This involves branching in several directions and prevents the centralization of the chapter on a single theme. Principally we need to follow up the general notions of adjustment, integration, etc.; the nature of ego and superego; the developmental stages by which these structures arise; the nature of the fifth and later dynamic crossroads, which are concerned with ultimate neurotic developments in the adjustment process; and to take an initial glance at the relations of conflict to society.

The important principles which have to be stated within the bounds of this chapter are based on an array of evidence from everyday life which cannot be briefly tabulated as can experimental data. Not only the supporting data, but also the sufficient multiplication of illustrations must therefore be left to the student's class discussion or individual thought, as well as to the ensuing chapters on particular aspects of personality, in which these general principles will henceforth be applied.

The attack on these problems can best begin with a closer examination of the nature of the ego and the superego structures.

**Clinical Account of Superego Development.** The psychoanalytic account of the origin of the superego is approximately as follows: The first "object-love" of the young child is his mother. His primary affection for her, however, has sensuous, sexual qualities, of the forbidden nature of which he soon becomes aware, perhaps at about three or four years, as he grows into general awareness of social taboos, particularly as they are represented by his father. Thereafter his affection becomes a normal boyish fondness, need, and dependence, shorn of the sexual elements, which are in turn repressed into the unconscious, becoming the Oedipus complex, to which we have already referred (Chap. 8).

In the patriarchal family the child gives up his primitive ergic demands under fear of the social taboos represented by the father,[1] but also, in the modern family, almost as much by the mother.  This fear, however, is partly motivated by love of the parents, *i.e.*, it is not, except perhaps in the first stages, a fear of parental punishment, but a fear of loss of the security guaranteed by parental affection.  As we have pointed out in connection with the characteristics of the unconscious, the id is "ambivalent," that is to say, hate and love for the same object can simultaneously arise from it and remain strong and unneutralized.  Some jealousy and hatred of the father is therefore not incompatible with profound admiration and fondness for him, and the same applies to the mother in her "forbidding," distant, and regal role.  Now it is considered a characteristic of libido, *i.e.*, of affection, that when an object is greatly loved the individual wants to possess it and make it part of himself.[2]  This is called identification in the initial process and finally, introjection.  Consequently the child at this stage "introjects" the parent into his own make-up.  He behaves as if he had said, "I want to be powerful and happy and admirable like father and mother, so I will punish myself if I behave in these stupid, childish ways."  He has become aware of himself as a source of unpleasant, monstrous, and uncontrolled impulses, and takes comfort in the possibility of having someone inside himself like his strong parents, who will protect him from these upsetting desires and their dangerous consequences.

**Reinforcements of the Superego Forces in Conscience.**  The psychoanalytic account of the origin of the superego thus began with the Oedipus complex and the introjection of the parents' images.  These introjected superego foundations have thus aptly been called the gravestone of the Oedipus complex.  But the superego as finally fashioned draws additional support from several distinct sources.

In the first place, the further clinical experience of the last twenty years has revealed that some superego formations occur earlier than the Oedipus

---

[1] To the abnormal fear and aggression against the father which sometimes arises when the child has difficulty in giving up the Oedipus relationship, the term "castration complex" has been given, from evidence of castration and castration substitutes having been applied at adolescence to potential breakers of the incest taboo among primitive people.

[2] This is tied up to some extent with the oral experience of swallowing what is good. The overfond individual sometimes says "I could eat you."

complex, in fact so early that some have argued for a degree of innateness of superego structure. The Oedipus attachment is formed in the second year and retreats into the form of a complex only toward the end of the nursery-school period. Those initial distress reactions toward wrongdoing that can be perceived vaguely in the first and second years of life must be due to a mere "conditioning" to fear, ostracism, and punishment, without introjection. But this can scarcely become a major component since, as any child-guidance clinician knows, punishment that emanates from other than a beloved person usually leads to escape from the whole field, rejection, and anger rather than remorse. One of the further puzzling features about the moral superego, in the early studies by clinicians, was its frequently savage and ruthless character, as we can see in cases where men "drive themselves to death" with perfectionist ideals, or flagellate and crucify themselves as in many religious sects, or torment themselves into insane depression, as do melancholics. Curiously enough, such cases seem to occur with greater frequency where the parents have been loving, protective, and considerate than where they have carelessly neglected or actively rejected the child during its early years.

MOTHER-CHILD RELATION*

| Attitude | Good, affectionate | | | Bad, rejecting | | |
|---|---|---|---|---|---|---|
| Intensity | Intense | Moderate | Weak | Intense | Moderate | Weak |
| Severe depressions............ | 6 | 11 | | | | |
| Mild depression.............. | 4 | .. | 3 | 7 | .. | 4 |
| No depression............... | .. | .. | 2 | 11 | 2 | 14 |

* Data from a study of 123 unselected nursery-school children by Spitz (17) showing incidence of definite depressive behavior, with loss of weight and increased susceptibility to colds, on temporary separation from mother, related to parent-child attitude.

The explanation appears to be that the superego is powered not only by (*a*) the love for the introjected parents, (*b*) early fear of punishment, as discussed above, (*c*) the primary narcistic libido, *i.e.*, love of self expressed as love of an ideal self (which we have discussed under the self-sentiment), but also by (*d*) aggression. The aggression against the parents who have frustrated him is here turned against himself (once the original frustration becomes accepted, through affection). Indeed self-assertive satisfactions may also be added to this pugnacious component of aggression, constituting a continuously active sadistic-masochistic[3] drive getting pleasure from dominating and dragooning oneself.

[3] Masochism is a sexual pleasure in being hurt, complementary to sadism as a sexual pleasure in hurting. It may be the origin of the self-submissive erg, as sadism is considered

**Superego Relation to Shame, Guilt, and Anxiety.** Augmented by additional drives, as described above, the superego normally becomes a powerful structure. Since this powerful structure has, as it were, a vested interest in punishment it is not surprising that we see, in the normal individual, behavior that seems to indicate a "need for punishment." Most parents have at some time seen a young child, who has just done something he knows is wrong, say to himself, "Naughty Johnny," or slap his own hand in a way he has seen done before. It is an almost universal reaction to experience relief by confession, even though confession brings punishment.

The quality of guilt feeling is that of a complex "derived emotion" because the drives involved in the conscience or superego are numerous. Thus we have indicated that primarily the superego begins with love of the parent, *i.e.*, a libidinal satisfaction. Later, with the substitution of the "gang" or group authority for the parental authority, the gregarious need (which may be a maturation out of libido, Diagram 30) becomes involved. The individual who does not do "what is done" is shunned by the rest of the group and experiences that dissatisfaction of gregarious drive that we call loneliness. On the whole, however, the basic moral values are imparted by the parents, while the values imparted later by the group shade off into merely conventional values; so that the breaking of conventional values brings an internal reaction of loneliness different from the sense of guilt, fear, and total loss which may accompany a consciousness of sin in a conscientious individual. The feeling quality of shame indicates a shift of emphasis to yet another drive—that of self-submission—and is connected more with that aspect of the superego which we shall call the self-regarding sentiment, described below.

The initial awareness of any one of these threats of punishment is probably experienced as anxiety. It will be obvious that the arousal of anxiety at the juncture of the third and fourth dynamic crossroads, which we have studied in some detail above, is normally the work of the superego; for the superego is the repository of the experiences of past punishment.

There are complications concerning the arousal of anxiety, however, notably through punishment occurring for unconscious evil *intentions* of the id as well as from conscious *transgressions* of the ego, as discussed above, and from anxiety arising through other than superego conflicts. These complications are best investigated in connection with ego-defense dynamisms, below.

**Abnormal Developments of the Superego.** Much about the structure of the superego can be better understood after studying those circumstances in

the origin of self-assertion (see Diagram 30). Self-punishment in the superego vs. ego relationship can thus provide satisfaction to two drives: assertion (sadism) operating through the superego, and self-submission (masochism) through the ego.

which its development goes astray—generally in the direction of excessive or defective magnitude of growth.

Excessive development in the psychotic, and inconsistent, vacillating action in the neurotic, have already been commented upon, when pointing out that the melancholic and the anxiety hysteric are suffering from undue or misdirected action of the superego. Excessive action may occur through greater than normal involvement of any one of the drives normally involved in the structure. For example, the parent attachment may have been unusually strong and the child may then take the moral values for which the parents stand even more seriously (and in more exacting ways) than did the parents themselves (partly also through his failure to perceive the real moral weaknesses of the parents). Or, as Freud has pointed out, the narcistic libido may be abnormally strengthened by the libido suddenly liberated when a loved person dies or proves unworthy. The melancholy of Tennyson's *In Memoriam* and its lofty demands upon the self illustrate how grief from such a loss may in this curious way "ennoble" the one who grieves. Again, some special failure or futility in directing aggression outward may end in its reinforcing the component of inward-turned aggression in the superego. This produces that excessively exacting, ruthless "conscience" which aims at perfection and may lead to suicide as a final act of aggression against the inadequate self.

Insufficient superego development, on the other hand, occurs in many inveterate criminals, moral imbeciles, and psychopaths. This defective moral sense appears so early and is so resistant to all attempts to influence it (as witness the disappointment both of benevolent prison visitors and of prison psychiatrists with a certain minority of cases) that psychiatrists have argued that it is innate. Undoubtedly, inability to integrate character is partly an innate disposition rigidity or incapacity to bring about or tolerate long-circuited, metanergic satisfaction, but the above observation is more likely to be explicable on the ground that the irremediable damage or deficiency occurs so early in life that it cannot readily be distinguished from something inborn. The superego, we have said, is the gravestone of the Oedipus complex. If there is no Oedipus to bury, there can be no gravestone. In other words, unless the first object attachment of affection was well formed, it is impossible later to arouse any reactions of remorse, contrition, or guilt. In the writer's own clinical experience it has been very striking that the individuals who have been referred as "morally incorrigible" have been precisely those who, in the first two years of life at least, were unwanted and rejected by mothers or stepmothers. Recently Jenkins (see (30), Chap. 16) has shown that the pattern of unsocialized aggressive delinquency (see Chap. 16) correlates more highly ($0.47 \pm 0.07$) with parental rejection than with any other situation in the individual's background.

Even when the early Oedipus relation has been sound, however, certain types of inadequacy in the superego may still arise. The first arises from a too-tyrannical or severe authority. Just as the individual who feels himself "underpunished" may punish himself, so the overpunished may absolve himself and strike back against authority without any hindering sense of guilt. But this is not usually a permanent cause of delinquency. More systematic weakness exists where the parent, having established a good emotional relationship, neglects, out of laziness, ignorance or, distraction, to use it to impart good moral standards. Several researches now clearly indicate that a large fraction of delinquency is due to nothing more psychologically complicated than this failure of parents to inculcate appropriate guilt sense and good civilized standards! The delinquency of the spoiled, insufficiently disciplined child, however, is easily distinguished from that of the first kind of superego-deficient individual, by the fact that in the former *some* strong moral inhibitions exist, but are very restricted in area. In his classical study of delinquency Burt found three home upbringing conditions (other than parental rejection itself) associated more with the delinquent than the control group: insufficient discipline (spoiling), harsh, oversevere discipline, and inconsistent discipline. The last, whether it be due to inconsistent parents, or to too many changes of authority among different parent substitutes, seems to have some relation to neurosis as well as to delinquency.

## 2. THE SENTIMENTS AND THE STRUCTURE OF THE SELF

**The Riddle of the Self.** The self is something very obvious to the man in the street but very illusive to psychologists. Introspectionists have tried to turn around so quickly as to introspect on what the introspecting self is; but all they return with is conflicting observations that the self is a conscious awareness of doing, or a set of muscle tensions and visceral sensations, or an act of willing. Three senses of self are defined in the detailed analyses of Chapter 21; the present discussion is largely about the last of these—the "structural self." Unfortunately, dynamic psychology, which deals with behavior, has not succeeded much better in its attempts to define, operationally and scientifically, what the self-structure is in terms of behavior.

The psychoanalytic concept of the ego is lacking in precision and has not been brought into relation with experimental psychology and the study of learning. Let us now, therefore, seek a definition of a more exact nature, to enable operational tests to be applied. First it is clear that the self or ego is not that which is responsible for (*i.e.*, the source of) all actions of the organism. If a man sneezes in your face and says "Pardon me" he is politely assuming responsibility for something not willed (not emanating from "me"), and if a man charged in court with manslaughter pleads that he was "beside himself" with terror at the time, he may be exonerated on the grounds that the action sprang from the organism and not the ego. Reflexes and drives operating in unintegrated isolation are not the ego.

On the other hand, anything that is deliberately willed comes from the ego: indeed in the history of psychology the psychology of the will and the psychology of the ego are themes which constantly interweave, suggesting that they are aspects of the same thing. The essential features of the psycho-analytic ego are that (*a*) it is a structure formed from several drives, attempting by confluence to achieve the greatest satisfaction of the greatest number; (*b*) it is guided in this action by intelligent perception of the situation and by access to memories of past experiences of punishment and reward, by which the integration of the drives is maintained. These memories give stability to behavior in spite of big fluctuations in the appetitive state of the organism. When a man is hungry he does not behave as if gaining food were his only aim: he is influenced also by the need to retain his self-respect, or by considerations of loss of other satisfactions if he spends too much money on food, and so on. The self is thus the integrated "pilot" of the organism, seeking for it the greatest possible long-term satisfaction.

**Alternative Concepts of the Main Integrated Structure.** The questions which immediately suggest themselves to anyone familiar with the field are: (*a*) Is it correct to assume that the ego is concerned only with conscious and available memories, since conceivably behavior could be affected by unconscious experiences? (*b*) Even if this distinction holds, is it justifiable to distinguish between ego and superego as radically as psychoanalysis does, since a good deal of the superego is conscious and integrated?

Whatever we may decide logically these questions in the end have to be settled empirically, mainly by factor analysis which will indicate how many functional unities exist here and what their boundaries are. In fact, we do not know enough to decide logically, except perhaps the first question. There the evidence is all to the effect that what is unconscious with respect to any mental system operates dynamically in independence of it. Consequently we can be reasonably certain that factor analysis will reveal a unity in all behavior that is controlled by available conscious memories, and that other behavior will not enter into this unity. In fact, as the evidence of Chapters 3 and 4 shows, there is already factor-analytic support for the concept of an ego structure in factors $C$ and $G$ with their loadings in integration, ability to accept deferred satisfactions, and ability to control impulses. It may be that one of these will prove to be an innate capacity to integrate and the other the pattern acquired by experience. The same covariational approach gives evidence also of a unitary superego pattern in the factor which has been labelled $K$, or "Trained, socialized mind."

The separation of the superego may, however, be questioned by some on the ground that the checks and modifications of behavior which spring from memories of moral considerations (the superego) and those which spring from memories of material considerations (the ego) are likely to become functionally bound together in the same field of integrated memory. It is just possible, however, that most conscious moral considerations are so dependent on the *unconscious* part of the superego which preceded them, that they partake of some degree of dependence on the unconscious and some degree of independence of the conscious universe of integrated ideas which guide the ego. They may be a more intransigent part of the conscious ideas—"moral prejudices"—less subject to reason, as psychoanalysis maintains. On the other hand a great number of general, conscious sentiments affecting the ego have unconscious roots and are just as slow to react to rational manipulation, so that the distinction may not prove functional.

If, as much evidence indicates, there are two relatively independent systems here, they could, logically, be either, first, (*a*) ego and (*b*) superego, or second, (*a*) ego and conscious superego and (*b*) unconscious superego. Each view has outstanding protagonists, in that Freud has propounded the first and McDougall the second. Let us examine McDougall's account of the *self-regarding sentiment*, as developed by himself and others, to cover what psychoanalysis would divide into the ego and the conscious superego (Diagram 36).

**The Development of Sentiments.** McDougall's concept of the self-regarding sentiment was historically approached through, and is best understood in the light of, his examination of the growth of sentiments. The student will realize that this approach differed from Freud's in making more use of analysis of everyday-life observations, of cultural anthropology, and of the comparative psychology of the mammals. Its strength lies in the breadth of its roots in general observation, and in those connections with general psychology which permit ready formulation and experimental investigation. Its weakness has been its failure to notice that appreciable role of unconscious mechanisms in ordinary sentiment formation, which clinical study reveals.

Sentiments were first perceived (Chap. 6) as structures producing interference with what was then called "instinctive" behavior. The ergic goals of behavior initiated in lower animals is first decided by the direct competition of stimuli, the more powerful stimulus producing the behavior of the correlative drive, with suppression (or, more generally, supercession) of its rival. But this does not account for all the suppressions even among animals. Yerkes (22) records instances of hungry male chimpanzees deferring to "an accepted custom" of the female eating first. Similar subordination of a strong drive to the stimulus of a learned symbol, indicating complexly a relatively remote alternative satisfaction, can be seen in dogs and other mammals.

As we have seen (Chap. 6) the term sentiment is applied to any habitual modification, due to learning, whether it be of a single drive or an aggregate of drives, having confluent satisfaction in the behavior concerned. It was McDougall's contention that the behavior of civilized man differed from the "instinctive" (purely ergic) behavior of natural man, by reason of sentiment formation, which acted by (a) draining off into sentiment structures the energy (readiness to react) which previously was invested in innate drives; (b) providing in these powerful aggregates forces strong enough to suppress any single drive with which they came into conflict.

However, he was soon compelled to recognize that the typical sentiments he had considered, *e.g.*, to home and family, to hobbies, professions, country, or religion, were not enough to account for the degree of integration observed. A man's sentiment to his family, satisfying drives of security, hunger, sex, etc., might suppress a powerful attraction to another woman, based on sex alone, while the sentiment of patriotism, based on gregariousness, fear, self-assertion, etc., might control the soldier's primitive drive to escape danger. Yet loyalties of this kind can be found strongly developed in unintegrated neurotics and criminals; while individuals whose loves and hates and admirations we know well may yet be unpredictable and undependable as regards the emotional stability with which they pursue the objects of these interests. It is even possible to find men with developed sentiments to high moral standards and abstract virtues of honesty, justice, or religious goodness, who have, intermittently, behaved like scoundrels.

McDougall's solution of the puzzle was the inference that all object sentiments of this kind are integrated in a single, larger *self-regarding sentiment* having the self as its object, the degree of integration of which determines the individual's ultimate stability of character.

**The Self-regarding Sentiment.** Since William James's lucid accounts of the development of the concept of self, it has been realized that among the mental objects about which we form sentiments (as readily as about physical objects) is the concept of one's self. The individual begins in infancy with an idea of his physical self. Soon after beginning to speak and understand words he learns that he has a name and begins to acquire an idea of himself, just as he does of his brother John, as a small boy, of a certain age and appearance, with particular excellences and disabilities, much loved by his mother, disliked by his cousin Jane, stronger than the little boy next door, and quite as good at drawing as his sister. He hears his name mentioned and is shy and sensitive, perhaps, to the implied praise or blame, in regard to that name, occurring in remarks of his parents or visitors. He experiences pleasure, through the satisfaction of self-assertive, gregarious, and appeal ergs, in so far as he is able to fit his conduct to this image of himself. Thus from earliest childhood a conception of the self is being attentively shaped and incorporated with other sentiments.

McDougall reasoned that this self-sentiment occupies a central position, about which the others become more organized as time proceeds; it is the keystone to the arch of sentiments. He argued that it defines for the individual an aspiration level in many fields, but particularly in moral matters, so that whenever a temptation or demand for persistent effort arises, of the kind not automatically met by our habits, the self-sentiment is brought into conscious awareness. What we call the will, *i.e.*, that which intervenes when a conscious decision or set has to be taken, McDougall considered to be the self-sentiment in action, and he brought some appreciable but not complete evidence that damage to, or failure of development in, the self-regarding sentiment accounts for defects of will.

**The Problem of Dynamics of the Self-sentiment.** Thus far McDougall's initial description. What remains to be explained and explored is how this concept of the self comes to occupy so powerful a position and what individual drives contribute to its dynamic potency. One can see at once that such a sentiment must draw heavily upon the drive of self-assertion, which gains its satisfaction from the individual's success, from his ability to maintain high moral standards, and so on. It also involves fear—fear for the individual's good reputation—along with acquisitiveness, deference toward one's ideal characters, and probably even gregariousness and sex.[4] The form of the self-regarding sentiment, and even its existence, must depend a good deal on the cultural form of society. In a lax society, where no particular consequences follow from a man's having an immoral reputation, why should fear be involved lest a good name be damaged? Further, in cases where an

---

[4] One of the most generally confirmed clinical observations of psychoanalysis is that of "secondary narcism." This is to the effect that fondness and interest (libido) in admired types frequently become withdrawn from these external objects and invested in the self—at the same time as one tries to incorporate their admired qualities in one's own personality. The young boy who admires some older athlete tries to incorporate the skill and fortitude of the beloved model in himself and, as he does so, comes to "love" these qualities in himself. Though self-love strikes us at first as a vice it is certainly too prevalent to be abnormal! In the higher forms of self-reverence and self-respect it seems to be an essential cement for the building of characters with high aspiration levels.

Sublimated sex drive, narcissistically directed, thus undoubtedly plays a part in the self-sentiment. The suggestion that gregariousness has some smaller role—that one can enjoy one's own company, *i.e.*, the furniture of ideas and people one has incorporated in the self—is more speculative. Whatever quantitative analysis eventually reveals about the composite satisfactions in the ego, it is at least clear that ego satisfaction is not to be identified merely with satisfaction of the self-assertive erg. Students should be watchful, therefore, of falling into the style of some recent popular writings on the ego which confuse "ego satisfaction" with self-assertion.

unreliability, a failure, or a misdemeanour will be known by no one but the doer, whence springs the powerful motive necessary to avoid it? These two situations seem to indicate that essentially the self-regarding sentiment must depend on some categorical, unquestionable, and, at least originally, unconscious demands of the superego.

Conceivably, integrated and moral conduct could arise from powerful sentiments and the superego without much conscious deliberation about the self. At least, in characters like those of Christ, Mohammed, Pasteur, St. Francis, Nelson, Lenin, Tolstoy, or Napoleon, the self and the things to which it is devoted seem blended completely in a single sentiment, which is throughout consistent with the demands of the superego. Here, unless we refer to the integrity of the self, the sentiment to the object seems to overtop the sentiment to the self—and even the self-integrity seems to be part of an abstract sentiment to Integrity.

Experimental and statistical investigation of the self is practically nonexistent, for the sufficient reason that to be effective at all it would have to be preceded by very vigorous and subtle thinking. Pending such investigation we must proceed with the contingent approximation that the self-regarding sentiment—hereafter called the self-sentiment—is a structure overlapping with the ego and the conscious superego (as shown in Diagram 36), for it is determined by both realistic and moral considerations. However, in the last chapter of this book we shall attempt to carry the analysis of the self beyond the present stage of clinical concepts to a more complete degree of definition. There we shall take up, for example, the question as to whether the self-sentiment (*i.e.*, organization *about* the self as object) has as much true dynamic functional unity as the ego (*i.e.*, organization *of* the self as willed action). A preliminary answer may be indicated by the above-mentioned findings of factor analysis, namely that there are *two* factors in the realm of character or personality integration (apart from the superego factor $K$) which have been labelled $C$ and $G$. $C$ is a dimension of inter-individual variation in emotional stability, dependability, and freedom from impulsiveness. $G$ loads these to some extent but also perseverance, conscientiousness, and other traits which might depend more on training or on influences from superego development. The hypothesis has already been presented that $C$ is a more innate stability or ease of integration (obverse of neurotic constitution) and that $G$ represents ego strength, but either, at this stage of experiment, could be considered a candidate for identification as the operating ego.

### 3. MALADJUSTMENT AND THE EGO DEFENSES

**Possible Consequences of Repression.** The integration of ego and superego in a single unified sentiment or dynamic structure (which may or may not best be called the self-sentiment), utilizing all the drives of the id, is, according to our present conception, the most favorable possible conclusion of the individual's adjustment process. Outstandingly well-adjusted characters present good examples of this achievement, but the majority achieve it only partially, while the neurotic and psychotic fall far short of such integration. Let us now turn back to the series of dynamic crossroads and, with the advantage of this close examination of ego and superego structure, see what happens when the conflict with rejected drives in the id proceeds farther.

Successful sublimations or supressions (paths δ1, δ3) require no further follow-up, but the path of repression (δ2) opens up several possible sequels, schematized in Diagram 37.

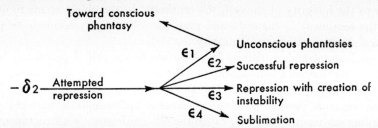

DIAGRAM 37. The fifth dynamic crossroad and the ε (Greek letter epsilon) sequels: attempted repression.

First, the repressed drive may continue to gain expression by "unconscious phantasy," as in path ε1, which may revert at any time to conscious phantasy. Some critics have objected to this use of the term phantasy, and since the phantasy is here an inferred rather than an observed activity, it may be that some other term should be used. The evidence is that the superego reacts *as if* forbidden phantasies were being enjoyed by the id, while at the same time one observes that the ego has repressed drives of the kind which might express themselves in phantasy. The ego is not directly aware of these phantasies but by free association and dream analysis it is sometimes possible to unearth them.

Second (ε2) the repression may be successful and absolute—a fact not realized in early studies which were wholly with neurotics in whom repression has generally failed as a final answer. In this case the only evidence of the act, other than the disappearance of a drive, is a certain loss of psychic energy and ego spontaneity due to the need to maintain an investing force, a censor, permanently on guard. It is possible also that some physiological repercussions occur and that occasionally changes take place in the physiological substrate of the "imprisoned" desire. The third possibility (ε3) is one in which the repressive measures fail to provide a permanent solution and set up, instead, a state of instability, requiring further measures to give the desired equilibrium. The causes and consequences of incomplete repression are studied further, below.

At the last of the epsilon alternatives, ($\epsilon$4), the drive may express itself in aim-inhibited, sublimated form, providing an acceptable adjustment.    Probably most sublimation is of the $\epsilon$4 type, *i.e.*, following an act of repression. The extent of $\delta$3 sublimation, *i.e.*, sublimation occurring without prior repression, simply through failure of direct expression, is still speculative, and it is possible that there are some qualitative differences between sublimations achieved by these two paths.

**Unstable, Inconclusive Repression.**    The path through $\epsilon$3 leads to a new series of problems which can now be studied at the $\zeta$ crossroads, as represented in Diagram 38.

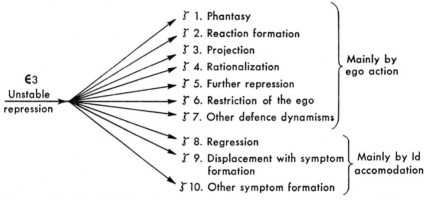

$\epsilon$3
Unstable
repression

$\zeta$ 1. Phantasy
$\zeta$ 2. Reaction formation
$\zeta$ 3. Projection
$\zeta$ 4. Rationalization
$\zeta$ 5. Further repression
$\zeta$ 6. Restriction of the ego
$\zeta$ 7. Other defence dynamisms
} Mainly by
ego action

$\zeta$ 8. Regression
$\zeta$ 9. Displacement with symptom formation
$\zeta$ 10. Other symptom formation
} Mainly by Id
accomodation

DIAGRAM 38.    The sixth dynamic crossroad and the $\zeta$ (Greek letter zeta) sequels: inconclusive repression leading to ego-defense dynamisms and symptoms.

To understand these sequels it is necessary now to take into account the three-cornered nature of the conflict, for some of these zeta sequels could no longer arise from conflict of two dynamic traits, as occurs in the situations $\alpha$ through $\epsilon$.    We have now to pay attention in any conflict to the internal economy of the whole dynamic structure.    The main conflicts occurring are: (*a*) between the ego and the id, typically in suppression and repression of id impulses by the ego.    However, the act vity of the ego in this censorship is not entirely of its own initiating but is partly due to (*b*) pressure on the ego from the superego when the former's actions, compromising with the id, conflict with the superego standards, and (*c*) that part of the conflict between the superego and the id which takes place directly, that is not mediated by the ego and is therefore unconscious.

*Possibilities of Ego Failure.*    As stated in Chapter 8, the ego, which is the only integrating and willing consciousness, is placed, as it were, between the devil of the id demands and the deep sea of the superego punishment, while on a third front it faces the intransigent facts of reality.    In these circumstances it may fail partially or completely in its functions, and indeed, in clinical experience most of the theoretically possible permutations of failure are known.  They include (*a*) withdrawal of the ego from reality contact, as in most insanity; (*b*) alliance of the ego with the id to suppress the superego, as in criminal and criminal insane behavior; (*c*) relinquishment of much of id control to the superego, as in melancholia and anxiety neurosis; (*d*) buttressing of the ego with artificial ego-defense dynamisms, to take the place of normal flexible control by the ego of the id, as in the "character neuroses."

It is resort to the unsatisfactory "solutions" (*c*) and (*d*)—the operations typically concerned with neurosis formation rather than delinquency or insanity—that we are now called to study.  These arise from a weakened ego rather than total abdication by the ego.  The weak development of the ego may arise from many causes, some of which we shall study later, but principally from *failure to utilize the forces of the id for its own development* (7). This is generally occasioned by undue rejection and repression of id forces, sometimes under the influence of a prematurely developed superego.  When the ego experiences difficulty in handling powerful id drives, it may, as it were, "fly into a panic" and begin wholesale repression—just as a minority government, and especially one making great demands on the people, may quickly resort to secret police and the concentration camp.

This resemblance between the social and individual organism is more than a remote analogy.  There is much evidence that, in addition to the sources of anxiety already described in connection with remembered punishment, the fear response occurs also as a primary response to the situation of "loss of control."  It is not only that loss of control by the ego may lead to punishment; it is also that loss of control comes under the heading of "the strange and unexpected" which we have set down (Chap. 7) as one of the primal stimuli for the erg of fear.  Thus instances are known clinically where anxiety has been provoked by bodily, physiological reactions proceeding abnormally, even with no pain or foreboding of consequences.  The present writer has referred elsewhere to a clinical case initially diagnosed as anxiety hysteria in which it turned out that a brain tumor was slowly causing interference with vision.  The strange experiences of failure of visual control here proved to be the real source of the prodromal anxiety.  To the other factors in anxiety discussed in the preceding chapter we must therefore add strangeness of internal experience and especially of impotence of the ego.  When the interferences of the superego, and especially, the volcanic forces of the id, become too strong, the ego is thus reinforced by fear and proceeds to the commonest form of ego defense, in face of dire threat, namely, attempts at rigid and absolute repression.  This exacerbates the situation, for the whole economy is thrown out of balance: the id remains overcharged with unexpressed drives and the ego is impoverished.  To buttress its control of an unstable situation the ego may then resort to further defense mechanisms.

Thus, essentially, imbalance arises either because the ego is unduly weak or because it has unwisely attempted to repress (instead of to incorporate) forces which are too strong. Without going too far into this aspect of the question one can see that they may both arise partly from a common source, namely, an upbringing which has rejected too many drives from the constitution of the ego.

Individuals of low dominance, defective ability, excessive superego development, and previously defective ego development tend to meet frustration at blocks by repressing the drive rather than by overcoming the block. Since what is rejected from the ego turns up in the id, we finally have the spectacle of a prim, rigid, insecure, and unadaptable ego sitting precariously on top of a dangerously overloaded id. But other causes, notably regression, may contribute to ego defect.

**Ego-defense Mechanisms or Dynamisms.** A classical account of defense mechanisms has been given by Anna Freud (6). Here we must confine the account to some of the most common forms, as shown in Diagram 38. A preliminary mention of these ego-defense dynamisms was made in Chapter 4 in connection with the construction of tests to measure the extent of such action. About phantasy and repression we need say no more, for their place in the search for adjustment has already been set out. The situation is now one where difficulty is experienced in maintaining the repression, and auxiliary devices must consequently be invoked.

Rationalization is a relatively superficial defense. The repressed drive is allowed some expression, but the individual saves the ego and superego from conflict by unrealistically refusing to admit that certain behavior is an expression of the undesirable drive. This he does by building up a fabric of reasoning safely imputing the behavior to other motives. Thus a man may be jealous of his son, but because his self-respect and conscience refuse to allow him aggression against the son, he may say that his severity is part of a theoretical plan of education, for the son's greatest good. The rationalizer fools himself totally; other people only partially.

Projection is a defense which may be seen from infancy onwards. The threat from the id is externalized as a threat from the outside world, where the individual feels that he can deal with it more safely. It may emanate from any drive. Thus, instead of acknowledging that he is bursting with aggressions, the individual believes that certain people are malignant or persecutory towards him and sets out to deal with them in the real world. Instead of realizing that his own drives are in a state of chaos, he may, like certain schizophrenics, believe that a cataclysm is about to bring chaos to the real world. As mentioned before, projection is probably, on finer analysis, a combination of three distinct processes.

In reaction formation the defense consists in vigorously adopting consciously a set of attitudes radically opposed to those of the unconscious drive.

The individual battling an unconscious "part instinct" to play with excrement will then show an exaggerated interest and care about cleanliness. Another with strong sadistic tendencies will show great alertness to instances of cruelty and will "protest too much" about the need for curbing such impulses. The case of the prude, in whom ill-managed sexual impulses are restrained by exaggerated care over sex morality and pruriency concerning the sex life of others, is well known. The individual who employs reaction formation is like a man who, finding a hole in the wall of his house, stops the hole by building on a whole new wing there.

The mechanism of overcompensation, as described so accurately by Adler (1) in connection with the "inferiority complex," is to be considered a variety of reaction formation. Here a sense of worthlessness, occasioned in childhood by some obvious physical or mental blemish, exacerbating the child's normal sense of dependence and ineffectiveness, is reacted to by an exaggerated striving for power. Security is sought, not through comradely union with the group, but by compensatory self-assertion, directed as a fictive goal of absolute power. Further symptoms then result from the necessity for reconciling this impossible, distorted ambition with the individual's mediocre talents. These maladjustments will be discussed later in connection with delinquency and abnormal behavior.

There are many other ego-defense dynamisms, such as identification, reversal, etc., but, for the purposes of a first survey, these may remain mere names. One device, "restriction of the ego," which is relevant to the Adlerian neurosis above, deserves mention, however, because it is rather prevalent. Here the individual acquires a habit of avoiding situations that might provoke the unconscious pressure. If his ego is in conflict with an exaggerated self-abasement drive, as in the Adlerian "inferiority complex" described above, he will rigidly avoid competitive or inferiority-provoking situations in which he might be tested and made to feel insecure. Or, if the sexual drive is the source of difficulty, he may, like the early anchorites, retire into the desert where no women can be seen. From the individual's standpoint, restriction of the ego is a relatively healthy and not too unrealistic defense: it is mostly socially that it offers difficulties and defects, through the social problems created in an attempt to organize in a common group people of restricted experience, sympathies, and habits.

The remaining $\zeta$ sequels are considered in the following section.

## 4. THE FORMATION OF NEUROTIC SYMPTOMS

**Ergic Regression and Personality Regression.** The next "defense" listed in Diagram 38, namely $\zeta 8$, is by regression. Actually $\zeta 8$, together with $\zeta 9$ and $\zeta 10$, is best placed a little apart from the other sequels since all three are as much due to "accommodation" by the id drives as to action by the ego.

Regression, as a turning back to earlier modes of expression in the maturation of a drive, may relieve the situation, when the conflict centers on the more developed, mature form of expression of the drive in question. For example, conflict over attempts at heterosexual satisfaction may be solved by a return to autoerotic satisfaction. Such regression, however, generally creates more problems than it solves: indeed, as we shall now see, regression is more frequently a *cause* of neurotic conflict than a *solution*.

It is necessary to distinguish clearly between ergic regression, *i.e.*, regression of a single drive, and regression of the total personality. The latter, which occurs through a number of diverse traumatic and degenerative conditions, and shows itself in undoing of integrations once attained and in return to childish ways of behaving and sense of responsibility, is not our main object of study here.[5] We are concerned instead with the reversal of those stages in innate maturation of drives which were studied in Chapter 6. Evidence of these phases of maturation has barely reached the experimental level and is mainly of a clinical nature, being clearest in relation to the maturation of the sex drive, through at least two object stages of three erogenous zones, as we have seen.

Now, in general, if the sex desires of the adult have either reverted to an earlier goal object (or erogenous zone) or have failed to advance normally during childhood and adolescence, additional adjustment problems of frustration and repression are created. It is hard enough to satisfy adult

---

[5] General regression is to be explained largely in terms of amnesia, *i.e.*, the forgetting and abandoning of acquired habits which have ceased—in the dismaying situation—to be rewarding or which have become burdensome. It is "regressive" merely in the sense that the abandoned habits happen to be those acquired *later* than habits that remain rewarding, though it may also be "regressive" in a sense involving moral or other values, *i.e.*, "a falling away from desirable norms." Ergic regression, on the other hand, is withering of a *maturation* stage, not the undoing of learning. Because ergic regression is a cause of neuroses and creates difficulties for any attempt to live on a highly integrated adult level, it is often associated, secondarily, with *general* personality regression; but in essential nature the two are different. If we consider logical possibilities, both ergic regression and total personality regression could be (*a*) the reversal of learning experience in personal history, (*b*) the reversal of a historical maturation process, (*c*) a falling away from some agreed standard of behavior, *e.g.*, of moral worth or efficient integration. But the last sense is arbitrary and better covered by other terms than regression, while there is no proof of all these theoretical possibilities actually existing. Freud (1916) pointed out that personality (ego) regression and ergic (libidinal) regression are normal, as transient, reversible processes. "In sleep the latter is carried to the point of restoring the primitive narcism, while the former goes back to the state of hallucinatory wish-fulfillment." Much normal recreation is also temporarily regressive in both senses.

sexuality under an exacting moral code; but it is in fact (if not in the neurotic's anticipation) still harder to satisfy infantile sexuality, for the behavior required not only conflicts more with conventions and morals, but may even be logically incompatible and physically impossible.[6]  The neurotic, indeed, as later clinical investigation has shown, is more often battling with infantile sexuality than adult sexuality.  Thus the conversion hysteric is typically fixated at the stage of the Oedipus complex and the obsessional neurotic seems to have adhered to the concentration of interest on excretory processes.  Although no detailed evidence yet exists, it is likely that similar failures of maturation to appropriate adult levels can occur in the preferred modes of satisfaction of other drives too.

**Causes of Regression.**  As indicated above, regression may be provoked by the conflicts and difficulties of the immediate adult situation; but it was

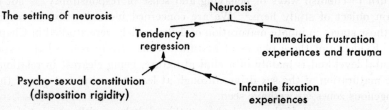

DIAGRAM 39.    Schematization of major factors in neurosis.

soon realized that generally the origins are deeper than this.  Freud's observations led him to believe they are partly hereditary—the inheritance of a "psychosexual constitution" with unusual "adherence" or lack of plasticity in the drive.  This may be the same as the measurable source trait of disposition rigidity discussed in Chapter 4.  Additional to this, however, is the actual intensity and satisfyingness of the infantile fixations experienced by the given individual during infancy.

Finally, regression is to some extent a self-perpetuating process.  If energy investments get tied up for any reason in infantile fixations, there is less energy to go on and the drive is more likely to recoil from difficulties it meets at later stages, and to stay arrested at those later but still infantile stages.  Freud likened the maturation process to the advance of an army: the more troops it has to leave besieging points on its line of communication, the less is it likely to get past points of difficulty met later on.

Apparently the importance of the actual difficulties encountered at the point where the individual ceases to go ahead is much less than common

[6] The various sexual perversions are attempts to satisfy the goals of infantile sexuality. It is from these, and from neurotic phantasies and symptoms, that the polymorphous perverse "part instincts" of the infantile sex erg are deduced.  Obviously, there are certain combinations of regressive goal and regressive erogenic zone which are almost inherently impossible of fulfillment.

sense would suppose. For example, an individual may show sexual regression and neurosis when encountering especial difficulties in an adult sex relation in marriage. The abnormal appeal and satisfyingness of the regressive phase, however, must generally be looked for in things happening before this "trauma" was encountered. Indeed, psychoanalysis gives the general formula for neurosis, *i.e.*, for especial difficulty in getting a stable equilibrium between ego and id, as shown in Diagram 39.

**The Role of Displacement.** Regression is thus the greatest single cause of neurosis, but many other conditions are necessary, and it is in terms of the operation of particular defense mechanisms that the final form of the neurosis is to be understood. An important condition is that defense or perhaps, better, "accommodation" mechanism, shown at ʃ9 in Diagram 38 which still remains to be discussed. This device—*displacement*—means the shifting of an emotional satisfaction from one object (usually difficult or denied) to another (usually innocuous or disguised, as a symbol of the first)—when the shift would not be logically, realistically made as part of a normal subsidiation development. The process has also been called transference, as when Freud originally called the common neuroses, *transference neuroses*, because they all showed this process in their symptom formation; but transference is now commonly applied to the emotional relation to the psychiatrist in psychoanalysis—a very special case of the general process. Displacement is possible in the first place through the relativity of that disposition rigidity which conditions all learning; indeed it may be that individuals of low rigidity will be found to utilize displacement more frequently. In sublimation and, indeed, all sentiment formation, plasticity (*i.e.*, relatively low rigidity) operates; but here it operates in defiance of logic. Displacement is thus properly employed in a restricted sense: to describe the unintentional, unrealized expression of a forbidden drive through some accidentally or symbolically associated response which usually operates as a neurotic symptom.

**"Equivalence" and "Subsidiation."** While describing displacement it is appropriate to define the term "equivalence" which refers to another aspect of the same relationship. It has been a common observation of neurosis, first made in conversion hysteria, that the disappearance of one symptom (except through true therapy) is generally immediately followed by the appearance of another. These symptoms could therefore be regarded as alternative displacements or "equivalents." It was this phenomenon which forced Freud to the practical conclusion that getting rid of symptoms by hypnotic suggestion must be abandoned in favor of getting at the deeper morbid drive seeking expression. It also led to the theoretical conclusion that psychic energy is indestructible.

This principle, first observed in neurosis, is, however, readily seen to be applicable to all mental life. A normal person, feeling lonely, may get into the habit of assuaging that loneliness by reading a companionable book or by taking a friend for a drink. These two habits or "trait-elements" can be demonstrated to be equivalents, *i.e.*, to draw upon the same (gregarious) erg, by the fact that they can be substituted for one another. Massive personality traits may thus be equivalents or substitute behavior forms, though more frequently only minor trait-elements or symptoms are involved.

Equivalence should be considered along with subsidiation (Chapter 7) for they constitute the two principles of organization covering the whole development of metanergic mental structures. It is by observing equivalence and tracing paths of subsidiation that we are able to map out the dynamic trait structure of any given individual. Diagram 40 illustrates both relationships, by indicating three equivalent subsidiation paths, *A*, *B*, and *C*.

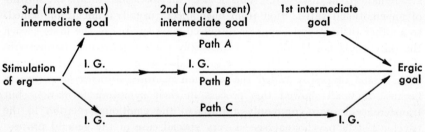

DIAGRAM 40.   Dynamic equivalence.

Returning with these concepts to survey the $\zeta$ crossroads and the problem of neurosis, we note that the typical history of neurosis begins with adjustment problems created by regression. The ego fails to handle the inexpressible drive constructively by sublimation (or any of the previous $\alpha$, $\beta$, $\gamma$, or $\delta$ paths) or alternatively to maintain conclusive repression, and is forced to resort to ego-defense dynamisms. Effective ego-defense dynamisms do not necessarily entail full-fledged neurotic symptoms, though they frequently produce odd beliefs (projection), unreasonableness (rationalization), silly avoidance behavior (restriction of the ego), or ill-balanced enthusiasm (reaction formation) which are recognizable as constituting "the neurotic personality" or a "character neurosis." The blocking of expression is itself responsible for the high general emotionality which, as we have seen in Chapter 3, is also an essential part of the general neuroticism factor (source trait *C*).

When the ego has lost effective contact with and control over the dissociated drive, the way is open for displacement to occur. The offensive desire disappears as a subject of conscious conflict and reappears as a neurotic symptom. The neurotic symptom may appear as part of a defense mechanism, but if it does it must be considered a broken-down, largely ineffectual defense mechanism; for the purpose of the latter device is to handle the errant drive without its being an abomination to the superego and a nuisance to the ego—and this it has failed to do in the case of a disabling and alarming symptom.

**The Nature of Neurotic Symptoms.**  A symptom is initially seen as a disablement in social adjustment or personal efficiency; but psychologically it is definable as a breakdown in the orderly tripartite structure of personality, including the auxiliary defenses used to bolster the ego.  For the symptom is at once a part of the ego, the id, and the superego.  The conflict has become a kind of mental hemorrhage from which a new structure has appeared —the symptom.  For the symptom is an *ad hoc*, disorderly device expediently trying to satisfy what the regular structures cannot satisfy.  It gives satisfaction at once (usually symbolically) to the escaped, imperfectly controlled id impulse, to the need for self-punishment originating in the outraged superego (which may have some perception of the true origin of the symptom), and to the attempted ego defense against the tension both of the id and the superego.

As the psychoanalysts have pointed out, the character of the symptom is explicable if one remembers that it is thus "overdetermined" by several causes.  It is indeed a necessary compromise (but not a planned, ego-controlled, middle-of-the-road expression) representing the "resolution of forces" from id, ego, and superego; *i.e.*, it is a confluence, but outside the regular, realistically subsidiated structure of personality.  As we shall see later, there may also be a "secondary gain," an unforeseen dynamic bonus, from the fact that the symptom enables the individual to avoid work or responsibility.  But this, like the above dynamic satisfactions in the symptom itself, is generally purposive rather than purposeful.

**A Case of Conversion Hysteria.**  These principles can be readily illustrated by reference to any compendium of case histories.  Let us first consider a typical conversion hysteria, a case of a girl suffering from deafness, without physiological cause and along with emotional superficiality and other signs of hysteria.  Free association eventually brings to the surface emotional connections which show (*a*) a strong Oedipus relation to the father, the sexual, id drives of which achieve expression by identification, for the father also suffered from deafness; (*b*) punishment by the superego for the forbidden wish, in that the deafness is really an affliction to the ego; (*c*) secondary gain in that she gets sympathy for her disability and is also able to avoid the drudgery of music lessons.

The reader should note there is no inconsistency in asserting that the gain and suffering do *not* cancel each other.  Different structures are involved: the superego profits by the punishment, the id profits by the sympathy.  The well-known application of these principles to the lesser amnesias, symptomatic slips of the pen and tongue in averagely adjusted people, illustrates the same point. The man who completely forgets a certain appointment, which he knows is going to be very humiliating but which is very important to him, may say, "It is absurd to say I *wanted* to forget. In the long run it will cost me a lot to have missed the appointment." This is true of the conscious ego; but the unconscious id, which in any case never barters immediate satisfaction for "in the long run," certainly wanted to arrange a forgetting. It may be objected that this supposes some splitting of the individual. This is true: all conflict presupposes separate dynamic foci; but it is only in the neurotic that this incompleteness of integration has reached dangerous proportions as a result of his operating by regression and other defense mechanisms, instead of by suppression and sublimation.

**Anxiety Hysteria.** Exactly the same principles are at work in any case of anxiety hysteria, the symptomatic difference from conversion hysteria depending partly on temperament and partly on the relative magnitude of the forces involved. In the anxiety hysteric the role of the superego is more powerful. The ego defends itself more by unconscious phantasy, by reaction formations and, in phobias, by projection. The id gains satisfaction from the unconscious or conscious phantasy, and the superego gains expression by punishing the ego with anxiety.

In one of the classical instances of phobia the individual had a dread of all small enclosed spaces. These symptoms vanished when the psychotherapist eventually dragged up from his unconscious a recollection of an early childhood experience in which he was greatly frightened by a large dog in a dark, narrow passageway. But this cannot be interpreted as a mere mechanical conditioning. We find that in fact the child was going down the dark passage for an immoral purpose—to steal something. The revival of phantasies of an immoral nature in the adult consequently reactivates the reinforced sense of guilt from the original experience. Unable to face this situation, the ego projects its own anxiety (the threat from the superego) on to external situations, the association being suggested by the early experience. In this way, at the cost of projection, rationalization and restriction of the ego, it "solves" the conflict, for by avoiding the places which cause the phobic reaction, the ego assumes that comparative "adjustment" can be enjoyed.

**Symbolic Disguise of Symptom.** The choice of symptom must be one which will satisfy the defense mechanisms operating at the time and also the id drive. To be permitted expression the id drive must disguise itself, and so it suffers transformation usually by the same devices as do the forbidden wishes in dreams, employing symbolism, displacement, and the significance gained through accidental association. This may be illustrated by a Freudian case of obsessional neurosis (7a). A girl of nineteen could not sleep unless she went through a ritual of gathering together the flower pots in her room on one table and arranging the bolster so that it nowhere touched the edge of the bed. When the psychoanalysis had brought unconscious trends to light and the symptoms had disappeared, it became clear that the flower pots symbolized her own sexual organs and the bolster and bed her father and mother, respectively. She wished to separate them, or at least prevent their coming together, so that she could have her father to herself. Thus the behavior gave symbolic comfort to the id, while the burden of the exacting ritual allayed a sense of guilt, for, as with most obsessional neurotics, the anxiety from the superego broke through only if she failed to carry out these "senseless" acts.

## 5. SOME MODIFICATIONS OF CLINICAL THEORY

**Neuroses in Perspective of Total Adjustment Process.** This is as far as the study of the neurotic can suitably be pursued in connection with the general course of adjustment and maladjustment. In Chapters 17 and 18, which make an over-all study of the abnormal personality, the dynamic processes here followed will be seen in the perspective of the whole picture of abnormality, including the psychoses, persistent delinquency, and the character neurosis. They will also be brought into relation with experimental work on neurosis.

Here it is important to realize that the development of neurotic symptoms is only *one* of several possible solutions, even when the individual has entered the third dynamic crossroads occurring at the unbreakable barrier. As will be seen from Diagram 41, which puts the various dynamic crossroads in proper sequence, neurosis is properly only a byway beyond the main highways of adjustment.

Thus, the basic principles to bear in mind in understanding the genesis of neurosis are (*a*) many neurotogenic processes have to intervene after the original frustration (indeed, if each path has an equal chance of being taken, the individual confronted with the $\beta$ crossroads (unbreakable barrier) has only a quarter of a third of a third of a chance, *i.e.*, one chance in thirty-six, of entering the path of unstable repression and neurosis); (*b*) the symptoms are not accidental but follow the same laws as do dynamic traits in general, being the outcome of id, superego, and ego demands; (*c*) since sex, especially incestuous or perverted sex, is most frequently the subject of horror and taboo, with aggression next in low repute, most neurotic symptoms are symbols of sex drive or aggression, and expressions also of the punishment anxiety which these wishes generate; (*d*) the neurosis is merely "*provoked*" *or precipitated* by a difficult situation in adult life. The more important cause is the preparation of the ground for neurosis by early-life trauma and fixations which cause regression and create faulty, unstable ego development.

**The Adlerian Modification.** It remains to conclude our clinical account of the final (internal-conflict) phases in the adjustment process, by critically

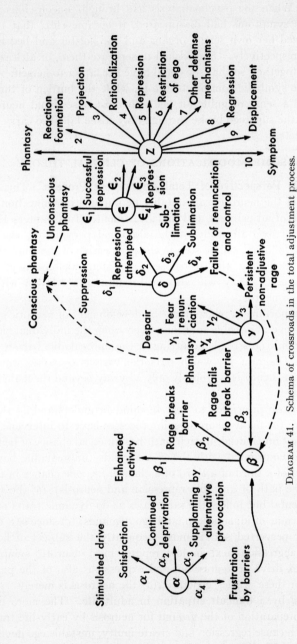

DIAGRAM 41.   Schema of crossroads in the total adjustment process.

reviewing some modifications put forward at various times with respect to psychoanalytic concepts. First among these, historically and in the radicalism of its modification, is, as mentioned earlier, the theory of the Viennese psychiatrist Adler, that deprivations and trauma of a nonsexual nature play an important role in maladjustment and that the self-assertive drive is particularly likely to be involved. Adlerian trauma (producing the "inferiority complex") and Adlerian mechanisms are considered by most clinicians to operate at later and more superficial levels than those examined in psychoanalysis, and to account better for the transient behavior problems of middle childhood than for the true neuroses of adults.

Adler found in many neurotics that the reactions seem to lead back to some traumatic experience in which the person had been made to feel desperately inferior and insecure. As discussed above, the individual attempts to wash out this hurtful feeling of inferiority by overcompensatory strivings for eminence and absolute power (1). Indeed he behaves as if the only security were in absolute power over others, and shows no sense of love and social solidarity with the group. A certain sense of inferiority is normal to the state of childhood, and the associated drive to independence is part of normal growing-up. The Adlerian psychologists found, however, undue frequency of physical defects and embarrassing peculiarities in the early life of neurotics, and concluded that by these scars the inferiority was exacerbated. Then the individual concentrates abnormally on correcting it and begets greater than normal strength (at the cost of distortion), as a broken bone grows thicker than one never damaged.

**Instances of Adlerian Response.** Unfortunately the individual does not generally have the capacity to reach such eminence. Except for a few geniuses, who possess special gifts which can be tortured into highest expression by this relentless drive to perfection, the goal of absolute eminences must remain a "fictional" one. The individual gets discouraged and finally drags in a neurotic response as the only way to adjust the fictional goal to the reality. He says, "I am really capable of outshining everyone, but owing to this unfortunate neurotic disability I have to be content with the realities of my present life."

Adler cites the case of a woman who developed such a phobia of open spaces that she was eventually unable to leave her home at all. An infantile inferiority had led to an overcompensation in the form of an intention to cut a resplendent figure in fashionable society. When it became apparent that she had not the talent for the latter she developed an anxiety neurosis which prevented her going out, and so permitted her to escape from the test of reality. Similarly, in a case known to the writer, a young man developed a palsy (conversion hysteric) of the right arm after a trivial accident. It developed in analysis that through a powerful sense of inferiority he had developed the overcompensation that he would be a great novelist. Failing, after years of effort, he did not adjust by using the talents he had, in the useful but ordinary occupation which he followed, but developed instead a palsy which prevented his writing at all. This saved him from further efforts toward the unrealistic goal, while permitting him to believe that he was equal to it. The symptom is thus always very simply determined by the Adlerian mechanism; in fact, what psychoanalysis regards as a mere "secondary gain" becomes the whole dynamic reward. The distinction between legitimate, native ambitiousness on the one hand and overcompensation on the other is made on the basis of whether the ambition is adjustive and ready to meet the tests of reality or, on the other hand, evasive and rigid.

**Jung's Modification.** The Swiss psychologist, Jung, has similarly departed from the psychoanalytic position by stressing that inadequacy and the need for emotional dependence are sometimes more important than sex needs in the causation of neurosis (12). Neurosis is regarded by him rather as a failure of self-realization due to a somewhat similar "lack of courage" to that invoked by Adler.

How is this to be reconciled with the motivation principles considered above in psychoanalysis? In the first place the Adlerian insecurity-inferiority is regarded by psychoanalysts as springing primarily from an unresolved Oedipus conflict. The individual has failed to give up the primary sexual object and to introject the father completely as a superego. Consequently his libido is not desexualized, *i.e.*, converted into sociability; his reaction to authority (father substitute) is rebellious and amoral, while he experiences constant guilt (insecurity-inferiority) as a result of clinging to the original id goal. This explains adequately the main characteristics of the inferiority case as described by Adler. Referring personal problems to a particular inferiority-provoking situation is then considered mainly as a projection of guilt-insecurity feeling already in existence upon a mere precipitating accident.

The reconciliation of the two theories has also been indicated in the above consideration of overcompensation as a special instance of the ego-defense mechanism of reaction formation. But the difficulty arises that a reaction formation normally has the quality of a *moral* course of behavior, overemphasized by the ego to subdue an opposing immoral desire in the id. The inferiority-complex behavior, on the other hand, is scarcely moral, though it may be considered as an attempt to hide a painful conflict between id and superego by emphasis of ego characteristics (self-regarding sentiment). It is possible also to consider the inferiority complex as a conflict simply between the drives of self-assertion and self-submission, in which the latter represses the former and sets up reaction formations. But in the normal personality self-submission is not painful and is healthily adjustive (as in reverence), so that the basic explanation must deal, as above, with why this need to repress submissiveness arises.

**View of Horney.** Among these writers, *descriptive* observations on the general nature of the neurotic are not in dispute. As Horney points out (10), the clinical characteristics of the neurotic, apart from the disintegration and symptom formation, are a disproportionate need for affection (compensated by a "don't care" attitude), an incapacity to give affection (compensated by a compulsive eagerness to help), a sense of inadequacy (sometimes compensated by self-assertive striving), and an inhibition of any normal amount of aggression or sexual expression (sometimes compensated by affected, domineering behavior and compulsive, affected sex behavior). But it could be argued that the sense of inadequacy found in the neurotic (see characteristics of source trait $C$, general neuroticism (page 60)) is a secondary result, not a primary cause of the real social awkwardness and maladaptation. The awkwardness would then be viewed as resulting from primary lack of an integrated, adapted, and adjusted personality. It is quite easy, as the writings of psychoanalysts, of Jung, Adler, Horney, and others show, to make a convincing argument, from a suitable collection of clinical cases, for any one of these alternative emphases on causation. Until present clinical methods are surpassed by more accurate observation, impersonal selection of case histories, and intelligent statistical treatment of measurements, we must admit that our preference for the Freudian concepts in psychoanalysis rests only on an over-all judgment of diversely accumulated case histories.

### 6. ADAPTATION, INTEGRATION, AND ADJUSTMENT OF THE PERSONALITY WITHIN SOCIETY

**Adaptation, Basically Biological, Involves Also Sociomoral Standards.** These terms—adjusted, adapted, and integrated—which are much used in dynamic psychology, and which we have so far been using with implicit definition, can now be examined and defined more exactly. They are not really restricted to dynamic traits alone, but refer to the whole personality. However, the burden of adjusting to nondynamic abnormalities, *e.g.*, an excitable temperament or low intelligence, eventually falls on the dynamic structure.

The term *adaptation* is best retained in the basic biological and social sense. The individual organism is well adapted to its environment when its behavior assures normal chances of survival to itself and to the society of which its offspring are part. To be realistic this must include adaptations to moral as well as physical facts; for a society of amoral people does not survive and a gangster may be shot by the police. Adaptation to morals is part of survival. It may then be objected that to examine the success of an individual's adaptation involves going beyond psychology, and indeed it does if our psychology is one which ignores society, morals, and biological survival. The fact that psychology is not competent to pass judgment on moral values or problems of biological survival, however, does not mean that it must ignore them, nor is it sufficient for psychologists to recommend a personality adjustment, however agreeable, which is not consistent with the survival of the individual or the species.

Parenthetically, it is necessary to comment here (in connection with both adaptation and integration) on the question of the relation of the individual to society, which is taken up more fully in Chapters 13, 14, and 15. Because the painful and often disastrous conflicts which clinicians seek to alleviate arise in part from prohibitions imposed by society, some lesser followers of psychoanalysis have demanded that every "irrational," *i.e.*, incomprehensible, moral restriction should be removed and in particular that Victorian rigidity of sex inhibition should be abolished. It is true that Freud's comments on the burden of civilization are sometimes sour and that Adler even explicity advocated avoiding the inferiority complex by outlawing economic and other competition. But sociopsychological research shows that the restrictions of civilization are mostly successful devices to maximize ergic satisfaction for everyone, *e.g.*, by eliminating famine, sexual jealousy, and sudden death. The task of education is to internalize these prohibitions of external society, and it is not the fault of the social prohibitions if this is sometimes done in a way which creates neurosis.

Finally, if we accept the desirability of the adaptation standard, we must recognize that for some psychological analyses it may be useful to distinguish between adaptation to the physical and social world (which are ego functions) and adaptation to moral values (which operates more through the superego), but total adaptation, *i.e.*, survival of the individual and society, requires cognizance of both. This concept of adaptation is worth stressing because it keeps in view aspects of therapy that are often quite lost from sight when discussing adjustment only.

**Adjustment.** In popular psychology this much-used term means anything from the passive toleration of the morally intolerable to the earning of a large income! To gain a concept that means something, let us begin by paring away the meanings that belong to other concepts. In the first place, it is possible for a person to be adjusted but not adapted. For example, a man may be free from conflicts or repressions so long as he expresses himself criminally, or takes opium, or maintains some dangerous, exciting hobby, none of which is compatible with survival. Or a well-to-do, voluntarily childless woman may be perfectly happy with the "sublimations" of social distraction into which her maternal interests have disappeared. But she is not adapted, for a society whose women were wholly of this type would perish.

Similarly, as we have seen, it is possible for a man to be adapted but not adjusted, as seen in many severe neurotics who nevertheless hold jobs. However, in this case the loss of energy by internal friction always to some extent detracts from the final soundness of the adaptation. Indeed, *in general*, adaptation and adjustment will tend to go together. If, for example, one has contemplated psychological adjustments and adaptations in relation to the recent war, he sees that the soldier who dies for his country in the complete faith of courage is both adapted and adjusted, whereas the neurotic is neither, for his internal adjustment is miserable and his external adaptation is not such as would permit his group to survive.

Is then "well-adjusted" nothing but a piece of jargon for "happy?" Not quite, because happiness is a state of consciousness, and psychology knows nothing about the measurement of conscious states. Adjustment describes the goodness of the internal arrangements by which an adaptation is maintained. Of those arrangements we can ask, "Does the adaptation, however good from the standpoint of society and personal survival, involve great internal conflict?" This may appear to have some relation to Shaffer's (16) definition of adjustment as "tension reduction." But even apart from the uncertainty of the term "tension"[7] this cannot be accepted because it would make the best adjusted man a dead man. An effective, adapted personality obviously requires considerable long-circuitings of drives, with the resultant maintenance of tension. In defining the degree of goodness of an adjustment, therefore, what we ask is, "In the maintenance of this level of adaptation how much mental energy is lost in 'internal friction'?" By internal friction we mean both conflict and the stalemate of opposing investments of drive, as in successful repression. Until mental energy and goodness of adaptation can be measured, it is thus not possible to measure, except in theory, the goodness of adjustment. Probably, too, most psychologists would want to have measurements on a second dimension of this adjustment, namely, its stability and likelihood of resistance to trauma.

**Integration.** In general, by extent of integration we mean the extent to which the individual's conscious purposes work together harmoniously or detract from one another. Does the person undo with his left hand the work done with his right? If, for example, a man states that his goals are to be a great athlete and to eat as much food as he can, or to contribute his utmost to science and to make a lot of money, we may suspect him of a certain lack of integration. Integration is initially independent of adaptation and adjustment. One can be very integrated about some very maladaptive goals,

---

[7] This use of "tension" was unfortunately born of the era when psychologists were trying to avoid the notion of drives. It tries, with the distortion and evasiveness typical of its parent era, to define that logical impossibility, a force without a direction. It also masquerades, sometimes as a conscious experience, sometimes as an inference from behavior.

as was, for example, Schopenhauer in his intention to have nothing to do with the general trend of human life, or as a single-minded criminal might be.

Integration concerns the extent to which all the drives and endowments of personality work to a single goal or harmonious set of goals. But this single goal need not be such a simple one as "to make a million dollars" or "to love Jane Doe": it may be the Epicurean one of "obtaining the maximum expression for all my desires," or some similar multiplicity in unity. If integration is made to include the unconscious as well as the conscious needs it becomes synonymous with adjustment, for good integration then implies organization with the minimum of friction. Usage makes it impossible to reject this meaning *of total dynamic integration*, but if integration is to have a meaning all its own we must use it with respect to conscious purposes and *external behavior* rather than internal conflict. It may be objected that this brings it near to intelligence, since only a fool allows his schemes to undo one another. Intelligence doubtless enters, but so also does capacity for long-circuited behavior, *i.e.*, the suppression of impulses.[8]

In the last resort these concepts have to be classified empirically, by correlation, etc., rather than logic alone. Common observation, however, indicates definitely that adaptation, integration, and adjustment will be considerably correlated. Yet the maladapted suicide may be integrated about the idea of death; the unintegrated, pampered youth of P. G. Wodehouse's stories, or a happy manic, may be well adjusted, and a courtesan may be adjusted but not adapted.

Finally, these concepts, like that of intelligence, are not normative, when this term is used in the sense that the average is the standard of perfection from which all are measured. One might have a whole community of maladjusted and maladapted neurotics and still recognize their deficiency. For, at least theoretically, we have a standard of a dynamically efficient mind, free from "kinks" and conflicts, and from which all actual minds fall short, as all machines fall short of being frictionless. Integration is examined more fully in Chapter 21.

**Conscious Integration and the Formation of Sentiment Structures.** This discussion of integration now permits us to perceive certain attributes of sentiments with which we have not previously complicated the picture. The general distinction made between complexes and sentiments has been that the latter are conscious and integrated. But this is only relative, and in the last resort an appreciable proportion of sentiments grow on the foundation of complexes, or at least through such processes as ego-defense dynamisms.

---

[8] The usual sequence, of course, will be for conflicting external courses of action to be thrown back eventually into the internal conflicts of maladjustment; but not with a sufficiently insensitive person, *e.g.*, a psychopath.

Some varied examples from the writer's clinical and general observation are as follows: A young man opens the Bible at random and, on the strength of the verse under his finger, takes up the career of a missionary, building in the course of the next thirty years a massive sentiment thereon.  A man with a phobia for small spaces has in consequence a distressing experience in a "cell" in a Gothic building.  He develops an antipathy for Gothic style, talks much about its "defects," and spreads the antipathy to include most of the works of the Middle Ages.  A youth who has been under psychotherapeutic examination for a disability which proves to rest on a mother fixation gets engaged soon after to a girl greatly resembling his mother (though he is very surprised when this is pointed out later).  He develops the powerful sentiments thereon of a stably married man to his wife.

In these cases we see, first, a displacement onto some object, springing from unconscious, repressed drives; followed by the development of a sequence of attitudes forming a conscious sentiment.  Or we see a development of a sentiment by reaction formation, rationalization, or some other defense dynamism.  Normally, as seen in the examination of sentiments in the dynamic lattice (page 158), a series of subsidiations in attitudes can be consciously traced, *i.e.*, the whole is integrated, until one reaches the basic drive concerned, at which the trail passes into the unconscious id.  This is to say, the individual, when you examine his sentiment to his sweetheart, comes to the end of his ability to answer when you ask him, "But why do you find the curve of her neck so attractive?"  Presumably one has come to an innate ergic response.  But in many cases the conscious subsidiation ends in something other than an ergic pattern, namely, in an irrational love, hate, or fear which is personal, peculiar, and evidently due to a complex, an unconscious displacement, of the mechanism of which the individual is not aware.  The subsidiation chains of sentiments also pass in *and* out of the unconscious at higher levels, due to complexes, but at the foundation of the sentiment they pass into the id, either to basic drives or, perhaps with equal frequency, to complexes.  One would expect that sentiments founded directly on drives would have a different quality and greater stability than those which stand on complexes.

**Modes of Sentiment Growth.**  With this addition it is now possible to summarize more completely the chief modes by which sentiments arise, as follows:

1. By accidental, repeated satisfaction of otherwise unsatisfied drives (or by conditioning), with respect to a particular object, a habit structure is induced.

2. Through similarity, contiguity, or by symbolic connection, a displacement to a particular sentiment object takes place from a repressed drive in an unconscious complex.

3. By reasoning from known needs or existing sentiments, the individual forms further, subsidiary, and subsidiated sentiments necessary to the better satisfaction of the first.

4. In the interests of ego defense, sentiments which happen to give increased feeling of ego security may be acquired largely without conscious recognition of purpose.

**Perspective on Psychodynamics and Personality.** Concentration on dynamic processes, which impress one with their extreme lability, their capacity to create new interests and skills, and the readiness of oscillation between equivalents, etc., can easily lead the student to overestimate the total fluidity of the personality. Indeed psychoanalysis, and particularly the Adlerian offshoot of it, has at times been as extreme as mechanical reflexology in predicting that any form of personality whatever can be fashioned out of a given personality by suitably readjusting the ergic flow, at conscious and unconscious levels. It is necessary to keep in mind, therefore, while in the midst of studying psychodynamics, that patterns of dynamic adjustment are limited for any given person, first by the increasing disposition rigidity or functional autonomy of drives with age;[9] second, by the fixed temperamental and ability dimensions of personality with which the dynamic traits have to operate, and third, by fixity of the cultural environment to which the person has to adjust.

The system of analyzing the processes of human adaptation, adjustment, and integration into six major crossroads, as given here, is thus primarily a qualitative analysis which needs to be implemented with quantitative data regarding specific dynamic, cognitive, or temperamental values in the solution of any individual problem. Further, it must be remembered that it formulates the fate of a single dynamic trait, or of a single trait in conflict with a second dynamic system, and that any actual problem requires simultaneous consideration of many traits. The traits which interact, even those which join in "confluence," may themselves be derivatives from very different stages in the crossroads series. For example, a course of action may satisfy at once a conscious ergic need as at $\alpha 1$, the phantasy from a different, frustrated erg, as at $\gamma 4$, and an unconscious "neurotic" trait, as at $\zeta 3$.

Although the system therefore clears the way for more quantitative treatment, the structural and quantitative facts required for the psychodynamic calculus which could ensue have to be found by further methods and involve further concepts.

### 7. SUMMARY

1. Our concepts of the final stages in mental conflict and internal equilibrium have to rest almost entirely on clinical evidence. The superego is a

---

[9] Freud, for instance has complained that successful outcome in psychoanalytic treatment is decidedly less in men after the age of fifty and women after the age of thirty.

structure, largely unconscious in functioning, largely based originally on the Oedipus attachments, but reinforced by internalized aggression and other drives.   It is the chief source of guilt and one of the chief sources of anxiety. It is subject to both under- and overdevelopment, favoring delinquency and neurosis respectively, due to conditions of upbringing.

2.  The development of stable sentiment structures is not enough to account for the consistency of behavior observable in more developed personalities, and it has been suggested that ultimate integration is to be accounted for only by a conscious sentiment centered on the self and including ego and conscious superego.   This structure can be perceived in observing clinical-type observations on normal and abnormal development, but there remain obscurities about its eventual role.   The self-sentiment is liable to vagaries of development related to those of the superego.

3.  A four-factor theory of anxiety is proposed, namely that it arises from fear of ego dissolution (the internally strange) and fear of punishment, these primary fear responses being modified by the uncertainty about the punishment threat which resides in its anticipatory character and by the stresses and uncertainties connected with responding to symbols instead of concrete stimuli.   Since anxiety is physiologically destructive and akin to pain it tends to provoke the extreme response by the organism which we call repression and which is carried out by the dominant dynamic system.

4.  The process of attempted repression ($\delta 2$ at the fourth crossroads) may result in several stable forms of adjustment already discussed, but opens up the possible requirement of several further internal readjustment processes. This occurs particularly when the ego is impoverished and the id overcharged, a condition likely to follow from regression and abnormal infantile experiences preceding adult trauma.

5.  Ergic regression is to be distinguished from personality regression, though they tend to occur in company.   The causes of ergic regression are not fully understood, but earlier fixations, the need to withdraw from difficulties in expressing matured forms, and contemporary trauma are most important among them.

6.  In this last situation the ego responds by defense mechanisms, which produce characteristic personality developments, and the total dynamic interplay may give rise to neurotic symptoms.   Symptoms are not accidental but are overdetermined by primary gains to the id and superego, and secondary gains to the ego.   The id gain has to be by way of disguises similar to those of dream content, principally leading to symbolic satisfaction.

Study of the neurotic responses brings out more clearly the dynamic processes of equivalence (or displacement), which are to be placed alongside subsidiation as basic necessities in describing dynamic structure and change.

7.  The clinical concepts of psychoanalysis are to be considered in the light

of various proposed modifications, *e.g.*, those of Adler, Jung, Horney; but in so far as these stand critical examination they are merely differences of emphasis nomenclature, leaving basic principles unchanged.

8. Adjustment, integration, and adaptation are related concepts in the sense that a personality high in one is likely to be high in the others, but they are logically distinguishable, adaptation being effectiveness of living, adjustment freedom from internal friction, and integration the extent to which behavior contributes harmoniously to a single life goal or consistent set of goals.

9. It is now seen that sentiments are not *wholly* conscious in their subsidiation chains and that they subsidiate eventually not only to (*a*) ergic satisfactions but also to (*b*) complexes—directly or in connection with ego defenses necessitated by complexes. Thus it follows that new sentiments can come into being in some four ways: by serving (*a*) ergs, (*b*) existing sentiments, (*c*) the displacements required by complexes, (*d*) the needs of ego defenses.

10. The almost unlimited number of dynamic adjustments initially possible for a person, and the continuation of appreciable plasticity to a late age, must not cause us to overestimate the role in personality determination of dynamic processes or to overlook the fact that relatively fixed temperament, ability, and physical characteristics definitely limit the number of possible dynamic adjustments.

### QUESTIONS AND EXERCISES

1. What causes the Oedipus attachment to become an Oedipus complex? Describe the changes in affectionate relations to the parents which occur at this point.

2. What are the conditions of identification and introjection? Describe the role of identification in bringing about self-punishment.

3. Describe the normal development of the self-sentiment and discuss its relation to the ego and superego structures.

4. Describe briefly three styles of upbringing responsible for *insufficient* superego action.

5. Enumerate the $\epsilon$ and $\zeta$ sequels that are possible following an attempted act of repression.

6. Describe the conditions, constitutional and otherwise, which are normally necessary for the onset of neurotic symptoms.

7. Define, and give three illustrations of, neurotic symptoms. How is the choice of a particular symptom determined? Illustrate (*a*) equivalence, and (*b*) subsidiation.

8. Debate the necessity for modification of psychoanalytic principles, in the light of the suggestions of Adler, Jung, and Horney, and of all available evidence.

9. Distinguish adjustment, integration, and adaptation, giving examples of behavior showing each, affected as little as possible by the others.

10. Describe with illustrations the four ways in which sentiment structures come into existence.

### BIBLIOGRAPHY

1. ADLER, A.: *The Practice and Theory of Individual Psychology*, Kegan Paul, Trench, Trubner & Co., London, 1924.

2. CATTELL, R. B.: *Crooked Personalities in Childhood and After*, Nisbet, New York, 1940.
3. ENGLISH, O. S., and G. H. J. PEARSON: *Common Neuroses in Children and Adults*, W. W. Norton & Company, New York, 1937.
4. FLUGEL, J. C.: *Man, Morals and Society: A Psychoanalytic Study*, Gerald Duckworth & Co., Ltd., London, 1945.
5. FLUGEL, J. C.: *Men and Their Motives*, International Universities Press, Inc., New York, 1927.
6. FREUD, A.: *The Ego and the Mechanisms of Defence*, Hogarth Press, London, 1937.
7. FREUD, S.: *The Ego and the Id*, Hogarth Press, London, 1927.
7a. FREUD, S.: The Meaning of Symptoms. In *New Introductory Lectures on Psychoanalysis*, Garden City Publishing Company, Inc., New York, 1933.
8. GUTHRIE, E. R.: *The Psychology of Human Conflict*, Harper & Brothers, New York, 1938.
9. HENDRICK, I.: *Facts and Theories of Psychoanalysis*, Alfred A. Knopf, Inc., New York, 1944.
10. HORNEY, K.: *New Ways in Psychoanalysis*, W. W. Norton & Company, New York, 1939.
11. ISAACS, S.: *Social Development in Young Children*, Harcourt, Brace & Company, Inc., New York, 1933.
12. JUNG, C. G.: *Collected Papers on Analytical Psychology*, Kegan Paul, Trench, Trubner & Co., London, 1920.
13. MEAD, G. H.: *Mind, Self and Society*, University of Chicago Press, Chicago, 1934.
14. MILLER, N., and DOLLARD, J.: *Social Learning and Imitation*, Yale University Press, New Haven, 1941.
15. PHILLIPS, M.: *The Education of the Emotions*, George Allen & Unwin, Ltd., London, 1937.
16. SHAFFER, L. F.: *The Psychology of Adjustment*, Houghton Mifflin Company, Boston, 1936.
17. SPITZ, R. A.: Anaclitic Depression, in *The Psychoanalytic Study of the Child*, International Universities Press, New York, 1947.
18. SYMONDS, P. M.: *The Dynamics of Human Adjustment*, Appleton-Century-Crofts, Inc., New York, 1946.
19. TOLMAN, E. C.: *Purposive Behavior in Man and Animals*, Appleton-Century-Crofts, Inc., New York, 1932.
20. TROLAND, L. T.: *The Fundamentals of Human Motivation*, D. Van Nostrand Company, Inc., New York, 1928.
21. VAUGHAN, W. F.: *The Lure of Superiority*, Henry Holt and Company, Incorporated, New York, 1928.
22. YERKES, R. M.: Conjugal Contrasts Among Chimpanzees, *J. abnorm. soc. Psychol.*, 36: 175–199, 1941.

# CHAPTER 10

## PSYCHOSOMATICS: I. KNOWN FUNCTIONAL PATTERNS

1. Organization of Study of Body-Mind Relations
2. The Role of the Central Nervous System
3. Special Functions of the Frontal Lobes
4. The Role of the Autonomic Nervous System
5. The Endocrine System and Personality
6. More Detailed Examination of the Endocrines
7. The Physiological Patterns of Emotion
8. The Physiology of Ergic Motivation
9. Summary

### 1. ORGANIZATION OF STUDY OF BODY-MIND RELATIONS

**Traditional Backgrounds.** That body and personality behave as aspects of a common, underlying unity has been a supposition in discussion for thousands of years. The particular conceptions and misconceptions that have arisen still influence our thinking, obliquely through our cultural value systems and more concretely through language. For example, most religions, to help combat the ever-present "old Adam" and the tyranny of physical appetites, have generally emphasized the independence of the spirit to the point of claiming its complete separability from the body.

Philosophers, though making no real progress in solving the riddle of matter and consciousness, have introduced verbal formulae, such as "epiphenomenalism," "preestablished harmony," "psychophysical parallelism," etc., the stereotypes in which to some extent affect scientific approaches. On the other hand, many scientists have approached the problem with the crass assumption imported from the physical sciences that all phenomena of consciousness and behavior can or will be understood in terms of laws already known through the investigation of matter. In investigating the correlation of the physical, physiological, and behavioral responses of the organism we must be open-minded to perceive relations of a new causal order.

**Organization of Presentation.** Competing claims to direct the arrangement of the present study are offered by categories of subject matter, by methods and fields of investigation, and by logical order of presentation. When a subject is well developed it is natural to plan exposition around functional units, which in this case might be physiological organs, such as the

270

brain, the autonomic nervous system, etc., or psychological processes, such as emotion, intelligence, drive, or learning. Fortunately, a rivalry of physiological and psychological functional unities is not forced upon us, because in most cases they suggest s'milar categories. On the other hand, with a subject where the evidence is clearer than the conclusions and still needs to be separated from theories of doubtful permanence, the classification of material is better done according to fields of evidence or even methods, *e.g.*, mental changes observed in physical disorders, results from the electroencephalographic method, etc.

From the student's point of view, if not from that of scientific method, it seems best to present first those areas in which some nucleus of order and understanding has already appeared and to organize them in terms of *physiological* functions. Thus, the first of these two chapters on psychosomatics will deal with the well-developed themes constituted by the central nervous system, the autonomic system (including the expression of emotion), the endocrines, etc., in relation to personality. The second chapter will deal with less ordered fields, which will accordingly be organized in terms of areas of evidence or method, *e.g.*, the mental changes observed in physical illnesses, the electroencephalogram, the evidences from artificially produced physiological changes, etc. It is hoped that the first chapter will aid the student in forming his own conclusions from the facts presented in the second.

**Range of Methods and Disciplines.** The variety of specific scientific methods and the range of professional fields of knowledge that are brought to bear here is very great. For example, the bodily associations of mental disease have been studied by methods ranging from those of clinical medicine to cytological microscopy and biochemical analytical methods. Similarly, the personality traits connected with specific physical disorders have been investigated by methods extending from casual, psychiatric personality-rating methods in the work of Dunbar to the more penetrating application of factor-analytic methods in $P$ technique (19,21) using objective mental testing along with biochemical analysis.

Consequently, although the student will be assumed to know only as much *psychology* as has been covered in this book and the preceding general psychology course, it will be necessary for him to read elsewhere such physics, chemistry, physiology, and anatomy as may be lacking in his background. It will also be necessary for him to realize, in view of the above-mentioned unevenness of exactitude in existing methods, where conclusions are obviously approximate because recognizably based on approximate methods, and where both the somatic and psychological data are on a more refined level. The absence of adequate teamwork in research, as well as the above-mentioned immaturity of methods, makes it impossible to arrive in this field at generalizations of sufficient depth to integrate the whole area of study. The student would be more realistic to prepare himself to perceive this realm through a number of relatively isolated, more or less successful exploratory penetrations, which are not yet ready for integration in methods or final concepts.

Recently a more popular wave of interest in the question of relating bodily conditions to personality has occurred through a medical, clinical realization that the effects of mental conflicts upon physiology are far-reaching. Disorders which were previously treated as entirely physical, *e.g.*, stomach ulceration, diabetes, heart disease, are regarded partly as the result of personality stresses and handled by psychotherapy. This has provided us with the new, convenient title of "psychosomatics" for the area we are now studying, but it must not mislead us into supposing that the clinical methods of "psychosomatic medicine" provide the only or even the chief methods and approaches to this broad area of contact of biology and psychology.

## 2. THE ROLE OF THE CENTRAL NERVOUS SYSTEM

**The Cerebral Cortex.** One might reasonably expect that the central nervous system, so obviously the instrument of organized behavior, would be the first to reveal relationships between its structure and the structures of personality. The actual historical course of discovery has, however, yielded most obvious personality relationships to the *autonomic* nervous system. Indeed, until recently, it was only the ability traits from among all the traits of personality that were shown to have any relationship to the central nervous system and cerebral cortex. The first discovered localizations in the cortex were largely areas of specific sensory sensitivity and areas of specific motor control, while the cerebellum was found to function in regard to general motor coordination and balance. Around the sensory areas were found areas of specific sensory associations necessary for apperception. The rest of the cortex was, by inference, a connecting system to provide higher-order associations and the perception of relations, though some areas, notably the frontal lobes, seemed to have little role even in these functions. That intelligence, which from the nature of *g*-saturated intelligence tests seems to be the general power to educe relations and correlate, should prove to be substantially correlated with the total mass of cells in the cortex, is therefore not surprising. Further advances, in the work of Lashley, Hebb, Penrose, and others, need to be made before this identification of intelligence with total cortical action can be expressed in a form free from objections, but in essence this is the trend of findings.

**The Hypothalamus.** General research, including comparative brain anatomy, has proved the cortex to be the seat of discriminative perception and memory (learning) as well as of certain powers of inhibiting and redirecting emotional response; but it points to the phylogenetically older structures —the hypothalamus and the midbrain—as responsible for emotional, vegetative, and ergic (instinctive) action.   Direct stimulation of these areas causes emotional reactions, *e.g.*, anger, or suggestions of drive activity, notably sleep, while injuries to the hypothalamic or thalamic region produce loss of drive, as in Brookhart and Dey's (12) demonstration of loss of sexual reactions in guinea pigs after obliteration (Horsley Clark technique) of part of the hypothalamus.   However, the psychologist who wishes to make further analysis of affective and conative response patterns in terms of neural pathways will find many complications to the above introductory picture.   For example, Harrison (36) found that "sleep drive" behavior was not produced by electric stimulation unless it was of a strength to produce tissue destruction, and Masserman has claimed from some suggestive experiments (56,57) that the hypothalamic theory of emotion is inadequate.   His argument that the emotional response is only a "sham" response, a mere physical grimace, is supported perhaps by the finding that it cannot be conditioned (in cats); that affective reactions can be made to external stimulus situation while the hypothalamus is directly stimulated; and that normal affective reactions can be made after quite extensive thalamic lesions.

Light has been thrown on this matter most recently by the systematic researches of Bard (4) which, however, have been exclusively on the rage response.   He points out that rage reactions persist—indeed with greatly lessened inhibition—in animals with the cerebral cortex removed, but the display of emotion is never adequate if the hypothalamus is removed. Partial, incomplete rage patterns may persist, however, when only mesencephalic, pontile, or bulbar levels remain intact.   He further showed that the usual hyperexcitability on removal of the cortex does not occur—in fact the animal is unusually inhibited and placid—if only the neocortex is removed, leaving the rest of the forebrain (gyrus cinguli, amydala, pyriform lobe, and hippocampus) intact.   From these studies it may be concluded that hypothalamic mechanisms *are* prepotent in expressing such emotion and that several distinct forebrain mechanisms act as a series of checks and balances in permitting emotional expression.

The particular parts of the hypothalamus that are concerned, the extent of possible substitution of new neural arcs for damaged ones, and the relative role of the hypothalamus respectively in affection and conation, thus remain unsettled.   (The last issue opens up the vast question of the relation of the mere "sham" emotion pattern to conative drive and the role of the hypothalamus in translating physiological states into drive.)   An acceptable summary, however, is found in Ingram's evaluation (42) which agrees that the hypothalamus acts first as an organizing, controlling center for vegetative, homeostatic processes of the organism.   These are: temperature regulation, energy metabolism, water and mineral balance, carbohydrate metabolism, and some control of endocrines, the alimentary tract, circulation, and breathing activities. Second, it controls emotional *expression* of all kinds, and the drive behavior at least of sex activity, sleep, and hunger. Some specific localization has been found in the cell group constituted by the *nucleus supra opticus*, but otherwise these functions cannot be located other than in the hypothalamus generally.

**Local Cortical Injuries.** Although, until recently, no specific localization of personality functions could be made in the cortex it was known that cortical injury in general affected more than the specific abilities of the zones concerned. In the first place, injury brings a loss of general mental capacity roughly proportional to the extent of lesions and independent of their locality, as might be expected from the above equation of intelligence with total cortical activity. But there is also general impairment of memory, concentration, and general interest, while the individual becomes easily fatigable, slow in thinking, more than normally affected by alcohol and toxins, unable to work steadily, somewhat depressed and irritable, sometimes sexually impotent, and probable more hysterical and lacking in emotional stability (11,71,72). The chief of these symptoms, it may be noticed, represent the central variables normally present in the *B* factor of personality. From both the pathological and the factor-analytic evidence we may infer the probability that the cortical cells responsible for general intelligence are also responsible for some powers of concentration, recall, and perseverance toward remoter objectives, *i.e.*, for characteristics that enter into behavior of a more dynamic nature.

In equating evidence from normal (*B*-factor) behavior with abnormal, it is to be expected that only the essential core will be the same, since loss of cortical power in an individual previously possessing it will bring social and superego readjustments of a temporary nature (depression, irritability, and perhaps impotence) not seen in the individual normally of lesser cortical capacity. Parenthetically we may note that severe concussion, bringing multiple minute hemorrhages throughout the cortex, produces essentially the same syndrome as in a more severe but more local lesion, as described above.

Cortical lesions produced in a controlled fashion in animals result in a similar picture of decreased intelligence and decreased power of learning or recall for more complex matters (64), but the inability to concentrate comes out more strongly as a general hyperactivity. Beach (6) found the running activity of rats increased more by anterior than posterior lesions and the previously less-active rats to be more affected. Kennard (45) found that ablations in monkeys and chimpanzees had to be extensive to produce hyperactivity. The hyperactivity (pacing around, being readily distracted, etc.) had no relation to internal tensions, hunger, etc., or to sound, but declined with absence of light or removal of the occipital lobes. Finan (34) found that frontal lobe injury in monkeys upset "delayed reaction" performance, but not complex discrimination tasks. The delayed reaction (30 seconds) lost by ablation would, however, be relearned, with difficulty. Other studies show that the operated monkeys suffer more from the distracting (retroactive inhibition) effect of intermediate stimuli.

Lashley (50) summarizes that after cortical loss specific activities such as "new combinations of movement, maze habits, visual memories, [items of] vocabulary, can be restored by persistent training with strong motivation after almost any degree of central nervous destruction. The fundamental changes are not sensorimotor disorders or amnesias but lower intelligence, decreased power of abstraction, slowed learning and reduced retentiveness, loss of interest and spontaneous motivation. There is little evidence that these improve, *i.e.*, become restored with time and training."

Further discussion of the role of the cortex requires concentration on a particular region—the frontal lobes—which, because of the volume of recent work, is best undertaken in a special section.

### 3. SPECIAL FUNCTIONS OF THE FRONTAL LOBES

**Sources of Information.** Evidence on the role of frontal lobes comes largely from (*a*) accidental injuries to human beings, (*b*) experiments on animals, (*c*) leucotomy (cutting of connecting fibers) or lobectomy (excision of brain matter) practiced therapeutically on psychopathological human subjects or animals. Accidental injuries were noticed to produce behavior disorders before exacter methods showed that they also produced some loss of *g*. In general, the individual showed no specific disabilities, but, when he had previously been a person of firm character and mature responsibility, he manifested, after the wounds had healed, a certain unreliability, lack of regard for social responsibilities, increased impulsiveness, a decreased initiative in matters of work and duty, and a decline in foresight.

Psychological measurements on psychologically normal individuals who have had frontal lobe operations, *e.g.*, for tumors, show similar results. There are no losses in specific abilities, but there is a decline in general ability proportional to the amount of tissue lost, a loss of restraint, and in general a more euphoric mood. Leucotomy and lobotomy have been performed on individuals suffering from ineradicable psychotic depressions, anxiety states, and schizophrenic psychoses of long standing, with results insufficiently psychologically distinguishable to justify separate enumeration. From a therapeutic point of view these operations have proved more successful with obsessional phobias and with manic-depressive conditions than with schizophrenia, and more effective with agitated melancholias than uncomplicated depressions, as the studies of Petrie (64a) and Porteus (67), for example, show.

**Conclusions from Frontal Lobotomy.** The changes in personality that ensue, additional to or as part of the general improvement in these pathological states are: a decline in abnormal degrees of self-consciousness (shyness and excessive reserve or egocentricity, limiting social adaptability); a change from depressed to euphoric mood; a change from tormenting anxiety to placidity; but also to lesser reliability; diminished control and inhibition of emotion; some restless excitability; reduced scrupulousness; more lying; less restraint; less response to social hints and more "crass" social behavior; less ability to supply spontaneous, fresh lines of attack on a problem; and less ability to keep several mental sets operative in parallel (41,72,73). As an example of a careful, detailed study in regard to a psychotic condition which typically improves, we may take Mixter's (59) report on bilateral frontal lobectomy in two agitated depressives. Symptoms of anxious agitation, negativism, perseveration, apathy, and laziness disappeared. There was a marked increase in weight and appetite, a partial return of a sense of humor, improved social relations, and a general placidity. Petrie, (64a) who was first to use objective personality tests on an adequate sample of patients before and after operation, found that results could be summarized as a clear-cut and significant change in *three* personality factors: (a) a decrease in general emotionality or neuroticism, *i.e.*, a rise in C factor; (b) an increase in surgency, *i.e.*, a rise in F-factor measures; and (c) the usual decline in B factor, *i.e.*, in general ability.

As there is a state of confusion, with disorientation and memory upset, for three to nine months following the operation, it is not easy to determine the exact nature of the "permanent" effects prior to relearning. Freeman and Watt (32), who have been largely responsible for developing leucotomy as a therapeutic measure, claim that some eighty-five per cent of a typical group of psychotics, including all kinds tried by this therapy, show marked or slight improvement. Sometimes the changes are dramatic, as in a case of chronic hypertension where the blood pressure fell 30 mms. and remained at this level. They have brought more exact evidence concerning the neurological boundaries of the operations on the frontal lobes, showing that the operation mainly consists in severing from the hypothalamus its projection areas on the cortex. By reason of degeneration of fibers back into the thalamus after prefontal lobotomy, they have been able to find the specific areas of the thalamic nuclei that correspond to specific frontal cortical areas.

Experiments on frontal lobes of animals yield a different picture from that of general cortical loss, but one which still does not have any very close relation to that in human beings. Richter and Hawkes (69), on removing the frontal lobes of rats, found behavior most similar to that of a human manic patient. They showed marked hyperactivity on the running wheel, and were savage and irritable, ate much more, and were sexually hyperactive.

The conclusion to be drawn from these changes of behavior, as well as from the neural anatomy, seems to be that the frontal lobes are the principal seat of the inhibitory powers and controlling associations, particularly those residing in memories of painful experience, that operate upon the diencephalon and centers of the hypothalamus expressing emotions and drives. The hypothalamus, in spite of the modifying evidence listed earlier, must be regarded as an organ for expressing ergic behavior in response to internal strength of appetite. The frontal lobes mediate the meaning of the external stimulus, in general inhibiting, but also at times initiating, by reminding of the remoter meaning attached to some immediate stimulus. This last mode of action is proved not only by the loss of initiative through frontal lobe loss but also by the relief from obsessional fears and the improvement of some schizophrenic hallucinations and delusions through lobotomy. In such individuals the past experiences have been unfortunate and constantly initiate wrong lines of conduct leading to an impasse. It is shown also by the decidedly greater success of the operation with agitated than simple depressions, for it is the former (see Chap. 19) that arise from guilt and aggression against the self, rather than from more physiologically determined conditions.

In human beings Freeman and Watt have attempted to summarize their findings by saying that loss of frontal lobe action reduces a "distressing and unyielding consciousness of self" and that the lobes are concerned with "the projection of the individual as a whole into the future," with self-criticism, anticipation, and social sense. This description implies something more than those past associations of drive experiences which we have just indicated above to be connected with the frontal lobes alike in men and animals. It implies foresight and fearsight, but also their connection with the specific idea of the self. It may simply mean that *all* major emotional control in man has to operate through the self-regarding sentiment or superego, and that consciousness of the self is accordingly located where control of emotion and anticipation of social and future punishment grows up. This will be discussed further in Chapter 21 on the psychological self.

### 4. THE ROLE OF THE AUTONOMIC NERVOUS SYSTEM

**Sympathetic and Parasympathetic Systems.** After the central nervous system the autonomic system needs next to be reviewed; for without correct appreciation of its action all the facts on body-mind relation, and especially on the somatics of emotion, cannot be integrated. As the student knows from his general psychology course, the autonomic nervous system is phylogenetically older than the central and is divisible into two functionally somewhat independent and definitely complementary sections, the sympathetic or thoracic-lumbar system, and the parasympathetic with preganglionic fibers from the cranial and sacral regions of the central nervous system.

The functions of the autonomic system are mainly those vegetative and emotional organization functions mentioned in connection with the hypothalamus, for the hypothalamus is the chief link between the autonomic and the central nervous system. The autonomic has control of heartbeat and breathing, of the vasomotor system and blood circulation generally, of most of the endocrine gland system and other glands such as the salivary and sweat glands, of the processes in the alimentary canal, the maintenance of body temperature, and the balance of chemicals in the blood stream. Among these the sympathetic system is most concerned with the "energy-spending" or catabolic process, chiefly in the adjustment of the body to emergency conditions such as are created by asphyxia, loss of blood, extreme cold, and to external emergency conditions creating fear or rage. The parasympathetic is anabolic, conserving and building up, favoring the normal processes of digestion and also such pleasurable emotions as those of sex. Attempts have been made to divide personalities into types according to the predominance of one of the two systems, but it is not certain that an individual could remain healthy with one continuously predominating, nor in fact has statistical evidence of such personality patterns being connected with physiological variables yet been presented.

Functionally the autonomic system differs from the central nervous system in having a comparatively rudimentary sensory service (in fact it is generally discussed as a motor system), and in tending to act as a whole and in a relatively all-or-nothing fashion (at least in the sympathetic branch). Anatomically it differs in having most of its synapses and ganglia outside the bony protection of the skull and cord, in having few of its nerves myelinated, and in being connected much more with smooth than striated muscle. The sympathetic and parasympathetic are connected to much the same organs but act in opposite senses. For example, the sympathetic accelerates the heartbeat, inhibits action of stomach, rectum, and bladder, and contracts arteries, whereas the parasympathetic inhibits heart action, causes stomach contraction and secretion, initiates urination and defecation, and dilates arteries.

**Physiological Associations.** Unlike the central nervous system, the autonomic in its action at synapses and end plates involves definite chemical transmission, an adrenalinlike substance being liberated by the sympathetic system and a substance called *acetylcholine* being liberated by action of the parasympathetic. For this reason the sympathetic system, which also liberates adrenalin directly from the gland, is called *adrenergic* and the parasympathetic *cholinergic,* though the former also has a few cholinergic nerve fibers. As Morgan (60) points out, the greater diffusibility of adrenalin without destruction (acetylcholine is destroyed by cholinesterase) conforms with the tendency of the sympathetic to act as a whole and with the tendency of the parasympathetic to act more specifically. In both, the action of the accompanying chemical is such as to further the direct action of the autonomic nerves themselves. Attempts to trace distinct sympathetic and parasympathetic arcs through the hypothalamus have not yet been successful. Cannon sectioned the midbrain at several levels and showed that at a level below the hypothalamus the individual reactions exist but the pattern is lost. Chang (22) stimulated afferent autonomic nerves and claimed that stimulation of the vagus caused liberation at synapses in the midbrain, of acetylcholine, which then stimulated secretion of adrenalin through the sympathetic response engendered; but anatomical and physiological knowledge is not yet at a sufficiently confirmed level here to suggest solutions, or pose new problems, to the psychologist.

**Personality Patterns and Autonomic Action.** Among the more thoroughgoing attempts to relate autonomic function to personality are those of Darling (27) and Darrow (28) based on the latter's suggestion that differential effects on the psychogalvanic reflex and on blood pressure will suffice to distinguish sympathetic and parasympathetic action. A factorization was made by eight autonomic reaction measures and six personality-trait ratings on fifty-eight children over eight years old. Four factors were found, one loading *H*-like personality traits (Chaps. 2, 3, and 4) but no physiological measures, a second loading hyperactivity and low skin resistance, and two loading autonomic variables as follows:

> 1. *Sympathetic (Adrenergic) Reactivity*
>    Conductance.............................. 0.70
>    P.G.R. minus systolic blood pressure......... 0.80
>    Systolic blood pressure..................... 0.54
> 2. *Parasympathetic (Cholinergic) Activity*
>    P.G.R. response (average).................. 0.71
>    Systolic blood pressure..................... 0.72
>    Conductance.............................. 0.30

It is reported additional to the ratings that the most alert individuals had low blood pressure and high psychogalvanic response (cholinergic pattern) and the most somnolent the converse, but that individuals with high cholinergic factor balanced by high sympathetic factor were also alert. In a further study, with psychotic patients, Darrow observed that those showing most hostility to the examiner and most confusion and delusion had small P.G.R. and high blood pressure responses.

There are puzzling features about the above factorization, and we shall turn to the elucidation of such factors by further researches. The studies of Herrington, Darrow and Heath, Freeman and Katzoff, Miller and Wenger summarized by the present writer elsewhere (20) give confirmation of only three factors in this realm, one labeled *Total Autonomic Activity*, another generally recognized as *Sympathetic Activity*, and another *Thyroid Activity*, the last matching the hyperactive, low resistant factor above, while the parasympathetic factor is poorly defined, and different in Miller's study from the above. The variables highly affected by the first two are as follows:

*General Autonomic Activity* (T. (SF) I in the standard series (20))
  Basal metabolic rate (per unit weight)
  Pulse rate
  Blood pressure
  Body temperature
  P.G.R. response magnitude
*Sympathetic, Adrenergic, Tension Pattern* (T. (SF) II in the standard series (20))
  Pulse rate
  Respiration rate
  P.G.R. minus systolic pressure
  Conductance

The first of these, in Herrington's careful study (38), was found positively correlated with several personality characteristics, specifically with activity level, aggression and drive, vigor in athletics, physical tempo, excitable speech and pressure for expression in social situations, energy and enthusiasm in work, and perhaps with greater professional success when intelligence is held constant.

**Evidence on Reaction Patterns from *P* Technique.** A more delicate method for revealing psycho-physiological patterns is that of *P* technique, in which a single individual is measured in many psychological and physiological variables each day for a hundred days or so. The series thus formed on the different variables are correlated to show degrees of covariation of those variables in response to inner trends and outer stimulus changes. The independent functional unities are then isolated by factor analysis. The study by Cattell and Luborsky yielded ten such factors of which the three following seem most likely to be connected largely with autonomic action. These have been confirmed also in the *P*-technique study by Williams (84), and the following loadings, where starred, show that the items occurred in both discovered patterns and are the mean for the two studies (21,84):

| *Factor 1* | *Approximate Loading* |
|---|---|
| Large P.G.R. deflection magnitude | 0.70* |
| High ratio of emotional to nonemotional words recalled | 0.70* |
| High pulse and blood pressure | 0.60 |
| Rating of "sociable" | 0.50* |
| High basal metabolic rate | 0.50* |
| Rating of "vigorous" | 0.50* |
| Large ratio of pupil to iris diameter | 0.50 |
| High skin resistance | 0.40* |
| High critical frequency of flicker fusion | 0.40 |
| Brief duration of after-images | 0.40 |

Factor 1 closely resembles Herrington's general autonomic activity factor mentioned above. The ratings indicate that in terms of behavior it is the *H* factor, contingently called "adventurous cyclothymia." We shall conclude that these patterns—the above physiological and the rating pattern—are the inward and outward expressions of the same "*H*" factor.

| *Factor 2* | *Approximate Loading* |
|---|---|
| Low skin resistance (high conductance) | 0.70* |
| High pulse pressure | 0.60* |
| High pH (alkalinity) of saliva | 0.60 |
| High irritable emotionality | 0.60* |
| Large performance upset by noise distraction | 0.50 |
| High glucose concentration in blood | 0.50 |
| High lymphocyte count | 0.40 |
| Long dark adaptation period of eye | 0.40 |
| High pulse rate | 0.40* |
| Moderately large P.G.R. deflections | 0.40 |

Factor 2 seems to be a more complete and, it might be argued, more carefully rotated, picture of the sympathetic, adrenergic factor in the above reported studies. Among the *P*-technique studies a third clear factor occurred, as follows:

| *Factor 3* | *Approximate Loading* |
|---|---|
| High skin resistance | 0.60* |
| Rating "relaxed" (and large skin resistance rise in relaxation period) | 0.60* |
| Low cholinesterase in the blood | 0.60 |
| P.G.R. response magnitude | 0.50* |
| Briefer dark adaptation period of the eye | 0.50 |
| Frequency of urination (and volume of urine) | 0.45 |
| Small difference in upward and downward flicker fusion frequency | 0.40 |
| Slow pulse rate | 0.40* |
| Low blood sugar (glucose) | 0.40 |

Factor 3 seems to be substantially what is generally described as the parasympathetic or vagotonic factor, some aspects of which have already appeared in the factorizations with fewer variables mentioned above. Additional *R*- and *P*-technique studies are now required, exploring a larger range of variables, to see what else belongs in these factors and to define the loadings of the pattern in the general population more precisely.

Meanwhile, whatever the ultimate interpretation in autonomic part-actions may be, there can be no doubt of the existence of psychosomatic factors or source traits defined in the first instance by (*a*) large P.G.R. response, high blood pressure, ratings of sociable and vigorous, and tests of "alertness," and emotional responsiveness; in the second by (*b*) low skin resistance, high pulse rate and pressure, and signs of irritability; and (*c*) high skin resistance, high proneness to relaxation, large P.G.R. responses, large urine production, and probably low cholinesterase. Contingently these may respectively be labeled *Autonomic Vigor, Sympathetic Overaction* and *Parasympathetic Inhibition or Relaxation.*

## 5. THE ENDOCRINE SYSTEM AND PERSONALITY

**Endocrines and the Nervous System.** It may be desirable to begin this section by stimulating the recollection of, but not repeating, the necessarily simplified description of the endocrine glands given to the student in general psychology. He may recall that the pancreas, the thyroid, the pituitary, the adrenal medulla, the adrenal cortex, the parathyroid, the thymus, the stomach, the intestines, and the gonads contain organs of internal secretion, whatever other functions they may have. Further, one may suspect that there are other hormones or enzymes not yet known to us, but functioning in the same catalytic fashion, from similar anatomically obscure internal gland cell sources.

The endocrines have important vegetative functions, such as the regulation of blood sugar, of oxygen consumption, of the water balance, of fat deposition, of calcium metabolism, and of ovulation, as well as exerting those influences on behavior which make them of especial interest to the psychologist. They form, with the autonomic nervous system, a codirectorship in these vegetative administration tasks which is peculiar in that no single controlling member stands at the head of it. Very few endocrine glands have any controlling innervation from the autonomic nervous system or, more directly, from the cortex. The adrenal medulla is strongly directly affected by the sympathetic nervous system, while the adrenal cortex and perhaps the stomach are also affected by sympathetic stress, and the pituitary may be affected directly by the brain. But the rest, as is well demonstrated in the case of the thyroid, "live their own lives," except in so far as they respond to chemical messengers in the blood stream from other endocrines or from other bodily products.

**Initial View of the Adrenal and Thyroid Glands.** Briefly, the specific functions of the glands may be recapitulated as follows: (*a*) the hormone insulin (from the pancreas) makes sugar available to the cells, and mental symptoms of confusion and eventually unconsciousness follow on its failure; (*b*) adrenalin from the adrenal medulla releases stored sugar from the liver, releases red corpuscles to increase the oxygen-carrying power of the blood, relaxes the smooth muscle of the alimentary canal and constricts that of certain blood vessels, increases the coagulability of the blood, etc. Deficiency of adrenalin is associated with effeminacy, partly because of secondary action on the sex glands, and with lack of vigor and inability to meet stress situations; (*c*) cortin, from the adrenal cortex, is a mixture of a dozen or more steroid hormones, which have been demonstrated to restrict the elimination of sodium and of water. Since sodium ions help maintain the sensitivity of the nervous system a defective cortin supply means a low level of general activity. Cortin specifically postpones the effects of fatigue; (*d*) thyroxin regulates the oxidation of sugar and the general metabolic rate, and perhaps through these the rate of growth and development. As is well known, deficient amounts, as in myxedema and cretinism, spell mental sluggishness and apathy, dulling of intelligence, and permanent defect of development if allowed to operate over a long period in the childhood development stages. Excess does not increase normal intelligence but brings irritability and tension; (*e*) parathormone, from the parathyroids, increases calcium in the blood, which decreases nerve excitability. Its lack causes excitability and convulsive tetany of muscles; (*f*) The gonads induce secondary sex characteristics, mental and physical. Males low in testosterone and androsterone are less dominant and less active, while the female low in estrin is also less active, and, if low in progesterone, is likely to lack maternal feeling.

**Initial View of the Pituitary Secretions.** The hormones of (*g*) the pituitary, need a little more discussion even in a brief recapitulation, because of the complexity of the gland and the importance of its hormones. The posterior lobe, which possesses nerve cells, secretes pituitrin (probably consisting of several distinct but related chemicals) which is responsible most obviously for inhibiting water excretion. The anterior hormone, also a combination of several hormones, controls, through the hormone phyone, the general growth, particularly affecting the long bones and the sexual organs, causing dwarfism, gigantism, acromegaly, and sexual infantilism. Through the diabetogenic hormone it acts oppositely to insulin, raising the blood sugar level. Finally, the anterior hormone includes a number of substances called "tropic" hormones, which act as chemical messengers stimulating the other endocrines. Thus the thyroid, the adrenal, the gonads, the parathyroid, and the pancreas are stimulated to secrete thereby and, conversely, tend to atrophy if the anterior pituitary fails. The psychological results of pituitary failure are obscure as far as abilities and reactivities are concerned, but very significant in regard to the total personality. Although the specific nature of the temperamental instability induced is not agreed upon, and although some distortions of personality may arise secondarily from the social effects of pituitary physical deformities, the association of pituitary dysfunction with behavior disorder is very real and direct.

**Endocrine Interaction.**  Of the known interactions of the endocrines in their interlocking directorate, the most systematic effects are those from the gonadotropic, adrenotropic, etc., hormones just mentioned and which place the pituitary in the position of the keystone in the endocrine structure. However, there exist other important interactions, such as that of the adrenal gland in stimulating the secretion of the gonads as well as the secretion of the thyroid.  In these interactions it is necessary to bear in mind that there occur both *direct* stimulation or suppression and *indirect* interaction through glands opposing one another's effects in the body or acting as substitutes in producing a common effect.

### 6. MORE DETAILED EXAMINATION OF THE ENDOCRINES

*Research on the Thyroid.*  More detailed, more recent, and less organized findings will now be considered separately for each of the glands, beginning with the thyroid.  Experiments on animals show that rats made hyperthyroid by being fed excess thyroxin are more excitable and active.  Sooner than the controls they learn to cross water (as an obstacle), to run a maze, and to make choice-box choices.  Some studies find that removal of the thyroid does not, however, affect learning, retention, or reversal of a habit. This, however, is a difficult operation to perform successfully.  In dogs, hyperthyroidism has been found to produce some stomach upset, greater stomach activity, and quicker passage of food through the intestine.  Hall and Lindsay found that the amount of voluntary activity in rats was proportional to basic metabolic rate.  Anderson (2) found a significant negative correlation of thyroid development and sexual activity in rats.  Collins (23) nevertheless found that thyroxin secretion level in hens was a significant factor in order of dominance as established at first encounter.

Clinical observations on human beings have suggested that thyroid activity should correlate with intelligence, but experiment shows the correlation of gland *size* to be only slightly positive in young children and absent in older people.  The clinical picture of hypothyroidism, as in myxedema, is one of depression, irascibility, suspiciousness, and delusion.  In milder cases there is abnormal fatigue, loss of initiative, nervousness, mental apathy, and abnormal desire to sleep (83).  Hyperthyroidism also presents a high incidence of people "difficult to live with," because of nervous restlessness, "unreasonableness," and alternating excitement and depression. A detailed study of an individual known to be definitely overdosed with thyroxin, but otherwise normal, has been presented by Thomson (82).

Studies (24,78) of series of hyperthyroid cases in Basedow's and Grave's diseases show that some constitutional factor exists (and women are twice as liable as men) and that these individuals were mother dependent, afraid of parental responsibilities, etc. But they also show that, despite the lack of thyroid innervation, the gland somehow responds to emotional stress, for a very high percentage showed a history of psychological trauma and stress.

**The Parathyroid.** The hypoparathyroid syndrome has a superficial resemblance to hyperthyroidism, being marked by restlessness and emotional instability. The work of Dda (30) indicates that the symptoms of calcium deficiency should be separated from those of hormone deficiency per se. The symptoms relieved by calcium gluconate feeding are: tetany and physical slowness, dullness and paresthesias of senses, poor balance, confusion, inability to express emotion, loss of initiative, fear, and depression. Symptoms apparently more dependent on the hormone are the extreme sensitivity which causes timidity, certain traits of overconscientiousness, and an over-acute sensitivity to impressions.

**More Detailed View of Adrenal Gland Action.** The physiological and psychological effects from the adrenal medulla and cortex have been extensively investigated with animals. Hartman and others have shown that adrenalectonized animals manifest ready fatigue, lack of activity, loss of appetite, and finally vomiting, coma, and death. The inactivity is partly due to sheer muscle asthenia, since muscle preparation ceases more quickly to respond without adrenalin. With adrenal hypofunction Benetato observed that (8) histamine causes a drop in blood pressure, and he inferred that repeated performance against fatigue, as in athletes, causes adrenal hyperfunction. He also found better glandular response in pyknics than in leptosomes. Administration of cortin tends to remove fatigue but does not raise the level of spontaneous activity and emotional excitement, as does adrenalin. The role of adrenalin in the level of emotionality is discussed in the next section.

Recent explorations have been concerned with the relation of adrenalin to acetylcholine, since the key to the understanding of certain mood states seems to be there. Burn (16) finds that though they are antagonistic in the autonomic nervous system, in nervous tissue itself a rising adrenalin concentration first augments and then reduces the facilitating action of acetylcholine (and therefore the general tonus of muscle). This is confirmed by Bülbring (15) and others. It has relevance to the theory of manic-depressive disorder put forward in Chapter 18.

**Evidence on Gonadal Hormones.** Animal studies on sex hormones are too numerous to mention individually, though those of C. P. Stone (79,80) and F. A. Beach (6) deserve especial reference for systematically continued advances. Through such studies it is known that sex patterns of behavior tend to be retained if castration occurs after puberty; that if lost they can be restored by testosterone injections; that in hens, rats, chimpanzees, etc., the dominance order is closely dependent upon and can be altered by changes in the male sex hormone level;[1] that male behavior patterns (singing, courtship, aggression) can be induced in females by testosterone; that general activity level, but not learning capacity, is affected by the animal having appropriate level of male or female sex hormones. The voluntary activity level in castrated rats does not, however, have a relation of simple proportionality to the amount of testosterone injected.

In human males testosterone injections have not been found to produce changes in most cases of impotence, homosexuality, or schizophrenia, where psychological causes for the sexual abnormality may therefore be assumed to predominate. However, with younger adults, and particularly with boys and girls just prior to puberty, personality changes both with respect to sex interests and to more general traits have been observed. Bize and Moricard (10) administered testosterone to a small group of boys over some months and believed they observed increased strength, intellectual curiosity, aggressiveness, self-assertion, and detachment from the family group. Sollenberger (76) had ten thirteen year-old boys rated for maturity of behavior, interests, and attitudes. Their maturity of interests, attitudes to girls and to personal appearance, as well as participation in strenuous sports, correlated more with amounts of androgen in the urine than with chronological age. There is still much room for research here, with larger groups, better personality measures, and a breakdown of gonadal hormones into half a dozen distinct contributors. There is also need for investigation of causality in the reverse direction—*i.e.*, of mental upon physical conditions. Steinach (77) isolated male rats from females for six to nine months and found distinct gonad atrophy, which disappeared on return to mating. The nervous and physiological mechanisms here need investigation.

**More Detailed Evidence on the Pituitary.** The pituitary still remains a considerable puzzle and, because of anatomical difficulties, is less investigated. Removal of the pituitary stops the inhibition of bladder action by emotional stress through the adrenal gland and seems to upset the action of other endocrines (60,61). It does not, however, seem to interfere with mental ability and learning in animals (or humans) providing the motivation can be retained. Conditioning and extinction of reflexes in dogs were actually found to proceed a little quicker. However, "temperamental" changes follow, for removal of the pituitary in puppies upsets their growth, causes them to be more easily fatigued, to show little or no play, and to be cranky

---

[1] Collins, (23) with hens, found (*a*) male hormone, (*b*) thyroxin, (*c*) social rank in home flock, and (*d*) body weight, important (in that order) in determining dominance, and that a multiple *r* of 0.75 with dominance could be obtained from these four factors.

and irritable.  Conversely, animals (rats) fed anterior pituitary in excess grow more rapidly and reach a greater final size of body, but not of nervous system, and are healthy and active.

Observations on human reactions are largely clinical.  Levy (52) studied thirty-three boys with Fröhlich's hypopituitary syndrome and found a preponderance of submissive behavior, in contrast to the antisocial action sometimes reported.  He believes this is not a consequence of psychological history or of psychological response to the social "stigma" of the physique.  Conversely, Brown (13) found that anterior pituitary excess seemed to be associated with boldness and lack of inhibition.  Molitch studied 269 boys in a behavior correction institution and found 25 per cent had endocrine disorders of which one-half were pituitary dysfunctions.  Such findings have occurred repeatedly, *e.g.*, Lurie (53), but would be more convincing if adequate control groups had been taken to show that certain exact degrees of pituitary dysfunction were statistically far less frequent in controls.  However, results all trend this way, and are in agreement with the high percentage of pituitary dysfunction found in psychotics generally.

Other endocrines have not been extensively investigated, though the finding of Bruner and Cunningham (14) on the thymus deserves mention as substantiating early views as to its antagonistic action to the gonads.  Although working on only seven female rats they obtained, through thymus injections, decided declines in copulation frequency, aggression, and ability to evoke male responses.

**Relation to General Endocrine Action.**  The general extent of the effects of endocrine disorder on personality may perhaps be gauged from Lurie's finding (53) in examining 1000 problem children that 20 per cent showed glandular disorders and most—46 per cent of these—were pituitary in nature, while thyroid disorders ranked second.  There is no doubt, however, that, over and above imbalances in individual glands, the *total effectiveness of the whole glandular system* relates to personality.  Yeakel and Rhoades (85) and Hall (35) have shown, for example in rats, that it is possible to breed selectively more and less emotional rats and they have then shown that the former have larger weight of adrenals, thyroid, and pituitary glands.  The same has been investigated with more sensitive methods by Anderson and Anderson (2) who found low correlations between sexual activity of rats and the weight of gonads and pituitary, more with adrenal, and a slight but significant negative correlation with thyroid.  Their results, indicating a slight *negative* correlation of emotionality with glands other than the adrenal and thyroid, suggest that the commonly accepted emotionality measure in rats is a measure of *fearful emotionality* only, and that the adrenal and thyroid weights must have predominated in the gland weight in the Yeakel and Rhoades studies.

In man, as a survey of the literature and the above specific endocrine accounts shows, the removal of part or all of almost any gland, at least of thyroid, pituitary, adrenal, or gonads, results in decreased activity. (The parathyroid is eccentric, but the increased activity is not permanent.) Large amounts of activity of the kind that the gland serves, *e.g.*, vigorous physical activity in the adrenal, sex activity in the gonads, tend to increase gland size—indeed adrenals and gonads increase under any increase of physical activity. But the main determiners of energy as such seem to be the thyroid and the adrenal gland, the former affecting the constant energy level, especially with respect to nervous metabolism, and the latter the emergency energy, especially of muscle and physical activity. Comparative anatomy and psychology bear out this summary, for man, with a larger brain, has a larger thyroid, whereas animals have larger adrenals, and, to a lesser degree the same difference holds, according to Crile (25), for civilized and natural man.

### 7. THE PHYSIOLOGICAL PATTERNS OF EMOTION

**Associations of Fear and Anxiety.** The apparatus of hypothalamus, autonomic nervous system, and endocrines so far discussed shows one of its most coordinated activities in the expression of emotion—indeed, as every student knows, it was through the bodily phenomena of emotion that attention was first called to many parts of these structures.

It seems to have been overlooked by many writers on emotion that practically all the psycho-physiological generalizations about emotion are actually on one only of the dozen or more possible primary emotions, namely, on fear. The concentration of experiment on fear, or less frequently, on anger, is a natural consequence of their being more easily aroused in experimental situation.

The typical physiological response pattern in fear is largely that of the sympathetic nervous system; a quickening of the heartbeat, rise of blood pressure, quicker breathing, dilation of the pupil, sweating, hair standing on end, blanching of the skin through closing of the capillaries, shifting of the blood from the viscera to the big muscles, an increase of adrenalin in the blood, an increase of blood sugar and red corpuscle concentrations through excretion from the liver and spleen, respectively, an increase of blood coagulability, and an arrest of stomach and intestinal movement. Some of these effects are produced by direct autonomic innervation, some, with a few seconds' delay, by adrenalin, and most by both acting in union. Most of the bodily changes are obviously useful, purposive emergency measures, and cannot be maintained for long periods without the organism suffering from digestive troubles, constipation, defective circulation and nutrition, high blood pressure, etc.

Studies on animals show that (in cats) in emotional responses to stress the blood-fat (cholesterol) level, as well as the blood sugar, is raised, that there is an increase in nonprotein nitrogen, in urea, creatinine, uric acid, and hemoglobin, but no change in amino acids, calcium, or chlorides (43). The metabolic rate increases sharply, proteins as well as carbohydrates being consumed, and histamine is produced. Benedict (7) observes that an intense emotional experience causes an increase of metabolism that may not subside for several days. There is loss of weight and loss of body protein. Prolonged emotion, indeed, produces in some cases—how infrequently or abnormally we do not know—a partially or totally irreversible increase in blood pressure or gland action.

Recent and more detailed studies may be represented by Ahronheit's finding in urine specimens from 388 combat fliers that albuminuria was common after stress, had no relation to age but was less in officers (1). Emotional stress in battle, as Podolsky (66) has observed, produces impotence more widely and quickly than any civilian stress and is not generally relieved by testosterone. Here is a mechanism, possibly related to the above discussed antagonism of thyroids and gonads, needing illumination. The detailed mechanisms of more long-established connections have in many cases become clearer; for example, the inhibition of urine secretion has been found to be brought about more immediately by splanchnic nerve action and, secondarily, by posterior pituitary antidiuretic hormone, though adrenalin tends to suppress the latter. The pituitary then plays some part in stress reactions, but whether through adrenal stimulation, as in the case of the thyroid, or more directly is uncertain.

**The Physiological Creation of Emotion.** Interest in the James-Lange theory, with its hypothesis that the consciousness of emotion is really consciousness of this physiological reverberation, has declined, as the impossibility of bringing consciousness scientifically into psychology has become apparent. But certain aspects of the problem, cast in new terms, require an answer, and can receive one partly from work done in response to the original introspective problem. For example, there is the question as to whether an emotion is defined and particularized by occurrences in the central nervous system or by occurrences in the viscera, and as to which of these patterns occurs first in response to the cognitive stimulus. Then there is the related problem of *what* particularizes and distinguishes one emotion from another. (Emotions are initially identified or labeled by the ergic activities and goals with which they are associated, though we must bear in mind that an emotion is not a drive.)

The question as to whether the injection of adrenalin alone will produce the conscious experience of emotions and the external bodily expressions of emotions as they appear from central excitation was originally answered by

Marañon and by Cannon in dubious vein, by saying that the subjects had a
"cold" emotion, "as if" afraid or sorrowful.   Repetition of the experiment
with more careful controls by Cantril and Hunt (18) on normals, and Landis
and Hunt (47) on psychotics, showed that genuine emotional responses,
chiefly of fear or anxiety but also of pleasurable excitement, with tremor,
heightened pulse, etc., appeared in many but not all subjects.   Parenthetically, the fact that schizophrenics showed decided reactions militates against
the notion that the incapacity to experience emotion is the basic condition
in schizophrenia.

**Specificity of Patterns of Emotion, Fatigue, Etc.**   Differentiation of emotional patterns is still incompletely understood.   Diethelm watched the
curves of blood-sugar "tolerance" and found that "acute sudden emotions
raise blood sugar more than strong emotions of long duration."   But in
moods of elation or depression unmixed with anxiety, no blood-sugar changes
akin to those in fear or rage could be found.   Diethelm (31) and others also
found some distinction between anxiety, resentment, and anger on the one
hand, and fear on the other, in that the former had more adrenergic, the
latter more cholinergic factors.   Depressed and elated states showed a
mixture of both.   Arnold (3), however, claims that fear is predominantly
sympathetic and that anger has a strong parasympathetic excitement.
Although the visceral patterns remain obscure, several experimenters have
shown a 60 to 90 per cent correct judgment of emotion from tones of voice
and about the same from photographs of facial-muscle movement.   Fay
and Middleton (33), however, found judgments of the trait of self-confidence,
from the voice alone, to correlate only $0.13 \pm 0.02$ with ratings.

One of the most clearly defined somatic patterns is that of the startle
reaction, as investigated by Hunt and Landis (40).   The patterns of rage,
fear, and affection as described by Watson and Morgan have not received
good confirmation from other studies, and Dennis has indeed shown that the
supposed specific stimuli for these emotions e.g., restriction of movement for
anger, were not correctly defined by Watson.   The external patterns of
these emotions are, however, stereotyped and recognizable in animals, e.g.,
rage in a cat by the arching of the back.

Whatever the differentiation ultimately obtained (and factor analysis of
visceral data seems the obvious way to obtain it), it is very probable that
some large factor will appear as a pattern common to many forms of emotion
—at least to the emotions roused by nocive stimuli.   For it has been observed
by many, from Cannon onwards, that fear, rage, pain, and severe physical
stress produce much the same visceral response.   The similarity of the effects
of this emotional core to the effects of fatigue also is noteworthy and suggests
some functional design in the production of cortin and adrenalin by the same
glandular organ.

Parode (63) observes that fatigability is high in hypofunction of the adrenals (and of the pituitary). Pincus and Hoagland (65) show that the stresses of flying induce hypersecretion by the adrenal cortex, increased still more by deficient oxygen, and that the cortical steroids (cortin) naturally produced (or the related chemical pregnenolone) and artificially administered reduce the fatigue effects of stress. Riess (70) has similarly shown that in moderately fatigued rats cortical steroids reduce errors and lower times in maze learning.

The "clearing up" process after the upsets produced by the sympathetic reaction is, however, not yet understood.

The importance of emotion study to personality lies immediately in the need to develop more accurate objective measures of emotional reaction and of specific emotions, secondly, in understanding the associations likely to be found with individual differences of emotionality (some studies suggest emotional instability is associated with physiological instabilities), and lastly, in understanding the chief connecting links in the chain from psychological disturbances to physical illness. This last has been extensively discussed by Landis and others (48).

## 8. THE PHYSIOLOGY OF ERGIC MOTIVATION

**Simple Appetitive Relationships.** Brief attention has already been given in Chapter 8 to the fact that ergs in man and instincts in animals can sometimes be definitely traced to special physiological conditions that operate whenever the drive operates. Although drives have been divided into appetitive or viscerogenic and nonappetitive ergs, the possibility has not been ruled out that the nonappetitive ergs also depend on physiological conditions, though of a more constant and more subtle nature and perhaps more active in the central nervous system than viscerally.

Let us first examine evidence on the extent of physiological determination of specific drives and then proceed to whatever general conclusions are possible. Correlations of drive with physical conditions were first proved in hunger, where the restless seeking for food was found to correspond with periodic stomach movements. However, it is now realized that stomach contractions are only an additional provocation to hunger, for food-seeking has been found to be almost normal in humans or animals deprived of the stomach or deprived of sensory connections with it. Bask (5) and Morgan (60), after experiments with insulin hypoglycemia, concluded that a chemical condition, determined by the amount of sugar stored in the body, is the common cause of stomach motility, consciousness of hunger, and food-seeking restlessness. Further evidence, including a lack of perfect correlation between blood-sugar level and hunger, along with the fact that *some* element in the blood stream determines hunger (transfusion from a starved to an unstarved dog, as Carlson showed, produces hunger), leads Morgan to the conclusion that a hunger hormone arises from the intestine under the influence of sugar lack.

**Detailed Evidence on the Hunger Drive.** Further evidence on the physiological basis of the hunger drive is provided by Margolin and Bunch's (55) experiments showing, in rats, a decline of the strength of the drive, relative to some other drives, with age, and a change in the deprivation time necessary for maximum strength in relation to age. Of special interest have been the researches of Richter (68) and of Young (87) which show that rats definitely seek specific foods, the need for which has been created by some internal chemical condition. For example, pancreatomized rats avoid sugar and seek fats, adrenalectomized rats drink much salt solution to preserve the balance upset by the adrenal function loss, and rats with loss of the pituitary drink large quantities of water to stave off the threatened dehydration. Similar specific, correct cravings have been clearly but less systematically observed in humans, while Davis has shown that young children eating freely automatically balance their diet. The theory of specific hungers put forward by Richter and Young may, however, have to admit limits to specificity.

A curious fact, independently observed by Drew and D. Katz, (44) is that a satiated animal will resume eating after some interpolated stimulus, *e.g.*, a sex stimulus, with no change in the physiological condition. This suggests some positively inhibitory action from the physiological satiation condition, which, like most inhibitions, can be lifted by distraction.

**Physiology of Sleep.** The erg of sleep has long been suspected to have a physiological basis and various waste products have been suggested as the internal provocation for the withdrawal behavior and specific sleep-seeking activities; but the evidence from animals having a common circulation, in which one slept and the other did not, is against the hypnotoxic theory. It is certain, however, that there is a "wakefulness" center in the hypothalamus and mesencephalon, as indicated in Section 2 above, the destruction of which causes constant somnolence. The physiological mechanism here, probably one of inhibition of cortical activity, is thus seemingly nonvisceral, though appetitive in the sense of having a cycle.

**The Parental Erg.** Overwhelming evidence, summarized by Seward (74) indicates that the parental, protective erg in the female animal is strongly conditioned by hormones, notably prolactin. Beach (6) points out that in some species prolactin and progesterone affect both parental behavior and nest-building, though contact with young reciprocally stimulates the physiological secretions. However, the work of Leblond (51) suggests that two distinct drives may be operative in this area, for, in the study of 250 mice, he found nest-building, brooding over the young, and defending the young to be typically physiological and independent of experience, but retrieving, licking, and cuddling of the young seemed to depend more on prolonged exposure to the young in the cage.

**The Sex Erg.** By far the most extensive work on the physiological relationships of drives has occurred with regard to the sex drive. Seward (75) has shown, analogously to hunger, that the drive is not due to afferent "sensory" reception from the sex organs and suggests that the sex hormones must act directly on the brain stem. The effect of testosterone in bringing on early masculine sex behavior in young males (79,80) as well as in inducing the activity in castrates (75) and in females is well known. It is also known that other physiological factors affect the activity; *e.g.*, both in men and in animals low nutrition reduces sex activity, as also does injury to the pituitary or adrenals. A particularly neat demonstration of the action of endocrines in bringing out a reaction pattern has been given by Berg (9) with respect to the appearance of the leg-raising micturition pattern in the male dog.

The role of the central nervous system has also been extensively investigated. Beach (6) found that in rats and some other animals, 50 per cent or more of the cortex could be removed without loss of sex behavior, but in rats and dogs there is reduction of excitability in proportion to amount of cortex removed. Injury to the human cortex, especially if it affects also the hypothalamus, reduces sex drive. Brookhart and others (12) have shown in guinea pigs that with properly placed lesions in the hypothalamus sex behavior practically ceases and cannot be restored by high hormone concentrations. The work of Davis and Domm (29), employing several specific sex hormones, shows pretty conclusively that the various male and female behavior patterns are common to the central nervous system (essentially the hypothalamus) of both sexes and that it is the specific hormone which brings out the appropriate behavior.

**General Physiological Mechanisms of Ergs.** This last observation agrees with the formulation of Lashley (49) on instincts in general: that they are neuron patterns, largely in the diencephalon, which become selectively sensitized by hormones, producing specific perceptual interests and recognitions and specific patterns of response. The *extent* of the behavior is largely determined by the hormone concentration for, as Richter points out, the size of a nest, for example, that a rat will build can be shown to depend on the extent of lowering of body temperature by thyroid removal. The Sewards (74,75) suggest a division of ergs into vegetative and emergency drives. The former involve more the craniosacral (parasympathetic) and begin with hormone or chemical conditions which sensitize a neural mechanism. The emergency drives (fear, anger, etc.) involve the sympathetic system and begin with a neural response through an external stimulus, which induces chemical conditions favoring the continuation of activity. This is adequate for the drives commonly considered experimentally, but leaves room for further explanations in connection with such putative ergs as those of exploration, gregariousness, self-assertion, self-abasement, hoarding, disgust, appeal, and laughter. No physiological basis, other than some neural structure probably located largely in the diencephalon, is indicated in these ergs, though it is, of course, possible, in view of the crudity of present experiment, that some hormonelike substance predisposing to easy reactivity in these directions will later be found.

## 9. SUMMARY

1. Our present knowledge of psychosomatic relations is derived from disparate methods of investigation developed in originally unrelated fields, as well as from methods of very different degrees of accuracy, so that any synoptic generalization has to rest on uneven evidence.

2. In the central nervous system the hypothalamus and midbrain generally have to do with organization of basic emotion and drive pattern, while the cortex is concerned with discrimination and adaptation, *i.e.*, the perception of relations, involving general mental capacity. Nevertheless, a pattern of personality characteristics—perseverance, ability to concentrate, conscientiousness, and self-control—are indicated, both by clinical evidence on brain injury, etc., and by factor analysis, to be a function of general cortical activity or intelligence.

3. The frontal lobes have some degree of specialization in control of emotional and dynamic activities by associations, principally from past punishment, that make the individual foresighted and particularly with respect to the individual's reputation (self-regarding sentiment).

4. The autonomic system handles vegetative and emergency internal bodily adjustments, by means of the adrenergic sympathetic system and the cholinergic parasympathetic. Factorization shows at least three distinct factors in autonomic responsiveness, two of which have definite personality associations.

5. Definite relations of temperamental characteristics to specific endocrine excesses and deficiencies can be recognized when the latter are extreme, but the interaction of endocrines complicates analysis of temperament in these terms.

6. The principal hormones with which personality characteristics as well as bodily functions have been found to correlate are: thyroxin, parathormone, adrenalin, cortin, androgen, estrogen, testosterone, anterior pituitary hormone, and pituitrin. In many cases these relations have not yet been demonstrated as correlations in a normal range.

7. Emotion is associated with a great variety of coordinated physical changes, some caused directly by hypothalamic action, others indirectly

through hormone action. Artificial production of the physical pattern in many cases creates an experience of emotion, different from the normal experience in being out of dynamic context. Differentiation of emotions by visceral patterns is still somewhat conjectural.

8. The emotions occurring in relation to nocive stimulus situations, *e.g.*, fear and anger, have been most studied experimentally. They are mainly responses of the sympathetic branch of the autonomic and have much in common with response to pain and stress. Intense or repeated emotion may leave physical symptoms of long or "permanent" duration.

9. The drive in appetitive ergs is demonstrably closely dependent on physiological factors, though in every investigated instance—hunger, thirst, sleep, sex, parental protection behavior—afferent impulses from the viscera are not adequate to account for the drive.

10. Although ergs vary in pattern, some being appetitive, others emergency, and others neither appetitive nor emergency, it seems that in most sufficiently investigated instances both a central nervous (hypothalamic) structure and a biochemical agent are necessary. The latter sensitizes special paths in the diencephalon, facilitating special perception and reaction. In the case of the sex drive, both sexes have sufficiently similar structure to permit either behavior pattern to emerge, according to the concentration of hormones.

## QUESTIONS AND EXERCISES

1. Enumerate six methodological approaches that have yielded important results in the field of psychosomatics.

2. Describe the effects of cortical lesions upon human and animal behavior, discussing the separation of primary effects from incidental effects and from secondary and adjustive developments.

3. Review evidence available up to the most recent date on the successes and failures of frontal lobectomy and leucotomy (lobotomy) in dealing with mental disorder, and deduce what is possible regarding the function of the frontal lobes.

4. Enumerate the physiological changes that occur in the functioning of sympathetic and parasympathetic nervous systems.

5. Describe mental characteristics found associated with hyperthyroidism, hypoadrenalism, and insufficiency of testosterone, in man.

6. Discuss the findings on activity, learning capacity, and health of animals experimentally subjected to endocrine abnormalities.

7. Describe the somatic reaction patterns that can perhaps be recognized as distinct for different emotions.

8. Discuss the possible origin of physical disorders through intense or prolonged emotions, with particular reference to the action of endocrine glands that are not directly innervated in emotion.

9. What is known about physiological influences underlying the ergic behavior of (*a*) hunger, and (*b*) sleep?

10. Discuss general physiological theories of drive, attempting to differentiate the action in appetitive ergs, emergency ergs, and other nonappetitive ergs.

## BIBLIOGRAPHY

1. AHRONHEIT, J. H.: Emotional Albuminuria in Combat, *Psychosom, Med.*, 9: 51–57, 1947.

2. ANDERSON, E. E., and S. F. ANDERSON: The Relation between the Weight of the Endocrine Glands and Measures of Sexual, Emotional, and Exploratory Behavior in the Male Albino Rat, *J. comp. Psychol.*, 26: 459–474, 1938.

3. ARNOLD, M. B.: Physiological Differentiation of Emotional States, *Psychol. Rev.*, 52: 35–48, 1945.

4. BARD, P.: Central Nervous Mechanisms for the Expression of Anger, *Mooseheart Symposium on Feelings and Emotions*, University of Chicago Press, Chicago, 1949.

5. BASK, K. W.: Contribution to a Theory of the Hunger Drive, *J. comp. Psychol.*, 28: 137–160, 1939.

6. BEACH, F. A.: *Hormones and Behavior*, Paul B. Hoeber, Inc., Medical Book Department of Harper & Brothers, New York, 1948.

7. BENEDICT, F. G.: Degree of Constancy in Human Basal Metabolism. *Amer. J. Physiol.*, 110: 521–530, 1935.

8. BENETATO, G.: The Effect of Repeated Physical Effort on the Level of Adrenal Functioning in Man, *Travail hum.*, 7: 153–162, 1931.

9. BERG, I. A.: Development of Behavior: The Micturition Pattern in the Dog, *J. exp. Psychol.*, 34: 343–368, 1944.

10. BIZE, P. R., and R. MORICARD: Psychic Changes Following Injection of Testosterone in Young Boys, *Bull. Soc. Pediat.*, 35: 38, 1937.

11. BLAU, A.: Mental Changes Following Head Trauma in Children, *Arch. Neurol. Psychiat.* Chicago, 35: 723–769, 1936.

12. BROOKHART, J. M., and F. L. DEY: Reduction of Sexual Behavior in Male Guinea Pigs by Hypothalamic Lesions, *Amer. J. Physiol.*, 133: 551–554, 1941.

13. BROWN, L.: Remarks on the Endocrines and Some Associated Psychoneuroses, *Brit. Med. J.*, Number 3709: 223–226, 1932.

14. BRUNER, J. S., and B. CUNNINGHAM: The Effect of Thymus Extract on the Sexual Behavior of the Female Rat: Preliminary Report, *J. comp. Psychol.*, 27: 69–77, 1939.

15. BÜLBRING, E.: The Action of Adrenalin on Transmission in the Superior Cervical Ganglion, *J. Physiol.*, 103: 57–67, 1944.

16. BURN, J. H.: The Relation of Adrenalin to Acetylcholine in the Nervous System, *Physiol. Rev.*, 25: 377–394, 1945.

17. COLMA, I., and S. WRIGHT: Action of Acetylcholine, Atropine, and Eserine on the Central Nervous System of the Decerebrate Cat, *J. Physiol.*, 103: 93–102, 1944.

18. CANTRIL, H., and W. A. HUNT: Emotional Effects Produced by the Injection of Adrenalin, *Amer. J. Psychol.*, 44: 300–307, 1932.

19. CATTELL, R. B., A. K. S. CATTELL, and R. M. RHYMER: *P*-technique Demonstrated in Determining Psychophysiological Source Traits in a Normal Individual, *Psychometrika*, 12: 267–288, 1947.

20. CATTELL, R. B.: *The Description and Measurement of Personality*, World Book Company, Yonkers, New York, 1946.

21. CATTELL, R. B., and L. B. LUBORSKY: *P*-technique illustrated as a new clinical method for determining personality and symptom structure, *J. of Gen. Psychol.* 42: 3–24, 1950.

22. CHANG, H. C., K. F. CHIA, C. H. HSE, and R. K. S. LUN: Humoral Transmission of Nerve Impulses at Central Synapses: I. Sinus and Vagus Afferent Nerves, *Chin. J. Physiol.*, 12: 1–36, 1937.

23. COLLINS, N. E.: Statistical Analysis of Factors which Make for Success as Initial Encounters between Hens, *Amer. Nat.*, 77: 519–538, 1943.

24. CONRAD, A.: The Psychiatric Study of Hyperthyroid Patients, *J. nerv. ment. Dis.*, 79: 505–529, 656–674, 1934.

25. CRILE, G.: A Neuro-endocrine Formula for Civilized Man, *Educ. Rec.*, 22: Suppl. 14, 57–76, 1941.

26. CURETON, T. K.: *Physical Fitness Appraisal and Guidance*, The C. V. Mosby Company, Medical Publishers, St. Louis, 1947.

27. DARLING, R. B.: Autonomic Action in Relation to Personality Traits of Children, *J. abnorm. soc. Psychol.*, 35: 246–260, 1940.

28. DARLING, R., and C. W. DARROW: Determining Activity of the Autonomic Nervous System from Measurements of Autonomic Change, *J. Psychol.*, 5: 85–89, 1938.

29. DAVIS, D. E., and L. V. DOMM: The Sexual Behavior of Hormonally Treated Domestic Fowl, *Proc. Soc. Exp. Biol.*, N. Y., 48: 667–669, 1941.

30. DDA, C. F.: Psychological States Resulting from Parathyroid Deficiency, *J. Abnorm. soc. Psychol.*, 34: 481–496, 1939.

31. DIETHELM, O., E. J. DOTY, and A. T. MILHORAT: Emotions and Adrenergic and Cholinergic Changes in the Blood, *Arch. Neurol. Psychiat.*, Chicago, 54: 110–115, 1945.

32. FREEMAN, W., and J. W. WATT: Retrograde Degeneration of the Thalamus Following Prefrontal Lobotomy, *J. comp. Neurol.*, 86: 65–93, 1947.

33. FAY, P. J., and W. C. MIDDLETON: Judgement of Confidence from Voice, *J. gen. Psychol.*, 30: 93–95, 1914.

34. FINAN, J. L.: Delayed Response with Pre-delay Reinforcement in Monkeys after the Removal of the Frontal Lobes, *Amer. J. Psychol.*, 55: 202–214, 1942.

35. HALL, C. S.: The Inheritance of Emotionality, *Sigma Xi Quart.* 26: 17–27, 1938.

36. HARRISON, F.: An Attempt to Produce Sleep by Diencephalic Stimulation, *J. Neurophysiol.*, 3: 156–165, 1940.

37. HEBB, D. O.: Man's Frontal Lobes, *Arch. Neurol. Psychiat.*, Chicago, 34: 10–24, 1945.

38. HERRINGTON, H. S., in MCNEMAR, Q., and M. A. MERRILL, *Studies in Personality*, McGraw-Hill Book Company, Inc., New York, 1942.

39. HINTON, R. T.: The Role of the Basal Metabolic Rate in the Intelligence of Ninety Grade School Students. *J. educ. Psychol.*, 27: 546–550, 1936.

40. HUNT, W. A., and C. LANDIS: The Overt Behavior Pattern in Startle. *J. exp. Psychol.*, 19: 312–320, 1936.

41. HUTTON, E. L.: Personality Changes after Leucotomy, *J. ment. Sci.*, 93: 31–42, 1947.

42. INGRAM, W. R.: The Hypothalamus: a Review of the Experimental Data, *Psychosom. Med.*, 1: 48–91, 1939.

43. KATZ, H. L., and L. B. NICE: Hematocril and blood volume in emotionally excited rabbits. *Amer. J: Physiol.*, 105: 75–76, 1933.

44. KATZ, D.: Psychological Needs, Chapter III in Cattell, R. B., and R. M. W. Travers, *Human Affairs*. Macmillan & Co., Ltd., London, 1937.

45. KENNARD, M. A., S. SPENCER, and G. FOUNTAIN, JR.: Hyperactivity in Monkeys Following Lesions of the Frontal Lobe, *J. Neurophysiol.*, 4: 512–524, 1941.

46. KLUVER, H.: The Nervous System and Behavior, *J. Psychol.*, 17: 209–227, 1944.

47. LANDIS, C., and W. A. HUNT: Adrenalin and Emotion, *Psychol. Rev.*, 39: 467–485, 1932.

48. LANDIS, C., S. FERRALL, and J. PAGE: Fear, Anger, and Disease: Their Inter-correlations in Normal and Abnormal People, *Amer. J. Psychol.*, 48: 585–597, 1936.

49. LASHLEY, K. S.: Experimental Analysis of Instinctive Behavior. *Psychol. Rev.*, 45: 445–472, 1938.

50. LASHLEY, K. S.: Factors Limiting Recovery after Central Nervous Lesions, *J. nerv. ment. Dis.*, 88: 733–755, 1938.

51. LEBLOND, C. P.: Nervous and Hormonal Factors in the Maternal Behavior of the Mouse, *J. Genet. Psychol.*, 57: 327–344, 1940.

52. Levy, D. M.: Aggressive-Submissive Behavior and the Fröhlich Syndrome, *Arch. Neurol. Psychiat.*, Chicago, 36: 991–1020, 1936.

53. Lurie, L. A.: Endocrinology and Behavior Disorders of Children: A Study of the Possible Causal Relationships between Endocrinopathic States and Behavior Disorders of Children, *Amer. J. Orthopsychiat.*, 5: 141–153, 1935.

54. Man, E. B., and E. Kahn: Thyroid Function of Manic-depressive Patients Evaluated by Determinations of the Serum Iodine, *Arch. Neurol. Psychiat.*, Chicago, 54: 51–56, 1945.

55. Margolin, S. E., and M. E. Bunch: The Relationship between Age and the Strength of Hunger Motivation, *Comp. Psychol. Monogr.*, 16: 34, 1940.

56. Masserman, J. H.: The Functions of the Hypothalamus in the Cat: Destruction Experiments (Film), Bethlehem, Pa., Psychological Cinema Register, 1940.

57. Masserman, J. H.: The Role of the Hypothalamus in Behavior and Neurosis (Film), University of Chicago, Chicago, Division of Psychiatry, 1943.

58. McKenzie, Kenneth G., and Lorne D. Proctor: Bilateral Frontal Lobe Leucotomy in the Treatment of Mental Disease, *Canad. Med. Ass. J.*, 55: 433–441, 1946.

59. Mixter, W. J., K. J. Tilloston, and D. Wies: Reports of Partial Frontal Lobectomy and Frontal Lobotomy Performed on Three Patients: One Chronic Epileptic and Two Cases of Chronic Agitated Depression, *Psychosom. Med.*, 3: 26–37, 1941.

60. Morgan, C. T.: *Physiological Psychology*, McGraw-Hill Book Company, Inc., New York, 1943.

61. O'Connor, W. J., and E. B. Verney: The Effect of Increased Activity of the Sympathetic System in the Inhibition of Water Diuresis by Emotional Stress, *Quart. J. exp. Physiol.*, 33: 77–90, 1945.

62. O'Connor, W. J., and E. B. Verney: The Effect of Removal of the Posterior Lobe of the Pituitary on the Inhibition of Water Diuresis by Emotional Stress, *Quart. J. exp. Physiol.*, Cognate *Med. Sci.*, 31: 393–408, 1942.

63. Parode, G. W.: Ermundung, *Dtsch. med. Wschr.*, 67: 1333–1337, 1941.

64. Pennington, L. A., and N. Berkovitz: Behavioral Effects of Cerebral Injury in Reiation to Change in Motivation, *J. comp. Psychol.*, 31: 243–254, 1941.

64a. Petrie, A.: Preliminary Report of Changes after Prefrontal Leucotomy. *J. ment. Sci.*, 95: 449–455, 1949.

65. Pincus, G., and H. Hoagland: Steroid Excretion and the Stress of Flying, *J. Aviat. Med.*, 14: 173–193, 1943.

66. Podolsky, E.: Sexual Neurosis in Soldiers Not an Uncommon Condition, *Med. World*, N. Y., 64: 15–17, 1946.

67. Porteus, S. D., and H. N. Peters: Maze Test Validation and Psychosurgery, *Genet. Psychol. Monogr.*, 36: 3–86, 1947.

68. Richter, C. P.: Biology of Drives, *Psychosom. Med.*, 3: 105–110, 1941.

69. Richter, C. P., and C. D. Hawkes: Increased Spontaneous Activity and Food Intake Produced in Rats by Removal of the Frontal Poles of the Brain, *J. Comp. Psychol.*, 41, 1948.

70. Riess, B. F.: Some Effects of Adren-cortical Steroid Hormones on the Maze Behavior of the Rat, *J. Comp. Physiol. Psychol.*, 40: 9–11, 1947.

71. Ruesch, J., R. E. Harris, and R. M. Bowman: Pre and Post-traumatic Personality in Head Injuries, *Res. Bull. Ass. Nerv. Ment. Dis.*, 24: 507–544, 1945.

72. Rylander, G.: Personality Changes after Operations on the Frontal Lobes, *Acta Psychiat. neurol.*, Suppl. 20, 1939.

73. Rylander, G.: Mental Changes after Excision of Cerebral Tissue, *Acta psychiat.*, Kbh., Suppl. 25, 1943.

74. SEWARD, G.: *Sex and the Social Order*, McGraw-Hill Book Company, Inc., New York, 1946.

75. SEWARD, J. P.: The Hormonal Induction of Behavior, *Psychol. Rev.*, 48: 302–315, 1941.

76. SOLLENBERGER, R. T.: Some Relationships between the Sexual Maturation of Boys and Their Expressed Interests and Attitudes, *J. Psychol.*, 9: 179–189, 1940.

77. STEINACH, E.: The History of the Male Sexual Hormone and Its Effects in Mammals and in Man, *Wien. klin. Wschr.*, 49: I. Zul., 161–172, 196–205, 1936.

78. STEINETZ, K.: Basedow nach Psychischen Traumen, *Arztl. sachv. Ztg.*, 38: 57–60, 71–79, 1932.

79. STONE, C. P.: Precocious Copulatory Activity Induced in Male Rats by Subcutaneous Injections by Testosterone Propionate, *Endocrinology*, 26: 511–515, 1940.

80. STONE, C. P.: Activation of Impotent Male Rats by Injection of Testosterone Propionate, *J. comp. Psychol.*, 25: 445–450, 1938.

81. STONE, C. P.: Copulatory Activity in Adult Male Rats Following Castration and Injections of Testosterone Propionate, *Endocrinology*, 24: 165–174, 1939.

82. THOMSON, G. N.: Psychiatric Factors Influencing Learning, *J. nerv. ment. Dis.*, 101: 347–356, 1945.

83. WATKINS, R. M.: Mild Hypothyroidism, *Ann. Intern. Med.*, 7: 1534–1539, 1934.

84. WILLIAMS, H.: An Exploration of Psychosomatic Source Traits by *P* technique, Ph.D. Thesis, University of Illinois Library, Urbana, Ill., 1949.

85. YEAKEL, E. H., and R. P. RHOADES: A Comparison of the Body and Endocrine Gland Weights of Emotional and Non-emotional Rats, *Endocrinology*, 28: 337–340, 1941.

86. YOUNG, P. T.: *Emotion in Man and Animal*, John Wiley & Sons, Inc., New York, 1943.

87. YOUNG, P. T.: Studies of Food Preference, Appetite and Dietary Habit: VIII. Food-Seeking Drives, Palatability, and Law of Effect, *J. Comp. Psychol.*, 41: 4–20, 1948.

# CHAPTER 11

## PSYCHOSOMATICS: II. METHODOLOGICAL AVENUES TO FURTHER EVIDENCE

1. Personality Concomitants of Definite Physical Disorders
2. Physiological Reactivities of the Total Organism in Relation to Personality
3. Biochemical and Health Differences in Relation to Personality
4. Biochemistry of the Nervous System in Relation to Personality
5. Effects of Experimentally Produced Abnormal Physiology
6. Effects of Specific Drugs
7. The Contribution of Electroencephalography
8. Summary

### 1. PERSONALITY CONCOMITANTS OF DEFINITE PHYSICAL DISORDERS

**History of This Approach: the Case of Tuberculosis.** In this chapter it is proposed to study methods and approaches now being exploited in psychosomatics and which are likely to lead to advances of importance in the next decade. The results to be considered are in part intelligible in terms of functional unities considered in the previous chapter, and they will augment the student's understanding of those functions. But they need to be considered apart from the systematic accounts of the last chapter because premature incorporation would distort their possible significance. It is best, therefore, to consider them as theoretically and practically important bodies of knowledge not yet entirely organizable in terms of the known psychophysiological structures discussed in that chapter.

A first, relatively obvious, approach toward obtaining knowledge of psychosomatic connections is that of observing departures from normal mentality in persons known to be suffering from physical diseases, and particularly from disorders whose physical influences are known. This "physical disease syndrome" approach yielded some of the basic understanding of endocrine action, since, as in cretinism, the gross physical abnormalities which gland malfunctioning occasions, are also accompanied by recognizable mental changes.

Good clinicians throughout the history of medicine have looked for personality characteristics in physical disease syndromes and many more or less inspired perceptions are on record. Galen and Hippocrates believed, for example, in a *spes phthisica*—a tendency to a high-strung unrealistic cheerfulness in lung tuberculosis—which more objective but more coarse per-

300

sonality assessment devices in modern times have not yet been able to verify. Tests show no systematic differences of patients in tuberculosis sanatoria from the general population, in intelligence, special aptitudes, and occupational interests (77,76). However, both from questionnaires and observers' ratings (76,77,80), there is evidence that tubercular patients are significantly more neurotic, lacking in self-confidence and self-sufficiency, more "introverted," more "neurasthenic," more anxious and depressed, more schizoid (with apathy), and more frequently of the mental pattern of lower social status groups. It is certainly noticeable that the highly gifted persons with tuberculosis—Emerson, Thoreau, Keats, Shelley, Chopin, Schiller—were of a schizoid temperament. Apart from the "sanatorium personality," however, there is no *type* syndrome here but only a number of slight and sometimes significant differences in means on certain factors.

**Direction of Causation in Observed Connections.** This instance brings out sharply the methodological problem throughout these observations on psychosomatic correlations. Does the physical disorder produce the mental symptoms physiologically or otherwise? Is the physical disorder the consequence of a way of life occasioned by the mental traits, when the individual stays in the pattern of our culture? Is some common organic failure the root of both the physical and the mental symptoms? And, last, are the mental symptoms the consequence of the psychological problems created for the individual by the physical illness? In the case of tuberculosis it is easy to see that the loss of family and occupation and the uncertain future might be enough to account for the difference in anxiety, depression, and, perhaps, neuroticism. But there is also the above suggestion of various functional insufficiencies of a schizoid type, reacted to by exhausting overcompensatory efforts or by death wishes. (One of the most famous tuberculosis sufferers wrote: "Now more than ever seems it sweet to die, to fade upon the midnight with no pain . . . ," and the role of a perfectionist death wish would bear examination in the writings of many victims of this disease.)

**Anemia and Diabetes.** Clinically it has long been recognized that there are personality characteristics associated with another physical disease—in this case of instability and even psychosis—namely, with anemia. De Natale (21), examining cases of pernicious anaemia, concludes that there is no specific personality trend, but that the disease brings out whatever neurotic or psychotic trend is latent in the personality. Morsier notes the prevalence of both neurosis and psychoses in anemics, and argues for a common origin of the anemia and mental disorder in some other source, possibly gastric achylia. Commonly reported traits are irritability, suspiciousness, lack of "sense of proportion," and paranoid delusions about the self. Since this pattern appears in other physiological conditions producing defective metabolism in the brain generally (see previous chapter on cerebral anoxia, etc.), we shall conclude that deficient brain metabolism brings out latent neurotic and psychotic trends, but in most people brings out generalized paranoid tendencies. Parenthetically, the last observation is an additional indication of the "normality" of paranoia and of the difficulty of drawing a sharp line anywhere between normal and paranoid systems of belief.

Diabetes has frequently been declared to be closely associated with personality characteristics of a maladjusted kind. McGavin (62) found no significant trait differences in I.Q. of patients and nonpatients but found the former to have a higher percentage of maladjustment. Various clinicians refer to traits of emotionality, depression, anxiety, moroseness, hypochondria, and insomnia, and mention the proximity of the emotional-expression center in the hypothalamus to the pancreas-control center as if some causal connection might lie there. Lindberg describes a "diabetic psychosis" observed in fourteen diabetics in middle age, but the paranoid and manic-depressive features, as well as neurological disturbances, suggest that this may be primarily a consequence of disturbed sugar metabolism reducing general cortical efficiency.

Meyer and others (64), following up the suggestion of "traumatic diabetes" brought on by psychological shock or stress, verify the observation and suggest that the personalities which respond in this way tend to be dependent, attention- and affection-demanding individuals, who grow hostile under frustration. The psychological evidence in general is consistent with the interpretation that the diabetes-prone person is naturally of high general emotionality ($C$ factor) and has a more than normal probability of a manic-depressive constitution. Environmentally he is likely to have had a "good" home upbringing but with overprotection, generating dependence. Possibly the pancreatic failure can be viewed as in part due to the strains on sugar metabolism created by an overemotional temperament, causing excessive adrenal action, with frequent outpourings of blood sugar undischarged by activity.

**Rheumatic Heart Disease and Arthritis.** Dunbar (25,26) who has most systematically collected in recent years evidence on psychological traits in physical disease, brings data, as yet insufficiently controlled for rating and sampling errors, that even rheumatism has its psychological type. She found that sufferers from rheumatism and rheumatic heart disease, compared with other (accident) patients, tend to have a generally poor health record and high liability to infections, while being more than averagely active and emotional, with sociability, talkativeness, adventuresomeness, and nervous restlessness. However, in contrast to diabetics, they contributed less than the average population quota to mental hospitals. Gregg finds, by way of confirmation, less arthritis in mental hospitals than in the general population, but ascribes this to more protected physical existence and lack of prolonged muscle tension through mental effort, the latter seeming a doubtful conclusion. Halliday (39) brings appreciable evidence for a single pattern of proneness to gastric ulcer, bronchitis, and rheumatism (especially nonarticular rheumatism). This pattern is favored by obsessional, energetic constitution in the subject, and by stress, *e.g.*, economic stress, in the environment (40). The recent finding of an association between rheumatism and exhaustion of the adrenal cortical steroids would, if confirmed, support its connection with the anxious, stressful, energetic personality.

Saul (72) and Despert (22) bring convincing evidence that the common cold is significantly more frequently caught by individuals under psychological stress or in emotional conflicts, or who are maladjusted. Gastrointestinal symptoms showed some parallelism also to proneness to infection, both presumably being conditioned by the exhaustion of emotional conflict.

**Hypertension.** Hypertension and heart disease, gastrointestinal disorders and allergies have such close psychological associations that it has seemed better to study them as "localized neuroses" under "neurosis" in Chapter 17. The remaining physical disorders with marked psychological correlates are those in which disease directly attacks the central nervous system as in general paresis and encephalitis. Encephalitis has produced the expression "postencephalitic ethical atrophy" because the most obvious symptom is general moral failure, and this is far more marked in children (seven to sixteen years) than in adult sufferers. The first signs are restlessness, contrariness, incapacity for social life, followed by irritability, temper tantrums, cruelty, stealing and lying, exaggerated uncontrolled erotic behavior, and general impulsiveness. If the disorder continues to more widespread brain destruction, behavior breaks down to a purely instinctive level, with antisocial reactions to attempts at restraint, but with transient periods of remorse and contrition which distinguish the pattern from the psychopathic personality. This behavior, occurring through brain lesions not specifically located in the frontal lobes, suggests that in children the whole cortex is more involved in emotional inhibition than it is in adults. Both in encephalitis in children and in general paresis in adults the cortical loss is widespread and is accompanied by marked declines in I.Q., as would be expected, but the personality changes in general paresis, though generally similar to those in encephalitis, have more emphasis on confusion and delusions and less on antisocial and unethical behavior—possibly because socialization and ethical behavior are only in process of being acquired and are not yet much cortically localized in the child victims of encephalitis.

Further advance in this approach now awaits more precise measurement and analysis of personality functions, most that can be done by clinical rating having been achieved.

## 2. PHYSIOLOGICAL REACTIVITIES OF THE TOTAL ORGANISM IN RELATION TO PERSONALITY

**Individual Differences in the Normal Range.**　As the logically complementary approach to that just presented above, one should study the somatic differences noted in well-defined *mental disorders*.　This methodological contribution, however, is better studied in Chapter 18, in connection with mental disorders generally, to which the student may turn in due course. Here, therefore, we shall proceed to the next of the logically possible approaches, namely, the relation of measured differences in the *normal* range of physiological qualities to personality qualities.　This approach will be spread over three sections: the first dealing with individual differences in certain reactivities of the total organism, notably of the autonomic system and in muscle tension; the second, with differences found in blood physiology; and the third, with differences noted in the physiology of the nervous system.

The relation of personality to metabolic rate and blood pressure has already been described in a general way in connection with the description of the autonomic nervous system in the previous chapter.　There it was pointed out that positive correlation exists between basal metabolic rate, on the one hand, and general energy and enthusiasm of personality, on the other.　It was also pointed out that the normal if not the basal rate is raised in emotion, and that marked emotionality results in a change that lasts for a long time.　Graham (37), studying 695 men in an armored brigade engaged in at least a year of desert warfare, found an abnormally high proportion (27 per cent) had blood pressure at a high level, but lacked neurotic symptoms and returned to normal in two or more months of rest.　Except in neurotics, autonomic activity level may thus be regarded as situational, though it depends in civil life partly on the individual, since he can to a considerable extent determine the degree to which he will get involved in situations.　A physiological variable probably related to metabolic rate is that of muscular tension.　Duffy (24), using twelve measures of muscular tension, found that it increased in mental and physical effort, that it could be resolved into some five factors by factor analysis, that one of these is a general tension factor which is a persistent character of the individual, and that persons who have a high general tension relative to the specific muscular tension required are either new to the task or of nervous disposition.

**The Galvanic Skin Reflex.**　Another measure that is a function of autonomic activity—specifically of the sympathetic system—but on which findings have accumulated in more extensive fields than for total sympathetic system reactivity as such, is the psychogalvanic reflex.　What follows applies to the *F* effect (the Féré effect—a decline of electrical skin resistance to a low-voltage external current, through mental stimulus) and not necessarily to the $T$ effect (the Tarchanoff effect, appearing as an actual emf at the body surface), since nearly all systematic research is concerned with the former.

Most studies have been concerned with the magnitude of the momentary decrease in skin resistance when a stimulus is perceived, but the absolute resistance level also has some psychological significance, being high in sleep, relaxation, boredom, and perhaps in suppressed states, sulking, and when feeling confident. It is high in conversion hysterics and low in anxiety hysterics and individuals with high emotionality. It is low in excitement, alertness, fear, etc., and subjects in a state of low resistance have higher fluency of association scores than when resistance is high (19). The expression

$$\text{Resistance} = \frac{\text{Constant} \times \text{available drive energy (freedom from fatigue)}}{\text{extent of release of energy occurring consciously}}$$

has been suggested as the determiner of resistance level (12).

The magnitude of the deflection or decrease is frequently roughly described as proportional to the amount of emotion, but careful analysis of many hundreds of introspective protocols shows that the true correlate of the reflex is *conation* (or effort and impulse to act). Thus the highest deflections are found with pain, tension, startle, excitement, acts of will, and exertion, while the smallest are found with pleasurable emotion, disappointment, cognitive processes, etc. (12).

For the same kind of stimulus—usually a shock or sudden sensory presentation demanding attention—there are marked individual differences in the magnitude of the deflection. In the normal range it has been found that the largest deflections occur with individuals rated high for forcefulness of personality, cheerful emotionality, desire to excel, rapidity of decision, ability to learn nonsense syllables, soundness of bodily constitution, and school success relative to intelligence (12). This pattern is strikingly similar to that found by Herrington (previous chapter) for general autonomic activity. Schizophrenics and, to a lesser extent depressives, give abnormally small deflections; conversion hysterics and manic-depressives in a manic phase give medium deflections, while anxiety hysterics or obsessional neurotics give the highest deflections among abnormals, and approximately the same as normals. Freeman and Katzoff (32) found a factor loading "recovery quotient" (the extent to which resistance is recovered after startle) which correlated appreciably with psychiatric ratings of maturity and self-control and somewhat with sheer magnitude of deflection.

An interesting observation on normal subjects, which fits in with the above observed general tendency to low deflections among psychotics, is that the extent to which a sensory experience is perceived as "objective," "out in the real world," as opposed to "subjective," "dreamlike," "part of the self," is proportional to the magnitude of the P.G.R. in the act of perception (9). It is the capacity to exert effort, apparently, which makes objects "real"; which was perhaps known to Dr. Johnson when, on hearing of Berkeley's theory (of the unreality of the external world) he kicked forcefully against a great stone, saying, "I refute it thus." This has importance in personality in connection with the phenomena of "depersonalization" and "feelings of unreality," which we may now suppose arise from *so disordered a dynamic organization that this "effort" (conation) in perception is no longer possible.* It may have bearing also on the middle of the exact meaning and manner of operation of that "reality principle" which breaks down in all psychosis.

**Personality Correlates of High Psychogalvanic Reactivity.** The essential personality correlate of deflection magnitude is thus seemingly a combination of conative energy and of willed control. Dynamic impulsiveness and emotionality *not checked* by will action (*i.e.*, presumably, autonomic activity without cortical control) does not, therefore, produce the largest deflections (12). Darrow (19) points out that such uncontrolled, subcortical emotionality tends to produce large blood-pressure changes but that in this condition the blood-pressure changes are no longer paralleled by psychogalvanic deflections. The galvanic response, as suggested earlier (12), is essentially proportional to the amount of control exerted on an impulse.

That the first of the two above factors—the conative energy, expressed in traits of "forcefulness," "cheerful emotionality," "rapidity of decision," etc. —is actually the *H* factor (Adventurous Cyclothymia) of personality (Chap. 3) is suggested both by the nature of the traits and by a *P*-technique study (11) in which the P.G.R. deflection was found largely in the *H* factor. This factor loaded also a high ratio of emotional to nonemotional words recalled, a high *frequency* of deflections, and other evidence of emotional "abundance." The P.G.R. was also loaded in this study by a second factor, *G* or "Persevering, Integrated Character," which agrees with the independent indication above of the role of will in accounting for larger P.G.R. response and with the finding of large galvanic response in the will-character factor, based on *R* technique, described in Chapter 4. The galvanic response is thus best understood as a two-factor phenomena.

In spite of certain technical difficulties (polarization, the problem of counting deflections as percentages, or as absolute resistance changes, etc.) the psychogalvanic reflex has been valuable to personality study both as a measure of individual differences in the above factors and as a means of tracing specific dynamic connections. Although Colman and McCrae (17) and others have found good correlations between P.G.R. deflection size and the conative valence of the stimulus object, the relationship is too complicated for the P.G.R. to be used in simple fashion in the exploration of dynamic trait strengths. For as Whately Smith showed (12) the height of deflection is related in a $U$ curve to the memory value of stimuli, indicating that the *direction* of ego response or some other directional factor has to be taken into account. Second—and this may ultimately prove to be the same thing— the magnitude of the P.G.R. has been found (*a*) to be much more closely correlated with the strength of hostile (anger, fear) attitudes to the stimulus than to the strength of more friendly or affectional interests (12), (*b*) to be no good as a measure of attitude strength except when used with statements *against* the attitude (see (4), Chap. 6). Consequently the use of the P.G.R. in exploring dynamic traits of personality is only possible with designs which convert the total interest energy of the trait into fears or pugnacities regarding the course of action concerned in it.

### 3. BIOCHEMICAL AND HEALTH DIFFERENCES IN RELATION TO PERSONALITY

**Supplementing Gross Observation by Measurement.** The present section continues the relations of abnormal physiology and abnormal personality into the range of normality, where precise measurements of individual differences are substituted for gross syndromes. Its findings are mainly such as supplement those already set out.

Supplementary findings to be discussed in connection with mental disorder include such finer biochemical analyses as those of Quastel and Wales (68), who found (by hippuric acid excretion test after benzoate administration) that the detoxication action of the liver in catatonic schizophrenics is significantly poorer than in schizophrenics generally, suggesting a toxic origin for catatonic rigidity. Again, there have been some rewarding studies on blood chemistry of sugar, calcium, etc., in abnormals. As indicated in Chapter 18, blood sugar is likely to be high in manic and depressed phases of manic-depressive disorder, presumably due to the emotional state, while in schizophrenics, as McCowan and Quastel's results (59) show, there is likely to be a low hyperglycemic index. Calcium level is slightly elevated in schizophrenia, is lower than normal in the depressed phase of manic-depressive disorder, and much higher in the manic, excited phase. It is also high in epileptics but normal in general paralytics. Hulbert (46) and others found doses of calcium gluconate exercised a calming effect on irritable and "fractious" subjects, on psychomotor overactivity, and on epilepsy. One may hypothesize that the "crowding out" of unpleasant associations in the manic phase (see page 15) is made possible by the action of calcium in reducing nervous sensitivity. On this hypothesis the manic is inwardly calmer: his conflict is externalized. There is much scope for further research into the complex interdependencies involved in the body's permitting these changes in blood calcium and blood sugar; for in every case it is necessary to explain not only an overproduction but the breakdown of balancing, checking systems.

**Distribution of Mortality Causes.** Another supplementary line of investigation of physiological associations of disordered mental conditions consists in making comparisons of the physical illnesses and causes of death of psychotics and normals. Chevens, examining 786 records of various psychoses, concluded (15) that schizophrenics have poor life expectation generally and display inability to react to chronic infections; paranoids are subject to an undue degree to malignant growths; epileptics and imbeciles have a high rate of pneumonia, colitis, and dysentery, while melancholiacs and paranoids are high in cardiac disease and chronic nephritis. Freeman (31) finds sufficiently similar results, summarizable as follows for three diverse diseases:

INCIDENCE PER MILLION PATIENTS

|  | Schizo-phrenics | Paranoids | Epileptics | Manic-depressives |
|---|---|---|---|---|
| Tuberculosis.......... | 317 | 20 | 60 | 24 |
| Syphilis.............. | 218 | 134 | 455 | 435 |
| Cancer............... | 43 | 136 | 10 | 112 |

Such results are only suggestive, for they need correction for age, I.Q. (which correlates, for example, negatively with syphilis infection), and perhaps social status. Further, since degenerative diseases seem less frequent in protected, institutionalized populations (8), some correction is necessary in other disorders. But the trend as regards tuberculosis will be recognized to be in accord with constitutional theories of schizophrenia, while the cancer incidence in paranoia and manic-depressive disorder is notably different and worthy of investigation.

**Biochemical Observations.** Among physiological, biochemical differences found within more normal ranges of personality the following are well or tolerably established: there is no discoverable relationship between blood groups (O, A, B, etc.) and intelligence, emotionality, or extraversion-introversion; individuals with greater variation of serum calcium show greater variability of mood, and low calcium is associated with depressed moods (Laird and Stephan in reporting this finding suggest it is due to role of calcium in autonomic visceral control); salivary pH (alkalinity) is slightly positively correlated with excitability, it is decreased by mental and emotional activity, and, according to one unconfirmed finding (3), it is positively correlated with intelligence. This last finding might be due to an indirect connection, namely, that low intelligence, in school and other fixed environments from which individuals were samples, is correlated with more effort and exhaustion.

Hamilton and Shock (41) show that some correlation exists between personality instability and respiratory irregularity, while Goldstein (36) claims the same for variability in a wide range of blood indexes—inorganic phosphorus, cholesterol, sugar, chlorides, creatinine and calcium (see above). It may be that the inability to maintain internal, physiological stability—homeostasis in the widest sense—is a prime cause of difficulty in maintaining constant relationships to the outer environment—*i.e.*, adjustment in the widest sense. A possible, but less likely, alternative is that the emotional upsets created by maladjustment to the environment are the cause of the high physiological instability.

### 4. BIOCHEMISTRY OF THE NERVOUS SYSTEM IN RELATION TO PERSONALITY

**Nerve Cell Chemistry.** Division of data between the preceding and the present section is not easy to arrange, but in the main we have gathered in this section those facts about blood chemistry which permit of being organized about existing knowledge of *the biochemical functions of the nervous system itself*.

Referring at this point to his courses in physiological psychology (see (60) Chap. 10) the student will recall that a nerve cell responds to stimulation with a local electrical potential which does not propagate. When stimulation reaches a certain intensity, however, a "spike potential" is created, which passes along the axon without loss. This "firing" of the nerve is an all-or-nothing phenomenon, accompanied by a depolarization of the nerve membrane (loss of the positive charge on the outside) and followed by a period of chemical action, accompanied by heat, in which the potential difference is restored. Any visible nerve in the body consists actually of a bundle of small filaments, of which an increasing number "fire" as the stimulation at one end of the nerve is increased. The larger filaments have thicker myelin sheaths, conduct faster, respond to weaker stimulation, and have a higher (negative) potential in the "spike" discharge. It is now realized that most nerves exist in a state of some instability even without obvious external stimulation. They fluctuate rhythmically in electrical potential (but short of the propagating spike potential) and therefore in excitability. With special conditions of mutual interaction these fluctuations may increase to the point of firing, which is believed to account for the rhythmic discharges observed in the electroencephalogram (see Section 7, p. 319) as well as in some convulsive conditions.

**Synapse Transmission.** The point of greatest obscurity in nerve physiology is now no longer the cell but the synapse where one cell meets another.

The synapse invariably delays, and sometimes blocks entirely, the transmission to a second nerve of a spike impulse started in the first. A synapse, moreover, transmits in one direction only. This is due to the fact that the transmitting nerve, through the joint convergence of its many additional, roundabout routes, usually has many terminal bulbs on the same region of the second nerve, whereby many incoming impulses can summate to cause a sufficient stimulus, whereas if an impulse arrived in the reverse direction it would appear as a single impulse split up among many terminal bulbs. The riddle of nerve physiology concerns whether the effect of one nerve in stimulating another at the synapse is a direct electrical stimulation or the creation of a chemical "irritant" substance which in turn stimulates the second nerve (the humoral theory of transmission). At present it seems either that both the electrical and humoral theories are true—in the sense that the effects occur and aid each other—or that one holds in some regions (the autonomic system) and the other in other special regions (the cortex).

These physiological issues may seem too remote at present to be the concern of the student of personality; but at any moment the discovery of certain missing links of knowledge may open up new realms of interconnectedness and explain puzzling phenomena in the total behavior of the organism. Most of the issues discussed in the present chapter concern relatively unstructured fields of knowledge, but they are fields of development with which the student of personality should be familiar if he is to see the import of advances now being made. And at the very least such knowledge will enable the student to reject some of the too facile physiological theories of personality that periodically become fashionable.

**Calcium, Potassium, Acetylcholine, and the Hormones.** At present the state of the blood is known to affect the functioning of nerve tissue as follows: A more acid condition (lower pH value), such as occurs through accumulation of the products of oxidation, lowers the excitability of the nerve cell, requiring more powerful stimuli to elicit action. A shortage of oxygen, apart from causing a momentary sensitive phase, acts in the same direction. A shortage of calcium ions, on the other hand, raises excitability. Potassium ion concentration, when low, causes a decline in excitability; indeed, the presence of sufficient potassium seems to be permissive—a necessary precondition—to any other chemicals exerting a sensitizing action. Lehmann (52) has shown that the effects of these diverse chemicals is, at least in grosser features, equivalent. The various changes in concentration that raise sensitivity alike produce a lower threshold (potential) of stimulation, a tendency to spontaneous discharge, and a rhythmic afterpotential.

From the previous section and chapter it will be obvious that the effects on the behavior of the total organism are very directly related to those on the single cell. Calcium, for example, acts as a sedative for "fractious" individuals, while individuals with low blood calcium, through parathormone deficiency for instance, are excitable, unstable, and "on edge." This is perhaps surprising, for the action of a single chemical on the neuron might be expected to be modified by some different action of the same chemical on the synapse, or by its action in bringing inhibitory centers more strongly into play at the same time as the centers of drive or stimulation. In some cases such complex resultants are seen, and in the example of surgency-desurgency below it is possible that action upon synapses is as important as that upon cells.

As indicated in the discussion on the autonomic nervous system, adrenalin and acetylcholine are formed at the synapses, nerve-end plates, and perhaps elsewhere, respectively in sympathetic and parasympathetic ganglia. (Potassium ions are also liberated and perhaps other substances.) Whether these chemicals are *the* necessary transmitters, or whether they are by-products playing some more lowly part is uncertain; but it is probable that they are important facilitators. In the central nervous system there is evidence that both appear as a result of, and facilitate still further, nervous action. Acetylcholine action is more marked in some parts of the central nervous system than in others. Adrenalin readily diffuses, but it seems that the nervous system has had to develop an enzyme, cholinesterase, to get rid of accumulating acetylcholine which, at least as far as present knowledge goes, could act to accelerate nervous transmission indefinitely. Cholinesterase is in turn partly controlled by the chemical eserine. Individual differences in eserine or cholinesterase are therefore likely to betoken differences also in acetylcholine concentration.

**Biochemical Basis of Surgency-Desurgency.** It is in connection with the neurochemistry discussed above that one of the most interesting temperamental differences arises—that distinguishing the surgent from the desurgent temperament. The $F$ factor, it will be recalled, is one of the most firmly established and clearly delineated personality factors, having first been discovered in 1932 (10) and frequently experimented upon since.

It loads principally such traits as cheerfulness, energy, and carefree unconcernedness at the positive pole, anxiousness, depression, rigidity and introspectiveness at the negative pole. Among the psychoses it probably distinguishes mania from melancholy, while Eysenck's (27) researches strongly suggest that among the neuroses it distinguishes conversion hysteria from anxiety hysteria.

Recently a good deal of evidence has accumulated indicating that this dimension is more closely associated with physiological differences than are most other personality factors, though whether this finding implies constitutional determination or merely that the whole body physiology alters in relation to psychological changes remains to be determined.

*P*-technique studies (11,13) relating the slight daily variations in surgency-desurgency to physiological measures, show that in surgency the saliva is decidedly more alkaline, the electrical skin resistance is high, the red-blood count is high, the cholinesterase is low, and the reaction time is long, while various other physiological items likewise give a general picture of physiological ease and good reserves. The factor is quite distinct from the factor of general fatigue, however. In Eysenck's *R*-technique study the same general trends emerge: he found the desurgents (dysthymics in the nomenclature of abnormal psychology) higher in cholinesterase concentration in the blood serum, lower in salivary output, etc. Other studies have shown that in alkaline states of the blood the individual is more good-tempered, while with acid states the individual feels "out of sorts" and irritable. Since acids are products of metabolism, these particular findings may deal primarily with a fatigue factor, whereas the indications here are that the correlations with fatigue variables are secondary and perhaps only late-appearing.

From these and other phenomena the hypothesis is presented here that the degree of surgency-desurgency is determined by the concentration of acetylcholine (and perhaps to some extent also of adrenalin) in the central nervous system, and perhaps more specifically in the frontal lobes. Certainly the surgent individual behaves like a person in whom synaptic conduction in the central nervous system is low, who is not deterred (and in some cases not spurred on) by thoughts that occur to the average person, and whose autonomic system is not strongly affected (through the hypothalamus) by emotional associations that occur to him (the superficial emotionality of hysteria). This complacency shows a distinct resemblance to slight alcoholic intoxication, and the notion that the surgent individual is "born one drink ahead" of the average person may be due to a real resemblance of physiological actions. For, as McDougall argued, alcohol may produce its effect by increasing resistance at synapses, though it could also do so by direct reduction of frontal lobe action by interference with oxygen metabolism.

On the other hand, the desurgent, depressed, anxious, more *profoundly* emotional individual is unable to keep out of consciousness an excess of considerations—especially those of "foresight and fearsight" due to frontal lobe associations. He is inhibited, tense, quick in reaction time, etc., as tests show. This is presumably due to the irradiating and widely facilitated nervous conduction made possible by accumulation of acetylcholine (28,29). Three facts may at first sight invalidate the theory. First, it is the cholinesterase level that we actually observe to be high in desurgency, but this we ascribe to a compensatory attempt to reduce the hypothesized excessive acetylcholine. Second, one clinical report (48) shows that daily injections of acetylcholine will *reduce* anxiety states and attacks—though with relapse on cessation of medication. Again this can be ascribed to a compensatory rise in cholinesterase which temporarily reduces the cortical concentration. Third, acetylcholine in the parasympathetic system should *reduce* anxious emotionality. But the hypothesis is that the concentration occurs in the central nervous system, due to local action there, and, as is well known, acetylcholine has little capacity for diffusion. There are thus certain missing links in the theory, but it suggests definite issues for experiment.

## 5. EFFECTS OF EXPERIMENTALLY PRODUCED ABNORMAL PHYSIOLOGY

**Changes in Oxygen Metabolism.** So far, the methods reviewed have employed observations on naturally occurring concomitant variations of mental and somatic phenomena, clinically observed or biochemically measured, as they are seen in nature. It is now time to augment the views thus obtained by deliberate experiment, controlling more variables and producing more extreme or abnormal conditions.

Some of the most extensive experiments on artificially produced, extreme physiological conditions—apart from that carried out on animals—have been concerned with the basic question of oxygen metabolism. Most of this work has been done by exposing subjects to low oxygen pressures in tanks, simulating the conditions of high altitudes.

Among the changes recorded are: decline in ocular efficiency and visual functions (intensity discrimination, dark adaptation, color perception, acuity); decline in reading speed and increase in frequency of eye fixations; decline in speed and legibility of writing, in problem solving, memory, sensory thresholds of all kinds (additional to vision), in reaction time (simple and choice), and neuromuscular coordination (*e.g.*, the mirror drawing test). There is also increase of variability of response. As the researches of McFarland and his coworkers (60) show, the decline in all these is a roughly linear function of the falling oxygen saturation. In some respects the changes are very similar to fatigue (and a 10 per cent reduction in oxygen produces a change in function equal to about one hour's hard work), which suggests a theory of fatigue as decline in oxygen availability.

Gellhorn (34) points out that normally the reduction of oxygen cannot be considered in its effects apart from the automatic compensatory activities of the autonomic system—which produces, for example, rise of blood pressure, lowering of body temperature, quickening of breathing, dilation of the pupil (which, incidentally, reduces the decline in retinal sensitivity), etc. He notes also that oxygenic and glycemic level are mutually compensatory, so that breathing pure oxygen will eliminate for the time the mental and physical defects from low sugar level. Gellhorn observes that reduction of cortical efficiency by either anoxia or hypoglycemia brings on a state of increased excitability in the autonomic centers. On the psychological side, Gellhorn notes, in addition to the above symptoms of deficiency, an increase in perseveration, in dissociation, in errors (*e.g.*, misspellings), in slowness of work, but he argues that memory (power of recall) is the most sensitive function (33). Kraines (50), however, shows that a very real decline in intelligence-test performance results. His observation that the loss is greater in asthenics suggests that differences might be found in all performances under anoxia, for pyknics and leptosomes, and that this might offer a key to the greater schizoid tendencies of leptosomes under the normal stresses of life.

Barach and Kagan (1) compared normals and anxiety neurotics under low oxygen pressure and found differences in emotional control. In general, lowering of oxygen pressure seems to bring out whatever neurotic or psychotic trends are present—once the first stage of "intoxication-like" lack of control, emotionality, and overconfidence is passed. Paranoid trends of irritability, disordered social judgment, and ideas of self-reference are frequently reported.

**Toxic and Deprivation States from Other Sources.** The changes in total personality reaction through experimentally produced hypoglycemia are, with present methods of personality assessment and perhaps even ultimately, indistinguishable from those of anoxia, and will therefore not be reviewed in detail. Experimenters report fatigue, memory loss, mental confusion, ocular and general sensory weakness, neurological-failure symptoms of a general kind, speech and writing disturbances, the development of tics, and various affective disturbances such as anxiety, manic excitement, and paranoid symptoms—eventually leading to stupor and coma. Perhaps the only specific symptom is the development of a sense of hunger, exaggerated by the poor cortical control to excessive expression.

The general symptom pattern just considered is also similar to that produced by various toxic and deprivation conditions such as uremia, carbon-monoxide poisoning, anemia, alcohol poisoning, lead poisoning, etc. Although the specific differences are sometimes well defined and instructive from the point of view of brain physiology, it is not appropriate to pursue such issues in much detail in this treatise.

**Vitamin Deficiencies.** Much experimental work has been done with vitamin deficiencies, specifically of the B-group vitamins, which apparently produce gradual deficiencies of nervous functioning visible in slighter, more subtle personality changes than those of anoxia, etc. The physiological cause is not fully understood except that it is known that vitamin-B deficiency interferes with sugar metabolism through inducing a failure to remove its products, namely lactic and pyruvic acids. It may be the irritating effect of these undisposed products rather than the slowing down of sugar metabolism which produces some symptoms, notably the tendency to neuritis (as in beri-beri) and the proneness of vitamin-B-deprived animals to fall into convulsions with strong sensory stimuli. Physiologically there is also an inter-ference with protein metabolism so that deprived animals show a loss of appetite generally, specifically for carbohydrates and proteins, with a relative increase of appetite for fats.

With animals subjected to the most severe vitamin-B deficiency, there is, as Poe and Muenzinger have shown, a general decline in learning capacity, especially when the deficiency occurs two to six weeks after birth. Bid and Wickens investigated the possibility that this is due merely to decline in drive or to poor muscular coordination, but found the same deficiency in a simple conditioning situation (eyelid reflex).

Experiments with human beings agree in indicating changes toward "neurasthenia," deficiencies in foresight and judgment (maze test)—but not toward lower I.Q., reasoning ability, or speed of coordination—fearful-ness, irritability and depression, decreased inclination to perform accustomed tasks and to make social adjustments, sleeplessness and sensitiveness to noise, uncooperativeness, and the failure of attitudes of good morale. Brozek and his coworkers (7) were first able to obtain these personality changes in measurable form, with the Minnesota Multiphasic, the Rorschach, and Cattell's Cursive Miniature Situation tests. The significant differences were an increase in the general emotionality $(C-)$ factor, along with increases in anxiety and timidity, *i.e.*, probably in desurgency $(F-)$. (Note this pat-tern is just the opposite of that found by Petrie in leucotomy (64a) Chap. 10). The increase in general emotionality, with its characteristic decline of perseverance and self-control is similar to the main change in anoxia, but the fearfulness and lack of self-confidence are new, and may be due either to the secondary physiological effect or to the guilt arising from the continu-ation of the poor performance and social clumsiness over a much longer period than in anoxia experiments.

**Neuroses of Malnutrition and Hunger Conflict.** The experiments of Brozek, Keys, Franklin, and Schiele (7,30) on the psychological effects of general malnutrition have also produced some results of decided psycho-logical interest. Thirty-six young men were kept on a 1,570 daily caloric diet for six months, during which they lost 24 per cent of body weight, suffered a decrease in basal metabolic and pulse rate, and various physical signs of malnutrition. Among "abilities," auditory acuity increased, intelli-gence, and other capacities remained constant. Physical movement became slower, and there was a decline in spontaneous activity. Weakness, fatigue, complete loss of sex drive, decline in sociability, loss of ambition, and a feeling of "growing old" were commonly experienced. Moods became unstable, depression being especially easily precipitated, but also occasionally elation, while irritability predominated. The men rated themselves as lacking in self-control, subject to indecisiveness, restlessness, inability to concentrate, sensitiveness to noise, and general nervousness. Observers noted a narrowing of the subjects' interests, deterioration of personal grooming, preoccupation with food interests, egocentricity and seclusiveness, loss of humor (except of an ironic, sarcastic variety), and a loss of enthusiasm and sociability, with a terminating condition of marked apathy.

Apart from the interests of the hunger drive and some conflicts specific to the situation, this picture has marked similarities to the early schizoid personality and suggests that the role of defective energy and defective metabolism in creating the initial conflict situation in schizophrenia has not been properly appreciated.

Nine of the thirty-six subjects developed neuroses or borderline psychosis. Their scores generally increased most markedly on the depression hysteria, psychasthenia, and schizophrenic components in the Minnesota Multiphasic Questionnaire; but the clinical description of the disorder corresponded most with trends already observable in the pre-stress personality. For example, a manic episode developed in an individual known to have cyclical insanity in the family. The conflict engendered in all subjects, by starving amidst plenty, arose to a slight extent from superego conflicts over the temptation to cheat by clandestine eating, partly from their failures to live up to their own ideals of "being able to take it," and partly from discrepancies between implicit standards of bodily and mental performance and the poorer standards which their condition gradually forced upon them.

If the argument put forward in Chapters 9 and 17, namely, that neurosis can only be effectively created when an *appetitive* drive, such as sex, hunger, or sleep, is brought in conflict with the ego or superego (because it is practically impossible to produce continuous conflict with a drive requiring constant external stimulation to maintain the continuity), the situation set up by Brozek and Schiele should have been highly neurotogenic. A close examination of their data indicates that the effects of starvation per se, attained early, consisted mainly of weakness, lack of drive, and depression, with no appreciable changes in intelligence or general efficiency of the central nervous system such as occur in anoxia, etc. The remaining symptoms developed as a result of prolonged conflict and may be considered to constitute one of the first true experimental neuroses produced in man. Even so, it is noticeable that the form of the neurosis was decided by prior, often constitutional, conditions, which suggests that in the uncontrolled, naturally occurring neuroses also, the determination of the neurosis as conversion hysteria or anxiety hysteria, or of a psychosis as schizophrenia or cycloid insanity, does not rest with the personal history of conflict as some psychoanalysts maintain, but with "temperamental" determiners in the personality. Fuller discussion of experimental neurosis, however, is deferred to Chapter 17.

## 6. EFFECTS OF SPECIFIC DRUGS

**Effects of Ethyl Alcohol.** The survey of biochemical associations of personality would not be complete without a glance at the effects of drugs that are known to have influence on general behavior, although the biologically artificial, extraneous nature of some of these drugs prevents generalizations in regard to normal physiology, except where the interaction with normal body chemistry is well understood. Available studies concern mainly alcohol, caffeine, benzedrine, sodium amytal, strychnine, phenobarbital, morphine, and mescal.

An enormous research and literature on alcohol has nevertheless not yielded reasonably complete answers to questions of personality change, because much of it was done before psychometrics became possible for personality traits as well as abilities. Broadly two kinds of change occur through small doses of alcohol; first, a loss of moral, social and general inhibitions, and foresights—accompanied by a pleasurable sense of release—and, second, by a decline in abilities of all kinds. The latter extends over all abilities—reaction time, manual dexterity, fluency of association, power of recall, and general intelligence (14). As Shakespeare pointed out in the porter's speech in Macbeth, this decline of powers to some extent reduces the damage that the individual might inflict through his loss of inhibition, but Shakespeare was unfamiliar with automobiles, automatic pistols, and other artificial sources of power. The loss of inhibition shows itself in an increase of general emotionality, with some specific emphasis on the drives that have been most under suppression in the individual concerned. This is experienced subjectively as an increase of strength of these drives; but, as Scott and others (75) have shown in the case of the apparent increase of appetite and hunger, there is no apparent change in the physiological processes normally determining the strength of the hunger drive. A review of the general field of research on alcohol has been most recently presented by Marshall (58).

An interesting new slant on the action of alcohol is provided by the work of Masserman (see (30), Chap. 21) as yet insufficiently extended and confirmed, that cats under alcohol do not acquire neuroses in those conflict situations that normally produce neuroses, and that cats in which neuroses have been produced in the normal conflict situation lose them under alcohol. The former situation may be understood in terms of reduction of the actual intensity of conflict, since the intoxicated cat is seemingly no longer afraid of the air blast. The latter might also be understood in terms of conflict reduction, by the elimination of fearful associations; but one would then expect certain consequences of the prolonged conflict (general reduction of nervous efficiency, as shown in Chap. 17) to persist even though the hesitant conflict behavior is lost.

**Caffeine, Strychnine, Bromides, Barbiturates.** Much research has been done upon the effects of drugs upon conditioning and habit acquisition. Skinner and Heron (78), Wentinck, and others have shown that caffeine and benzedrine increase the rate of conditioned responses and restore the rate in a response declining to extinction. Petrova and various researchers in the Russian school find both caffeine and bromides restore responses and power of inhibition in dogs subjected to "neurotic" disintegration of discriminating powers. Culler (18) has shown that a conditioned response established under curare disappeared when the effect of the drug wore off, and vice versa. These results suggest that the action of hormones in sensitizing specific inborn neural structures may perhaps be extended to biochemical action generally and with respect to learned patterns acquired under particular conditions. They suggest farther that the phenomena of multiple personality (see Chap. 21) should be examined not only for dynamic causation through the predominance of particular stimuli and inner repressions, but also for biochemical causation, by the action of specific sensitizers.

Strychnine and caffeine in most psychological effects are very similar, except that the former is more powerful. They are opposed in action to the depressant drugs and sedatives, either because they stimulate nerve metabolism or because they lower resistance at synapses. The tendency of strychnine with slightly increased dosage to produce convulsions has suggested the latter action. There arises, under these stimulants, an increase in power of recall, but no increase of intelligence except in fatigued or depressed subjects, a quickening of reaction time, a decline in errors, an increase in speed in psychomotor performances, and an increased rate of fluctuation in the reversible perspective test. Caffeine has a specific effect in increasing red-orange color sensitivity. The action of other alkaloids—morphine, cocaine, mescal, etc.—is too complex for discussion here and relatively unrewarding, as yet, in bringing new light on personality.

In general, the depressant drugs have opposite effects to the above, the general pattern of which has been described with respect to alcohol, but there are certain specific influences also, notably in the barbiturate group which includes phenobarbital and sodium amytal. The use of sodium amytal in inducing a slightly intoxicated, uninhibited state, but with apparently little loss in powers of recall, has been utilized in psychotherapy to bring into consciousness material otherwise sharply repressed, as described, for example, in the work of Grinker and Spiegel (Chap. 17). Phenobarbital, first used as a depressant of epileptic seizures, produces first some degree of exhilaration and then sleepiness. Ikemi (47) found some slight increases in memory ability and a suggestion of decline in ability to reason and calculate.

Animals show no change in learning ability at the time of injection, but a decline in the days following the experiment (63). Henry (42) reports from a study of fourteen "problem" children that self-control and behavior generally are adversely affected by phenobarbital.

**Benzedrine.** Some of the most striking effects of a drug upon personality have been found with the chemical amphetamine or isomyn (trade name, benzedrine) which is similar in chemical structure to adrenalin but does not occur naturally in the body. No improvements of abilities result in men or animals from this drug unless the organism is already fatigued or depressed. Thus, while it fails to produce changes in intelligence-test scores with student subjects, it produces marked increases, as Sargent and Blackburn have shown (71), with psychotics and neurotics, mostly among depressives.

With the drug almost all the effects are ascribable to changes in drive and "values." Its most striking effect is in reducing the subjective sense of fatigue, irritability, boredom, and depression, but this is demonstrable objectively, first, in changes in optimism score on questionnaires (81) and, as regards fatigue, in a lowering of perseveration (increased speed of flicker fusion), postponement of the drop in output curves, increased steadiness and strength of maintained handgrip, etc. The change in mood and values is also shown by the greater interest of children in schoolwork, a striking improvement in such tasks as those of arithmetical computation (4), and a marked improvement in school achievement tests.

Further, as Lindsley (55) and two other researchers have independently shown, there is in problem children an improvement of behavior, a calming and steadying effect without loss of drive (contrasted in two studies with deterioration from phenobarbital). In clinical work generally, however, the most marked improvement has occurred with chronic nervous exhaustion, next with depression (except the deepest kind), and next with psychoneurosis. In such subjects the change is easily outwardly observable in increased motor activity and talkativeness.

It will be noticed that the general nature of the change is almost exactly that which could be described as a shift from desurgency toward surgency. Physiological discussion has favored the view that benzedrine acts in the region of the cerebral peduncle or the midbrain and that it is antagonistic to the action of acetylcholine in the central nervous system. This would be in agreement with the theory of surgency-desurgency propounded above.

### 7. THE CONTRIBUTION OF ELECTROENCEPHALOGRAPHY

**Analysis of E.E.G. Wave Forms.** Berger, who discovered that faint potential variations at the brain cortex (1 to 10 millivolts) could be picked up and magnified from the scalp, and who, single-handed, carried out a surprising amount of the more fundamental research on the matter, suggested the terms $\alpha$, $\beta$, etc., to describe certain wave frequencies that are most prominent in the pulsing variations of potential that occur. The $\alpha$ waves have a frequency of about 10 per second; the $\beta$ waves, a frequency centering on 25 per second; the less-defined $\gamma$ waves, a frequency centering upon 40 per second; while the more recently studied $\delta$ waves are large, slow waves of about 3 per second.

The tendency for the principal rhythms to occur at these frequencies was first noticed by simple inspection of electroencephalograms (E.E.G's); but has since been confirmed by Fourier wave analysis, indicating the greatest energy expression to occur at peaks constituted by these several frequencies. However, when the rhythms have been well described the further problem arises as to whether certain frequencies are functionally related and others not. For example, there has long been speculation as to whether the slower $\alpha$ rhythm could be an interference effect from $\beta$ or $\gamma$ frequencies which scatter over a slight range of frequency under certain conditions. If so, one should observe some inverse correlations between emphasis on these rhythms, and one might expect to demonstrate a cause for the tendency of frequency to disperse slightly to create the interference.

It was not until quite late in E.E.G. study that this question of functional relations was fundamentally attacked by Hsü and Sherman (45) who inter-correlated measures of some twenty-two aspects of the E.E.G., factorized and obtained six factors, as follows: (*a*) an epileptiform pattern, of the spike and other forms previously observed separately for grand and petit mal; (*b*) a group of waves previously called "psychomotor epileptiform" with a flat-topped appearance and which were shown here to belong with certain 6-per-second frequency waves; (*c*) a factor of slow waves of all kinds—delta waves—below the alpha frequency; (*d*) a pattern of upset of alpha waves occurring in some people with hyperventilation—excessive deep breathing; (*e*) a set of frequencies all in the beta wave range, a pattern possibly associated with age, and (*f*), of course, the dominant $\alpha$ frequency. This factorization still awaits confirmation. Generally, in measuring the individual E.E.G., the practice has been followed of recording any one rhythm (or pattern of rhythms, as resulting from the above factorization) with respect to the "percentage time," *i.e.*, the amount of the record which it covers, and also with regard to its departure from the mean frequency or amplitude for that form. More recent work again shows that these may be functionally related in single patterns. Thus, for example, Brazier and Finesinger (5) found with 500 seventeen- to forty-seven-year-olds that the "percent time alpha" is appreciably negatively correlated with the alpha frequency.

**Anatomical Distributions.** Further matters which need to be settled before the significant aspects of the E.E.G. can be related to personality, concern changes with physiological conditions, age, etc. Lindsley (56) demonstrated that there are actually four ·foci of E.E.G.'s—the occipital, the temporal, and two other cortical regions—which are not identical in pattern or phase. He suggests that these may be cortical projection areas from a thalamic center. The rhythm in the thalamus seems to be more basic, in that the cortical rhythm disappears in adverse conditions (*e.g.*, anoxia) when that of the thalamus does not. In children, after the age of three months, regular rhythms begin to appear in two areas—the precentral and the occipital, both being slower than the alpha in adults, particularly the occipital. Between nine and twelve years (the age of completion of myelination) the frequencies and forms take on adult values.

**Psychological and Physiological Associations.** Most of the studies underlying the generalizations that follow have been on the well-defined occipital rhythms. The relation to psychological events is as follows: the perception of light (or, in the case of other cortical sense areas, the perception of other stimuli) blots out the dominant alpha rhythm. A pulsating stimulus, however, if near the frequency of the alpha rhythm will tend to constrain the rhythm to its own frequency, and Livanov has shown that this dominant rhythm will spread from visual to auditory areas, etc. The $\alpha$ rhythm is blotted out also by sudden concentration, emotion, and, especially, fear; and there is usually an increase of beta and gamma waves in these circumstances. Strong emotion also brings on the large, somewhat uneven delta waves. The possible parallelism of E.E.G. and P.G.R. suggested by these observations has been investigated by Jurgens (49) who found greatest upset of the alpha rhythm by those stimuli which produced greatest P.G.R. and vegetative change. Darrow found similarly (19) that stimulation reduced alpha and increased beta, and he gives correlations of these with autonomic measures. Williams (82,83), however, points out a neglected phenomenon, nevertheless confirmed by one or two other workers, in the form of a *strengthening* of the alpha rhythm by a stimulus (instead of a blocking) when the stimulus is expected. Adoption of a mental set seems to steady the alpha rhythm and stimuli, especially familiar stimuli, then augment the cortical process. The alpha frequency declines slightly in periods of rest and accelerates slightly during periods of high activity. In hypnotic "sleep" the alpha rhythm does not disappear as in normal sleep, though when the subject is instructed to "see" a nonexistent object the rhythm interrupts as in a real perception. The outstanding "mental process" change, apart from alpha interruption on perception, is the outbreak of delta rhythms in emotion, in brain injuries and infections, in unconsciousness, in anoxia, and wherever cortical action is replaced by emergency, hypothalamic activity.

Physiological research shows that the alpha rhythm is responsive to efficiency of brain metabolism, its amplitude and frequency being reduced by alcohol, oxygen deficiency, or hypoglycemia. Hyperthyroid conditions, a rise in blood acidity or in temperature, or ingestion of caffeine have the opposite effect.   In Addison's disease (deficiency of adrenal cortex) the beta rhythm is impaired.   Moruzzi (66) found that weak injections of acetylcholine into the brains of rabbits enhanced the amplitudes of rhythms and showed various phenomena of cerebral spread and facilitation.

**Relations of E.E.G. to Personality.**   The above findings already indicate some relations to personality, but more direct evidence exists.   In the first place, the E.E.G. is observed to be highly characteristic of the individual, quite as characteristic as handwriting.   Most workers comment that related persons are similar and that identical twins are indistinguishable, while Lennox and Gibbs (53) have shown that in 90 per cent of cases the E.E.G. reveals correctly whether twins are monozygotic or dizygotic.   But there are changes with age and perhaps experience, for Greenblatt (38) has shown that delta incidence and slow rhythms generally decline to a minimum in the 45 to 55 age range and that the very fast rhythms increase to 55 years and perhaps later.

Most studies relating normal ranges of personality in such variables as intelligence, dominance, introversion, neuroticism, etc., to the E.E.G. have obtained negligible or conflicting finds, doubtless partly due to the poor definition and modes of measurement of such variables as "extraversion." However, a correlation of $+0.5$ between intelligence and alpha frequency has been demonstrated in young children (homogeneous in age), though by twelve years of age it has already declined to $+0.12$.   There is an increase of frequency also with chronological age.

"Per cent time alpha" was found by Berger to be high in mental defectives, which he ascribed to their freedom from interrupting ideas.   It seems, however, also and more definitely to have a connection with another dimension of personality, for it is lower in tense, emotional, and schizoid individuals and perhaps higher in cyclothymics and manic-depressives (particularly depressives).   It was found to be longer in passive, good-tempered persons with records of having held jobs longer (55).   Rubin and Bowman (69), however, found large per cent time alpha also in peptic ulcer patients and asthmatics, and argued—from their theory that these are passive, dependent people—that such an E.E.G. goes with mother-dependent, overprotected, "good" as well as passive personalities.

In schizophrenics the alpha is not only somewhat short but also lacking in amplitude, highly variable over different parts of the cortex normally similar and more variable from day to day than among normals.   There is a disproportionate amount of energy in the beta rhythm (35).   A similar relative predominance of beta and deficiency of alpha is reported in various anxiety states. Schizophrenics, however, also show an excess of slow delta rhythms, such as are commonly associated with poor cortical function, e.g., around tumors.

As Lindsley has shown (55) the E.E.G. of "problem" children tends to differ perceptibly from normals, first in the high percentage (70 to 90 in different groups) of abnormalities of all kinds, but principally epileptiform curves and especially the high incidence of delta waves.    These abnormalities appear with hyperventilation much earlier than in control cases.    Psychopathic personalities in adults also (44,57) show excessive delta—at about six per second.    Among minor "behavior disorders" the most abnormal E.E.G. is found in enuretics (65).    The general findings with problem behavior have impressed Lindsley with the role of abnormal constitutional conditions (55) in what has frequently been considered a largely sociological problem.

The most striking personality imprints in the E.E.G. occur in connection with epilepsy—indeed a conservative writer like Walker argues that the only indubitable associations are with brain lesions, with catatonic and hebephrenic schizophrenia, and with epilepsy.    A specific spike pattern in normal conditions and flat-topped and high frequency, high amplitude patterns in fits are found in epileptics.    The spike and other epileptiform patterns are found over 100 times as frequently among people who have fits as among others (84).    They are also present six times more frequently in the relatives of epileptics than in the general population.

Further advance in understanding of the electroencephalogram depends both on finer concepts in measuring personality and more complete, factorial means of picking out independent patterns among the rhythms.

### 8. SUMMARY

This chapter would normally terminate with a discussion of the relation of personality to somatic structure, to physical build and form and those aspects of physique that are largely fixed and constitutional.    This whole matter, however, has already been substantially dealt with in Section 4 of Chapter 5 on heredity, in a manner not different from that required here. The student should therefore refresh his memory there, seeing new connections in the light of the present chapter, particularly regarding the associations of certain physiques with trends in physiological and psychological test results and with proneness to specific mental disorders.

Physique also affects personality indirectly, as a possession of the individual to which the social and physical environment responds in certain ways. This aspect, or at least the effect of "social stimulus value" of physique, is more appropriately considered in the ensuing chapter on growing up.

The direct associations of personality and physical organism discussed in this chapter may be briefly summarized as follows:

1. The method of approaching psychosomatic relations by noting mental traits developed in specific physical illnesses has the disadvantage that

various secondary effects have first to be discounted. However, with proper control, it yields definite findings in quite a variety of illnesses, *e.g.*, diabetes and other endocrine disorders, hypertension, encephalitis, anemia, and perhaps rheumatism and tuberculosis. These may not at present indicate entirely new mechanisms but they add to the understanding of psychophysiological mechanisms already studied.

2. Various indices of the physiological reaction of the total organism, notably metabolic rate, electrical skin resistance, magnitude of the psychogalvanic response to stimulation, level of muscle tension, have decided relation to personality, the level of activity being greater in individuals rated energetic, enthusiastic, bold, and ambitious and in individuals who do well relative to their endowment in intelligence.

3. Researches on individual biochemistry not directly related to nervous metabolism reveal quite a number of sporadic but significant findings, notably on glycemic level, calcium level, and pH value of the blood, which cannot yet be completed organized. There is also evidence of large differences in the incidence of various causes of death among individuals suffering from various psychoses.

4. Physiological instability seems to be correlated with behavior instability. Since causation in both directions can readily be hypothesized, further research is required into this relationship.

5. The chemistry and physics of the individual nerve cell are now tolerably understood, though action at the synapse is still obscure. Nevertheless the reaction of the nervous system as a whole to changes in concentration of calcium, potassium, oxygen, etc., is essentially that which would be predicted from our knowledge of the single cell.

6. The action of adrenalin and acetylcholine, and of the enzymes cholinesterase and eserine, in facilitating and controlling nervous activity in different regions is suggestive of a physiological theory to account for the important personality factor $F$ or surgency-desurgency, but the absence of certain links of information prevents a detailed articulation of the theory.

7. Anoxia, hypoglycemia, and other simple reducers of nerve metabolism rate have essentially similar results on behavior; reducing intelligence, speed and other abilities, emotional control and judgment, and tending to bring out whatever neurotic or psychotic trends are latent, but usually bringing out paranoid trends. Individuals of asthenic build seem less able than others to adjust autonomically to such physiological insults as have been studied here.

8. Nutritional deficiencies produce most rapid mental change when occurring in the B vitamin complex. Lack of vitamin B produces convulsive hypersensitivity in animals and in man brings on a neurasthenialike condition, with depression, irritability, timidity, and lack of emotional control.

General malnutrition also causes depression and schizoid symptoms, but may, through the psychological conflicts engendered, produce in addition a typical "artificial" neurosis, which fact supports the "appetitive drive" theory of neurosis.

9. Most drugs, *i.e.*, chemicals not normally found in the body, fall either into the group of stimulants, which accelerate response and improve recall slightly, or depressants, which have a converse effect on abilities (but proceed further and affect intelligence too) as well as emotional control and foresight. However, there are also effects specific to any particular chemical group of depressants and even to particular members of the chemical family. Benzedrine is one of the few known drugs which also have a direct effect upon drives, producing a change of mood and values, which is reflected in goals and general behavior.

10. Electroencephalography is valuable in diagnosing some functional mental abnormalities, as well as in locating organic conditions in the brain, but the relation of brain rhythm patterns to normal personality differences is not yet very clear. Its use confirms and extends what was known about the relation of brain metabolism to behavior, and suggests a more constitutional emphasis in many "behavior problem" cases than has usually been supposed.

11. Certain indubitable relations exist between temperamental traits and racial genetic factors as well as the leptosomatic and other factors in body build. These are discussed in Chapter 5.

## QUESTIONS AND EXERCISES

1. Describe briefly the personality picture associated with (*a*) anemia, (*b*) diabetes, (*c*) encephalitis, and discuss the direction and manner of causal connection in each.

2. Outline what is known about the relation of (*a*) level of skin resistance, (*b*) magnitude of the psychogalvanic reflex, to, first, mental state at the moment and, second, persistent personality traits.

3. Examine the theory that physiological stability and psychological stability are related, with reference to biochemical and total organic reactions in normals, psychoneurotics, and psychotics. Discuss causation.

4. Describe the behavior of the ordinary nerve cell under stimulation, stating what is known about the action of acid-base equilibrium, and concentration of calcium and potassium ions.

5. Outline the theory that bases human variation along the surgency-desurgency continuum upon variations in acetylcholine concentration in the central nervous system.

6. Describe in detail the changes of capacity and behavior observed to take place with decreasing oxygen supply to the brain. Discuss the causes of individual differences in response.

7. What are the proved immediate effects of severe general and specific (vitamin-B) deficiencies? Describe the symptoms of neurosis, as obtained in the experiments of Brozek, with reference to general theories of neurosis.

8. Describe the psychological effects of (*a*) a typical depressant drug, and (*b*) benzedrine, speculating about the locus and manner of their action.

9. What is known about the patterns and functional unities in the human encephalogram, and the relation of these patterns to brain maturation and metabolism?

10. Discuss the value of the encephalogram in clinical diagnosis. Examine the evidence of relation of wave patterns to normal personality differences as well as to pathological conditions.

## BIBLIOGRAPHY

1. BARACH, A. L., and J. KAGAN: Disorders of Mental Functioning Produced by Varying the Oxygen Tension of the Atmosphere: I. Effects of Low Oxygen Atmospheres on Normal Individuals and Patients with Psychoneurotic Disease, *Psychosom. Med.*, 2: 53–67, 1940.

2. BERNHARD, CARL G., and C. R. SKAGLUND: On the Blocking Time of the Cortical Alpha Rhythm in Children, *Acta. psychiat.*, Kbh., 18: 159–170, 1943.

3. BLONSKY, P. P.: The Alkalinity of the Saliva as Indicator of Intelligence and Mental Concentration of Attention, *Psychol. u. Med.*, 4: 22–26, 1929.

4. BRADLEY, C., and M. BOWEN: School Performance of Children Receiving Amphetamine (Benzedrine) Sulfate, *Amer. J. Orthopsychiat.*, 10: 782–789, 1940.

5. BRAZIER, M. A. B., and J. E. FINESINGER: Characteristics of the Normal Electroencephalogram: I. A Study of the Occipital Cortical Potentials in 500 Normal Adults, *J. clin. Invest.*, 23: 303–311, 1944.

6. BROWN, C. H.: The Relation of Magnitude of Galvanic Skin Responses and Resistance Levels to the Rate of Learning, *J. exp. Psychol.*, 20: 262–278, 1937.

7. BROZEK, J., H. GUETZKOW, A. KEYS, R. B. CATTELL, and M. HARROWER: A Study of Personality of Normal Young Men Maintained on Restricted Intakes of Vitamins of the B Complex, *Psychosom. Med.*, 8: 89, 1946.

8. CAPRIO, F. S.: The Morbidity Incidence of Degenerative Somatic Diseases in Psychotics in Comparison with the Same Type of Disease in Comparable Age Groups in Civil Life, *Amer. J. Psychiat.*, 95: 185–192, 1938

9. CATTELL, R. B.: The Subjective Character of Cognition, *Brit. J. Psychol. Monogr. Suppl.*, No. 14, 1930.

10. CATTELL, R. B.: *The Description and Measurement of Personality*, World Book Company, Yonkers, New York, 1946.

11. CATTELL, R. B., A. K. S. CATTELL, and RUE M. RHYMER: P-technique Demonstrated in Determining Psychophysiological Source Traits in a Normal Individual, *Psychometrika*, 12: 267–288, 1947.

12. CATTELL, R. B.: Experiments on the Psychical Correlate of the Psychogalvanic Reflex, *Brit. J. Psychol.*, 19: 357–383, 1929.

13. CATTELL, R. B., and L. B. LUBORSKY: P-technique Demonstrated as a New Clinical Method for Determining Symptom Structure, *J. gen. Psychol.*, 42: 3–24, 1950.

14. CATTELL, R. B.: The Effects of Alcohol and Caffeine upon Intelligent and Associative Performance, *Brit. J. med. Psychol.*, 10: 20–23, 1930.

15. CHEVENS, L. C. F.: The Correlation of Cause of Death with Types of Insanity, *J. ment. Sci.*, 77: 562–572, 1931.

16. COHEN, R. L., and A. WIKLER: Effects of Morphine on Cortical Electrical Activity of the Rat, *Yale J. Biol. Med.*, 16: 239–243, 1944.

17. COLMAN, R. D., and C. R. McCRAE: An Attempt to Measure the Strength of Instincts, *Forum. Educ.*, 3: 171–181, 1927.

18. CULLER, E., J. D. COAKLEY, P. S. SHURRAGER, and H. W. ADES: Differential Effects of Curare upon Higher and Lower Levels of the Central Nervous System, *Amer. J. Psychol.*, 52: 266–273, 1939.

19. DARROW, C. W.: The Galvanic Skin Reflex and Blood Pressure as Preparatory and Facilitative Functions, *Psychol. Bull.*, 33: 73–94, 1936.

20. DARROW, C. W., H. JOST, A. P. SOLOMON, and J. C. MERGENER: Autonomic Indications of Excitatory and Homeostatic Effects on the Electroencephalogram, *J. Psychol.*, 14: 115–130, 1942.

21. DE NATALE, F. J.: Psychotic Manifestations Associated with Pernicious Anemia, *Psychiat. Quart.*, 15: 143–158, 1941.

22. DESPERT, J. L.: Emotional Factors in Some Young Children's Colds, *Med. Clin. N. Amer.*, 28: 603–614, 1944.

23. DIAZ-GUERRERO, ROGEHO, S. JACQUES GOTTLIEB, and J. R. KNOTT: The Sleep of Patients with Manic-depressive Psychosis, Depressive Type; an Electroencephalographic Study, *Psychosom. Med.*, 8: 399–404, 1946.

24. DUFFY, E.: Level of Muscular Tension as an Aspect of Personality, *J. gen. Psychol.*, 35: 161–171, 1946.

25. DUNBAR, H. F.: *Emotions and Bodily Changes*, Columbia University Press, New York, 1946.

26. DUNBAR, H. F.: *Psychosomatic Diagnosis*, Paul B. Hoeber, Inc., New York, 1943.

27. EYSENCK, H. J.: *The Dimensions of Personality*, Kegan Paul, Trench, Trubner & Co., London, 1947.

28. FELDBERG, W.: Present Views on the Mode of Action of Acetylcholine in the Central Nervous System, *Physiol. Rev.*, 25: 596–642, 1945.

29. FORSTER, F. M.: Action of Acetylcholine on Motor Cortex; Correlation of Effects of Acetylcholine and Epilepsy, *Arch. Neurol. Psychiat.*, Chicago, 54: 391–394, 1945.

30. FRANKLIN, J. C., B. C. SCHIELE, J. BROZEK, and A. KEYS: Observations on Human Behavior in Experimental Semi-starvation and Rehabilitation, *J. Clin. Psychol.*, 4: 28–45, 1948.

31. FREEMAN, A.: Biometrical Studies in Psychiatry: VII. Tuberculosis, Syphilis, and Cancer, *Hum. Biol.*, 4: 208–238, 1932.

32. FREEMAN, G. L., and E. T. KATZOFF: Individual Differences in Physiological Reactions to Stimulation and Their Relation to Other Measures of Emotionality, *J. exp. Psychol.*, 31: 527–537, 1942.

32a. FREEMAN, G. L.: *The Energetics of Human Behavior*, Cornell University Press, Ithaca, 1948.

33. GELLHORN, E.: The Influence of Carbon Dioxide in Combating the Effect of Oxygen Deficiency on Psychic Processes, with Remarks on the Fundamental Relationship between Psychic and Physiologic Reactions, *Amer. J. Psychiat.*, 93: 1413–1434, 1937.

34. GELLHORN, E.: Anoxia in Relation to the Visual System, in Kluver, H., *Visual Mechanisms*, Science Press, Lancaster, Pa., 73–85, 1942.

35. GIBBS, F. A.: Spectra from Eight Cortical Areas of Normal Adults, Epileptic, Parents of Epileptic and Schizophrenic Patients, *Trans. Amer. neurol. Ass.*, 66: 211–212, 1940.

36. GOLDSTEIN, H.: The Biochemical Variability of the Individual in Relation to Personality and Intelligence, *J. exp. Psychol.*, 18: 348–371, 1935.

37. GRAHAM, J. D. P.: High Blood Pressure after Battle, *Lancet*, 248: 239–240, 1945.

38. GREENBLATT, M.: Age and Encephalographic Abnormality: a Study of 1593 Neuropsychiatric Patients, *Amer. J. Psychiat.*, 101: 82–90, 1944.

39. HALLIDAY, J. R.: Psychological Factors in Rheumatism: a Preliminary Study, *Brit. J. Med.*, 17: 213–217, 264–310, 1937.

40. HALLIDAY, J. R.: The Concept of Psychosomatic Rheumatism, *Ann. Intern. Med.* 15: 661–671, 1941.

41. HAMILTON, J., and N. W. SHOCK: An Experimental Study of Personality, Physique, and the Acid Base Equilibrium of the Blood, *Amer. J. Psychiat.*, 48: 467–473, 1936.

42. HENRY, C. E.: The Effect of Drugs on Behavior and the Electroencephalogram of Children with Behavior Disorders, *Psychol. Bull.*, 38: 590, 1941.

43. Henry, C. E.: Electroencephalograms of Normal Children, *Monogr. Soc. Res. Child Developm.*, 9: (No. 3) 1944.

44. Hodge, R. S.: The Impulsive Psychopath: a Clinical and Electrophysiological Study, *J. ment. Sci.*, 91: 472–476, 1945.

45. Hsü, E. H., and M. Sherman: The Factorial Analysis of the Electroencephalogram, *J. Psychol.*, 21: 189–196, 1946.

46. Hulbert, H. S.: Calcium (Soluble) for "Fractiousness," *J. crim. Law Criminol.*, 34: 233–235, 1943.

47. Ikemi, T.: Intoxication of Phenobarbital, *Nagoya J. Med. Sci.*, 50: 487–494, 1939.

48. Jones, M.: The Effect of Acetylcholine on the Somatic Symptoms of Anxiety, *J. ment. Sci.*, 82: 785–790, 1936.

49. Jurgens, B.: Uber Vegetative Reaktionen Heim Menschen in Ihner Abhangizheit von Verschiedenen, *Reizen. Arch. Psychiat.*, *Nervenkr.*, 111: 88–114, 1940.

50. Kraines, S. H.: The Correlation of Oxygen Deprivation with Intelligence, Constitution, and Blood Pressure, *Amer. J. Psychiat.*, 93: 1435–1446, 1937.

51. Laird, D., and J. M. Stephan: The Relation of Emotional Tone to Blood Calcium, *Med. J. and Rec.*, 138: 223–224, 1933.

52. Lehmann, J. E.: The Effect of Changes in the Potassium-Calcium Balance on the Action of Mammalian Nerve Fibers, *Amer. J. Physiol.*, 118: 613–619, 1937.

53. Lennox, W. G., E. L. Gibbs, and F. A. Gibbs: The Brain-wave Pattern, an Hereditary Trait; Evidence from 74 "Normal" Pairs of Twins, *J. Hered.*, 36: 233–243, 1945.

54. Liberson, W. T., and C. A. Seguin: Brain Waves and Clinical Features in Arteriosclerotic and Senile Mental Patients, *Psychosom. Med.*, 7: 30–35, 1945.

55. Lindsley, D. B., and C. E. Henry: The Effect of Drugs on Behavior and the Electroencephalograms of Children with Behavior Disorders, *Psychosom. Med.*, 4: 140–149, 1942.

56. Lindsley, D. B.: Electroencephalography, Chapter 33 in J. McV. Hunt, *Personality and the Behavior Disorders*, The Ronald Press Company, New York, 1944.

57. Marsh, C.: Electroencephalographic Changes Due to Cerebral Trauma, *Bull. Los Angeles Neurol. Soc.*, 9: 38–45, 1944.

58. Marshall, H.: Alcohol: a Critical Review of the Literature, 1929–1940, *Psychol. Bull.*, 38: 193–217, 1941.

59. McCowan, P. K., and J. H. Quastel: Blood Sugar Studies in Abnormal Mental States, *Lancet*, 221: 731–736, 1931.

60. McFarland, R. A.: Psycho-physiological Studies at High Altitude in the Andes: I. The Effect of Rapid Ascents by Aeroplane and Train, *J. comp. Psychol.*, 23: 191–225, 1937.

61. McFarland, R. A.: Psycho-physiological Studies at High Altitude in the Andes: II. Sensory and Motor Responses during Acclimatization, *J. comp. Psychol.*, 23: 277–285, 1937.

62. McGavin, A. P., E. Schultz, G. W. Peden, and S. D. Brown: The Physical Growth, the Degree of Intelligence, and the Personality Adjustment of a Group of Diabetic Children, *New Engl. J. Med.*, 223: 119–127, 1940.

63. Mendenhall, M. C.: The Effect of Sodium Phenobarbitol on Learning and Reasoning in White Rats, *J. comp. Psychol.*, 29: 257–276, 1940.

64. Meyer, A., L. N. Ballmeier, and F. Alexander: Correlation between Emotions and Carbohydrate Metabolism in Two Cases of Diabetes Mellitus, *Psychosom. Med.*, 7: 335–341, 1945.

65. Michaels, J. J.: The Relationship of Antisocial Traits to the E.E.G. in Children with Behavior Disorders, *Psychosom. Med.*, 7: 41–44, 1945.

66. MORUZZI, G.: The Phenomena of Facilitation in the Cerebral Cortex and the Hypothesis of Chemical Mediation in Nerve Impulse, *C. R. Soc. Biol.*, Paris, 129: 27–32, 1938.

67. MURPHY, J. P., and E. GELLHORN: Hypothalamic Facilitation of the Motor Cortex, *Proc. Soc. exp. Biol.*, N. Y., 58: 115–116, 1945.

68. QUASTEL, J. H., and W. T. WALES: Faulty Detoxication in Schizophrenia, *Lancet.*, 235: 301–305, 1938.

69. RUBIN, S., and K. M. BOWMAN: Electroencephalographic and Personality Correlates in Peptic Ulcers, *Psychosom. Med.*, 4: 309–318, 1942.

70. RUBIN, S., and L. MOSES: Electroencephalographic Studies in Asthma with Some Personality Correlates, *Psychosom. Med.*, 6: 31–39, 1944.

71. SARGENT, W., and J. M. BLACKBURN: The Effects of Benzedrine on Intelligence Scores, *Lancet.*, 1385–1393, 1936.

72. SAUL, L. J.: Psychogenic Factors in the Etiology of the Common Cold and Related Symptoms, *Int. J. Psycho-Anal.*, 19: 451–470, 1938.

73. SCHIELE, B. C., and J. BROZEK: Experimental Neurosis Resulting from Semi-Starvation in Man, *Psychosom. Med.*, 10: 31–50, 1948.

74. SCHWAB, R. S., J. E. FINESINGER, and M. A. B. BRAZIER: Psychoneuroses Precipitated by Combat, *Nav. med. Bull.*, Washington, 42:.535–544, 1944.

75. SCOTT, C. C., W. W. SCOTT, and A. B. LUCKHARDT: The Effect of Alcohol on the Hunger Sense, *Amer. J. Physiol.*, 123: 248–255, 1938.

76. SEIDENFELD, M. A.: A Comparative Study of the Responses of Turberculous and Non-tuberculous Subjects on the Maller Personality Sketches, *J. Psychol.*, 9: 247–258, 1940.

77. SHULZ, I. T.: The Emotions of the Tubercular: a Review and an Analysis, *J. abnorm. soc. Psychol.*, 37: 260–300, 1942.

78. SKINNER, B. F., and W. T. HERON: Effects of Caffeine and Benzedrine upon Conditioning and Extinction, *Psychol. Rec.*, 1: 340–346, 1937.

79. SPRAGG, S. D. S.: The Effect of Certain Drugs on Mental and Motor Efficiency, *Psychol. Bull.*, 38: 354–363, 1941.

80. STRECKER, E. A., F. J. BRACELAND, and B. GORDON: Mental Attitudes of Tuberculous Patients *Ment. Hyg.*, 22: 529–543, 1938.

81. TURNER, W. D., and G. P. CARL: Temporary Changes in Affect and Attitude Following Ingestion of Various Amounts of Benzedrine Sulfate (Amphetanime Sulfate), *J, Psychol.*, 8: 415–482, 1939.

82. WILLIAMS, A. C.: Facilitation of the Alpha Rhythm of the Electroencephalogram, *J. exp. Psychol.*, 26: 413–422, 1940.

83. WILLIAMS, A. C.: Some Psychological Correlates of the Electroencephalogram, *Arch. Psychol.* New York, No. 240: 42, 1939.

84. WILLIAMS, D.: The Nature of Transient Outbursts in the Electroencephalogram of Epileptics, *Brain.*, 67: 10–37, 1944.

# CHAPTER 12

## PERSONALITY AND THE CULTURAL MATRIX:
## I. THE FAMILY, ITS STRUCTURE AND SETTING

1. The Changing Family in a Changing Society
2. The Typical Family and Its Variants
3. The Psychological Dimensions of the Family Syntality
4. Factors in the Stability of Marriage
5. The Dynamics of the Total Marital Situation
6. Scheme for the Analysis of Intrafamilial Attitudes
7. Methodology of Intrafamilial Attitude Measurement
8. Summary

### 1. THE CHANGING FAMILY IN A CHANGING SOCIETY

The inquiry up to this point has dealt with the nature of the organism and the principles of its adjustment in terms of the most general things that can happen to it. It has dealt with psychological and physiological universals. Thus we have analyzed the broad adjustment processes but not the particular cultural events in the environmental background occasioning adjustments or the specific modifications of adjustment that suit them. The cultural environment, in other words, was taken for granted, as far as its detailed variations are concerned, or was "held constant" while the development processes common to most cultures were considered. It is now necessary to focus the cultural demands more sharply, to examine in more detail the mechanisms through which they act, and to see what individual differences of personality arise through variations in the strength and pattern of the cultural experience.

Apart from the influences of geographical and climatic environment alone, which are small, our study is concerned with the influences of social institutions such as the family, the school, the church, the social class, the play group, the literary heritage, the government, and the traditions involved in the national culture pattern. These influences are interlocking and interdependent in complex ways which it is the business of social psychology to unravel. In the next chapter we shall take brief account of what social psychology has to say about these relations, but since the present chapter is wholly concerned with one institution, the family, no interrelations need yet be discussed.

The family is of such paramount importance because it operates upon personality in the earliest years of its formation, because its control is well-nigh complete, and because, to a greater extent than any other institution, it is a model of the whole culture pattern, reflecting with great fidelity the mental furniture, emotional values, and moral laws of the larger society. In this chapter we shall study the formation of the family from the parental personalities, the structure of the family, and its setting in society, leaving to the second chapter on the family the study of effects on the growing child personality.

**Trends in the Form of the Family.** Even though at this point we do not pursue the psychodynamic connections of the family with other institutions, it is necessary to recognize that the family has changed greatly with time and cultural locus and that it is necessary to define the kind of family on which the experiments are carried out and to which the generalizations apply. On the social, historical, and anthropological comparisons of the family the student should read Baber (2), Burgess (5), Briffault (4), Westermarck (31) and others.

The family in democratic, Christian countries—on which most psychological data have been gathered—is in a process of transition. The chief trends over the last century or half-century that are of importance to the psychologist are:

1. A decline in patriarchal, authoritarian structure and rise in feminine control, due partly to democratic idealism, partly to the improved status of women through economic, educational, and legal changes, and partly to business competition withdrawing the father from parental duties.

2. A sharp decrease in typical family size, both through reduction of the number of children (from an average of 5.28 in 1860 to 3.4 in 1930) and of the custom of having grandparents and other in-laws living in the same family.

3. An increased urbanization, leading to (a) decline of dependent neighborliness, (b) increased possibilities of recreational and emotional satisfaction outside the family, (c) decreased selectivity in marriage, due to ignorance of social and family backgrounds, (d) decreased social control through "anonymity."

4. A shift of some responsibilities from the family to the local community or the state, e.g., education, health supervision, recreation, and others to commercial organizations, such as substitution of radio for conversation, of prepared foods for those previously made at home.

5. A decrease in durability of marriage. (In America between 1867 and 1929 the population increased by 300 per cent; the annual number of divorces by 2,000 per cent.)

While these changes have not abolished the family or even made it a categorically different thing from the family of a hundred years ago, they have somewhat reduced its role as a transmitter of culture, as a school of social experience and as a center of emotional and economic security—at least beyond the level of infancy.   This has coincided with what may be most briefly described as a rise of psychological individualism on the one hand and a decline of family-community distinctness, *i.e.*, an increase of state paternalism, on the other.   Nevertheless, the main functions of the family remain: (*a*) To provide a controlled, secure environment, economically and emotionally, during childhood; (*b*) to express through a stable institution the sexual and companionable and other needs of adults; (*c*) to help transmit the culture pattern, especially its basic moral values and taboos; (*d*) to provide social-emotional learning in a microcosm of the outer world.   These and other functions receive fuller discussion in Section 8, below.

## 2. THE TYPICAL FAMILY AND ITS VARIANTS

**Definition of the Syntality of a Family.**   Most of our knowledge of personality structure and much of our insight into psychological causation arise from the study of the ways in which individuals differ—from others and from themselves at other times.   In such study we *measure* people and find how the various measures correlate with others or how they change under certain influences.   Thus we discover the functional unities which it is important that we measure.   Similarly, if progress is to occur in the psychology of the family, we must measure the family instead of attempting to define it by some loose typology or looser adjectives.   As with the individual personality, however, meaningful measurement can proceed only after we have discovered the dimensions that need to be measured.

**Syntality, Structure, and Population.**   Properly to design research and formulate conclusions in this field it is necessary to realize that the family, like any other group, can be measured from three aspects: (*a*) in regard to its behavior as a single organism, as when we speak of a capable, or well-knit, or peaceful, or sociable family.   Then we describe the total family atmosphere and its reactions as a unitary group.   It has been suggested (6) that we describe this as the *syntality* of the family, just as we would refer to the *personality* of an individual.   Thus we might say the Smith family has an aggressive but stable and well-knit syntality; (*b*) with regard to the nature of its *structure*, *i.e.*, the "form of government" and inter-individual attitudes that hold it together, *e.g.*, is degree of patriarchalism, and (*c*) with regard to the single elements out of which the structure is formed, namely, the nature of the individual personalities among whom the structuring attitudes exist *e.g.*, the average intelligence of the siblings in the family.   Just so, in any team, we may describe the individuals, the way they are organized, and the resulting performance of the team as a team.

**The Normal Family Described.**   Since the question of the dimensions of the family group is a complex one, not yet objectively solved, we shall postpone its discussion awhile and attempt to describe the existing, typical family in terms and "dimensions" already available in common speech. For it is surely necessary to verify that we are all talking about the same thing when we begin with generalizations concerning the psychology of "the average family." How big is the average family? (The "dimensions" of vital statistics at least are clear—size, death rate, duration, etc.) And what is the usual difference of age between parents and children? What is the most common mode of control of children by parents? Are the siblings normally jealous of each other? What percentage of families last or break up, or are composed of one or more stepparents, etc.? How much leisure is typically spent in intrafamilial activities? What is the normal amount of parental protection of children and what amounts to overprotection? And so on with respect to income, capital, health, cultural level, community surroundings, etc.

The definition of the normal family is still in some essentials unknown, and only in a few respects do we have also the norms whereby we can state how extreme in deviation a particular family is in any particular trait. The failure to develop such norms is a serious defect both in sociology and in such fields as clinical psychology. When the clinical psychologist generalizes that parental conflict is the cause of defective character development in children, or a psychiatrist states in a given clinical case that the child is suffering from parental rejection, a scientifically disposed psychologist may well question the statements. He will demand proof of what is a normal degree of intraparental conflict, or ask at what point on the continuum of "affection for the child" rejection may be said to operate.

Some available facts, however, may help a little toward the desired perspective. We know (14) that at the present time about 10 or 15 per cent of families consist of husband and wife alone, 40 per cent consist of parents and children with no other relatives, 8 per cent consist of husband and wife with in-laws, and the remainder are largely families with children and in-laws together or with children and unrelated people (lodgers) living in the home. Thus what many think of as the typical family actually constitutes only 40 per cent of families.

As to size of family, we know that in America the birth rate dropped 22 per cent between 1925 and 1935 and in Britain a little less in the same period. The average size of family in 1950 lies between two and three children in America, about two in Britain, less than two in France and Germany, and about three and a half in Russia. Urban families are smaller than rural ones and upper-class smaller than lower-class. At the moment, unfortunately, intelligence holds a closer association than either of these variables with size of family. The smaller families are found to average higher in intelligence. Or, put in causal order, the intelligent have smaller families, so that parents with an I.Q. of 130 are found to average about

1½ children and those of I.Q. 80 average 4½ children (8).    The death rate between birth and eighteen years of age reduces the child population by about 7.1 per cent and the reduction operates somewhat more strongly both on lower social-status groups and on lower intelligence groups.    The average difference in age between parents and children is greater for higher than lower social-status groups and decidedly greater for more intelligent than less intelligent or less educated parents.

**Effect of Information about Family upon Psychological Interpretations.** All these sociological considerations need to be taken into account in interpreting the psychological effects of family situation.    For example, the finding that the only child is somewhat above average intelligence might be interpreted as the result of his greater association with adults if one did not know that restriction of family correlates with family intelligence.    Again, psychoanalysts have interpreted the fact that schizophrenics have experienced more sibling deaths to mean that the schizophrenic is suffering from guilt because his unconscious aggressive death wishes have issued in the death of those near to him.    But schizophrenia is more prevalent with lower social status, just like sibling deaths, which suggests the alternative interpretation that both are the result of some more stressful conditions associated with the lower social status of the family.

The durability of the typical family is limited by divorce, separation, desertion, and death of parents, as to the frequency of which some findings can be presented.    In 1940 there were 40,286,770 children under eighteen in the United States of whom 4,518,000, or about one in nine, lived in broken homes (1).    Of these, 1,196,000 were in homes headed by men and 3,322,000 in homes constituted by mother or stepmother.    Of the total "broken homes" (with children in them) 2½ times as many were broken by death of father, mother, or both as by divorce.    Thus it is evident that of the one in five or six (18 per cent at present) marriages that end in divorce a disproportionate number come from the childless marriages.

The experiences of having to adjust to parental separation or to the making of a new home with stepparents or to a home lacking one parent fortunately befall only a minority of children, but it is not a negligible minority.    The frequency of experience of the death of a parent appears to be, with our present conditions, that 3 per cent of children under five, 7 per cent between five and seven, 12½ per cent from ten to fourteen, and 17 per cent from fifteen to seventeen have lost either one or both parents by death.

### 3. THE PSYCHOLOGICAL DIMENSIONS OF THE FAMILY SYNTALITY

**Family Characteristics.**    As to what is normal in the less tangible characteristics of families with which psychologists deal, practically no data can yet be presented, nor have the measuring instruments yet been invented

—save for the intrafamilial attitude measures presented in Section 6 below— by which such variables could be assessed. The great need in this field is a comprehensive study intercorrelating measures on the intrafamilial attitudes, on economic status, size of family, health of family, the personality characteristics of the parents, the interaction of the family with the neighborhood, etc. By a skillful factor analysis of these intercorrelations we could then arrive at the primary dimensions—the unitary traits—in terms of which all families, as units, are most aptly measured and described for comparative purposes.

As usual, where dimensions for measuring and defining a psychological entity are lacking, we tend to deal with the more primitive descriptive counters provided by types. Sociologists and psychologists have used such rubrics as "the oversolicitous home," "the companionable home," "the father-dominated home," "the autocratic home," "the democratic home," "the favored-child home," "the divided home," "the community service home," "the nomadic home," "the disgraced family," "the small-town home," "the materialistic home," "the invalid home," "the suddenly wealthy home," and so on, indefinitely.

**Some Probable Dimensions for Measurement of the Family.** Although a more comprehensive factor-analytic study of the family has not been done, it is probable that dimensions found by Cattell and Wispe (11) for the description of the behavior of small groups (6 members) will prove to hold with slight modification for the family also. Most of the performances of which small groups are capable, namely, common constructive work, friendliness or hostility to other groups, self-criticism, persistence in difficulties, honesty, internal dissension, etc., are the same regardless of whether the component individuals are or are not relatives. The Cattell and Wispe study (11) observed twenty-one groups of six students each in their performances or reaction *as groups* in some forty performances. Factorization of the intercorrelations revealed six or more factors, contingently described as follows:

*Factor* 1.[1]  *Extravert Responsiveness vs. Withdrawal.* This loaded ability to show speedy, flexible performance, practicality in achieving goals, some tendency to be emotionally suggestible and responsive, and a liking for art and music. At the negative pole the loadings were in tendency of the group members to like solitary activity, for the group to have an impracticably high group aspiration level, and to have a tendency to instability of attitudes. In the positively endowed groups there seemed to be more good will among members, and in the negative, more frigidity. There is considerable resemblance to the *A* factor in *individual* personality dimensions.

---

[1] The numbers are not the same as in the original article, since the order there had little relation to relative psychological importance. The labels, however, are retained.

*Factor* 2. *Intelligent Esprit de Corps.* Groups high in this solved puzzles more quickly, liked intellectual problems, and were confident and effective generally. It corresponds to the factor *B* of general mental capacity in the individual.

*Factor* 3. *Realism, Dependability vs. Instability, Evasiveness.* Groups at the positive pole were high in performances requiring persistence, determination, dependability, and freedom from unfairness and dishonesty. The members of these groups seemed considerate of each other and integrated in purposes. The high negative loadings were in vacillation of attitudes, lack of realism about group performance, and attempts to avoid the whole field of group interaction. There was confusion and the anarchy of too many bosses in these latter groups. This is strikingly similar to the *C* or *G* factors of individual integration and might be called the primary morale factor in small groups.

*Factor* 4. *Informed, Realistic Relaxedness vs. Industrious Rigid Aggressiveness.* Groups high in this factor scored higher in realism of estimates about the group, in interest in physical recreation, and in goodness of judgments requiring general information. At the opposite pole were groups high in engineering skill, in arithmetical performance, in rigidity of aspiration level, and in proneness to challenging other groups (to tug of war). The positive groups seemed to show more talkativeness and interaction in their members, the negative to be more quiet and serious. This has some resemblance to the individual factor *F*, surgency-desurgency, and a little to submissiveness-dominance, *E*, but its striking resemblance is to the "cultural pressure" factor in the national patterns (9).

*Factor* 5. *Practical Shrewdness, Doggedness vs. Autism, Dynamic Lability.* This loads positively emotional responsiveness to competition, length of resistive deliberation when under persuasion, and good judgment based on general information; and, negatively, attitude vacillation, high aspiration level, and interest in individualized activities. On one side, a closeness of the members, on the other, a social distance and independence. This resembles the second cyclothyme—schizothyme factor, *H*, in individuals.

*Factor* 6. *Fortitude vs. Easy Verbal Activity.* Groups positive here showed more preference for, and better performance in, a variety of tough, painful, or laborious tasks. There was evidence of a more stern intragroup discipline here. At the opposite pole were found verbal facility, general information, and liking for discussion. It has some resemblance to *J* and *M* in individual factors. Gibb believes this factor (which was regarded as a third dimension of morale) to be identical with one found in his study, loading high degree of group organization, "democratic" leadership, and orderliness of behavior individually maintained, *i.e.*, within a permissive atmosphere.

*Factor 7. Friendly Urbanity and Savior-faire vs. Lack of Group Self-possession.* The upper groups were self-possessed in their dealings with other groups, secure enough to have a larger volume of self-criticism, friendly to other groups and, socially skillful in transactions with them. At the opposite end were groups prone to solitary performances, unrealistic in aspiration level, and naively susceptible to emotional appeals. This has clear resemblances to the individual personality factor *K*.

Gibb's further studies again bring out this dimension and show it to be related to well integrated behavior, a high degree of expressed satisfaction with being a group member, a low degree of reported frustration and a feeling of security in the group. He also found that the average individual personality scores in the groups high in this factor were significantly higher in *C* factor (Emotional Stability) and *I* factor (Self-sufficiency).

Though these patterns may be slightly different for the more dispersed age groups and more traditional structure of the family, one can readily see that they provide dimensions with respect to which it is quite practicable to measure families. The psychiatric social worker often uses terms to describe the differences of families with respect to Factor 1—the cohesiveness and responsiveness as opposed to dispersedness and withdrawingness of families. Families also differ obviously in their total intelligence in solving family problems (Factor 2), while the realities of economic difficulty reveal striking differences on the "fortitude" dimension of Factor 5. Perhaps the most important dimension of all is the "morale" or "family adjustment" score possible through Factor 3. For we know that nothing is so far-reaching among environmental influences on the child's personality as the level of the family in regard to consistency or emotional integration, as opposed to conflict and anarchy.

**Clustering of Family Characteristics.** A suggestive and comprehensive study aiming at determination of the important dimensions of the family, is that of Baldwin, Kallhorn, and Breese (3). They intercorrelated for a sufficient sample of families some twenty-nine variables from the Champney rating scales for the family, including such syntality characteristics as adjustment of the home, activity, sociability of the family, and such intrafamilial parent-child attitudes as protectiveness, solicitousness, and acceptance. Unfortunately the analysis stopped short of a factorization for independent dimensions; but a number of distinct correlation clusters were isolated, some of which may turn out to be expressions of the above factors, as follows:

1. *Indulgence vs. Nonchalance.* Positive in protectiveness, solicitousness, babying. This has resemblance to our Factor 1 of emotional warmth as opposed to withdrawal.

2. *Intellectuality vs. Lack of Intellectuality.*   Positive in clarity of policy, readiness of parental explanation, etc.   This has resemblance to our Factor 2, of intelligent esprit de corps.

3. *Personal Adjustment vs. Lack of Personal Adjustment.*   The variables which correlated in this cluster were absence of discord, adjustment of the home, and understanding of the child, which make it clearly similar to our Factor 3 above.

4. *Hustling vs. Non-hustling.*   Positive in activities of home, coordination, and attempts to accelerate child education.   This is like the negative end of Factor 4.

5. *Acceptance vs. Rejection.*   Positive in affectionateness to child, rapport, absence of disciplinary friction.   This is much like our Factor 5, with the autism, dynamic lability end of that factor corresponding to rejection here.

6. *Severity vs. Easy Casualness.*   Positive in readiness of enforcement of rules and severity of penalties.   This is probably our Factor 6, which shows itself outwardly in the fortitude and self-punishment of the group.

7. *Democratic vs. Autocratic.*   Positive in readiness of explanation, clarity of policy, nonrestrictiveness of regulations, etc.   This might be our Factor 7.

8. *Nagging vs. Absence of Friction.*   Positive in disciplinary friction, readiness of criticism, and emotionality.

That the Democratic vs. Autocratic dimension (which might be better labeled by terms with fewer prejudicial implications) came out one of the largest clusters here and only weakly in the student groups is probably due to the fact that elected leadership, as in the student groups, has only a small possible range of increasing domination compared with the hierarchical family and the range of relative autocracy which different cultural traditions sanction.   Actually both our Factor 4 and the Baldwin-Kallhorn-Breese cluster 8 (nagging) have as much claim to the "autocratic" label as No. 7.

Study of the effects of the family endowment in these "unitary traits" upon the child personality, however, is relegated to later sections of this chapter.   Here it suffices to clarify the description of the family per se. Using the term syntality (6) to describe the totality of behavior for the group, as personality does for the individual, we must conclude with two propositions regarding group syntality: (*a*) the half-dozen or so dimensions of syntality set out above are not exhaustive or more than suggestive.   Furthermore, there are many traits of a dynamic kind—interests, traditions, ideals— which, by the experimenters' choice of variables, would not be represented in the above dimensions; (*b*) the above dimensions refer to the group syntality, *i.e.*, to the behavior issuing from the group as a unit and not primarily or directly to its internal dynamic structure, *i.e.*, the attitudes and relations existing among the members.   The thesis propounded elsewhere (6,11) is that the group syntality is a function of the personalities of the group members and the structural relation that exists among them.   But our study will be more complete if we examine the influence of all three—syntality, structure, and individual personalities—upon the personality of an individual—specifically the growing child—in the family. For instance, we may suspect that a high negative manifestation of Factor 4 (above) in the family syntality is associated with high dominance attitude of father toward mother and of mother toward children in a hierarchical structure. But we cannot yet assume these concomitants of "dictatorship." Accordingly the next two sections will discuss independently the structure of attitudes, (a) between the parents, and (b) among parents and children.

## 4. FACTORS IN THE STABILITY OF MARRIAGE

**Analysis of Ergic Satisfactions in Marriage.** If we are to study the influence of the family upon the child we must begin with the formation of the family itself. As any novel reminds us, marriage also has formative or destructive influences on the personalities of the adult parties involved, and that also is a necessary aspect of the present study, but the main emphasis here is on marriage as it determines the family that affects the individual during the most fateful years of his personality formation.

Marriage is undertaken under a combination of impulsions which differ in relative importance from culture to culture. In our own culture we recognize that the satisfaction of the ergs of mating, gregariousness, protectiveness, fear (seeking for security), and self-assertion (pride in the possession of another person, as approved by society) is most prominent. We also recognize that these and other ergs operate through certain institutions and their associated sentiments, as when we say that a person marries for money, to aid a career, to avoid the responsibility of a career, to gain social status, to escape from under an unhappy parental roof, and so on.

Obviously the ergic composition—the vectorial direction—of the individual's attitude to marriage is likely to determine both the degree of success of marriage and the reactions that shape the personalities of the children born of the marriage. (This applies both to the ergic composition of the premarital attitude to marriage and to the ergic composition of the satisfaction that the marriage in fact ultimately offers.) Since the ergic analysis of attitudes is in its infancy, however, no quantitative data yet exist on the relative success, etc., of marriages undertaken under various motivations.

**The Principle of Assortative Mating.** What we *do* possess already is an excellent collection of data and generalizations about the *personalities* of marriage partners in relation to marital success. In the first place, it is known that mating is selective and assortative. It is *selective* in that individuals of defective personality tend to remain unmarried, as much or more so than those of defective physique. There is no evidence that this is true of intelligence—indeed over some upper ranges the more intelligent may less frequently be married—but there is sufficient evidence that greater frequency of stable marriage is significantly related to the personality factors of emotional stability (factor $C$), surgency-desurgency (factor $F$) and cyclothymia-schizothymia (Factors $A$ and $H$), as described in Chapters 2 to 4. Evidence as to the direction and extent of the relationship is scattered and indirect; but it is reasonably certain that individuals of low emotional maturity and integration less frequently marry (low marriage rate, for example, in criminals and clinic patients); that highly surgent, hysteroid individuals tend to remain gay bachelors (among 600 neurotics Eysenck (10) found anxious, depressive desurgents more frequently married than their opposites—hysterics); and that schizothymes and the relatives of schizophrenics have less than the average family attachments (see Chap. 18).

Matings are *assortative* in that partners resemble each other to a degree far above chance expectation in physical and mental characteristics—and this has been found both with engaged and with married couples. The correlations range from about +0.3 to +0.7 for such traits as weight, height, hair and eye color, health (even degree of hearing acuity!), intelligence, surgency, cyclothyme tendency, length of education, and measured attitudes and interests. This resemblance has many implications. It argues for the truth of the psychoanalytic view that a certain amount of narcism enters into normal sexual libido; it suggests that this narcism has the biological purpose of avoiding the infertility found in matings of biologically very remote types;[2] it suggests that sex plays a lesser role than congenial gregariousness in marital satisfactions, and it may indicate that the image of the opposite-sex parent exercises some influence in the choice of a mate.

It seems likely that the assortativeness of matings *increases* as extraneous influences—*e.g.*, parental control of marriage choice, marriage for material considerations—*decrease*, and it is also likely that the perfection of assortativeness increases with later marriages, less constrained by accidents of locality, local upbringing, and defective integration of personality. It is certain that, as Terman's results (30) first showed, the correlations are higher for happily married than for unhappily married or divorced couples. On the correlations so far available one can only conclude that the resemblance is about the same for physical as for mental traits, for constitutional temperament as for acquired interests and accomplishments, and that it holds for practically every trait investigated. One of the rare exceptions is dominance—submission (source trait $E$) in which the correlations (Allport's Ascendance-

---

[2] When the gap between biological types amounts to a species difference matings are usually neither attempted nor fertile. Lesser differences, in animal breeds, are associated with relative infertility or with the production of offspring that are sterile. Scattered evidence yet available indicates no difference in this respect of human breeds from mammalian breeds generally.

Submission test) have been zero or slightly negative (see Chap. 5, examination of hereditary similarities).

**Background Factors in Marital Success.** Beyond assortativeness of mating the following factors in personality and background have been found to be the most important predictors of marital happiness and stability. The ten most important background factors found in Terman's study and receiving general confirmation from other studies, show the happier married individuals to have:

1. Higher record of happier marriages in their own parents
2. Higher level of reported happiness in childhood
3. Less conflict with mother
4. Home discipline that was neither careless nor harsh
5. Stronger attachment to mother
6. Stronger attachment to father
7. Less conflict with father
8. Frankness by parents on sex education
9. Infrequent and not severe punishment in childhood
10. Premarital attitude to sex free from disgust and aversion

Terman's study as well as those of Hamilton (23) (after critical examination by Ferguson (15)), Kirkpatrick (27), Burgess and Cottrell (see (5)), E. L. Kelley, and others confirm the above and add: a greater probability of successful marriage in those without premarital sex experience; with acquaintance of several years before marriage; with equal fondness for their own parents; with more education; with desire for children; with neither too few nor too many female friends in the husband's history; and with steady employment for the husband. Economic level, age at marriage or differences of age, positive or negative, had no relation to success of marital adjustment. Differences of education and intelligence were associated, as one might expect from the correlations found in assortative mating, with greater likelihood of unhappy marriage or divorce.

**Consciously Realized Marital Difficulties.** The most frequent complaints of married people were found in Terman's study to be as follows:

| *Husbands* | *Wives* |
|---|---|
| 1. Insufficient income for wife's expenditures | 1. Insufficient income obtained by husband |
| 2. Wife too sensitive, feelings too easily hurt | 2. Disagreement with in-laws |
| 3. Wife criticizes me | 3. Husband nervous, irritable, impatient |
| 4. Disagreement with in-laws | 4. Expenditure of husband's income is poorly managed by him |
| 5. Wife is nervous and emotional | 5. Husband criticizes me |
| 6. Expenditure of income poorly managed by wife | 6. Husband prefers different kind of recreations and amusements from those preferred by wife |
| 7. Lack of freedom | |

These conscious complaints would not be expected necessarily to bear much relation to the real causes of marital maladjustment. Thus, although the restrictive influence of comparative poverty is most complained about here, and is popularly regarded as a major factor in marital discord, the fact is that no significant difference exists between the reported happiness or recorded stability of marriage at different socioeconomic levels. The quality of ergic satisfaction may differ systematically with class status. We should expect more ego satisfaction at the upper levels and more sex satisfaction at the lower cultural levels, as the Kinsey study of sex activity demonstrates (26) and the Freudian theory of cultural sublimation requires. But the evidence is as yet too scant and the space here too limited to explore the variations of marriage as a form of personality expression, with regard to social status, sex, age, and other dimensions.

The most noteworthy fact about the above list of complaints is their similarity in the two sexes. They are essentially the complaints that would arise in any two or more human beings in a joint undertaking—against the difficulties of the environment, the enforced contacts with less congenial people (in-laws), the mental limitations and emotional instability of the partner, and resentment at the reciprocal criticisms of that partner. The only differences that seem sex-specific are the woman's complaint about incompatible ideas of recreation and the man's lament about his loss of freedom.

**Findings on Unhappy Marriage.** The evidence on significant differences in personality between happy spouses and unhappy or divorced spouses is in agreement with that inferred above from the nature of selection in marriage. Terman found the unhappy and divorced more frequently to have personalities that were moody, emotionally unstable, suffering from a sense of social inferiority, reporting a dislike of being methodical, and showing more radical opinions on politics, religion, and sex. They showed also more evidence of parent fixation and infantilism of personality. The women manifested in addition, specifically, greater ambition and a greater tendency to be "joiners" of societies than did the happily married.

The findings clearly suggest that unsuccessful marriage springs from three main groups of causes, as follows: (*a*) lack of assortativeness of selection, *i.e.*, intrinsic dissimilarities and incompatibilities, sexual and general, as between the specific partners involved; (*b*) defectiveness of personality stability, integration, and adjustment, of a kind that would be hazardous for adjustments of any kind (social, occupational, material); (*c*) a dynamic adjustment which makes other interests predominate considerably over marriage as such. Strong cultural sublimations in religion, art, politics, or science (mostly included in the above observations under "ambition") are notoriously inimical to marriage and best pursued in celibacy, except where the interests of the partner or the sanctions of the culture pattern favor this attenuation of one partner's attention to the other.

## 5. THE DYNAMICS OF THE TOTAL MARITAL SITUATION

**Social Maturity and Assortativeness Not Enough.**   The above studies of marriage in general and of contrasted successful and unsuccessful marriage indicate that available findings can best be summarized in terms of (*a*) the personalities per se, (*b*) the relations of the personality characteristics of partners, and (*c*) the nature of the dynamic satisfactions sought in the total marital situation.

*Personality.*   As to personality per se, nothing further can be said except that personality "defect" operates adversely and that as far as marriage is concerned the handicap is probably greatest for low $C$ factor (emotional instability), low $A$ and $H$ factors (schizothyme temperament), and perhaps high $E$ factor (dominance) and high $F$ factor (surgent, hysteroid tendency).

*Relation of Partner's Personalities, the Assortative Principle.*   Psychometric evidence points to marriage, like friendship, being more stable, and happy with individuals of like abilities, temperaments, and dynamic traits, with the exception of dominance, where a primary similarity may be overlaid by a secondary complementariness.   These similarities are not due to "growing together."   Indeed it is possible that though time brings some convergence of interests it also causes some growing complementariness and specialization.   The similarities exist at the time of courtship and marriage: present measurements are not exact enough to say whether they increase or decrease afterwards.

*The Completion Principle.*   Clinical evidence, as presented in the arguments of Jung, for example, has pointed to the existence of a second selective tendency, in some respects contrary to assortative mating, namely one toward complementariness or "completion."   One must analyze this into at least three distinct dynamic satisfactions if it is to fit present knowledge.   First there is a desire to satisfy self-assertion and gain social or inner approval by "possessing" in the beloved some admired qualities that the lover does not possess.   Second, in actually living together, if not in the falling-in-love situation, it is rewarding to all drives to have one partner do well what the other cannot do, as in any business or group enterprise.   Third, there may be an *immediate* satisfaction in enjoying in another qualities one does not possess oneself, *e.g.*, wit, geniality, immunity to anxiety.   Sex satisfaction itself comes in this category.   These three independent causes of complementariness we may call "social competition," "adjustment of the partnership to reality," and "psychic satisfaction."

That these do not in fact succeed in neutralizing the primary assortative tendency, except for a few special characteristics, must be ascribed to the external situation which may be called the "marketing situation." If men like physically healthy women and women like physically healthy men, the exchange, from the laws of supply and demand, will result in more healthy men obtaining more healthy women, and the less healthy will become mated to the less healthy. In short, two of the complementary tendencies, social competition for admired, but unpossessed, qualities, and psychic satisfaction through contact with unpossessed qualities, will be changed by the competitive "field" into assortative tendencies. Whether complementariness, *i.e.*, actual negative correlation, will finally remain, as this hypothesis suggests, only in traits involved in "adjustment of the partnership to reality," and in "immediate satisfaction in complementariness," remains for research to discover.

Some aspects of the Principle of Completion, though not under that concept, have recently been discussed by Fromm (18). Where the principle operates with respect to gaining social approval and prestige (the first of the three sources of the search for completion), as shown for example in Negroes seeking partners lighter than themselves, or in the general search for partners of higher social status or greater beauty or intelligence, it should be possible in later research to work out "exchange rates" among these commodities.

*Dynamic Satisfactions.* It is obvious that in dynamic terms the marriage satisfactions must fit into the scheme of total life satisfactions enjoyed by the individual and that the dynamic gains in the total marriage situation must be greater than the losses. Thus the extent of satisfaction of gregariousness required outside marriage will be inversely related to the extent of companionableness within the marriage, and so on. The preceding principle or principles, incidentally, might be subsumed under this third principle of total dynamic satisfaction. For example, the gaining of social approval which is part of the principle of completion above is part of the more general principle that the marriage administers to any and all needs existent in the individual. However, at this stage, when some principles are more investigated and investigable than others, it will be well to give them the distinction of separate statement.

**Ergic Analysis of Marital Satisfactions.** For lack of precise, quantitative research on attitudes and sentiments, particularly of vectorial, ergic analysis, very little can yet be said about the relative strength of various satisfactions in marriage or about the principles of their growth, decline, interrelationship, etc. In the first rosy dawn of psychoanalysis and emancipation from Victorianism, many writers took the high correlations found between sexual adjustment and total marital adjustment to mean that the former was the cause of the latter, and that the sex drive must therefore be the most important satisfaction in marriage. Scattered evidence which cannot be readily summarized now inclines most psychologists to the opposite view: that sex satisfaction fails where the total adjustment of ego satisfactions and general affection has first broken down.

In so far as such a complex matter can be briefly summarized we may say that the chief dynamic components in the interspouse sentiment are the ergs of sex (direct and sublimated), protectiveness, gregariousness, self-assertion and self-submission, and perhaps fear[3] as can be seen, for example, in the substitute behavior when the widowed or divorced grope for adjustment.

In interparental attitudes generally we must recognize that the ergs operate both through conscious and unconscious channels. Clinical studies insist on this and point out that the unconscious component in the attitude is typically the attitude that the marriage partner built up early in life to his or her opposite-sex parent. It is the unconscious and therefore unmodifiable and unrealistic character of this searching for a mother or a father in the marriage bond that brings many possibilities of maladjustment.

The psychological analysis of marriage, prior to the appearance of children, whose personalities will affect and be affected by the interparental relationship existing, can thus be summarized as follows: Marital partners are initially selected by (*a*) a principle of assortativeness, (*b*) a principle of completion, both of which operate within a field of (*c*) necessary total dynamic satisfactions through marriage, the nature and variability of which has not yet been quantitatively mapped.

### 6. SCHEME FOR THE ANALYSIS OF INTRAFAMILIAL ATTITUDES

**The Fourteen Interpersonal Attitude Situations of the Family.** The problem of the effect of the marriage adjustment upon the personality of the child is conceived in its most essential form when we ask what changes in the interparental attitudes necessitate changes in the dynamic composition of the attitude to the child. For example, a father's inability to take pride in his wife (or himself) may lead to undue attempts to satisfy self-assertion through his children. Or a wife's failure to obtain sexual satisfaction through her husband may lead to an overloading with sexual elements of the affectional relation to her son, tending to fixate the Oedipus attachment in his personality development. But "dynamic drainage" relations of this kind are not the only relations that can exist between interparental and parent-child attitudes, as will be evident from the following section.

In order that measurement may be introduced, to provide data for the formulation of laws concerning intrafamilial dynamics, it is necessary to settle upon the field of attitudes requiring measurement. Diagram 42 offers

[3] The role of escape, fear, the craving for security in the marriage attitude is very differently estimated by different writers. While it may enter powerfully into the children's attitude to the *family*, it is almost certain a minor component in attracting the adult, especially the male, to *marriage*.

the paradigm for the typical family, showing that there are eight basic interpersonal relations, if we take account of the basic differences resident in sex differences. Each relation, except No. 7 and No. 8, permits asymmetric attitudes, so that fourteen formal interpersonal attitudes, or, rather, situations for possible attitudes, have to be considered in any family complete with father and mother, sons and daughters.

Each formal interpersonal attitude, however, can have many different psychological qualities. For example the attitude of a father to a daughter

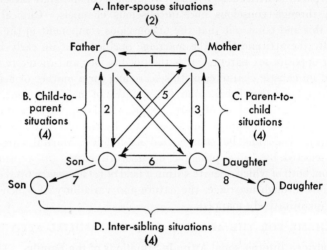

DIAGRAM 42. Classification of two-way intrafamilial attitude relations. (Showing eight interpersonal "relations" and fourteen interpersonal situations, each of which can be estimated, for several dynamic qualities.)

may be one of affection, companionship, overprotectiveness, hate, or rejection, and the attitude of a sister to a brother may be one of companionship, protection, admiration, pride in, hate toward, or affectional indifference. Generally the ultimate attitude will be a combination of these in various strengths, for the misleading feature of the psychoanalytic term *ambivalent* is that it indicates attitudes to be combinations of only love and hate, whereas in fact a good many more constituents can enter into any single attitude, *e.g.*, curiosity, submissiveness.

**Dimensions for the Definition of Any One Intrafamilial Attitude.** This amounts to saying that each of the fourteen interpersonal attitudes will in any given instance, have a specific vectorial direction, defined with respect to a system of coordinates presented by the basic ergs or independent dimensions of emotional satisfaction, as described in Chapters 6 and 7. What these independent directions are we do not yet know, and the following tentative analysis is offered only as a means of proceeding until systematized, confirmed factorial research defines them. These contingent dimensions are based on clinical experience and were worked out by the present writer with the aid of P. S. de Q. Cabot, director of the Cambridge Somerville Youth Study, from ten years of clinical records in that study, reflecting the efforts of psychologists and psychiatric social workers to describe intrafamilial attitudes in a wide range of homes. The dimensions independently arrived at by psychologists at the Fels Research Institute agree with many of the main categories presented here. The clinical records indicate the necessity for certain different dimensions of attitude in specific relations, though most are common, so they are set out below in four groups, *A, B, C,* and *D* as indicated in Diagram 42.

### A. *Interspouse Attitude Dimensions*

| | |
|---|---|
| Affectionate | vs. Indifferent |
| Dependent | vs. Self-sustained |
| Hostile | vs. Indifferent |
| Dominant | vs. Submissive |
| Jealous of | vs. Confident in relation to |
| Proud of | vs. Ashamed of |
| Sexually attracted | vs. Sexually indifferent |
| Protective | vs. Indifferent |
| Respecting | vs. Being contemptuous of |

### B. *Parent-to-child Attitudes*

| | |
|---|---|
| Affectionate (Fond, devoted, kind) | vs. Cold (Heartless, uninterested) |
| Accepting (Responsible, loyal, having vigorous contact) | vs. Rejecting vs. (Neglecting, disowning, begrudging, impatient) |
| Hostile-sadistic (Bullying, severe, censorious, callous) | vs. Lacking aggression |
| Dominant-nurturant (Supervisory, imperious, commanding, coercive) | vs. Submissive (Self-effacing, lax, diffident) |
| Jealous of (Competitive towards, insecure in regard to, feeling frustrated by) | vs. Trusting (Secure in relation to, grateful towards, friendly) |
| Proud of (Admiring, exhibitionistic about) | vs. Ashamed of (Guilty or depressed about) |
| Comradely (Close in emotional rapport and sympathy, affiliative, seeking social contact with) | vs. Socially distant (Out of touch, merely dutiful or official) |

Protective-solicitous            vs. Adventurous about
  (Succorant,  anxious  about,       (Allowing child unconsciously to
  overcareful, sheltering, babying)      get his own experience)
Claimant-appealing               vs. Independent
  (Demanding affection, emotion-
  ally dependent on child)

## C. *Child-to-parent Attitudes*

Affectionate                     vs. Cold
Dependent-appealing              vs. Confident-adventurous
  (Claimant, identifying)              (Independent, assured)
Hostile-aggressive               vs. Lacking aggression
Fearful-submissive               vs. Bold towards ("Fresh")
  (Respectful, awestruck)              (Independent, not respectful to)
Jealous of                       vs. Trusting
                                       (Grateful towards, not rivalrous)
Proud of                         vs. Ashamed of
  (Admiring, worshiping)               (Critical of)
Rebellious                       vs. Docile
  (Negativistic, rude towards, dis-    (Obedient, tractable)
  obedient)
Exhibitionistic                  vs. Effacing
  (Attention-seeking)
Comradely                        vs. Socially distant
  (Sociable, confiding, close emo-     (Independent)
  tional rapport)

## D. *Intersibling Attitudes*

Affectionate                     vs. Cold
                                       (Rejecting)
Dependent                        vs. Independent
  (Following,  subordinate,  de-       (Self-assured)
  manding protection)
Hostile-sadistic                 vs. Indifferent
  (Bullying,  destroying,  critical,
  spiteful)
Dominant                         vs. Submissive
  (Ascendant,  exploitative,  lead-    (Diffident)
  ing)
Jealous of                       vs. Trusting
  (Competitive for affection, feel-    (Grateful and helpful towards)
  ing frustrated by)
Proud of                         vs. Ashamed of
  (Admiring, possessive)               (Guilty about disowning)

Comradely            vs. Socially distant

(Sociable, confiding, constant     (Withdrawn, lacking in sympa-
emotional rapport)           thy and harmony, isolative)

Protective            vs. Adventurous, unconcerned

(Sheltering, babying, doting on)

Dutiful about          vs. Ignoring any responsibility about

(Anxious over, reponsible for)

## 7. METHODOLOGY OF INTERFAMILIAL ATTITUDE MEASUREMENT

**Behavioral Indicators of Attitudes.** Some ten scales for measuring the above attitudes, in terms of actual behavior, have been made available in the present writer's *Guide to Mental Testing* (7). A reproduction of one will suffice for illustration.

**Scale 1. Formal Relation: Parent-to-child. Dimension: Affectionate to Indifferent.** The psychiatric social worker checks each of the following 24 items present or absent, summing, with due regard to negative items, to a single score.

*Scale 1. Parent-to-child. Affection–Indifference.*

1. Parent rarely speaks to child without smiling.
2. Parent tries to put himself in child's position when discussing child's behavior.
3. Parent brings child small presents other than seasonal ones.
4. Parent takes child with him on trips at some personal inconvenience.
5. Parent complains boy is wearing him out and constantly criticizes him. (Negative contribution to total score.)
6. Parent constantly compels child to keep out of the house and out of his way. (Negative.)
7. Parent does not deliberately plan definite periods of companionship with child. (Negative.)
8. Parent does not kiss or greet child after long absence. (Negative.)
9. Parent fails to reciprocate son's friendly advances, *e.g.*, to sit on parent's knee. (Negative.)
10. Father shares child's creative play activities, *e.g.*, drawing, erector sets, schoolwork, favorite reading.
11. Parent romps with child and encourages physical development.
12. Parent does not inquire about child's whereabouts, his needs, or his activities. (Negative.)
13. Parent denies himself—*e.g.*, food, clothing, amusement—in order that child may have equivalent satisfactions instead of himself, *e.g.*, has no time to play with friends but plays with child.
14. Parent anticipates child's physical, mental, and emotional needs—*e.g.*, prophylaxis for cold, need for holiday, new hobby clothing—before child is fully aware of it himself, *e.g.*, planning meals with regard to child's likes and dislikes.

15. Parent ignores and is indifferent to child, despite cries and appeals for something which by the standards of his environment he ought to have. (Negative.)
16. Parent smiles and praises child at latter's successes.
17. Parent's first reaction is to resent criticism of child.
18. Parent accepts irksome, aggressive, or anger-provoking behavior from the child without being ruffled or retaliating.
19. Parent sacrifices energy, time, and money to enable child to have better start in life than he himself had.
20. Parent shows he is ready to listen to child's account of his exploits, hobbies, interests, and friends.
21. Parent sides with and shows favoritism for this particular child in contrast with siblings or others with whom quarrels arise.
22. Parent allows child to use family property without stint, restriction, or inquiry.
23. Parent errs on the side of allowing child excessive satisfaction of his impulses, even though detrimental by the parent's own standards, *e.g.*, eating candy to excess, destroying furniture, defacing rooms, showing disrespect to other people.
24. Parent shows little remorse or feeling when child's property—*e.g.*, favorite doll, book, or toys—is accidentally destroyed. (Negative.)

**Intrafamilial Attitudes in Terms of the Ergic Theory of Attitudes.** The principle of measuring the total interpersonal attitude in terms of its separate, independent components—such as the affectional component above—is likely to provide the most useful data both for generalization about family dynamics and for laws about the effect of family dynamics upon the dynamics of the individual personality. However, it would also be possible to make scales for measuring directly the *strength* of attitude of one person to another, (what has been called in Chapter 6 the total *interest*) in terms of an already defined composite direction, *i.e.*, some unitary course of action dictated by a mixture of end satisfactions. (Assuming the direction to be the same as that established by factorial analysis of a typical population of families.) It should not be overlooked, also, that strictly an attitude is *about* and not *toward* an object: "I want so much to do this with that." When we speak of a parent's attitude of fondness toward a child, therefore, it is strictly, "I want so much to make this child happy, or secure, or healthy, etc.," and the attitude is in large part inferred from attitudes and opinions about other objects, *e.g.*, toys, school, medical care, etc.

This technical point must be mentioned lest inconsistency be imagined to exist between Diagram 42 above, showing interpersonal attitudes and the original Diagram 27 showing the dynamic lattice. The interpersonal attitude is an attitude that has reached the magnitude of a sentiment. It is the investment of a whole set of attitude satisfactions in a single object.

General Relations Possible between Personality and Intrafamilial Attitudes. About general familial dynamics we as yet have virtually no systematic exact evidence though the whole of psychoanalysis offers suggestive generalizations about what happens in particular corners of the family. It is reasonably safe, however, to infer, first, that important relations exist between intrafamilial attitudes and the total family performances as discussed in Section 2 above. For example, clinical observation suggests that the family, like most groups, has a hierarchical dominance order, and that situation of masculine parental domination, with its related dominance attitudes of mother to children, is more marked in families that are ambitious as a whole or under economic stress,[4] *i.e.*, high in negative loading of a Factor 4 above.

Second, we can safely assume that important relations exist between intrafamilial attitudes and the personality adjustment of every individual. For example, clinical evidence suggests that a relation exists between the degree of that stunting of ego development occurring in the youngest child and this same emphasis on hierarchical dominance within the family.

In addition to the almost innumerable specific relations which could be suggested between single attitudes and single personalities in the style just mentioned, there are obviously relations to be explored between personality and certain *constellations* of intrafamilial attitudes. For example, we frequently see special alliances developing, sometimes defenses shared by the children against overstrict parents, sometimes between the opposite-sex parent and child as in the Freudian notion of Oedipus and Electra complexes, sometimes of oldest and youngest sibling against the middle children, and frequently, of all children with the mother against an errant father. These dynamic constellations, if they persist for any length of time, are likely to shape the child's personality, as discussed in Sections 2 through 5 of Chapter 13.

## 8. SUMMARY

1. The family is in a state of transition, partly through economic and cultural changes, partly through the shift of population from rural to urban living. The chief trends concern family size, degree of authority, degree of recreational and emotional investment in the family, balance of economic dependence between the family and the state, and the lessened stability of the family.

2. The typical family can be defined as to size, expenditure, age differences, stability, etc., by existing social statistics, but exact *psychological* norms on family life do not yet exist.

[4] It has been claimed by one analyst-anthropologist, Roheim, that, for example, the masculine dominance of the Australian aboriginal male accounts for the severity with which women in turn dominate the children, and the older dominate the younger children.

3. The psychological characteristics of the family need to be measured at three levels, (*a*) personality traits of members, (*b*) structure among them (intrafamilial attitudes and positions), (*c*) syntality (total climate and behavior as a unitary group), the last being theoretically derivable from the two first.

4. The psychological dimensions involved in family syntality cannot yet be reliably stated. Lists of terms employed in social workers' descriptions of the family are presented. However, from correlation studies of the family and factor-analytic studies of the behavior of small groups it is possible roughly to estimate the nature of some seven or eight primary dimensions.

5. Substantial advance has been made in defining the determiners of marital stability, which are, principally, (*a*) certain relationships between the personality characteristics of the partners, as expressed largely by, first, the principle of assortative similarity, and second, the principle of completion; (*b*) a sufficient level of general effectiveness of personality as defined by much the same source-trait loadings as make for effectiveness in many general social and occupational situations. The loading emphasis seems to be on emotional stability (*C*), absence of schizoid tendencies (*A* and *H*) and absence of excessive surgency (*F* factor). Along with these personal traits may be considered the backgrounds of the individuals, among which stable parental home, normal affection for parents, and intelligent sex education are important; (*c*) a satisfactory fit of the dynamics of the marriage into the total dynamic goal situation of the individual's life.

6. The ergic composition of the satisfactions sought and found in marriage is probably largely: sex drive, self-assertive drive, gregariousness, parental protective drive, fear, and appeal (dependence); but the measurement of the direction of the attitude vectors (conscious and unconscious) in regard to marriage, necessary to give an exact answer concerning the nature of the dynamic satisfactions, has not yet been carried out.

7. There are fourteen attitude relations from eight possible paradigms of interpersonal relationship in the family and each relationship can hold in a wide variety of dynamic dimensions, *i.e.*, be made of varied emotional qualities. Each of these attitudes needs to be measured for strength and for dynamic direction, if the family constellation is to be understood. By dynamic direction is meant the angle of the attitude vector with respect to rectangular coordinates constituted by the dozen or more possible ergic components in the human dynamic constitution.

8. Although the ergic analysis of attitudes is in its infancy it is possible to indicate some seven or eight dimensions of dynamic quality that have proved clinically useful in defining the character of the attitude of one member of a family to another, and illustrations of scales for measuring in these dimensions are given.

## QUESTIONS AND EXERCISES

1. Illustrate in detail the nature of some four trends of change in the family during the past century.

2. Describe the average family of today with respect to vital and economic,. *i.e.*, nonpsychological statistics.

3. Distinguish between dynamic and nondynamic aspects of syntality. In what way is the syntality of a family or small group likely to be derived from the personalities of the members?

4. Name six dimensions of family syntality suggested by intercorrelations of family traits and factor analysis of the performances of small groups. Speculate as to how high scores in each may affect the personality of the child reared in families with such syntalities.

5. Define two principles that operate to determine the relationship of partners' personalities in successful marriage and give examples of successful and abortive actions of each.

6. Describe two personality factors and two personal background factors that favor stable marriage in the case both of men and of women.

7. Discuss the ergic composition of a husband's attitude to the family, *i.e.*, the relative strength of the different ergs that normally achieve satisfaction through the family.

8. Point out differences, on the basis of available clinical-type information, between the attitudes of husband and wife with regard to ergic composition, and indicate what light this throws on the importance of the family in the life of each.

9. Draw a diagram showing the basic possible intrafamilial attitude relations and list ten dynamic dimensions of these attitudes that have been found important in clinical and social work. (Not all ten need apply to any one relationship.)

10. List half a dozen items in an intrafamilial attitude scale designed to measure the dimension of Affection vs. Indifference in the attitude of a mother to a daughter.

## BIBLIOGRAPHY

1. ANON.: One Child in Nine in a Broken Family, *Statist. Bull. Metrop. Life Insur.*, 25: (No. 3) 3–6, 1944.

2. BABER, R. E.: *Marriage and the Family*, McGraw-Hill Book Company, Inc., New York, 1939.

3. BALDWIN, A. L., J. KALLHORN, and F. H. BREESE: Patterns of Parent Behavior, *Psychol. Monogr.*, 58: (No. 3) 1945.

4. BRIFFAULT, R.: *The Mothers*, Macmillan & Co., Ltd., London, 1934.

5. BURGESS, E. W.: *The Family: from Institution to Companionship*, Harvey Locke, New York, 1945.

6. CATTELL, R. B.: The Concept of Group Syntality, *Psychol. Rev.*, 55: 48–63, 1948.

7. CATTELL, R. B.: *A Guide to Mental Testing*, (2nd Ed.), University of London Press, Ltd., London, 1948.

8. CATTELL, R. B.: *The Fight for Our National Intelligence*, P. S. King & Sons, Ltd., London, 1937.

9. CATTELL, R. B.: The Dimensions of Culture Patterns by Factorization of National Characters, *J. abnorm. soc. Psychol.*, 44: 443–469, 1949.

10. CATTELL, R. B.: The Diagnosis and Classification of Neurotic States; a Reinterpretation of Eysenck's Factors, *J. nerv. ment. Dis.*, 102: 576–587, 1945.

11. CATTELL, R. B., and L. G. WISPE: The Dimensions of Syntality in Small Groups, *J. soc. Psychol.*, 28: 57–78, 1948.

12. CROOK, M. N., and M. THOMAS: Family Relationships in Ascendance-submission, *Univ. Calif. Publ. in Educ. Phil. and Psychol.*, 1: 189–192, 1942.
13. CROSBY, S. B.: A Study of Alameda County Delinquent Boy, with Special Reference to Broken Homes, *J. juv. Res.*, 13: 220–230, 1929.
14. CUNNINGHAM, B. V.: *Family Behavior*, W. B. Saunders Company, Philadelphia, 1936.
15. FERGUSON, W.: Correlates of Marital Happiness, *J. Psychol.*, 6: 285–294, 1938.
16. FITZ-SIMONS, M. J.: Some Parent-child Relationships as Shown in Clinical Case Studies, *J. exp. Educ.* 2: 170–196, 1933.
17. FLUGEL, J. C.: *The Psycho-Analytic Study of the Family*, Hogarth Press, London, 1939.
18. FROMM, E.: *Escape from Freedom*, Farrar and Rinehart, Inc., New York, 1941.
19. GARDNER, L. P.: An Analysis of Children's Attitudes toward Fathers, *J. genet. Psychol.*, 70: 3–28, 1947.
20. GEDEON, S.: The Problem of Obedience, in C. Bohler's *The Child and His Family*, Harper & Brothers, New York, 1939.
21. GOLDFARB, W.: Psychological Privation in Infancy and Subsequent Adjustment, *Amer. J. Orthopsychiat.*, 15: 247–255, 1945.
22. HALL, D. E.: Domestic Conflict and Its Effect on Children, *Smith Coll. Stud. soc. Work*, 1: 403–404, 1930.
23. HAMILTON, G. V.: *A Research in Marriage*, Albert & Charles Boni, Inc., New York, 1929.
24. HATTWICK, B. W.: Interrelations between the Pre-school Child's Behavior and Certain Factors in the Home, *Child Develm.*, 7: 201–226, 1936.
25. HATTWICK, B. W., and M. STOWELL: The Relation of Parental Over-attentiveness to Work Habits and Social Adjustment in Kindergarten and the First Six Grades, *J. educ. Res.*, 30: 169–176, 1936.
26. KINSEY, A. C.: *The Sex Life of the Human Male*, W. B. Saunders Company, Philadelphia, 1948.
27. KIRKPATRICK, G.: Factors in Marital Adjustment, *Amer. J. Sociol.*, 43: 270–283, 1937.
28. KOMAROVSKY, M.: *The Unemployed Man and His Family*, The Dryden Press, Inc., New York, 1940.
29. REICH, T.: *The Psychology of Sex Relations*, Rinehart & Company, Inc., New York, 1948.
30. TERMAN, L. M., with P. BUTTENWIESER, L. W. FERGUSON, W. B. JOHNSON, and D. P. WILSON: *Psychological Factors in Marital Happiness*, McGraw-Hill Book Company, Inc., New York, 1930.
31. WESTERMARCK, E. A.: *Three Essays on Sex and Marriage*, Macmillan & Co. Ltd., London, 1934.

# CHAPTER 13

## PERSONALITY AND THE CULTURAL MATRIX:
## II. THE FAMILY, ITS RELATION TO CHILD PERSONALITY

1. Origins of Initial Parent-Child Attitudes
2. Effects of Parental Attitudes on the Child
3. The Development of Child-Parent Attitudes
4. The Effects of Intersibling Attitudes and Relative Positions
5. The Effects of the Family Syntality Traits
6. The General Functions of the Family Relative to Society
7. The General Functions of the Family Relative to the Individual
8. Summary

### 1. ORIGINS OF INITIAL PARENT-CHILD ATTITUDES

**The Meaning of the Child to the Parents.** As the preceding chapter has discussed the family created by the parental personalities, their relations, and their general social setting, so the present chapter discusses its effects upon and influence by the personalities of the children growing up in it. This division, primarily for convenience of exposition, does not deny that for all members of the family the interaction of the personality and the family syntality is mutual, but it does imply that the comparatively formed and settled personalities of the parents do most to determine the dimensions of the family syntality, and that the family syntality in the main shapes rather than is shaped by the personality of the child.

Most evidence yet available on family dynamics and the child personality has so far not been based on measures of syntality—which have not existed— but has accumulated specifically with regard to the effects of parent-child relations.[1]

To the parents the arrival of the child means a major development in the emotional satisfactions existing in the marriage. It brings ego satisfactions[2] to both, evokes deeper expressions of the protective erg, satisfies the gre-

---

[1] A bibliography up to 1932 is available in F. M. Thurston (40).

[2] The extent to which the parents may justifiably say "my child," by virtue of the sacrifices made on its behalf, is, however, less, as a result of the recent social trends discussed at the beginning of the chapter, by which the state shares these sacrifices and responsibilities. But the child remains a major ego satisfaction whatever the communal system, in that it is part of the parents' "immortality" and an extension of the ego.

garious erg, both through the child's company and through giving the parents a greater sense of having a stake in the community, and gives greater scope for play and healthily regressive, recreational ergic satisfactions generally.

**Ambivalence of Parental Attitudes.** As indicated in discussing inter-parental relations it is necessary in all the deep and complex intrafamilial attitudes to reckon with attitudes operating at both conscious and unconscious levels, and commonly with some ambivalence in terms of love and hate for the same person. This ambivalence is normally least in the parent-child attitudes, yet the restrictions and responsibilities brought by the child do nevertheless frequently develop hostilities in the parent, commonly repressed, sometimes given rationalized expression (severity of "discipline") and, in a few cases of violent rejection, expressed quite overtly. This is most readily seen in the stepparent, who has less naturally stimulated affection to submerge the hostility. But perhaps some "jealousy" of the child is normal, for all parents must feel at some time that the "hungry generations tread thee down."

With the normally adjusted parent there may develop, if not hostility, at least a period of internal conflict of various kinds, due to the considerable readjustment of habits that the new motivations and circumstances require, and in this age of careers for women, if not in all ages, the greater burden of readjustment falls to the wife. With maladjusted and neurotic parents the very fact of the child's birth has been known frequently to bring symptoms of neurosis, anxiety, and depression. Clinically this depression is explained as guilt due to an unconscious revival of the castration complex, for where sex has been strongly associated with guilt and Oedipal wishes, the child's existence is overpowering evidence of "sin."

**Some Causes of Parental Attitudes.** While this section does not set out to deal systematically with the *causes* of parental attitudes, in addition to the effects—mainly because empirical studies of causes are lacking—yet the present brief glance at causes must be carried a little further. Probably the most frequent single cause of a parental attitude of rejection of a child is a rejection of the marriage itself, in an unhappy marital adjustment. On the other hand, as pointed out when discussing the Oedipus complex, a disappointment of one parent with respect to the other may lead to an *increase* of affection for the child. This can usually be distinguished from strong affection in the normal family situation, however, by an overstrained quality and often by sexual coloring.

In Symonds's studies (39) certain personality characteristics were noted to connect with certain attitudes. The mothers showing defective acceptance or active rejection of their children were on an average emotionally immature, timid, and dependent, often dominated by their husbands and lacking in attempts at self-realization. The oversolicitous, anxious attitudes were found in mothers who were insecure but who compensated for insecurity-inferiority by striving and obsessional overactivity, frequently dominating both husband and children.   Other clinicians have observed that fussy oversolicitousness is fairly commonly an attempt at domination through anxiety.   Numerous clinical examples could be brought to show how deprivations, indulgences, and trauma in the life of the mother have induced an instability and immaturity which cause the presence of the child to constitute an inappropriate and resented task.   The study of every childhood behavior problem therefore goes back necessarily to the grandparents.[3]

As to overindulgent attitudes, Flugel (14) points out the large role played by unconscious identification with the child.   Realistic thinking, the super-ego, and public opinion may prevent the individual indulging his narcism with respect to himself.   But even public opinion sometimes condones a man's pampering or demanding absurd advantages for his offspring.   And those indulgences which are not evident to society but only to the individual's own superego can nevertheless be freely expressed despite the superego, by the defense of identification with the child.   The role of self-assertion, involving the child as an extension of the parent's ego, is a more normal and healthy reaction, but it brings its own distortion.   Stogdill (36), for example, notes that parents rate their children significantly more well behaved than general observers do, and that those parents who do so strongly, also rate themselves as more patient, consistent, and less abrupt in their treatment of the children than others do.

Among other unconscious mechanisms and attitudes of the parent in relation to the child are the unconscious agreement of two parents to use the child as a scapegoat for their own difficulties, rationalizing this response to their frustrations as necessary discipline.   Equally unconscious is the tendency of the parents to build the attitudes to their children on the attitudes they have to their own parents or to younger siblings.   Flugel points out the latter procedure as a normal and necessary one, for the attitudes to the children cannot have much strength if they are developed *de novo* and without roots in the more powerful emotions normally resident in the stereotyped attachments formed in the early years.   The present writer has several times seen this unconscious identification illustrated, in others and himself,

---

[3] Roheim (27) develops the observation that parental frustration leads to infantile trauma: for he shows how sexual and other frustrations of the parents result in aggression against the child or overloading of the child relation with sexual components, both of which produce eventually emotional disturbance.   In particular he argues that "the infantile trauma in any group is conditioned by unsatisfied components in the normal sexual lives of the adults."   The infants thus traumatized are compelled to seek sublimated outlets which constitute culture itself.   For culture, as a deviation from biological satisfactions, is one vast sublimation or even a collection of neurotic symptoms.   Thus the situation we are now discussing has in it the germ of all cultural developments.

by slips of the tongue which call the child by the names of the parent's younger brother or sister. Unconscious identification of the child with the parent's parent, in what psychoanalysts call the "reversal of generations," can also be seen operating in lesser degree, especially as the child grows up and the parents grow smaller.

The effects upon the child of the parent's experience in the families in which they were children, although clearly formulated from clinical work and in psychoanalytic theory, has not yet received nearly enough empirical checking. Terman's study of marital happiness establishes such causal connections with respect to husband and wife adjustments, but apart from Baruch's study (3) there is little evidence in regard to attitudes to children. The latter research showed relations to exist between poor adjustment of the child (as well as poor marital happiness) and antagonism of the mother to her own father, discord between mother's parents and antagonism of father to his own mother. The mother's family situation was more important than the father's. The child's adjustment seemed to have no relation, on the other hand, to degree of positive attachment of the father to his mother or of antagonism to his father, or to the marital happiness of his parents, or to any change in social status of either of the child's parents at the marriage.

Symonds presents evidence that in regard at least to dominance attitudes "a person adopts an attitude as a parent similar to that held toward him by the parent of the same sex."

Regarding the initial attitude of the child to the parents, if attitude it may be said to have in the early months before its libidinal attachment at the Oedipus stage is formed, it is primarily an enhancement of its own narcism. "If I am so loved and valued, how important I must be!" One experimenter who asked somewhat older children why their parents loved them was able to get only such completely egocentric answers as "Because they're my parents," or "Because mothers love their children."

## 2. EFFECTS OF PARENTAL ATTITUDES ON THE CHILD

**Consequences of Parental Rejection.** Through the work of Symonds, (39), Levy (22), Stogdill (36), Gedeon (16), Hattwick and Stowell (20) Carpenter and Eisenberg (5), Fitz-Simons, Mueller (26), and others a good deal of direct evidence has now accumulated on the relation of measured parental attitudes to child behavior and personality. However, it is still far from completeness or adequate confirmation and has been restricted to relatively few attitudes—chiefly affectionateness, hostility, rejection, dominance, jealousy and overprotection—from among the possible range of basic parent-child and child-parent attitudes listed on pages 347 and 348.

Clinical work early drew attention to the strong effect on personality of parental rejection. Fathers may feel jealous of their children or reject them for more basic reasons. Some mothers may *never* truly accept, emotionally, the fact of their child's existence. With the causes, whatever they are, we are not immediately concerned. Our study is directed rather to the baffling situation presented to the child who finds rejection where he needs emotional nearness and warmth.[4] Clinically one can sometimes see that such a situation generates tensions of frustration and anxiety that are almost too much for the immature ego to handle. Its most direct effect is to undermine self-esteem and produce pervasive feelings of helplessness. Its chief indirect effect is even more important, namely, a failure of the Oedipus object attachment to achieve normal development, especially if rejection occurs in the first year or two of the child's life.

Since the superego is formed on the Oedipus complex, (by its normal dissolution, *i.e.*, since the child will adopt the moral inhibitions only of people he loves) we should expect the child rejected at this age to show conspicuous failure of conscience and altruism. The hypothesis that psychopathic, criminal personalities—other than those with the hereditary syndrome—are largely products of this situation, has not yet been sufficiently investigated, but the undoubted evidence that milder degrees of such personality disorder are associated with milder or later rejection is clearly in line with this hypothesis. Symonds (39) summarizes studies (ninety-eight clinical case histories) which show that the rejected child manifests an undue frequency of behavior recorded as aggressiveness, rebelliousness, hostility, truancy, some daydreaming, and, especially, lying and stealing. Gedeon (16) studying the matter from the standpoint of disobedience, found a correlation of 0.75 between instances of disobedience and instances of harsh parental attitude. A glimpse at the persisting effects into adolescence and later of early rejection and lack of close parental affection is offered by Goldfarb's (17) comparison of fifteen adolescents brought up institutionally with others brought up in foster homes. The observations suggest that infant deprivation of affection tends to produce passivity and emotional apathy. Perhaps the primary antisocial behavior either persists or is disciplined into conformity accompanied by apathy.

**Overprotection—Cause or Consequence of Child Traits?** At this last observation we do well to raise one or two questions which may have been uppermost in the student's mind in studying the above evidence. First, is it possible that the child's personality provokes the parental attitude rather than vice versa? Does the pugnacious, disobedient, uncontrollable child get rejected, the delicate, shy child overprotected? The controls are not good enough to rule this out, but it seems unlikely that more than a minor part of the variance springs from the child's personality as stimulus. Second, one

---

[4] For a discussion specifically of effects of lack of maternal affection in the first years of life the student is referred to the reference to Ribble and others in Chap. 19.

may wonder whether common heredity of general emotionality ($C$ factor) may make the child more disobedient and the parents more harsh and unreasonable. This question of analyzing out causes among associations will be taken up generally at the end of the chapters on cultural influences.

**Ambivalent Indulgent Attitudes.** A third attitude that has come in for study is the overindulgent (or oversolicitous) attitude, defined as laxness of discipline, giving the child all he asks, heaping material luxuries upon him (usually in lieu of attention and time), and neglecting to make the child face moral realities. Psychoanalysts, *e.g.*, Flugel (14), have stressed the strong ambivalence in this attitude. It is apt to be connected with an unstable alternation of irrational indulgence and severity or rejection, suggesting the probability that the indulgence is really a reaction formation in consciousness against basic rejection in the unconscious. This clinical hypothesis is well born out by statistical records for, as Symonds points out (39), the behavior pattern of children with overindulgent parents is distinctly like that found among rejected children, but with stealing and lying conspicuously low and temper-tantrums, stubbornenss, and feeding problems relatively higher. Other studies show overprotected children more frequently (41 per cent as against 7 per cent of controls) to have had more prolonged breast feeding (to twelve months or longer) and to be slightly earlier in walking, talking, and bladder control. In school they seem less likely to react to a problem with increased "fighting" zeal as it becomes more difficult. More tonsillectomies and fewer fractures are recorded for them, and they show more interest and acceleration in reading activities. There is no evidence of a more difficult sex adjustment in later life in the "indulged-overprotected" but some in the "dominated-overprotected."

**Parental Dominance.** As to dominance in parents, the evidence is somewhat obscure, largely because the present dearth of factorial analyses of attitudes leaves doubt regarding the role of dominance in various merely clinically defined attitudes, *e.g.*, overprotection. J. S. Mill expressed the popular view on direct dominance when he said, "Strong-willed parents make weak-willed children," though we should note that $E$ factor has little to do with perseverance and strength of will but only with aggressiveness, conceit, and social insensitivity. The results of Crook and Thomas, using the A-S test, show that at least through childhood and adolescence the correlation of parent-child dominance, as a personality characteristic if not as a specific attitude, is zero or slightly negative (correlation of mother and daughter = $-0.07$ to $-0.16$, $n = 71$; correlation of father and daughter = $-0.04$, $n = 47$). Since in every investigated trait there is *some* degree of inheritance it would seem that in this case the positive correlation of true inheritance is suppressed by a stronger negative correlation from environment, and that John Stuart Mill was indeed correct in his generalization.

Further light is thrown on this by Mueller (26) who studied twenty-five dominant fathers in relation to twenty-six sons, intensively. The dominance was judged to have a neurotic compensatory function or a consolation for unfulfilled ambitions of the father or to belong to an authoritarian cultural background. A majority of the children (fifteen) reacted by being passive, dependent, and obedient, six were openly rebellious and resentful, and five were passively resistant. Watson (43) found adult students excessively disciplined as children to show some resentment to the parents, to be socially maladjusted and given to quarreling with associates, to be overconscientious, anxious, and depressed.

It is possible that parental dominance produces a bimodal distribution of dominance-submission in the children, with most turning out submissive. Carpenter and Eisenberg (5), studying dominance in young women, found that the more dominant were allowed more freedom and independence at home, were allowed to visit away from home, and were given allowances and allowed to solve their own problems. They resembled and were close to the father (emotionally and in age) more than to the mother, relative to the less dominant, and they tended to have weak and demonstrative mothers. Levy (22) found submissive mothers have a tendency to create dominating children, who seem to depend, however, on having someone to dominate. He also found greater general submissiveness in the offspring of dominant mothers. Clinical observation suggests, however, that though high-dominance attitudes in the parents produce low dominance in the offspring through childhood and adolescence, there is a tendency for delayed maturation of dominance in the offspring of dominant individuals, such that they also become of above average dominance in later life. There seems also to be some slight correlation of high dominance with high character standards, presumably because the parental dominance is useful in the transmission of the cultural standards which are less readily adopted by the child.

Symonds found, from questionnaire responses made by observers of his subjects, that dominated children tended to be humble and shy, to feel more inferiority and inadequacy, to be somewhat more confused in social situations, more tolerant of others (in youth), and more fair and broad-minded, while there were indications that they were more sexually inhibited as adults. The children were rated significantly more courteous, obedient, interested in school, neat, reliable, and responsible. The clinical cases were relatively high in truancy from school, running away from home, failure in school, and unhappiness and quarreling. This last is the picture of dominance when other circumstances, e.g., low intelligence, are added, forcing maladjustment.

By contrast the children of "submissive" parents were found to be significantly more talkative, independent, disobedient, antagonistic, given to food fads, lacking interest in school, not neat or punctual, lazy, stubborn, self-confident, careless, and selfish. The clinical case history group showed relatively more feeding problems, temper-tantrums, enuresis, and disobedience. Evidently a certain amount of dominance on the part of the parent and submissive deference on the part of the child is psychologically more adjusted to their true relationship of greater and less knowledge and powers, and to *the necessity for transmitting the culture pattern*. It is an illustration of compensatory dynamics that the children more suppressed at home accept the school and its tasks more readily as an interesting outlet (except where their incapacities cause them to truant). Research on the measurement of the optimum age at which to impose particular cultural restraints and complexities is still lacking. Possibly the dominated group is reliable, courteous, and restrained at too early an age: certainly the group lacking parental pressure is obviously deficient in acquiring the culture pattern, apart from other, more specific personality characteristics.

### 3. THE DEVELOPMENT OF CHILD-PARENT ATTITUDES

**Changes in Parent-Child Attitudes with Age and Sibling Multiplication.**
Regarding general trends and relations in parental attitudes to children we may note first that they change with the sex of the child and the parent, often in ways that are so "normal" and taken for granted that we do not notice them. Baldwin (1) obtained ratings on the thirty Fels Parent Behavior Rating Scales for seventy-four three-year-old and seventy-nine nine-year-old children and found significant age trends notably in that the older children are treated with less warmth and indulgence, fewer deliberate attempts to stimulate their intellectual development and more applications of restrictions. Some parents diverged from the general trend by showing, with the decline in indulgence, an increase in solicitousness ("anxiety about").

Baldwin also investigated (2) the changes in the mother's attitude to children during pregnancy and at the birth of a new sibling. The most significant changes were: (*a*) temporarily during pregnancy a decrease, with recovery afterwards, in the "activity level in the home" variable and the "quantity of suggestion" (general directives to child) variable; (*b*) permanently, a decrease in a set of warmth-indulgence variables (child-centeredness, affection), some decrease in the understanding variable (insight into child's needs and point of view), and an increase, less significant, in a bunch of restrictive variables (restrictions, coercion penalties). These changes are greater at the birth of the second child than of later children, suggesting, as we find in the following section, that sib antipathies might consequently be greater between the first two than later children. The changes observed on the arrival of a new child are strikingly similar to those observed between the three- and the nine-year level above, suggesting that part of the age change is really due to new arrivals (a crucial experiment has not yet been done here to separate these influences).

**Other Associations of Parent-Child Attitudes.** In the natural sequence of study we should now turn to the relations of parent-child attitudes to economic level, religious philosophy, parental age, illness, unconscious identifications, sexual and general emotional relations between the parents, and changes in the personality of the child, but research still leaves this field largely unexplored.

A matter obliquely related to intrafamilial attitudes is that studied under the somewhat vague notion of "social distance." Duball studied (by a questionnaire to 458 children aged twelve to seventeen) the "social distance" between parents and children (presumably degree of identification and approachability) and found that it was smaller (*a*) for adjusted than unadjusted children; (*b*) from child to mother than child to father; (*c*) for daughters than for sons; (*d*) for younger than older children; (*e*) for smaller than for larger families. This study also found that for daughters *and* sons the mother was more frequently taken for a model and guide than the father—a finding that agrees with the correlations found in moral values, attitudes, etc., of the personality.

On the reciprocal relation—the attitudes of children toward parents—surprisingly little experimental data exist. The psychoanalytic view—that the children are first bound by affection to the mother and then to the opposite-sex parent, with an ambivalent attitude of admiration and resentment toward the same-sex parent, has already been amply described. Gardner's study (15) of 388 fifth- and sixth-grade children bears out some of these relations, though the crudity of the questionnaire method (he presented a 45-item questionnaire) compared with the clinical approach leaves something to be desired. This study found that by both sexes the mother was given about twice the preference rating of the father and that both preferred the mother for services. Though there was no clear evidence of special affection for the opposite-sex parents, the boys were somewhat more critical of the father than were the girls, though both criticized the same sorts of things. In this "normal" sample of children neither sex reported a desire for more affection from either parent. With regard to ego ideal, each sex gave more ways in which it desired to resemble the same sex than the opposite-sex parent, but nevertheless rated the opposite parent somewhat higher in disposition and character. It is possible that this last is really an indication of that special fondness which could not be revealed by direct questionnaire, since "overvaluation of the object" is a characteristic of libidinal investment of an object.

**Attitudes to Opposite- and Same-sex Parent.** Differences in children's attitudes to father and mother, as far as can be seen from evidence of the above nature, seem to be more related to differences of parental role than to differences of sex. In industrial societies, and many others, the father is an almost unseen provider, a more rigorous disciplinarian and one with less experience of the children's idiosyncrasies. The mother, showing more intimate personal care and cherishing, is likely in any case to be considered by the younger child as more affectionate. Fondness and fair play are the most constantly demanded requirements by children of those who control their lives, and what the greater emotionality of the mother loses to fair play is more than made up by what she presents in fondness.

Chang (12), studying the attitudes of six- to fifteen-year-old children in Northern China (186 boys, 168 girls) by the method of paired comparisons, found preferential affection ratings as follows: mother, 2.08; father, 1.63; grandmother, 0.71; elder sister, 0.64; younger brother, 0.62; elder brother, 0.56; grandfather, 0.40; younger sister 0.40. It is noticeable that except for "younger sister" the female always stands higher than the corresponding male.

The studies of Stagner (33) and Stagner and Krout (34) deal partly with attitudes of parents to children, but as the evidence is obtained by asking college students about their parents it may be essentially best classified under attitudes of children to parents. In the first study comparing personality traits measured by questionnaire with attitudes to parents the most clearly significant finding was a tendency for students with higher general emotionality to show more attachment to the mother and less to the father than in the more stable. This might indicate that unresolved Oedipus attachments upset emotional integration or that high emotionality leads to difficulty in accepting superego discipline. The later study found that children who feel "distant" from the parents are likely to report them as emotionally unstable. The remaining findings are best presented without attempts at interpretation at this stage, though they are very provocative. Boys who were father's favorite report distant relations with the mother, but girls do not do so. Boys who report more distant relations to the father are somewhat more inclined to be forgetful, to worry, and to have suicidal thoughts. Girls reporting distant relations to the father, on the other hand, show neuroticism, carelessness with money, somatic, digestive upsets, dizzy spells, and headaches more frequently, while those reporting more punishment by the father show more neurotic somatic symptoms, dizzy spells, daydreams. It is noteworthy that the girls' symptoms are nearer those of conversion, and the boys' nearer anxiety hysteria.

Children were found to report as more emotionally stable the parent with whom they identified more. Identification occurs more where the child feels he is the favorite: thus a coefficient of association of 0.54 was found between girl's identification with the father and mother's preference for the boy. When the mother prefers the child of opposite sex to the respondent, the father is reported unstable, and, in general, rejection of a child by the mother led both to more expectations from and more criticism of the father.    Girls were somewhat more predictably influenced by the family pattern than were boys (*i.e.*, the correlations are higher) suggesting that from an early age the boy gets somewhat more of his emotional relations from outside the immediate family circle.

Symonds sums up several studies to the conclusion that personality in boys tends to show feminine traits when the mother is a forceful, dominating person, and to show masculinity and tomboyishness in girls when the mother is inadequate or rejecting.    Terman finds that sons of very religious mothers are likely to score rather feminine on the masculinity-femininity of interests test, and that masculinity occurs in girls whose fathers have strong mechanical interests—a somewhat obscure connection.

**Changes of Child-Parent Attitude with Age and Other Variables.**    The children's attitudes to the parents will change with age not only because of the changing personalities and attitudes of the parents (see above), which are slight, but because of the changing personality of the child and particularly his changing powers of perceiving the parent for what he really is. Probably, though no systematic data can be brought to show it, the parents suffer in some respects a loss of prestige as the child grows older.    At least it would scarcely be the norm for an adolescent to lack criticisms of his parents, and is part of a realistic evaluation associated with lessened emotional need for dependence.

But if this "disillusionment" occurs at an early age, through gross, real defects of the parent, personality difficulties in the child are likely to ensue. In the Oedipus period the attitude of the child to the parent conditions the introjection of the parent values into the superego, and assists the growth of the ego.    Clinicians report two principal effects from defective attitudes to the parent at this time: (*a*) a devaluation of the self along with the parent, causing a "narcistic wound" to the ego, leading to oversensitiveness, pessimism, and lack of confidence; and (*b*) the formation of an overrigid, infantile exacting superego, through too early an acceptance of superego responsibility by the child and the elimination of later, modifying, "humanizing" processes normally imitated also from the parent.

In general, as Stott's study (37) on a 64-item test of confidence in and affection for parents shows, there is a decided correlation (+0.61 in this sample of 490 children of thirteen to twenty years) between a favorable attitude to parents and general goodness of personal and social adjustment. Oscar Wilde summarized the attitude transition here by his aphorism.

"Children begin by loving their parents; as they grow older they judge them; sometimes they forgive them." Presumably, from the above findings, these last are the well-adjusted!

## 4. THE EFFECTS OF INTERSIBLING ATTITUDES AND RELATIVE POSITIONS

**What Adult Attitudes Are Founded on Intersibling Attitudes?** As indicated in the schema of intrafamilial attitudes (Section 3 above) the principal attitudes to be considered among siblings are affection, jealousy, admiration (identification), protectiveness, dependence, aggressiveness toward, fear of, indulgence, solicitousness, companionableness, etc., mostly in complex and ambivalent[5] forms.

Although the parents, particularly the mother, constitute the first and most permanent objects with regard to which the child has the experience of forming powerful attitudes, a part of the energy expressed in those attitudes soon becomes shifted to siblings (if they exist) and the education of those attitudes proceeds through experience with the siblings. The parents initially stand both for what later becomes specifically "cultural authority" and "sociable society," and doubtless the child's later attitudes both to authority and to friends are primarily formed by this initial experience. Nevertheless, the attitudes to friends, largely, and the attitudes to authority, partly, receive much further molding, into stereotypes from which they are likely to depart little in later life, through the *early experience with siblings*. All of clinical psychology points to the tremendous formative power of these early relations in shaping the strength and manner of the later capacities to love, to be jealous, to be dominant or submissive, cautious or open-handed in later relations with equals, subordinates, or leaders.

**Attitude Development in the Only Child.** The role of intersibling attitudes may perhaps best be initially indicated by considering the only child, in whose experience they are absent. The only child is in some ways maligned by popular rumor. Experimental evidence indicates that he is typically somewhat above average intelligence and still somewhat more advanced in scholastic attainment, especially verbal attainment. He is likely also to show more adult standards of behavior and to have fewer listed misdemeanors in school and out, except negativism and temper-tantrums. Later he may show a proneness to neurasthenic syndrome symptoms and a somewhat greater likelihood to neurosis generally, while in childhood he is brought with greater frequency than other children to a child guidance clinic. Indeed on closer inspection one sees that the outer signs of good adjustment are a shell of good training hiding a somewhat pervasive emotional defect. This defect centers on the capacity to give

---

[5] Ambivalent, of course, means more than complex. Most attitudes are complex blends of primary ergs. Ambivalent connotes in addition a degree of dissociation in the combination; some parts being conscious and some unconscious and therefore independent and unintegrated.

affection and to make psychological exchanges with others. Lacking contact with coevals in the primary group constituted by the family, he has no real basis of experience and "emotional practice" for linking into the larger secondary group constituted by society. For intelligence, particularly the intelligence of a child, is not sufficient to indicate how the attitudes learned toward the parents need modifying in dealing with the comparatively disorderly world of one's peers. Naturally, the intelligent parent gives the only child plentiful contacts with other children, but, judging by the results, it is only in special circumstances that this extrafamilial contact has the same force as a true or foster sibling in exercising the persistent emotional dependencies, aggressions, and satisfactions that generally obtain within the family.

Much has been written on the effect of sibling position, particularly by the Adlerians in relation to the development of inferiority overcompensations. Since it is an easy, tangible matter for direct experimentation much factual evidence has accumulated—too much for more than an over-all interpretative summary to be given here.

**Effect of Sibling Position.** In the main, the oldest and youngest children seem to occupy the positions of greatest psychological difficulty.

The first-born is slightly more prone to suffer from psychosis as an adult and to require clinical consultation as a child. A trace of this difference may be due to the greater liability of the first-born to birth injuries, notably anoxia in a long delivery (see Chapter 16), but most is probably due to the fact that the parents have to practice the skills of child-rearing for the first time on the first-born. The only specific directions of personality difference yet found to have statistical significance are the tendency of the first-born to be less active and assertive (probably because more secure) and to have some resemblance to the only child, notably in greater frequency of temper-tantrums. The Adlerian view is that the oldest child is likely to be more conservative, because the principal change he has known—loss of full possession of the parents through the arrival of the second child—has been for the worse. But attitude scale studies actually show the youngest child to be the only one significantly deviant—and he is so in a conservative direction. Nevertheless, it is probable that the second most important peculiarity of personality of the oldest child (the first being that due to parental inexperience and some experience of being an only child) arises from the trauma occasioned by the birth of a rival. To this deprivation he frequently responds by directly attacking the new sibling or by developing anxiety symptoms through the repression of aggression. But in the end he may gain in maturity relative to other sibs through experience of responsibility and the stimulation of affectionate protectiveness and possessiveness by their juvenility.

That the second (or the middle children in a larger family) tend to show overcompensatory striving, as required by the Adlerian theory in response to the inferiority of position is tolerably borne out. (The oldest child is *born* to a command position; the youngest *retains* the strongest appeal to the parents). Ratings indicate in the middle child a lack of passive or easy-going qualities and a tendency to be overambitious. This, of course, is only an *average* tendency in many families.

The youngest child faces psychological hazards greater even than those of the first-born, if we judge by the outcome. He shows a greater than average tendency to neurosis and this increases with the number of older children under whom he is "buried." In source-trait terms, it seems that the various results can be simply explained by saying that the youngest tends to be lowest in $C$ and $G$ source traits, the principal factors in character integration. For example, the youngest is significantly the highest in tests of disposition rigidity (7,8), which are expressions of poor integration of character and proneness to neurosis. These findings are probably to be explained by (*a*) the comparative inability of the youngest to assert himself directly and build up a strong self-regarding sentiment (ego structure); (*b*) the necessity he experiences to gain his ends more by appeals to the parents, which interferes with normal maturation; (*c*) the fact that much of his upbringing necessarily occurs through the erratic discipline imposed by older children rather than by the somewhat more skilled upbringing from parents.

One must preserve perspective on the above findings by comparing the variance due to family position with that due to all other causes. Then it will be seen that the former accounts for little when compared to differences between families, or to sib differences in heredity, or to differences from specific emotional experiences. Further, the generalizations about sib position have to be modified according to differences in age, sex, intelligence, etc., of the sibs involved.

**Effects of Sib Rivalry and Affection.** However, though *mere age* position has relatively small systematic influences, the specific *emotional, historical* sib relationship may affect the whole personality very powerfully. The important thing to bear in mind, as Flugel indicates (14), is that the clinical evidence shows the normal initial attitudes among sibs to be one of hostility or jealousy, upon which affection and companionship are later grafted. (This does not mean that affection may not finally outweigh hostility, especially if "identification" occurs.) The primary affection is directed to the mother, and sibs are at first only interlopers in this field of mutual affection.

Recently some experimental and statistical evidence has become available on intersib hostility and jealousy attitudes. Sewall (30) studied forty boys and thirty girls of two to eight years of age, each having a younger sib. More than half (thirty-nine children) were hostile to the younger sib as evidenced by physical attacks, ignoring his needs, or by showing personality changes (usually regressive) when the younger child enters the scene. Jealousy had no relation to sex or I.Q., but was greater in small families, oversolicitous families, and families with inconsistent discipline and mal-adjustment of or conflict between parents. Levy (22) discusses similar findings in a group of 844 child-guidance cases, which, however are naturally not as representative as the smaller group, but show the trend with family size more smoothly.

| Children in family | Number of families | Percentage with problem of sibling rivalry |
|---|---|---|
| 2 | 339 | 37 |
| 3 | 218 | 33 |
| 4 | 141 | 24 |
| 5 | 55 | 15 |
| 6 or more | 91 | 14 |
| Total........ | 844 | 30* |

* The mean percentage is calculated from 252 cases out of 844.

Sewall found that overt jealousy (recorded by the behavior mentioned above) by the older sib was high when the age difference of the sibs ran from thirteen to thirty-six months and declined steadily with greater differences. Levy points out that the curve is similar to that of resistive, contra-suggestible, obstinate behavior (see Chapter 19). If this proves true with fuller statistics we might infer that the frustration is primarily one of ego wounding.

An attempt to study sib rivalry on the assumption that phantasy in a play situation would have constant relation to real-life behavior was made by Levy (22), who introduced children with a younger sib to a mother doll, a baby doll, and an older sib doll. The children seemed to identify appropriately in most cases, but no new generalizations emerged except that the phantasies became less inhibited with repetition and the children showed attempts at self-punishment (at three and four years old) along with their aggression.

Ackerson's analysis of a clinical population showed hatred or jealousy of a sibling to be manifested by personalities having the following clinical assessments of traits (presented as correlations of traits with jealousy as a symptom):

| | Boys | Girls |
|---|---|---|
| Defective personality integration........... | 0.43 | 0.45 |
| Inferiority feelings...................... | 0.36 | 0.43 |
| Destructiveness......................... | 0.35 | 0.29 |
| Egocentric traits........................ | 0.32 | 0.32 |
| Queerness.............................. | 0.30 | 0.21 |
| Daydreaming........................... | 0.30 | 0.07 |
| Spoiled child........................... | 0.28 | 0.19 |

This suggests schizoid endowment to have some influence, in addition to spoiling and general instability.

Other studies, such as that of Smalley who found in a sample of twenty-seven families, eleven jealous, seven friendly, and nine protective, agree with the above studies and indicate such additional points as that jealousy is greater in girl-girl pairs and least in boy-girl, and that it is greater with differences in I.Q. On the other hand clinical studies often show greater jealousy with more similarity of personality traits and especially of interests and ambitions. This is probably the cause of the trend often seen, even in twins, for children to seek their ego-involved ambitions in quite different fields.

Nevertheless, it is clear that with the children as with the parents greater personality similarity brings more closeness than hostility, as shown in high frequency of harmonious association in identical twins. Considering the above facts apart from the personality characteristics aspect, and noting especially the increase of jealousy with smaller families, oversolicitous parents, and younger age, we must obviously conclude that hostility arises most where there exists more parental attention to lose, though, as commented above, the greater blow from this loss may be eventually to ego needs rather than to libidinal ones. However, one must not lose sight of a second general principle that operates here: namely, that with children, as with parents, frustration of the family needs *per se* tends to increase internal bickering and aggression. For this reason it would seem likely that there would be more conflict among rejected children than those receiving much attention, though no proof of this is available.

**Causes and Effects in Other Intersib Attitudes.** Studies along the above lines of establishing norms and causal connections are badly needed with respect to other intersibling attitudes, such as dominance-submission (admiration), protectiveness, gregariousness, dependence, etc. Carpenter and Eisenberg (5) found in their study of dominant and nondominant women that the former had experienced more admiration from siblings, particularly brothers. They had also experienced more companionship from children older than themselves.

What indications are yet available in clinical and general studies suggest that the effects of sib attitudes resemble those of the same attitudes in parents, but that they are weaker and more liable to compensation through the parents. Hostility and rejection lead to more antisocial behavior and precocity; oversolicitous older siblings provoke dependence; admiring, submissive sibs induce traits of dominance, and so on.

### 5. THE EFFECTS OF THE FAMILY SYNTALITY TRAITS

**Dimensions for Which Evidence Is Available.** The whole treatment of the family in this chapter, as indicated in Section 2, calls for measurement with respect to three aspects: (*a*) The syntality, as expressed in certain "atmospheres," psychological climates, or dimensions of the *total* family behavior, regarding the family as an organic unity; (*b*) the intrafamilial attitudes, especially those between parents and children, which, along with positions of the members, define the internal structure of the family, dynamically; (*c*) the individual personalities of the members, in which the attitudes are embedded and which affect the growth of any other given personality by their temperamental, dynamic, and cognitive realities.

These three aspects are presumably so related that, if we knew enough psychology, we could deduce the third from any two, *e.g.*, syntality from internal structural pattern and knowledge of the component personalities. Even so, it would be most convenient to have laws separately relating the family effects on personality to data in each of the three fields. Evidence has been given above on the effects of family attitudes and personalities: here we shall turn to the less-surveyed field of relations to total family climate or syntality.

Since, as Section 2 above shows, psychology has only recently turned to the problem of determining the important dimensions of syntality, the available evidence is frequently on the effects of an obscure combination of dimensions and pure influences could not be confidently sorted out even if the dimensions were known with more confidence than the tentative conclusions of Section 2 permit. Most reliably we have evidence on Dimension 3, above, that of family integration, adjustment, or morale. Next we have some evidence on Factor 4, which refers essentially to the extent of psycho-economic pressure as opposed to leisure and relaxedness. Then there is evidence on severity of disciplinary atmosphere (Factor 6) also on so-called democratic vs. autocratic ways of imposing discipline (Factor 7), on indulgence or child-centeredness (Factor 1), on acceptance-rejection (Factor 5), and some on family-intelligence level (Factor 2).

**Effects of Degree of Integration.** Morale or integration has been studied principally by comparisons of normal with abnormally *low* endowments, namely, with that found in homes having acute parental and general dissension or damaged by disgrace or broken membership. Unfortunately the data on so-called "broken homes" have been gathered regardless of the fact that data under that rubric include two distinct phenomena: the physically broken home, by death or distance, and the psychologically broken home, by divorce, separation, or desertion. Conceivably the former might affect only the efficiency of cultural transmission or create a slight deprivation of affection and attention. The latter, on the other hand, presents an extreme of the dimension (Factor 3) of conflict, dissension, and disintegration of the family.

Perspective on the incidence of the broken home in the unanalyzed sense has been given in Section 2 above, when reviewing the durability of the family. Wallenstein (42) gives the percentage of broken homes in the United States as eighteen to twenty-five, and states that it is decidedly lower in some natio-racial and class minorities than in others. Early and nonstatistical writers on the subject of broken homes have gratuitously assumed effects that they should have proved, and have probably created exaggerated conceptions. Thus Mead (25) speaks of the "shattering and disastrous" effects on the child, while other writers have "viewed with alarm" the insecurity, chronic depression, inferiority, insufficiency, apathy and "functional disturbances" created.

From studies of delinquency, notably the surveys of Burt (see (8) Chap. 16), Healy (see (24) Chap. 16), and Maller (24), it has long been known that broken homes are a causative factor, and such studies as that of Crosby show that delinquency from this source is more often tied up with personality problems than is delinquency in general. But the magnitude of the association is not great. Shaw and McKay (31), for example, in a survey of several thousand delinquents and control nondelinquents, found, in two groups, that the rate of delinquency from broken homes only exceeded that from nonbroken by 6.4 per cent and 5.9 per cent, though the difference was statistically significant. Other studies show a very slight loss of school attainment (A.Q.), a slightly lower rating in obedience, desirable habits, and personality adjustment, and a nonsignificant difference in the direction of social aggressiveness and emotional instability in children from broken homes.

A study outstanding for its scientific control is that of Wallenstein (42) who was aware of the double sense of "broken home," who matched groups for national and class origin, C.A., M.A., and sex, and who used objective personality tests. He found the highest incidence of broken homes in the Negro group, next in the Slavic. He confirmed that a just statistically significant difference exists, such that children from homes not broken (by divorce, desertion, and separation) are superior in school achievement, character standards, and emotional stability. There was no consistent difference in dominance-submission. By holding social status and I.Q. constant the difference was less than that usually found, because the incidence of broken homes is negatively correlated with these. The Slavic group showed more ill effects from broken homes than did Mediterranean, Nordic, Jewish, or Negro. Girls showed fewer ill effects than boys.

A comparison on a smaller scale at the college level, by Torrance (41), showed children from broken homes to rate higher in proneness to anger, self-centeredness, insensitivity to social approval, lack of self-control, and proneness·to depression. They had more problems with the college and more dismissals. Matched for I.Q. and C.A. with the controls, they showed more extreme (high and low) achievement, a fact noted in other studies and regarded as an indication of the existence in many cases of a compensatory overreaction to the trauma.   This study also separated physically broken from psychologically broken homes and found that the former had in a lesser degree the same effects as the latter.   Hall (18) compared the incidence of personality difficulties, habit-formation problems, lying, etc., in children from the fifty most harmonious families known to the home visitor with the fifty having most domestic conflict.   Personality difficulties were found in 28 per cent of children in the former and 48 per cent of the latter. Habit problems were less clearly distributed.   When divided in liars and nonliars (presumably with regard only to habitual lying!) 90 per cent of the nonliars came from the harmonious homes, and *all* nonliars were definitely children "wanted" by the parents.

The clear conclusion is that families high in dissension cause a corresponding lack of emotional integration (presumably $C$ factor) in the child, and perhaps also schizoid tendencies and proneness to secrecy and deception. Most experimenters agree that in the broken home the worst effect is temporary, and limited to the breaking period, and that thereafter comparatively slight effects persist.   The indications are that broken homes are significantly less deleterious to character formation than homes with systematic conflict and maladjustment.   Needless, perhaps, to add, the remark that family conflict is a *cause* of defective integration in the child, means that it may be a cause both through inheritance from the parents of that emotional instability which is a factor in family conflict, and through the inimical environment being unfavorable to ego and superego formation.   Until the measurement of unitary personality traits is more advanced and the statistical techniques are more refined than in available researches, the partialing out of distinct influences is not possible.

**Effects of Degrees of Factors 1 and 5.**   Regarding Factor 1, the dimension ranging from an atmosphere of indulgence, protectiveness, easygoingness, and emotional responsiveness to one of indifference, withdrawal, nonchalance, Baldwin's findings are that the high scoring home "is a warm, friendly place with emphasis on the social virtues.   Children from such a home tend in nursery school to be friendly and sociable but somewhat inactive.   At school age, children from these homes seem less well adjusted, they are emotionally insecure, they are somewhat shy.   They are still inactive and unaggressive, but the friendly tenor of their behavior has disappeared" (see reference in (1)).   The findings suggest that a parental overprotective attitude is an integral part of this general family atmosphere.

Concerning Dimension 5—acceptance, affection, emotional rapport, practical shrewdness vs. distance, rejection, "autism in the group," Baldwin and his coworkers find, for the low-scoring families in the same group of 150 families, that the children show at all ages a more highly emotional, nonconforming personality. They refuse to accept the necessary inhibitions of the environment. Also a significantly poorer intellectual performance, notably in originality and creativity, was found relative to I.Q.

**Effects of Less Defined Dimensions.** In several studies made before preliminary research had been undertaken to determine the dimensions of family syntality, the attempts to define and label the family atmospheres studied are scientifically quite inadequate. Strictness and harshness, for example, were evidently used as synonyms for the dimension of rejection here studied. Gedeon's intensive study of eight children (16) found disobedience strongly positively correlated with the harsher atmosphere, but also found that children outside the family responded best to the methods, intrinsically poorly effective though they might be, to which they were accustomed. Correlations of −0.43 and 0.21 (if one may report correlations for eight children) suggest that with children for whom lenient treatment is effective, harsh treatment is ineffective and that if normally strictly treated, strict treatment is still slightly more effective. On larger groups the same relations were found, and it was observed also that the greater effectiveness of lenient treatment was more marked for boys than girls (is this because boys rebel, or because, as indicated elsewhere in this chapter, there is still a tendency for them to receive greater attention and valuation?). Gedeon also studied the modes of disobedience (negative arguments, ignoring, avoidance, defense) and found (*a*) girls more given to ignoring, boys to avoidance, (*b*) ignoring an order is more characteristic of younger children, while negative arguments correlate 0.90 with age. Avoidance of the instruction also correlates somewhat with age and is a device of those least given to disobedience. In its totality this evidence shows that affection (acceptance) and the rewards it brings are necessary to keep the child "in the field" if he is to learn in face of the punishments (nonrewards) necessary for learning social regulations.

The same study also brought evidence on the effects of what was there called the democratic-autocratic dimension, but which covers only a fraction of what democracy implies and is perhaps best called simply "Factor" 7. Clinicians have argued that authoritarianism is associated with strong tendencies of the child to identify with the parent; a development of narcism through which the individual perceives himself as practically always right; an emphasis on rules, with exact analysis of ethics and an exploitation of the rules by those who happen to exercise dominance, as rationalization for self-assertion. But Gibb (10) has shown that individuals report less frustration with firmer leadership—up to a point.

On the experimental side, if we combine the findings of Baldwin, Kallhorn, and Breese (see (3), Chap. 12) with those of Cattell and Wispe (see (11), Chap. 12), we conclude that families that are positive in this dimension (*i.e.*, nonauthoritarian) show readiness to explain behavior, a clarity of policies and perhaps also objective self-criticism, social skill, and self-possessed friendliness in dealing with other groups.

In nursery school, children from such "rational" homes are rated rather solitary and shy but interested and capable in intellectual tasks. Later, in school, social development progresses markedly, and they become rated highly for popularity and leadership. They are also emotionally stable and secure and unexcitable. The descriptions suggest high endowment in the personality factor called $K$ and also in $C$ and $G$. The study quoted here also measured "change of I.Q.," *i.e.*, change in intelligence test performance, which may be interpreted as progress in the skills that become learned especially through the application of innate intelligence ($K$ factor again). This change was greatest in the "democratic" group, *i.e.*, those high in the factor just described, but it was also great in the indulgent and least in the rejectant.

Some light is also thrown by the above study on the wider associations of three of these family dimensions (Factors 1, 5, and 7). More years of education in the parent conduced to a more democratic-skillful-self-criticizing atmosphere (Factor 7) and, less strongly, to a more accepting-emotional-rapport atmosphere (Factor 5), though it was only in the upper half of the education range that the correlation was marked. Higher income was similarly related to Factors 7 and 5, and was negatively correlated to the "indulgence" end of Factor 1, which last may not be so much of a surprise to observant social workers as to economic theorists who make low income and "underprivileged" synonymous terms. The only occupational breakdown, into farmers, "others," and college teachers, showed decreasing autocracy of atmosphere, in that order. I.Q. level (parents and children) was related to Factors 7 and 5 precisely in the same way as level of education.

## 6. THE GENERAL FUNCTIONS OF THE FAMILY RELATIVE TO SOCIETY

**The Family as Intermediary for Individual and Society.** Our preparation is now perhaps as complete as present data will permit for viewing the functions of the family as a whole, and even so we shall have to fill in the gaps with evidence from merely sporadic experiment and unsystematized clinical and sociological observation.

Without anticipating the analysis of the larger society and culture pattern to be made in the next chapter, we can yet see that the family has important dynamic and cognitive exchanges with this outer world which condition in turn the family's exchanges with the individual personality on the "inner side" of the home surface. The individual, the family, and the society form a triangle—though other social subgroups, *e.g.*, the school, could also be studied as operating in the third angle where we now place the family. Our present purpose is to look chiefly at two arms in the triangle—very briefly and summarily at that constituted by the relation of family to society, and, in the light of the whole chapter, at that constituted by the family and the individual.

**Main Principles of Interaction of Family and Society.** Basic propositions as to the interaction of family and society will therefore merely be presented as bold statements.

1. The family acts as a smaller organizational unit within society, for the collection and distribution of economic, psychological, legal, and moral powers and responsibilities (see (44)).

2. The family and the larger culture pattern exercise mutual influence not only through the transfer of habits of emotional response and thought but also through direct dynamic exchanges, whereby the dimensions of the culture pattern and of the family are likely to change with reciprocal responsiveness. Important special examples of this dynamic exchange and transfer are:

*a.* The observation that countries with persistent inclinations to totalitarian forms of political structure also persistently produce a family structure more extreme in the dimension of autocracy, with the accompanying hierarchy of dominance from the father down and the necessarily reduced status of the wife (and ultimately of women generally) relative to the husband.

*b.* Countries with many conflicting subcultures and with high mobility (like the United States) are likely to have a higher rate of family instability. However, the sympathetic relation of family and culture pattern need not always be in the isomorphic pattern suggested by this and the preceding example, as the following further instances show.

*c.* As noted in the above reference to historical trends (Section 1), the closeness of the family group, *i.e.*, the magnitude of the satisfactions obtained through it and which determine its cohesiveness, will vary *inversely* with the degree of security and interaction in the larger society, *e.g.*, with the degree of urbanization, socialization or paternalistic government (see evidence on Urban Emancipation (Factor 9)).

*d.* The stability of the family depends partly, but not wholly, upon the ability of the larger society or religious community stably to maintain certain restrictions—law and order, outlawing of sexual promiscuity, higher taxation of bachelors, etc. This amounts to compensating for the natural burdens of the family by binding dynamic (including economic) satisfactions more closely to the family.

3. The family is also influenced by physical (and therefore economic) features of the environment as well as by society. If the family lives in a one-room hut, the child's development in sexual and social attitudes will necessarily be very different from that in a family more highly developed in privacy. (Roheim's emphasis (27) on what he calls the trauma of "the

primal scene," *i.e.*, early misperception of the parental sexual act, is most important here.) Again the numerical size of the family and magnitude of "real income" in goods and services will influence personality development. For example, much of the growth of "progressive education" with its demands on time and security is not due to greater intelligence and enlightenment of present-day educators, but simply to economic permission. Increased "democratic" and "indulgent" atmospheres, operating at once as ideals and as social perils, have in fact occurred principally with decline in the size of the family. Again, the frequency of rejective attitudes to children is partly a function of the economic burden of the child relative to parental earnings.

4. The interactions described in items 1, 2, and 3 above will vary among families according to the position of those families within society, *e.g.*, their social status.

In discussions of family function there is danger of becoming involved, quite unnecessarily at this stage, in questions as to whether the family exists for the state or the state for the family, and similarly for the third item in the triangle—the individual. Some questions of dynamic subsidiation (but not of these ultimate ethical values) within society are attached in the next chapter (see Diagram 43). When we say that a function of the family is to transmit the cultural values of society this carries no implications as to whether this is for the ultimate ends of the state, the individual, or the family.

## 7. THE GENERAL FUNCTIONS OF THE FAMILY RELATIVE TO THE INDIVIDUAL

**The Family as a Stabilizer of Ergic Investments.** From what has been said in the present and preceding chapter it is possible to put in perspective the functions of the family which bear most on its relation to the individual as follows:

1. The family operates as a convenient, realistic, stable mode of expression for an appreciable fraction of the total ergic needs of the individual. How big that fraction is, and what its ergic composition may be, can only be guessed at until more comprehensive vectorial studies of attitudes have been made. The vector composition of the attitude to the family will naturally be somewhat different for the typical father, mother, son, and daughter. For example, the parent's attitude will normally include a higher loading in sex drive and the child's a higher loading in the erg of escape, *i.e.*, the drive to security. Certain subpropositions follow:

*a.* The vectorial sum of the various attitudes of the members to the family (expressing their canalized dynamic habits) provides the force that keeps the family together and determines its dynamic relations to all other groups, including the main society.

*b.* Some of these dynamic exchanges, like dynamic exchanges in general, take place through money, *e.g.*, the father expresses his affection by giving money which permits his family certain dynamic satisfactions, the family expresses its appreciation of the services of society by paying taxes. But it is a mistake to assume that all dynamic exchanges, or even most, require this mediation by tokens.

The best data yet available on the extent of cohesiveness and control operating through money are those showing the amount of breakdown when money disappears. The studies by Komarovsky (21) and others of the family during unemployment and in the depression show that the unemployed father tended to lose *some* control, particularly of the adolescent, and that this was most marked with sons when they were still working. Stouffer and Lazarsfeld (38) stated, further, first, that the father can lose authority with children and not with wife, but not vice versa; second, his companionship and authority with young children increase; third, hard times, which do not actually result in the father losing employment, in fact strengthen the family and particularly increase control over sons if the latter are unemployed. Contrary to Komarovsky, the investigators believed father-son conflict was highest when both were unemployed, a secondary result, probably, of general frustration.

From such data one may conclude that the cohesion and control of the family as far as father, mother, and young children are concerned, is more through immediate dynamic satisfactions (affection, need for security, companionship, etc) which, for the children, normally come more through the mother[6] than through the father.

But with older children, whose immediate dynamic satisfactions reside more with the peer group, and with the prospects of their own future, a surprising amount of control actually comes through economic control, and this is probably more stark in the authoritarian family.

**The Family as a Transmitter of Culture.** This brings us to the second main function of the family toward the individual:

2. By virtue of the security, stability, and other satisfiers provided for the children, it is able to reward and punish sufficiently to transmit the major parts of the culture pattern, dynamic and cognitive, to the child. The school does this also, but complementarily, with less emphasis on major personality adjustments and moral inhibitions and more on cognitive skills.

Incidentally, the school is more open to social control and permits ready

---

[6] The gamut of drives that a mother may seek to reward and punish in exercising this control is illustrated by a recorded statement in a child-guidance-clinic report. "I tried explaining, reasoning, smiling my approval, rewarding with candy, coaxing, bribing with promises of a holiday, cajoling, shaming, ridiculing, spanking, threatening with father's displeasure, sending to bed, standing in a room in the dark—"

transmission of new demands of the culture pattern, but the home, because it transmits powerful *dynamic* patterns that are often subconscious or wholly unconscious, cannot so readily be tampered with. It presents a less interruptible cycle, making for social conservatism and stability.

Appreciation of the role of the family in transmitting the culture pattern has got somewhat out of perspective with various specialists. Psychiatrists tend to criticize the family for damaging the personality of the child for the "trivial" purpose of transmitting the culture pattern, particularly its inhibitions. Certain sociologists, on the other hand, see the personality as the whole transmitted culture pattern and nothing but the culture pattern (repeating the old *tabula rosa* error of Locke and underrating the importance of that ergic and temperamental inheritance that conflicts with the culture pattern.[7]) To them the family is suspect only in so far as it is a crude and conservative transmitter. If parents heeded these one-track theorists the possibilities of family conflicts over the nature, purposes, and methods of family culture transmission would be increased!

**The Family as a Socioemotional Learning Ground and as a Shelter.**
3. It acts as a training ground for the emotional attitudes of the child to other people and society generally, but especially for the social skills in dealing with a range of older and younger people. Though this training is in the main sound and well shaped for later society, there are also systematic ways in which it is maladapted, producing modes of behavior which, if not appropriately modified, lead to maladjustment in society. These maladjustments arise principally because society is less ordered, less paternal, and less secure (for most children) than the family. Children who are submissive, conscientious, altruistic, and repressed, for example, are likely to suffer more in rough-and-tumble society by their expectations of justice and altruism. This psychological observation does not deny that society may need people with high expectation and aspiration levels in these matters.

Naturally these modifications of the attitudes normally built up within the shelter of the family have to be made not only to society but to the larger external world in all its aspects. Not only must the individual beware of encouraging political dictatorsnip by carrying over childhood attitudes of complete dependence on authority, but also he needs to recognize economic

---

[7] Stogdill (35), Laycock (see (32) Chap. 16) and many others have pointed out that in evaluating the seriousness of abnormal behavior psychiatrists seize on neurotic, depressive, and withdrawing reactions (the results of "superstitious moral codes"), whereas parents and teachers tend to rate most serious the offenses against morals, *e.g.*, stealing, masturbation, lying, "and those behavior patterns most interfering with their own affairs." Compared to psychiatrists they are reluctant to grant children responsibility in social contacts, love affairs, and freedom from parental curiosity and dominance. While experts lose perspective in this way the parent continues to attempt to discharge the responsibilities of the family correctly to society, the child, and the family.

and physical truths with which he had no cause to concern himself in the family. All that goes under animistic or, at least anthropomorphic, thinking is encouraged by early family experience. For example, psychiatrists have commented that children in indulgent but highly stable and moral families, who have repressed, religious, perfectionist personalities, are apt to react to the "punishment" of physical illness with guilt (shown in anxiety, depression, and compulsive-obsessional expiatory performances). Here is a mode of response, like that of primitive peoples to natural calamities, which is ineffective. Naturally many minor, systematic adjustments of this kind have to be made to adapt family training to society training.

4. The family also acts as a training ground—indeed may we say as a "finishing school"—in which the personalities of the young marriage partners are either matured to true adult stature or subjected to another psychological trauma.

5. It acts as an asylum, a sheltered psychological area, in which emotional satisfactions can be more readily obtained, with less need for constant readjustments, than in the larger society. Here play and trial-and-error learning are possible with fewer risks. A smaller range of adjustments is required because the parent personalities are similar by selection, and the child personalities by heredity, in comparison with the wider range of personalities, values, and interests, to be adjusted to in the world at large.

**Possible Systematic Defects in Education in the Family.** From society's point of view this "walling-in" of the family may in some aspects be regrettable. First, although pride in the family and close identification of self-assertion with the family may help hold the individual to high family standards, it may at the same time separate him from loyalty to the general culture pattern, *e.g.*, as in Napoleon's family, typical of the strong Corsican family, trying to assimilate the French Republic to the family instead of the family to the ideals of the Republic. Second, the protectiveness of the family may shield the individual unduly from making general social adjustments. Thus schizophrenics come from more than averagely overprotected homes (see Chap. 18).

In this connection one may ask, "How far is the difficulty in growing out of the family at adolescence due to this too-sheltered atmosphere?" Admitting some responsibility of the too-segregated family one may still argue that it is desirable to have some asylum from the full stresses of society, and that if the family provides such sanctuary society does not have to make other and special provisions. Suicide, neurosis, and crime rates are in general lower for married than for unmarried adults. This is in part because the family offers clear-cut "institutionalized" dynamic expressions for drives otherwise not easily expressed, but it is probably also due to the shelter offered by the family "wall." Secondly the family offers for society a large number of comparatively watertight compartments, which, when undesirable social or political fashions threaten to sweep the ship of state, provide some possibility of resistance. Resistance to Nazism in Germany, for example, was often tied up with the morale of the resistant family per se.

The suggestion that the similarity of members within a family lessens, in a desirable way, the problems of adjustment among its members has sometimes been criticized. Bernard Shaw has argued that members of the same family, by virtue of this similarity of personality defects, are the last people one should reasonably expect to live happily together (32). But the learning of adjustment and about personality may actually proceed better for this very reason. Rationalizations are penetrated most readily by those who would be prone to show similar ones so that stage scenery in the façade of personality is more at a discount in the family than in the more transient and less penetrating contacts of social life generally. At the same time the older members of the family are more likely to have faced the same personality problems than would be unrelated mentors and are consequently likely, if affection prevails, to show more sympathetic insight in aiding the younger member to a substantial solution of any given personality problem. (Though "When I was a boy . . . " may also suffer from poor memory and unawareness of cultural change.)

Consideration of the defects of "education" between individuals thus remote in age calls us to look again more closely at the point made in discussion of function 3 above—that social training in the family has the advantage of being a training with respect to the whole age range of human life. In general, outside the family, interest in mutual aid in personal adjustment comes only from people facing the same problems at the same time and coming together like partners in misfortune. It is a matter of common clinical observation that there is either marked sympathy or marked hostility between individuals with similar complexes, adjustment problems, or ambitions. The former predominates, accounting for the emotional closeness of children in the same age groups. Normally, therefore, people with strange dynamic problems, different from our own, will react with indifference and even impatience. The common bond of the family affections forces us to learn to pay attention to individuals of different age and sex, thus developing broader sympathies and understandings than the gang or the school or the professional group can engender.

The most important general fact about the training influence of the family upon personality is, after all, that it presents a continuous series of social and general learning situations in adjustments of a very varied nature, most of which could be evaded in other social situations for a longer time, even though with more disastrous end-results. The personalities of a group of growing children have to fit together like brazil nuts in the larger shell.

Exercise is given for adjustments in attitudes of dominance-submission and protection-dependence and to personality traits of dependability or insta-bility and so on. Sooner or later a number of principles are explicitly learned or implicitly incorporated in personality, *e.g.*, the principle of seeking non-overlapping areas of excellence when competition is severe; the principles of maintaining fair play as ultimately most rewarding; the habit of thinking and acting altruistically, in terms of responsibility to the community; the habit of thinking in terms of the value of real personal reputation; the princi-ple of solving problems through group discussions and allied action; and the habit of expending energy to maintain and recapture individual rights. These personal skills and sentiments, properly developed in a balanced group of siblings, are no mean gift from the family toward the successful integration of the adult society later formed by the children of the generation concerned.

## 8. SUMMARY

1. Parental attitudes to the child develop initially from the parents' atti-tudes to the marriage and from their life values generally, rooted in their own early experience and constitution. Most attitudes are partly uncon-scious and shaped on attitudes to siblings or parents in the parents' own family.

2. Systematic relations have been found between parental attitudes and child personality, overprotection leading to withdrawing personalities, rejec-tion to antisocial, rebellious personality, dominance to restrained personality, and so on.

3. The child's initial attitude to himself and the parents depends on their valuation of him. Children show greater attachment to the mother, and a general decline of dependence, reciprocated by declining parental warmth, with age.

4. Among intersibling attitudes hostility is often primary and ambivalence the rule. Jealousy is less in larger families.

5. Sibling position slightly but significantly favors certain personality developments, notably in the first and last child.

6. The effects of family syntality on child personality arise principally from the syntality traits or dimensions of Integration (Morale) vs. Dissen-sion, Easygoing Responsiveness vs. Nonchalance and Warmth, Emotional-rapport vs. Rejection, Group Autism. They are associated respectively with personality traits of emotional stability, of friendliness and of obedience with altruism. The similarity to parent-attitude effects suggests that these aspects of syntality are largely determined by parental attitudes.

7. The family, the individual, and the total culture pattern form a tri-angle of functional exchanges, among which, however, it is not necessary to intrude value judgments attempting to say for which function everything is

finally designed. In relations to society the family functions as a transmitter of the culture pattern, as a distributing and collecting unit, and as a developer of attitudes that have to be consistent with those also required in society; for the family and society buttress each other and share stability or instability.

8. In relation to the individual the family functions as a stable institution for the canalized expression of a certain combination of ergs; as a means of building moral and other habits contributing to adjustment in the larger culture pattern; as an asylum from excessive demands on adjustment; and as a training ground for emotional development.

## QUESTIONS AND EXERCISES

1. Describe four ways in which parental attitudes to the child arise from attitude to the marriage and from earlier family experiences.

2. Discuss two dimensions of the constitutional aspect of the parent personality, *e.g.*, intelligence, in regard to their effect on attitudes to the child.

3. Name three parent-child attitudes that have been found important for child personality and describe the personality developments that have been found in the child associated with extreme developments of each.

4. Discuss, with regard both to clinical observation and statistical data, the attitudes of children to the same- and opposite-sex parent, with regard to (*a*) ergic composition of the attitude, (*b*) the development of the ego ideal and superego, and (*c*) the changes of attitude with age.

5. Discuss intersibling hostility, in relation to family position, age, family atmosphere, and the nature of the personalities involved.

6. What personality characteristics have been found associated to any extent with sibling position?

7. What dimensions of family syntality are most clearly shown to affect the personality of the child? Discuss possible mechanisms for this action.

8. List the functions which the family may be said to maintain in relation to (*a*) the needs of society, and (*b*) the needs of the individual.

9. Discuss the special value of the family learning situation in regard to development of (*a*) the capacity to form attachments and the pattern of emotional expression therein, (*b*) moral sense or conscience, (*c*) social skills, (*d*) stability and security, illustrating the value in each case by instances of failure of these functions.

10. Attempt a quantitative statement of the ergic composition of attitudes to the home with respect to various members, and show how the rewarding of the component ergs is used to maintain family cohesion and hierarchical control. Illustrate deterioration of family cohesion and control through (*a*) failure of the father to gain an income, and (*b*) failure of some more direct ergic satisfaction to take place in the family exchanges.

## BIBLIOGRAPHY

1. BALDWIN, A. L.: Differences in Parent Behavior toward Three and Nine Year Old Children, *J. Person. Res.*, 15: 143–165, 1946.

2. BALDWIN, A. L.: Changes in Parent Behavior During Pregnancy, *Child Develpm.*, 18: 29–39, 1947.

3. BARUCH, D. W.: A Study of Reported Tension in Intermarital Relationship as Coexistent with Behavior Adjustment in Young Children, *J. exp. Educ.* 6: 187–204, 1937.

4. BRUNK, C.: The Effects of Maternal Overprotection in the Early Development and Habits of Children, *Smith Coll. Stud. soc. Work*, 3: 261–273, 1932.

5. CARPENTER, J., and P. EISENBERG: Some Relations between Family Background and Personality, *J. Psych.*, 6: 115–136, 1938.

6. CATTELL, R. B.: The Assessment of Teaching Ability, *Brit. J. educ. Psychol.*, 1: 48–72, 1931.

7. CATTELL, R. B.: The Riddle of Perseveration; I. Creative Effort and Disposition Rigidity, *J. Person. Res.*, 14: 229–238, 1946.

8. CATTELL, R. B.: The Riddle of Perseveration: II. Solution in Terms of Personality Structure, *J. Person. Res.*, 14: 239–267, 1946.

9. CATTELL, R. B.: The Dimensions of Culture Patterns by Factorization of National Characters, *J. abnorm. soc. Psychol.*, 44: 443–469, 1949.

10. CATTELL, R. B.: *Social Psychology* (in press).

11. CHAMPNEY, H.: The Variables of Parent Behavior, *J. abnorm. soc. Psychol.*, 36: 525–542, 1941.

12. CHANG, S. T.: The Ethical Sentiment in Children, *Educ. Rev.* (Chinese), 27 (No. 3): 63–68, 1937.

13. DAVIS, W. A., and R. J. HAVIGHURST: *Father of the Man*, Houghton Mifflin Company, Boston, 1947.

14. FLUGEL, J. C.: *The Psycho-Analytic Study of the Family*, Hogarth Press, London, 1939.

15. GARDNER, L. P.: An Analysis of Children's Attitudes toward Fathers. *J. genet. Psychol.*, 70: 3–28, 1947.

16. GEDEON, S.: The Problem of Obedience, in C. Bohlar's *The Child and His Family*, Harper & Brothers, New York, 1939.

17. GOLDFARB, W.: Psychological Privation in Infancy and Subsequent Adjustment, *Amer. J. Orthopsychiat.*, 15: 247–255, 1945.

18. HALL, D. E.: Domestic Conflict and Its Effect on Children: *Smith Coll. Stud. soc. Work*, 1: 403–404, 1930.

19. HATTWICK, B. W.: Interrelations between the Pre-school Child's Behavior and Certain Factors in the Home, *Child Develpm.*, 7: 201–226, 1936.

20. HATTWICK, W. W., and M. STOWELL: The Relation to Parental Overattentiveness to Work Habits and Social Adjustment in Kindergarten and the First Six Grades, *J. educ. Res.*, 1936, 30: 169–176, 1936.

21. KOMAROVSKY, M.: *The Unemployed Man and His Family*, The Dryden Press, Inc., New York, 1940.

22. LEVY, D. M.: Studies in Sibling Rivalry, *Am. Orthopsychiat. Ass.*, New York, 1937.

23. LINTON, R.: A Neglected Aspect of Social Organization, *Amer. J. Sociol.*, 45: 870–886, 1940.

24. MALLER, J. B.: Broken Homes and Juvenile Delinquency, *Social Forces*, 10: 531–533, 1932.

25. MEAD, M.: Broken Homes, *Nation*, 128: 253–255, 1929.

26. MUELLER, D. D.: Paternal Domination: Its Influence on Child Guidance Results, *Smith Coll. Stud. soc. Work*, 15: 184–215, 1945.

27. ROHEIM, G.: *The Riddle of the Sphinx*, Hogarth Press, London, 1934.

28. SEARS, R. R.: Personality Development in Contemporary Culture, *Proc. Amer. phil. Soc.*, (in press).

29. SEARS, R. R.: *Survey of Objective Studies of Psychoanalytic Theory*, Bull. 51, Social Science Research Council, Committee on Public Administration, Washington, D.C., 1945.

30. SEWALL, M.: Some Causes of Jealousy in Young Children, *Smith Coll. Stud. soc. Work*, 1: 6–22, 1930.

31. SHAW, C., and H. D. McKAY: Are Broken Homes a Causative Factor in Juvenile Delinquency? *Social Forces*, 10: 514–524, 1932.

32. SHAW, G. B.: Parents and Children, preface to *Misalliance*, Brentano's, New York, 1914.
33. STAGNER, R.: The Role of Parents in the Development of Emotional Instability, *Amer. J. Orthopsychiat.*, 8: 122–129, 1938.
34. STAGNER, R., and M. H. KROUT: The Study of Personality Development and Structure, *J. abnorm. soc. Psychol.*, 35: 340–355, 1940.
35. STOGDILL, R. M.: Experiments in the Measurement of Attitudes Towards Children, 1899–1935, *Child Develpm.*, 7: 31–36, 1936.
36. STOGDILL, R. M.: Parental Attitudes and Mental Hygiene Standards, *Men. Hyg.*, N.Y., 15: 813–827, 1931.
37. STOTT, L. H.: Parent-Adolescent Adjustment, Its Measurement and Significance, *Character & Pers.*, 10: 140–150, 1941.
38. STOUFFER, S. A., and P. F. LAZARSFELD: Research Memorandum on the Family in the Depression, *N.Y. Soc. Sci. Res. Council Bull.*, 29: 1937.
39. SYMONDS, P. M.: *Diagnosing Personality and Conduct*, Appleton-Century Crofts, Inc., New York, 1931.
40. THURSTON, F. M.: *Survey of Literature on Parent-Child Relations*, The National Council of Parent Education, Century Company, New York, 1932.
41. TORRANCE, P.: The Influence of the Broken Home on Adolescent Adjustment, *J. educ. Sociol.*, 18: 359–364, 1945.
42. WALLENSTEIN, N.: Character and Personality of Children from Broken Home, *Teach. Coll. Contr. Educ.*, 721: 1937.
43. WATSON, G.: A Comparison of the Effects of Lax versus Strict Home Training, *J. soc. Psychol.*, 5: 102–105, 1934.
44. ZIMMERMAN, C.: *On the Family*, D. Van Nostrand Company, Inc., New York, 1935.

## CHAPTER 14

## PERSONALITY AND THE CULTURAL MATRIX: III. GROUP DYNAMICS AND PERSONALITY

1. The Psychodynamics of Overlapping Groups
2. Cultural Anthropology and the Definition of Syntality
3. Nine Fundamental Principles of Personality-culture Interaction
4. The Interactions of Social Organs and Institutions through Personality
5. The Methodology of Relating Personality to Culture Pattern
6. Social Status and Its Relation to Measured Personality Traits
7. Social Status: Wider Associations and Interpretations
8. Summary

### 1. THE PSYCHODYNAMICS OF OVERLAPPING GROUPS

**The Definition of a Psychological Group.** Before any effective methodology can be applied or any meaning can be given to the interpretation of present data concerning culture pattern relations to personality, it is necessary to take up more systematically than we have yet done the social psychology of groups themselves. Because so little of a confirmed and systematic nature on the psychology of groups has yet been published, the attempt in the first part of this chapter to present a condensed account of the principles and factual bases of the social aspect of our problem must necessarily seem somewhat dogmatic and abstract, as indeed it is approximate and tentative. For fuller discussion the reader is referred to Cattell and Gibb's textbook (12) on social psychology and to social psychology readings generally.

Effective formulation of the relation of personality to cultural group requires, in regard to the latter, essentially (a) an understanding of the first principles concerning the formation and functioning of groups, (b) an acquaintance with the varieties of group culture patterns and the methods of describing and measuring them.

A number of people constitute a group when all are instrumental in the gaining of satisfactions for each and all members. That is to say, the group exists psychologically only in so far as its physical existence makes possible satisfactions not otherwise obtainable.[1]

---

[1] Sorokin, Zimmerman, and Golpin (47) distinguish between "systems" and "congeries." A mere collection of individuals, even when having common features to permit a logical

386

**The Concepts of Effective and Maintenance Synergies.** The sum total of individual interest-energies going into the group activities we may call the group synergy. This can be divided into two parts, the *effective synergy* that actually issues in the group action, and the *maintenance synergy* that is absorbed in the internal group activities. For example, a group of men may band together to make money as an investment company. Some of the psychological energy and money of each is absorbed in internal debates in the manner of investment, in office expenses, in the determination of internal structure, so that the actions that eventually issue for the company as such do not represent all the synergy of the group. Always some energy—some time and money—is lost in overcoming internal friction and in nothing more than the maintaining of the cohesion and structure of the group. This issue of the relation of effective to maintenance synergy has been recently dealt with by Merton (43), though not with the aid of these definitions. He points out that internal struggles for power in bureaucracies and government organs seem to draw most of the available energy inwards, so that the effective synergy—the execution of their true functions—may be temporarily acutely impaired.

Chapter 6 has shown how the dynamic traits of the individual—his pattern of attitudes and sentiments—can be most accurately represented by a diagram called the *dynamic lattice,* showing how interests subsidiate one to another. Although no emphasis was placed in that introduction on the role of groups, it is true that for most individuals some of the more important chains of dynamic subsidiation run through social institutions or groups. A considerable proportion of individual ends are gained through belonging to groups. This is illustrated by Diagram 43 representing twelve social groups and showing (*a*) by continuous lines the subsidiation chains of individual persons "using" groups and (*b*) by dotted lines the subsidiation chain of *the dynamic purposes of groups considered as individual entities.* With the latter we are not so immediately concerned. The subsidiation of individuals can be illustrated by the line beginning at 3, Diagram 43. Here a high-school boy, very keen on football, debating at the moment whether to leave school and get married, decides to stay under the parental roof (group 1), in order that he may be supported at the university (group 2), in order that he may get on the university football team (group 3). Another sequence of groups can be illustrated at 1. Here an *émigré* doctor may acquire citizen-

---

group classification, *e.g.,* all wearing top hats or all owning Chrysler automobiles, does not make them a true group, but only a "congeries." Nor does the criterion accepted by some psychologists—that there is "internal interaction"—seem satisfactory, for a number of nations at war then constitute a "group." Internal interaction, of a special "group" kind, arises secondarily from the primary fact of the group's acting *to satisfy common purposes of the individuals in it.*

ship (group 1), in order that he may belong to a professional body (group 2), in order that he may support his family (group 3). Probably the most common subsidiation pattern of all is one in which attitudes to individual persons and objects alternate in the same chain with groups. For example, at 2 let us suppose a sailor who wants to reach his girl friend across the sea and who joins a trade union (group 1), in order that he may join a ship's company (group 2), in order that he may reach his girl.

**Dynamic Subsidiation of the Purposes of Groups.** That a group, through its effective synergy, needs and uses other groups is shown by the dotted

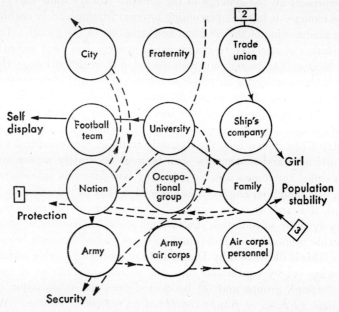

DIAGRAM 43. Dynamic subsidiation of groups with regard to other groups and to individuals.

lines in Diagram 43. Thus the family belongs to the nation in order that it may get certain services, one of which is defense. So the subsidiation (Diagram 43) runs on to the army and in turn to some adjunct to the army—the air corps—and so to yet another group, the air corps personnel service. In general, since most of the transactions among groups per se are in money, the dynamic subsidiation path is followed by economic arteries. Thus in the example given the family is taxed to support national government, which in turn supports the army, which supports an air corps, which creates a personnel service. It is not necessary that every link in such a chain be intimately understood by the original group, which it serves. No more is the single individual always conscious of the links of satisfaction in his own dynamic lattice. What *is* important for their persistence as habits is that those ways of behaving continue to bring the group or the individual the satisfactions demanded.

**Individual Sentiments in Relation to "Pure" and "Overlapping" Groups.** A common error in discussing groups is to think of them as autonomous, independent entities, like opposing football teams. Such groups do exist but most groups with which social psychology has to deal overlap in their personnel. A man belongs to a family, but also to a city, a profession or trade union, a hobby club, a religious organization, and a nation. He is divided among groups and the membership roll of any group can therefore be divided many times over with respect to the membership of other groups. Even pure groups, however, are rarely to be understood entirely in terms of the psychology of the individuals who compose them. For those individuals either bring mental furniture from other groups to which they *have* belonged or are the bearers of traditions from earlier life phases of the same group, as it was carried on by other generations.

Unless the groups to which a man belongs work harmoniously together in an accepted hierarchy of control and specialization, the man is unintegrated (as integration has already been defined) in that his own various attempts at satisfaction will mutually interfere. Sociologists have classified groups in various ways, notably into primary groups, such as the family into which a person is born and with whose members he has immediate contact, and secondary groups, which do not have this immediacy and tend to serve the primary groups. But from a psychological point of view other classifications are at least as fundamental; *e.g.*, classification according to the amount of the individual's total dynamic energy absorbed by the group, according to predominant subsidiation order of the groups, according to the individual's order of preferential loyalty, according to the nature of the ergs satisfied through the group, etc.

It follows from the above that there will exist a certain isomorphism between the structures of overlapping groups, on the one hand, and the structure of attitudes and sentiments within the mind of the individual, on the other. A powerful sentiment will correspond to a powerful institution and an order of loyalty will be related to an order of dynamic subsidiation. This isomorphism will be determined originally by the law of effect. Groups, like individuals, acquire dynamic traits (habits of ergic expression) through reward and deprivation (punishment) of trial responses. That these rewards are passed on at second hand (and transmuted in various ways) to the component individuals accounts for some of the slowness and inefficiency of group learning, *e.g.*, in avoiding wars. But through the reward and punishment of the individual he learns to invest energies and loyalties in groups to the extent that they succeed in supplying his needs. This harmony is aided in stable historical periods and harmed in times of rapid social change by the disposition rigidity of the organism. For without disposition rigidity habits would always be slipping back to short-circuited but dangerous paths, by the usual process of extinction. Indeed the stability of social institutions is partly dependent on internal psychological conditions—notably individual disposition rigidity and soundness of dynamic integration—which maintain individual sentiments in their correct relationships. On the other hand, these internal brakes on the responsiveness of habit structures to reward and punishment can bring dangerous degrees of conservative maladjustment in times of rapid change.

**Treating a Group as a Unitary Organism.** Whether a group is a "pure" or an "overlapping" group, the question arises as to whether it has sufficient persistence, consistency, and uniformity of behavior to be treated as a single psychological entity in social psychological predictions and calculations. The economy of recognizing the "wholeness" of a group arises from such group characteristics as its showing learning and remembering *as a whole*, its capacity to respond *as a whole* to stimuli applied to its parts, its susceptibility to moods, the unitary character of its collective deliberations, etc., but principally and primarily from the demonstration (12) (see (9), Chap. 13) that the traits of its "syntality" have comparable reliability coefficients and predictive values to those found for traits of the individual personality. For this unitary character, as explained in Chapter 11, the term syntality has been suggested, analogous to personality for the integrated behavior of the individual.

## 2. CULTURAL ANTHROPOLOGY AND THE DEFINITION OF SYNTALITY

**The Contribution of Cultural Anthropology.** In describing any social group, *e.g.*, a nation or a family, it is necessary, as indicated in discussing the family, to describe the characteristics of its syntality, of its mode of internal structure, and of its component personalities or population. Thus the aggressiveness of a national syntality need not have any close or simple relation to the average aggressiveness of its citizens, because the syntality is also a function of its internal structure. With one type of internal structure a population of a certain average level of intelligence will show more intelligent syntal behavior than with another form of internal organization, and so on. A necessary but, until recently, much neglected foundation for a true source of social psychology is the development of a morphology of groups—an understanding of the ways in which groups differ and of the ways in which those differences, *i.e.*, culture pattern differences, may be expressed in terms of measured quantities. We need a great many factor-analytic studies on different sizes and kinds of groups to determine the principal dimensions with regard to which their syntalities can be readily and meaningfully expressed.

Anthropologists have already given us a survey of syntalities, national characters, and wider culture patterns at the verbal descriptive level. Spengler, Dilthey, Keyserling (31), and others have analyzed the more "advanced" culture patterns. Malinowski presented a sharp contrast to these in the very divergent culture patterns of primitives, notably the Trobriand Islanders (38). There followed Mead's (40) study of Samoa and New Guinea, Benedict's (2) American Indians and the Melanesians, Linton (36) on the Marquesans and Madagascans, Dennis on the Hopi culture (14), Whiting on the Kwoma (53), DuBois on the Alonese (16), Gorer (20) on Himalayan, American, and Japanese cultures, and so on.

**The Inadequate Methodology of Cultural Anthropology.** It has to be confessed that the usefulness of these studies to a scientific social psychology is limited. Dennis and a few others have approached the problem with the eye of an empirical psychologist but most, being untrained in psychology, have accepted uncritically the more elaborate of psychoanalytic interpretive theories and failed further to distinguish between observation and interpretation. At best the data have the validity of observations by a single observer, with no reliability coefficient offered. The fine insight and objectivity of a Malinowski in anthropology may match that of a Freud in clinical psychology, but this cannot be expected of all followers. Good observations by this method are at the level of, and may integrate with, a premetric clinical psychology—except that the anthropologists' evidence is clinical psychology restricted to generalizations from a single instance and usually by a single observer! At its poorest this method of "analyzing culture patterns" descends to the level of unchecked travelers' tales, journalistically interesting but scientifically to be done over again.[2]

These oversimplified, distorted descriptions, stillborn from an infantile methodology, tell us, for example, that the Northwest Coast Indians have a "paranoid" culture in which all is subordinated to self-assertion; that the Marquesans reject their children because there is "insecurity in their hearts," and because the shortage of women causes an overemphasis on sex activities, and so on. In no case are these correlations established; still less is there any demonstration of the necessary direction of causal links.

It uses terms like Apollonian-Dionysian (after Spengler) in describing the Zuni culture, where temperate, controlled, and modest habits is all that is implied, and when it proceeds beyond description to interpretation it claims

[2] A similar warning to the uncritical enthusiasm of some psychologists for the present methods of cultural anthropology has been raised by the editor of the *Journal of Personality* —"the relatively scanty use of satistical methods and the likelihood of some coloring of reports in terms of the field investigator's theoretical bias point toward the desirability of *independent repetition* . . . " (55). The same writer also asks for "functional equivalents . . . in our own culture," *i.e.*, the detection of uniform dimensions possible by factor-analytic methods.

that these methods "have demonstrated quite convincingly that the diffuse, suspicious, unambitious personality of the adult Alonese is more than usually connected with the fact that the infants of this group are nursed at irregular intervals, disciplined in an unsystematic manner—as the parent or nurse feels the mood."[3]

**Dynamic and General Dimensions of Culture Patterns.** If a comparative psychology of cultures and their influence on personality is to be built up— and intrinsically this is an excellent, almost indispensable avenue to verifying hypotheses about the dynamic exchanges and personality interactions in any single culture—it will be done only on a foundation of measurement, based on discovery of the important dimensions along which syntalities can be measured. These dimensions[4] have already been tentatively indicated by a factor analysis of sixty-nine national cultures (see (9), Chap. 13) with respect to measured variables. They must include in the end an adequate refinement of dimensions for measuring the dynamic as well as the tempera-

---

[3] As Chesterton claims, with equal conviction, the modern child is, through distraction of mothers by careers, "For mother, dear mother, is turning a crank, increasing the balance at somebody's bank."

[4] The most important of them may be briefly defined as follows:

1. *Magnitude of Population.* In addition to sheer size variables, *e.g.*, area, population, number of large cities, this loads variables of poor organization, rebellion, assassinations, internal cultural differences, and other indicators of the difficulty of integrating larger national communities.

2. *Cultural Pressure.* This seems to express degree of long-circuiting of expression maintained in the community and affects high cultural output, complication of occupations (industrialization and urbanization), high interaction with other countries (treaties, wars, diplomatic clashes), high complexity of social and governmental organization, and high suicide rate.

3. *Affluence.* This indicates the general wealth level and loads real standard of living, freedom from tuberculosis and malnutritional diseases, level of expenditure on education, low death rate, high luxury and travel expenditure.

4. *Conservative Patriarchalism.* This is evidenced by restrictiveness of customs, *e.g.*, difficulty of divorce, emphasis on masculine customs, preeminence of religious and military control and values, infrequency of telephones, industrialization, low unemployment, and little cultural invention.

5. *Order and Control.* This factor, seeming to indicate a vigorous, self-willed, deliberate control of the cultural ways, affects principally high standard of living, high development of railroads, etc., low birth and death rates, infrequency of revolutions, and low homicide rate.

6. *Cultural Integration and Morale.* This is evidenced by correlations of low death rates from syphilis, alcoholism, tuberculosis, typhoid fever, etc., absence of publicly licensed prostitution, "progressive" divorce laws, low birth rate, high percentage of eminent men eminent in fields outside politics, etc.

These and six other factors described in detail elsewhere (12) suffice to account for about three quarters of the international variation of culture patterns as evidenced in any available measurable features of existing nations. Through these twelve factors the essential outline of the syntality of any given nation could thus be expressed in measured terms comparable to the culture patterns obtaining in other countries.

mental and cognitive traits of a culture. That is to say, the vector quantity constituted by the effective synergy of any group must be definable.

Most of the groups of importance to the individual are overlapping groups within the larger culture pattern of the society, and it is with respect to the effective synergy of these groups and the energy put into them by the individual that one last social psychological theorem has to be stated. This states that, since the mental energy of the individual is not an unlimited quantity, the growth of one (overlapping) group synergy will be at the cost of the synergies of overlapping groups in the same culture. Thus, even if there were no rivalry on logical grounds, we could predict psychological rivalry between, for example, family and club, or religion and totalitarian patriotism.

With this necessarily sketchy survey of the dynamic psychology of group functioning—sparsely explored as this psychology still is—we must turn to the relation of the culture pattern to personality.

### 3. NINE FUNDAMENTAL PRINCIPLES OF PERSONALITY-CULTURE INTERACTION

**Classification of Major Aspects of the Individual's Environment.** Since many of the principles governing interaction of personality with special subgroups and institutions repeat those found in exchanges between personality and the whole society, it is most economical first to consider interactions with the total pattern. Also we need to explore a little more the articulation of the constituent institutions in the total culture in order not to lose sight of the way their individual effects on personality are conditioned by the whole.

Let us first, however, clarify some terms proposed for defining aspects of the culture pattern and the total environment. For various psychological purposes it is sometimes convenient to deal with one or another of the three following conceptual abstractions from the individual's total environment:

*Cosmic Environment.* This is the set of facts and principles (called "universal" by Kluckhohn and Mowrer (33)) common to all cultures, e.g., heat and cold, gravity, parentage, death, and mathematical principles. This is the measure of outward reality to which all men everywhere have to adjust. It includes not only the common physical realities but also the least common denominator of social realities among all cultures.

*Regional Environment.* This defines circumstances peculiar to a region, including (*a*) the *climatic environment*, which covers the physical peculiarities, atmospheric and geographical, and (*b*) the *culture pattern* or common social environment affecting all in that region. Kluckhohn and Mowrer (33) call this the "communal environment" and Kimball Young calls it the "personal-social experience." Whatever we label it we should note that it includes (*i*) that environment created within the group by the comparatively immutable heredity of all concerned in it, and (*ii*) the group environment constituted by changeable attitudes, traditions, and skills. The actual regional environment has elements in it, of course, which are in the cosmic environment, but when we define it as an abstraction we are interested only in the elements peculiar to the environment.

*Idiosyncratic or Purely Personal Cultural Environment.* This is that selected section of the cosmic and regional environment that has been brought to bear on the individual and constitutes his personal life history. It is the experience residing in the peculiar selectiveness, accidents, trauma, and opportunities of his own life. Kimball Young's "personal-social" experience is meant by the term social to be distinguished from this purely personal, but perhaps the terms regional and idiosyncratic bring this out more clearly.

Only for certain purposes is it helpful to trace environmentally acquired personality traits to these separate sources. In principle this can be done easily enough. For example we can see that an individual's ability as a runner or a basic skill in dealing with people are adjustments to the cosmic environment, largely comparable anywhere on earth. On the other hand, an ingrained habit of taking an afternoon siesta may arise from the climatic environment; a sentiment toward democratic government would arise from the cultural environment; and a neurotic fear of bushes could arise from idiosyncratic environment. The chief practical object in making this division would be to discover how much of environment we need to control in order to affect certain aspects of personality. However the practical methodology of determining the divisions might prove difficult, having to proceed by analyzing the total variance of personality traits into (*a*) the variance between cultures, (*b*) the variance between "climates," and (*c*) the variance of individuals within cultures and climates. At this stage we need pursue such problems no further, since the data available have not been gathered with such attention to proof of environmental source, and practically everything discussed in this chapter is generally regarded as a function of the culture pattern only.

**Nine Principles of Culture Pattern Interaction with Personality.** With this delimitation of the chief influences to be considered, we can proceed to a survey of basic generalizations about the interaction of culture pattern and personality.

The facts supporting these principles reside in general experience and the substance of earlier chapters. Some are truisms requiring bare enunciation and not justifying the elaborate verbiage frequently accorded to them, but a few require wider illustrations and subtler analysis.

1. *Personality and Culture Pattern Isomorphism.* Each culture pattern tends to be associated with the predominance of a particular personality

pattern, deliberately inculcated. (Conversely the approved personality pattern demands that the culture pattern develop characteristics that fit it.) This matching shows itself most in the dynamic structure of the personality, particularly in the ego, the self-ideal, and the investments of energy in particular social institutions. Probably the superego pattern is one of the most vital links between personality and the culture pattern, but, as the second principle indicates, its formation may be neither direct nor isomorphous.

2. *Cultural Molding by Indirect Determination.* This adjustment of personality to culture applies not only to the conscious structure, but also to the unconscious (often complementary to the conscious content, as Jung has stressed)—and particularly, as indicated, to the unconscious superego (and the values in consciousness irrationally developing therefrom). Consequently it is inadequate to speak of the shaping of personality by culture entirely in terms of isomorphism. For there are many personality characteristics due to a culture pattern which are not *directly* molded by the culture and which at first sight, or by reasoning alone, one would never suspect of being connected with the culture pattern.

Thus, in Lippitt's (37) study of child personalities under so-called "democratic" and "totalitarian" regimes the conversations in the more dominated group had more hostile, resistant, attention-demanding, and idea-defending items. It is not self-evident that a culture pattern idealizing dominance and obedience will develop more attention-demanding behavior or obstinacy. These are personality traits which are unintended by-products of that pattern which the society deliberately seeks to inculcate. Thus the culture pattern determines other traits than those consciously cherished and molded through the pattern.

3. *Rewarding of Conformity, and Conflict with Eccentricity.* Deviant individuals, *e.g.*, neurotics, defectives, individuals of radically different temperament, eccentrics, geniuses, criminals, engage in mutual conflict with society, because there is an attempt to exclude from society those who cannot or will not stay within a subliminal degree of deviation. The rewarding of conformity and punishment of nonconformity that results in the molding effect described in item 1 is accomplished by granting varying access to the total dynamic satisfactions made possible by the group. In the formation of the superego, and to a less extent of the ego, the ergic composition of this controlling force is weighted with gregarious, self-assertive ergs. (In civilized societies hunger and other ergs can generally be satisfied in spite of group disapproval of the individual.) That is to say, the ego ideal is shaped largely under the drive to gain group approval and to avoid the loneliness of nonparticipation.

4. *Provision of Order to Reward Habitual Expectations.* One of the most rewarding features of the culture pattern occurs with respect to the need to

save energy. The failure of the schizothyme to deal with people when he is quite capable of dealing with the nonhuman world, indicates that the predictability of (nonhuman) natural objects is more satisfactory than of human beings—when both have no imposed order. The culture pattern reduces the unpredictability—and the associated demands for unlimited adaptability—of man. It provides expectations of what people in certain roles will do and makes a more rewarding order out of a less rewarding chaos. This psychological saving through order has to be considered further in the light of modifying principles 6 and 7 below. From the point of view of the individual personality the principle accounts for much cultural learning and for individual differences of personality between those who do and do not acquire the highest understanding of the culture pattern ways.

5. *Conditions Imposed by the Pressure to Satisfy the Total Ergic Nature of Man.* Culture pattern often begins historically as fragmentary socializations of particular human needs. Other needs may for a time be neglected as regards any social, *group* provisions and regulations. With even a moderately high degree of social organization, however, it becomes necessary for the culture pattern to develop institutions to satisfy ergic needs, which are mere by-products and residues of the ergic needs with which the more urgent cultural institutions are primarily concerned. For example, the complication of the work of breadwinning may create the need for recreational institutions, and the more rigid institutionalizing of monogamous marriage may give rise in some communities to institutionalized prostitution.

In general, so long as the culture pattern is an integrated one, catering for the total ergic nature of man, institutions have to maintain an ergic complementariness, *i.e.*, the strong satisfaction of a drive in one particular institution reduces its participation in others. The social dynamics of the personality, therefore, is to be understood in terms of the individual and society seeking, on parallel courses, to balance the expression of ergs through alternative institutions.

6. *Personality Disorganization by Cultural Change.* Severe problems of individual personality adjustment may be caused by the change, growth, and decay that normally occur in the history of otherwise well-integrated and adjustment-helping culture patterns. In rapid growth individuals may be trained for roles that do not exist when they become adult. Historical accidents, *e.g.*, the loss of a generation in Germany through the First World War, may cause loss of contact between generations, with failure of cultural transmission. Again, in a culture collapsing through decay or the external impact of indigestible ideas and institutions, the complex pattern of normal anticipations is broken, and individuals seem to suffer a common frustration and sense of insecurity manifested in depression and loss of morale, self-confidence, and self-respect. Spengler notes this repeatedly in the cycles of

past cultures. Gilbert Murray, the famous classical scholar, spoke of the "failure of nerve" in citizens of ancient Greece; and W. H. Rivers, observing the white impact in Melanesia, noted the apathy, indifference, and loss of interest of those who felt that the vessel of their culture was broken.[5]

7. *Cultural Complication as a Psychological Burden on Personality.* Despite the gains mentioned in principle 4 above, the imposition of the cultural pattern produces also a psychological burden for the individual. The culture complication may provide a longer, richer, more physically comfortable life, with greater over-all ergic satisfaction, but it does so at the cost of more restraint, more deferring of satisfactions, and more tension from "long-circuiting" of dynamic habits. The innate nature of man is therefore in conflict with the culture pattern, especially during early life and education, and undergoes modification only through the rewarding process discussed in 3 above. In some cultures certain periods of life and certain aspects of culture bring especial conflict, *e.g.*, the adolescent period in our own culture and the complications of sex expression in many. Most culture patterns therefore provide, deliberately or accidentally, for relief from cultural pressure, (*a*) by recreational institutions, *e.g.*, days of special license and by groups concerned wholly with recreation, (*b*) by periodic regressions of the whole culture, as in war, (*c*) by allowing a gap to exist between the stated ideals of the culture and its practices, *e.g.*, in our culture full sexual expression before marriage is forbidden, yet the recent study by Kinsey, Pomeroy, and Martin (32) shows that approximately 60 per cent of unmarried men at seventeen years of age and 80 per cent of unmarried men at twenty-five years of age fall short of this standard.

Without attempting, with existing exiguous research, any systematic analysis of different ways in which culture is a burden, it is yet possible to see that several distinct psychological strains for the individual personality are involved. First, there are the strains of restraint (suppression, repression) under which the neurotic staggers, and which Freud has discussed in *Civilization and its Discontents* (17). There are also stresses from demands on intelligence and discrimination which, if the studies of Pavlov, Liddell, and others on animals are strictly applicable, also issue in a form of neurotic disorder. Further, there are strains of emotional adaptability, relative to the disposition rigidity of the organism. This stress is tied up particularly with the social phenomenon of playing many different roles, requiring the maintenance of very different emotional attitudes with proper regarding for broad contexts and purposes. For example, the individual may properly

---

[5] In our own culture the effects of a temporary disorganization were more closely observed by Rundquist and Sletto (46), who noted that the unemployed in the depression of 1929 showed both loss of faith in the values and leaders of their culture and loss of personality integration and will power.

play a dominant role in his family but not in his profession, be easygoing with his friend as a friend but not as a court judge, kill another human being in war but not murder him for personal ends, and so on. There is a double emotional difficulty, in fact from (a) having to adopt too many roles oneself, and (b) having to recognize cues which indicate the different roles being played by any one other person.

It is this stress of constantly reorganizing behavior in terms of many diverse broad mental sets that the present writer would argue to be the essential psychological burden constituted by the sociological component in the etiology of schizophrenia. A sociological theory of schizophrenia was first put forward by Devereux (15), who pointed out that though mental disease occurs among primitives, schizophrenia is relatively uncommon and also is "refusal to grow up." (Much more examination of schizophrenia death rates under primitive conditions needs to be made before this can be finally accepted.) He ascribes this to "the higher number of ultimate traits" in the more complex culture pattern and instances also the data of Faris showing a higher schizophrenia in culturally more disorganized (or diversified) areas in our own society. Other evidence could be cited along the same lines from the apparent increased rate among natives when new cultures infringe upon and complicate their lives, as has occurred in Africa (27).

The specific relation of this form of culture stress to schizophrenia probably resides in the following connection. First, the schizothyme is a person poor at maintaining over-all mental sets, *e.g.*, the main drift of a conversation, while adjusting minor sets within it, and also shows undue rigidity. Second, the demand of a more complex culture is precisely for these missing qualities. It has many groups and institutions (see the following section) the appropriate behavior within which cannot be simply inferred from any one. The expedient and resourceful cyclothyme can adjust to these differences: the schizothyme craves a unifying role suited to his own feelings, and if he cannot get this, through religious or other systems, he is apt to give up under "the weary weight of the intolerable world."

8. *Variation of Personality with Position in Culture Pattern.* If this interpretation is correct, incidentally, we should expect the commonly observed phenomenon of "an individual's personality varying according to the group in which he finds himself" to be relatively pronounced in cyclothymes—an issue which can be taken up in more detail in discussing the ego in Chapter 21. Although it is conceptually incorrect to say the individual's personality varies (as pointed out in Chap. 21, it is the same personality manifesting different behavior through new stimuli) we may say that the overt personality will show itself differently, by emphasis on different sets of latent possibilities of reaction, in different groups within the same culture pattern. The culture pattern thus impresses not only a general pattern but patterns adapted to each institution. This is taken up further in Section 4.

9. *Dependence of Cultural Change on Individual Personality Change.* The fact that the individual mental structure tends to be isomorphous with the cultural structure, as stated in 1 above carries the implication that changes in the group structure will to some extent be dependent on the properties of the individual mind and vice versa. For example, the degree of natural disposition rigidity will partly determine the rate of cultural change, the degree of emotional stability will partly determine the stability of culture pattern structures to transient pressures, and the constancy of the sum total of individual mental energy will cause certain complementary relationships to hold among diverse aspects of the culture pattern. These are better discussed as principles concerning the relationships of personality and specific "organ" groups within the culture—in Section 4 below.

## 4. THE INTERACTION OF SOCIAL ORGANS AND INSTITUTIONS THROUGH PERSONALITY

**Social Organs and Social Customs.** In the remaining sections of this chapter and in Chapter 15 individual cultural institutions will be examined more closely as to their roles in creating and expressing the individual personality. But in this section it is necessary first to persevere a little further with clarifying the purely social psychology of their own interaction and also to work out the method whereby their relative roles in personality formation can be expressed. This must be done for such important institutions as the family, the class division, the clan or totem group, the neighborhood community, the sex and age groups, the school, the play group or gang, the political party, and the religious congregation—together with the customs and values belonging to each of these.

The most effective and realistic way of classifying and dealing with such "cultural elements" has yet to be worked out. Sociologists have used the term "institution" to apply both to groups (*e.g.*, the family) and to customs (*e.g.*, property customs) so that it becomes the most generic of all terms for cultural elements. Within this generic concept it will suffice for our purely psychological purpose if we distinguish *organs* and *customs*. An organ is a group—not any group, but what we have previously called an overlapping group and which could now be defined more precisely as a group in such constant dynamic exchange with other groups within a larger group that *it could not exist alone.* A school, a city, a class, a family are examples of such social organs.

What we shall call a social *custom*, on the other hand, is a habit, *i.e.*, a stereotyped mode of individual dynamic satisfaction, ergic or metanergic, *having relation to habits possessed by others and frequently expressed in a group situation.* The formulation "having relation to" instead of "similar to" the habits of other group members is necessary because in many situations the necessary roles of different members in the same social activity, *e.g.*, a religious ritual, a war expedition, the running of a business, are quite distinct.

**Social Customs and Roles Subserve Organs.** Just as the dynamic and nondynamic traits of the individual are inferred from his general behavior so the nonindividual, social sentiments are distinctly recognized and inferred from that behavior which is common to all in a particular group, *i.e.*, from customs. Thus we infer a sentiment of patriotism partly from such customs as saluting the national flag or buying war bonds. Some group sentiments may be partly unconscious, behaving like common complexes, as in celebrating birthdays, the religious custom of exhibiting alcheringa sticks, the sacrificing of animals at the altar. The moral customs concerned with preserving a group, *e.g.*, resenting atypical people, subscribing to a police force, enacting laws, practicing group marriage, conducting feuds, may also be as unconscious in operation as the individual superego, being thus expressive of prejudices (*i.e.*, attitudes not possessing known rational sources) rather than attitudes.

For further clarity of nomenclature we shall join the sociologist in distinguishing within the general class of "customs" the special subclass of roles. What social psychologists call "roles" are those group-sanctioned customs which require a change of emphasis of the whole personality in response to a standard situation—usually a new subgroup situation. Naturally this is no radical restructuring of personality but rather the wearing of a new mask, made easy by stimuli which suppress some of the more usual reactions and call for others perhaps normally seldom provoked. It is in this specific sense that the term role is used in Principle 7 of the previous section, imputing the cultural burden and schizophrenic breakdown to the multiplicity of roles. Institutions of the culture pattern can thus be considered as *organs* when we concentrate on the constituent groups and their dynamic organization or as *customs and roles* when we concentrate on patterns of individual social behavior, *i.e.*, on actual functioning of groups. Such social behavior is often studied by the sociologist purely descriptively (see *e.g.*, Warner and Lunt (50,51)), without immediate regard to the underlying dynamic unities of groups. But one may generalize that all customs have dynamic utility to the group and are concerned either to preserve the group (expressing the maintenance synergy)—if only, on occasion, by discharging harmlessly energy denied expression elsewhere by the culture pattern—or to carry out the purposes of the group as a unit (expressing the effective synergy).

However, the analysis of observed customs in terms of the dynamics of existing social organs is only just beginning. Social psychology gropes toward the most economical ways of formulating the interaction of cultural organs with one another and with the personality of individuals—indeed, there does not exist a tried system for even describing and classifying the modes of social-organ interaction.

**The Effect of Roles upon Personality.** Before asking what these changes of role do to the dynamic exchanges among groups it is desirable to ask precisely what they do to the individual personality directly. The problem is discussed more fully in Chapter 21 in connection with the meaning of "the self" and the possibility of representing "conditional personalities" by a particular formula in the specification equation, so the present discussion is of a preliminary nature and has to do only with the conditional personalities arising from roles.

Much has been said by sociologists about the transformation of personality occasioned by adopting a special social role, but surprisingly little has been gained in the way of exact concepts and methods of investigation or prediction. It is evident that when a man puts on a uniform, or steps into a pulpit, or stops playing with his children on the hearthrug and steps into his office as a big business executive, he undergoes some systematic change in his reactivities and mental sets, often of a very striking kind. But it is questionable whether we should say that his personality has changed, unless we can prove some degree of dissociation, *i.e.*, of failure of certain past experiences and needs to be intelligently integrated in response to present demands. The fact is that civilization causes us to be acting in roles *all* the time, though some are more striking than others, and that it is a normal part of personality adjustment to be temporarily denying expression completely to some drives and giving special expression to others.

These massive "conditional mental sets" which condition the response to each current stimulus situation while the role is "on" are themselves a response to an over-all stimulus situation which acts upon the one and only essential personality. They are adopted because they are rewarding to the dynamic make-up of the essential personality—commonly to the self-sentiment but sometimes to the pocket. And the extent to which the role is successfully adopted depends on the personality. The sociologist speaks of roles as if a given role were the same for all individuals—a cloak put on and off—but the figure shows through the cloak. Citizens become soldiers, but there are still brave and cowardly, punctual and unpunctual, imaginative and dull soldiers. And though there may be some reduction of variance when the demands of the role are very rigorous, the observed reduction must be considered partly accounted for by selection—for people do not long adopt roles which their personalities make impossible of attainment.

A review of experimental studies carried out on the influence of social expectations on personality and performance has been presented by Dashiell ((14), Chap. 21). An experiment of some interest in view of claims made for permanent effects from *simple* play therapy is that of Timmons ((51),

Chap. 21).  Each of several subjects acted for five weeks of rehearsals in the play "Hedda Gabler."  A succession of eighteen dominant individuals were cast in submissive roles and fifteen submissive personalities in dominant roles.  No changes could be detected over this period by the Bernreuter questionnaire in the out-of-play personalities—except a very slight increase in self-sufficiency among dominants cast in submissive roles.  It would have been of further interest to know how successfully the dominant individuals were able to assume the submissive role in the play (and vice versa) and what compensations appeared off the stage.  Psychologically, therefore, the adoption of roles is not the creation of new personalities but simply a part of the general adjustment to changing aspiration levels and self-conceptions which goes on all the time, is pursued with varying enthusiasm and success according to personality and provokes varying compensatory adjustments among the roles themselves.

**Three Principles of Social-organ Interaction via Personality.**  As indicated in the first section of this chapter, wherever social organs have a persistent and vital functional existence, it is probably more economical to formulate laws as to their functions primarily in terms of the dynamics of such groups, rather than in the stuff of customs, which are merely more numerous, detailed, and transient indicators of the group dynamics.  In general, such formulation means aiming at generalizations about the syntalities of groups in relation to the personalities of individuals.  We shall now attempt a few basic generalizations which will be illustrated by material in the remainder of this chapter, though if we had space also to discuss more debatable generalizations illustrated more tentatively in that material, a more extensive set of principles could already be made available.

*Social-organ Similarity through Transfer of Personality Structure.*  First, we note instances where the formation of personality in a certain manner by one group tends to shape similarly the pattern of a second group to which the person also belongs.  For although the overt personality *does* change slightly from group to group the individual carries the more massive and unconscious aspects of his personality with him.  For example, we find a tendency for patriarchal, authoritarian family structure to exist in politically totalitarian states; a tendency for children who are given more freedom in school to rebel in a too "directive" home; a tendency for those raised in a charitable religion to attempt to extend this behavior to international relations, and so on.

This relationship of groups, which we may call "the principle of similarity or convergence through transfer of personality structure" is actually planned, deliberately and systematically to take place between the social organ we call the school and the total culture pattern, as represented especially by national government and religion.  The school specifically operates to produce individuals with the personality stereotype required to run the adult culture group, wherefore society shapes the school and the school, society, in a converging process. However, most of these interactions, which are sometimes productive of conflict and sometimes of harmony for the individuals involved, are neither conscious nor deliberate. For example, few people foresaw that the introduction of free and universal education in the nineteenth century in Prussia would result in the culturally uninterested army also acquiring devastating standards of efficiency compared with the other armies it met in 1860 and 1870, thereby rewarding the values of military glory rather than the values which gave birth to education.

*The Principle of Ergic Complementariness of Social Organs.* Second, we encounter what is in some respects an opposing tendency to the above. Like the covergence principle, it operates on the whole range of dynamic traits but in this case is probably more active among the more superficial interests and attitudes. Here the individual tends to seek or shape a second subgroup (overlapping group) to give expression to the ergic needs denied in the first—as a man might seek action for unused muscles. This accounts for the generation of certain groups and roles, notably those numerous organs under the heading of recreational groups, which could not be accounted for by any logical demand on the part of the larger group for such attendant groups. A special case of this has been observed by Bateson (1) among the Iatmul of New Guinea. Here normally the male is dominant and competitive while the woman is passive and subservient. As if for relief from the latter role, the women on certain ritualistic occasions, put on the men's martial gear and the men then adopt a complementary passive role. Such "cleavage roles," *i.e.*, the splitting of ergic satisfactions among different groups, are naturally very varied, as also are the varieties of new personal relationships, symmetrical, unsymmetrical, adjusted, strained, etc., occasioned among people as they change their groups and roles. A related process is the intermittent change of roles for almost everyone, in the major society, as when escape is sought from monotony by holidays and carnivals or from the tension and long-circuiting of peace by going to war.

*Transfer of Stability.* A third important proposition, or set of propositions that arise from that isomorphism of group structure and individual sentiment structure, already glanced at in basic principle 9 of the preceding section, concern what may be called the *transfer of stability*. It is frequently loosely remarked that the integration, disorganization, complexity, and stability of the group culture reflect themselves in parallel qualities in the individual personalities in the group. As argued in more detail in Section 6 below, this is not precisely true of the first two characters, though it seems to be in regard to the last two.

Concerning stability, the following propositions on interorgan influence can be seen to hold, additional to the direct relation stated in principle 9 above that social conservatism is a function of individual rigidity: (*a*) organs which, for various reasons, decrease the stability of the individual ego, will tend to decrease the stability of other organs supported by the same individuals; (*b*) organs which make very fluctuant demands on the individual's investments of interest are likely, by the principle of ergic complementariness, to cause fluctuations in other organs and instability in the whole cultural pattern; (*c*) organs that mutually support or oppose one another in ways conforming to the dynamic subsidiation in the individual personality, assist general cultural stability, and vice versa.

As examples of these we may take (*a*) Murphy's (44) observation that the Roman family structure and values were such as to produce marked conflict between father and son. In several historical instances this cleavage in the family led to upsets in other social organs and crises for the whole community; (*b*) communities with individuals in occupations that are relatively steady in their psychological demands seem to enjoy greater stability in family life, political organization, etc., than those having many occupations with strong seasonal or erratic variation; (*c*) if the individual joins the army in order to defend his country, instability will be created in so far as the army takes other attitudes to the country than that of defending it. The symbiosis of the church and the family, each attempting to generate attitudes that are fitting to the other, is an example of the converse direction of action of the principle, *i.e.*, of stability induced at once in the individual personality and the larger group.

## 5. THE METHODOLOGY OF RELATING PERSONALITY TO CULTURE PATTERN

**The Quantification of Person-Organ Relationships.** The above generalizations, indicating the type of formulation at which we can hope to aim with respect to relations of institutions to personality, cannot safely be carried further by clinical-or anthropological-type observation alone. Let us therefore now face the problems of the methodology of measurement. Organ groups themselves, by means of well-planned factorial research, can have the dimensions of their syntalities discovered and measured. The problem that remains is to express the relations between the dimensions of these syntalities and the dimensions of the personality affected by them. It may be illustrated by Hartshorne and May's (22) attempt to discover the relative potencies of family, school, play group, etc., in shaping the moral values of the individual personality. Their figures, not yet improved upon by any research of adequate scale, are as follows: correspondence of child's moral judgments with parents', $r = .545$; correspondence of child's moral judgments with friends in play group, $r = .353$; correspondence of child's moral judgments with club leaders, $r = .137$; correspondence of child's moral judgments with day-school teacher, $r = .028$; correspondence of child's moral judgments with Sunday-school teacher, $r = .002$; showing, incidentally, the overwhelming importance of the home and the appreciable importance of friends relative to those institutions which society specifically sets up to form values.

Now, the manner in which one will interpret such correlations will depend on the extent to which the effects of other institutions than those named have been "partialed out." For it is uneconomical and unreal to treat as separate entities two supposedly different institutions that correlate too highly together to be independent. For example, if a certain personality trait correlates 0.5 with a dimension of social class status and 0.7 with a dimension of family, we want to know how much of the family effect is already accounted for by the family being of a certain social status. Possibly, among families of the same social status the personality-family correlation is much lower.

**The Choice of Independent Organs.** Reflection on this problem will show at once that since most social organs are likely to be intercorrelated in their influences and characteristics our first task is to decide which organs are to be considered basic and "independent" and which mere functions or ancillaries of others. The factorization of variables representing many institutions will indicate, far more comprehensively and quickly than unsystematic experiments with "partialing out," which organs offer the stable, relatively independent unities best adopted as independent "institutions." But even so it will reveal complications, *e.g.*, possibilities of alternative sets of factors, second-order factors, reflecting the undeniable truth that causal systems lie depth beyond depth and that alternative systems can always be found, one more convenient to some purposes, another more relevant to a certain system of philosophy or applied work, and so on. Functional unities can then only be sorted out with respect to "degrees of efficacy" (9) and it is probable that such sorting of factors will leave us with much the same functional unities, *e.g.*, the family, the social class, the religious community, as common sense already indicates.

**Goals of Research Methods Investigating Relations of Organs and Personalities.** Granted that we have thus chosen the most useful, "efficacious" reference organs, the methodology of research and expression of findings calls for (*a*) determination of the correlations among these organs, with respect to their various dimensions, *e.g.*, the relation between degree of democracy in society and degree of father-dominance in the family, or degree of sexual repression in the religious community and degree of academic achievement in the schools, and (*b*) determination of the correlations between personality traits in the individual and the dimensions of those culture organs in which he has been embedded, *e.g.*, the correlation between delinquency-proneness in the individual and stability of the family, or paranoid tendencies and the form of the economic system.

### 6. SOCIAL STATUS AND ITS RELATION TO MEASURED PERSONALITY TRAITS

**Definition of Social Status.** Most data now to be discussed concern social class, but class includes a good deal of what is due to occupation and neighborhood. All known human and most animal societies exhibit some sort of stratification according to prestige or dominance, sometimes "institutionalized," sometimes appearing merely in behavior but not in any formal ideational system. In the industrial societies on which our interest naturally concentrates it has been usual to speak of economic or socioeconomic classes, but it is easy to show that wealth is only a tool of psychological stratification, so that even without economic differences class stratification can persist.

Psychologically one realizes that there could be as many "dimensions" of status as there are things to admire. (Hyman, for example, mentions economic levels, intellectual levels, cultural status, social—presumably social attractiveness—levels, degree of handsomeness, etc.) But it is possible that socially some of these correlate, so that relatively few real, organically functional dimensions of status exist. No study of this matter exists on an adequate scale, but the present writer (8), using a sample of twenty-six occupations as reference points, correlated, with respect to these entries, (*a*) mean intelligence of followers of the occupations, (*b*) mean income, (*c*) prestige as rated by paired comparisons by many judges, (*d*) birth rate, (*e*) length of education, and found most *r*'s strongly positive (0.81 to 0.95).

Although the scale of the study was insufficient to justify an attempt to determine the number of possible dimensions (factors) it was at least clear that most variance could be conceived as due to one paramount dimension, of general social status, with respect to which *prestige rating* and *intelligence level* were the most central and significant variables. Other variables which general sociological observation and measurements regard as affected in some degree by this social-status dimension are: property, social titles, social status of friends, code of manners, dress, etc., neighborhood of residence, interests and values, political and religious affiliations, death rates, number of people by whom known, etc.

In covering the effects of social status on personality it is necessary to consider the influence of (*a*) the very existence of stratification, (*b*) the individual's typical status, and (*c*) the individual's movement through strata. The first is best considered last, in a summary. The reality of the second— the effect of status—is shown by persistent findings of personality correlates, even though the crudity of present measures fails to reveal such correlates for other social divisions that have been investigated. For example, Brown (6) found the relation of emotional stability (as determined by questionnaire) to race or rural-urban differences to be undetectable, but found a definite positive relation to socioeconomic status.

**Relation of Status to Personal Abilities.** Let us consider the evidence under four headings: abilities; general personality factors; interests, sentiments; psychotic and neurotic conditions. *Abilities*, notably education level and intelligence level, are correlated with social status to the extent of about 0.5 and 0.3 respectively. This is obvious also from the relations of I.Q. to occupational complexity. Thus, examining American Army Classification test scores for civilian occupations, the Harrells (21) found accountants, lawyers, and engineers highest, and lumberjacks, farmhands, miners, and teamsters lowest, in a long range of occupations. Among British civilian occupations the present writer (11) found the following mean I.Q.s: university teachers, 151; physicians, 146.5; stenographers, 129; precision fitter, 114; carpenters, 98; machine operators, 96; hairdressers, 89; packers and sorters, 78. The study of British occupational groups by Himmelweit and Whitfield (24) in the Second World War draftees gives almost exactly the same order of occupational mean intelligences. These differences are found also with culture-free, perpetual intelligence tests, and exist, as Robert Thorndike has shown for neighborhoods, when educational level is partialed out. The exact means to be accepted have recently been examined by Johnson, using the standard score I.Q. (29).

*Relation of Status to Personality Stability and Integration Factors.* Among personality factors, the *C* and *G* factors of emotional stability and conscientiousness have been most studied. The miniature-situation experiments of Hartshorne and May (22) showed honesty and conscientiousness among children to be slightly but definitely positively related to social status. Jones found the same (30). Harrower found the moral development of children, as judged by levels of reaction to cheating and punishment defined by Piaget, to be more advanced in children of higher social status (12). Slaght found truthfulness positively related to status (12). Using questionnaire methods, Hoffeditz (12), Meltzer (42), and Wrightstone (12) found, in widely different samples, lower emotional stability with lower social status. Character defect is, in any case, only one factor in delinquency, but some studies, *e.g.*, the extensive studies of Burt (see (8), Chap. 16), Sullenger (see (46), Chap. 16.), and the Gluecks (see (21), Chap. 16) find more delinquency with lower status. Others, *e.g.*, Healy and Bronner (see (24), Chap. 16) find no such connection but only a poorer chance of recovery from delinquency in lower status homes. Kvaraceus's (35) study of 761 delinquents in Passaic compared occupational frequencies and found fewer delinquent children in families of parents who were professional workers, working proprietors, clerks, sales personnel, craftsmen, and in nondomestic service. Some evidence of less successful discipline and control in lower status homes is found in DuVall's survey of children's views of parents, those from poorer homes more frequently rating parent discipline as too strict. Meltzer's (42) careful study calls attention to the possible confusion in class comparisons arising from a nonlinearity of relations, the trend from lowest, through lower, lower-middle, and upper-middle tending to reverse itself in the strictly "upper" class. His index of total "healthiness" of parent-child relations (mainly of least child-parent conflict and hostility) increased through most of the population range to the middle class and then decreased slightly for the small percentage consisting of the uppermost class.

A closer analysis, by Francis, of the possible factors associated with defective integration showed that crowding, unhygienic homes, poor aesthetic standards, inadequate play space, and parents' soundness of spending control had no conspicuous relation to child adjustment; but parents' attitudes to child's health, to sex problems, to choice of schoolmates, to community activities, and especially to discipline were closely correlated with adjustment and accounted for part of the class correlation found in most studies. Ulton (see (47), Chap. 15) in a study of seventy-four seven- and eight-year-olds, observed diminishing mean emotional stability and "social integration" with lower social status and noted that estimates of parental understanding of discipline problems as well as their own integration fell in the same order.

**Status and Dispositional Traits.** Most of the disposition and temperament studies are concerned with dominance-submission and sociability-withdrawal. Questionnaire methods (48) and Hoffeditz, Carpenter and Eisenberg, Pallister, Ridenour, Stagner and Smith in (12) show, among adults, more dominant traits with higher social status, but no such clear trend with children. Indeed, referrals of children to clinics show more aggressiveness and delinquency in lower status and more withdrawal, shyness, etc., in higher status. A single formula to cover this might be that the adult culture pattern, and its adult bearers, exercise less dominance in lower status groups.

The evidence on sociability, self-sufficiency, extraversion-introversion, etc., is as conflicting as might be expected from the confusion of test concepts that has prevailed. In personality factor terms it seems that self-sufficiency and the acquired element in the schizothyme tendency ($A$ factor), as well as, perhaps, desurgency ($F$ factor), increase slightly with social status, perhaps as a result of more extensive inhibitions and more individualistic training. There is insufficient but cumulative evidence (see (7,8), Chap. 13) that disposition rigidity (perseveration) is greater with lower social status. The connotation of lesser integration, adaptability, and drive agrees with indirect evidence on these qualities. A good analytic study of personality in relation to status has yet to be made.

**Status and Dynamic Investments.** On interests and sentiments there again are little reliable data. Politically the lower status groups are more favorable to social change and left-wing views, but, as Kornhauser (12) has shown, from *Fortune* and Gallup poll data, the differences are slight and less than popularly supposed, so that he concludes, "a simple, automatic, economic determinism of social opinion is psychologically pure fiction." Stagner (48) finds most left-wing views in the middling low income groups and argues that what he calls "Fascist" views are curvilinearly related to income levels—high at the top and the bottom of the range. Against the tendency for such a distribution to occur stands the tendency for more progressive opinions to be associated with greater intelligence, *e.g.*, as in Carlson's data (7). Kornhauser stresses the greater role of personal maladjustment than of social status in determining "Agin' the government" attitudes, saying "the personally dissatisfied at the upper income levels tend to hold views approaching those more commonly held by the economically less favored." However, as Kornhauser points out and Super (12) confirms, personal dissatisfaction, as revealed by questionnaire responses, consistently rises with declining social status, whether the latter is expressed in economic categories or in complexity of occupation. This is clearest in regard to job satisfaction, but extends to satisfaction with society as a whole. Rundquist and Sletto (46) found similarly, with unemployed during the depression, that "general maladjustment was greater among the men from the lower occupational strata, among older men, and among the men with the least education."

If attitude measurement had progressed further and been carried into more basic aspects of interest and libido investment, we might expect to find from general clinical evidence, as is already indicated by such studies as those of Thorndike (49) and Kinsey (32), that more time is spent, in the lower classes, in general, casual sociability, in simple ergic satisfactions, and in collective recreation, and more in the upper status members in reading, individual hobbies, and cultural activities. We should expect generally better informed minds and fewer random prejudices with upper status. What few researches have been carried out in this region support common observation and repute. Zapf (54), for example, in his study of superstitious beliefs, found $r$'s of $-0.20$ with intelligence, $-0.11$ with emotional-social adjustment, and $-0.22$ with socioeconomic level.

Among children play interests show less connection with social status than do other aspects of culture. This we might expect if play is in part an escape from culture, based on needs rooted in the biological nature of man. Boynton and Wang (5) presented a 108-item play inventory to 1800 children in the fourth, fifth, and sixth grades, and found class differences significant in only 19 of them.

The most massive difference in interest trend, however, is probably the greater participation in sex satisfaction at the lower status and ego satisfactions at the higher status. The common observation that unskilled workers as compared with professional workers spend more time in sex conversation and activity is clearly borne out, as regards activity, by Kinsey's findings, *e.g.*, that total frequency of orgasm decreases with educational level and social status (except for the very small "most well-to-do" group); that relative frequency of masturbation and other aim-inhibited expressions increases; that frequency of premarital intercourse for twenty-year-olds is about twice as great in the lowest as in the highest educational group. Higher status is thus associated with more sex sublimation and more direct ego satisfaction, *i.e.*, of self-assertive and security ergs. It is also probable, though not easy to demonstrate except by reference to statistics for physical assault and pugnacity of recreation, that lower status is associated with more "aggressive," pugnacious interests.

### 7. SOCIAL STATUS: WIDER ASSOCIATIONS AND INTERPRETATIONS

**Status and Psychosis.** In this section we continue exploration of the association of social status by taking up the fourth category of evidence, that from life-record statistics, and work towards some tentative interpretations of the whole.

The distributions of definite psychoses and of neuroses with respect to social status have been established from records of the past twenty years with tolerable reliability. These records show that psychosis in general increases with lower social status, though individual types of disorders may show a different trend. The chief exception to the general trend is manic-depressive disorder, admissions for which are either evenly distributed or slightly concentrated in the upper class—probably the latter if we allow for the fact that fewer upper-class borderline psychotics get hospitalized. Schizophrenia; arteriosclerotic, degenerative psychoses, and especially the alcoholic psychoses, however, definitely occur more frequently with lower status. Among schizophrenics, relative to their general trend of increase with lower status, the paranoid form is more upper and the catatonic more lower class in distribution.

**Status and Neurosis.** The general trend in neuroses is less clear, since clinical opinion expects on theoretical grounds somewhat more neurosis with more exacting upper-class upbringing, but not all surveys indicate this. In a British sample, with children, Neustatter (12) found more neurosis with upper status, but Stagner (12) and others in America, using questionnaire methods, conclude the converse. However, the evidence of Hirsch (25) on actual neurotic referrals in America leaves no doubt that the correct interpretation is somewhat more neurosis with upper status. Hirsch also instances the greater frequency of neurosis in the army among officers than among enlisted men (five to one in the British and three to one in the American army). Hyde and Kingsley (28) examined the class distinction of diagnosis at a New England induction center and found that the *total* incidence of major mental disorders increased from 7.3 per cent in upper socioeconomic group to 16.6 per cent in the lowest. As one might anticipate from other research approaches, the greatest percentage increase was in mental defect (0.9 to 6.9 per cent) but the diagnosis of psychopathic personality also increased strongly (2.4 to 6.9 per cent), and the psychoses in general significantly. By contrast the neurosis showed no increase with lower status and it is probable, therefore, that if all psychosis could have been screened out from neurosis the latter would have shown the reverse tendency, *i.e.*, that described by Hirsch.

Bowman and Ruesch (4) find psychosomatic disorders properly regarded as "localized neurosis" (Chapter 17) to occur more frequently in individuals of higher-than-average intelligence and social status (namely, in the so-called "middle class"). In regard to neurosis generally, therefore, it seems that the more exacting superego and ego standards of upper status, as well as the lesser sexual expression and greater social competition, impose greater psychological strains. These take effect in spite of the better endowment in intelligence and emotional stability in meeting strains which the upper-status groups possess.

**Status and Types of Neurosis.** Regarding specific neuroses the evidence increasingly throws its weight in support of the original findings of Hollingworth (see (12)) and McDougall (39) that neurasthenia and psychasthenia (obsessional-compulsive neuroses) are more common with upper and conversion hysteria with lower status. (Intelligence and army rank follow the same pattern as civilian status.) Smith and Culpin (see (12)), comparing executives with lower ranks in industry, again found more obsessional neurosis at upper levels, but described anxiety neuroses as more prevalent lower down.

General clinical evidence, *e.g.*, Hirsch summarizing the results of Maddy, agrees with the last observation, finding more suppressive, self-disciplinary obsessions in upper-status children and more worries in children of semi-skilled parents. Levy (12) found undue introversion, temper-tantrums, and negativisms in upper-status children and stealing, lying, and incorrigibility in lower; Pisula (see (12)) and Mathews (see (12)) likewise report less aggression and more withdrawal in upper-class children. Adler finds feeding problems more prevalent in upper-class children, and, regarding delinquency, points out that upper-class parents can more easily save their children from the damaged reputation and ensuing vicious circle of aggressive-delinquent behavior than can parents with less influence; but other data show this cannot be the whole explanation for instability showing itself more readily in delinquency in lower-status groups.

More miscellaneous associations, not classifiable under the above five rubrics, are to be found in such studies as that of Bonney (see (5), Chap. 15) on popularity or "social success," where a correlation of this "success" in children was found to the extent of 0.31 with intelligence and 0.39 with socioeconomic status. A high socioetric "tele" score, *i.e.*, being the recipient of many friendship pledges, has repeatedly been found commoner with upper-status in mixed-status children's groups.

**Perspective on Personality and Social Status.** In discussing for summarization we note, first, that the personality differences found to correlate with social status are by no means negligible, and, though some belong to superficial features of training and attitude, others go deeper into subtle orientations of the whole personality. The scientific analysis agrees, with common experience that one of the first things recognizable in any newly encountered personality is the status and background of his upbringing. Nevertheless, present testing methods indicate only dimly some relations that may be suspected on other grounds. For example, the findings of higher intelligence, dominance, more integrated will, etc., with higher status agree with what might reasonably be expected when social climbing is opened to competition. But it is also observable that when lifted beyond a certain modest level of comfort and security intelligent men begin to pursue other goals than wealth, while even below this level men of the finest character, *e.g.*, missionaries, cease to compete on the socioeconomic ladder. Consequently, we might expect correlation of "desirable" or "competent" personality traits with social status to hold over the lower range, whereas in the upper-class levels (especially as economically defined) we might expect even a reversal to set in as regards certain character qualities and perhaps as regards intelligence. Thus antisocial selfish traits sometimes accumulate, in high economic levels, as Fisher (12), Burt, and the present writer (8,12) have shown with respect to the trait of infertility. Such departures from linearity of correlation at the top of the social range are indicated in some of the data above. How far down this reversal of trend will run will depend on the conditions of the social stratification, *e.g.*, whether eminence depends mainly on wealth, on intelligence, on social service, as well as on the conditions of competition or promotion.

If we pursue the present search for causes of the discovered associations more systematically, we shall find instances of status engendering trait and of trait being responsible for status. We shall also find some of the traits to be largely hereditary and others largely environmental. And throughout all instances we shall find the same subtle ambiguity of moral valuation of the traits associated with status—depending on the psychological nature of the status dimension and the conditions by which people move in a given society up the status gradient.

Among the more constitutional associations of social status we must place intelligence, emotional stability, and relative freedom from psychosis, as well as some obscure temperament quality underlying proneness to obsessional rather than anxiety neurosis. These qualities, along with some physical ones, *e.g.*, stature and perhaps good looks (26), tend further to become mutually associated by what has been called (12) "genetic adhesion." Though initially genetically and psychologically independent, they come together with greater than chance expectation in the total inheritance, because each favors a rising social status and the class-assortative mating brings the promoted carriers of these various genes together. It is possible that the appreciable correlation (0.4) of the psychological independent factors intelligence ($B$ factor) and emotional stability ($C$ factor) arises through the operation of this sociogenetic law, "genetic adhesion" (12) in the culture pattern.

As to whether cyclothyme-schizothyme ($A$ factor) status differences should be included in the hereditary block, no clear answer can be given. For in spite of the greater lower-class incidence of schizophrenia there is actually a suggestion that the leptosomatic build, commonly considered appreciably correlated with schizothyme constitution, is more prevalent with upper status. The greater frustrations, especially ego frustrations, associated with lower social status, could themselves be enough to account for the greater incidence of schizophrenia. Nevertheless, the schizothyme's well-known lack of energy and resourcefulness also indicates a constitutional reason for his lower status. To the environmental influence of higher status we must almost certainly assign the greater $K$ factor, the greater dominance ($E$ factor), the better character integration ($G$ factor) and some of the freedom from delinquency, as well as the somewhat greater proneness found in the upper class to neurosis.

Finally, it is necessary to keep in mind that for reasons discussed in this section many correlations will be curvilinear; that some associations will be specific to the middle range of status where competition is strongest and mobility highest; and that the very existence of social status, or at least of certain conditions of competition upon the social ladder, does more to shape personality than does any position on the ladder as such.

## 8. SUMMARY

1. Groups exist in virtue of the synergy derived from the individual purposes they are able to satisfy.

2. There exists an isomorphism between the overlapping and often subsidiated group structures in a community and the attitude and sentiment structures in the typical individual.

3. A group is defined and measured through its syntality which is a function of (*a*) the group structure, and (*b*) the personality characteristics

of the population. Cultural anthropology now attempts to define such syntalities, but it is necessary for social psychology to develop exact methods.

4. The individual's environment may be divided into a universal, cosmic environment, a climatic environment, a cultural environment (or pattern), and an idiosyncratic environment.

5. The main functions of the culture pattern in relation to personality can be stated in some nine generalizations covering approved personality pattern, indirect personality molding (superego), reaction to deviants, provision of order, necessity for satisfying ergic constitution, effects of disorganization, adjustment to the psychological burden, variation of personality with role, and dependence of culture change on disposition rigidity, and the like.

6. In regard to method the object of science is to determine the relative contribution of the various dimensions of various social organs (which are inferred from and embodied in their customs) to the variance of individual personality dimensions. This involves partialing out the effects of functionally correlated organs, after the unitarily functioning organs have been located by factor analysis and other wholistic methods.

7. Social organs exert mutual influence not only through general social dynamic interchanges (see Section 1) but also via the individual personality, notably by the principle of convergence, the principle of dynamic complementariness, and the principle of stability.

8. Of all social organs the home makes the greatest contribution to personality variance, with friendship group, school, etc., following in descending order.

9. Social status is a dimension demonstrable among occupations and individuals by factor analysis. It loads most highly prestige, but also mental capacity, income, years of education, and many other variables.

10. Social status correlates significantly with personality factors of general ability, character integration, dominance, low perseveration, patterns of interests (more ego, less sex expression), and with lower incidence of delinquency and mental disorder. Relations are curvilinear, are directed sometimes more to mobility than to status as such, they arise from causal action in both directions. In addition to manifesting associations with *individual* traits, social status creates and associates itself with what may be termed *status-oriented patterns* of personality. These arise both by convergence of environmental influences and by "genetic adhesion" of class-selected genes through class-assortative mating.

## QUESTIONS AND EXERCISES

1. Distinguish between the effective and the intrinsic synergy of a group and illustrate by a simple example how one of these operates in the subsidiation of groups in a dynamic lattice.

2. Illustrate, by reference on the one hand to a modern industrial nation and on the other to a primitive tribe, the isomorphism of the culture pattern and the sentiment structure in the individual personality.

3. Mention two or three dimensions with respect to which culture patterns may differ, and illustrate by citing patterns studied by social psychologists or cultural anthropologists.

4. What generalizations can be made about the action of the culture pattern upon personality with respect to (*a*) deviant personalities, (*b*) superego formation, (*c*) the provision of order in relation to habitual expectations?

5. Discuss the sense in which the culture pattern is a psychological burden, in spite of being desired by the majority. Illustrate by the theory relating cultural complexity to incidence of schizophrenia.

6. On what basis is it possible to select from numerous possible conceptions of culture elements or institutions those particular concepts of organs which make the best reference points from which to predict, by multiple correlation, the effect of the culture pattern elements upon personality?

7. Describe three ways in which culture organs influence one another by way of their effects on individual personality.

8. Discuss the various attempts to define social status, and show how the factorial approach provides an answer. What features of status seem likely to persist through a wide variety of cultures?

9. Name some individual personality associates of social status, giving evidence as to the closeness of association.

10. Discuss the interpretation of relations found between personality and social status, with particular reference to hereditary and environmental determinations and to the curvilinear nature of certain associations.

## BIBLIOGRAPHY

1. BATESON, G.: *Naven*, The University Press, Cambridge, England, 1936.

2. BENEDICT, R.: *Patterns of Culture*, Houghton Mifflin Company, Boston, 1934.

3. BONNEY, M. E.: Relationships between Social Success, Family Size, Socio-economic Home Background, and Intelligence among School Children in Grades 3 to 5, *Sociometry*, 7: 26–39, 1944.

4. BOWMAN, K. M., and J. RUESCH: Prolonged Post-traumatic Syndromes Following Head Injury, *Amer. J. Psychiat.*, 102: 145–164, 1945.

5. BOYNTON, P. L., and J. D. WANG: Relation of the Play Interests of Children to Their Economic Status, *J. genet. Psychol.*, 64: 129–138, 1944.

6. BROWN, F.: A Comparative Study of the Influence of Race and Locale upon Emotional Stability of Children, *J. genet. Psychol.*, 49: 325–342, 1936.

7. CARLSON, H. B.: Attitudes of Undergraduate Students, *J. soc. Psychol.*, 5: 18–28, 1934.

8. CATTELL, R. B.: The Concept of Social Status, *J. soc. Psychol.*, 15: 293–308, 1942.

9. CATTELL, R. B.: *The Description and Measurement of Personality*, World Book Company, Yonkers, New York, 1946.

10. CATTELL, R. B.: Concepts and Methods in the Measurement of Group Syntality, *Psychol. Rev.* 55: 48–63, 1948.

11. CATTELL, R. B.: *A Guide to Mental Testing*, University of London Press, Ltd., London, 1948.

12. CATTELL, R. B.: *Social Psychology* (in press).

13. DAVIS, A.: American Status Systems and the Socialization of the Child, *Amer. sociol. Rev.*, 6: 345–354, 1941.

14. DENNIS, W.: *The Hopi Child*, Appleton-Century-Crofts, Inc., New York, 1940.

15. DEVEREUX, G. A.: A Sociological Theory of Schizophrenia, *Psychoanal. Rev.*, 26: 315–342, 1939.

16. DU BOIS, C.: *The People of Alor*, University of Minn. Press, Minneapolis, 1944.

16a. FARIS, R. E. L., and DUNHAM, W.: *Mental Disorders in Urban Areas*, University of Chicago Press, Chicago, 1939.

17. FREUD, S.: *Civilization and Its Discontents*, Hogarth Press, London, 1930.

18. FRYER, D.: Occupational Intelligence Levels, *Sch. & Soc.*, 16: 273–277, 1922.

19. GILLIN, J.: Personality Formation from the Comparative Cultural Point of View, *Sociological Foundations of the Psychiatric Disorders of Childhood*, Woods Schools Proceedings, Woods School, Langhorne, Pa., 1945.

20. GORER, G.: *The American People*, W. W. Norton & Company, New York, 1948.

20a. GORER, G.: *Japanese Character Structure*, Institute for Intercultural Studies, New York, 1942.

21. HARRELL, T. W., and M. S. HARRELL: Army General Classification Test Scores for Civilian Occupations, *Educ. psychol. Measmt*, 5: 229–239, 1945.

22. HARTSHORNE, H., and M. A. MAY: Testing the Knowledge of Right and Wrong, *Relig. Educ.*, 539–554, Oct., 1926.

23. HEALY, W., A. BRONNER, and A. M. BOWERS: *Structure and Meaning of Psychoanalysis*, Alfred A. Knopf, Inc., New York, 1930.

24. HIMMELWEIT, H. T., and J. W. WHITFIELD: Mean Intelligence Scores of a Random Sample of Occupations, *Brit. J. Indust. Med.*, 1: 224–226, 1944.

25. HIRSCH, N. D. M.: *Mental Deviants in the Population of the United States*, Private Circulation, 1939.

26. HOLLINGWORTH, L. S.: The Comparative Beauty of the Faces of Highly Intelligent Adolescents, *J. genet. Psychol.*, 47: 268–281, 1935.

27. HUXLEY, J. S.: *Africa View*, Harper & Brothers, New York, 1931.

28. HYDE, R. W., and L. V. KINGSLEY: Studies in Medical Sociology I and II; with Chisholm III, *New Engl. J. Med.*, 231: 543–548, 571–577, and 612–618, 1944.

29. JOHNSON, D. M.: Applications of the Standard Score IQ to Social Statistics, *J. soc. Psychol.*, 27: 217–227, 1948.

30. JONES, V.: *Character and Citizenship Training in the Public School*, University of Chicago Press, Chicago, 1936.

31. KEYSERLING, H.: *The World in the Making*, Harcourt, Brace & Company, Inc., New York, 1927.

32. KINSEY, A. C., W. B. POMEROY, and C. E. MARTIN: *Sexual Behavior in the Human Male*, W. B. Saunders Company, Philadelphia, 1948.

33. KLUCKHOHN, C., and O. H. MOWRER: "Culture and Personality," a Conceptual Scheme, *Amer. Anthrop.*, 46: 1–29, 1944.

34. KLUCKHOHN, C., and H. MURRAY: *Personality in Nature, Society, and Culture*, Alfred A. Knopf, Inc., New York, 1948.

35. KVARACEUS, W. C.: Juvenile Delinquency and Social Class, *J. educ. Sociol.*, 18: 51–54, 1944.

36. LINTON, R.: *The Tanala, a Hill Tribe of Madagascar*, Marshall Field Expedition to Madagascar, 1926, University of Chicago Press, Chicago, 1933.

37. LIPPITT, R.: Field Theory and Experiment in Social Psychology; Autocratic and Democratic Group Atmospheres, *Amer. J. Sociol.*, 45: 26–49, 1939.

38. MALINOWSKI, B.: *Sex and Repression in Savage Society*, Harcourt, Brace & Company, Inc., New York, 1927.

39. McDOUGALL, W.: *Outline of Abnormal Psychology*, Charles Scribner's Sons, New York, 1926.

40. MEAD, M.: *Coming of Age in Samoa*, William Morrow and Co.; New York, 1930.
41. MEAD, M.: *Growing Up in New Guinea*, William Morrow and Co., New York, 1930.
42. MELTZER, H.: Economic Security and Children's Attitudes to Parents, *Amer. J. Orthopsychiat.*, 6: 590–608, 1936.
43. MERTON, R. K.: Bureaucratic Structure and Personality, *Social Forces*, 18: 560–568, 1940.
44. MURPHY, G.: *Personality*, Harper & Brothers, New York, 1947.
45. PARSONS, T.: Age and Sex in the Social Structure of the United States, *Amer. sociol. Rev.*, 7: 604–616, 1942.
46. RUNDQUIST, E. A., and R. F. SLETTO: *Personality in the Depression*, University of Minn. Press, Minneapolis, 1936.
47. SOROKIN, R. A., C. C. ZIMMERMAN, and C. G. GOLPIN: A *Systematic Source Book in Rural Sociology*, University of Minn. Press, Minneapolis, 1930.
48. STAGNER, R.: Fascist Attitudes: Their Determining Conditions, *J. soc. Psychol.*, 7: 438–454, 1936.
49. THORNDIKE, E. L.: On Spending Leisure, *Sci. Mon.*, 44: 464–467, 1937.
50. WARNER, W. L., and P. S. LUNT: *The Social Life of a Modern Community*, Yale University Press, New Haven, 1941.
51. WARNER, W. L., and P. S. LUNT: *The Status System of a Modern Community*, Yale University Press, New Haven, 1942.
52. WARNER, W. L., and L. SROLE: *The Social Systems of American Ethnic Groups*, Yale University Press, New Haven, 1945.
53. WHITING, J. W. M.: *Becoming a Kwoma*, Yale University Press, New Haven, 1941.
54. ZAPF, R. M.: Relationship between Belief in Superstitions and Other Factors, *J. educ. Res.*, 38: 561–579, 1945.
55. ZENER, K.: *Sociological Foundations of the Psychiatric Disorders of Childhood*, Woods Schools Proceedings, Woods School, Langhorne, Pa., November, 1945, p. 32.

# CHAPTER 15

## PERSONALITY AND THE CULTURAL MATRIX:
## IV. PERSONALITY AND SPECIFIC SOCIAL ORGANS

### 1. PERSONALITY AND OCCUPATION

**Intelligence and Occupation.** Our inquiry now proceeds to investigate the mutual effects of personality and specific cultural institutions, begun in the preceding chapter with certain general observations and the study of a particular institution—social status. The institution naturally calling for study after social status is occupation, with which status is correlated.

It is a sad illustration of the meager harvest accruing to pure science from comparatively heavy expenditures on applied science that, in spite of the enormous attention vouchsafed in the last forty years to the psychology of vocational guidance, we still have no figures even for the *means* of occupations with regard to the principal personality factors. In only one factor— general intelligence—do any dependable data exist and these reside in exactly four articles appearing in thirty years (7,16a,23) (see (21), Chap. 14). As mentioned in the previous chapter, an attempt to bring these to a common standard score has recently been made by Johnson, who shows that in different countries and regions there is considerable similarity in the occupational I.Q. levels. Consequently, although it is a commonplace that a man's occupation appears in his personality, we cannot document this with precision or ask how much of the convergence is due to vocation being selected to personality and how much to personality being shaped to a life-long occupation.

This much, however, is probable: that personality, apart from special skills, is less correlated with job than with status, for in day-to-day contacts we cannot so surely place a man's occupation as his class.   The intelligence test data show a very great range within each occupation, *e.g.*, in a typical sample of trained nurses the mean I.Q. was 122, with the upper and lower quartiles standing at 136.5 and 101.5.   Within these quartiles lie, among other occupational means, such diverse complexities of occupations as may be illustrated by general managers in business, standing at 136 and sheet-metal workers with a mean at 102.   Evidently in our society it is not possible to make much of an estimate of the complexity of a person's occupation from his intelligence, or vice versa.

**Surgency, Cyclothymia, and Dominance in Relation to Occupation.**   With respect to two or three other factors—*A*, cyclothymia-schizothymia, *E*, dominance-submission, and *F*, surgency-desurgency—some shreds of evidence exist.   On the Allport A-S Test foremen are found to be significantly more dominant than workmen, and salesmen than the average of our populations.   Now that such occupational interest blanks as those of Strong (42) and Kuder (26) have been factorized and related to more direct measures of personality factors, it is possible to see personality trends at least in occupational preference.   For example, greater surgency seems to go with an occupational choice of advertising man, lawyer, and school superintendent, and greater desurgency with the choice of physicist, farmer, artist, mathematician, and accountant.

Kretschmer (see (38), Chap. 5) has made a good case from the clinical standpoint for the powerful role of *A*-factor endowment (cyclothymia-schizothymia) in determining occupation among individuals of the same general ability.   The cyclothyme (*A*+) individual tends to choose business occupations requiring good administrative contact with men and constant adjustment to practicalities of the total situation.   The schizothyme, on the other hand, prefers ideas, is more likely to go into the academic world, into hierarchies with regular rules of conduct, and into occupations where the word rather than the thing, or still more the person, has to be dealt with.

**Interests and Occupation.**   Unless investigation of the relation of personality to occupation is to attempt the hopeless task of exploring the relationships found in countless specific occupations, it will be necessary to put occupations in certain groupings.   This can be done either with respect to characteristics of the occupations *per se*, *e.g.*, complexity, length of training, indoor-outdoor, in which case we finish with generalizations similar to those about social status, or with respect to psychological traits required (or found) in the occupation.   The latter sort of classification is already to some extent available with regard to Strong's classification of occupations according to similarity of interests involved in them.   Some four factors have been found in Strong's test (42), of which the two below are the most clear.   They contrast the following sets of occupations:

1. *Sociable Activity vs. Detached Creative Interests*

| | |
|---|---|
| Salesman | Artist |
| YMCA Secretary | Doctor |
| School teacher | Mathematician |

2. *Philistine Go-getting vs. Aesthetic Interest*

| | |
|---|---|
| Lawyer | Farmer |
| Purchasing agent | Artist |
| Accountant | |

Perhaps the dimensions of personality which distinguish the person fitted to the occupations on the left from those whose interests fit occupations on the right will turn out to be primary personality factors, *i.e.*, the classification of occupations thus attained will be essentially a classification according to personality demands. Until these facts are clearer it is idle to discuss how far occupation molds personality or personality selects occupation.

As to the weighting to be assigned to personal and situation factors in the matching of person and career, we have the survey of Wren (53) on 871 male clients at a guidance and adjustment service. He concluded that the level (social and economic) of occupations at which an individual aims is determined by (*a*) dominance and persistence as a personality factor, (*b*) the level of occupations attained by relatives, (*c*) present income, (*d*) abilities and educational proficiency. He found no relation to age, marital status, stability of employment, and length of special supplementary education. This interesting survey needs to be repeated on better samples and with more sensitive categorization and calculation methods.

## 2. ECOLOGY: THE EFFECTS OF REGION AND MOBILITY

**The Meaning of Locality and the Evidence of General Observation.** Both common observation and exact statistics show significant relationship between personality and the regions (within any one nation) in which people live. The neighborhood in which a person is brought up and his later experience of change or immobility obviously affect some aspects of his personality. First, it is necessary to note that sociologists who study human ecology have concluded that the important varieties of region to consider are: the big city, the small town, the farming countryside, as well as the urban subdistricts constituted by the downtown region, the middle-class suburbs, the factory region, the slums, and the rooming-house areas, each of which has its characteristic economic level, way of life, recreational possibilities, and mode of government. That such regions, as well as the various provincial regions of a country, turn out personalities to some extent recognizable in origin, and not merely by an accent either, is common knowledge. It was remarked by an induction center psychologist in the last war that a common danger of misclassification for inexperienced examiners was that of writing down the slow, taciturn rustic from Kentucky as a mental defective and the man from Brooklyn as a paranoid. Certainly a considerable ecological variance of personality has to be discounted everywhere if we are to make sound comparisons with respect to the rest of personality.

**Statistical Evidence And Test Data.** Those ecological patterns that have to do with interests and attitudes, *e.g.*, the tendency of a Vermonter to be a Republican, a Georgian to be a Democrat, or a citizen of Salt Lake City to have the viewpoint of Mormonism, are so obvious as to need no further comment. Demonstration of the further and more obscure differences rests at present more on life-record data, showing the incidence of this and that, than on personality measurement, and such data generally leave us undue latitude in drawing inferences. For example, relative to their populations the small towns produced in the last war more good infantry officers than the large cities, a fact ascribed to the training in community responsibility and initiative offered by small towns, but open also to a variety of other interpretations. On the other hand, the number of men of genius, per 100,000 of the population, is three or four times higher for middle-class suburban regions than for small towns and especially for general farm country. This may admit explanation by hereditary selection or by environmental stimulus. Or again, we find that Burt showed the highest juvenile delinquency rates to occur, not in the poorest city districts of all, but in those poor districts that abut on well-to-do ones. Is this due to greater prevalence of provocation or to some distorting influence of the situation on the whole personality?

Stott (41) compared 695 farm children, 640 town children, and 520 city children, finding the usual order for I.Q., but adding the indication that in personality qualities—honesty, initiative, responsibility, etc.—the city group was highest. How significant this difference will be when objectively measured, and whether its origins are in school-efficiency and social-status differences, remains to be checked. An interesting study on values, by Woodruff, shows, in student samples, that the relative admiration for and interest in wealth, society, and political power tend to increase with the size of town from which they come, whereas social service, personal comfort, and religious interest tend to drop. Robert Thorndike (46) and Johnson (23) have been able to demonstrate some slight but significant differences in average I.Q. and average level of verbal skill between different regions of the United States. The evidence of army drafts and of poll sampling agree in placing the Far-western states highest, some New England states next, followed by the Midwest and finally the South. How far these slight differences represent educational levels or real sociobiological selection effects on the population is unknown. Whether the distribution about these means is the same in different regions is also unknown, but it seems probable that they are fairly normal, since Thorndike's (44*a*) findings on the percentages of eminent men from various states agree pretty closely with the level of the average I.Q.

**Integration of Findings on "Social Area" Effects.** Perhaps the most important—because the most generally applicable—of ecological divisions is that into city center, suburb, slum, small town, and farming areas. This is primarily neither a class, a racial, nor a climatic division, but one according to the areas that typically develop in industrial nations.

One of the most successful attempts to integrate such data is that of Faris (15), who points out the following: "The slum sections [of cities], usually but not always near the central parts of the city, inhabited by low-paid working people, with a high proportion of foreign and Negro populations, have relatively very high rates [of delinquency]. The outlying residential sections, inhabited by native-born, business, and professional population, have very low rates." He then attempts to show, from the work of Shaw and McKay (37), that this is due to "community disorganization" and occurs to *any* groups that get into very culturally mixed and residentially transient neighborhoods. The distribution of suicide frequencies follows much the same pattern, but occurs somewhat more in the rooming-house and hobo districts where settled family life is rare.

It has long been known that psychosis is significantly more frequent in urban than rural areas, even when all differences of standard and hospitalization facility are properly discounted. (These could not in any case have major influence, for the distribution of mental defect is just the opposite.) It can now be shown that the frequency even of *variety* of psychosis differs systematically with city ecology. Manic-depressive disorder is not common in the poorer and more disorganized areas, but schizophrenia is. Catatonic schizophrenia has low rates in the rooming-house, transient areas but high rates in the foreign-born slum areas. Paranoid schizophrenia, on the other hand, correlates $+0.82$ with an index of hotel and rooming-house concentration (15). The psychoses associated with alcohol and venereal disease (general paralysis) are highest in hobo and rooming-house areas, in the Negro area, and the foreign-born slum areas, the former especially being associated with low income.

The tendency of sociologists has been to interpret these results as showing that income level and racial or cultural subgroup as such do not correlate with crime or psychosis. They argue that social disorganization—the unintegrated kaleidoscope of culture-pattern fragments thrown together in certain areas—is the baleful glare which constitutes the primary cause of personality disintegration. From this it has been easy to slip into the error of supposing that no other factors, biological, familial, psychological, etc., have any role. Again it is necessary to remind the psychologist to think in terms of "contribution to the variance" in analyzing causal influences. The sociologists have been guilty in the first place of forgetting the world outside Chicago, the unusual city where these five ecological studies have been made. Amsterdam has delinquency—admittedly less than Chicago—without any problem of racial and cultural mixture, and Edinburgh has psychosis—again somewhat less than Chicago—despite the absence of the transient population. Again, in looking at the above correlation of $+0.82$ one should, of course, remember first, that it is a correlation of *group means*, always higher than for the individuals in the groups, and second, that its probable error is very great since so few groups enter into the correlation series.

**Interpretation of Associations.** Finally, we should question that the results prove that any lasting disorganization of personality results from social disorganization. The odd behavior may be that of entirely *normal* personalities to the odd (and temporary) stimulus of social disorganization. Or it may be that poorly integrated, disordered personalities, *e.g.*, those of hoboes, tend to drift into and help create disorderly communities. Psychologists have long realized that the behavior of the normal personality under special group conditions is very different from, and not readily usable as a predictor of, the reactions of the same personalities under other conditions. The social disorganization of an earthquake or great fire has commonly produced in a law-abiding community a host of looters, murderers, and sexual delinquents. During the demobilization of American troops in France, Gen. J. T. McNarney (*New York Times*, April 26, 1946) issued an order pointing out that the "rapid demobilization and frequent change of station of units" had resulted in "the firm ties of unit pride" being weakened, as a result of which abnormally high rates prevailed in the following: black market participation, going AWOL, automobile accidents, venereal disease, lack of observance of military courtesy, and standards of dress.

In short, the tendency for increase of manifestations of delinquency, neurosis, and all that goes under poor character integration to take place in disorganized communities is well-nigh universal. Although such change is generally temporary and specific to the situation, it must be admitted that living in a disorganized society in the first six years of life would tend to produce more permanent changes in personality integration *per se*. On the other hand, the child is to some extent cushioned against the effects of disorganization of society as such. He lives in the protecting womb of the family and is likely to be affected only by such social disorganization as disorganizes or distorts the family. However, at adolescence, as discussed in Chapter 20, disorganization of the community as such creates real personality maladjustments.

With present knowledge each of these three directions of causal connection—personality disorganizing society, society disorganizing personality, and temporarily disorganized society bringing out odd behavior in normal personality—must be given about equal weight. As to the first, we recognize that poor adaptability of the schizoid personality favors his getting into a low socioeconomic group, just as the obstinate eccentricity of the paranoid favors his ending his days in a rooming house, perhaps by suicide through loneliness, rather than amidst a family. As to the second, we must recognize in so far as high crime and psychosis rates are ascribable to the regional character, as much weight must be given to poverty and the poor family discipline of low status as to the community disorganization itself. In the adult the heaped-up ego frustrations of poverty and the isolation of rooming-house existence favor, respectively, the ego-obliteration of schizophrenia and the unchecked delusional systems of paranoia. For the developing child the patchwork-quilt culture of regions having diverse foreign-born groups undoubtedly favors both delinquency and schizoid breakdown. If one standard of morals is maintained here and quite another there, perhaps all moral standards are suspect. And if the child is laughed at outside the family for behavior well inculcated by solicitous parents, a possible response is a schizoid withdrawal from the larger society.

**Personality and Mobility.** The effects of mobility—either of high geographical mobility or of social mobility, *i.e.*, rapid change of status or cultural setting—are closely akin to those of community disorganization, namely, a tendency to the production of maladjustment and the disregard of moral values. Again the effects of selection must be heeded, for excessive efforts at social climbing are often signs of felt inferiority and insecurity, while the world wanderer may also be an escapist. To whatever maladjustment the mobile individual thus felt in his original class or culture are added, however, the results of the suspicions and rejections of the new in-group into which the individual enters. A certain amount of frustration from lack of unity with the group, a certain schizoid withdrawal or self-sufficiency, and some degree of weakening of moral inhibitions are thus, as various clinical and sociological data show, the average characteristics of the person who has experienced excessive mobility of class or clime.

With regard to local, regional influences in general, it is noteworthy that the variety of patterns that may impress themselves is not endless, for certain necessary connections exist, precluding some combinations and making some order and generalization possible. In his classical study of more than 200 American cities (44) Thorndike showed that certain groups of "good" and "bad" features tend to go together. For example, comparing the five highest with the five lowest in the goodness-of-living index, he found that in the former:

1. The frequency of death from homicide is one-twelfth as great.
2. The library circulation is three times as great.

3. The frequency of high-school graduation is twice as great.

4. The frequency of death from syphilis is one-twelfth as great.

It is thus to be expected that the "citizen of no mean city" will have a tendency to show a personality pattern which differs from that of the dweller in less morally developed communities, not in isolated respects but in the simultaneously greater impress of a whole pattern of "civilized" habits and values.

## 3. ORGANIZED SCHOOLING

**The School and Society.** Psychologists scarcely need to be reminded that the school, which is society's "official" and explicit institution for shaping personality to the culture pattern ("to communicate the type and to provide for growth beyond the type"), does not in fact have the potency which that definition assigns to it. As we have seen from the correlations of personality values with background institutions, the popular impression of the school's capacity to influence personality has to be discounted heavily in favor of the family, the play group, and possibly other institutions.

However, despite the seemingly great amount of research in educational psychology and the lip service paid by educators to training character as distinct from imparting skills and information, we still have surprisingly little exact knowledge of the magnitude of the effect on personality of the average school or of different school systems (*e.g.*, day and boarding schools). Historically one can point to the inauguration of certain school systems, *e.g.*, the seven famous English public schools, being followed by the development of a way of life and new values and movements in the culture pattern which seem to be the consequence of the personality values set by the schools, but such evidence cannot yet meet the standards of scientific method.

Incidentally, the relation of the school to society has varied a good deal in one important respect: that it is sometimes "ahead" of society and sometimes only a faithful servant trailing behind society, teaching rigidly the existing values of society. Obviously, the school in fact has to educate in part for citizenship in a state which does not at the time exist. In any historical or sociological analysis of personality and the school it is important to take note of the extent to which the school follows the dictates of society or is, alternatively, allowed to lead, to the experimental and critical of existing values, following minorities which are supposed to be "advanced."

**The Three Chief Influences in the School.** In school the child is subjected to the stimuli constituted by (*a*) the personalities of other children, (*b*) the personalities of the teachers, and (*c*) the personality training through the vicarious experience offered in reading and other symbolic reference to the remote. "Academic" thinking about education, *e.g.*, the thinking of the French encyclopedists, of Herbart, of Comenius, as contrasted with so-called progressive education or the English public school with their emphasis on student government (*vide* Kipling's *Stalky and Co.*), has under-estimated the role of the first of these.  The Boy Scout movement, and others which recognized the inevitable power and possible usefulness of the natural gang situation, have helped to bring into state education in the last half-century organized pupil government and values otherwise found only in the above-mentioned special experiments.  Consequently, the study of the influence of the school is partly a study of the gang or play group and is properly considered in organic connection with these.

The nursery school, necessarily largely concerned with social and emotional development, also brings to bear to a marked extent the influence of the child's age group.  Bonham-Sargent claims that the following traits are influenced by the nursery school: "sociability, initiative, independence, good nature, orderliness, curiosity, self-assertion, self-reliance, sympathy, and willingness to talk."  Since there is no difficulty in finding a control group of children not exposed to the nursery school, its influence can be scientifically determined; but this is not true of the school generally, and until ingenious indirect methods have brought a harvest of results the extremely important question of the total influence of the school cannot be psychologically evaluated or answered.

**Evidence on Influences.**  Of the influence of the teacher personality, and the teacher's ways of handling problems, upon child personality, practically nothing has been established, for lack of valid personality measurement techniques.  H. H. Anderson (3) has demonstrated that the degree of dominance shown by the teacher has much the same relation to interchild criticism and to the development of hierarchies of aggression and dominance among children as has been shown by Lippitt with club groups.  But there is no evidence as to the duration and generalization of the response habits thus established.

That the world opened up by books does have an appreciable influence on personality has been shown with respect to moral values by Jones (see (30), Chap. 14) who demonstrated improvements in honesty and possibly courage following admiration of book heroes with these traits.  Child, Potter, and Levine (10) analyzed 914 stories in school texts to see whether any consistent personality model could be said to be operative and found definite patterns, *e.g.*, girls and women presented as sociable, kind, cautious, contented, and unambitious (perhaps also as uncreative!).  They also found repeated patterns of encouragement of some traits and discouragement of others.

As one might expect, the school tends to produce greater uniformity of personality (11), being more uniform than the families from which children come.  It is notable that some, the more egocentric, the more divergent in intelligence, and those from outstandingly good or bad homes, show least of this convergent change. Newcomb (32) observes somewhat the same at the college level, with respect to adoption of college sociopolitical opinions. But it is easy to see in clinical work that the school also produces special compensatory developments. Children who are lacking sufficient affection from the parents tend to respond more strongly to the encouragement offered them by the teacher. Children with no particular social gifts may discover talents in school subjects, about which their ego development becomes strongly entwined. Page (33) and Jack (21) show that in very young children, where personality change occurs more readily, changes in dominance-submission of a measurable degree occur in response to acquisition of skills. Children low in dominance, trained in a skill until they surpassed the skill of more dominant children, showed an appreciable increase in dominance (*E* factor) traits, though the extent and permanence of transfer beyond the specific situation was not ascertained. Conversely, children poor at schoolwork or spoiled in the home may tend to become spiteful or discouraged and uncooperative in school. For most children the teacher inherits some of the parental role, and the school may become so much a second, protected home environment that the same problems arise in growing out of it into the world as with the family. Nevertheless, in the main the personality that the child shows in school is most predictive of that which he will show in the world afterwards, and the school can correctly be regarded as a microcosm of the total culture.

The role of the children themselves has been in general to shape personality toward somewhat different ideals from those formally proposed for the school by adults. An acute observer of the English public school in relation to society, Robert Graves, has described it as a "self-governing republic" of boys demanding "the Spartan virtues of modesty, reticence, endurance, courage, generosity, loyalty, personal cleanliness, and general decency (unwillingness to take unfair advantage)" coupled with "the Spartan prejudice against all things artistic, eccentric, abstract, poetic, studious, foreign, or feminine." Since one result of the decline in the authoritative, well-knit, supervisory family has been to shift, relatively, socioemotional education to the child's age group, it becomes a matter of considerable practical as well as theoretical importance to understand the action of the "play" group of coevals.

To appreciate the action of the child group in shaping the personalities of individual children—an action normally much modified in school by the greater authority of the adult—it is best to consider it in the untrammeled operation of the "gang," the play group, or the "friendship group." At about six years of age the child normally achieves sufficient self-assurance and control of its environment to have some confidence in breaking out in some degree from the parental shelter. From this time until the individual responsibly accepts and is accepted by the adult world at mid-adolescence, he persists in an ambivalent attitude to culture that has, not inaptly, been called "the little savage" stage. It is at this stage that the revolt against the burden of the culture pattern, which has already been discussed as a normal, inevitable psychological experience, comes nearest to a total, undistorted expression, both because the impact of the culture pressure is most sharp during the years of growth and because the family-school situation gives most opportunity. Let us study the social organ expressing this partial revolt.

### 4. THE GANG AND THE FRIENDSHIP GROUP

**Psychological Definition of the Antisocial Gang.** From one angle a gang is essentially a more or less tacit agreement of a group of individuals, each of whom experiences a need to evade the full demands of the culture pattern, to sustain one another in an agreed degree of evasion. Jameson (22) points out that the members of a gang are not primarily delinquents nor do they show necessarily the poor integration and defective superego of the typical individual delinquent. Gangs, especially among adolescent girls (22), are formed or joined by individuals with unsatisfactory home or community opportunities for expression, who find therein a congenial gregariousness, through which they are led, perhaps only in that situation, to join in delinquency. Thrasher (47), whose study of boy gangs in Chicago is unmatched in thoroughness, concludes, "Gangs represent the spontaneous effort of boys to create a society for themselves where none adequate to their needs exists."

Freud (16) and others have pointed out what has been defined as the "horde" structure in a group, wherein a patriarchal leader or the group itself abrogates the functions of the individual's conscience. The individual's superego is the introjected parent or group authority and it can be handed back to the group, relieving the individual of responsibility for his own behavior. Much crowd and mob behavior as described by Le Bon, McDougall, and others, is most readily explicable in this way. Similarly, the gang gives the individual sanction and moral courage to defy the outer culture pattern, to the extent most congenial to the perhaps regressive or immature level attained at that time by the individual.

It is characteristic of the gang that, in providing relief from suppressions and distasteful requirements, it engenders some hostility to the main culture group. It generally demands reversal of a few of the adult cultural standards that have specifically provoked its bravado, though it unconsciously preserves a great many. Thus, a lad who is well mannered or shows regard for public property may be ostracized. "Our first loyalties" as one of Thrasher's subjects reported "were to protect each other against our parents." The discipline of the gang is characteristically more harsh, and its edicts less open to reasoning and examination, than those of most parents, but they are in general more adapted to the natural inclinations and values of the age level concerned. Many of them are not primarily anticultural but designed to stabilize and protect the often unconsciously needed satisfactions of the age. For example, in many of Thrasher's gangs the youth who went out with girls was ostracized, because psychologically the gang belongs to the stage of homosexual sublimation prior to full adult sexuality.

**The Nonantisocial Gang.** Perspicacious educators—from Baden Powell to A. S. Neil—have often observed that the gang has valuable educational functions. For example, it has been noticed in experimental schools that delinquents who through various personal maladjustments have developed rooted antipathies to order and authority as such, after experiencing the miseries of chaos in an uncontrolled group of fellow rebels, will begin to form gang law, which, through being of their own devising and sanction, is emotionally supported. The gang also offers an intermediate training step in transition from complete dependence on parental guidance to cooperation in government with a community of one's peers. Incidentally, except when the morale of the main culture is poor, considerable development and utilization of such "immature groups" can be safely tolerated. Nor is a single, maladjusted leader likely to develop such groups excessively, for, as the studies of Thrasher show, the gang forms *before* the leader, who is only thrown up later as an appendage.

Personalities that have experienced no gang stage of "break-away" from parental authority may thus be expected to be unduly dependent, to be rigidly dominated by the superego, to have insufficient emotional sense of the basis of social order, to be too conforming to offer necessary criticism of social institutions, and perhaps to show greater suppressed, displaced hostility. On the other hand, too early, too prolonged, and too complete an experience of gang revolt against authority may dispel the guilt tension necessary for a high level of cultural adaptation and accomplishment. Every second case of genius can be cited as an instance of overstrict, successfully repressive upbringing, and the same is doubtless true of many less eminent but socially essential citizens. On the other hand, such contributions to cultural impetus among successful gang graduates are hard to cite, except perhaps in the realm of politics and military performance.

The gang that is not antisocial is essentially the peer group or neighborhood friendship group and as such its dynamics have a different emphasis from the antisocial gang. The motivations of escape from the cultural burden and of hostility to those who impose it play a much smaller role, while the larger role is taken by the gang as a doorway from the family to the larger adult society. As we have seen from the chapter on the family, there is definite evidence that the parental affection or, at least "concern" for the child, declines as it grows up, while critical attitudes increase. There comes a point in the decline of the family attachment and the rise of the importance of approval from the peer group where the youth is drawn in some respects more to the peer group than to the home. For it must not be forgotten that, as a result of the homosexual sublimation occurring in this period, there is a very real affection to be obtained from the gang. Where affection is greater, there will disciplinary restrictions be more willingly accepted.

Under the influence of this affection and his need for prestige and status in his peer group, the individual may actually have more dynamic support for the acceptance of "cultural burdens" from his peer group than from his parents. Hence in these circumstances it becomes incorrect to speak of the gang as an "escape" from the culture burden, for indeed the individual is prepared to accept far more onerous and exacting conditions in the gang than he would in the family and in everyday life. The often very strict discipline of the peer group is accepted because the growing individual senses more understanding there than he gets, in certain fields, even in the best of families, and because he perceives the approval of this group as a precursor of establishment in the adult world.

### 5. RECREATIONS AND PLAY

**The Three Chief Functions of Play.** Examination of the friendship group or gang and analysis of the extent to which it is motivated by desire to escape from the complexities of the main culture pattern, raise the kindred issue of the whole influence of recreational "escapes" and play in the development of personality. As pointed out in the above section on the behavior of groups, the culture pattern has to allow for escapes from its psychologically more exacting (long-circuited, highly discriminating) tasks in the form of (a) systematic approved recreations, involving especially physical exercise and phantasy, which constitute continuous institutions, (b) periodic abolition of cultural restrictions, deliberately in "holidays," "feast day," "saturnalia," etc., and unconsciously in war and revolution, (c) certain admixtures of the cultural task with hidden regressive satisfactions, (resembling the neurotic symptoms of the individual) in which the approved culture pattern obliquely gives symbolic satisfaction at a lower level, e.g., offering scope for sadism in cultural initiation ceremonies.

The function of "play," as seen in areas (a) and (b) above, is primarily, as any textbook on educational psychology will remind us, first, to provide learning, by trial and error in the less fateful conditions of an agreed make-believe situation, e.g., as the kitten fighting a ball of wool; second, to provide recreation by regression to earlier, more primitive behavior, also in a "fenced in" protected situation, *e.g.*, boxing and football; and third, perhaps to provide a ready channel for the discharge of superfluous energy. The individual who, by mental habits or by opportunity, fails to achieve sufficient play proverbially becomes dull. He lives drily and rigidly by the will rather than adaptively and resourcefully by the imagination; for the latter is a function of phantasy. From the standpoint of creativity, moreover, it also seems that the individual who does not feel the need to give frequent vent to his unconscious is "inefficient." Much evidence on neurasthenia and the character neurosis of the inhibited character (*e.g.*, their association with upper social status and their symptom similarity to fatigue from continued long-circuiting) suggests that these "colorless" conditions of personality are associated with lack of ability or opportunity to play.

As to the effect on the personality of too much play, we have no measurements; but observations suggest increased surgency along with diminished contact with reality. If defective character integration is also an observed associate one must reflect that to play excessively in a world where there is much work to be done requires a certain irresponsibility in the first place. That is to say, defective emotional integration could be a selective rather than a functional correlate of play. The major unhealthy personality correlate of play—namely, poor contact with reality—arises from the intrinsic, ergic connection of play with make-believe, which runs through most games, through music, through wit and humor, and *the* play at the theater. The person who can enter readily into make-believe has a valuable cushion against the pressure of the culture pattern, but if he begins excessively to enter into phantasy, like certain adolescents or the schizophrenic, we have a sign that he is not adjusting properly to the load of the culture pattern.[1]

However, these emphases on the role of play as escape or regression on the one hand or mere discharge of superfluous energy on the other must not cause us to lose sight of the equally essential function of play in trial-and-error learning and particularly in permitting the individual to empathize, by mimicry and make-believe, into personality roles other than his own. The broadening of personality and the conferment of increased adaptability through such experiences of empathy is well shown by the inclusion of drama and literature in education of the so-called sociodrama in psychotherapy.

*Incidence of Play.* Both the study of the amount and of the nature of the recreation that the individual takes is therefore essential to the understanding of personality. At present we have practically no norms. The standard working week (Brookings Institute figures) shifted from fifty-seven hours in 1900 to fifty in 1929 and forty in 1935, and the five-day week is now

---

[1] An interesting sidelight on the amount of emotion discharged in phantasy is the observation of Kleitman (25) that motion-picture audiences show a significant increase in muscle tension and a rise of body temperature of from $\frac{1}{2}$ to 1 degree!

followed by 45 per cent of automobile and other industrial workers, 60 per cent of workers in the building industry, and probably a majority of clerical workers. But the saturation point for play activities is evidently not yet reached! As to how leisure is spent we have such norms as that of Lundberg, Komarovsky, and McInery (31) who found that suburbanite leisure was spent 21 per cent in visiting, 13 per cent in reading, 9 per cent in entertainment (movies, etc.), 9 per cent in sports, 8 per cent in radio, 3 per cent in motoring, 25 per cent in eating, and 12 per cent in other activities. E. L. Thorndike, in a similar survey for New York clerical workers, also found "visiting" or relaxed, playful gossiping about nothing in particular was the favorite recreation. Wallace (51), studying 161 college women in the ten years after graduation, found decidedly more leisure spent in organizations (social, professional, cultural, general, church, in diminishing order) than in hobbies.

**Varieties of Recreation.** As to preferences in recreation or hobbies, we have the beginnings of information in the work of Super (43). He found that the "compensatory" theory of hobbies does not always hold and that the most frequent hobby of engineers is model engineering! As might be expected there were as great differences in intelligence and other personality factors among followers of avocations as among people in different vocations. For example, stamp collectors are high in intelligence and in emotional stability, while the most maladjusted were found in those whose principal hobby was music. Frequently a hobby was the gravestone of a once-desired vocation. These studies as yet have made very small inroads, however, into the whole relationship of personality to recreation.

**Assortative Selection in Friendship.** While considering recreation, the play group, club group, or circle of friends, it is appropriate also to deal with the general question of friendship in relation to personality. With regard to the personalities that make friends we have to consider (*a*) the laws governing matching of friends, and (*b*) the laws governing popularity. Evidence on the former is overwhelmingly to the effect that in friendship, as we have already seen in marriage, similarity brings congeniality.

The evidence of some forty researches have recently been reviewed by Richardson (35), who shows that in addition to the decidedly positive correlations found for age (especially in the young) and sex, positive correlations of the following magnitude occur for general personality factors:

| | |
|---|---|
| Intelligence | 0.10–0.50 |
| Neurotic tendency (Thurstone) | 0.11–0.32 |
| Introversion-extraversion (Laird) | 0.13–0.56 |
| Popularity (pleasingness rating) | 0.34–0.53 |
| Social adjustment | 0.38–0.42 |
| Emotional steadiness | 0.17–0.20 |

There are indications that the correlations on opinions run higher for men than women, and on all aspects run higher with increasing age, increasing powers of discrimination, and decreasing role of mere propinquity and accidental community of purpose. Thus Richardson's (35) correlations on the Allport-Vernon study of values were about $+0.20 \pm 0.04$ for undergraduate and $+0.30 \pm 0.06$ for adult women. The correlations on temperament, and with more objective measures, run somewhat higher.

**Personality and Friendship Popularity.** Popularity was measured by the present writer by asking individuals to name friends, recording the number of options each individual received (9), a device which has since come to be called the "sociometric score," in an unfortunate attempt to narrow to a specific use the general term sociometry. As thus measured, popularity was found to correlate most with the $C$ and $G$ factors of emotional stability and integration. It was inversely related to measures of disposition rigidity or perseveration, which is not surprising in view of the connection we have seen between perseveration and neuroticism or poor integration.

Surgent individuals were slightly more popular than desurgent, but the chief effect of surgency seems to be to increase "catalytically," or by "advertising," whatever tendencies to popularity or unattractiveness previously exist in the personality. Other studies on popularity show similar trends. Bonney (5) who measured popularity both by the above friend-choice technique and by number of gifts and valentines received, stressed the highness of loading in two factorlike syndromes, one like character factors $C$ and $G$ (quiet, tidy, friendly, etc.) and one that seems a cluster of surgency ($F+$) with some cyclothyme ($A+$) factor traits, namely, active, energetic, enthusiastic.

**Field Conditions of Friendship.** The definite findings of the above (and other studies listed in Bonney's extensive bibliography) must not blind us to the fact that a good deal of the individual variance in social popularity rises from factors right outside personality, notably from capacity to reward others materially, from position in the social field, *e.g.*, social status (see last section), and from physical characteristics, *e.g.*, athletic prowess and good looks. Regarding the last named, Young and Cooper (54) found that no psychological characteristic distinguished "popular" from "isolated" children so significantly as personal appearance and that the face was more important in this complex than clothes or voice.

This third aspect of friendship—the field conditions and personality conditions that favor its appearance and disappearance—has been insufficiently investigated to permit any really established generalizations. General clinical evidence indicates that the friendships of schizothymes are fewer and more sensitively determined than those of cyclothymes. In general the dynamics of need satisfaction are likely, *mutatis mutandis*, to be similar to those discussed in marriage. Some inverse relationship between the strength and frequency of friendship relations on the one hand and family ties and cultural sublimations on the other can be expected. Changes in family and cultural investments will accordingly be correlated—generally inversely—with the rise and decline of friendship attachments.

**Personality and Leadership Activities.** It is psychologically appropriate to glance here at the relation of personality to group leadership. Common misconceptions to be discarded here are the assumptions that popularity and leadership are identical; that there is a necessary similarity between the leadership personality for all kinds of leadership situations; and that leadership inheres in personality rather than the group situation. Regarding the first, it is true that rating studies show considerable resemblance of the leader personality (in face-to-face situations) and the popular person, namely, in high character integration ($G$ factor), high emotional maturity ($C$ factor), and high surgency ($F$ factor), but they also show high dominance ($E$ factor) and intelligence ($B$ factor) which do not correlate markedly with mere popularity. Together, these four factors imply high correlation of leadership (5,13) with such trait elements as persistence, cooperativeness, emotional stability, kindness on principle, originality, aggressiveness, and self-confidence.

The relation to leadership found with the more accurately measurable factor of intelligence—namely, that the leader should be brighter but not too much brighter than the led—might also be found with some other traits if measurement could be accurately pursued. Regarding all traits it is evident that the correlations will vary with the type and field of leadership, *e.g.*, dominance is not likely to play a role in leadership in literature, while in "removed" (*i.e.*, not face-to-face) leadership, sociability may play a lower and intelligence a higher part than elsewhere.

Regarding the third point, Gibb (17) has brought out clearly, as have the historians (Turner, Beard, Wells), that the leader is chosen and created by the group need. Whoever can provide a solution to the group problem becomes, at least momentarily, a leader (*cf.* the "simple Breton pilot, Herve Riel," in Browning's well-known poem). Few specific problem solvers, however, have the remaining personality qualities necessary to give confidence in them as permanent problem solvers, particularly as to that common core of skills in managing men which is needed in all varieties of leadership. Fewer still, judging from history, have those personality qualities necessary to resist certain deteriorative effects which more permanent leadership produces in personality and which are illustrated most simply by the god-emperors of Rome. The factorial relationships between the syntality of groups, especially the dynamic syntality, and the personality of the leader, remain, however, in need of extensive experimental investigation, particularly since the effectiveness of leadership is only to be objectively judged by measures of the effectiveness of the syntality of the groups led.

## 6. ORGANIZED RELIGION

**Religion Defined as to Social Functions.** In spite of some isolated attempts (4,6) to organize a psychology of religion, psychologists of the last decade have fought shy of the issue in comparison with psychologists of the generation earlier, largely, one hopes, through an awareness that existing methods are incapable of grappling with the main problems. To any student of humanity it is obvious that some of the deepest and also the most socially important aspects of personality are tied up with the individual's religious sentiments, his philosophy of life, and his final adjustment or lack of adjustment to the cosmos.

What we actually have data upon is the individual's association with the church or with some social organ of a religious nature, rather than with aspects of this basic philosophy of life. In considering the relation of personality to religious membership, as in considering relations to each and all of the social organs reviewed in this chapter, we really have four distinct questions to ask *seriatim:* (*a*) A social psychology question: what is the nature and function of religious institutions in and for society? (*b*) A question of empirical observation only: what distinguishes the personalities of those who are religious from those who are not? (*c*) What distinguishes the personalities of those belonging to the cultural subpatterns of different religious sects? (*d*) To what extent do the above differences arise from the effect of religions on personality, and from the choice of religions being based on prior personality characteristics?

**Religious Interest and Personality.** As to the functions and dynamic relations of religion and the total culture pattern the reader must be referred to social psychology texts. The writer has summarized elsewhere (6) the evidence that religion serves for the individual the functions of (*a*) providing satisfaction for the basic infantile dependent attitudes to the parent image in the unconscious; (*b*) providing, as Freud expressed it, a group "obsessional neurosis" of agreed rituals for the discharge of guilt; (*c*) providing sublimations for repressed libido; (*d*) providing, through the symbol of deity (expressing the goal of the culture pattern), a real, if "irrational," connection between ethical striving and the maintenance and forward momentum of the culture pattern (see (6)).

Admission of the role of infantile dependence is not necessarily to be regarded as any disparagement of the religious adjustment. To admit powers greater than man in the universe is psychologically a more realistic adjustment than not to do so. And the individual who admits no emotional dependence on the universe or on society may be either a lunatic or a criminal. In fact, if we had space to examine the dynamics in more detail it could be shown that the integration indicated at (*d*) is in part dependent on the persistence of some emotional dependence of the kind indicated at (*a*).

Processes (*b*) and (*c*) have been discussed at length by Freud.  He questions, as others have done, whether the sublimations so conveniently provided by religion for the repressed drives whose repression it sanctions are always the most desirable sublimations.  The expression of repressed sex as sublimated homosexuality, *i.e.*, as general altruism, undoubtedly provides an indispensable cement for binding large societies; but the discharge of guilt in elaborate religious rituals may be less defensible.  Unwin, whose research (see (19), Chap. 8) showing, in a hundred societies, an appreciable correlation between extent of sexual suppression and degree of religious elaboration, as mentioned in the previous chapter, has provided the most valuable evidence yet available for assessing this dynamic relationship.  He shows also that sexual repression generates a phase of sociopolitical expansion and ultimately of cultural progress and rationalism.  (This is the "cultural-pressure" factor demonstrated elsewhere (Chapter 14).)  Thus, although religion and scientific rationalism may later part company and clash, they spring from the same stem.  For the qualities of social stability, impersonal devotion to a task and of regard for remote future satisfactions of society which are built up by religion are also the necessary social and ethical foundations for the growth of science.

**The Religious Personality.**  The traits distinguishing the religious personality in a social-transition period, such as the present, with its conflict of authoritarian religion and scientific empiricism may therefore be different from those in more settled periods.  As Thurstone's analysis of attitude interrelations has shown, the general factor of Radicalism-Conservatism becomes considerably involved in religious belief or nonbelief and, as Chapter 3 has shown, this factor is practically identical with the personality factor which Guilford called "Liking Thinking."  The wider roots of the *LT* factor are not yet understood.

In general, the personality traits distinguishing religious and nonreligious are far from explored and many of the data are misleading because they contrast traditionally, socially religious (church-belonging) individuals with others, rather than those with and without religious sentiments.  Carlson (see (7), Chap. 14) on an unselected sample of students found a significant correlation of $-0.19$ between traditional religious belief and score on an intelligence test.  He also found a correlation of $-0.42$ between such belief and a group of attitudes constituting a syndrome of "progressiveness" (Radicalism-Conservatism above) in social and political beliefs.  These findings are typical, and there is also some suggestion that religious interests (again mainly church interests) are higher in the more inhibited, the more aged, and those of female sex.  In temperament measurements clear associations are indicated between high perseveration, as associated with Mediterranean physical constitution, and religious interest (see (10), Chap. 4), though the meaning of this association is obscure. A central feature of the high perseveration and rigidity syndrome is resignation, emotionality, and a tendency to depression, and it is easily seen that this might conduce to a religious philosophy. Psychological research has so far, however, only provided a fragment of the data necessary to understanding dynamics, and it is a fragment that could easily lead to very distorted conclusions.

Some definite associations have been found between sex life and religious membership, in the Kinsey study (see (32), Chap 14). Incidence of premarital intercourse as well as frequency of marital intercourse were found consistently lower in each religious group for "devout" as contrasted with casual members of the church concerned. This is clearly in accord with the cultural aims of religion, but it might also arise selectively from more conforming individuals being lower in dominance and in that sexual activity which enters into the dominance syndrome.

**Personality and Variety of Religious Affiliation.** Even less is known about average personality structure in different religious groups. In America some groups, *e.g.*, Roman Catholics, consistently show a higher percentage of delinquents than others, such as, the Presbyterians, but insufficient evidence exists to parcel the probable influence of racial differences and social-status differences. When the association is proved it would remain to discover whether a religion is associated with high delinquency for the same reason that fire engines are associated with fire.

McDougall (27) made a good case for the theory that, apart from historical counter-influences, the choice of religion is tied up with temperamental aspects of personality and that the surgent (hysteroid) Mediterranean race tends to Catholicism while the desurgent but more dominant Nordic favors Protestantism. In this study the correlation of the racial patterns and the religious affiliations depended on showing that certain traits, *e.g.*, low suicide, low divorce, high impulsive bodily wounding, low drunkenness, and membership in the Catholic religion followed the geographical distribution of the Mediterranean physical race characteristics, rather than the national, historical, and cultural boundaries. This very suggestive lead by McDougall needs further definition through exact research.

A contribution to this further definition comes from the study of culture patterns through the syntalities of seventy nations, as already described (see (9), Chap. 12). Correlating the percentage of population belonging to a certain religion with a wide array of other measurable characteristics the following significant correlations were obtained for four major religions:

*Catholicism.* Low death rate from cancer, 0.58; high index of divorce restriction, 0.48; high frequency of typhoid fever deaths, 0.45; state supervision and licensing of prostitution, 0.44; high musical creativity, 0.43; high frequency of revolutions, 0.41; low legal marriage age limit, 0.38.

*Protestantism.* High sugar consumption per head, *i.e.*, luxury standards in relation to world at large, 0.72; high association with Nordic race areas, 0.68; low birth rate, 0.60; high cancer death rate, 0.60; low general death rate, 0.58; high caloric consumption per head, 0.57; high legal marriage age limit, 0.55; low percentage of population illiterate, 0.54; high creativity in science, 0.53; low degree of censorship of press, etc., 0.50.

*Mohammedanism.* Nonrestrictive divorce laws, 0.53; low death rate from alcoholism, 0.50; absence of legalized sterilization and similar laws, 0.50; high illiteracy, 0.40; belated onset of industrialization, 0.40; low sugar consumption per head, 0.40; low estimated general standard of living, 0.35; high fraction of men generally rated eminent found eminent in field of politics, 0.35.

*Buddhism.* High percentage of nation of Mongolian race, 0.52; low frequency of attainment of Nobel prizes (per million) in science, literature, etc., 0.50; low musical creativity, 0.50; tendency of workers to save from earnings, 0.50; low frequency of legalized sterilization, 0.50; low frequency of telephones, 0.40; low percentage of Nordic race, 0.39; high degree of censorship of newspapers, etc., 0.30.

There are many other *significant* correlations which space does not permit; but the only large correlations omitted are those showing inverse correlations between the religions, *e.g.*, the percentage of Catholics in a country correlates −0.55 (for seventy nations) with percentage of Protestants, as one might expect from their being alternatives. Naturally, since the above patterns are established in international statistics that were *available* rather than those which the experimenter would ideally *choose*, the reader is left with a task of interpretation. For example, from the picture of Protestantism in terms of measured statistics, showing high scientific creativity, low birth and death rates, high caloric consumption, and high cancer death rate, etc., the reader needs to do much to reconstruct the causal connections and remaining culture-pattern items which constitute what this pattern *means* in terms of social life values and molding of the individual personality. But it is better to have uncertainties about interpretation than about fact, and the interpretations of culture patterns in terms of ideal constructs come close to being based on phantasy.

Studies of the characteristic associations of religious patterns within cultures need to be supplemented by investigations on individuals. Of the very few studies here the research on some social attitudes by Sappenfield (35a,35b) is most helpful. Using measures of attitudes to foreigners (Chinese, Germans), to punishment of criminals, to communism, to the constitution of the United States, and to war, he found significant (1 per cent level) differences in that Catholics and persons of Jewish religion were less favorable to war than Protestants, while the "Jewish group was more favorable toward communism, less favorable toward the Germans, than were either the Catholics or the Protestants." The above differences are partly accounted for by differences of race and intelligence as well as the religious pattern itself, and at present, in the absence of factorial results, the contribution of the various distinct institutions here cannot be decided.

## 7. POLITICAL PARTY AND NATION

**Personalities with Strong Political Interest.** Considering the same question for political parties as for religious faiths we again find most pieces of the jigsaw puzzle missing. As to what differentiates personalities with political affiliations from those with weak political interests, we have only evidence resting largely on questionnaires and self-ratings. Thus Whisler (52) found a factor in questionnaire material in which high interest in politics went with preference for working with people (rather than things), awareness of differences of interest from those of people considered friends, a dislike of seeing codes of behavior violated, and a disinclination for "philosophical" thought. With Strong's interest test a factor is found tying interest in occupations of salesman, personnel worker, school superintendent, with interest in politics, welfare work, general sociability, and travel (see (42)). From a factorial survey (see (5), Chap. 4) it is evident that political interest is not to be accounted for by less than three factors and the evidence suggests the personality factors of cyclothymia $(A+)$, surgency $(F+)$, and dominance $(E+)$ as being most important.

**Personality and Particular Political Viewpoint.** Regarding political parties, it is perhaps necessary to point out that popular left- or right-wing talk overlooks the fact that these political differences also involve and confuse several other dimensions than that of Radicalism-Conservatism. Radicalism-Conservatism is nevertheless the most important of the dimensions found in sociopolitical attitudes, though it would be a mistake to suppose that what is here demonstrated and labeled is logically the same as Progressive-Unprogressive or even exactly the same as political radicalism-conservatism. The findings on the character of this dimension, for many researches, summarized by the writer elsewhere (see (5), Chap. 4), show the radical as more politically left, in favor of easier divorce, birth control, belief in evolution, international control of national soverignty, eugenics, equality of sexes, and departure from traditional church beliefs. He tends to be more intelligent and well informed, slower in speed of decision, more introvert, less athletic and more scientific in interests, and less frequently from small towns (see p. 87). This picture is taken at twenty years of age, leaving doubt as to how the constellation alters with years. It has been said that if a man is not a communist at twenty he has no heart, but that if he is still a communist at forty he has no head!

When we ask whether the personality creates the political attitudes found associated with it, or vice versa, there can be little doubt in answering that the direction of causation lies mostly in personality determining political views, and, second, in some common mold, *e.g.*, social status or family, determining both, as Newcomb has shown (32). Nevertheless, like any other canalized outlet for a drive, the political sentiments, by the further experience of conflicts and of rewards which they bring, can affect the total personality. These relationships have been very adequately investigated by the social psychologist just mentioned (32) who showed the great power of family loyalties over later pressures and who illuminated the nature of the personality stresses in the impact of different political groups. Personality relationships and developments have also been shown by Diamond (12) in connection with political sentiments. He observed shifts in "extraversion" —probably, as tested, a mixture of dominance, surgency, and cyclothymia— and found radicals less stable than the average. But those who were active in the Communist party shifted (every one of 140 subjects) considerably in the "extravert" direction during their period of enthusiasm for this minority viewpoint.

**Personality and the National Culture Pattern.** In view of the very obvious importance of the national culture pattern in shaping personality it is at first surprising that no quantitative, scientific results exist to show what the patterns are and what the magnitude of their influence is compared with that of religion, social class, etc.

A moment's reflection on the fact that few tests are internationally standardized and few psychologists ready to gather subjects in many countries, even if they were available, explains this dearth. In the Middle Ages and even later it is easy to see that common religion or common class meant more, in terms of personality resemblance, than common country. A Frenchman and a German of the same social class (*e.g.*, Voltaire and Frederick the Great, of the "royal court" class) shared more values than they did with their countrymen of a different class or religion. But the rise of truly organized nationalism since the French Revolution has brought greater emphasis on and integration of natio-racial culture patterns, and it may be that the self-containedness of personality patterns developed by national systems of education are now greater than those produced by any other group difference.

Between such similar countries as Britain, America, and Australia the differences are too slight to admit of ready recognitions of nationals by behavior. The British may complain in regard to Hollywood movies of an American accent or an excessive surgency which precludes thoughtful dialogue: the American may be aware, conversely, of a slowness of action and a casualness of manner. But between, say, an American, a German, an Arab, a

Russian, and a Burmese there are differences of value regarding personal freedom, morals, social adjustment, and family organization which reach down into the general dynamics of personality, the nature of the ego, and the roots of the superego.

Whereas individual similarities of intelligence, constitutional temperament, etc., may elsewhere contribute to final similarities of individual personality, where a strong cultural impress of this kind is at work upon such individual constitutions the result may be an even greater divergence than between individuals of no constitutional similarity. The more intelligent the individual, the quicker he learns the national cultural values. Newcomb, (32) for example, in comparing the attitudes of students in a conservative college with those in a more radical institution found that the better-informed (and perhaps the more intelligent) were more conservative in the former and more radical in the latter. Indeed, we may on general principles expect that positive qualities of intelligence and stability or potential power of personality integration will favor more effective adoption of the refinements of national (or any other) culture patterns and, accordingly, clearer manifestation of the greater divergence presented by their peculiarities.

At present we have to leave this field in the position that though no adequate studies exist showing the impress of the pattern on individual personalities, some data can already be presented defining factorially the national syntality patterns to which individual personalities are exposed. The diagrams below show the profiles of nine widely sampled nations with respect to their endowments in the six syntality factors mentioned in the previous chapter. (The values in the diagrams are set out in the footnote below.[2]) The estimates are made by unweighted addition of the highest variables in each factor and apply to the century ending in the Second World War. It will be noticed that certain nations, *e.g.*, Britain, United States, Australia, show a distinct family resemblance relative to the general range of

[2] Table of national endowments in defined cultural dimensions.

| | 1 | 2 | 3 | 4 | 7 | 12 |
|---|---|---|---|---|---|---|
| United States.......... | 1.675 | 2.644 | 2.514 | −0.322 | 1.853 | −0.005 |
| United Kingdom........ | −0.817 | 5.760 | 1.737 | −0.286 | 1.352 | −0.956 |
| Australia............. | 0.143 | −0.129 | 2.114 | −0.270 | 1.850 | −0.102 |
| China................ | 4.487 | −0.560 | −1.169 | −1.640 | −1.342 | −1.655 |
| India................ | 3.278 | −0.425 | −1.233 | −1.629 | −0.539 | −1.445 |
| Liberia.............. | −0.321 | −0.519 | −0.999 | 1.333 | 1.041 | −0.502 |
| U.S.S.R.............. | 4.835 | 0.238 | 1.092 | 0.638 | −0.591 | 1.375 |
| Argent............... | −0.328 | 0.052 | 0.839 | 0.438 | 1.175 | 2.177 |
| Arabia............... | −0.185 | −0.545 | −1.310 | −0.264 | 0.054 | −0.050 |

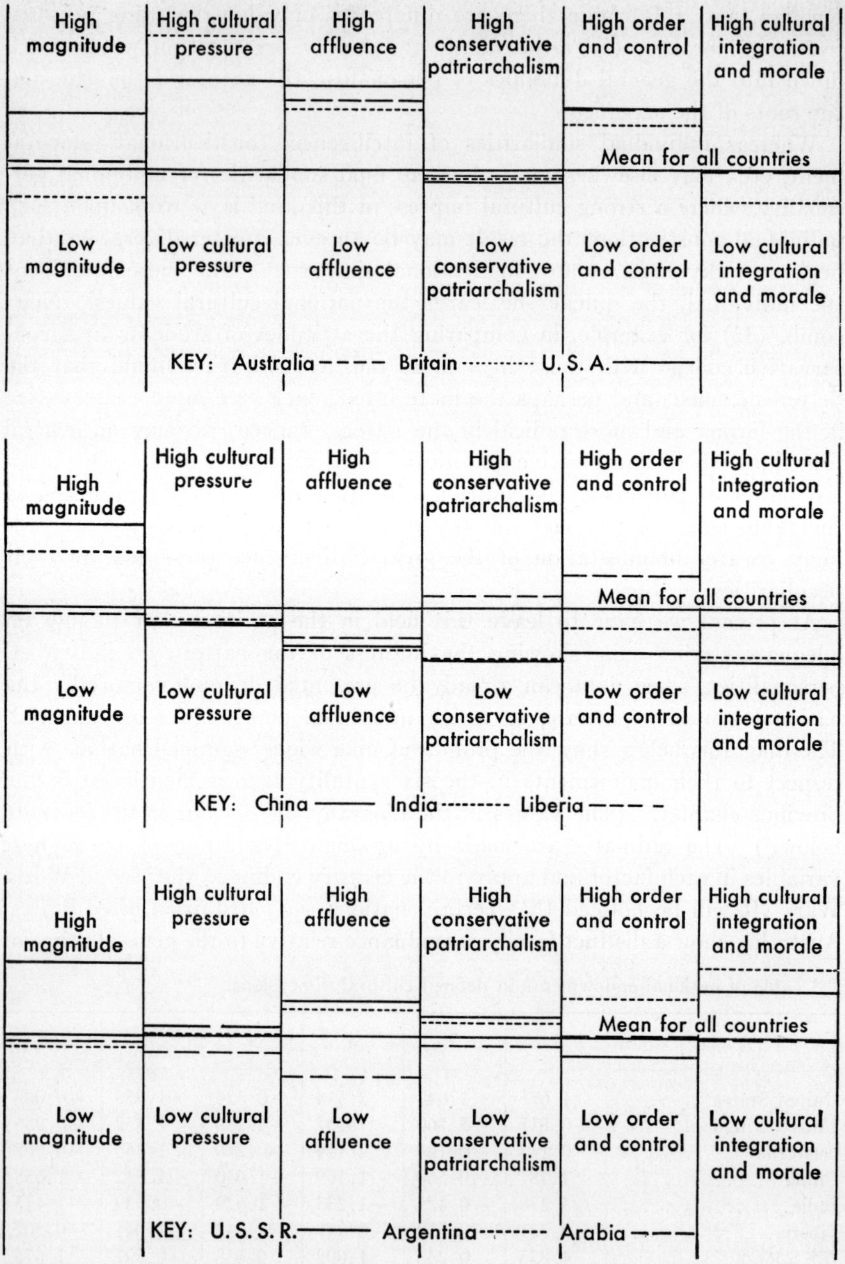

DIAGRAM 44. Profiles of the syntality patterns of nine nations showing three types of culture pattern (I, II, and III).

national profiles. Such resemblances, marking the belonging of groups of nations to a single broader culture pattern, can be shown by correlation of profiles to exist with respect to about eight broad groupings (9a), as Toynbee has pointed out independently on historical grounds. We should expect correspondingly—though no direct data yet exist—that some eight broad patterns of personality pattern, particularly as to sentiments and attitudes structures, would be found among the population of the world.

## 8. GENERAL RELATIONS OF INSTITUTIONAL TO PERSONAL PATTERNS

**Three Modes of Relation of Personality Pattern to Society.** There remain now for discussion only certain general issues in the relation of personality to culture pattern. First, the above examples will have brought out that society produces not only the personality patterns (ideal forms) it intends to produce, but also others, as inevitable by-products. For example, the organized groups or institutions of school, religion, nation, etc., produce their types, but so also do groups according to sex, age, social status, social region, etc., which are, as it were, culturally fortuitous and due to psychological laws acting on unintended, functionless groupings.

Again, as we have seen, the deliberate creation of personality roles by the necessities of occupational training or the approved cultural pattern of the schools also produce, by psychological (mainly compensatory) laws, the rise of secondary personality roles not primarily foreseen or desired. Thus it is questionable whether college faculties foresaw or desired the social eminence of college football and its effect on the personality roles of the student. Another topical instance is the enshrinement by American mental hygienists in the last generation of the "extravert" as the desired, adjusted personality type, regardless of the fact that much that characterizes or is valued by our culture, *e.g.*, the writing, the mechanical invention, is the expression of introverts who did not dissipate their energies socially. (Compare the output of diaries, philosophical thought, novels, and mechanical invention of introvert, repressive New England of the nineteenth century with that of more extraverted cultural climes.)

One can thus recognize, in preliminary study, three types of personality roles related to the culture pattern: (*a*) the "directly impressed" pattern of the "ideal" promoted by an institution or the whole pattern; (*b*) the "situational" or "ecological" pattern due to living in a particular location or group not intended, by education or propaganda, as a pattern; (*c*) the "psychologically necessary" pattern created by psychological laws as an immediate by-product of the patterns created by the culture in (*a*) and (*b*). The "psychologically necessary" pattern, of (*c*) arises mainly from the need to satisfy drives not given expression by the culture. In some fields, *e.g.*, recreation, after these by-product patterns have enforced themselves as modes of expression, they in turn become institutionalized and part of the culture pattern. In other fields, notably in the drives of sex (in the adolescent) and pugnacity, the culture pattern says only how they shall *not* be expressed. With such drives, especially if the individual is induced also to practice true repression, effective contact between the conscious ego and drive is lost and it is free to reappear in a bewildering variety of rank or perverted forms.

**Criteria of Origin of Patterns.** When methods of determining more exactly the relation of personality forms to culture pattern have been developed, it is possible that additional or intermediate forms to the above three types of relation will be revealed. One useful method of investigation has been developed by Schanck (36), who points out that when a mode of behavior is institutionally determined (our (*a*) type) it tends to follow a *J*-shaped distribution curve, *i.e.*, the majority of people approach the institutional ideal and none exceed it, whereas other patterns—presumably our patterns (*b*) and (*c*) above—follow the usual Gaussian distribution as for biological measures. Probably (*c*) could be distinguished from (*b*) in part by the greater standard deviation of such distributions and by sympathetic variation with the (*a*) and (*b*) patterns with which they are organically connected.

In his study of Elm Hollow (36), Schanck found that on many issues there was for each person both a public and a private attitude, the former—partly owing to "pluralistic ignorance" whereby none knew what his fellows privately thought—following the institutionalized *J*-curve distribution and the latter a normal distribution. It may be that "directly impressed" patterns, because they represent a powerfully motivated aspiration level, will generally be differentiable, by a *J*-curve, and by such features as greater conflict with the rest of the personality, greater ego involvement, etc., from patterns due to ecological effects or personal psychological needs. But these are matters for future research.

**Social Patterns Expressed in Personality Structure and Mode of Perception.** It has been sufficiently illustrated in this and the three preceding chapters that different social institutions are associated, by selection effects or by the pattern of behavior they reward, with differential cognitive, temperamental, or dynamic structure characteristics in personality.

What remains to be stressed is that these connote differences also in the meaning of perceptions, as experienced by the individuals concerned, and that some of the more obvious social and individual differences arise in the area of perception.

It is a truism, dating from the earliest days of psychology and beyond, that all aspects of personality (not merely those derived from social conditioning) influence perception and can be inferred from perception. A person accustomed to seeing physical objects in a certain perspective may not recognize them from another perspective or may wrongly identify other objects which present a similar perspective. This intrusion of personal experience is well demonstrated by the optical illusions studied by German psychologists in the late nineteenth century and by Ames and Cantril more recently, as well as by the inventions of generations of conjurors. Herbart's concept of "apperception," *i.e.*, of that which the person brings to the sense impressions to give them meaning, remains a useful reminder of the substantial role of "additions" to any sense data in the act of perception.

As the discussion of Misperception tests and Ego-defense Dynamism tests in Chapter 4 illustrates, it is the *dynamic* state of the perceiver which has the greatest effect on perception. The depressed person is more likely to feel that people neglect or slight him, the terrified person sees hostility where none exists, the poor person, as Bruner and Postman show, is more likely to see coins as larger than they are, while it is well known that the hallucinations of the insane operate mainly as wish fulfillments.

Groups of personalities with a common institutional purpose are very prone to perceiving events in terms of their interests. The behavior which they see as "license" in other countries they see as "freedom" in their own, while a gallant war of independence on one side is a dastardly revolution on the other. Cognitive equipment, however, also plays its part, and groups of similar dynamic make-up may see things very differently because each has been subjected for years to a different selective process in the news which reaches it.

In general to say that an individual has a certain personality structure is the same as saying that he sees things in such and such a way, while to say that "He came to see the matter differently" is equivalent to "His personality structure underwent some modification." But the problem of systematically relating meaning to personality is nevertheless still little formulated. However, it is clear that *the pattern of loadings of source traits for a given performance situation constitutes the psychological meaning of that situation.* For example, if a situation has a high loading[1] in intelligence, a low loading in dominance, and a high loading in the fear drive, we should describe it as a complex and terrifying situation (with no appeal to dominance). This, of course, is the *common* meaning of that situation, if the loadings are from $R$ technique and the *individual* meaning is from $P$ technique. The difference of one person's perception of a situation from that of another is represented, therefore, in terms of meaning, as the differences of their corresponding source traits, each weighted by the situational index.

---

[1] For simplicity we have spoken of loadings or situational indices, but the mean involvement of a drive in a situation represents a measure of mean strength to be obtained after loadings have been calculated and used as weights.

For example, if reaction to a certain situation is estimated by a specification equation in which the only large loading is for intelligence, the only individuals for whom it will have a substantially different meaning will be those differing appreciably in intelligence.

### 9. PERSONALITY RELATED TO SOCIAL "COMPLEXITY," "INTEGRATION," AND "ORGANIZATION"

**Confusion of Concepts in This Area.** In discussions above on cultural anthropology in relation to social psychology, reference has been made to the effects on personality of having to play a multiplicity of cultural roles and to notions of cultural disorganization and complexity. Much has been written by cultural anthropologists apparently on the implicit assumption that "complexity" and "disorganization" of culture are somehow simply related to complexity and disorganization of the individual personalities in the culture concerned. Thus Blumer (see (12), Chap. 14) for example, says that social disorganization is an extension of individual disorganization, while in Section 2 above we have met the view of Devereux that schizophrenia develops through an excess of culture elements and in Section 5 the argument of Faris that social disorganization is largely responsible for delinquency and mental disorder.

Is complexity different from disorganization and what does each mean? It has been said that the schizophrenic is more sensitive than most to the fact that what you have to do in one part of a culture cannot be "logically" inferred from what you do in another. It is questionable whether this use of "logically" has any meaning and it is certain that "logical cohesion" is not a touchstone for testing the soundness of organization of societies. It may seem strange that our friend Mr. Smith, the grocer, gives us apples over his garden wall one day as a friend and charges us for apples the next day in his store, or that Professor Jones treats us very authoritatively in mathematics class but refuses to advise us with equally confident authority on marital affairs, or that society regards a man with horror for murder yet decorates him for killing in war. But only the psychologically deficient, *e.g.*, the paranoid, would argue that what is incomprehensible is necessarily illogical. The incomprehensibility of society is no different from the incomprehensibility of nature (we pour one liquid on a fire and it puts it out, we pour on another and it increases the conflagration), and it is perhaps not surprising that the schizothyme Voltaire, who somewhat overdrew social irrationality in *Candide* also protested "in the name of reason" against the Madrid earthquake!

**Integration Distinguished from Complexity.** The true scientific substitute for "logicality" is *integration*, defined analogously to its definition in the individual, *i.e.*, as the extent to which society achieves its various satisfactions (goals) without mutual interference. Our argument will be that poor integration of society affects primarily the wealth and vitality of society, and the individual personality only through these. What presents immediate difficulties for the individual personality is complexity, and by complexity we mean (*a*) having to make constant fine discriminations according to situation (as with the grocer above), (*b*) having to accept postponed satisfactions and adopt long-circuited behavior, (*c*) having to adopt many different roles. There is not space to discuss whether (*c*) can be resolved wholly into (*a*) or whether it involves dynamic ability to maintain mental sets as well as special ego developments additional to (*a*), so it is best listed separately. The evidence yet available suggests that it is (*a*) and (*c*), and perhaps (*b*) also, that are responsible for the schizophrenia-producing quality of a culture.

**The Further Concept of Cultural Disorganization.** Granted that there are at least indications that the "complexity" of a culture, as defined, tends to produce schizophrenia and perhaps other related personality disorders, what is the role and meaning of cultural "disorganization"? The demands made upon the individual by "disorganization" as defined by Faris are in part demands of *complexity* and in part those of trying to adjust to a culture which simply does not remain consistently the same from day to day. This fluctuation and inconsistency does not primarily present problems of discrimination in attaining an agreed goal under different conditions. Rather must it be recognized as an alteration in the very goals and values of living. The child who is rewarded for honesty today is punished for it tomorrow, with no consistency of cues. Such situations in an area of conflicting culture patterns, *e.g.*, a Chicago slum, are essentially the same as those in a unitary culture pattern in a state of rapid change or deterioration, *e.g.*, the rapid change from rural to urban conditions, with their profound influence on the role of the family (previous chapter), or, on a smaller scale, the introduction of commercial credit systems, with their greater demand on foresight, to people used to dealing in cash.

**Effects of Cultural Disorganization.** The term cultural disorganization would have clear meaning if restricted to this element in the total situation described by Faris. As we have seen, cultural disorganization, especially in discussing the sixth principle of community and personality interaction (page 396), if acting upon the young, seems to have its most powerful effect upon character integration and the formation of the superego. For shorter periods and upon personalities already formed the effects may be more temporary—a reaction to the situation rather than an irreversible change of personality. Data are beginning to fit together already regarding the effects of social disorganization on adults, notably with regard to economic depressions to social catastrophe of the kind that overtakes citizens thrown into concentration camps, and in regard to war, and cultural decline.

Economic depressions begin with widespread anxiety reactions, shown tangibly, for example, in a sharp increase of incidence of stomach ulcers. There follows a lowering of aspiration level (security replaces the goals of ambition), a loss of respect for superiors, authority, and patriotism, an increase in drunkenness, and a loss of solidarity among the workers, with mutual hostility and individualism of the "sauve qui peut" variety. Rundquist and Sletto (see (46), Chap. 14), in their extensive (3,000 cases) attitude studies among unemployed of the depression of 1929, found that discontent with the socioeconomic system, poor morale, and general maladjustment distinguished unemployed (of all ranks and previous occupations) from the employed. The difference was less in those living at home, and for women, who did not seem to canalize their discontent into political attitudes. Though the effects on adults are less marked than in the impact of sociofamilial disorganization upon children, their central character—a decline of morale and superego vitality—is the same. Along with the decline of loyalty to authority and of solidarity with fellow sufferers one can detect also many symptoms of a general personality regression, e.g., a lowering of aspiration and of personal behavior standards, a turning back to the family, and a narcistic withdrawal into the self.

Allport, Bruner, and Jandorf (2) studied individuals uprooted by the Nazi revolution, obtaining estimates of their personalities both before the catastrophe and some years afterwards. Their outstanding conclusion was that the main outlines of personality were not altered though, at the time, aggression was stimulated, followed by resignation, regression (including increased conformity), and lowered aspiration. Such studies remind one (see Chapter 9) that normally the individual obtains much satisfaction of the self-assertive erg and therefore much of his self-respect through belonging to a group. If the group suffers disorganization he loses much of this satisfaction, especially if he has been of any social status above the lowest. Bettelheim (4a) observes the attempts of men when first removed to concentration camps to grasp at anything "which might prove helpful in supporting their badly shaken self-esteem," but adds that "members of the lower class derived a certain satisfaction from the absence of differences among the prisoners." He notes again the strong tendency to regression to infantile levels shown in loss of standards in morals, self-respect, and interests. There is also a tendency to preserve the prison and the preprison personalities as distinct concepts, resenting and repressing associations between the two.

As to the effect of the social disorganization constituted by the unprecedented demands of war upon the personality few exact data exist. In the noncombatants, who suffer the least disorganization, the increased sense of in-group solidarity seems actually to produce a psychological simplification, and some observers point to temporary declines of rates of neurosis and psychosis. Similarly, only rough generalizations can be made about the effect of cultural decline and disintegration. Since a man's self-respect is tied up with that of the group to which he belongs, it is not surprising that some observations suggest that the break-up of the over-all society is first accompanied by the turning of individuals to various minority in-groups and increased shaping of their personalities on the minority patterns. Destructions of groups could thus lead to a whole series of escapes to different personality identifications.

The decline of a whole culture with which the individual is inescapably identified may well prove to be associated with some degree of maladjustment, depression, and demoralization of the participating personalities. Available accounts suggest that this was true equally of the cultured Roman of the fourth century A.D. and of the American Indian at the time of the Ghost Dance. On the other hand, it is possible that some cultures pass into disorganization and perdition in high spirits.

## 10. SUMMARY

1. Although practically nothing is statistically proved concerning the relation of most personality factors to occupation there exists systematic information about intelligence. Significant differences in mean intelligence level exist with respect to most occupations. However, the overlap among occupations with respect to intelligence is considerable, and it is not known whether this is due to the large element of chance in job selection or to the compensatory action of other personality factors in determining efficiency level.

2. Ecological research shows definite relationships of personality to area of upbringing, with regard to interests and attitudes and the incidence of mental defect, genius, delinquency, and mental disorder. The two last are highest in zones of disorganization and of high mobility and are probably consequences, not causes.

3. As among different cities a pattern of "general goodness" of civic life can be demonstrated to affect simultaneously freedom from crime and disease, level of education, circulation of libraries, etc. Presumably this whole pattern impresses itself in varying depth on different citizens, creating ecological differences.

4. The school operates on personality through the teacher, the world of books, and the children, each of which can be demonstrated to have some effect, the first affecting skills and information most, and the last, personality. Books aim to create a certain personality type and to a measurable extent succeed in doing so.

5. The action of the friendship group in school is a limited version of the action of the "gang." The latter, based on the congeniality of coevals,

largely serves the function of defending the immature against culture pressure, but also of enabling the individual to grow out of the family into the responsibilities of the adult world.

6. Friendships influence attitudes and personality traits appreciably and are founded primarily on an initial degree of similarity in personality and interests. Popularity and leadership are functions of the group situation but show some consistent dependence on personality factors.

7. Play, *i.e.*, recreation in the widest sense, has three major functions in personality formation. Insufficient play may be associated with deficient spontaneity and creativity, but excessive play, involving phantasy, may be a symptom of inability to adjust to the cultural load.

8. Certain personality traits distinguish the religious from the irreligious, as well as the followers of different religious sects. The same is true of political interests. The causal direction is still obscure, though in some traits it is fairly certain that the temperament and ability traits determine the religious or political affiliation. Nevertheless, long exposure to a religious or political loyalty obviously affects more than attitudes; and the pattern of personality affected can perhaps best be inferred at present from the known cultural association pattern of the religion concerned.

9. The ways in which personality is shaped by the culture pattern can be reduced to three: (*a*) "direct impress" of part or whole of the culture pattern by more or less deliberate communication; (*b*) "situational effects" due to the individual's position in the culture; and (*c*) "psychological necessity" in which secondary patterns arise by psychological laws of individual need resulting from the demands of the patterns more directly impressed on personality. They show themselves equally in modes of behavior and modes of perception (apperception). A methodology is developing whereby these sources of personality patterns can be distinguished.

10. Three general qualities or dimensions of all culture patterns can be defined, namely, "complexity-simplicity," "integration-disintegration," and "organization-disorganization," and the first and last of these can already be shown to have effects on personality. Complexity may be related to the incidence of schizophrenia, while disorganization produces poor individual morale and antisocial behavior.

### QUESTIONS AND EXERCISES

1. Enumerate instances of known association of personality (including intelligence) test scores and occupation. Discuss the basis and utility of various classifications of occupations.

2. Contrast the personality associates of (*a*) rural areas, (*b*) suburban regions, and (*c*) the central slum regions of large cities. Suggest which associations are largely due to environmental influence and which to selection.

3. Mention two or more studies showing the personality correlates of high geographical and social mobility and discuss causes for these associations.

4. Discuss the manner and extent to which the school achieves its aim of forming personality and note ways in which school and home influences conflict with and aid each other.

5. Give evidence for what you consider the main motives in gang formation. In the light of this motivation discuss the possibilities and limitations of treating the gang as an educational influence.

6. Describe the personality characteristics of (a) a friend, (b) a popular person, and (c) a leader, in relation also to the extent to which they are determined by other personalities and the situation.

7. Define the essential psychological functions of recreation and indicate what is known about the relation of specific choices of recreation (hobbies) to personality.

8. What types of personality show strong (a) religious, and (b) political affiliations?

9. Describe some evidence on the methodological possibilities of defining national culture patterns, giving illustrations. What fraction of interpersonal variation do you think is ascribable to this source?

10. Define cultural complexity and cultural disorganization. Assemble what evidence you can, either observational or statistical, to determine the nature of their effects on personality.

## BIBLIOGRAPHY

1. ADLER, A.: Influence of Social Level on Psychiatric Symptomatology of Childhood Difficulties, *Proc. 12th Instit. of Child Res. Clin., Woods Schools*, Duke University, Woods Schools, Langerhorn, Pa., 1945.

2. ALLPORT, G. W., J. BRUNER, and E. M. JANDORF: Personality under Social Catastrophe, *Character & Pers.*, 10: 1–22, 1941.

3. ANDERSON, H. H.: *Dominance and Social Interest in Behavior of Kindergarten Children*, The Journal Press, Provincetown, Mass., 1939.

4. BACKHOUSE, W. H.: *Religion and Adolescent Character*, Lutterworth Press, London, 1947.

4a. BETTELHEIM, B.: Individual and Mass Behavior in Extreme Situations. *J. abnorm. soc. Psychol.*, 38: 417–452, 1943.

5. BONNEY, M. E.: Personality Traits of Socially Successful and Socially Unsuccessful Children, *J. educ. Psychol.*, 34: 449–472, 1943.

6. CATTELL, R. B.: *Psychology and the Religious Quest*, Thomas Nelson & Sons, New York, 1938.

7. CATTELL, R. B.: Occupational Levels of Intelligence and the Standardization of an Adult Intelligence Test, *Brit. J. Psychol.*, 25: 1–28, 1934.

8. CATTELL, R. B.: The Cultural Functions of Social Stratification: II. Regarding Individual and Group Dynamics, *J. soc. Psychol.*, 21: 25–55, 1945.

9. CATTELL, R. B.: Friends and Enemies: A Psychological Study of Character and Temperament, *Character & Pers.*, 3: 54–63, 1934.

9a. CATTELL, R. B.: The Principle Culture Patterns Discoverable in the Syntal Dimensions of Existing Nations (In Press: *J. soc. Psychol.*)

10. CHILD, J. L., E. H. POTTER, and E. M. LEVINE: Children's Text Books and Personality Development, *Psychol. Monogr.*, 60 (No. 3): 1946.

11. DAMBACK, K.: Typologische Beobachtungen in Schulneulingen, *Z. padag. Psychol.*, 38: 81–87, 1937.

12. DIAMOND, S.: A Study of the Influence of Political Radicalism on Personality Development, *Arch. Psychol.* (No. 203): 1936.

13. DRAKE, R. M.: A Study of Leadership, *Character & Pers.*, 12: 285–289, 1944.

14. DUVALL, E.: Child-Parent Social Distance, *Sociol. Soc. Rev.*, 21: 458–463, 1937.

15. FARIS, R. E. L.: Ecological Factors in Human Behavior, in Hunt, J. McV., *Personality and Behavior Disorders*, Ronald Press, New York, 1944.

16. FREUD, S.: *Group Psychology and the Ego*, International Psychoanalytic Press, London, 1922.

16a. FRYER, D.: Occupational Intelligence Standards, *Sch. & Soc.*, 16: 273–285, 1922.

17. GIBB, C. A.: The Principal Traits of Leadership, *J. abnorm. soc. Psychol.*, 42: 267–284, 1947.

18. GRAVES, ROBERT, and A. HODGE: *The Long Week End*, The Macmillan Company, New York, 1941.

19. HUNTINGTON, E.: *Mainsprings of Civilization*, John Wiley & Sons, Inc., New York, 1945.

20. HYMAN, H. H.: The Psychology of Status, *Arch. Psychol.*, N.Y., No. 269, 1942.

21. JACK, L. M.: An Experimental Study of Ascendance Behavior in Pre-school Children, *Univ. Ia., Stud. Child Welf.*, 9 (No. 3): 1934.

22. JAMESON, A. T.: Factors Contributing to the Delinquency of Girls, *J. Juv. Res.*, 22: 25–32, 1938.

23. JOHNSON, D. M.: Applications of the Standard-score I.Q. to Social Statistics, *J. soc. Psychol.*, 27: 217–227, 1948.

24. KARDINER, A.: *The Individual and His Society*, University of California Press, Berkeley, 1939.

25. KLEITMAN, N.: The Effects of Motion Pictures on Body Temperature, *Science*, 101: 507–508, 1945.

26. KUDER, G. F.: *Preference Record*, Science Res. Assn., Chicago, Illinois, rev. ed., 1942.

27. McDOUGALL, W.: *National Welfare and National Decay*, Methuen & Co. Ltd., London, 1921.

28. MERTON, R. K.: Bureaucratic Structure and Personality, *Social Forces*, 18: 560–568, 1940.

29. MORENO, J. L.: *Who Shall Survive?*, Nerve and Mental Disease Publishing Co., Washington, D. C., 1934.

30. MURPHY, G.: *Personality*. Harper & Brothers, New York, 1947.

31. LUNDBERG, G. A., M. KOMAROVSKY, and M. A. McINERY: *Leisure, a Suburban Study*, Columbia University Press, New York, 1933.

32. NEWCOMB, T.: *Personality and Social Change*, The Dryden Press, Inc., New York, 1943.

33. PAGE, M. L.: The Modification of Ascendant Behavior in Pre-school Children, *Univ. Ia. Stud. Child Welf.*, 12: (No. 3) 1936.

34. PINTNER, R., G. TORLANO, and H. FRIEDMAN: Personality and Attitudinal Similarity among Classroom Friends, *J. appl. Psychol.*, 21: 48–65, 1937.

35. RICHARDSON, H. M.: Community of Values as a Factor in Friendships of College and Adult Women, *J. soc. Psychol.*, 11: 303–312, 1940.

35a. SAPPENFIELD, B. R.: The Attitudes and Attitude Estimates of Catholic, Protestant and Jewish Students, *J. soc. Psychol.*, 16: 173–197, 1942.

35b. SAPPENFIELD, B. R.: The Responses of Catholic, Protestant and Jewish Students to the Menace Check List, *J. soc. Psychol.*, 20: 295–299, 1944.

36. SCHANCK, R. L.: A Study of a Community, Its Groups and Institutions Conceived of as Behavior of Individuals. *Psychol. Monogr.*, 43: (No. 195), 1–133, 1932.

37. SHAW, C. R., and H. D. McKAY: *Report on the Causes of Crime*, National Commission of Law Observance and Enforcement, Washington, 1931.

38. SHERIF, M., and H. CANTRIL: *The Psychology of Ego-Involvement*, John Wiley & Sons, Inc., New York, 1947.

39. SOROKIN, P.: *Society, Culture, and Personality*, Harper & Brothers, New York, 1947.

40. STAGNER, R.: Fascist Attitudes; Their Determining Conditions, *J. soc. Psychol.*, 7: 438–454, 1936.
41. STOTT, L. H.: Personality Development in Farm, Smalltown and City Children, *Res. Bull. Nebr. Agric. Exp. Sta.*, 36 (No. 114): 1939.
42. STRONG, E. K.: *Vocational Interests of Men and Women*, Stanford University Press, Stanford University, 1943.
43. SUPER, D. E.: *Avocational Interest Patterns: A Study in the Psychology of Avocations*, Stanford University Press, Stanford University, 1940.
44. THORNDIKE, E. L.: *Your City*, Harcourt, Brace & Company, New York, 1939.
44a. THORNDIKE, E. L.: The Origin of Superior Men, *Sci. Mon.*, 56: 424–433, 1943.
45. THORNDIKE, E. L.: *The Psychology of Wants, Interests, Attitudes*, Appleton-Century-Crofts, Inc., New York, 1935.
46. THORNDIKE, R. L., and G. H. GALLUP: Verbal Intelligence of the American Adult, *J. genet. Psychol.*, 30: 75–85, 1944.
47. THRASHER, F. M.: *The Gang*, University of Chicago Press, Chicago, 1927.
48. ULTON, P.: A Study of Parent-Child Relationships, *Center Res. Child Develpm. Monogr.*, 1 (No. 4): 1936.
49. UNWIN, J. D.: *Hopousia; or the Sexual and Economic Foundations of a New Society*, George Allen & Unwin, Ltd., London, 1940.
50. UNWIN, J. D.: *Sex and Culture*, Oxford University Press, New York, 1934.
51. WALLACE, J. K.: Women's use of leisure, *J. higher Educ.*, 14: 301–306, 1943.
52. WHISLER, L. D.: A Multiple-factor Analysis of Generalized Attitudes, *J. soc. Psychol.*, 5: 283–297, 1934.
53. WREN, H. A.: Vocational Aspiration Levels of Adults, *Teach. Coll. Contr. Educ.* (No. 855): vi and 150, 1942.
54. YOUNG, L. L., and D. H. COOPER: Some Factors Associated with Popularity, *J. educ. Psychol.*, 35: 513–535, 1944.

# CHAPTER 16

## THE ABNORMAL AND UNADAPTED PERSONALITY:
## I. EVIDENCE FROM THE SCHOOL MISFIT, THE DELINQUENT, AND THE CRIMINAL

1. Abnormality: Its Meaning and Role in Personality Study
2. Delinquency and Personality: Review of Incidence and Associations
3. Delinquency: Study of Direct Evidence on Personality Associations
4. Delinquency: Inferences on Personality from Environmental Associations
5. Delinquency: Perspective on Influences
6. Intelligence Abnormality in School and Adult Life
7. Intelligence and the Abnormal Personality
8. Summary

## 1. ABNORMALITY: ITS MEANING AND ROLE IN PERSONALITY STUDY

**The Correlation of "Deviant" Abnormality and "Inefficient" Abnormality.**
The term abnormal is used, consciously or unconsciously, in two quite distinct logical senses: (*a*) deviant from the social or biological average, and (*b*) unhealthy, defective when judged by some standard of possible or absolute efficiency. That so little confusion arises from the commonly ambiguous usage is due to the fact that these two characteristics tend to be very highly correlated in biological matters and moderately correlated in social matters.

By reason of millions of years of biological selection the organically average, normal type or form tends strongly to be the most efficient form known, in terms of vital processes; but the very fact of evolution shows that novel, deviant, forms are occasionally found that are more effective for living than the existing "normal" form.

The association of statistical normality with effectiveness in the *social* world is less close because central tendencies in social norms are less tested and more changeable, though the correlation is raised somewhat by the tendency of society in its turn to make the life of eccentrics and deviants difficult and ineffective. Even when the normal is not unhealthy through bad social norms, or from the wear and tear of that chance error which affects the majority, the standard of normality, *e.g.*, of law abidingness, though it becomes the standard of highest efficiency, is still not the standard of highest possible efficiency. Helmholtz pointed out, for example, that the human eye, even when entirely normal and free from chance damage, has most of the weaknesses that an optical instrument can possess. In short, it falls far short of a definable standard of perfect optical efficiency.

**Directions of Abnormality and Limits of Abnormality.** Confusion on the meaning of abnormal arises also from a third source—the failure to distinguish *the nature of the dimension* from *the nature of the limit.* When dealing with neurosis, instability, delinquency, etc., it is entirely practicable to deal either with the dimension of "statistical normality" or with that of "absolute efficiency," providing we explicitly state which we are using. In the latter the individual is measured by the extent to which he falls short of, say, giving absolutely no neurotic responses in a stress situation, or displaying no emotional instability, or committing absolutely no offenses against society. In either scale abnormality is defined by a limit or boundary as well as by a direction. And the point along this dimension at which we decide to draw the line and say, "This man must be hospitalized as a neurotic, or committed to an institution as feebleminded,[1] or put in the "custody of the law" is generally decided by normative standards. The norms of different societies draw the line differently with respect to the degree of inefficiency or eccentricity which they will tolerate.

Other considerations needed to avoid confusion over the practical use and theoretical meaning of abnormality are (*a*) that the use of the term *social* or *moral norm* is ambiguous. A moral norm is usually something to which no one gets very close! That is to say, it is only a norm in the sense that it is the average viewpoint in that community of what people *should* do: it is not the norm of what people do, and is really a standard of efficiency rather than a statistical norm; (*b*) that whereas "chance errors" tend to scatter people equally on either side of a statistical norm they generally tend to push the distribution to one side only—the lower side—of an efficiency norm.

Another distinct influence which reduces the degree of coincidence between the statistically and the functionally normal is "chance error." Such error —the accumulation of small, unsystematic influences—causes the central tendency in a set of measures to be that associated with the average amount of error (as much positive as negative). But from the point of view of greatest efficiency all error is loss. The average automobile on the road may have had 2½ years of wear, but the most efficient is that which has had none. And in man, though the average hereditary bodily proportions and relations of organs may be more efficient than most "sports," yet the average has suffered such chance errors of growth that perfect health is the

---

[1] That the legal definition of the limit is couched in terms of efficiency—"ability to manage one's affairs"—should not deceive us. For, as history and common observation remind us, no one is able to manage his affairs, even with the intellect of a Napoleon or a Lavoisier. And, conversely, in a primitive society many of our mental defectives, normal save for a prehistoric level of mental capacity, would be considered able to manage their affairs.

possession of the exceptional rather than the normal individual. In other words, most people have substandard health either by the standard of the healthiest possible man or by the standard of absolute freedom from sickness.

From the above discussion it might seem that we should do best to shift all psychological measures of abnormality on to an efficiency-morbidity scale rather than a scale of eccentricity or departure from the statistical norm, though in most "healthy" societies it may be practicable to accept the extent of deviation from the statistical norm (in one direction only, the inefficient direction) as a guide to fixing the limits for legal abnormality, treatment, etc. Unfortunately for this simplification there are many characteristics, some biological, most social, in which knowledge of the standards and directions of efficiency does not exist. Biologically we see that the tallest stature is not the best stature, since mankind has repeatedly evolved away from tallness. There must be some biologically optimum stature for man somewhere within the range of stature of human races. The average may here be the standard also of efficiency. Again, in cultural matters the norm of eating three meals a day or having one wife may or may not be the most efficient custom. Until social psychology is more developed and a science of ethics is available our best guides remain, in practice, social experience and revealed religious ethics.

**In Practice, Abnormality Is Generally Deviation.** The consequence of the lack of absolute standards of personal or, especially, of social efficiency is that no dimension of abnormality is possible except as deviation from the statistical norm. Theoretically it is still possible in these instances to conceive a dimension of efficiency—efficiency for survival or total adaptation as defined in Chapter 9, but since an increase in most psychological functions—*e.g.*, emotional reactivity—brings efficiency in some matters at the cost of others, the psychologist attempting thus to define abnormality becomes involved, as indicated, in profound problems of social psychology and in questions of ethics lying beyond his scope. Legal and practical definitions of abnormality often remain compromises of "deviant" or "eccentric" and "deficient" or "morbid" dimensions, or of a "deficiency" dimension with a limit fixed by consensus, *i.e.*, as a statistical norm.

Our present chapter must pursue the study of the abnormal under this compromise definition. But in those psychological functions where a distinction between deviant and deficient can be made on a firm basis it is generally valuable, and avoids much confusion, to preserve the distinction. Considered in the broadest context the meaning of deficient or inefficient is, in the last resort, unadapted to survival. Consequently, if we wish to specialize two terms for what has previously been covered ambiguously by "abnormal" we may refer to those who are extreme in deviation or in deficiency, respectively, as the "eccentric" and the "unadapted."

Our purpose here is to study eccentric, abnormal personalities and unadapted, morbid personalities for the light they are often peculiarly capable of throwing upon the normal. The emphasis will differ, therefore, from that of the overwhelming majority of writings on the subject, which are oriented to practical purposes of treatment. Psychotherapeutic matters will be considered, but only for the sake of their illumination of the nature of the abnormal processes they seek to rectify.

**Varieties of Abnormality to Be Studied.** The principal forms of abnormality to be studied are the psychoses, the neuroses, and delinquency, though many observations on more specific forms of behavior, *e.g.*, stammering, alcoholism, suicide, mental defect, homosexuality, must also be briefly examined for possible revelation of mechanisms unperceived in the normal personality. Although the treatment in this chapter naturally links up with and depends upon numerous incidental references to abnormality in other chapters, it has substantial dependence only upon (*a*) Chapter 1, through which it will be assumed that little further need be said here about the purely descriptive aspects of neurosis, psychosis, etc., and (*b*) Chapter 9, which has already gathered the first harvest of generalization, *e.g.*, concerning the personality structure of the unconscious, the superego, the processes of repression, and ego defense, that arises from the initial study of the abnormal personality.

The present chapter will deal with those personality disorders—mainly delinquency and neurosis—that fall short of psychosis.

## 2. DELINQUENCY AND PERSONALITY: REVIEW OF INCIDENCE AND ASSOCIATIONS

**Does Criminal Behavior Constitute a Personality Syndrome?** Delinquents and criminals are, respectively, children and adults whose behavior at some moment has amounted to committing an indictable offense against society's laws—either a minor offense, in which case it is called a "misdemeanor," or a major offense, which is legally styled a "felony." Parenthetically, many of the psychological data on these antisocial persons are restricted to observations on those who not only break the law but who are caught in doing so!

By reason of the great variety of possible offenses, as well as their specificity to a culture pattern or even a local set of bylaws, it has seemed to some psychologists an *a priori* conclusion that no "criminal type" of personality would be found. Consequently the repeated empirical evidence of such a syndrome, in studies from that of Lombroso to that of Lange mentioned in Chapter 5 on heredity, has met, in academic circles, a constant fire of doctrinaire criticism. But, as a little thought would show, there are certain psychological qualities in common to most offenses against law, whether it is wise law or eccentric law, namely, an inability to brook restraint, such as arises from poor self-control or powerful impulses, and an egocentricity or lack of altruism—not to mention sheer stupidity—which fails to perceive acts as transgressions.  Nevertheless, although the work of Ackerson (1), Berg (4,5), Hewitt and Jenkins (26), Sanford (40) and others even points to personality syndromes specific to particular types of crime, it must be admitted that these personality syndromes, both for crime generally and for specific branches of crime, are loose and shadowy patterns compared with the syndromes of psychosis and neurosis.  Indeed, it is more convenient and profitable to measure and define the delinquent personality with respect to deviation on a number of factors rather than in terms of types.

**Evidence on the Delinquent Personality as Such.**  The evidence of delinquency comes about equally from psychological and sociological studies, and though many psychologists have worked with uniform methods in both fields, it seems best, because of the different levels of inference, to deal in the present section with direct data on personality and in the second with data on the social interactions of personality and social factors in delinquency. Since the psychology of the delinquent personality is an old and established field of study, it is unnecessary to document all generalizations, and it seems best to set out the most important of them (resting substantially on such classical studies as those of Burt (7,8), Glueck (21), Healy and Bronner (24)) in brief systematic fashion and then to enlarge on such individual generalizations as need qualification and development.

**Incidence of Delinquencies.**  The forms of antisocial behavior to which the coming generalizations apply are (with frequencies indicated in Erkkila's study of 395 criminals aged thirteen to seventy-four years): violence against persons, 31 per cent; sex offenses, 6 per cent; against property (mainly stealing), 40 per cent; arson, 14 per cent.  These groupings include some thirty-two different categories according to law and leave some 9 per cent of crimes unclassified.  In child delinquency or "problem behavior," as dealt with by child-guidance clinics, we find also truancy, incorrigibility, swearing, willful property damage, and persistent lying.  Burt gives the following frequencies of child offenses in the London area:

|                                                              | Boys | Girls |
|--------------------------------------------------------------|------|-------|
| Sex offenses (heterosexual)                                  | 13.8 | 36.5* |
| Sex offenses (obscenity, masturbation, homosexuality)        | 9.8  | 13.1  |
| Bodily violence to persons                                   | 19.5 | 8.4   |
| Incorrigibility (to authority or associates without violence) | 11.2 | 26.7  |
| Damage to property                                           | 10.6 | 1.4   |
| Stealing, begging, swindling                                 | 91.9 | 46.0  |
| Truancy from home and school                                 | 39.9 | 19.8  |
| Attempted or achieved suicide                                | 0.0  | 4.1   |
| Persistent lying                                             | 4.9  | 13.6  |

* The great discrepancy of boys and girls here is almost certainly due to "the double standard" of morality which defines an "offense" differently in the two sexes.

These figures are per 100 children under sixteen years, and do not add to 100 per cent because one delinquent may have committed several offenses.

Laycock (32) gives a teacher's-eye view of the meaning of delinquency, presenting percentages of behavior listed as undesirable by some hundreds of elementary school teachers.

|  | Canadian study | American study |
|---|---|---|
| Violation of general standards of morality......... | 21.6 | 18.1 |
| Transgressions against authority................. | 7.4 | 6.4 |
| Violation of school regulations................... | 5.4 | 7.1 |
| Violation of classroom rules..................... | 6.6 | 16.7 |
| Violation of schoolwork demands................ | 18.6 | 9.8 |
| Offenses against other children.................. | 10.8 | 9.1 |
| Undesirable personality traits................... | 29.1 | 32.5 |

The incidence of delinquency (as defined by Burt's list above) varies from about one in one hundred to one in twenty of the child population, the London results being nearer the lower limit and the upper limit being reached in some American studies. Adult frequencies may be gauged from Cleckley's (see (23), Chap. 18) figures that, in 1944, there were 1,356,655 major crimes in the United States, *i.e.*, one for every hundred persons. Unless we assume that the average adult criminal, with an adult life span of fifty years, commits two major crimes every year, the criminal incidence is very much higher than one in a hundred persons.

**Personality Associates of Delinquency.** The personality factors found associated with delinquency are: (*a*) masculine sex; (*b*) youthfulness and the adolescent age range; (*c*) lower intelligence; (*d*) backwardness in school-work, absolute and relative to ability; (*e*) high score on performance tests (mechanical) relative to general ability; (*f*) some tendency to high dominance (*E*+ factor); (*g*) marked tendency to emotional instability (*C*− factor); (*h*) tendency to poor character integration (*G*− factor); (*i*) possibly an over-strong endowment in some one emotional disposition; (*j*) physique and presence below average; (*k*) presence of debilitating and chronically irritating physical disorders; (*l*) possibly some neurotic disorder, but only of a special type, *i.e.*, most neuroses have no greater than chance association with delinquency. Several clinical-type approaches have independently suggested a division of criminal personalities into egocentric, antisocial types, and unstable, psychopathic types, but this offers only an indication of factors which might be demonstrated by study.

## 3. DELINQUENCY: STUDY OF DIRECT EVIDENCE
## ON PERSONALITY ASSOCIATIONS

**Age and Sex Factors.** Expanding on the above factors, in the order given, we may note first that the excess of men over women criminals seems to be considerable in most culture patterns and for all offenses, except sex offenses. The influence of age is complex, but, in general, delinquency decreases with age after early or mid-adolescence. Blatz and Bott (see (6), Chap. 17) found a rather sharp increase around seven, eight, and nine years and a distinct peak in early adolescence (fourteen years). Burt points out that the incidence of first offenses shows a bulge at adolescence, paralleling that for tuberculosis and schizophrenia, but Carr-Saunders, Mannheim, and Rhodes (11), in a wide sampling of delinquency in Britain, find the high years (not first offenses, but all offenses) to be through twelve to sixteen for boys and fifteen through nineteen for girls. The chances of a first offense after thirty-five or forty are small. Hartman and Schroeder (23), analyzing 4,188 cases in Joliet prison, find the age percentages to be indistinguishable from those of the general population, which is what might be expected with a recidivist population that turns criminal early and stays criminal. They note that the proportion of psychopaths and individuals of low intelligence increases in older groups. There the finding is not typical for intelligence, and may be peculiar to the age range studied. In general, the individual of low intelligence is more likely than others to get into difficulties initially, through not foreseeing punishment. But, being punished, he is more likely[2] to learn than the more intelligent individual who foresaw the consequences of his actions from the beginning, but who commits crime through some systematic personality defect. Below a certain very low level of intelligence, however, even this learning by experience may fail, so one could expect low intelligence as well as psychopathic personalities to accumulate in the older, recidivist group.

**Intelligence and Crime.** As to the third factor, ability, some complications of the initial generalization also occur on closer study. The high incidences of mental defect and borderline defect in earlier studies are questioned now, on the grounds that individuals with low intelligence are more likely to get caught and also more likely to be sent to an institution, because of the poorness of general prognosis if left uninstitutionalized. Tulchin (50) studied 10,415 prisoners in all Illinois penal and correctional institutions and found a distribution no different from that of the Army draft (which, however, was not a true sample of the general population). It may be that in societies with a fair degree of cultural disorganization and a high delinquency rate the association of delinquency and low intelligence is reduced to a slight or

[2] Hartman (22) found recidivists more intelligent than first offenders in most crimes except sex offenses. Others have found them of the same intelligence distribution as the general population, but lower in *C* factor and in surgency.

even a negligible one; but the European studies, notably those of Burt and the studies in Scandinavian countries, unquestionably show the association, and most studies with children, especially those in a uniform and good environment, also show it.

Significant intelligence differences have been found between different types of crimes, the highest level having been found with fraud, running down through robbery, larceny, burglary, murder, and sex crimes, rape being the lowest. Burkey (6) found among child delinquents that stealing predominated in the more intelligent and sex offenses in the less intelligent, while the less intelligent, especially if they begin with truancy or incorrigibility, are less likely to vary in the form of their antisocial behavior.

**Delinquency and Practical, Mechanical Ability.** The peculiar tie-up of delinquency with performance test ability is instanced by Hirsch (27) finding that 95 per cent of 445 delinquents exceeded their age median on the Ferguson Form Board, whereas only 28 per cent passed the median on the Binet. (There was practically zero correlation of the two tests in this group.) This result on mechanical-type test performances is confirmed by Slawson, Daugherty, Jessup, and others. One is inclined to look for the explanation in some masculinity factor of personality, *e.g.*, dominance, self-reliance ($E+$) or $H+$ factor (since boys do better on these tests and boys are more delinquent); or in the poor school attendance and low verbal attainment of the delinquent (assuming the Binet measure contaminated with school skills); or in the greater need of the delinquent for social approval (since performance tests are more susceptible than others to a strong effort to please the examiner); or, if we consider school failure to be a serious emotional trauma, we may seek the explanation in the fact that since so much of schoolwork depends on ability to read, a relative backwardness in reading would be disproportionately frustrating. Gerlach (20) obtained a similar difference on verbal and nonverbal abilities, between normals and sixty-one clinic cases of various kinds. He divided the latter into "asocial" and "aggressive" problem children and noted the former were slightly younger and lower in I.Q. Although both showed verbal deficiency relative to normals the aggressives showed it more, and increasingly with age.

**Personality Measures and Delinquency.** As to the personality factors, we have evidence of the following kind: a tendency to score high on the "general maladjustment" factor, $C-$, (see (7), Chap. 3), and "dominance," "self-confidence," "self-sufficiency" factors in so-called neurotic questionnaires; on a general questionnaire, more worries, (desurgency) wider distribution of interests, more emotionality, and an awareness of fewer kinds of behavior as being wrong (ethical-knowledge test); higher ratings in laziness, disobedience, resentment toward discipline, unattentiveness, quarrelsomeness, lying, swearing, instability of mood, and bullying; a higher incidence of enuresis, of "hyperactivity," accident proneness, "extraverted" tendencies[3]; on the Pressey interest test an undue preoccupation with death, dying, sins, and in general interests an emphasis on hectic amusements (joy riding, movies, tap dancing); in their choice of admired characteristics in others an attraction to wealthy, husky, handsome, well-dressed rather than to cooperative, etc.; on objective tests delinquents show larger overstatement scores, more infringements of rules on the C.M.S. Test (see (4), Chap. 4), and higher (and more deviant) perseveration (disposition rigidity) scores (see (10), Chap. 4).

**Associations of Special Delinquencies.** Ackerson (1) found total conduct disorder (score as number out of 40 possible conduct problems checked; therefore, practically an index of delinquency) correlated 0.8 to 0.35 with the following in boys: disturbing influence in the home, swearing and other disregard of authority, a psychiatric rating of "psychopathic," destructiveness, truanting from home, disobedient, stealing, begging, using violence, being cruel to animals and to children, smoking, unpopular, truanting from school, exhibitionistic, homosexual, fire-setting, gluttonous, restless. The order for girls places violence and swearing higher, *i.e.*, as more diagnostic, which might be expected from their being more deviant from the approved feminine pattern.

Just as special delinquencies—what we might call "special delinquent occupations"—have their characteristic intelligence level, so also they have characteristic personality associations. Thus Ackerson found stealing to correlate most with truancy, lying, gang and bad companions, and with oversuggestibility and interest in the opposite sex. Violence, on the other hand, lacked these social and sexual interest associations and showed significant correlation with temper-tantrums, disobedience, quarrelsomeness, sullenness, hatred of siblings, emotional instability, and egocentricity. Frosch and Bromberg (18), studying adult sex offenders, found a low rate of recidivism but a high rate of psychopathy and neuroticism and reported strong religious affiliations. Ackerson found sex offenses in children correlated with mental conflict, daydreaming, bashfulness, oversuggestibility, and sulkiness.

Truancy falls partly in the same syndrome as stealing, but Ackerson found additional associations with loitering, incorrigibility, disobedience, and fantastical lying, while in adult recidivists with migratory tendencies Hovey (29) found early family and school maladjustment, antisocial behavior at adolescence, and deficient heterosexual interests. Speer (45) found significant differences between truants and thieves in that the latter showed insecurity and objected only to specific uncongenial tasks, whereas the

---

[3] In adult criminals there is a swing to introvert relative to the general population, *i.e.*, a significantly higher score on desurgency or depression-anxiety.

former were generally maladjusted, disliked work of any kind, were interested in recreation, adventure, fame, and "importance," but avoided risks. Comparing recidivists with nonrepeaters (fifty adults in each group) Tolman (49) found the former had statistically higher scores on opposition to the government (political insurgency), antagonism to immediate authority (chip-on-the-shoulder attitude), antagonism or reserve toward the father, reserve to the mother, and awareness of lack of integration in their own personality ideal. Doubtless, as more data become available, the analysis of personality in regard to proneness to particular kinds of crime will prove more profitable than establishing relations to delinquency in general.

**Delinquency and Neurosis.** As to the relation of delinquency to neurosis the findings are few and not too consistent. Bromberg and Thomson find about 7 per cent of definite neuroses in a large (7,000) prison population, which is not, apparently, different from the general population. Some results suggest a slightly lower incidence than in the general population. With young delinquents there is evidence of more than average neurosis in the *parents*. Psychoanalytic examinations of delinquents stress unconscious, if not neurotic, motivations in the form of "need for punishment," displaced aggressions (usually from a parent image), and various other displaced, irrational, unconscious needs. Factor-analytic results, partly inferred from individual traits and syndromes, point to low emotional stability $(C-)$, dominance $(E+)$, desurgency $(F-)$ and schizoid $(A-)$ factor tendencies in the egocentric, violent type; surgency $(F+)$ and cyclothymia $(H+)$ in the gang type, and lack of integration $(G-)$ in all.

Snyder and Snyder (44) analyzing the background of 275 child-guidance-clinic cases, found that with a history of illness, psychoneurotic, and particularly psychosomatic complaints were more frequent, while delinquencies, notably sex and stealing, were less frequent. Likewise, as reported in the study of intelligence (Section 7) below, those below I.Q. 80 had more delinquencies (especially sex) and more reading and speech difficulties, while the cases above I.Q. 109 had more feelings of inadequacy and personality difficulties.

Probably it is already safe to generalize that delinquents show more dominance, more surgency, more rejection in the home background, less intelligence, less history of illness and dependence, lower social and moral standards in the home background than do neurotics. But both tend to possess low emotional stability (*e.g.*, as Burt's clinical studies and Mosier's (36) questionnaire data show) *i.e.*, "general neurotic maladjustment," either by constitution or through inconsistent, traumatizing early upbringing. However, the traumatic home background situation (parental dissension, etc.) which might contribute to such maladjustment is more evident in the history of both than in that of normals. It is clear that the relation of the delinquent and the neurotic may be summed up with greatest brevity by pointing out that they share an abnormal position on the dimension of instability, but are differentiated by opposite positions on some second dimension of repressibility.   Both have conflict with society initially, partly by reason of emotional instability but some secondary personality dimensions of surgency, dominance, or even low intelligence cause the delinquent to continue his conflict without repression, whereas the neurotic brings higher superego standards to bear upon his instability.

**Delinquency and Somatic Features.**   As to the physique of delinquents, a typical finding is that of the Anthropometric Committee of the British Association (11) who found boys in correctional institutions five pounds lighter and three inches shorter than controls, and the same relation for girls. Morrison (11) considers physical inferiority one of the "most important" factors in delinquency.   Burt's thorough study of the individual delinquent found that both undersized and oversized children were unduly frequent delinquents but with predominance of undersized.   He also found chronic illnesses, bad teeth, verminous conditions, constant colds, etc., to be provocative factors.

### 4. DELINQUENCY: INFERENCES ON PERSONALITY FROM ENVIRONMENTAL ASSOCIATIONS

**List of Discovered Associations.**   Significant associations are found between delinquency and the following: (*a*) poverty and lower social status; (*b*) defective discipline—neglected moral training, inconsistent training, or harsh discipline—in the home; (*c*) inverted moral discipline, *i.e.*, education by parents with antisocial attitudes; (*d*) living in a disorganized area or one showing extremes of wealth, living customs, and culture pattern; (*e*) having high mobility; (*f*) living in a period of rapid social change, *e.g.*, war, economic depression; (*g*) dissension between parents, and broken homes; (*h*) neurotic parents; (*i*) absence of recreational facilities; (*j*) bad companions or gang associations; (*k*) unemployment (but not unemployment of the parent, which sometimes improves home supervision); (*l*) exposure to alcohol and drugs.

**Economic Factors, Living Space, and Mobility.**   As to poverty, in Bagot's recent study (3) 50 per cent of the families of delinquents were below the "poverty line," and he adds that unemployment percentages constituted "the most outstanding difference between delinquents and nondelinquents discovered in this study."   Other regions and researches, as discussed in the following section on interpretations do not show such marked correlations, but poverty remains high among delinquents in most studies, the principal exceptions being those of Faris and Shaw, which sometimes suggest that the *social disorganization* often found with poverty is the real factor.   Carr-Saunders, Mannheim, and Rhodes (11) in their exceptionally comprehensive studies throughout Britain find poverty, as such, correlated only 0.05 with delinquency, while Burt's figure of 0.15 is central for most studies. There are figures suggesting that density of population is more important than poverty, a finding with which the higher rates for urban contrasted with rural areas may also align itself. Actual crowding of the home is also a factor, the Carr-Saunders study finding slightly higher (delinquent-non-delinquent) ratios for such conditions.

Typical data on sheer density of population, as well as on mobility, can well be instanced by Sullenger's study of the city of Omaha, where crowded housing was found more definitely related to delinquency than density of population as such, and where the following relations appeared between mobility and delinquency rates for various wards of the city (46):

| Ward | Per cent of city delinquency | Per cent mobility |
|------|------------------------------|-------------------|
| 1 | 5.0 | 8.2 |
| 2 | 15.4 | 9.0 |
| 3 | 12.3 | 10.8 |
| 4 | 5.3 | 9.1 |
| 5 | 13.3 | 11.8 |
| 6 | 6.4 | 4.5 |
| 7 | 16.8 | 11.6 |
| 8 | 4.7 | 7.5 |
| 9 | 5.6 | 7.3 |
| 10 | 2.3 | 8.0 |
| 11 | 7.4 | 6.2 |
| 12 | 5.5 | 6.0 |

Although unemployment of youths is uniformly associated with delinquency, unemployment of their fathers is not so consistently related, and in young children and with fathers unemployed through little fault of their own (economic depression) rates are actually lower for children of unemployed. Similarly the Carr-Saunders study (11) found delinquency rates slightly higher for homes with employed mothers.

**Factors in the Home.** The role of the defective home background is complex. In the first place, the data show that homes broken by death, desertion, separation, and divorce have higher than expected rates of delinquency. For example, Carr-Saunders study (11) points out that 39 per cent of the entire population of juvenile correctional institutions have lost one or both parents—a figure decidedly higher than the average home (Chap. 12). Illegitimacy is also a factor in delinquency. The frequency of stepparents has been found significantly higher for delinquents, but the careful statistical evaluation of the last-mentioned research is that the association is slight.

Undoubtedly the really powerful factor in the home is the parental *morale* —no matter who the parents are or whether both are present. Burt's results (7,8) indicate parental dissension, neuroticism, ill-health, or delinquency to be decidedly worse in effect than a broken home. The study of Carr-Saunders, Mannheim, and Rhodes, with its large samples and careful analyses, showed that in the homes of delinquents the presence of delinquency in another member of the family is about *ten times* as frequent as in the homes of the control cases. We are dealing here with the tone of the family syntality, with the dimension of the morale of the family as a group, and this far exceeds in potency the sociological factors yet discussed.

**Influences of the Peer Group.** With the role of companionship outside the family and with the gang, Chapters 13 and 14 have already dealt. In the widespread British studies (3,7,11) some 50 per cent of thefts committed by boys and practically all thefts by girls were committed alone; but American results seem to show more sociable delinquents! Shaw and McKay (41) found 80 to 90 per cent of the juvenile offenses committed in the county they studied to be committed by boys in groups. This figure is unusually high but it shows roughly the magnitude of group influence. Much of the delinquency, under this heading, is merely "situational" as defined above, arising from the well-known social psychological effect of horde delegation of conscience. As to that horde influence toward delinquency which has more permanent personality effects, *e.g.*, in "inversion of conscience," Shaw (41) says some "who had the longest careers in delinquency were the ones who possessed personality traits usually regarded as most desirable!" Within the values of their group they were persevering, dependable natures! There is, incidentally, evidence in Healy, Bronner, and Bowers (25) that delinquents tend to be more gregarious generally than the controls, but whether this is due to compensation for an unsatisfactory home or to cyclothymia of temperament is unknown. Certainly many delinquents may say, like Shakespeare's King Henry IV (Act III, Scene 3) "Company, villainous company, hath been the ruin of me," but evidently this applies more to social reputation than to character as such.

Generally, therefore, the delinquencies of the gang do not indicate or produce serious or permanent personality defects, other than suggestibility and excessive extraversion. Actually the more chronic delinquents, in general, show slightly less tendency to join clubs, etc., than do controls. Their greatest difference in this field, however, concerns their ability to get interested in wholesome hobbies and recreations. The difference found in the British study (11) in *availability* of recreation for delinquents and controls was slight, but the difference in *interest in actual hobbies*, their frequency and nature, was considerable, as shown by the following London data:

|  | Delinquents | Controls |
|---|---|---|
| Reading (alone) | 13.4 | 15.9 |
| Reading and sport | 0.7 | 11.4 |
| Reading and other interests | 5.1 | 6.3 |
| Sport (alone) | 8.7 | 25.7 |
| Sport and other interests | 0.4 | 2.0 |
| Handicrafts | 4.0 | 10.6 |
| Music | 1.4 | 1.4 |
| Games and other interests | 8.3 | 10.3 |
| Cinema, etc | 1.8 | 1.1 |
| None | 56.2 | 15.2 |
|  | 100.0 | 100.0 |

Thus both sport and handicrafts occupy the nondelinquent far more—a fact which may reconcile us to some of the excesses of present-day sport.

*Delinquency and Social Values or Trends.* Religious affiliations show significant differences in groups otherwise in a similar cultural environment, social class, etc. Thus, Royd's (see (11)) study of the industrial city of Oldham found that 31 per cent of offenders and 47 per cent of controls were nominally attendants at some place of worship, and similar results have been found for recorded attendance, *e.g.,* Carr-Saunders' study (11) found that 9.1 per cent of delinquents and 16.9 per cent of controls had previous attendance records at church.

A review of the social, environmental associations of delinquency would not be complete without noting the effects of social trends and spasmodic changes. Crime of most kinds shows an increase during economic depression. Doob, Miller, and others have made a case for the aggressive crimes, at least for lynchings and possibly gang crimes, increasing most markedly through economic frustration (16a). War produces a reduction in adult crime and an increase in juvenile crime, and it seems improbable that the former is due to any proneness of the armed forces to take crime-prone individuals. After a war both juvenile and adult crime remain high for some years. Carr-Saunders, Mannheim, and Rhodes examined the general secular trend in crime over the first part of this century in Britain. In a period comparatively unaffected by wars—1929 to 1935—they show that adult crime steadily decreased. In this particular era of cultural relaxation juvenile delinquency showed a steady increase throughout the period, ranging from 16 per cent for certain modes of delinquency to 60 per cent for others (11).

### 5. DELINQUENCY: PERSPECTIVE ON INFLUENCE

**Broad Divisions of Influences.** For soundness of conceptualization, as well as for many practical purposes, the above discussed associations of delinquency are best interpreted in terms of three classes of factors: (*a*) personality factors of hereditary origin; (*b*) personality factors of environmental origin; and (*c*) environmental situations—the social "field" or group syntality—prone to incite delinquency, even in well-adjusted personalities. Both (*b*) and (*c*) are covered in the preceding section and it is not easy to draw the line between them, for the anomalous situation that provokes a temporary delinquency, *e.g.*, a gang situation, a breakdown of society in war, may also act, when prolonged, as an environmental agent to produce more permanent changes of personality as such.

**Modes of Action and Interaction of Influences.** Much could be written from the files of present day information by way of special qualification and elaboration of the above statements on known influences in delinquency; only the briefest comments are possible in this review. Most of the influences can operate independently, but a few act only together (low intelligence, absence of organized recreation) or catalytically (high dominance, emotional instability). Most factors have a tolerably linear relation to incidence of delinquency, but a few are decidedly curvilinear, *e.g.*, severity of parental discipline, perseveration (rigidity), age, physique, and possibly parental wealth or poverty.

For complete interpretation, most of the broad, macroscopic, sociological associations need to be explored in terms of intervening psychological mechanisms. For example, "unsatisfactory homes" breaks down into immoral education by parental precept and example, moral education pursued with "unsatisfactory discipline," and the effects of parental dissension and neurosis in forcing premature development of the ego and a poorly integrated or developed superego.

"Unsatisfactory discipline" as Burt has shown, amounts generally to lax attitudes, overindulgent attitudes, and oversevere attitudes. The first, a powerful factor in present-day delinquency, amounts to a sheer neglect of the effort, tact, and firmness required to inculcate good habits and values in the child and may spring either from weak parental character and morale or from preoccupation with social and economic competition, etc. Overindulgent and oversevere attitudes are almost certainly the outward signs of that emotional rejection (Chap. 13) which, as we saw, either rationalizes its sadistic dominance as strong discipline or overcompensates for it by indulgence. Some indulgence may also be the projected narcism of an unrealistic, neurotic parent. It would be interesting to know how much of what appears as "capricious home discipline" is an oscillation between these alternate expressions of rejection and how much springs from the inheritable emotional instability manifesting itself in the parent. The psychology of superego formation (Chap. 9) would lead us to expect that rejection would be far more destructive—perhaps amounting to one of the main causes of psychopathic personality—if occurring in the earliest years.

**Manifestations of Superego Defect.** If the environmental evidence points strongly in any one direction it points to the delinquent being defective in superego development—a somewhat obvious conclusion yet one frequently overlooked in favor of more complicated theories of neurotic delinquency. Confirmation of this comes from direct tests, *e.g.*, those showing defective ethical knowledge and a tendency to consider fewer items of behavior as wrong. An interesting sidelight on this matter is thrown by the study of Rubinstein (39) who matched 271 institutionalized "problem children" with 271 normals on a 100-item questionnaire on reactions to behavior. He found that "the well-adjusted criticized themselves for not doing as well or as much as they could of things they *should* do and criticized other boys severely for shortcomings," but the delinquents showed far less concern for moral standards or duty, either in themselves or others.

Whatever the particular mechanisms through which home and parents operate in ego and in superego formation, it is clear from the accumulated evidence that the home is extremely powerful. That a great deal of the weight ascribed to the home must be attached to its environmental influence rather than heredity is shown by Healy's study of 500 delinquents, where transference to good foster homes brought 80 per cent of success as against 40 per cent by all other child guidance influences without change of home (24). This accords well with the experience of most child guidance workers.

The main associations of delinquency with directly observed personality traits, *e.g.*, with emotionality instability ($C-$ factor) or dominance ($E+$ factor) require no explanation, though they add to our appreciation of the meaning of these factors for personality. The association with low intelligence, however, illustrates some of the oblique, causal connections to which one needs to be alert even with more obvious personality traits. Some four hypotheses, in fact, need to be investigated here, leading perhaps to four distinct weightings of the effect of intelligence, according to circumstances. They are: (*a*) that low intelligence means poor foresight both as to the anti-social consequences of behavior and the certainty of detection, as seen in mental defectives; (*b*) that low intelligence increases the individual's frustrations, at least relative to the levels of satisfaction he sees in others, and thus engenders pugnacity; (*c*) that low intelligence reduces the individual's capacity to enjoy the sublimated activities, *e.g.*, reading, which culture presents in compensation for ergic renunciations; (*d*) that the same relation-perceiving capacity which operates in intelligence tests is probably also involved in learning effective emotional integration of impulses. This is suggested by the positive correlation found between the $B$ (mental capacity) and $G$ (character integration) factors of personality.

**Scientific Predictive Formulae in the Field of Delinquency.** The ultimate objective in understanding personality in delinquency is not only to see causal connections clearly but also to be able to use in predictions of onset and recovery from delinquency proper formulae and weightings for the various factors involved. This presents a special instance of the general problem, discussed in the previous chapter, of choosing the most efficacious factor unities in the total situation, and of determining their regression coefficients. It is precisely this maintenance of perspective that is still most deficient in current writings, for sociologists, anthropologists, and psychologists in special fields continue to ignore the necessity for a methodology which embraces other fields than their own. Occasionally this lack of sense for the whole field occurs through an innocent absence of mind, as when an experimenter matches delinquent and control groups for certain conditions and then concludes that one or another of the excluded influences has no real role in delinquency! But mostly these special emphases are less ludicrous than scientifically ugly.

One of the commonest disputes concerns the relative importance of the delinquent personality, inherited and acquired, vs. that of the sociological factors of poverty, or social disorganization—regarded as "field" or syntality factors rather than agents of personality formation. Bagot's high estimate of poverty and unemployment (3) and Faris's emphasis on social disorganization have already been mentioned. In criticism of the former, Burt (7) points out that only 15 per cent of the London delinquents were below the poverty line, in contrast with Bagot's 50 per cent; that in Bagot's Liverpool study a large number of nondelinquents were also below the agreed poverty line, and that a proper analysis of Bagot's own data shows the correlation of delinquency with low intelligence to be actually greater than that with poverty (3). Even the remaining correlation of poverty would vanish if intelligence were partialed out, justifying the conclusion that low intelligence is causal both for poverty and delinquency. This in fact is the direction of Burt's ultimate conclusion, for he adds that though low intelligence and emotional instability occur in every class "they are found twenty to forty times as often in families who drift into the slums as in families from the middle or professional classes" (7). Carr-Saunders, Mannheim, and Rhodes (11) similarly conclude that "when we find an association between delinquency and low economic status we may have to recognize that some deficiency in character (including intelligence) may be the reason why the status of the family is low."

When influences are correlated in this way only exact correlation and factor analysis can give indications of which factors are more primary in a given complex of influences. At present the elaborate treatment of the wide range of data necessary for assigning relative independence and degree of "depth" to causes, and relative weights to the contribution of the above factors to delinquency *in general*, scarcely exists. Still less can one hope to get exact estimates with respect to *special* areas, periods, and varieties of crime.

In an intensively studied group of 123 boys and 74 girls brought before London courts Burt has attempted to work out coefficients of association for various influences, which he presents systematically as follows:

*Coefficient of*
*Association*

*A. Factors beyond the Immediate Personality*
  (*a*) *Hereditary* Physical............................................................ 0.17
               Intellectual............................................................ 0.34
               Temperamental (pathological)............................ 0.24
               Temperamental (delinquent symptom).................... 0.41
  (*b*) *Environmental* (i) Home.  Poverty.................................. 0.15
               Defective family relations.......................... 0.33
               Defective discipline.............................. 0.55
               Vicious home...................................... 0.39
        (ii) Outside home (peer group, neighborhood)............ 0.29

Average 0.34

*B. Factors Directly Observable in the Personality*
  (*a*) *Physical personal condition*
      Developmental.................................................... 0.37
      Pathological...................................................... 0.15
  (*b*) *Psychological personal condition*
      Intellectual...................................................... 0.41
      Emotional (i) *Inborn,* disposition................................ 0.53
               General emotionality................................ 0.46
    *Acquired* (ii) Interests, sentiments.................................. 0.40
               Complexes........................................................ 0.45

Average 0.45

This is in tolerable agreement with what one would conclude on general grounds, namely, that the immediate influence of the family outranks the general social setting, the school, the age group, associates, etc., and that among personality traits intelligence and emotional stability, both with considerable hereditary determination, surpass in influence most other personality traits. Further, one might add that, except for transient crime (which may nevertheless be socially serious) the influence of companions in the gang is more dramatic than deep seated.

From the standpoint of the psychology of personality the study of delinquency presents us with valuable additional orientation, notably an added proof of the potency of the family in character formation; a demonstration of the possibility of establishing "inverted" moral values; an indication of the magnitude of compensatory needs created by failure in school; further evidence on recreational needs and the ready transition of play into delinquency; a revelation of the powerful dynamic effects possible from a purely cognitive endowment—general ability—and the suggestion that the potent hereditary influence which Lange and others demonstrated in crime may reside in a factor of constitutional emotional instability.

## 6. INTELLIGENCE ABNORMALITY IN SCHOOL AND ADULT LIFE

**Study of Eccentrics Needed in All Personality Factors.** As stated initially, our study in these chapters on the abnormal is to include both the abnormally deviant and the abnormally unadapted, in the expectation that the special attention given to these salient personalities and their unusual mechanisms may throw new light on the normal. Theoretically, a valuable approach would be systematically to study outstandingly high and low deviant behavior in each of the twelve or more primary personality factors. But since evidence on deviants, as distinct from maladapted personalities, is available with respect only to one factor, namely, general intelligence, these three chapters concern themselves almost entirely with abnormality as maladaptation and only the present two sections deal directly with deviation— in intelligence. And even so these sections will concern themselves largely with this deviation in relation to maladaptation, the first section with that maladaptation in school and occupation related to low intelligence, and the second, with the relation of intelligence to all the kinds of maladaptation covered in the three chapters.

**Eccentricity in Intelligence.** Personality study has in general paid insufficient attention to the role of abilities, as distinct from dynamic traits, in personality. There is ample evidence that the individual's level of general intelligence powerfully affects the pattern of personality outside the boundaries of what is commonly thought of as cognitive activity. This is illustrated, for example, by contrasting the field of research inquiry pursued by researchers thinking of general ability in terms of the stereotype $g$, in its purely intellectual context, with the field that opens up when we think of it here as $B$, *i.e.*, as a personality factor among personality factors, with its demonstrated relation to such personality manifestations as conscientiousness, character integration, breadth of interests, etc. (see page 59).

It is appropriate at this point for the student to collate and reorganize what he knows about various personality correlations with intelligence in terms of the over-all question of the role of intelligence in personality. In this book the issues are handled most systematically, first, in introducing the data on the factor of General Intelligence in Personality ($B$) in Chapter 4, again in studying heredity in Chapter 5, in Chapter 10 in connection with cerebral function, and finally in the present study of the abnormal. It is here that we may hope to draw the various threads together and emerge with some general principles concerning the interaction of general ability with the rest of personality.

**Manifestations of Intelligence Deviation.** The study of deviation in intelligence requires attention to both high and low deviants. Far more research attention has been devoted to the latter, and it is convenient to deal with this larger mass of integrated evidence first. Historically this work begins with interest in backwardness in school, a form of abnormality which, except for delinquency and neurosis, has provoked more systematic study at least among those concerned with pre-adult population, than any other abnormality. The classical work of Burt (9) covers most that is known about the incidence of causes of defective adjustment to the scholarship aspects of school life.

Defining the backward child as one with an educational ratio of 0.85 or less (average of all school subjects), *i.e.*, as one unable at ten years to do the work of a class one year below that normal for his age, Burt finds such backwardness (of the degree requiring special educational provisions) to occur in about 10 per cent of children. This makes backwardness about seven times as frequent as mental defectiveness, but its frequency varies from one area to another far more than does mental defect, which tends only to increase somewhat with rural conditions and with lower social status.

**Factors in School Backwardness.** In the final analysis Burt points to the multiplicity of causes and summarizes their frequency for the London area as follows: "Three-quarters of the [backward] children were found to be suffering from unfavorable *physical* conditions; two-thirds from unfavorable *social* conditions; three-quarters from unfavorable *intellectual* (*i.e.*, ability) conditions; about one-third from unfavorable temperamental conditions; and only one-sixth from unfavorable school conditions" ((9), p. 565).

However, the largest single correlation of low school achievement in almost all samples and conditions is with general intelligence, and averages about 0.7. When the influence of intelligence is partialed out, the next highest correlations are with poor long-distance memory (0.55) and irregular attendance (0.52). The former is probably partly an index of those temperamental, dynamic factors mentioned above which determine the child's acceptance of the school and his interest in the success of his own school activities, and partly an index of general physical fitness.

Many investigations have been made of the factors in school performance other than intelligence by means of comparisons of children with high and low achievement quotients (ratio of educational age to mental age). The achievement quotient remains only moderately constant from year to year. One extensive investigation finds a correlation of only 0.38 between the achievement quotients of the same children separated by a year. The general findings—that character qualities of stability and perseverance, as well as some introvert qualities, are related to performance—agree with the common observations of teachers. Oates (see (15)) found that persistence on the June-Downey test correlated significantly with school achievement when intelligence was partialed out. Wolff (see (86), Chap. 19) studied 1,078 children and found superior achievement related to more desirable personality traits, an interest in intellectual matters, less interest in motor activities, and better social and emotional status of homes.  Cohler noted the same but brought out the interesting fact that the achievement quotient tends to be higher for children near the mean in intelligence, and concluded, "School instruction, as well as social demands and opportunities, come nearer to exploiting one's fullest capacities, the closer these capacities approach the mean."  Presumably this leveling effect would exist less in well-run school systems which sort children better, according to intellectual capacities, in appropriate classes.

The correlations of intelligence with school attainment among the backward show much the same relations as are found in normal ranges and in older age groups also, namely, values of about 0.5 to 0.7 for such subjects as arithmetic problems and composition, of about 0.4 for geography, history, etc., and of no more than 0.1 or 0.2 for handwork, drawing, and athletics.

**The Backward Group in Society.**  The similarity between the group that is backward in schoolwork and the group that fails in occupations, falls to the less skilled ranks, and is intermittently or constantly unemployed in normal economic times, is considerable.  Indeed, Burt's follow-up studies show that the adult perennially unemployed group is largely fed by the school backward and maladjusted group.  In holding an occupation, however, there is almost certainly more emphasis on emotional stability and freedom from neurosis, and less on intellectual capacity; for the demand for relatively unskilled workers, of low intelligence and low degrees of literacy, remains high in expanding countries, in agricultural countries, in reconstruction after wars, and wherever much material construction has to be done.  Nevertheless, practically all occupational-intelligence surveys or related studies including unemployed persons show the latter to be distinctly below the intelligence level of the employed.  Parenthetically, owing to the high degree of inheritance of mental capacity, this shows itself also in the children of unemployed, as the diagram on page 475 illustrates.

As Spearman pointed out long ago, since there are a large number of special abilities, and since the variance in many of them is largely accounted for by specific factors, every man could be, by sheer chances of distribution, a near-genius at some one thing.  This holds, to a lesser degree, for Thurstone's primary abilities, which permit an individual low in the second-order general-ability factor nevertheless to be fairly outstanding in some one ability, *e.g.*, verbal, number, or fluency performances.  Since the ego need, especially in a competitive society, for the individual to claim high ability in *some* direction is very urgent, it is not surprising that the individual of low general intelligence will sometimes perform prodigies of skill through concentration in a field where general ability is not important.  (The *idiot savant*, however, generally turns out on examination to be a prodigy relative to his intelligence group rather than to the general population.)

**Personality Traits Associated with Low General Ability.** As to the distribution of various compensations for low general ability, and their origin in environmental circumstances and temperament, little is yet known. Among normal subjects, as indicated earlier, high verbal ability ($V$ factor) tends to be associated with schizoid and desurgent factors, while high numerical ability seems to be a direction of expression of general ability more favored by the emotionally stable, and high drawing ability is found more in surgent individuals.

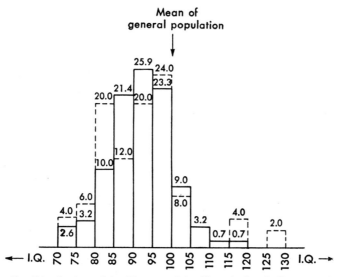

DIAGRAM 45. Distribution of intelligence of families of chronically unemployed men (broken line, country population; solid line, city). (*From The Fight for Our National Intelligence, P. S. King & Staples, Ltd., London, 1937.*)

However, the chances seem to be that the individual of abnormally low ability generally will acquire also personality traits of apathy or maladjustment which militate against effective use even of the ability that he has. The factor found by the present writer (12) in Eysenck's correlations on 700 neurotic adults, which loaded personal history of unemployment, 0.67; lack of initiative, 0.61; history of unskilled occupation, 0.53; narrow interests, 0.50; apathy and retardation, 0.34; and poor organization of personality 0.33 (as well as having the only factor loading found in the intelligence test), can almost certainly be identified as a factor depicting the realm of influence of (low) general ability. Other studies (see (7,14), Chap. 3) have also generally shown an appreciable loading of "character" factors—such as lack of perseverance, indolence, unreliability, lack of self-discipline, impulsiveness, and irresponsibility in the general-ability factor, while Chassell's exhaustive study (16) sets the true correlation between intelligence and such character qualities (in reverse) as high as 0.6.

It has long been observed by authorities on mental defect, *e.g.*, Tredgold,

Burt, Goddard, Terman, Doll, that the characteristic traits of the mental defective are lack of initiative, suggestibility, impulsiveness and lack of foresight, apathy, and unreliability. The syndrome of true mental defect affects only some 1 to 2 per cent of the population, but it constitutes a largely inherited condition, as do higher levels of intelligence, and grades into the general intelligence distribution. Consequently, the personality associates of merely subaverage intelligence would be expected to be less extreme degrees of those revealed by this approach through the extreme, abnormal case, and the above factorial analyses confirm this interpretation.

Laycock (31) compared defective aspects of personality adjustment in fifty-one children above I.Q. 110 (median 121) with fifty-one others below I.Q. 90 (median 78.8). He found that lower intelligence was significantly more associated (in declining order) with ratings of grouchiness, peevishness, depression, mocking others, cheating, spitefulness, gossiping, truancy, tempertantrums, being too dependent, showing feelings of inferiority, failing to join group activities—in short, with signs of ergic frustration and defective superego development. High intelligence, on the other hand, was related significantly to defects of overimaginativeness, overconscientiousness, conceit, overconfidence, and craving for sympathy.

**Interpretation of Associations.** The causes for some of these associations have already been discussed in this chapter, under delinquency. A small part may be due to genetic adhesion (Chap. 14), another part—that residing in the positive correlation of $B$ and $C$ factors (Chap. 4)—may be due to individuals of low intelligence being very likely to have their personality training badly organized by parents of low intelligence and low social status. But probably most of the correlation must be interpreted as due to the effects of low intelligence directly upon the experience of the individual. That the feeling of worthlessness and ego frustration seem so often associated with low intelligence is partly a consequence of the individual's initial experience being in an environment—the school—which necessarily places much emphasis on intelligence and assigns great prestige to learning ability. But the ergic frustration existing alongside the ego frustration arises from the inevitably greater failure in seeking for satisfaction generally, either in dealing with the nonhuman environment or through the almost inevitably relative failure in a competitive human society. Whether these frustrations and defects of training lead more to delinquency on the one hand or to apathy and lack of initiative on the other will depend on the factors discussed under delinquency.

**Personality Associates of Abnormally High Intelligence.** The effects of the opposite "abnormal" deviation—high intelligence—have been very thoroughly studied by Terman and his coworkers (47,48). Fortunately it is possible to put the essence of these findings, concerned with the top

1 per cent or ½ of 1 per cent of the intelligence distribution, very briefly by saying that the majority of personality traits found are the complete opposite of those found for mental defect. The deviant individual tends to have better than average physique and good looks, greater freedom from illness, outstanding school performance, more than average emotional stability, high conscientiousness and perseverance (47), and tends to come from a home with better attitudes on home and child. (See (50), Chap. 17.) Only in a certain withdrawal from social life (lower rating for "fondness for groups," "popularity," and "leadership") does he resemble the defective; he prefers to read and have intelligent hobbies rather than "go with the crowd"—for both the highly intelligent and the defective are deviants and share certain characteristics created by frustration of gregariousness (47,48).

The highly intelligent child, as shown both by Terman's and by Hollingworth's studies, tends to get habits of nonconformity and sometimes of almost unhealthy withdrawal from social adaptation into the world of books and phantasy. He chooses companions among older people. If put in class with children of the same actual age he is reported as "restless," "lacking in interest," and "daydreaming." Fales (17) with a scale of "vigorousness of play" found the more vigorous children were those of lower actual age or of lower mental age (compared to the group average). In athletic interests and social and religious activities the more intelligent rates lower than the low intelligence deviates (43), he dislikes competitive games, but exceeds the averagely as well as the subaveragely intelligent child in total range of interests, consistent development of interests, and in social and quiet games (48). At college some of the relative social disabilities of childhood disappear. Miller found the college student of high intelligence to be lower in athletic interests, higher in extracurricular activities generally, especially in dramatics, publication (including journalism), and particularly debating, and to appear more frequently in public office.

In later life the highly intelligent deviant is opposite to the defective in having a greater than average constancy of employment, of representation in skilled, professional occupations and in occupations (e.g., moral education, research) which are constructive rather than destructive of the community.

## 7. INTELLIGENCE AND THE ABNORMAL PERSONALITY

**Interpreting Intelligence-test Findings in Other Abnormalities.** The last section has studied directly the influence of high or low intelligence of an extreme kind upon personality, with certain definite findings. But, because intelligence is a readily measurable personality factor, much evidence has accumulated also on the relation of intelligence to all kinds of personality abnormalities, and this evidence is worthy of consideration for the additional clarifications it produces with regard both to the meaning of intelligence and the nature or sources of these abnormalities.

To comprehend results in this and similar areas it is necessary to bear in mind that performance on speeded intelligence tests declines from the age of about twenty-two, but not on unspeeded tests, and that the decline is less in verbal intelligence than in the perception of *new* relations. The saturation of special performances with general ability, whether it is taken out as a first-order ($g$) or a second-order factor ($G$), declines after childhood. These facts, and others on brain injury (Chap. 10) have been organized elsewhere under the *theory of fluid and crystallized ability* (13). This hypothesis supposes that after adolescence two overlapping general abilities are operative, (*a*) *fluid ability* which has to do with the perception of complex relations, which is measured in speeded tests, which continues to preserve its unitary function, and declines with age; and (*b*) *crystallized ability*, which remains at the level of the original fluid ability, suffers loss of speed with age, has to do with acquired powers of discrimination, and does not preserve its unity except in a passive historical sense, *e.g.*, brain injury may affect one area only of the crystallized ability but not of fluid ability (13). This problem of age trends in ability is discussed in more detail in Chapter 20.

**Intelligence, Psychosis, and Neurosis.** Many studies have been made on the relation of intelligence to psychosis and neurosis with indefinite or conflicting results. The first study adequate in scale and method to clear up the problem seems to be that of Roe and Shakow (38) who finished with the following Binet scores (uncorrected for age) for various groups.

|  | *Months of mental age* |
|---|---|
| Psychoneuroses | 169.1 |
| Manic-depressive psychoses | 166.4 |
| Catatonic schizophrenic psychoses | 164.8 |
| Paranoid schizophrenic psychoses | 164.7 |
| Normal controls | 163.6 |
| Psychopathic personality | 163.0 |
| Simple schizophrenia | 154.8 |
| Chronic alcoholism | 145.9 |
| Unclassified schizophrenics | 144.0 |
| General paresis | 132.1 |
| Feeblemindedness | 104.4 |

Nearly all the differences from normals were significant, but there was considerable overlap and dispersion in all groups.

Considerable doubt will always arise in the minds of readers as to how far intelligence testing of persons in psychotic states represents the full powers of the psychotic and especially of the less accessible schizophrenics. Even with accessibility and cooperation it has long been suspected that states of mental conflict and emotionality may actually temporarily reduce general intelligence, and the careful studies of Stone with schizophrenics who showed recovery indicates that in acute stages such reductions occur. Nevertheless the Roe and Shakow findings deserve confidence because the experimenters were very careful to avoid cases where emotional states upset performance.

Another possibility of distortion arises through selection. Some of the early studies obtaining very low intelligence levels for psychotic populations took inmates of state institutions, mainly serving groups of low socio-economic status. Furthermore, it might be argued that selection goes on with respect to commitment to mental hospitals because the more intelligent, even when deranged, are more capable of managing their affairs so as to avoid commitment. At least in the last generation, the more well-to-do neurotic or psychotic was cared for at home and did not come into the area of state-hospital surveys.

**Interpretation of Intelligence Level Differences among Psychotic Types.** Many questions could be asked, but the most important seem to be: (*a*) Do the intelligence levels represent differing degrees of deterioration under different psychoses, or differing degrees of liability among various intelligence levels to certain psychoses? (*b*) If the latter, is the association due to hereditary correlations or to the ability of the more intelligent to avoid, relatively, certain kinds of frustration or stress?

Studies of "psychological deficit" show that almost all psychotic groups, relative to normals, are better on vocabulary tests than other intelligence subtests. Much of the supposed "deterioration" in schizophrenics turns out not to be a real and irreversible loss of intelligence but a loss, perhaps largely permanent, in dynamic power to maintain a mental set long enough to solve a problem. However, the results of Roe and Shakow seem substantially borne out by other studies (30) and it seems likely that the above figures represent most nearly *the intelligence levels of individuals prone to the various psychoses*.

From the frequencies of geniuses with various mental disorders, as well as from other oblique sources of information, one would suspect, as the above averages show, that the manic-depressive has a slight tendency to be congenitally above average intelligence. Similarly general paretics, even apart from the deteriorative process, are likely to be well below average, because it is known that the incidence of syphilis in the population is decidedly higher in the lower social groups.

It is also known that both schizophrenia and alcoholism (Chap. 14) are more frequent with lower social status. But the prepsychotic schizophrenic tends to be an unusually steady, orderly individual and probably shows, like the alcoholic, a likelihood of having been overprotected. Granted good intelligence these individuals would probably have made fine citizens: without it, their very rigidity, persistence, and dependence on authority are likely to make the resulting relative failure seem worse and less bearable. In short, low intelligence may create situations which the schizoid is peculiarly unable to bear. On the other hand, manic-depressive disorder seems to have so high a hereditary determination (Chap. 5) that no amount of intelligence and success is likely to avoid it—and it happens further that it has some hereditary association with high ability.

**Intelligence and Neurotic Syndromes.** Concerning intelligence and neurosis there has also been prolonged vacillation of opinion, principally between the view that high intelligence, and the complex attitudes which it makes possible, predisposes the intelligent person to neurosis, and the opposite view that the less intelligent, exposed to more severe emotional trauma and frustrations, are more frequently neurotic. Most of the more extensive studies show a mean and scatter barely significantly different from the normal population, but the deviation is almost always above the normal, as in the Roe and Shakow study. Thus Hunt (30) lists six studies, the mean of the average values found being 164.5, a little above the mean (160 to 164) for the general population. Eysenck (see (22), Chap. 17), however, with military neurotics, finds a slight inferiority of neurotics in means, but favors the view that the only significant difference from normals is in standard deviation, the neurotics being more scattered.

The failure to find any consistent trend in the difference of neurotic group from normal group means may indicate that the difference is a function of the organization of various social groups. But the consistent finding of greater standard deviation suggests that the stress of *being different from the average* is a constant factor in neurosis. However, there is no doubt but that differences of mean intelligence exist between different *kinds* of neurotics. The means of the studies by Hollingworth (28), Roe and Shakow (38), and Malamud and Gottlieb (34) pooled, with equal weight, give the following:

|  | *Mental age in months* |
|---|---|
| Psychasthenia (obsessional neurosis) | 177.6 |
| Anxiety neurosis (hysteria) | 172.0 |
| (Conversion) hysteria | 163.6 |
| Neurasthenia | 155.8 |

Apart from the unduly low position of neurasthenia, these averages agree with other scattered results, *e.g.*, of McDougall (35) and, as far as anxiety and conversion hysteria are concerned, receive confirmation from Eysenck's far more extensive data. They agree also with what is disclosed in the next chapter about social status distribution of neurosis. Indeed, it is most likely that the above rank order according to intelligence is produced by social status and would therefore stand out more emphatically if years of education or measures of typical attitudes of families in different social groups were inserted instead of intelligence-test scores.

In general, the evidence of this chapter and the next would lead us to expect, in regard to personality disturbances of *all* kinds, that low intelligence is rather strongly associated with delinquency and higher intelligence or social status slightly associated with particular forms of psychosis and neurosis. The evidence for children, who generally offer more representative sampling, tends to confirm this conclusion. Levy (33) surveying 700 children with psychological problems (aged three to eighteen years) found more personality and nervous, emotional problems in the higher I.Q.'s and more antisocial conduct problems in the lower I.Q.'s. Such results might be queried on the grounds that neurosis is probably somewhat more associated with higher social status and education than I.Q., and that parents of such status would be more likely to refer nervous children for treatment. However, Levy reports, perhaps with insufficient statistical basis, that the connection of personality disorders is closer with I.Q. than with social status. Burt (9), on the other hand, found problems of nervous disorder reaching about 12 per cent among children in the less intelligent ranges, compared with about 4 per cent in the general, average population. Probably the solution, at least in regard to adult findings, lies in Eysenck's observation that neurosis increases with deviation from the mean intelligence, so that experimentation with high- or low-skewed samples get different results.

### 8. SUMMARY

1. "Abnormality" means both "deviation" and "defect." In some cases the second has meaning only in regard to normative standards and in most cases the *extent of defect* defining an abnormal limit depends on statistical standards. But, intrinsically, "defective" (or pathological) is a different dimension from "deviant" or statistically abnormal. "Eccentric" and "unadapted" are suggested as correct terms for these logically distinct but practically correlated dimensions.

2. Some twelve or more personality factors or traits have been found with respect to which significant differences exist between delinquents and nondelinquents in our society.

3. Some twelve or more family, social, and experimental background factors have been found which are significantly different for delinquents and nondelinquents in our society.

4. The determination of delinquency by these factors is complex, some operating directly, others through secondary factors; some having a simple linear relation, some a curvilinear relation. However, it is possible roughly to pick out factors of more outstanding potency than others, *e.g.*, low intelligence and high general emotionality among hereditary factors; parental

rejection and lack of discipline among environmental, experiential factors, and social disorganization among environmental field factors or syntality conditions.

5. Maladaptation as shown in poor school performance is related to maladaptation in regard to occupational success. Low intelligence and inadequacy of personal character operate in both, but poor school performance is more strongly related to low intelligence. The personality qualities associated with extremely low intelligence, *e.g.*, lack of initiative and confidence, antisocial attitudes, are in part opposite to those found with extremely high intelligence, but both extremes share traits arising from a certain withdrawal from the life of the group.

6. Abnormal personalities with respect to psychosis and psychoneurosis do not deviate from the intelligence average as clearly as do those who are delinquent. Psychotics, particularly schizophrenics and depressives, show defective intelligence-test performance while in psychotic states; but the prepsychotic intelligence of psychotics appears to be distributed similarly to that of normals and only slightly below it. Of the functional psychoses, the schizophrenias occur more in individuals of lower intelligence, while manic-depressive disorder seems hereditarily associated with greater than average intelligence. Psychoneurotics average the same as normals but are more dispersed. Among neurotics, psychasthenics and anxiety hysterics tend to be more intelligent than neurasthenics or conversion hysterics.

## QUESTIONS AND EXERCISES

1. Discuss the different use of the two meanings of abnormal (eccentric and unadapted) with respect to the definition of (*a*) a delinquent, (*b*) a mental defective, and (*c*) a neurotic.

2. State the incidence of delinquency generally and of specific forms in the general population. How does it vary with sex, age, social status, intelligence, ecology, and national culture pattern?

3. Describe six personality characteristics related to delinquency and indicate the nature of the evidence for these connections.

4. Describe six characteristics of the environment and personal history (including the individual's physique) associated with delinquency and indicate the nature of the evidence for the association.

5. Analyze the various factors in parental condition and behavior that tend to result in child delinquency, and state definite hypotheses as to how each operates.

6. Attempt to rank in order, in our society, the potency of some ten factors in delinquency. Choose six of these as being relatively independent of one another and describe the interdependence which caused you to reject the remaining four as independent factors.

7. Describe the incidence of abnormal backwardness in school performance and discuss its personal and environmental associations.

8. Describe the personality characteristics that tend to differentiate, respectively, extreme high and low deviates in intelligence from the average person. What are the causes for the appearances of these traits?

9. Discuss the intelligence of psychotics and particular varieties of psychotics, dealing with methodological difficulties and the interpretation of the results.

10. What is known about the intelligence of neurotics? Mention some alternative possibilities to the notion that the observed connections are due to the effect of intelligence level directly upon personality development.

## BIBLIOGRAPHY

1. ACKERSON, L.: *Childrens' Behavior Problems:* Vol. II. *Relative Importance and Interrelations Among Traits*, University of Chicago Press, Chicago, 1942–1943.
2. ALEXANDER, F., and W. HEALY: *Roots of Crime*, Alfred A. Knopf, Inc., New York, 1935.
3. BAGOT, J. H.: *Juvenile Delinquency: A Comparative Study of the Position in Liverpool and England and Wales*, Jonathan Cape, Ltd., London, 1941.
4. BERG, I.: A Comparative Study of Car Thieves, *J. crim. Law Criminol.*, 34: 392–396, 1944.
5. BERG, I.: A Comparative Study of Forgery. *J. appl. Psychol.*, 28: 232–238, 1944.
6. BURKEY, R. E.: A Statistical Study of the Sequence of Successive Delinquencies, *J. juv. Res.*, 16: 133–144 1932.
7. BURT, C. L.: Critical Notice of Juvenile Delinquency by J. H. Bagot, *Brit. J. educ. Psychol.* 11: 138–142, 1941.
8. BURT, C. L.: *The Young Delinquent*, University of London Press Ltd., London, 1948.
9. BURT, C. L.: *The Backward Child*, Appleton-Century-Crofts, Inc., New York, 1937.
10. CABOT, P. S. Q.: *Juvenile Delinquency*, The H. W. Wilson Company, New York, 1946.
11. CARR-SAUNDERS, A. M., H. MANNHEIM, and E. C. RHODES: *Young Offenders*, The Macmillan Company, New York, 1944.
12. CATTELL, R. B.: The Diagnosis and Classification of Neurotic States, *J. nerv. ment. Dis.* 102: 576–589, 1945.
13. CATTELL, R. B.: The Measurement of Adult Intelligence, *Psychol. Bull.*, 3: 153–193, 1943.
14. CATTELL, R. B.: Some Changes in Social Life in a Community with a Falling Intelligence Quotient, *Brit. J. Psychol.*, 28: 430–450, 1938.
15. CATTELL, R. B.: *A Guide to Mental Testing*, 2d ed., University of London Press, Ltd., London, 1947.
15a. CATTELL, R. B.: *Crooked Personalities in Childhood and After: An Outline of Psychotherapy*, Cambridge University Press, London, 1938.
16. CHASSELL, C. F.: The Relation Between Morality and Intellect, *Teachers Coll. Contrib. Educ.* No. 607, 1935.
16a. DOOB, L. W., J. DOLLARD, N. E. MILLER, O. H. MOWRER, and R. R. SEARS: *Frustration and Aggression*, Yale University Press, New Haven, 1939.
17. FALES, E.: A Comparison of the Vigorousness of Play Activities of Preschool Boys and Girls, *Child Develpm.* 8: 144–158, 1937.
18. FROSCH, J., and W. BROMBERG: The Sex Offender; a Psychiatric Study, *Amer. J. Orthpsychiat.*, 9: 761–777, 1939.
19. GARRETT, H. E.: *Great Experiments in Psychology*, Appleton-Century-Crofts, Inc., New York, 1930.
20. GERLACH, M.: A Study of the Relationship between Psychometric Patterns and Personality Types, *Child Develpm.* 10: 269–278, 1939.
21. GLUECK, S.: Types of Delinquent Careers, *Nat. Comm. for Ment. Hygiene*, N.Y., 1917.
22. HARTMAN, A. A.: Recidivism and Intelligence. *J. crim. Law Criminol.*, 31: 417–426, 1940.

23. HARTMANN, A. A., and P. L. SCHROEDER: Criminality and the Age Factor, *J. crim. Psychopath.* 5: 351–362, 1943.
24. HEALY, W., and A. F. BRONNER: *New Light on Delinquency and Its Treatment*, Yale University Press, New Haven, 1936.
25. HEALY, W., A. F. BRONNER, and A. M. BOWERS: *Structure and Meaning of Psychoanalysis*, Alfred A. Knopf, Inc., New York, 1930.
26. HEWITT, L. E., and R. L. JENKINS: *Fundamental Patterns in Maladjustment, and the Dynamics of Their Origin*, State of Illinois, Springfield, 1946.
27. HIRSCH, N.: *Dynamic Causes of Juvenile Crime*, Sci-Art Publishers, Cambridge, 1937.
28. HOLLINGWORTH, H. L.: *Psychology of Functional Neurosis*, Appleton-Century-Crofts, Inc., New York, 1920.
29. HOVEY, H. B.: Behavior Characteristics of Antisocial Recidivists, *J. crim. Law Criminol.*, 32: 635–642, 1942.
30. HUNT, J. Mc V., and C. W. COFER: Psychological Deficit; in *Personality and the Behavior Disorders*, Vol. II, The Ronald Press Company, New York, 1944.
31. LAYCOCK, S. R.: Adjustments of Superior and Inferior School Children, *J. soc. Psychol.*, 4: 353–366, 1933.
32. LAYCOCK, S. R.: Teachers' Reactions to Maladjustments of School Children, *Brit. J. educ. Psychol.* 4: 11–29, 1934.
33. LEVY, D.: A Quantitative Study of the Relationship between Intelligence and Economic Status as Factors in the Etiology of Children's Behavior Problems, *Amer. J. Orthopsychiat.*, 1: 152–167, 1931.
34. MALAMUD, W., and J. GOTTLIEB: *Therapeutic Results in Psycho-neurosis*, 1944 (unpublished)
35. McDOUGALL, W.: *Outline of Abnormal Psychology*, Charles Scribner's Sons, New York, 1926.
36. MOSIER, C. I.: On the Validity of Neurotic Questionnaires, *J. soc. Psychol.*, 9: 3–16, 1938.
37. MYERSON, A.: Neuroses and Psychoneuroses: the Relationship of Symptom Groups, *Amer. J. Psychiat.*, 93: 263–301, 1936.
38. ROE, A., and D. SHAKOW: Intelligence in Mental Disorder, *Ann. N.Y. Acad. Sci.*, 42: 361–490, 1942.
39. RUBENSTEIN, L.: Personal Attitudes of Maladjusted boys, *Arch. Psychol.*, N.Y., 250, 101, 1940.
40. SANFORD, R. N.: Psychological Approaches to the Young Delinquent, *J. consult. Psychol.*, 7: 223–229, 1943.
41. SHAW, C. R., and H. D. McKAY: *Juvenile Delinquency and Urban Areas*, University of Chicago Press, Chicago, 1942.
42. SLATER, P.: Scores of Different Types of Neurotics on Tests of Intelligence, *Brit. J. Psychol.*, 35: 40–42, 1945.
43. SMITH, G. B.: Intelligence and the Extra-curriculum Activities Selected in High School and College, *Sch. Rev.*, 44: 681–688, 1936.
44. SNYDER, B. J., and W. U. SNYDER: Some Relationships between Childrens' Symptoms of Maladjustment and Background Factors, *J. clin. Psychol.*, 2: 13–22, 1946.
45. SPEER, G. S.: Wishes, Fears, Interests, and Identifications of Delinquent Boys, *Child Develpm.*, 8: 289–294, 1937.
46. SULLENGER, T. E.: *Social Determinants in Juvenile Delinquency*, John Wiley & Sons, Inc., New York, 1936.
47. TERMAN, L.: *Genetic Studies of Genius, Vol. III*, Stanford University Press, Stanford University, Calif., 1925–1930.

48. TERMAN, L., and M. H. ODEN: *The Gifted Child Grows Up: Twenty-five Years Follow-up of a Superior Group*, Stanford University Press, Stanford University, Calif., 1947.
49. TOLMAN, R. S.: Some Differences in Attitudes between Groups of Repeating Criminals and of First Offenders, *J. crim. Law Criminol.*, 30: 196–203, 1939.
50. TULCHIN, S. H.: *Intelligence and Crime*, University of Chicago Press, Chicago, 1939.
51. WEGROCKI, H. J.: A Critique of Cultural and Statistical Concepts of Abnormality, *J. abnorm. Psychol.*, 34: 166–178, 1939.

## CHAPTER 17

## THE ABNORMAL AND UNADAPTED PERSONALITY:
## II. THE NEUROTIC

### 1. THE DESCRIPTION OF NEUROTICISM

**General Neuroticism Defined as a Factor or Source Trait.** The nature of such specific syndromes as conversion hysteria, obsessional neurosis (psychasthenia), neurasthenia, and anxiety hysteria, as well as the nature of their general differentiation from psychoses, has already been set out in Chapter 1. Our task is now to penetrate beyond these syndrome descriptions to ask about the essential nature and interpretation of neurosis in general. The more recent, exact, and detailed evidence now to be studied will not, however, permit of formulation only in such simple generalizations as those of conflict, repression, and unconscious action, obtainable at the first level of nonmetric, clinical observation, as set out in Chapter 9. It belongs in part to a new era of clinical calculus which is likely to surpass present clinical control as much as a modern engineer's bridge surpasses the first log felled across a stream.

Although a common *syndrome* of general neurosis is not easily perceived and defined clinically, the more refined methods of factor analysis reveal that neuroses do have in common a *factor* which shows itself in a wide variety of behavior manifestations and is common to the different syndromes. As indicated in Chapter 4, a factor sometimes called Depression or General Neurotic Maladjustment is found in questionnaire material which shows itself in reports of "feeling lonesome even with others," "feeling worried and tense with little cause," "feeling miserable and in low spirits," "feeling not well adjusted to life," "suffering from insomnia," etc. But the identification of this with neurotic tendencies may be wrong, for it has no significant

486

relation to the $C$ $(-)$ factor or Emotional Maturity and Stability, which, in its negative loading, determines the traits "unrealistic," "changeable," "emotional and restless," "irritable," "self-pitying," "evasive," "dissatisfied," and "subjective." This, which from its description more closely corresponds to neurosis, correlates with a questionnaire factor of "being unable to keep emotions under control," "getting overexcited and rattled easily," etc., as discussed in Chapter 4. Precise factor measurements now being applied to neurotics should soon clear up the question of the roles of these two factors in clinical neurosis.

Eysenck's correlation of symptoms and background data on 700 male neurotics is one of the most extensive studies attempting to get at the nature of general neuroticism and, as rotated by the present writer (see (12), Chap. 16), yields a general factor loading such variables as badly organized, unadaptable, unstable personality, 0.75; symptoms of nervous disorder since childhood, 0.68; abnormal personality in the parents, 0.66; depressive or hypomanic mood, 0.62; seclusiveness, 0.58; stress of wartime regimentation and separation not sustained, 0.55; weak, dependent attitudes, 0.54; and poor muscle tone and posture 0.53. Eysenck also adds (22) narrow interests, dyspepsia, little energy, and hypochondriasis. Evidence of a neuroticism factor in objective-test data is discussed below.

**Clinical Description of General Neuroticism.** The impressions of clinicians as to what constitutes general neuroticism may be illustrated by Myerson's account of civilian neuroses and Grinker and Spiegel's (30) account of war neuroses. The former points to fatigue or energy disturbance (sudden loss of energy, low energy, fitfulness of energy, with physical symptoms such as violent heart action on slight exertion), distractability (obsessive and irrelevant memories), overreaction to stimuli (getting excited too easily, agitation over little, uncontrolled reflexes), overconsciousness of bodily processes (paresthesias, hypochondria) anhedonia (failure of desire, especially of appetite for food, sex, sleep, sociability), increased doubt in making decisions, etc., and feelings of unreality about the external world and the self.

Slater's study of 1233 war neurotics (67) found sexual impotence or inadequacy prominent[1] and significant differences also in the direction of a general sense of inadequacy in childhood, in poor physical habits, and incidence of amnesic tendencies. Other writers confirm the above list of essential items and add to the general neurotic picture stammering, enuresis, instability of emotion, nail-biting, vertigo, chronic low back pain, globus hystericus and inability to swallow pills, frequent headaches, desire to be alone, feelings of unreality and depersonalization, increased pulse pressure, dilated pupils, frequent micturition, and transient glycosuria.

---

[1] In several hundred civilian neurotics Reich (60) found about 50 per cent to be sexually abstinent, and serious disorder of potency in most of the remainder.

Grinker and Spiegel (30) list symptoms in military hospitalization (combat failure) in the following order of frequency:

Restlessness
Irritability and aggression
Fatigue and lethargy on arising
Difficulty in falling asleep
Sense of anxiety and tension
Ready fatigue
Excessive startle reaction
Depression and seclusiveness
Memory disturbances and failures with personality change
Tremor (loss of muscular coordination) and sympathetic overreactivity
Difficulty in concentration, mental confusion
Increased alcoholism
Decreased appetite
Preoccupation with combat experiences, nightmares, and battle dreams
Psychosomatic symptoms, *e.g.*, increased frequency of urination
Irrational fears and suspicions

When the emphasis in the causation of the war neurosis is on a traumatic war event rather than on the trauma of childhood there is evidence that the neurotic syndrome shows more overt guilt, nightmares, exaggerated startle reaction, tremors, gastric disturbance, and a reactive emotion in the recall of the event.

In children Ackerson defines a syndrome of nervousness, restlessness, and irritability which had significant correlations in his large clinic sample with changeableness of moods, restlessness in sleep, queer, irrational behavior, worrisomeness, distractability, temper, and daydreaming.

**Objective-test Evidence on the General-neuroticism Factor.** The agreement of these pictures of general neuroticism, despite differences of age, provocative situation, sample, and method of analysis is too striking to require that we present any single list of the common features. It remains, however, to see what experimental measurement can add to the definition. A summary of experimental findings on general neurosis, unless it is to drop much of the available data, must include samples somewhat biased toward particular forms of neurosis. The associations that are found, to a reasonable reliability, are with perseveration (disposition rigidity; neuroticism with extreme scores but especially high scores); high suggestibility on body-sway test; low fluency of association; low persistence in miniature-situation tests of endurance; poor dark vision (vision in faint light after half-an-hour of adaptation); high static ataxia in a blindfold, standing test; a tendency to more eccentric associations to ink blots (judged by the statistical norm on a selective-answer test); a tendency for greater fluctuation of attitudes (see

(21), Chap. 18); a tendency for matching to be carried out more by color than by form; high ratio of mistakes to score in a motor or other test requiring care; slow personal tempo; poor mirror-image performance; poor maze performance (Porteus) when intelligence is partialed out; more amnesia for early childhood events (questioned in some studies); more annoyances indicated on an annoyance inventory (Bennett); and fewer objective interests.

Many of the above associations have been established by the extensive factorizations of abnormal populations by Eysenck (22) and his coworkers; some by the present writer's experiments with a hundred varied objective personality tests (see (7,12a), Chap. 4); and a few, *e.g.*, the associations with perseveration, with mirror drawing, with persistence tests, with color preference, etc., by one or more individual investigators in special fields. But the majority of the associations have been confirmed·by at least two researches.

In addition to showing the decline in will power (ego strength, persistence, and inhibition) and the increased fluctuation and instability which are in line with general clinical observation, these results indicate somewhat surprisingly an equally emphatic basic impairment of energy and even of general physical fitness. They show, for example, more fatigue in arithmetical calculation or in any learning process, poorer sensory acuity (night vision), slower tempo, ataxia, poorer physical and general muscular endurance,[2] lack of reserves for even small strains, defective autonomic efficiency, and neurocirculatory instability.[3] On the other hand Ruesch (65), by taking a lactic acid index of true degree of exhaustion, concluded that the typical neurotic's complaints of fatigue and inability to face strain are not the result of defective physical fitness. The lack of fitness is in the lack of coordination of a still essentially unimpaired physical apparatus. Presumably these failures are the ultimate consequences of central nervous fatigue, through prolonged maintenance of tensions.

## 2. THE INCIDENCE AND DISTRIBUTION OF NEUROTICISM

**Neurosis in Civil and Military Populations.** To understand the above syndrome more fully by studying its incidence is not easy, for unlike delinquency, where police arrest and indictment constitute a sufficiently abrupt line of demarcation, the accepted levels of neurosis, in the absence of developed measurements, differ considerably from observer to observer.

Perhaps the best estimate of civilian incidence is that of Hirsch (36) who placed it at 3 per cent if conservatively and 4 per cent if more liberally

[2] With anxiety and effort syndrome neurotics, Jones and Mellersh (40) found a significantly poorer exercise response—lactate rise, pulse change, additional oxygen uptake.

[3] Osborne and Cohen (58), in a study of circulatory disorders—"peripheral vasoneuropathy"—in men suffering from exposure, concluded "the man of unstable personality [was found] particularly liable to severe effects from cold." Others report more vascular upset (increase in arm volume) in neurotics when making mental effort.

defined, in the United States. According to Dorcus (17), "The Surgeon General reported in 1947 that there are 8,000,000 Americans in need of care for mental disability." If we set aside the 500,000 in mental hospitals as the psychotic fraction, and another equivalent fraction for mental defect, we are left with a liberal estimate of 7,000,000 psychoneurotics, *i.e.*, about 5 per cent of the population.

On the other hand, the screening examination of selective service men in the last war rejected 1.5 per cent as suffering from definite neurosis (17). But it is well known that many neurotics had to be rejected in the later training period and that some of the psychiatric casualties in combat were previously neurotic. Presumably, therefore, in the United States, neurotic conditions severe enough partially to disable the individual, *e.g.*, to restrict him to occupations of low strain, affect between 2 and 5 per cent of the population, the true value being probably near the latter figure.

**Neurosis among Children.** Burt (8,9) studying neurosis in children, where its syndromes and forms are less defined than in adults, found the incidence to be 17 per cent in normal conditions but as high as 25 per cent among evacuees in wartime. He found neurasthenic syndromes about twice as prevalent as hysteria, and anxiety states about twice as prevalent as neurasthenia. Burt's standard of "neurotic behavior needing attention" in children is obviously higher than the above estimate of "disabling" neurosis in adults. Similar figures—one in five—have, however, been suggested for incidence of *noticeable neurotic symptoms* in adults.

**Incidence under Various Social Conditions.** The nonmetric, clinical-type estimates at present available, therefore, suggest an incidence of one in five for mild, recognizable neurosis and one in twenty for more severe,[4] disabling neurosis. This helps define the neurotic personality as discussed here; but, as indicated in Chapters 14 and 15, on the culture pattern, figures on the *relative* incidence of neurosis in different cultures, occupations, age groups, etc., would be more helpful in throwing light on the interpretation of neurosis. The indications are at present (59) that neurosis declines slightly in frequency after adolescence, except in those who remain unmarried, in whom it tends to increase. However, it is possible that there are increases for all in middle age in general nervousness, as some results show. On neurotic questionnaires women tend to show more neurotic reactions than men, at all ages studied. Farr and Stewart (23) in one- to sixteen-year follow-ups of 200 neurotics found 55 per cent had achieved tolerable adjustment,

---

[4] This rate is also in accord with Terman's estimate of 5 per cent of definite neurosis in school children; with the Lloyd survey of school children in Birmingham, England, which arrived at 6 per cent ((8) p. 336), with Burt's estimate of 4 per cent showing "urgent need for treatment" among children in a London borough (8) and with Culpin and Smith's finding, in 1,000 interviewed workers in industry, that 6 per cent had symptoms serious enough to call for treatment (15).

13 per cent eventually became psychotic, 24 per cent had not changed and 8 per cent committed suicide.

Crook, with neurotic questionnaires, retesting students after a five-year lapse, found a correlation of neuroticism score of 0.5—which indicates considerable persistence of neurotic trends. Good data—*i.e.*, extensive, representative, and objectively gathered data—on the incidence of recovery or change of form of neurosis are, however, still unavailable.

Stagner and Willoughby found questionnaire results bearing out clinical records indicating a higher incidence of neurosis among women. Items dealing with social feelings and situations were actually more frequently "morbid" in men; but most items, and those especially dealing with abnormal fears, compulsions, affects and moods, were higher in women.

As to the changing incidence of neurosis with social change there is clear evidence that it is on the increase, that the increase is most marked in psychosomatic disorders, and that conversion hysteria is, at least relative to other disorders, less common than formerly. Contrasting psychiatric casualties in draftees of the First World War with those of the Second World War, Hadfield (31) found in 700 of the latter more psychosomatic disorders, more low intelligence, more psychopathic personalities, and fewer conversion hysterics.

## 3. FACTORS IN NEUROTICISM AS SEEN THROUGH EXPERIMENTATION

**Limitations of Available Evidence.** Evidence on the origins of neuroses, apart from the preexperimental and prestatistical evidence of general clinical observation, as in psychoanalysis, comes largely from two sources: experimental studies on animals, and statistical data on hereditary and environmental frequencies in the background of human neurotics. The human statistical and experimental data are poor and unorganized compared with the evidence on delinquency, and we shall therefore start with the laboratory studies of animals.

As is well known, the first experimental studies on neurosis in animals were made by Pavlov, who trained dogs to expect food when one signal appeared (shown by salivation), and not to expect it when another signal appeared. He then made the signals more similar until the dogs' powers of discrimination no longer permitted them to tell with certainty whether their hunger would or would not be satisfied. Liddell (42*a*), Stockard (70), Gantt (26), Divorkin, Masserman (see (30), Chap. 21), Anderson and Parmenter (1) successfully repeated the experiment with sheep, pigs, cats, and goats. Maier (47) presented rats with discrimination problems and obtained markedly abnormal behavior when their expectations were upset, but he used an air blast as well as hunger to force them to choose, and it was later shown by Morgan (see (59), Chap. 10) and others that the high-pitched sound of the air blast alone accounted for the rats' behavior, which has since been named "audiogenic seizure."

The first criticism that must be applied to the current wholesale application of these results to the problem of human neurosis has to be directed to the unscientific, question-begging practice of referring to these disturbances as "animal neurosis" or "experimental neurosis." The behavior of the disturbed rat—wild, blind running, tonic and clonic fits, waxy flexibility, exhaustion, and failure to learn or respond normally for a time thereafter—resembles in human experience, first, epilepsy and, second, catatonic episodes, but neurosis scarcely at all. On the other hand, it is true that Hunt and Schlosberg (37), by causing rats to get an electric shock whenever they went to drink, produced a syndrome of flight, huddling, unpredictable aggressive behavior, and incontinence, which more nearly resembled that of neurosis.

**The Neurosis Syndrome in Animals.** The greatest bulk of research so far done in this area, on rats, must thus be set aside as concerned with "audiogenic seizure," peculiar apparently to the constitution of rodents (though human beings are also put "on edge" by certain high-pitched notes). The syndrome of disturbance in cats, dogs, sheep, goats, and pigs has far more definite resemblance to neurosis. We find therein abnormal excitability or depression in the test situation; autonomic upset (overrapid heartbeat and breathing in the choice situation); quarrelsomeness and unexpected aggression; an attempt to withdraw from the whole laboratory situation, with apparent anxiety and hostility toward the experimenter; refusal to eat; loss of whatever test discriminations have been acquired, with refusal or inability to be conditioned to new stimuli; and exaggerated reflex action. In some experiments, or to some extent, this behavior generalizes to situations outside the laboratory. This is shown with decline in eating; excessive sensitivity toward, or, more frequently, failure to respond to sexual stimuli; restless hyperactivity; marked startle reaction; general autonomic activity; and changed social attitudes to human beings and animal cage mates in the experiment.

Pavlov, Liddell (42a), Anderson and Parmenter (1), Gantt (26), and others report that the disturbances in dogs, sheep, etc., last for years, but that a complete change of scene brings some restoration of normality. Masserman (see (30), Chap. 21) on the other hand, was able to recondition a disturbed cat comparatively soon. He also showed that alcohol ingestion at the time of the conflict experience reduced its effect and, ingested later, reduced its consequences, at least temporarily.[5]

The number of higher mammals, *i.e.*, other than rats, on which experi-

---

[5] The same is true of audiogenic seizures in the rat, which are reduced by alcohol, morphine, etc., and increased by strychnine. They are also reduced by opportunity for vigorous bodily activity, notably of an exploratory nature (3,24).

ments have been systematically carried out is still too few to justify much confidence in the details of the syndrome. (For example, Gantt describes an excess of sexual activity in neurotic animals; Masserman, Liddell, and others a loss.) The contrast between the crudeness of measurement of the neurotic behavior (as well as the statistical treatment of the syndrome) on the one hand, the meticulous exactness of the conditioning technique that is supposed to produce it, on the other, betokens a preoccupation with the apparatus rather than the rat, such as stems from the reflexological, pre-organismic tradition. Hebb (35), in pointing out that there is "nothing in the literature that remotely justifies calling rat behavior neurotic," questions also the evidence as to the spread of the neurotic behavior outside the laboratory, in dogs, etc. His own observations on chimpanzees (35), on the other hand, show undoubted similarity to human neuroses, in the form of phobias, excessive emotionality, sexual impairment, agitated anxiety, and seclusiveness. Of the syndrome in cat, dog, sheep, and goat—and possibly of the rat in the Hunt and Schlosberg situation—it can only be said that it presents a truncated human neurosis syndrome, with restlessness, some autonomic and sexual dysfunction, and disorder of memory and learning. The fatigue, inability to sleep, and to some extent the anxiety (and possibly the hypochondriacal paresthesia) appear less definitely than in the human syndrome, or cannot be established.

**Definition of Neurotogenic Situations Found in the Laboratory.** The second and more serious source of doubts regarding present trends in applying these findings to human neurosis concerns the interpretation of the causal action. The situations in the Pavlov-type, reflexological experimentation that have been found to induce "neurosis" are (a) demanding too fine a discrimination between stimuli; (b) attempting to establish progressively longer delayed conditioned reflexes; (c) reversing the expectations, irregularly, on long-familiar positive and negative conditioned stimuli; (d) demanding response to stimuli too faint for definite perception; (e) monotonously repeating, without respite, a nocive conditioned stimulus.

The attempt to explain their action has taken the form of some unitary principle. It is not surprising, since the affects were first noticed in the course of reflexological experiments, that this has been a reflexological principle, rather than a dynamic one, *i.e.*, in terms of $R = f(S)$ instead of $R = f(O,S)$, where $O$ represents the organism and, in this case, its dynamic states. Such explanations not only left a gulf between theories of human and animal neurosis but also kept the design of experiments in a rigid and unfruitful pattern.

More recently attempts have been made to reinterpret the experiments of Pavlov, Liddell, Maier, and others in dynamic terms, and Mowrer, Masserman, and others have redesigned neurotogenic experiments on the hypothesis that the essential cause of the neurosis is conflict. Thus, as we have seen, Masserman (see (30), Chap. 21) set up a conflict in cats between a hunger and a fear drive and produced neurotic symptoms, but his contribution is limited by insufficient statistical control. If it is reasonable to suggest that one swallow does not make a summer, it is also good sense that one cat cannot create a confirmed principle! Liddell (42a), despite a physiological and reflexological frame of reference, has been alert to recognize that the total situation and the animal's dynamic needs are really involved. He cites both his own and Pavlov's extralaboratory observation that dogs develop neuroses from prolonged fear situations in which no escape response can be made; he points out that being imprisoned in the Pavlov apparatus is one factor in the development of the "conditioning" neuroses, and that the "domestication" of the animal, *i.e.*, its dependence upon and emotional attachments to the human experimenter (who then provokes ambivalent dynamic responses, like a sadistic parent) is a necessary factor in neurosis.

Mowrer (54) took two groups of rats and trained one, in a pain situation, to avoid danger by habit $A$. Both were then placed in the same danger situation and trained to avoid it by habit $B$. (Naturally, in the first group there was some difficulty in replacing $A$ by $B$.) Habit $B$ was then inconsistently rewarded (as in the neurosis situations) by a punishment being attached to its use. In these circumstances the first group "regressed" to habit $A$. As we have seen in discussing regression (Chap. 7), it can be either ergic regression or regression of the total personality and each can be conceived as (a) retracing a historical learning sequence; (b) retracing a historical maturation sequence; and (c) regressing in terms of some objective standard of integration or efficiency. Mowrer's experiment shows, in contradiction of the hypothesis of Lewin, that regression in conflict situations is historically determined.

Mowrer also observed an analogue to reaction formation in the above situation. The animals escaped the shock of an electric grill by pressing a pedal. When this was also electrified to give a lesser shock the rats pressed it, though with some conflict and reluctance. Mowrer observed that the first effect of the grill shock was to cause rats to retreat from the pedal, *i.e.*, they experienced, as it were, a feeling of guilt about the pedal, when this desire to escape became insistent, and actually retreated from it, though, like the human sinner, they eventually touched it. Mowrer has also shown similar effects in drives to those previously supposed due to reflexes, in that he demonstrated neurosis through a prolonged waiting period between the cue and the reward (54), analogous to the neurotogenic effect of delayed or trace conditioned reflexes.

**Possibility of Two Dynamic Causes of Neurosis.** Both the dynamic and the reflexologically designed experiments admit some degree of explanation on the hypothesis that sustained mental conflict, *i.e.*, stimulation by cues with incompatible motor outlets, is the cause of neurosis. This explains what we may label the sixth of the descriptively different neurotogenic situations. Sustained conflict occurs in the Mowrer and Masserman results as well as those of Maier, while it may explain the reflexological findings labeled (*a*), (*c*), and (*d*) among the five neurotogenic situations on page 493, for they all involved ambiguity of cues and therefore, presumably, a cognitively determined inability to discharge either drive.

However, the neurotogenic delayed response and the effect of monotonously repeated conditioned nocive stimuli are not more readily brought under the principle than some others. In this connection more observation is needed, of the kind made by Liddell (42*b*) as to possibilities of distinct neurotic patterns following from some, but not all, distinct modes of experimental neurosis production. He observed that whereas the discrimination problem, the delayed response and certain kinds of monotonous repetition produced in the sheep a neurosis characterized by hyperactivity, anxiety, and sleeplessness, other kinds of monotonous repetition produced immobility, withdrawal, and rigidity. (Repetition of a ten-minute anticipatory cue to a shock, followed by foot withdrawal from the shock did the former; a two-minute interval the latter.) It is possible to stretch the conflict theory to meet this, too, since the inhibition of the movement in the interval between the cue to danger and the time for response supposes a second drive (avoidance of effort?) inhibiting the first. But, on the other hand, we need to be alert, having regard to differences in the neurotic pattern, to the possible role of some second principle, perhaps one concerned purely with the economics of neural energy and dependent on levels of excitation reached and amount of neural activity in a given time. From a neurological viewpoint as pointed out by McCulloch (49*a*) the most promising explanation of neurosis is that it is the result of tying up too much energy in closed nervous circuits, from which no discharge can be made. In these the outside stimulus is no longer necessary to provoke the chain of reaction, which proceeds circularly.

## 4. FACTORS IN NEUROTICISM AS SEEN THROUGH STATISTICAL ANALYSIS

**Analysis of Precipitating Causes.** There is not space here to pursue further, in its present state of indefinite formulation and results, the animal experimentation undertaken to throw light on human abnormal behavior. The results show that conflict has essentially the same results as in humans, supporting the conflict theory of neurosis; but the small power of symbolization in the animal and its consequent inability to organize its drives about ego and superego structures of any magnitude, does not permit it to "enjoy its troubles" when physically removed from the conflict situation, as man constantly does, or to experience such prolonged and powerful conflicts. It is possible also that the restriction of animal experimentation largely to the conflict of two particular drives—fear and hunger—instead of the wide gamut involved in the human situations, produces results of restricted generalization.

The statistical analysis of causation in human neurosis, as indicated earlier, is very little developed, partly because the important influences are not such as can be recorded without more advanced measurement of psychological variables, *e.g.*, attitudes, strength of repression, ego integration, than has yet been achieved, and partly because clinical observation alone has uncritically been assumed to give a final understanding. However, there have recently become available statistical data on adequate samples, as in Slater's (67) study of 2,000 neurotic soldiers. These studies show among precipitating strains in the army group such items as separation from home and family, home worries, and the hardship of daily demands on energy. In civilian life, as Myerson points out, there are the strains of competition, of social control of appetitive, visceral drives, of concealment-revealment, *i.e.*, of having to sort behavior into public and private fields, and of constantly integrating behavior to more distant goals than the individual would naturally like.

**Analysis of Background Causes.** But beyond the precipitating circumstances we find early-environment history in many ways similar to that of the delinquent, *i.e.*, a high frequency of parental dissension and vacillating discipline, early problems of feeding and toilet training, etc. The tendency of prison populations to report more worries and to score higher on general neuroticism (or at least, the general emotionality that underlies neuroticism) has already been documented above. Baruch (4) found that maladjustment in preschool children, of the kind that leads in later life to neurosis, was related to parental tensions over sex, dominance-submission, double standards of discipline, insufficient affection, extramarital relations, work, friends, and relatives; but not over leisure habits, criticalness of the partner, tastes, and finances.

Needles (55) studying 100 army neurotic casualties, found, in comparison with 100 controls, poorer family background, socially and emotionally; a history of being more timid, inclined to worry and to be seclusive; fewer than average conflicts with the law, and less drinking, more religious affiliations; more discontent with the army and with society in general, and more reluctance to talk over experiences and difficulties.

Much of the above evidence adds up to the neurotic as an individual who has been exposed to, and has introjected, higher and more exacting standards of superego and sometimes of ego development. Much also points to early emotional trauma, temperamental emotionality, poor constitutional stability (high rigidity or *p* score), and disintegrative influences such as operate in many delinquents. Some writers have attempted to bring both delinquency and neurosis into the general formula of a failure of socialization occasioned by undue discrepancy between roles taught in childhood and the required adult role, but this at once includes too little to be comprehensive and too much to be analytically helpful. Here we face basically a defective ego structure and an excessive superego. Arguing that excessive superego demands are preeminent, Goodwin Watson applied a questionnaire to 250 older students, and found that those with more strict upbringing showed more guilt, worry, and anxiety as well as more dependence on the home and its standards. There were more in the strict than the less strict who showed antipathy to parents, sometimes carried over to teachers. Huschka claimed to find, in 213 cases, a relation between neurosis and strictness of early toilet training, constipation being a feature of these neuroses. But in general the clinical emphasis on importance of early bowel training has been only moderately confirmed, while as to feeding most studies report no relation of neurosis to time of weaning. The general formula for neurosis seems to be higher than average cultural demands combined with lower than average emotional stability. However, as indicated above, any attempt to assign correct relative weightings to these influences is premature and must await advances in personality measurement.

Hebb has recently done well to remind psychologists that syndromes indistinguishable from neurosis are found in a fair percentage of cases where nothing but a *physical* factor can be demonstrated in the background, notably vitamin-B deficiency, thyroid disorder, mild encephalitis, birth injury, hypoglycemia, and concussion, some mental effects of which were considered in Chapter 11.

The data on human neuroticism from laboratory experimentation lie as much in the infancy of our science as do meaningful statistical analyses. Both could be greatly advanced. Lundholm (46) and others, by implanting posthypnotic suggestions, have produced hallucinations accompanying rationalizations, as well as various symptoms of neurotic conflict, but these exploratory studies have not yet produced results sufficiently systematic and widely confirmed for consideration here. The important experiments of Brozek showing that "artificial" neuroses in human beings are possible have been described in Chapter 11.

### 5. FACTORS IN CONVERSION AND ANXIETY HYSTERIA

**The Frequencies of Specific Syndromes.** To pursue the factors in neurosis as thoroughly as our space may permit it is necessary now to study the associations of specific neuroses. The number of specific neuroses—or rather psychoneuroses—is to some extent arbitrary. Syndromes cannot always be tested by correlation, in view of the absence of a sharp limit between a well-defined as contrasted with a poorly defined correlation cluster. But most syndromes of well-defined form are covered by the labels: conversion hysteria, anxiety hysteria, psychasthenia, neurasthenia, effort syndrome, the hostile-reaction syndrome, and the character neuroses, the majority of which have been dealt with descriptively in Chapter 1. The last two are omitted from discussion here, because the character neuroses are better defined in personality factors than in syndromes and are properly discussed as modifications of normal personality, while the hostile-reaction syndrome is too recent and perhaps too transient a concept to have generated much evidence.[6]

As to the relative frequency of various special neurotic syndromes among adults there seem to be few reliable data, since no single therapeutic service caters for all cases, but from child-guidance-clinic data, providing a large sample of intensively studied cases, Burt arrived at the following relative frequencies among all nervous disorders:

|  | Boys | Girls |
|---|---|---|
| Neurasthenia | 12.3 | 8.1 |
| Anxiety states (various) | 16.1 | 30.8 |
| Anxiety neurosis | 4.5 | 5.3 |
| Anxiety hysteria | 3.2 | 6.0 |
| Compulsion neurosis | 7.0 | 4.6 |
| Conversion hysteria | 2.8 | 5.0 |
| Anger neurosis | 10.6 | 6.5 |
| Nervous habits (enuresis, nail-biting) | 14.6 | 9.3 |
| Speech difficulties (stammering) | 8.7 | 4.9 |
| Others (assertiveness in relation to authority, masturbation, etc.) | 20.2 | 19.3 |
|  | 100.0 | 100.0 |

These proportions are well in accord with those obtained by Isaacs (38) with a very different method, namely, listing symptoms reported by parents in asking for advice on difficult children.

[6] Burt (9) first used the category of "anger neuroses" in children, referring to temper-tantrum behavior on abnormally slight provocation and with displacement of anger from its real object. (He stressed panic insecurity as its primary cause.) Grinker and Spiegel (30) make aggressive, hostility neuroses one of their five major categories in war neuroses. They point to the generation of hostility by the special frustrations of the army, which reactivates and causes regression to the attempts to express aggression in childhood frustrations. The usual defense mechanisms—rationalization, projection, etc.—operate in making these abnormal expressions of hostility possible with ego safety and equanimity. Thus, high-ranking officers were often the recipients of this originally parent-directed hostility, or it went to inflate special prejudices and paranoid attitudes. Grinker and Spiegel note a rather high incidence of repressed homosexuality in the hostility neuroses, as in paranoia.

**Factors in Conversion Hysteria.** Conversion hysteria, formerly one of the commonest neuroses, is, according to general clinical observation, of diminishing incidence. Presumably this results from some trend in our culture pattern; perhaps the trend away from the conditions that characterized lower social status; for it has greater frequency in lower status groups. It is more frequent in women than men—as the origin of the name might indicate. Dorcus (17) cites suggestibility, inadequate synthesis of central functions, repression of sexual trauma, dissociation and redintegration as proposed but not entirely adequate explanations. Psychoanalysts point to a particular level of regression of libido and to problems encountered at the comparatively late level of Oedipus fixation. Eysenck (22) found that the conversion hysteric was significantly differentiated from the anxiety neurotic, in terms of precise factor measurements, by small vocabulary relative to intelligence, accident proneness, stammering, poor persistence in exacting work, high ratio of speed to accuracy, a low aspiration level (but high self-rating of his past performances), and high personal variability. This extensive study also shows a tendency to relatively stocky physique, good physical effort response (low oxygen uptake, lactate level, and pulse rate), and a low cholinesterase concentration in the blood.

Undoubtedly a constitutional difference plays a considerable part in determining that a neurosis shall take this form—a difference associated with high resistance at neuron synapses, a certain insensitivity to trauma, and capacity to dissociate conflicting, unpleasant, dynamic trends. Secondly, we have to recognize (Chapter 1) that the whole personality has marks of immaturity, dependence, and irresponsibility. It is in the context of these two conditions that the tendency to a conversion hysteric outcome of a traumatic infantile experience and a precipitating adult circumstance is to be understood.

More speculative questions concern (*a*) whether the immaturity and slowness to learn emotionally are a result of the primary temperamental condition, *i.e.*, whether all can be reduced to a single factor and (*b*) whether this temperamental condition, basically a proneness[7] to amnesia, especially of unpleasant associations, may not be a genetic variant favoring reduction of internal conflict and avoidance of neurosis. For although the hysteric shows greater than average proneness to getting into difficulties (note, for example, Eysenck's finding of accident proneness, above, and Kanzer's finding (41) that in seventy-one hysterics with amnesic symptoms, most had marital rifts, unfortunate love affairs, alcoholism, and financial difficulties) there is

---

[7] The philosophy of the surgent, conversion hysteria temperament has been expressed by the poet Masefield:

> "Laugh and be merry, remember, better the world with a song,
> Better the world with a blow in the teeth of a wrong."

It is assured, from Chapter 1, that the *F* factor is common to both conversion hysteric and hypomanic tendencies.

evidence that he shows a more robust resistance than average to mental conflict and exhaustion. Until the conversion hysteric *temperament* (the surgent, $F+$ temperament) can be measured, the relative proneness of this and other temperaments to conversion and other *neuroses*, at the same intelligence level and under equal difficulties, cannot be assessed; but the general evidence suggests that the conversion hysteria response is one made under more extreme difficulties than others.

**Factors in Anxiety Hysteria.** Anxiety hysteria blends so readily into normal behavior—into the behavior of a normal person with common phobias and superstitions and somewhat high capacity to worry—that the line for study is not easily drawn. Lunger and Page with an inventory of worries, covering the common areas found in previous studies—health, contemporary affairs, sexual matter, social relations, etc.—found no difference for men and women on the gross total, and noted that worriers were lower on general self-confidence (dominance) and higher on general maladjustment. In children, however, more worries have been found among girls than among boys. The fears of four-year-olds, notably fears of dogs, doctors, storms, and deep water, have been found to correlate with those of their mothers (Hagman). The most common worries of children concern health, the safety of members of their own families, and their school and social standing. Fears increase in number with age, up to fifteen years in boys and eighteen years in girls— particularly after the age of about five years—and then tend to decline. Means's study of 1,000 college women showed only 38 per cent of fears were of known origin and that 70 per cent of those that were of known origin came from firsthand personal experience. The scope for particular phobias is evidently very great. The less intelligent tended to have more fears.

The general course of events in anxieties that amount to a neurosis is indicated by Harris's survey (34), which in a follow-up of clinical cases found 31 per cent quite recovered, 49 per cent still suffering more or less severe anxiety, 7 per cent developed into psychosis, and 13 per cent dead.

There is little doubt that most anxiety neurosis arises from the repression of hostility and sexual libido, primarily in childhood, as in other neuroses. But, in this neurosis, to a far greater extent than others, the generation of anxiety must also be ascribed to suppression and repression of excitement (sexual and aggressive, particularly) evolved by the existing adult situation. In children, as indicated by child guidance clinic data, anxiety neuroses are particularly frequent in the lower middle class and groups under financial insecurity aiming at higher levels of status or "respectability." Kasanin (42) found children with marked anxieties usually had parents with marked anxiety, and though there is some element of pure heredity (Chapter 5) in proneness to anxiety neurosis, there is little doubt that this is situational. He found best therapy results when at least one parent was free of anxiety neurosis, and noticed, as other studies have done, that outright rejection of the child is not a common cause of anxiety, though ambivalent attitudes and overprotection are frequent.

Characteristically the anxiety neurotic develops in a home with high super-ego standards, and high regard for social respectability, but some underlying instability and tendency to early overprotection and libidinal satisfaction. The *psychoneurosis* of anxiety tends to leave behind, when the mental situation is changed, a physiological (true) neurosis of anxiety. Indeed, the habit or condition of autonomic overreactivity produced by the psychic anxiety may often set up such a vicious circle. For the endocrine alterations produce disturbance of metabolism, loss of body weight, fatigue, and insomnia which in turn cause the individual to be less able to meet the demands on his personality about which he is already anxious.

Anxiety hysteria, therefore, shades off in one direction into plain, neurological anxiety neurosis—bodily symptoms of excessive autonomic fear response to real but slight external stimuli but with no truly mental symptoms—and in another into effort syndrome or neurasthenia, where fatigue is the prominent symptom. All of these syndromes may be sequelae[8] of anxiety hysteria, but they all have existence also in their own right, through special causal circumstances, and it behooves us to glance at neurasthenia and effort syndrome in regard to these circumstances.

## 6. FACTORS IN FATIGUE NEUROSES AND PSYCHASTHENIA

**Nervous Fatigue in Peace and War.** Neurasthenia, with its general nervous fatigue, irritability, paresthesia, difficulty in making decisions, and poorness of memory, was ascribed by Freud to an endocrine condition produced by sexual overactivity. This is clear in certain cases but it does not suffice for all that is usually classified as neurasthenia. The syndrome undoubtedly needs more exact analysis than it has yet received. It has been noted most clearly in connection with conditions of endocrine and metabolic disorder, *e.g.*, adrenal insufficiency, poor muscular tone and visceroptosis, convalescence after infection, and status lymphaticus. What evidence exists on background factors suggests that the more educated, the more civilized, the more inhibitedly raised (dominant fathers are indicated in one study), and the more subjected to high character standards are more prone to neurasthenia.

"Effort syndrome" might be called the neurasthenia of war, and was first

---

[8] The transition of anxiety hysteria into neurasthenia seems to be indicated on an adequate sample by Greenhill's (29) observation on 700 psychiatric casualties of the Second World War as they returned to civilian life. He found a *decrease* of the following symptoms: anxiety, nightmares, insomnia, nausea, tremor, backache, and palpitation and an *increase* in irritability, sensitivity to noise, dislike of crowds, weakness, depression, headache, restlessness, and fatigability.

noted in the American Civil War among soldiers with mental symptoms.
It is sometimes called "combat fatigue" (when the latter is not used euphe-
mistically for all sorts of psychiatric casualty) and arises from the stresses of
battle which are shorter and sharper than the civilian stresses producing
neurasthenia. Its central feature is breathlessness, palpitation tremor, and
intolerance of effort, while the mental symptoms—insomnia, apathy, restlessness—are slight, but reminiscent of neurasthenia.

A somewhat different syndrome, closer to anxiety hysteria, has been noted
in men similarly exposed to shell shock, constant danger, inadequate sleep,
and loss of comrades. Ludwig (45), for example, notes a slow increase of
anxiety over months, and finally the onset of a reactive depression with

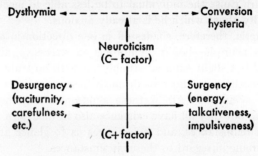

DIAGRAM 46. A schematic diagram of the hysteric-dysthymic dimension, as named by
Eysenck.

apathy, emptiness, and sense of guilt (but suicidal trends are rare). The
same pattern is evident in the cases of Grinker and Spiegel (30). Both of
these war syndromes show little or no association with earlier neurotic symptoms. They are direct responses to the stress of environment and show high
recovery rates (95 per cent) when the stress ends.

In all these syndromes in the anxiety hysteria group, showing small
emphasis on early neurotic maladjustment, a pattern of high aspiration and
good family integration, an association with immediate but prolonged stress
and exorbitant demand, there is a combination of anxiety, depression, and
fatigue. This is recognizable as the pattern demonstrated in the desurgent
endowment of the Surgency-Desurgency factor in normal persons (Chaps.
3 and 4). The work of the Maudsley Hospital Research Unit leaves little
doubt that it is essentially this Surgency-Desurgency dimension, continued
beyond the normal range and mixed with general neuroticism which essentially distinguishes the conversion hysteric from the anxiety hysteric. (In
the abnormal realm this factor has been named by Eysenck the "hysteric-
dysthymic" dimension) as indicated schematically in diagram 46.

As indicated above, the present writer favors the theory that this dimension is primarily a physiologically, temperamentally determined one. For

example, evidence of a reliable kind indicates that the desurgent or hysteric has a broader body build, a lower cholinesterase concentration in the blood, a more dissociative, insensitive nervous system, a longer reaction time, and perhaps a more alkaline physiological condition. But theories have also been advanced (22) that the difference is one of greater or lesser superego activity. Undoubtedly the desurgent individual shows greater signs of care, responsibility, guilt, and persistence, but there is no evidence that he has been subjected to training better calculated to build up such attitudes and such a dynamic structure. At present, the conclusion seems more likely that his greater sensitivity causes him to accept in more wholesale fashion the inhibitory associations of the superego, as part of a tendency to acquire more integrated and inhibitory associations of all kinds.

**The Obsessional-Compulsive Neuroses (Psychasthenia).** The obsessional neurosis syndrome, described in Chapter 1, probably lies in a direction of departure from conversion hysteria different from that of anxiety hysteria. A new dimension or factor seems to be involved, which prevents the inhibitions of the anxiety neurotic from expressing themselves in overt anxiety. It is a dimension of transition from free-floating anxiety to rationalized phobias, and so to the anancasms (ritualistic, expiatory, obsessional-compulsive habits) of psychasthenia. Culpin and Smith (15), it will be remembered (Chapter 14), obtained evidence that psychasthenics are found with greater frequency in upper executive and social positions than are anxiety hysterics. Both of these types, compared with conversion hysterics, show evidence of well-integrated home background, good social standards, and high conscientiousness; but the psychasthenic also shows some qualities of dominance or toughness along a dimension of personality not yet identifiable.

Lion (43) studied sixteen patients with obsessions, associated with depression as they frequently are. He found common characters of perfectionism and meticulousness, self-sufficiency, intolerance, morbid doubts, indecision and perplexity, superstitious beliefs, anxiety in recurring moods, rigidity of thought, tenseness, irritability, and resistance to therapy. Rickles (63) notes similarly overconscientiousness, shyness with exhibitionism, unsatisfactory heterosexual adjustment, and an economic attainment "below that of their group," but whether this last is real or the patient's own criticism of his performance is not clear.

The similarity of the rigidity and obsessional behavior of the psychasthenic to the onset of certain schizophrenias, (and secondly, to that of involutional melancholia) but notably paranoid schizophrenia, still leaves some doubt as to whether psychasthenia may sometimes occur as an intermediate stage of development of schizophrenia. The onset of psychasthenia is generally relatively sudden and occurs commonly in late childhood or adolescence. The prognosis is poor compared with all other neuroses and if psychotherapy succeeds, there is still likelihood of recurrences.

Psychoanalysts have stressed anal-erotic causation, *i.e.*, conflicts, trauma, and fixations over toilet training, with sadism (and masochism) and hostility to parents. As an observation of phenomenological associations this is unquestionable. Moreover, one would expect perfectionist, dominating, rigid parents to produce hostility, to pass on or generate dominant, sadistic attitudes, and to cause the child to encounter more severe problems over toilet training. What remains quite undecided is the priority or weight of these different factors, namely, of the inheritance of a dominant, tough disposition, of the constant exposure to a family tradition of perfectionism, and of the suffering of specific regressions at the toilet-training stage and later. These influences work in a single, self-sustaining circle, and though psychoanalysis may point to one only, their true roles remain, scientifically speaking, to be unraveled.

### 7. FACTORS IN LOCALIZED NEUROSES: STAMMERING, TICS, ENURESIS, ETC

**Organic, Localized Neuroses.** Just as neurosis is more psychologically localized than psychosis (even in the character neuroses), in the sense that the individual's contact with reality remains firm and he recognizes the aberrations as a local, uncontrolled feature in his total dynamic and cognitive functioning, so there exists a class of disorders showing even more localized disturbance than the typical neuroses. These disorders, such as enuresis, stammering, tics, and some psychosomatic disorders, are frequently centered on the function of a particular organ, but must not be confused with the pseudo-organic manifestations of conversion hysteria. To the casual observer—and indeed to generations of physicians—no conspicuous general personality disorder is related to these disturbances. Only by finer measurement and statistical treatment has it been possible to show that there are in fact personality correlates, which further research may trace either to genetic, temperamental linkages or to purposive connections in a dynamic response to environmental experience.

**Stuttering, Stammering, and Related Speech Disorders.** Disorders of speech, of the stuttering and stammering form, are not well defined before six years, but begin before eight years in 85 per cent of cases, are about four times more frequent in boys than girls (ratio between two and ten to one in different studies), decline somewhat in frequency with age and educational level, and affect about one in sixty to one in one hundred (in different samples) of the general population. Bender found indications that at the college level stutterers are of more leptosomatic body build and higher mental capacity than nonstutterers. Card (11) brings evidence on forty stutterers that they have more than an expected frequency of allergy difficulties and that their allergies and stuttering tend to increase and decrease at the same times. It is well known that stutterers have trouble with particular words, usually those demanding restriction of the resonating cavity and rapid precise articulation. But the elimination of such words leads to stuttering (though less marked) on substitute and associated words. They also show decreasing stuttering on slowing of speech, raising of pitch, singsong utterance, rhythmic speaking, and singing—in that order of effectiveness. There are also stutterers who do not stutter in another language or with particular sets of people, *e.g.*, coevals instead of parents or parent substitutes.

The ancient controversy over left-handedness and stuttering, started by the findings about Broca's speech area in the left prefrontal lobe, is still not entirely settled, but it is clear that there is no more than a trifling correlation between stammering and being trained to right-handedness when naturally left-handed. It has been suggested that the only cause for the association is the inferiority trauma occasioned by the child finding itself different from other children and that if the transfer of handedness is made tactfully no harm results. But there is probably some more basic feature in the connection. For example, Bryngelson comparing seventy-eight stutterers with seventy-eight nonstutterers found the former more frequently ambidexterous, more frequently with a history of changed handedness, and with generally less *definite* handedness. Similarly Travis found stutterers more left-eyed and poorer on right-handed mirror-image drawing than nonstutterers. There is some evidence that motor control is poorer generally, for the above experimenter found stutterers failed more on mirror drawing with *either* hand, and other observers have frequently noted their handwriting to be poor, arhythmic, convulsive, tumbling over itself, and tremorous.

Although much of the above clearly suggests temperamental associations, the low validity of present personality-measuring devices has not permitted any very definite conclusions. Meltzer noted (49) that stutterers are more talkative (agreeing with the surgency, conversion-hysteria association mentioned above), and Eisenson (20) in confirming this, observed that this excess fluency is of a "trial-and-error" nature and disappears when measured in situations where thoughts have to be combined and arranged, as in an essay. Eisenson and Pastel (21) have also shown, and their work has been confirmed, that stutterers are high on speed tests and on perseveration (disposition rigidity) measures. This points to a constitutional tendency to high emotionality and neurosis. Ackerson's correlations (tetrachoric—on presence or absence) of stammering (see (1), Chap. 16) with other characteristics in a large sample of child guidance clinic children yielded the following significant correlations:

| Positive associations | | Negative associations | |
|---|---|---|---|
| With rating of psychoneurosis... | 0.29 ± .07 | Bad companion............... | −0.27 |
| With conduct prognosis bad..... | 0.29 | Gang membership............. | −0.24 |
| With mental conflict............ | 0.22 | Irregular school attendance..... | −0.20 |
| With lack of initiative.......... | 0.17 | Leading others astray.......... | −0.20 |
| With inefficiency in work and play | 0.16 | Sex delinquency............... | −0.20 |
| With being object of teasing..... | 0.16 | Brother in penal institute...... | −0.20 |
| With inferiority feelings......... | 0.16 | | |
| With unpopularity.............. | 0.13 | | |
| With rating of sensitive (to criticism, etc.).................... | 0.12 | | |

The negative association with bad environment (which would tend to zero in a normal group) and the striking resemblance of the pattern on the left to that of the high perseveration syndrome (see (7,8), Chap. 13) points clearly to *a general* neurotic emotionality and defect of ego development, deep seated in early development or in constitution. The association with physique, with a family tendency to twinning (61), with a higher incidence of stuttering in ancestors (61), and with left-handedness or ambidextrousness, suggests a constitutional origin of some or all of this pattern, and one associated with more primitive racial strains. The particular trauma may itself be responsible for directing the general neurotic tendency to expression in the speech area or the neurotic constitution may inherently manifest itself by breakdown in speech rather than elsewhere.

**The Enuretic Syndrome.** Enuresis, either in the form of nocturnal bedwetting beyond infancy (three years) or of complete incontinence, occurs, according to Thorne's recent survey of 1,000 Army selectees, in about one in six of the male population (16 per cent after five years; and 2.5 per cent remaining nocturnally enuretic until the age of eighteen years) and is about three times more frequent (and harder to cure) in boys than girls. Weber (74) found 16 per cent of bedwetters in German children and found it increased to 20 per cent with the war and air raids. A small fraction of it is due to physical disorders and lack of training. (Gill, studying evacuated children in war (27), noted two-thirds of the enuretics were backward in schoolwork and from homes with "low social standards," though other studies show small association with lower intelligence—except that true defectives frequently tend to be enuretic—or with lower social status.) But most has a less obvious origin.

There is overwhelming evidence that enuresis is associated with personality maladaptation and there is fair consensus as to the particular forms taken by the latter. Hirsch (36*a*) found 32 per cent of enuresis in 367 delinquents, and noted that the personality traits particularly associated with it were emotional immaturity in 61 per cent of cases; hypersuggestibility, 42 per cent; instability, 40 per cent; inferiority and insecurity, 39 per cent; overintense fear reactions, 26 per cent; and sex perversions, 14 per cent. In actual delinquent manifestations, incorrigibility, sex offense, and destructiveness of property exceeded, in enuretics, the *general* frequency among delinquents by three times, more than twice, and twice, respectively. Larceny was below the normal frequency and Hirsch suggests that the enuretic favors pointless "crimes of instability."

Of Ackerson's 3,000 child clinic population 23 per cent were enuretic beyond three years, showing irritability and seclusiveness and yielding the following specific correlations:

| | Boys | Girls |
|---|---|---|
| Restlessness in sleep | $0.26 \pm 0.3$ | $0.31 \pm 0.4$ |
| Masturbation admitted | 0.24 | 0.19 |
| Temper-tantrums | 0.20 | 0.27 |
| General nervous symptoms | 0.11 | 0.32 |
| Fighting | 0.13 | 0.28 |
| Swearing | 0.15 | 0.28 |
| Sensitiveness (over some issue) | 0.22 | 0.09 |
| Nail-biting | 0.18 | 0.24 |
| Stubbornness | 0.10 | 0.23 |
| Quarrelsomeness | 0.18 | 0.22 |

There was also a low negative correlation with intelligence and slight positive correlation with daydreaming and preference for younger children. Michaels and Goodman (52) found no association of early enuresis with psychosis, but an appreciable association with enuresis after ten years. It did not tie up with any very specific syndrome, which parallels the finding in normals of most consistent association with "general conduct disorders." Their findings (52) regarding individual neuropathic traits are generally in accordance with the above.

General clinical observation on enuresis include such contributions as Goldfarb's stress on immaturity, aggression, and fearful withdrawal; Michaels' suggestion that the lack of guilt shown by enuretics is a paradigm of general psychopathic behavior, such as some show later; that enuresis, showing inability to renounce and sublimate urethral erotic components, indicates some *general* inability to renounce; that it is associated with somnambulism, nightmares, severe nail-biting, and nervousness (in Navy men); that stubbornness and antisocial traits are common; that sexual excitement, anxiety, and defiance are central; that anxiety over suppression of aggression in ineffectual personalities (100 soldiers twenty to thirty years) is central; and that enuresis declines when parent, teacher, or doctor is about to return after an absence, as well as at the contemplation of such holidays as Christmas.

Whether this picture of emotional immaturity, with a dispositional emphasis on fear and pugnacity, is a single syndrome or several we do not yet know. Conceivably there is one factor pattern due to heredity, for the hereditary influence in enuresis is considerable (Chap. 5), upon which one or more factors of environmental background—notably insecurity—are superposed, but the evidence of a substantial nature about the environmental factors is still lacking.

**Tics and Nervous Restlessness.** Nervous habits and tics constitute a comparatively trivial area of abnormal, unadapted behavior which may nevertheless throw some light on personality. Olson (57) in a general survey of tics and habits such as thumb-sucking in 700 five- to fifteen-year-olds began by showing positive correlations (0.06 to 0.88, obtained by time sampling observation, on thirty cases in the classroom) among all of the following varieties—oral (thumb-sucking, biting nails), nasal, hirsutal, irritational, manual, ocular, aural, facial, genital. Oral and nasal nervous habits were most highly correlated and the consistency of oral nervous habits was 0.87, falling to 0.46 when observed at times a year apart. Similarity of proneness to nervous habits in relatives was shown by correlations of 0.83 for identical twins; 0.46, fraternal twins; sisters, 0.32; brothers, 0.16 (eighty pairs); and neighbors in class, 0.28.

The suggestion of considerable hereditary influence conveyed by the contrasting figures for the two types of twins is somewhat discounted by the small resemblance of siblings in relation to that of unrelated but associated children. However, the latter may be due to a purely temporary contagion of nervous habits and fidgeting between children placed in sight of one another (the siblings, on the other hand, were generally in different classes). There is a distinct tendency, for children around seven years, for greater nervousness of this kind to be correlated with lower pondeval indices (weight over height), which is in keeping with the known tendency of leptosomes (Chap. 11) to be more high strung. However, Olson found in older children (eleven onwards) that extremely heavy children also showed more nervous habits, possibly due to the environmental influence of being abnormal in appearance.

The finding of Malmo (48) that experimentally induced emotional stress in patients produced more correlated voluntary muscle than autonomic reactions argues for the importance of this line of research. His finding that early schizophrenics and anxiety hysterics show the greatest reaction also supports the above indication of greatest effects with leptosomatic constitutions.

There seems to be no relation of nervous habits and tics to age, but girls show significantly more than boys.   Fatigue or mental conflict causes increasing manifestations.   In rats it has been shown that an irritant applied to the outer ear causes movements of ear cleaning to persist, as an avenue of motor discharge, from three to twenty-two days after irritation has actually ceased.   Olson found a slight tendency for the very high and the very low scorers in thumb-sucking to have had prolonged breast feeding, relative to those with average thumb-sucking.

Tics have a somewhat different distribution and perhaps etiology from nervous movement habits in general.   Blatz and Ringland (6) found them to increase from two to seven years, and that sex differences do not exist, but that a temporary situation of restriction of body movement increases them.   This parallels Wechsler's findings (75) on nail-biting, which increases from two to six, remains constant till puberty (girls twelve, boys fourteen), rises for two years, and then declines.   Some studies indicate a rather lower I.Q. and higher neurotic-questionnaire score among nail-biters than their associates.   Ackerson found the following associations of nail-biting in clinical records (see (1), Chap. 16):

|  | Boys | Girls |
|---|---|---|
| Slovenly................... | 0.31 | 0.12 |
| Restless in sleep........... | 0.27 | 0.40 |
| Nervous................... | 0.26 | 0.29 |
| Restless................... | 0.25 | 0.27 |
| Unhappy.................. | 0.25 | 0.07 |
| Fantastical lying........... | 0.21 | 0.16 |
| Masturbation.............. | 0.21 | 0.26 |

There is frequently a history of chorea and rheumatic infection in children with tics, and Creak and Guttmann (14) point out the similarity to compulsive utterances (note also nystagmus) and give instances of choreic movements persisting as tics.   A traumatic experience and the resulting form of mental conflict may account for the particular localization of a tic (usually historically rather than symbolically), but this direction of conflict expression seems determined most by a general disposition and local physical stimulation, the former closely resembling the rheumatic, overactive, restless type described by Dunbar (see Chapter 11).

### 8. FACTORS IN FURTHER "LOCALIZED NEUROSES," THE SPECIFICALLY PSYCHOSOMATIC DISTURBANCES

**Definition and Incidence.**   Evidence presented below indicates that somatic disorders directly traceable to mental stress are on the increase, absolutely and in relation to other neuroses.   They are to be classified as neuroses because they show unintegrated nervous action—behavior not in accordance with the organic wholeness or conscious intentions of the personality—and because in *fact* they tend to occur in individuals showing other signs of general neuroticism. However, the general neuroticism is not always marked, and it seems best to consider the chief specific psychosomatic disorders as "localized neuroses," *i.e.*, as associated with a minimum of total personality disturbance.

The relative frequency of these disorders can be gathered from the following analysis of 330 psychiatric war casualties with psychosomatic disorder made by Grinker and Spiegel (30):

|  | *Per cent* |
|---|---|
| Gastrointestinal | 46.6 |
| Cardiac | 14.4 |
| Dermatological | 12.1 |
| Joint and muscle | 11.5 |
| Urological | 6.3 |
| Headaches and vertigo | 5.7 |
| Hypertensive | 2.3 |
| Chest | 1.1 |

The present section will be confined to the most common civilian forms: stomach and duodenal ulcer, hypertension, colitis, and allergies (skin and asthmatic).

**Allergic and Asthmatic Reactions.** Allergies in general are known to increase with mental conflict and particularly with undischarged emotion. Thus, there are several convincing individual clinical studies showing migraine attacks at the point where the patient wanted to, but could not, run away from an intolerable situation, and attacks of hives as substitutes for weeping fits. Asthma has been observed to coincide with phases of depression at frustration. Wittkower (76), contrasting fifty hay fever patients with fifty surgical controls, considered the former to show "self-absorption, dreaminess, and overweening ambition." Riess and De Cillis (64) came out with the not too easily reconciled conclusion that allergic children are more ascendant, extraverted, and emotionally unstable. French and Alexander put forward the psychoanalytic view that the central problem in asthmatics is separation from the mother and they suggest that most asthmatics have difficulty in deciding to marry. They describe the personality as overanxious, cautious, and given (in childhood) to intense sibling rivalry. R. L. Thorndike (71), with questionnaire methods, confirmed the finding of Kling of a correlation of 0.20 to 0.50 between allergy and neurasthenic traits, and concluded that feelings of personal inadequacy are central. Gordon (28) found allergies more common among boys with enuresis and stammering than among 200 controls. The association with the above and nightmares was greater for migraine allergy and least for asthma.

The core of agreement in these observations seems to be (*a*) some constitutional weakness in the direction of general emotionality and instaiblity, as in neurosis generally (*C*− factor); (*b*) a tendency to high dominance (*E*+ factor); (*c*) good contact with parents and a training toward high character standards (*G*+ factor; superego). Faced with difficulties or temptations, the individual reacts in a strong positive fashion, but with a sense of inadequacy and anxiety through the discrepancy between the high self-regard standards and the sensed dispositional weakness. There is what Gayley has called "hyperfunctioning of the effort syndrome" and mobilization of adrenalin and somatic resources for an activity which cannot be made or is abortive. This ultimately results perhaps through the changed combining reaction of serum globulin in relation to foreign protein or through histamine reactions, in various allergic reactions.

**Hypertension.** Other failures of adaptation that are of psychological interest are those concerned with the alimentary tract (stomach ulcers, colitis) and with the circulatory system (heart disease, hypertension). Hypertension is predominantly a disease of European races and cultures, showing itself most clearly in the forty to sixty age range. Ever since research on the autonomic nervous system showed that blood pressure could be raised transiently by emotional states, speculation has continued freely that much chronic high blood pressure could be due to chronic psychological conflict rather than to physiological causes. Jacobson (39) describes a "neuromuscular hypertension" syndrome, with abnormal excitability of heart and respiratory system, spastic conditions of smooth muscle, insomnia, and general excitability, including both sympathetic and vagotonic symptoms, but has not demonstrated by correlation that this is to be regarded as the typical syndrome of high blood pressure. High blood pressure, of course, can result from other than psychological causes, *e.g.*, chronic infection, gastrointestinal disorders, vitamin deficicncy, poisoning.

As to personality, Darrow and Solomon (16) found larger blood pressure *changes* in persons described as irritable, aggressive, given to temper, and moody. Rennie (62) found perfectionism, ambition, hypochondria, and predominant emotions of resentment in subjects with chronic high pressure. Among psychotics high pressure is noted most in depressives and paranoids. Saul (66), on relatively few cases psychoanalytically examined, found individuals with submissive, accepting attitudes to dominant parents (chiefly mother), who had high standards of restraint in sex and self-assertion but who continued to harbor strong, half-repressed hostility toward the sources of restraint. The suggestion of submissiveness with high standards of restraint is in agreement with Hamilton's (33) study of 102 students. These studies also agree in finding the hypertensive less given to physical and social recreation and more to hard work.

**Gastro-intestinal Reactions.**   Excess acid secretion is the immediate cause of stomach ulceration and this may be brought about by vagus nerve stimulation, *i.e.*, hypothalamic activity, by prolonged absorption of histamine, and by repeated "sham" feeding.   Studies on human subjects with gastric fistulas have shown hyperacidity and stomach movement definitely stimulated by anxiety, hostility, resentment, homesickness, and emotional restlessness.   Wolf and Wolff (77) made a careful study of acid secretion and color of mucosa in the stomach of one individual under a moderate range of emotions.   They found that fear and sadness reduced secretion, but that anxiety, hostility, and resentment increased it—particularly when of long duration.

Estimates of the amount of existing general digestive disorder due to nonorganic (and presumably psychological) causes vary from about 25 to 50 per cent.   Stomach ulceration has increased significantly in frequency in the last generation and, as Dunn shows (19), it increases in time of war, in financial-stress periods, and during air raids.   He points out that it became "the most important medical problem of the Second World War" in the military forces, seeming to have climbed to first position with a decline of the anxiety and conversion hysterias more prevalent in the First World War.   If this substitutive relation could be proved, by wider statistical data, certain advances in theory could be made.   Stewart and Winser (69) present data for 1937–1940 with regard to sixteen London hospitals and show a statistically significant increase in perforated peptic ulcers occurring during the first two months of heavy air raids.   Ninety-three per cent of these were in men.

The incidence of neuroticism is high for victims of stomach ulcers, who, as Draper (18) noticed (see Chaps. 5 and 11) are generally, leptosomatic, androgynic, vagotonic, narrow-faced, and with a narrow jaw angle. The precipitating emotions, as clinically described are tension, anxiety, guilt, or depression, reacted to with rigidity.   Increases of responsibility, financial, health, and family worries predominate in the situations and it is suggested that individuals with strong need for dependence and avoidance of responsibility are most affected.   From consideration of both the social and individual evidence it seems that long-circuiting of behavior as such, *i.e.*, withheld action, under the influence of anxiety, acting upon the naturally reactive, dynamic, rigid, leptosomatic constitutional type, initially brought up with overprotection or dependence, is the essential cause of ulceration.

The studies of Bean, Brown, Cobb, Jones, White, and others on colitis present a picture of factors in parasympathetic system overactivity too similar to the above to justify any assertion at present of a difference.   They mention conscientiousness, sensitivity, low energy and tendency to give up in difficulties, dependence, and emotional reactions of anxiety and resentment.

With present reliabilities of statistics and measurements a single formula could cover all the above psychosomatic "neuroses," namely, some tendency constitutionally to general emotionality and to schizothyme, leptosomatic constitution; an upbringing with good parental relationships, some over-protection, overdependence, and strong superego development (conscientious-ness, perfectionism); and a precipitating situation of anxiety in which action has to be long-circuited. It is a picture more of stressful, willed activity than of disorganization, conflict, and repression as in the major neuroses.

### 9. SUMMARY

1. A general factor of neuroticism, called in normals $C(-)$ factor, or Demoralized General Emotionality, can be demonstrated in ratings, ques-tionnaire data, and objective tests. What clinicians have defined, by an accumulation of observations, as the essentials in general neurosis, approach closely to the items loaded in this factor. The items center on defective-will actions, instability of mood, memory defect, and overreactive autonomic system with general fatigue.

2. A clinically significant and unmistakable degree of neurosis exists in about 20 per cent of our population, but an appreciably disabling degree of neurosis exists in only 5 per cent and probably only 1 to 2 per cent is actually impelled to seek treatment.

3. Neuroses clearly resembling human patterns are found in chimpanzees; the same with omissions or different emphasis can be produced experimen-tally in dogs, cats, sheep, goats, and pigs; but in rats the pattern is less clear and in the most prevalent experiments radically different. Prolonged conflict of major drives seems necessary to produce typical neurosis and this is occasioned by using appetitive drives, by restraining all other possible modes of expression and by stimulating the drives through internal symbols or external stimuli made uncertain by complexity. Other neurosis-like patterns are produced merely by monotonous repetition of nocive condi-tioned stimuli, especially with delay in response. By conflict experiments in animals it is possible not only to produce general neurotic conditions but also various clinically recognizable defense mechanisms.

4. Statistical analyses of background conditions in human neuroses have not been sufficiently directed to real influences—largely through lack of measuring instruments—to throw light on anything but the most gross fac-tors, and laboratory experimentation with human neurotic responses is also in its infancy.

5. Anxiety hysteria is associated with evidence of greater acceptance of superego demands than is found in conversion hysteria, and is more affected by repression of hostility and sexual drive in the contemporary situation. However, anxiety hysteria differs from conversion hysteria most with respect to objective-test results suggesting a constitutional difference of nervous

reactivity and capacity for dissociations, as in surgency-desurgency among normals.

6. Neurasthenia and effort syndrome emphasize exhaustion in the general syndrome of anxiety, fatigue, and depression and are found with considerable frequency as aftermaths of anxiety hysteria or stress of fear, as well as through metabolic upsets.

7. Obsessional neuroses have a background more like anxiety than conversion hysteria, but seem associated with dominance and schizoid paranoid dispositions and a low rate of recovery.

8. Specific symptom groups, which may be called "localized neuroses" (because gross personality associations, *e.g.*, instability, are not obvious) are examined in the case of enuresis, stammering and stuttering, tics, and restricted nervous habits, and found to have definite, though more subtle, personality background associations of a specific nature.

9. There has been a tendency in this generation for conversion hysteria to decline and "localized neuroses" with psychomatic expression to increase. The etiology of gastrointestinal disorders, asthma, and hypertension, in the psychological field, is becoming more clear.

## QUESTIONS AND EXERCISES

1. List six variables highly involved in the factor of general neuroticism, in each of the areas (*a*) behavior ratings, (*b*) questionnaire responses (mental interiors), and (*c*) objective personality tests.

2. Describe three kinds of situations in conditioned reflex experiments which have been found to produce neurotic reactions in dogs. Show how they are more effectively interpreted in dynamic terms, in a way which integrates findings with those of Liddell, Masserman, and Mowrer, and with general clinical observation.

3. Summarize the features of the "neurotic syndrome" produced in dogs, cats, and sheep, and contrast it with that of audiogenic seizures in rats. Point out, and attempt to account for, the differences from human neuroticism.

4. Set out, approximately, the statistical findings on the general and specific, *e.g.*, class, incidences of neuroses, and of the background and hereditary influences associated therewith.

5. Contrast the expression of neurosis in conversion and in anxiety hysteria with respect to psychoanalytic views on childhood fixations, statistical findings on background, clinical findings on the course of the disorder, and the results of objective tests on performance, physiology, and physique.

6. Speculate on the data asked for in Question 5, with regard to two or more possible hypotheses accounting for the difference in expression.

7. Discuss the relationship (in the light of etiology, prognosis, etc.) of anxiety hysteria, anxiety neurosis, neurasthenia, and effort syndrome.

8. Discuss the anal-erotic theory of obsessional neurosis, especially in regard to the latter's occupational distribution, relationship to paranoid trends and rigidity, and prognosis.

9. What is known about the distribution of nervous habits with respect to age, background influences, emotional stress, physical illness, and heredity. Taking nail-biting as a specific example, discuss its possible dynamic etiology.

10. What is the evidence as to the extent and nature of psychological causation in gastrointestinal disorders?

## BIBLIOGRAPHY

1. ANDERSON, O. D., and R. PARMENTER: A Long-term Study of the Experimental Neurosis in the Sheep and the Dog, *Psychosom. Med. Monogr.*, Nos. 3 and 4, 1941.
2. ALTUS, W. D.: Some Correlates of Enuresis among Illiterate Soldiers, *J. consult. Psychol.*, 10: 246–259, 1946.
3. ARNOLD, M. B.: Emotional Factors in Experimental Neuroses, *J. exp. Psychol.*, 34: 257–281, 1944.
4. BARUCH, D. W.: A Study of Reported Tension in Interparental Relationships as Co-existent with Behavior Adjustment in Young Children, *J. exp. Educ.*, 6: 187–204, 1937.
5. BENNETT, E.: Some Tests for the Discrimination of Neurotic from Normal Subjects, *Br. J. med. Psychol.*, 20: 271–277, 1945.
6. BLATZ, W., and M. C. RINGLAND: The Study of Tics in Preschool Children, *Univ. Toronto Stud. Child Develpm.* (Ser. No. 3) 58, 1935.
7. BURT, C. L.: The Incidence of Neurotic Symptoms among Evacuated School Children. *Brit. J. educ. Psychol.*, 10: 8–15, 1940.
8. BURT, C. L.: War Neurosis in British Children, *Nerv. Child*, 2: 324–337, 1943.
9. BURT, C. L.: *The Subnormal Mind*, Oxford University Press, New York, 1935.
10. CAMERON, D. E.: *Objective and Experimental Psychiatry*, The Macmillan Company, New York, 1941.
11. CARD, R. E.: A Study of Allergy in Relation to Stuttering, *J. Speech Disorders.*, 4: 223–230, 1939.
12. CATTELL, R. B.: An Objective Test of Character Temperament: II., *J. soc. Psychol.*, 19: 99–114, 1944.
13. CATTELL, R. B.: The Riddle of Perseveration, *J. Pers. Res.*, 14: 229–267, 1946.
14. CREAK, M., and E. GUTTMANN: A Follow-up Study of Hyperkinetic Children, *J. ment. Sci.*, 86: 624–631, 1940.
15. CULPIN, M., and M. SMITH: The Nervous Temperament, *Industrial Health Res. Board Rept.*, No. 61, H.M.S.O., London, 1934.
16. DARROW, C. M., and A. P. SOLOMON: Mutism and Resistance Behavior in Psychotic Patients, *Amer. J. Psychiat.*, 96: 1441–1454, 1940.
17. DORCUS, R. M.: The Psychoses and the Psychoneuroses, Chapter 13 in Pennington and Berg, *An Introduction to Clinical Psychology*, The Ronald Press Company, New York, 1948.
18. DRAPER, G. W.: The Emotional Component of the Ulcer Susceptible Constitution, *Ann. intern. Med.*, 16: 633–658, 1942.
19. DUNN, W. H.: Gastroduodenal Disorders: an Important Wartime Medical Problem, *War Medicine*, 2: 967–983, 1942.
20. EISENSON, J.: *The Psychology of Speech*, F. S. Crofts & Co., New York, 1938.
21. EISENSON, J., and E. PASTEL: A Study of the Perseverating Tendency in Stutterers, *Quart. J. Speech.*, 22: 626–631, 1936.
22. EYSENCK, H. J.: *Dimensions of Personality*, Kegan Paul, Trench & Trubner, London, 1947.
23. FARR, C. B., and G. M. STEWART: Psychoneurosis in a Hospital for Mental Disease: a Statistical Study of 100 Men and 100 Women, *J. nerv. ment. Dis.*, 95: 133–145, 1942.
24. FINGER, F. W.: Experimental Behavior Disorders in the Rat, in J. McV. Hunt, *Personality and the Behavior Disorder*, The Ronald Press Company, New York, 1944.
25. FRENCH, F., and F. ALEXANDER: Psychogenic Factors in Bronchial Asthma: Part I., *Psychosom. Med. Monogr.*, 1 (No. 4): 92, 1941.
26. GANTT, H.: The Origin and Development of Nervous Disturbances Experimentally Produced, *Amer. J. Psychiat.*, 98: 418–424, 1942.

27. GILL, S. E.: Nocturnal Enuresis; Experiences with Evacuated Children, *Brit. Med. J.*, *Part II*, 199–200, 1940.
28. GORDON, I.: Allergy, Enuresis, and Stammering, *Brit. Med. J.*, *Part I*, 357–358, 1942.
29. GREENHILL, M.: Clinical Features of the Psychoneuroses in World War II Veterans, *N.C. Med. J.*, 7: 585–590, 1946.
30. GRINKER, R. R., and J. P. SPIEGEL: *Men Under Stress* The Blakiston Company, Philadelphia, 1945.
31. HADFIELD, J. A.: War Neuroses: a Year in a Neuropathic Hospital, *Brit. Med. J.*, *Part I*, 281–285, 320–323, 1942.
32. HAGMAN, E. R.: A Study of Fears of Children of Preschool Age, *J. exp. Educ.*, 1: 110–130, 1932.
33. HAMILTON, J. A.: Psychophysiology of Blood Pressure: I. Personality and Behavior Ratings, *Psychosom. Med.*, 4: 125–133, 1942.
34. HARRIS, A.: The Prognosis of Anxiety States, *Brit. Med. J.*, *Part II*, 649–654, 1938.
35. HEBB, D. O.: Spontaneous Neurosis in Chimpanzees; Theoretical Relations with Clinical and Experimental Phenomena, *Psychosom. Med.*, 9: 3–19, 1947.
36. HIRSCH, N. D. M.: Mental Deviants in the Population of the United States, Division of Health and Disability Studies, Bureau of Research, Social Security Board, 1940. (Unpublished Report.)
36a. HIRSCH, N. D. M.: *Dynamic Causes of Juvenile Crime*, Sci-Art Co., Cambridge, 1937.
37. HUNT, J. McV., and H. S. SCHLOSBERG: General Activity in the Male White Rat, *J. comp. Psychol.*, 28: 23–38, 1939.
38. ISAACS, S.: Some Notes on the Incidence of Neurotic Difficulties in Young Children, *Brit. J. educ. Psychol.*, 2: 71–91, 1932.
39. JACOBSON, E.: *Progressive Relaxation*, University of Chicago Press, Chicago, 1929.
40. JONES, M., and V. MELLERSH: A Comparison of the Exercise Response in Anxiety States and Normal Controls, *Psychosom. Med.*, 8: 180–187, 1946.
41. KANZER, M.: Amnesia: a Statistical Study, *Amer. J. Psychiat.*, 96: 711–716, 1939.
42. KASANIN, J., J. SOLOMON, and P. AXELROD: Extrinsic Factors in the Treatment of Anxiety States in Children, *Amer. J. Orthopsychiat.*, 12: 439–456, 1942.
42a. LIDDELL, H. S.: Conditioned Reflex Methods and Experimental Neurosis, in J. McV. Hunt: *Personality and the Behavior Disorders*, Ronald Press, New York, 1944.
42b. LIDDELL, H. S.: The Experimental Neurosis, *Annu. Rev. Physiol.*, 9: 569–580, 1947.
43. LION, E. G.: Anancastic Depression, *J. nerv. ment. Dis.*, 95: 730–738, 1942.
44. LIPTON, HARRY R.: Anxiety States and Their Intramural Management, in Lindner, R. M., and R. V. Seliger, *Handbook of Correctional Psychology*, Philosophical Library, Inc., New York, 499–509, 1947.
45. LUDWIG, A. O.: Neuroses Occurring in Soldiers after Prolonged Combat Exposure, *Bull. Menninger Clin.*, 11: 15–23, 1947.
46. LUNDHOLM, H.: A New Laboratory Neurosis, *Character & Pers.*, 9: 11–120, 1940.
47. MAIER, N. R. F.: *Studies of Abnormal Behavior in the Rat: The Neurotic Pattern and an Analysis of the Situation Which Produces It.* Harper & Brothers, New York, 1939.
48. MALMO, R. M.: *Experimental Studies of Mental Patients under Stress: Moosehart Symposium on Feelings and Emotions*, University of Chicago Press, Chicago, 1949.
49. MELTZER, H.: Talkativeness in Stuttering and Nonstuttering Children, *J. genet. Psychol.*, 46: 371–390, 1935.
49a. McCULLOCH, W. S.: Modes of Functional Organization ot the Cerebral Cortex, *Fed. Proc. Amer. Soc. exp. Biol.*, 6: 448–452, 1947.
50. McGEHEE, W., and W. D. LEWIS: Parental Attitudes of Mentally Superior, Average, and Retarded Children, *Sch. & Soc.*, 51: 556–559, 1940.

51. MEANS, M. H.: Fears of One Thousand College Women, *J. abnorm. soc. Psychol.*, 31: 291–311, 1936.
52. MICHAELS, J. J., and S. GOODMAN: Incidence and Intercorrelations of Enuresis and Other Neuropathic Traits, *Amer. J. Orthopsychiat.*, IV: (No. 1) 1934.
53. MICHAELS, J. J., and S. GOODMAN: Enuresis and Other Factors in Normal and in Psychotic Persons, *Arch. Neurol. Psychiat.*, Chicago, 40: 699–706, 1938.
54. MOWRER, O. H.: An Experimental Analogue of Regression, with Incidental Observation on Reaction Formation, *J. abnorm. soc. Psychol.*, 35: 454–478, 1940.
55. NEEDLES, W.: A Statistical Study of 100 Neuropsychiatric Casualties from the Normandy Campaign, *Amer. J. Psychiat.*, 102: 214–221, 1945.
56. OLSON, W. C.: *The Measurement of Nervous Habits in Normal Children*, University of Minn. Press, Minneapolis, 1929.
57. OLSON, W. C.: The Incidence of Nervous Habits in Children, *J. abnorm. soc. Psychol.*, 25: 75–92, 1930.
58. OSBORNE, J. W., and J. COHEN: Psychiatric Factors in Peripheral Vasoneuropathy after Chilling, *Lancet*, 249: 204–206, 1945.
59. PHILLIPS, W. S., and J. E. GREENE: A Preliminary Study of the Relationship of Age, Hobbies, and Civil Status to Neuroticism among Women Teachers, *J. educ. Psychol.*, 30: 440–444, 1939.
60. REICH, W.: Die Rolle der Genitalität in der Neurosentherapie, *Allg. arzt Zseh. f. Psychiotherap. u. psych. Hygiene*, 1: 672–681, 1928.
61. REID, L. D.: Some Facts about Stuttering, *J. Speech Disorders*, 11: 3–12, 1946.
62. RENNIE, T. A. C.: The Role of Personality in Certain Hyper-tensive States, *New Engl. J. Med.*, 22: 448–456, 1939.
63. RICKLES, N. K.: Exhibitionism, *J. nerv. ment. Dis.*, 95: 11–17, 1942.
64. RIESS, B. F., and O. E. DE CILLIS: Personality Differences in Allergic and Non-allergic Children, *J. abnorm. soc. Psychol.*, 20: 381–390, 1945.
65. RUESCH, J.: Personality Structure, Lactic Acid Production and Work Performance in Psychiatric Patients, *J. Psychol.*, 20: 381–390, 1945.
66. SAUL, L. J.: Hostility in Cases of Essential Hypertension, *Psychosom. Med.*, 1: 212–222, 1939.
67. SLATER, E.: Neurosis and Sexuality, *J. Neurol. Psychiat.*, 8: 12–14, 1945.
68. SLATER, E.: The Neurotic Constitution: a Statistical Study of 2000 Neurotic Soldiers, *J. Neurol. Psychiat.*, 6: 1–16, 1943.
69. STEWART, D. N., and D. M. DE R. WINSER: Incidence of Perforated Peptic Ulcer; Effect of Heavy Air-raids, *Lancet*, 242: 259–260, 1942.
70. STOCKARD, C. R.: *The Physical Basis of Personality*, W. W. Norton & Company, New York, 1931.
71. THORNDIKE, R. L.: A Note on the Relationship of Allergy to Neurasthenic Traits, *J. gen. Psychol.*, 17: 153–155, 1937.
72. THORNE, F. C.: The Incidence of Nocturnal Enuresis after Age 5. *Amer. J. Psychiat.*, 100: 686–689, 1944.
73. VINSON, D. B., JR.: Neurotic Behavior Patterns Arising Out of the Combat Situation, *Dis. nerv. Syst.*, 7: 19–22, 1946.
74. WEBER, A.: Uber die Enuresis Nocturna des Kinder, *Mschr. Psychiat. Neurol.*, 111: 144–176, 1945–1946.
75. WECHSLER, D.: The Incidence and Significance of Fingernail Biting in Children, *Psychoanal. Rev.*, 18: 201–209, 1931.
76. WITTKOWER, E.: Studies in Hay-fever Patients (the Allergic Personality), *J. ment. Sci.*, 84: 352–369, 1938.
77. WOLF, S., and H. G. WOLFF: Evidence on the Genesis of Peptic Ulcer in Man. *J. Amer. med. Ass.*, 120: 163–174, 1942.

# CHAPTER 18

## THE ABNORMAL AND UNADAPTED PERSONALITY: III. THE PSYCHOTIC

1. Incidences, Varieties, and Prognoses of the Psychoses
2. The Differentiation of Psychosis from Normality
3. The Psychological and Physiological Nature of Schizophrenia
4. The Background and Course of Schizophrenia
5. Theories of Personality in Schizophrenia
6. The Psychological and Physiological Nature of Dysthymic Psychoses
7. The Background and Course of Dysthymic Psychoses
8. Theories of Personality in Dysthymia
9. Personality in Relation to Other Psychoses
10. Summary

## 1. INCIDENCES, VARIETIES, AND PROGNOSES OF THE PSYCHOSES

**The Classification of Mental Disorders.** Although the study of psychosis has not yet led to such improved insight into the normal personality as have the data on neurosis and delinquency, it seems likely that the near future may see some radical contributions from this source, particularly in regard to the nature of temperament differences and the relation of physiological conditions to learning. Let us, however, begin by studying the psychoses in their own right, noting first, as with the other abnormalities, their nature and distribution.

In Chapter 1 the division of the psychoses into organic and functional varieties has been explained, and a description of the syndromes of the most important of the functional forms has been given. It is instructive, however, to realize how varied the forms and circumstances of mental disorder can be, beyond these central syndromes, even though this variety be indicated no more fully than by the following list:

*Classification of Mental Disorders (Approved by Council of American Psychiatric Association)*

1. Psychoses with syphilic meningoencephalitis (general paresis)
2. Psychoses with other forms of syphilis of the central nervous system
3. Psychoses with epidemic encephalitis
4. Psychoses with other infectious diseases
   *a.* With tuberculous meningitis
   *b.* With meningitis (unspecified)

    *c.* With acute chorea (Sydenham's)
    *d.* With other infectious disease
    *e.* Postinfectious psychoses
  5. Psychoses due to alcohol
  6. Psychoses due to a drug or other exogenous poison
    *a.* Due to a metal
    *b.* Due to a gas
    *c.* Due to opium or a derivative
  7. Psychoses due to trauma
    *a.* Delirium due to trauma
    *b.* Personality disorder due to trauma
    *c.* Mental deterioration due to trauma
  8. Psychoses with cerebral arteriosclerosis
  9. Psychoses with other disturbances of circulation
    *a.* With cerebral embolism
    *b.* With cardiorenal disease
10. Psychoses due to convulsive disorder (epilepsy)
    *a.* Epileptic deterioration
    *b.* Epileptic clouded states
    *c.* Other epileptic types
11. Senile psychoses
12. Involutional psychoses
    *a.* Melancholia
    *b.* Paranoid types
13. Psychoses due to other metabolic, etc., diseases
    *a.* With glandular disorder
    *b.* Exhaustion delirium
    *c.* Alzheimer's disease (presenile sclerosis)
    *d.* With pellagra
    *e.* With other somatic disease
14. Psychoses due to new growth
    *a.* With intracranial neoplasm
    *b.* With other neoplasms
15. Psychoses due to unknown or hereditary cause but associated with organic change
    *a.* With multiple sclerosis
    *b.* With paralysis agitans
    *c.* With Huntington's chorea
    *d.* With other disease of the brain or nervous system
16. Manic-depressive psychoses
    *a.* Manic type
    *b.* Depressive type
    *c.* Circular type
    *d.* Mixed type
17. Dementia praecox (schizophrenia)
    *a.* Simple type

     *b.* Hebephrenic type

     *c.* Catatonic type

     *d.* Paranoid type

18. Paranoia and paranoid conditions

     *a.* Paranoia

     *b.* Paranoid conditions

19. Psychoses with psychopathic personality

20. Psychoses with mental deficiency

21. Psychoneuroses

     *a.* Hysteria (anxiety hysteria, conversion hysteria, and subgroups)

     *b.* Psychasthenia or compulsive states (and subgroups)

     *c.* Neurasthenia

     *d.* Hypochondriasis

     *e.* Reactive depression (simple situational reaction, others)

     *f.* Anxiety state

     *g.* Anorexia nervosa

     *h.* Mixed psychoneurosis

22. Without mental disorder

     *a.* Epilepsy

     *b.* Alcoholism

     *c.* Drug addiction

     *d.* Mental deficiency

     *e.* Disorders of personality due to epidemic encephalitis

     *f.* Psychopathic personality

        With pathologic sexuality

        With pathologic emotionality

        With asocial or amoral trends

        Mixed types

**Incidences of Mental Disorders at the Psychotic Level.** The relative frequency of these varieties (in the United States) is as indicated on page 521. It will be seen that the functional disorders predominate, to an extent not easily realized when considering the numerous organic and other *possibilities* listed.

Attempts to compare the incidence in different racial and cultural groups, which would throw light on genetic and cultural determinants, have generally foundered on the fact that somewhat different syndrome definitions or recording systems are used in different countries, and even districts, and that there is a tendency to count the number of insane according to the hospital accommodation available! For that reason the German and Swiss column in the first table opposite is to be only roughly compared with United States categories to which it is adapted. However, Lemkan, Tietze, and Cooper (47), after careful comparisons of results and methods, give the following expectancies per 1,000 born, for the following three major psychoses,

FREQUENCY OF MENTAL DISORDERS

A comparison among ten psychoses of first admissions to state mental hospitals and to private mental hospitals, 1936*

| Psychosis | State hospitals, per cent | Distribution, private hospitals | German and Swiss records† |
|---|---|---|---|
| General paresis............................ | 8.1 | 2.0 | 11.0 |
| Cerebral arteriosclerosis.................... | 12.5 | 4.2 | 2.0 |
| Senile...................................... | 8.6 | 5.6 | 2.0 |
| Dementia praecox........................ | 20.1 | 13.6 | 24.0 |
| With mental deficiency.................... | 3.6 | 0.8 | (no category) |
| Alcoholic.................................. | 4.6 | 5.3 | 9.0 |
| With epilepsy............................. | 2.2 | 0.4 | 12.0 |
| Manic-depressive.......................... | 11.7 | 14.6 | 7.0 |
| Involutional psychoses..................... | 2.8 | 4.4 | 2.0 |
| Paranoia and paranoid condition............ | 1.5 | 2.5 | (no category) |
| With psychopathic personality.............. | 1.7 | 1.8 | 13.0‡ |
| Alcoholism without psychosis............... | 5.2 | 15.8 | 18.0 |

* United States Bureau of the Census, *Patients in Hospitals for Mental Diseases:* 1936 (Washington, 1938), page 14 (Table 10).

† The German and Swiss data are from the incidence among 10,684 siblings of 2,090 propositi chosen to present a stratified sample, and express percentages relative to total after mental defectives and noninstitutionalized psychopathic personalities have been deducted. Senile and arteriosclerotic are lower because the sample has a normal age distribution (47).

‡ And hysteria.

NOTE: Figures represent percentage of total group of mentally disordered which includes mental defectives and organic psychoses.

SEX DISTRIBUTION OF MENTAL DISORDERS*

| Psychosis | Male | Female |
|---|---|---|
| Involutional...................... | 1 | 2.5 |
| Manic-depressive................. | 1 | 1.25 |
| Psychoneurosis.................... | 1 | 1.75 |
| Dementia praecox................. | 1 | 0.87 |
| Cerebral arteriosclerosis........... | 1 | 0.60 |
| General paresis................... | 1 | 0.28 |
| Alcoholic psychosis............... | 1 | 0.14 |

* *Mental Deviants in the Population of the United States*, Nathaniel D. M. Hirsch, Division of Health and Disability Studies, Bureau of Research and Statistics, Social Security Board, Federal Security Agency.

in Germany and in New York State—two regions for which records are very complete:

|  | Germany | New York |
|---|---|---|
| Schizophrenia............... | 6.8 | 16.0 |
| Manic-depressive............ | 2.0 | 5.0 |
| General paresis.............. | 2.9 | 4.4 |

As to total incidence, in the United States, Landis and Page (46) estimate that at any one time 1.5 per cent of the adult population (considering figures for New York State most accurate) is in mental hospitals. Metropolitan Life Insurance Company figures suggest that 5 per cent of individuals spend some part of their lives in mental hospitals, which is compatible with the above figure of about 1 per cent at any one time. The above figures do not take account of a number, estimated from 20 per cent of the hospitalized patients in states with good hospital accommodation (10) to 100 per cent in poor areas, of extra, nonhospitalized cases. Thus psychosis is generally considered to be, at some time in the life cycle, a problem for between one in ten and one in twenty of the population. Its incidence is higher in urban than rural areas, higher for old than young, and is increasing, according to Hirsch's careful survey, at the rate of about 16,000 cases annually in the United States.

Until accurate knowledge of these rates of incidence exists also for individual mental disorder syndromes, however, we cannot proceed to any precise inferences from this source as to the power of various influences in mental disorder.

Carothers (18) has recently attempted to estimate the total impact of civilized inhibitions by investigating, with fairly dependable methods, the insanity rate among Kenya natives. In spite of poor food and debilitating diseases their rate appears to be about 3.4 per 100,000 whereas it is 57 for England and Wales, 72 to 86 for the United States (Massachusetts) and 161 per 100,000 among Negroes in the United States (Massachusetts figures). It is likely that *all* forms of mental disorder are increased by the pace of life, by crowding, and by increasing complexity in the emotional control and responsiveness expected by civilization. We may also infer that the physiological changes of age, including arteriosclerosis, reduce those powers of mental adaptation that make for sanity; but here again alternative explanations, *e.g.*, conflicts of later with earlier learning, maladaptation through social change, cannot yet be ruled out.

**Prognoses in the Psychoses.** The recovery rates for psychosis in general seem to have changed little in a hundred years, save for the slight recent gains from shock therapy, early psychotherapy, and frontal lobotomy. Thus

Carter gives for a large group of varied adolescent psychotics 38 per cent complete recovery, 8 per cent social recovery, 5 per cent recurrent, and 49 per cent deteriorating. As a fair example of the typical trend in specific psychoses we may take the following results of Bond and Braceland (12)

| | Recovered | Improved | Unchanged | Died | Suicided or Lost |
|---|---|---|---|---|---|
| 171 Manic-depressives............ | 86 | 19 | 30 | 24 | 12 |
| 116 Dementia praecox cases....... | 12 | 25 | 66 | 10 | 3 |
| 38 General paretics.............. | 13 | 8 | 5 | 12 | 0 |

## 2. THE DIFFERENTIATION OF PSYCHOSIS FROM NORMALITY

**The Defective Vitality of Psychotics Generally.** The evidence through which we may arrive at some clearer hypothesis as to the nature and causes of psychosis is very widely scattered, but will be reviewed sectionally—without any necessary sequence of the sections—before attempting interpretation. Such sections will include: their reactions to experimental tests when compared with normals; their heredity, of their physiology and anatomy; their histories and prepsychotic personalities; the situations which provoke psychosis; and the effects of various therapeutic procedures. A few of these can best be glanced at in relation to psychosis generally, but it is more profitable to study most in relation to specific psychoses, principally the functional disorders of schizophrenia and manic-depression, to which our survey will largely be restricted.

The tendency of psychosis, with the exception of cyclic insanity, to be more prevalent with lower social status has already been remarked. There is also some tendency for psychotics to be below normal from the standpoint of vital statistics. The average age at death of 1,379 psychotics was found (5) to be 56.5 years compared with 61.5 (60 for men, 63 for women) for the general population. This breaks down into 74 years for seniles, 61 to 70 for manic-depressives, 63 for alcoholics, 58 for psychopaths, 51 for general paretics, and 47 for schizophrenics. Organic nervous disorders and epilepsy show an even shorter life expectation than schizophrenics. The relatives of the latter show a somewhat lower life expectation and a decidedly lower fertility than the general population—all of which seems to point to some generalized and constitutional poor adaptation in the schizophrenic. Barry (7) found orphanhood in about 28 per cent of psychotics as against 20 per cent of normals, but it has also been shown that the life expectation of psychotics is less than that of their parents. This is probably not due to higher accident rate, for they are more protected, but to the somatic wear and tear of psychotic emotionality. Alstrom shows that the death rate of mental hospital patients (from all causes) is from 4 to 4.5 times that of the general population (2). It is still higher when age, sex, social class, etc., are correctly matched.

Parenthetically we may note that the death rate is abnormally high also for various grades of mental defective (53) and that tuberculosis and pneumonia have the same abnormally high rank as causes of death among them as they do among schizophrenics. Whether this is due to a similar inadequacy in meeting the socioeconomic environment or to a genetic linkage similar to that claimed for schizophrenia is uncertain.

**Defective Adaptation of Psychotics Generally.** The mental efficiency of psychotics shows itself to be below normal in most experimental test situations, indicating that the obvious social maladaptation is only a specific aspect of a general deficiency. On mental capacity alone, as seen from the previous chapter's study of the results of Roe and Shakow and others, it seems that the psychotic is only slightly inferior to the normal, presumably because lesser intelligence slightly increases the likelihood of getting into stressful emotional situations. The schizophrenic is significantly below the manic-depressive, while the alcoholic and the paretic are decidedly below the schizophrenic; but these last are possibly low in intelligence as a result of brain-cell damage. The maladaptation of the psychotic is thus not to be sought in defect of the relation-perceiving apparatus as such, but in the distortions of perception and of behavior control through dynamic causes.

This defect shows itself most readily in such experimental situations as that of the Cursive Miniature Situation Test, where the subject has to make "wise," foresightful judgments, restrain overexcitement, and keep a number of mental sets in a proper hierarchical relationship. With such tests there is very little overlap of normal and psychotic populations. Psychotics resemble neurotics in showing a general tendency to poor short-distance memory performance and a somewhat general poor physiological efficiency. In regard to the former, Rabin (62) showed, in conformity with other studies, that psychotics are as good as normals on those aspects of intelligence tests requiring verbal ability[1] or general information, but poorer in perception of relations and adaptability in new situations and in tests such as the symbol-digit, requiring good short-distance memory, control of associations, and steady concentration.

These experimental findings, summarizable as defective dynamic inte-

[1] However, one must distinguish between $V$ factor, which is largely a knowledge of vocabulary and grammatical forms, and effective use of language in new situations. Cameron (17) presented incomplete sentences with causal sequence of arguments to twenty-five schizophrenics, twenty-two seniles, twenty-five normal children, and twenty normal adults. The use of language to convey meaning and causal argument was poorer in psychotic adults, especially the schizophrenics, than in the children.

gration of mental sets, defective emotional control, defective memory and control of associations, do not immediately connote, however, a further characteristic that is even more conspicuous in the general observation of the psychotic—namely, his failure to "maintain contact with reality," shown also in his hallucinations and misperceptions. This rise of subjective beliefs and images into primary importance and autonomy, as well as the breakdown of the distinction between external and internal worlds, is something which cannot yet be expressed in experimental terms and reduced to any simpler definition or conceptualization.

With this degree of differentiation of the general class of psychotics from normals we shall turn to special syndromes, beginning with that which claims a higher percentage of psychotics than any other, namely schizophrenia.

## 3. THE PSYCHOLOGICAL AND PHYSIOLOGICAL NATURE OF SCHIZOPHRENIA

**Experimental Studies of Schizophrenic Performance.** As indicated in the descriptive introduction (Chap. 1), it is usual to recognize four sub-syndromes within the major syndrome of schizophrenia. Central to all is a withdrawal from social accessibility, hallucinations, poorly organized delusions, breakdown of emotional-cognitive integration, and bizarre verbal and motor habits. Introspectively the schizophrenic has experiences of ideas being out of control, strange, and therefore interpretable as coming from outside himself (*cf.* dream consciousness). The features *common* to the four subsyndromes will alone be studied intensively here.

The experimental study of the schizophrenic shows him to be generally slow in mental processes, *e.g.*, symbol substitution, tapping tempo, and reaction time. Even the reaction times of wholly cooperative subjects are longer and less regular; the reflex latency period is longer (in the knee jerk); unlike normals, the time for regularly forewarned reaction times is no better than irregular (inability to maintain mental set). Panara (58) found the schizophrenic reactions more variable and he also found frequent abrupt changes of rhythm on the ergograph. Schizophrenics are more likely to stop a task of their own accord than normals, and less likely to resume after an interruption. They have difficulty in maintaining a mental set, or, as Rickers-Ovsiankina (63) expresses the results of her experiments, there is inability to maintain "sufficiently firm segregated tension systems, to result in the execution of a goal-directed activity." All psychotics, but especially schizophrenics, according to Mischenko, fail to behave according to Pavlov's "principle of energy of the stimulus," *i.e.*, reacting more powerfully to a more powerful sensory stimulus (55). More than most psychotics they also show, on the Pressey X-O test, a high concern with "self"-interests relative to sex interests. On the body-sway test of suggestibility two independent studies show all schizophrenics except paranoids to have negative, contrasuggestible response instead of the normal positive direction.

The extensive studies of Shakow may be summarized as showing the schizophrenic to be most defective where the stimulus situation demands constant voluntary readjustment, but adequate, almost to normal level, on prolonged, unchanging performances. Parenthetically, it can readily be seen that most of the mannerisms and perseverations of the schizophrenic are due to this paucity of willed activity, for repetition and perseveration are normally not indications of perseverance but rather of failure of the will to inhibit, integrate, or modify localized, continuing neural activity. Compared with normals, however, the schizophrenic is unable to keep a mental set a normal length of time, takes the easiest, least will-demanding path when buffeted by circumstances, readily lowers his level of aspiration, and shifts from situation to situation without any plan. This is least evident in the paranoid subsyndrome.

On the other hand, the schizophrenic shows considerable improvement (compared with other psychotics) on repeated exposure to a task and more than average "consolidation" (due to less retroactive inhibition?) when practice is separated by long intervals (three months). In final comparison of the normal with the schizophrenic groups Shakow found the latter *least* deteriorated in vocabulary, the recall of overlearned material of long standing, and *most* deteriorated in "ability to function quickly at one's real level of ability," immediate memory recall, speed of movement in self-initiated activities, associative thinking, and ability to handle problems at the conceptual level rather than the concrete level. The present writer, comparing schizophrenics with normals and manic-depressives on the Cursive Miniature Situation Test found results concurrent with the above with respect to the schizophrenics' inability to marshal their powers to meet a situation. On the steady, repetitive tasks they performed normally, but failed on tasks demanding maintenance of mutually qualifying mental sets, or when a speeded test demanded a sudden stepping-up of performance.

**The Language Habits of the Schizophrenic, and Their Causes.** Clinically, one of the most obvious and frequently discussed features of schizophrenia is the bizarre thought association and speech. This strangeness seems to be in part due to the maintenance of a vocabulary normally rich in concepts and universals along with a dynamic disability which rules out the possibility of the complex mental sets necessary to applying a general concept. This is well shown in the inquiry on sentence structure, etc., by Kanner (38). And although the speech of the schizophrenic often appears metaphorical and abstract, actually, as White (76) has pointed out, "the language of schizophrenia is of a lower level of abstraction than normal adult language." Further, in the "word salad" of the schizophrenic there is a tendency to use words mechanically, as mere counters, without their full entourage of associations. Part of this is a literal or "limited context" application of ideas, as in a schizophrenic known to the writer who wore calluses on his scalp through standing on his head "because the world is upside down nowadays!"

Finally, the schizophrenic's central emotional apathy and hostility, by which he breaks his social contact with others, results necessarily in a disregard of the social character of language, so that, like Humpty Dumpty in Lewis Carroll's insightful *Through the Looking Glass* he may imply, "When I use a word it means just what I choose it to mean." Woods (79) made a special study of schizophrenic language and showed a poverty of precise thought, a tendency to empty phrases and platitudes eccentrically juxtaposed, and a stiff and rigid retention of the form of language when the meaning was lost.

**Physiological Differences.** Experimental studies of schizophrenia at the physiological level have produced an enormous literature, at the main conclusions of which we must briefly glance if we are to obtain as complete a picture as possible of the essential nature of this disorder. Most of the early literature points to a wide variety of subnormal conditions, defective endocrines, especially gonads, defective circulatory system, poor autonomic power of maintaining homeostasis, and defective resistance to disease. Many claim to observe neurological deterioration of the cerebral cortex, but the most recent neurological opinion is that these lesions are no greater than in a chance control group and must be put down to age and other secondary effects. There is no doubt, however, that the schizophrenic tends to be below average size, asthenic in build, poor in circulatory development (heart size small relative to body), and generally lacking in physiological "robustness" and perhaps maturity.

A more detailed statement of findings is as follows: Betz (9) confirmed the smaller and more asthenic build, poorer handgrip strength, and more variable pulse rate, suggesting autonomic instability; while several studies show an undue proportion of individuals with thyroid subnormality. Hoskins and Sleeper (35) found, in a wide array of variables, significant differences for schizophrenics only in a lower metabolic rate, increased urinary volume, moderate secondary anaemia, and leukocytosis. Freeman found the arm-to-carotid circulation time abnormally slow, along with general vascular hypotension. Others find breathing quicker and shallower than normals and conclude there is an inner muscular tension. Poor ability to maintain bodily temperature constant and a general "intravegetative ataxia" and autonomic inability to maintain homeostasis recur in many studies. Rodnick (64), for example, experimented with gradual blocking, through humidity and high temperature, of heat and evaporation loss from the lungs. The response in blood pressure change, heart rate, and P.G.R. was larger for normals than schizophrenics. Similarly, Angyal and Blackman (4) showed in fifty-eight schizophrenics that the vestibular reactivity to rotation was markedly subnormal. Although hypothyroidism, hyperadrenalism, and hypogonadism are the only endocrine defects reported consistently there is scattered evidence of a somewhat excessive proneness to still more general endocrine defect. A greater than normal proneness to childhood illness has frequently been asserted, but except for tuberculosis and encephalitis the results have not yet been presented in statistically convincing form. Kasanin and Kaufman (40) observe that tuberculosis in children leads to a "schizoid-ization" of the personality and describe a typical schizophrenia in a boy with disseminated tuberculosis. Cases are also reported of schizophrenia following severe infections such as typhoid and puerperal fever and brain damage. These instances of schizophrenia following major illness may not be frequent enough to require any explanation additional to that of a common lack of physiological integration and vitality being responsible for both.

The extensive work of Hoskins and his coworkers gives confirmation to most of the above and adds further that the attempt to remedy thyroid, adrenal, and gonadal deficiencies produces some real improvement in psychological and physiological efficiency but does not, in general, remove the central mental disorder. Since endocrine effects, *e.g.*, the maturation of secondary sex characters, usually require years of continuous action, it is still possible, though unlikely, that the endocrine deficiency is responsible for the main disorder. The gonad atrophy, which goes with deficiency of androgen secretion, has been found to be correlated with the severity of the psychosis, rather than with age or nutritional status. Hoskins presents neat evidence that the tissues are, furthermore, defective in their *reaction* to normal amounts of thyroid, adrenal steroids, etc. This may be related to the consistently subnormal oxygen consumption of the schizophrenic tissues and the low metabolic rate. Hoskins (34), Angyal (4), and Rodnick (64) note poor vestibular sense and marked ataxia, which again indicates some resemblance to severe neurotic conditions, since Eysenck found this defective sensitivity of balance with institutionalized neurotics, while the present writer observed it in lesser degree with low character integration (factor $C-$) in normals. The recent studies of Grenell at Yale in studying electric potentials directly generated by the body show schizophrenics to average about 65 microvolts, compared with about 10 for normals. While the exact meaning of this measurement is still obscure—possibly it is a function of muscle tensions—at least it indicates again a radical difference of general metabolism or bodily habitat from that of normals.

An important question that remains unanswered here is whether all of these defects arise through the prolonged conflict of the mental disorder or whether the difficulties in autonomic response, in mustering energy, in preserving balance, and in maintaining cortical activity existed in the prepsychotic and acted as disorganizing burdens in his attempts at normal adjustment.

#### 4. THE BACKGROUND AND COURSE OF SCHIZOPHRENIA

**Prepsychotic Personality and Background.** The extent of hereditary determination of schizophrenia has already been discussed (page 127). It is not high and leaves decidedly more to be accounted for by environmental variations, which we shall now examine. There is, in the first place, practically complete agreement that a certain prepsychotic personality is typically found in individuals who later become schizophrenic. It is true, however, of psychoses in general that certain personality characteristics of an unusual kind manifest themselves in childhood. Yerbury and Newell (80) studied a typical cross section of 75 per cent dementia praecox patients, 4 per cent manic-depressives, and 21 per cent organic insanities, and noted that in all the *functional* cases there seemed to be a prehistory of high general emotionality and/or social immaturity. They rated seclusiveness, perfectionism, and undue aggressiveness as most frequent and reported, incidentally, that 60 per cent had serious illness in early life, and 55 per cent had adverse sociocultural factors in the family environment.

The prepsychotic personality of those schizophrenics who are not indistinguishable, as children, from normals is very clearly one characterized in childhood by shyness, sensitiveness, a tendency to few friends and solitary amusements, and in adulthood, in addition by taciturnity. Kasanin and Rosen (41) found correlated with these cardinal traits, in the prehistory of 151 schizophrenics, also the reputation of a model child, general neurotic traits, no sense of humor, close attachment to the family, difficulties of emancipation from parents, great ambition but little self-assertiveness, frequent daydreaming and, in adult life, nonsmoking, total abstention, feelings of inferiority, an inability to discuss personal affairs and even affairs in general, a tendency to fuss over pain or illness, more churchgoing, unusually close attachment to some member or members of the family, and a low output of energy. Fits of violent temper are also common in the prehistory of catatonics.

Later, Kasanin and Veo (42) attempted to classify another series of patients with investigated prehistories into five natural groupings, one being normals and the other (*a*) odd, queer, peculiar children, (*b*) maladjusted neurotic, (*c*) unusually brilliant, ambitious, successful, and (*d*) shy, passive, backward "nobodies." Differences of intelligence or some other factor may account for variations on what is probably a single fundamental factor or two factors (see Chap. 4). Friedlander, out of 900 psychotics (schizophrenics and psychopaths), found twenty-seven who had also been in child clinics and for whom data were available.   The schizophrenics had been daydreamers, lacking in self-confidence, depressed, and showing marked irregularity of the home background and more interparental friction.   Lundholm attempts to sum up his observations on the personality of the schizophrenic by saying that he is overwhelmingly egocentric and with deficient altruistic interests.   Schumacher (65) and other writers stress also excessive industry and ambition without rational control, a tendency to pedantry, fanatical honor (sensitivity), accentuated self-consciousness, and sexual coldness.   They observe also among imminently schizophrenic children, irritability at interference with seclusiveness and daydreaming, a diminution of interests and a shift to those of younger children, sensitivity to criticism, often associated with violent outbursts, and a reduction of physical activity.

**Home and General Background.**   In the home background of the schizophrenic Kasanin and Rosen (41) found, with statistically undue frequency, maternal overprotection, paternal neglect, overattachment to the family, physical defects and anomalies, and, later, a history of unsatisfactory heterosexual attachments.   Sullivan (74) mentions the preponderance of fear experiences and, less definitely, of anger experiences, in the records of schizophrenic histories, as well as of "panic" experiences of disastrous destruction of self-esteem.   Henley's famous poem "Beyond this place of wrath and tears . . . ," with its compensatory emphasis on the inviolability of the ego, brings definite illumination of the schizophrenic situation. Despert (26) in a study of schizophrenia in children found the mothers to be aggressive, oversolicitous, and overanxious compared with those of normal children.   Others show a definitely higher than normal incidence of homosexuality, in patients and their relatives; of cerebral trauma, and early fright experiences.   Most studies show that schizophrenics and psychoneurotics have a higher frequency of unsatisfactory marital and sex relationships than do manic-depressives or the normal population.   McFie Campbell stresses *environmental* conditions that block sex adjustment and that upset social intercourse generally.

**Course and Prognostic Signs in Various Schizophrenic Syndromes.**   Background conditions will now be studied further in connection with differential prognoses.   Many studies converge on the notion that there are two main types, which may turn out to correspond to distinct factors, in schizophrenia. On the one hand we see cases characterized by asthenic body build, the typical prepsychotic personality, an early, insidious, gradual onset, low general recovery rate, and a rate, moreover, that shows no change through shock therapy.   On the other hand we see individuals without the typical constitutional features or personality prehistory in whom the onset is sudden and stormy, where precipitative stresses are readily visible, where stupor, states of ecstasy, confusion, and suicide predominate in the psychosis, and where the chances of remission, either naturally or through shock treatment, are much higher. Kant (39) found real psychological precipitating circumstances, immediate major stresses and frustrations, five times as frequent in recovering as in nonrecovering schizophrenics. Nonrecovering cases more frequently had conflicts arising *apparently* from single events and from events to which they had irrationally given excessive symbolic meaning and they also more frequently showed sudden loss of rapport with those around them.

These patterns will be more evident as we now study the typical course of schizophrenia. A typical analysis of the average ages of onset (67) yields twenty-six years for simple and hebephrenic forms, twenty-nine years for catatonia, and forty-two for paranoid schizophrenia. A follow-up of 100 cases of schizophrenia after six to ten years, by Langfeldt, showed sixty-six unchanged or worse, thirteen improved, four cured, and seventeen dead. Stalker (71) followed up 129 first admissions and 3,551 cases in the literature and found, in both, 12 per cent with a relatively complete recovery, while 71 per cent and 69 per cent in the respective populations were unimproved or relapsed after remissions. (The remaining 17 to 19 per cent were unclassifiable.)

It is generally agreed by clinical observers that the early stages of onset are characterized by anxiety and by pseudo neurasthenic states rather than by the emotional indifference that is so conspicuous later. Polatin and Hoch (60) point out that this disorder is often confused in early stages with neurosis, particularly obsessional neurosis and anxiety hysteria, but that there are also complaints of being unable to reach others emotionally, there are no attempts at logical explanation of the compulsive and hysteric symptoms as in neurotics, and there are marked mood fluctuations and ideas of persecution and self-reference. At this time there is noticeable a general indolence, a slovenliness in dress and social habits, a marked decline in the quality of the individual's regular work, a tendency to suspicious misinterpretation of simple acts and sudden deteriorations in the reliability of judgment. Bender (8) adds that in every case there is, initially, disturbance of vaso-vegetative functions and poor posture, with subjective sense of anxiety as the central feature. Others describe the course toward development of hostility to formerly loved members of the family, the outbreak of irrational, impulsive behavior, the expression of antisocial and immoral acts, the negative resistivity, and aggressive violence.

Lepel (49) describes the true psychosis as heralded by character changes, improper behavior, queer pranks, irritability, obstinacy, prejudices, feelings of insufficiency, inability to concentrate, and inability to learn new things. The presence of paresthesias and increased awareness of bodily sensation, similar to but more marked than those in the neurosis, is also evident in the prodromal period. Yet other clinical reports emphasize along with the anxiety a regression to more primitive forms of instinctual satisfaction; a preponderance of regressive phantasy contrasting with the external "good" behavior, preoccupation with ritualistic and "magical" thinking, and such special symptoms as difficulty in waking, the presence of half-waking dreams, and of the patient's dreaming that he dreams; changes in perception of faces and forms and disorders of time sense.

The next stage—the syndrome of the fully developed psychosis to which these symptoms lead—has already been described (page 14) and need not be repeated. Bleuler pointed out as far back as 1911 that the hallucinations, delusions, mannerisms, negativism, etc., in this syndrome are almost certainly only the adjustive compromises of a personality already handicapped by the primary symptoms of affective withdrawal, loss of energy, and cognitive confusion.

A sudden onset—present in about 40 per cent of cases—indicates a chance of recovery about twice as good as an insidious one. Better recoveries occur with pyknic body build (though this constitution is also more frequent in paranoid than simple or catatonic schizophrenia), with a single attack rather than a history of several attacks, with disturbances of movement and speech rather than of affect, with short duration of the illness, with an onset in the twenties rather than later or earlier, and with an absence of a history of adverse conditions in the first years of life. Stalker (71) found favorable prognosis also for: absence of disharmony between affect and thought; an acute mixed syndrome not readily classifiable in one of the conventional four types, and for a preponderance of environmental, psychogenic over organic factors. Bigelow (10) found unfavorable prognosis associated, in psychoanalytic terms, with anal-erotic trends, hypochondria, inflexibility, irritability, colorlessness, and infantile patterns of reaction.

Sokolskaya, attempting to "type" schizophrenics (69) regardless of the usual four-syndrome division, concluded that there are essentially two forms of personality, one rigid, narrow, but persistent, dynamic, and inclined to take itself very seriously, the other shut in and extremely sensitive. This shows good correspondence with our $A-$ and $H-$ factors. Zehnder observes that if the prepsychotic personality was more vital, active, and cheerful, the patient tends to remain more accessible, more colorful, and also more given to delusions and hallucinations. It has already been pointed out that the course of the disorder and its response to treatment suggests that patients differ with respect to two factors. The discovery that there are two schizothyme-like factors in the normal range of personalities—namely factor $A$ with its rigidity, assertiveness and hostility and factor $H$ with its sensitive withdrawal (page 62)—adds some statistical support to this clinical impression.

**Evidence from Outcome of Modes of Therapy.**  Psychoanalytic therapy of schizophrenia has generally failed, presumably through inability to obtain "transference." Some studies claim that patients improve, if any degree of accessibility exists, in an atmosphere of kindly sociability in which the individual is allowed to express aggression without fear of punishment, and in which there are opportunities to make atonement for a sense of guilt. Claims are also made for psychological shock. The only widely attempted therapy, other than frontal lobotomy, that has definitely produced a remission rate better than chance is that of physiological shock, through insulin, metrazol, camphor, or electric shock to the cortex. Sporadic cases also exist of apparent cure through endocrine therapy, especially gonadal, while improvement on mental tests alone has been produced, of a clearly significant degree, even by vitamin therapy. The course of recovery through repeated shocks and unconsciousness is described by Glueck and Ackermann (32) as proceeding first through increased accessibility, reduced fixity and confusion of delusions and hallucinations, reduction of anxiety, and increase of emotional plasticity. A later stage brings signs of "toxicity," confusion, true grasp on reality. A comparison (54) of psychological test measures, psychiatric evaluations and physiological measurements shows that they improve together in the course of shock therapy, but the psychological and psychiatric observations show more of a common trend than does either with the physiological measures.

## 5. THEORIES OF PERSONALITY IN SCHIZOPHRENIA

**Psychoanalytic Theories.**  A considerable number of theories concerning schizophrenia exist, though none is yet entirely adequate. The very names of the disorder imply theories, "dementia praecox" for example, explaining the condition as a premature senile psychosis—to which it has much resemblance[2]—and "schizophrenia" as a splitting or disintegration of dynamic organization which would account for the resulting cognitive and behavioral defects.

The psychoanalytic theory explains schizophrenia, first, as a personality regression but basically as a libidinal regression beyond the earliest object attachments, to the narcistic level. This agrees with the observed incapacity to maintain affectional relations to others; the preoccupation with the patient's own body and consciousness, and the tendency for object attachments, if any, to reach only the homosexual level. The libido has presumably experienced some very early trauma, through which it fails to advance to the heterosexual level. Spaer (70), comparing the analysis of eighteen schizophrenics with ninety-two nonschizophrenics, found a pre-

---

[2] As Lange points out, however, the senile dement has frequently been an autistic, suspicious, loveless, quarrelsome personality in earlier years, and it may be rather that the schizoid dements than that dement is schizoid.

dominance of early Oedipus attachment difficulties in the former; but this can be said of many neurotic syndromes also, *e.g.*, conversion hysteria, and, in the absence of more cogent evidence of the specific effect of the traumatizing influence, the psychoanalytic account of regression remains more of a description than an explanation.

The disorder has also been expressed in psychoanalytic terms as a destruction of the ego. In neurosis the ego props itself up against the stresses of id and superego by defense mechanisms, but in this case they fail. The highly conforming early behavior of the schizophrenic and his tendency to acute anxiety suggest that the defective ego development arises partly from a too perfectionistically developed superego, and that the main conflict arises from guilt from this source.

In seeking to account for the predominance of guilt Blum and Rosenzweig (11) have stressed the phantasy satisfactions of aggression, notably against siblings. The latter has shown that schizophrenics experience in childhood nearly twice as many sibling deaths as do normal controls (manic-depressives experience fewer than controls), and argues that they unconsciously interpret this as due to the death wishes arising from their own jealousy and aggression. They also experience more parental deaths, the females more deaths of mothers and the males more deaths of fathers. The question arises as to whether these undoubted death associations are not due rather to the above-mentioned lesser vitality of the schizophrenic constitution, *i.e.*, consequences rather than causes of the schizophrenic's condition. If they have an environmental, traumatic effect in addition, this could be as much through fear or grief as through phantasied aggression. Moreover, sibling *position* has been shown to have no relation to schizophrenia, which throws some doubt on sibling relations being of much importance.

**Physiological Theories.** The resemblance of schizophrenia to a physiologically toxic condition has often been noted. Schmidt points out that a septic tooth or the daily administration of half a grain of veronal can produce schizophrenia-like mental conditions, while bromide intoxication is often indistinguishable. Is it possible that some toxin or toxic by-product of excessive conflict in the central nervous system produces the main symptoms?

Still closer resemblance, perhaps, exists between the schizophrenic and the normal individual when dreaming and half asleep. There is the same confusion of real and not real, the same confused symbolic and literal thinking, the same inaccessibility and narcistic concentration of libido. Lorenz (50) and many others have shown that schizophrenics inhaling a mixture of $CO_2$ and $O_2$, which stimulates the oxygen uptake of the blood and presumably the brain cells, show muscular relaxation (loss of catatonia) and disappearance of negativism and mutism, followed by temporary lucid intervals, as if waking from a dream. One study (59) even reports mental improvement in ten out of twelve cases subjected to artificial respiration without exertion. Since the manner in which sleep supervenes through the action of hypothalamic centers and blood oxygenation levels is still not clearly understood, however, this similarity cannot yet be exploited.

Among other physiological and biological theories is that which considers schizophrenia as an allergy—an immoderate biological defense reaction—for which there is some provocative evidence. Also there is the old, constantly revived theory that it is due to a diffused dystrophy or degeneration in the brain cells, especially those at the base of the brain, similar to that occurring through X-rays or radium, or some toxic substance (1,14,68). The possibility of considering schizophrenia as a parasympathetic overactivity is a less common and less promising proposition among physiological theories. The "explanation" of "general biological and vital inferiority" has repeatedly been put forward. It organizes much of the evidence—for example, Kasanin points out that the parental overprotective behavior could arise from appreciation of this inferiority—but in this form it does not explain the actual psychosis.

**Social Psychological Theories.** The sociological theories of complexity and disorganization of culture have already been considered (Chap. 15). Other writers, following Faris, have stressed the effect of "cultural isolation," *i.e.*, of peculiarities of culture or obstacles to social contact causing the individual to turn in upon himself. That is to say, through the cultural situation the individual develops early in life an acute self-consciousness, which in turn makes it more difficult for him to fit into society and gain social satisfactions. Clark (22), on the other hand, argues that our culture as a whole, in the last hundred years, has developed in such a way as to provoke maladjustment in the schizoid individual. He points out that the schizothyme would be better catered for if (a) literary and religious values were given more prestige, and (b) there were more tolerance of individuality, of freely chosen values, and even of some degrees of eccentricity. One of the few clinical studies of sociological conflict is that of Hunt (36) who studied fifteen boys engaged in gang behavior and sexual perversions and later involved in a strong religious revival movement. Only those five who were exposed to these conflicting values in a strong degree (and none of those adhering to one viewpoint only) became psychotic. Other evidence (Chap. 15) also points to the conflict of social-induced sentiments being more important a factor than social isolation.

**An "Inadequacy and Overcompensation" Theory of Schizophrenia.** It should be obvious from the evidence now available that a multifactor theory of schizophrenia is necessary. Several distinct adverse influences add up to a specific bankruptcy. These are influences that operate to some extent in every normal individual and the only major problem that remains to be solved is why at a certain degree of accumulation their effects become irreversible.  Probably at some point we have to look for a self-sustaining cycle.

In the first place, we must admit a general biological inferiority, probably that which shows itself psychologically in the $H$ factor of personality with its low energy and poor powers of adaptability, and appears physiologically in the inefficiencies described by Hoskins.  Secondarily, this produces through social experience a high degree of frustration and a consciousness of inferiority.  To this the individual reacts either with hostility, egotism, and tenacious perseverance, or with a complete discouragement.

At this point a riddle appears as to why the experience of inadequacy thus leads to tenacity and to the self-controlled, conforming, persevering character which is characteristic of about half of the prepsychotic schizoids. The remaining half show discouragement from the beginning, without any compensatory assertion and persistence.  They are described as passive, immature, and sullen, and they begin even in childhood to become drifters, indolent, feckless, and withdrawn.  It is apparently these who pass into the early, insidious, quietly supervening form of schizophrenia.  Again the distinction approached by the clinician seems to be precisely that between our $H$ and $A$ schizothyme factors (Chap. 4).  Presumably some element of constitutional strength or dominance causes the $A$ type of reaction to develop in certain cases (to some variable degree in all).  If this is so we should expect the $H$ factor to be the primary schizothyme inadequacy and the $A$ factor to develop as an added, environmentally determined, reaction in some of those who show the $H$ factor.  Actually the correlation of $A$ and $H$ factors is marked—higher than for any personality factors except $B$ and $C$ (Chap. 4).

Let us then explore the sequence, however, in the inadequate ($H$ factor) individuals who also react with egotism and hostility ($A$ factor).  A second-order factor, largely in $A$ factor, and labeled, from its nature, "tenacity tension" (see (7), Chap. 3) seems to indicate the temperamental quality here involved.  It is well known from Kretschmer's work and more recent experiments that schizothymes on tests do better on willed activities, e.g., on concentrated compared with dispersed attention, as well as on academic work generally.

This "will quality" of tenacity-tension may be an aspect of the high-strung leptosome constitution, but it could equally be explained as a result of the close rapport between the schizothyme mother and child, the overprotection of the former being responded to by greater dependence, through social inadequacy, on the part of the child.  This bond enables adult character inhibitions and standards to be imposed relatively early.  In this connection we should not overlook the evidence of an undue number of fright experiences in the schizoid childhood, which may be another way of saying that the schizothyme's biological inadequacy includes timidity of disposition and a proneness to being frightened. This would increase the dependence on the parent and the willingness to forego behavior not in line with the approved character pattern.

Presumably this early "finished" character formation with its threatening superego necessarily leads to the handling of errant impulses by an undue use of repression, which impoverishes the ego still further and leads to the resemblance between early schizophrenia and neurosis. What the psycho-analysts have called "traumatization of the libido" is a central feature in this description and one which distinguishes it from the more superficial trauma of neurosis. From the beginning the inadequate schizothyme has sacrificed libido to security and to compensatory egotistic satisfactions. This egotism and hostility produce reactions in others which frustrate the need for social contact[3] and, at adolescence, the sex drive also. These frustrations, together with the decline of the capacity of the parents to reward good behavior, occur most sharply as the individual grows into adolescence and explain some of the difficulties in becoming emancipated from the parents. However, if the "good" character of the schizothyme were one based on altruism, sufficient reward would still continue to strengthen its integration against the conflicts now engendered by dissatisfied gregariousness and sexuality. But the altruistic libidinal drives were not developed and were not responsible for or part of the "goodness" of this character. It is not surprising that at this point many disintegrating schizophrenics direct their hostility against the parent dimly perceived to be responsible for the ersatz "character integration."

If the individual achieves religious interests, a parent substitute may continue to reward the good character, and the retreat from sex and society can be institutionally stabilized. Otherwise the frustrated drives of sex and sociability, to which frustrated ego satisfactions may now be added, insofar as they depend on social approval, bend the whole individual to an undisciplined phantasy satisfaction. Thus, whether the individual's inadequacy leads to loss of self-respect immediately or by this roundabout road by way of the ultimate breakdown of an overcompensatory egotistic striving, the final result is essentially the same—the failure of the ego to sustain itself. The more roundabout course, however, might be expected to yield more rigidity and hostility, as in catatonia and paranoid schizophrenia, because the individual has had time to formulate his general frustration as a frus-

[3] The sheer effect of frustration of gregarious need is much overlooked in the discussions on schizophrenic dynamics. Hoskins (34) suggests this frustration is not a secondary consequence but due to "innate primary defect . . . of inadequate empathy." This is an interesting proposition, for "inadequate empathy," a seeming inability to share the mental life of others, with all the educative influences which that would bring, is early prominent in the schizophrenic.

tration of a specific object—his ego—which clear view of frustration is necessary to arousal of hostility.

With the individual thus finally blocked in attempts to satisfy major drives—self-assertion (social approval), gregariousness, and sex—and with added difficulties from early repressions, some three new developments may take place, the first of which is certain and invariable.

First, the pressure on the reality function (whether this be an innate or an acquired habit of thought) finally breaks it and the individual is unable to distinguish any longer between daydreaming and reality. Second, the fragmenting attempts at repression of libido may penetrate even to repression of basic bodily reflexes, to refusal to eat, urinate, etc. Third, the prolonged conflict may conceivably develop some nervous-fatigue toxin, of the kind supposed by the physiologists, which accounts for some of the deteriorated nervous and general functioning. In regard to this last Danziger (25) has suggested a toxic substance which depresses oxygen consumption, perhaps by inhibiting one of the respiratory enzymes. Clear indications that the final pattern of schizophrenia is determined by the failure of a chemical pacemaker in brain metabolism have also been obtained by Hoagland.

The irreversibility of the disorder arises from these last three processes. First, the breakdown of the reality principle no longer permits ordinary learning reward to operate to reinstate good habits; second, the toxic fatigue condition prevents effective energy, contact and attention; and, third, the deep repression of basic dynamic needs leaves insufficient motivation by which to establish learning. The success of shock therapy is sometimes ascribed to its preferentially breaking down recent patterns of learning, which have been wrong; but it is not proved that this happens nor is it shown how it happens. Moreover, most of the habits that are "wrong" in schizophrenia—all except the final compromises and adjustive symptoms—are quite old habits. Possibly shock operates in this sense in so far as it damages brain cells, produces a diffuse "lobotomy" and interferes with *all* established habits. The possibility must also be considered, however, that shock creates out of the fragments of futile motivation a single powerful drive—fear—through whose operation attention can be gained for the new, salubrious, psychotherapeutic atmosphere in which the patient now moves. A third, but less likely alternative, is that the physiological shock of electric shock or insulin acts at the physiological level, stimulating processes which remove the toxic condition.

### 6. THE PSYCHOLOGICAL AND PHYSIOLOGICAL NATURE OF DYSTHYMIC PSYCHOSES

**Varieties of Dysthymic Psychosis.** Although there is a family resemblance in all dysthymic psychoses, *i.e.*, those psychoses in which the primary abnormality is a disorder of emotional tone, one must distinguish the typical cyclical insanity from related forms. In the most representative cyclic insanity, as described in Chapter 1, manic and depressive episodes alternate with each other, with or without normal periods between, or one of them alternates with normality. In addition to this dysthymic form, however, one must recognize, first, reactive depression, in which a real calamity is responsible for grief, but in which the reaction becomes excessive, and, secondly, involutional melancholia, which occurs specifically late in life and has some rigid, schizoid characteristics; while some psychiatrists would distinguish also an agitated melancholia, similar to involutional melancholia in symptoms, but not occurring through the specific bodily and mental situations of middle age.

As the form of the $F$ $(-)$ factor pattern shows, anxiety and depression are usually correlated, perhaps because both are normally provoked simultaneously in the irremediable type of frustrating situation which precedes all repression (see $\gamma 1$ and $\gamma 2$ in dynamic crossroads 3, Chap. 8). But, as Cameron (16) points out, anxiety is also present, scarcely beneath the surface, in manic conditions. Indeed, what distinguishes manic-depressive depression from the agitated or involutional depression is the far greater role of anxiety in the latter. The former is an almost pure depression in which inhibition and retardation are central and physiological signs are prevalent, whereas the latter brings tension and guilt in addition, suggesting a more purely psychological origin.

**Psychological and Physiological Peculiarities of the Manic-Depressive.** The experimental evidence on manic-depressive disorder divides into comparisons of normals with manic-depressives in a normal phase, *i.e.*, an attempt to distinguish the cycloid constitution *per se*, and comparisons of normals with individuals specifically in a manic phase or a depressive phase. Cycloids show a higher motor perseveration (disposition rigidity); a significantly slower reversible perspective rate (27,37); a tendency to attend to color rather than form, and to sort cards into categories on color rather than form (45); a tendency to higher dispersion of attention when instructed to attend to one particular thing; a higher fluctuation of attitudes when measured from day to day (21); a greater ability to put on spurts and reach momentarily high levels of performance (20). Leontera (48) comparing the work habits of schizophrenics and cycloids, found the former to be slower, slow in mastering technical detail, stereotyped, inefficient, and given to long interruptions without cause; whereas cycloids had a brisker pace, but liked change of work and were given to frequent brief interruption. This and other scattered data not yet sufficiently confirmed to mention, do not yet admit formulation, except as a general tendency to relaxation rather than tension, to more emotion in mental life, and to less highly integrated dynamic structure.

The manic state is described experimentally by higher speed, but especially by higher scores on fluency-of-association tests (73), lower perseveration (disposition rigidity) but still only reaching the average for normals, and quicker reversible perspective. The depressive state shows subnormal performance on speed tests; but, especially in agitated depression, the decline in fluency of association is far greater than in willed speed (ideomotor speed, cancellation, reading, etc.) Escalona (27) observed that depressives with most retardation in the motor field had a different history, onset, and course from those with most retardation in speed of decision. He found depressives to differ from manics also in having a more rigid aspiration level in the experimental tasks undertaken, manics being more responsive to immediate success or failure. Both mania and depression show decline in intelligence-test performance, judgment being generally impaired, but the nature of this decline and the degree of its dependence on defective attention have not been so clearly established as with the ability changes in schizophrenia.

It is doubtful whether any physiological connections specific to the cycloid condition as such can be considered established, though the correlation of the pyknic, endomorphic physique with cycloid disposition is certain, and probably reaches about +0.4. Clegg, however, in a study of 200 patients, found that manic-depressives tended to have a pituitary deficiency of late onset, while Richter cites at least one clear instance of an apparent manic-depressive who was found to be suffering from parathyroid deficiency and in whom the abnormal mood variation ceased after calcium therapy. Possibly any endocrine condition upsetting the physiological expression of emotion is a factor favoring the appearance of latent manic-depressive tendencies. This is suggested, for example, by the prevalence of manic-depressive episodes at the menopause.

However, the most frequent physiological finding in manic-depressives is specifically disorder of calcium metabolism. Most of the established physiological connections have appeared with respect specifically to manic or depressive conditions rather than to the proneness to either, *i.e.*, with cycloid temperament. In both there are autonomic-system and blood-content changes consistent with a picture of continued high emotionality, *e.g.*, high blood sugar and high adrenalin. The blood-sugar changes are more marked with agitated melancholia. Baird (6), for example, took whole blood from normals and manic-depressives and transfused it to adrenalectomized cats and rats. The cats lived 2.7 times and the rats 8 times as long with blood from patients as from normals and in one animal there was distinct mania-like behavior. Hemphill and Reiss (33) found, in thirty women depressives, instances of simple hypo-ovarianism but also the same condition combined with hyperthyroidism and hypoadrenalism or with hypothyroidism only. They suggest that disturbed anterior pituitary function is primarily responsible. In depressives there is a tendency for most glandular secretions to fall below normal, and Strongin and Hinsie (72) have shown that in the parotid gland this is so marked and so early in relation to other symptoms that it forms a good diagnostic item. They note also that it is lower in manic-depressive depressions than in other depressions and that the rise may be very sudden when depression ends. Eysenck and Yap (29) confirm this, noting that secretion in schizophrenics is 1.4 times as great as in patients with affective psychoses. They find about the same ratio also for dysthymic *neuroses* (as compared with conversion hysteria and nonaffective neuroses) and they point out the inhibition of secretion by mental effort in normals. The study of depressives also shows retardation in other general physiological processes, such as digestion and peristalsis.

## 7. THE BACKGROUND AND COURSE OF DYSTHYMIC PSYCHOSES

**Provocation and Outcome.** Clinicians have long pointed out that environmental provocation is far more commonly found in manic-depressive disorder and melancholia than in schizophrenia. In view of the known greater total environmental influence (see Chap. 5) in schizophrenia, this simply means that the provocations here are of a more obvious or sudden kind. Sherman (66) found stress situations in 47 per cent of schizophrenics and in 70 per cent of manic-depressives. For example, severe physical illness, accidents, glandular disturbances, organic lesions and brain injuries, encephalitis, operations, and pregnancy occurred with undue frequency and within a year of the psychotic episode. Melancholia and depression are reported to be associated with stresses of longer duration than those preceding mania.

The general outcome may be illustrated by Lundquist's inquiry (52) which followed up 319 manic-depressives from eleven to thirty years after first admissions and found that 92 per cent of the manics and 80 per cent of the depressives recover from the first attack and that 7 per cent gradually develop in a schizoid direction. Recovery is more complete if the first attack occurs when young. (Lundholm notes that middle-aged depressions pass more quickly when the patient has had prior experience of a depression.) Normally, later attacks are longer attacks. The presence of delusions and paranoid trends brings a bad prognosis but the presence of mental confusion augurs well. Sudden onset gives a better prognosis, while intense emotionality indicates a poorer chance of recovery. Depressions are decidedly more common than manic states in dysthymic disorders.

A study of mild depressive attacks brings out that associated physical complaints are generally emphasized by the patient more than the depression itself, and this suggests that many obscure physical disorders should be included when trying to obtain a true estimate of the incidence of depressive states. A follow-up of eighty-four mild depressions by Ziegler and Heersema

(81) after fourteen years, showed twenty-one dead, seven from suicide (which is many times the expected rate for this age group), four reclassified as schizophrenics, and fifty-nine working. Deaths from pneumonia and heart disease were above normal. Neurotic and hypochondriacal features were found indicative of more chronic depression. Lower rates of recovery (about 50 per cent) are found for agitated involutional melancholia than for depressions. Self-accusation and depreciation, with suicidal threats are found to predominate in those who got well, while definitely schizophrenic traits—hallucinations, ideas of persecution, catatonia—appear with a poor prognosis.

Parenthetically, it is a mistake to assume that all or even a majority of suicides are depressives. What proportion of suicides are psychotic cannot be accurately assessed, but certainly the rate is high for most psychoses. The depressive and the melancholic most frequently are preoccupied with ideas of suicide, but apparently the rate is practically as high in early schizophrenia. How high it is in schizophrenia cannot be determined as readily as among depressives because the uncertain insidious onset of the former disorder precludes prior diagnosis and many "normal" suicides may be early schizophrenics.

**Background and Prepsychotic Personality.** The family background of those suffering from dysthymic psychoses—especially manic-depressive psychosis—shows, as indicated in the chapter on heredity, a rather high proportion of emotionally unstable, neurotic, or even manic-depressive parents. This high incidence of personality disorders in the family naturally means that environmental trauma in early life are also more prevalent. Thus, whereas manic-depressive offspring of schizophrenics rarely occur, the converse is more common. Unless arguments can be brought for hereditary, Mendelian dominance of the latter, this indicates that being brought up with dysthymic parents is more severely traumatic. Nevertheless, the attitude of the parents is warmer and Witmer (77) found ambivalent attitudes far more frequent in the parents of schizophrenics. Both schizophrenics and manic-depressives show more overprotection from parents than occurs with normals, but this was found by Witmer nearly twice as frequently in dysthymics as in schizophrenics.

The prepsychotic personality of the manic-depressive shows principally a rather high degree of emotional instability and a tendency to get into social difficulties and to have difficulties in earning a living. But getting into difficulties is not so evident in the depressives and, indeed, the findings with reactive depressions and with melancholia, though they still indicate emotionality, emphasize either an excellent character or, at least, a narrow, dutiful personality. Curran and Mallinson (24) noted an increase of depressive cases in naval hospitals, under the demands of war (reaching 13 per cent of all admissions) and describe them as previously "men of a fine type and excellent morale." Titley (75) claimed that melancholics presented a somewhat different and more consistent picture than that found in manic-depressives, namely, a limited capacity for sociability and friendliness, a narrow range of interests, rigid adherence to a high ethical code, anxiety and stubborness, restriction of the ego, meticulousness, and a marked proclivity for saving. Myers and Von Koch (56) concluded, from 100 consecutive reactive depression cases in war, that the typical individual was of more than average ability, of the rank of sergeant or more, with traits of rigidity, unso-ciability, dependence on higher authority, high ethical standards, and strong family attachments. They concluded also that psychotic depression could not be sharply divided from the neuroses, particularly anxiety hysteria.

A list of common precipitating physical stresses in manic-depressive dis-order has been given above in connection with the work of Sherman. Brew (13) attempts to categorize the chief stresses as (*a*) insecurity and worry after financial difficulties; (*b*) social disapproval; (*c*) physical illness or irre-movable physical handicaps; (*d*) conflicts over some issue involving guilt; (*e*) self-pity over thwarting. However, there are also many instances of depression through what would normally be regarded as a matter for con-gratulation, *e.g.*, a professional promotion, the birth of offspring, and the stress here appears to arise from added responsibility or guilt at undeserved reward.

**Course and Therapy.** The disorder normally begins with some degree of confusion, and, in the case of depression, with physical exhaustion or hypo-chondria. After experience of one psychotic episode the patient usually has insight from initial symptoms that a relapse is on the way and often, but not always, may voluntarily seek hospital care. No adequate explanation can be given for the turning point toward normality occurring when it does in the psychotic period. Even before the day of shock therapy, however, it was noted that manic-depressive conditions would improve through inter-current somatic disease, widely divergent physiological upsets being about equally effective (78). Without such extraneous factors the disorder nor-mally clears up in a period from a few days to a year or two, the norm being at about six months and manic periods tending to be shorter than depressive ones. Psychoanalysis has been effective when undertaken in phases of insight and especially with melancholy. A definitely better recovery rate has also shown for shock therapy, especially in depressions, for lobotomy in some severe and complicated cases, and for endocrine therapy. The last is directed to improving calcium metabolism and stabilizing endocrine balance (removing "dysendocriniasis") and has been most effective in involutional melancholia at the menopause.

### 8. THEORIES OF PERSONALITY IN DYSTHYMIA

**General and Psychoanalytic Theories.** The less ambitious and more descriptive theories of manic-depressive disorder and melancholia tend to

consider them as a single disorder—melancholia being a depression colored
by local features of the time of onset and occurring only once.  They suggest that both mania and depression are reactions to insurmountable difficulties, in which confidence and security are lost, and in which aggression
and anxiety are developed in overwhelming amounts.  At this level also are
the theories which link mania and depression by the notion that both represent a reaction to the same internal conflict—typically a sense of guilt or
failure—but that in depression the situation is accepted whereas the manic
activity is an attempt to crowd it out of consciousness by other activities.

Psychoanalytic theories vary.  Palmer and Sherman, from an analysis of
fifty cases, conclude that anal-erotic fixations are primary, but others, *e.g.*,
Rosenzweig, have argued for oral-erotic levels of fixation.  Most agree that
excessive investment of the superego has occurred and that the ego suffers
from threats on the part of the superego.  The most acceptable general
formulation is probably that of Flugel (30), which follows on the basic contribution of Freud to understanding melancholia (31).  The loss of a loved
object, accompanied by mourning, is followed by an attempt to introject
the object—to set up its standards—within the self (see Tennyson's *In
Memoriam*).  Normally this happens to every child in connection with the
Oedipus love of the parent and the necessary end of that attachment, as we
have seen in Chapter 9.  Klein (44) has brought evidence that this introjection occurs also through the child's fear of its own explosive aggression,
which can only be handled by the strong parent, and has shown that the
apparent introjection of the Oedipus object is actually a more prolonged
procedure of alternating introjection and projection.  Since the young child's
attitudes are almost all ambivalent, the introjection brings also introjection
of aggression, which must be turned against the self.  Thus the superego is
dynamically sustained not only by primary narcism but also by secondary
narcism—object love that has returned to the self—and by aggression,
usually at the oral and anal levels.  So far we are mainly summarizing
what was said in Chapter 9; the application to melancholia requires closer
attention to the aggressive aspects.

The superego, the aggressive trends of which have the ruthless, all-or-none
character of early childhood, is obviously a device in which aggression can
spiral to alarming heights.  For frustration begets aggression, which provokes counteraggression from the superego, which heightens frustration—
and all these provoked aggressions have in the end to be directed against
the self.  Further, the psychoanalysts claim to observe the operation of an
additional process of sadomasochism or algolagnia, whereby the individual
obtains some sexual, libidinal pleasure in the active role of hurting himself
and also in enjoying the suffering inflicted.  In short the algolagnic need
perceives in the ego-superego conflict and persecution an unusual opportunity
for its own two-edged satisfaction, and parasitically encourages the dynamic

exchange. The melancholic or depressive is thus caught not only in the excessive action of an out-of-control superego, but also by an internal sexual perversion which clings to the suffering of the ego. The explanation of the manic phase—as an identification of the ego with the superego—is less convincing, because the conditions for this inflation do not seem sufficiently specific.

**Physiological Theories.** The marked hereditary determination of this disorder, the frequent physiological findings, and the good response frequently found to endocrine and chemical therapy (Lowenbach and Greenhill (51) have recently shown more than 50 per cent of rapid remissions in depressives, from the oral administration of lactic acid) combine to suggest some special condition of brain chemistry underlying the disorder. Sufficient convergence of evidence on any single physiological process does not yet exist, though the discovery of specific antidepressives such as amphetamine (benzedrine) is suggestive.

An explanation in terms of some biochemical deficiency, of course, would not rule out psychological stress theory but would only indicate more clearly why the psychological stress produces confusion and alternating mania and depression in some individuals sooner than in others. Possibly their greater emotionality causes them to use up some chemical reserve earlier or they are less endowed with resources to produce this chemical. In this connection the possibility must again be considered that mania and depression are not due to wholly opposite influences. Some chemical change might occur which in small amounts produces manic excitement and in larger amounts retardation and stupor. This is seen, for example, with increasing fatigue in children and in increasing dosages of alcohol and other "depressive" drugs. Actually, the clinical observers have pointed to the incidence of transient depressive phases in the course of onset of mania rather than the converse. It is conceivable that some decline of hypothalamic or cortical efficiency produces depression, by provoking compensatory attempts at greater inhibition on the part of the effective cortex available, while a still greater decline of effectiveness of cortical powers would remove all possibilities of inhibition and produce mania. The links in the chain of production of such a physiological agent are not clear. However, as Cameron (15) has shown, an inhibitory state resembling depression can be induced in guinea pigs by long frustration in face of a stimulating situation. And this is accompanied in time by loss of weight, lowered respiratory rate, and other physiological changes suggestive of patients with depressions. Physiological investigation of animals may thus throw light on the body chemistry of depression as well as on the dynamic conditions essential to producing it.

**A Theory of Manic-depressive Disorder through Unrealism of Self-sentiment.** Fewer theoretical difficulties are encountered if we consider melancholia as in some important respects different from manic-depressive disorder. The former seems to yield essentially to the psychoanalytic explanation offered above—powerful superego development, the inward turning of aggression, and resultant anxiety and depression. It occurs in a wider variety of constitutional temperament types and has symptoms not found in manic-depressive depression. Manic-depression, on the other hand, besides having constitutional associations, seems more explicable, at the psychological level, as the results of defects in the ego structure itself, coming primarily from the defects of reality testing that arise in a strongly emotional disposition. As a result of these reality-testing defects the self-concept (in the self-sentiment) is inflated, so that, especially in self-assertive moods, the individual takes on megalomanic tasks and accepts ego (not superego) standards which he cannot really hope to meet. Attempting to meet them he gradually becomes exhausted.

The physiological exhaustion shows itself first in poor inhibition and still more in overactivity, in poorer judgment, and eventually confusion. If physical exhaustion does not coexist, the individual may now escape into mania. If general fatigue, as well as specific cortical fatigue, exists, however, the tasks and standards which he has taken on in the assertive, energetic mood, now become obviously too great and, indeed, insuperable, precipitating a depression, in which he remains until ego standards are lowered or until the reduced activity has built up sufficient reserves to repeat the cycle. This theory, therefore, stresses changes in the self-assertive and self-submissive drives, occasioned by inner cues of fatigue, rather than of fear and guilt as in melancholia. It places the initial cause in a chronic defect of the reality principle, which permits self-assertion to achieve undue expression in the self-sentiment.

#### 9. PERSONALITY IN RELATION TO OTHER PSYCHOSES

**Psychoses Associated with General Physiological Impairment of Brain Metabolism.** To review the implications, for the understanding of personality, of the numerous less common psychoses would be too great an undertaking for the space here available, were it not that many of them, *e.g.*, Huntington's chorea, drug addictions, epilepsies, toxic psychoses, are too specific in nature to illuminate general processes, while others, *e.g.*, brain trauma disorders, are considered in special fields, in other chapters. Moreover, a large group of apparently disparate disorders, those with arteriosclerosis and circulatory disorder, with renal disorder, anemia, vitamin deficiency, and with general paralysis of syphilitic origin, teach us what they have to teach through revealing an effect which is common to them all, namely, defective metabolism of the brain cells.

In cell disorders of defective metabolism, though there may be specific defects, *e.g.*, the ataxia of general paresis or peripheral neuritis of pellagra, certain symptoms are common, notably, lowering of general intelligence, decline of memory, more especially for recent events, inability to concentrate, poorness of judgment, confusion, and emotional instability. In addition, there may be more specific disorders, such as manic states with delusions of grandeur, depressive states, agitated depressions, and anxiety neuroses, and various schizophrenic states with withdrawal or with paranoid delusions of persecution.

As indicated in Chapter 11, on physiological associations, most of these symptoms can be induced simply by lowering the oxygen pressure. Thus, in testing pilots in pressure tanks the general decline in intelligence, motor control, memory, judgment, etc., is sometimes accompanied by transient psychosis-like states, *e.g.*, paranoia. But it is probable that the disabilities have to operate over a longer period to bring out the unhealthy secondary adjustive habits which often accompany prolonged reduced metabolism in the brain from such organic causes as poor circulation, anemia, and the syphilitic destruction of chemical pacemaking enzymes.

That impairment of intelligence and resulting decline of judgment does not produce psychosis is already obvious from many lines of evidence. It now becomes evident, further, that general impairment of cortical action, reducing at once intelligence, power of recall, and emotional control, also does not necessarily at least produce any specific psychosis. The process seems only to bring out weaknesses already in existence, constitutional or acquired. (Possibly the reason that general paresis tends to have some specific associations with grandiose rather than other delusions is due to the disease being more frequently contracted by ascendant, unrestrained adventurous individuals.) It may be, therefore, that the decreased powers of emotional control and the interference with good dynamic integration occasioned by impaired memory, induce strains which *increase* psychotic expressions, or bring them from latent to patent manifestation, but the form of the psychosis is determined by prior conditions and follows syndromes found in the typical psychoses usually arising in other ways.

**Psychopathic Personality.** Although the syndrome category of "moral imbecile" expired at the turn of the century, swept away by the theoretical assertions of sociologists that innate moral defect was inconceivable, clinicians have repeatedly attempted to describe something of this nature and the idea has been strongly revived in recent years under the rubric of psychopathic personality. It is questionable, however, whether the many persons now in mental hospitals with this diagnosis present a single syndrome and it is time that correlation studies attempted to define the nature of the cluster more sharply.

Preu (61) claims that it is used "as a scrap-basket" but that "it serves a useful purpose in reminding psychiatrists that personality problems cannot be explained in environmental terms exclusively." The core of agreement in various clinical opinions seems to be that the syndrome presents: an absence of intelligence defect; a lack of responsiveness to social demands for good behavior and small responsiveness to the usual social punishments; some emotional instability and impulsiveness; and evidence that these have been life-long personality characteristics of the individual concerned. Cleckley (23) adds such touches as that the individual is a good, plausible talker, shows no anxiety, delusions, or other neurotic or psychotic features, has no lack of understanding and apparent foresight, yet commits endless delinquencies and follies, is callous and unfeeling for friends and relatives, but is not addicted to the graver felonies, is egocentric, sexually promiscuous, but infantile and lacking adequate sex drive.

Many of these traits are such as could be produced by a combination of certain personality factors, notably $F+$, *i.e.*, the surgent, hysteric factor with its inability to develop deep and serious emotions, $A-$, the schizothyme factor, with its asocial and antisocial behavior pattern, and the $G-$ or defective character integration factor with its lack of perseverance and regard for moral standards. It is in conformity with this analysis that some clinicians have diagnosed psychopaths, especially those involved in cold, emotionally incomprehensible crimes, as schizophrenic, while it has also repeatedly happened that disputes have arisen as to whether the happy, guiltless confabulator is a psychopath or a conversion hysteric. The reader will notice that in the table on page 521, earlier in this chapter, the German classification of mental disorders actually places hysterics and psychopathic personalities in the same category. If these clinical hesitations may be taken as evidence, in the absence of actual factor studies, it seems likely that the psychopathic syndrome is indeed a correlation cluster combining the defective character integration factor with varying amounts of surgency and schizothymia. In this combination of somewhat opposing qualities, the surgent $(F+)$ qualities would neutralize the withdrawing qualities normally found in the schizothyme, leaving only those traits of irresponsibility and emotional shallowness we find in psychopath.

The more accurate measurement of personality factors now possible may enable this hypothesis to be tested. If true it would seem that a good deal of the psychopathic pattern is constitutional, since $A$ and $F$ factors seem to be considerably hereditarily determined. The low $G$ factor, however, would presumably arise from failure of early parent attachment, with resulting Oedipus and superego defect, as discussed in connection with delinquency and conscience (page 238). The small statistical chance of finding one individual simultaneously extreme in three distinct factors would account for the rarity of what clinicians are willing to admit as a true psychopathic syndrome.

## 10. SUMMARY

1. Between one person in ten and one in twenty of the population of modern industrial societies spends some time in a mental hospital. The psychosis rates are higher with urban residence, age, and lower social status, and the different psychoses, functional and organic, retain approximately constant proportions.

2. Several miniature-situation, function-testing, and other objective, experimental measurements are now known which, as diagnostic tests, will almost completely separate normal from psychotic populations. They do not include verbal intelligence tests, in which psychotics are normal, but such measures as those of short-distance memory, control of mental sets, and normality of associations. However, an unmeasurable "inclination to maintain contact with reality" is the basic differentiator.

3. Schizophrenia is recognizable by (in addition to the clinical observations on the general-behavior syndrome) poor performance in adaptive tests, inability to maintain a mental set, low frequency of resuming tasks, high egocentric scores on interest tests, poor ability to marshal powers possessed in response to a sudden demand, and a large verbal ability poorly employed.

4. Physiological and anatomical associations of schizophrenia include defective endocrine secretions, degenerative changes in the testes, slow blood circulation, poor tissue response to hormones, defective autonomic ability to maintain homeostasis, heat production, etc., besides constitutionally asthenic build.

5. Schizophrenics have a background of poor marital stability in the parents but of some degree of overprotection from the mother. They have a personal history of good behavior, being withdrawn, oversensitive and emotionally unstable, of experiencing many physical illnesses and defects, of depending too much on the parents, and of making poor sex and marital adjustments. One can distinguish, however, two "types" here, with different prognosis.

6. Theories of schizophrenia—physiological, sociological, and psychological—are very numerous. A theory of initial biological inadequacy, leading to asocial ego formation, which fails by inducing frustration simultaneously in sex, society, and ego satisfaction and so leads to breakdown of the reality function, meets the facts most completely.

7. The definition of dysthymic psychoses requires investigation of the manic-depressive personality, as well as of the syndromes of mania, melancholia, and depression. Some psychological tests have moderate validity in measuring cycloid personality, but more success has been achieved with measuring and differentiating the syndromes.

8. Physiological and somatic studies show an association of pyknic, endo-

morphic body-build, and of the concomitants of high sympathetic activity in cycloids. There is dysendocriniasis also, mainly of calcium metabolism, with anterior pituitary defect. Depressives show a slowing down of glandular and general bodily activity.

9. Dysthymics tend to come from affectionate but emotionally turbulent homes, to have been parentally overprotected, and to have a history of emotional but good prepsychotic character. The psychosis requires certain hereditary and physiological conditions, on which psychological stresses are always found to have been imposed. The psychological structure seems to be primarily an abnormally inflated "unrealistic" ego formation in manic-depression and an abnormal superego formation in agitated melancholia. In the former the cycle may be viewed as one of exhaustion and recuperation.

10. The organic psychoses also throw some light on personality, showing that poor brain metabolism may reduce intelligence and emotional control without bringing on any specific psychosis. Specific psychoses, however, more readily develop in these circumstances. The claim that the psychopathic personality offers a definite psychotic condition or syndrome is questionable and it is better conceived as a combination of extreme endowments in certain personality factors.

## QUESTIONS AND EXERCISES

1. Set down all you know about the incidence and distribution of psychosis.
2. Describe in some detail two tests in each of three areas of personality expression that show significant differences between psychotics and normals.
3. Describe similarly six test performances which distinguish significantly, or to a considerable extent, the schizophrenic from the normal and the manic-depressive.
4. Outline three physiological and three anatomical or histological differences found to distinguish schizophrenics. Discuss also three other physical differences about which there is uncertainty, pointing out possible reasons for ambiguous findings.
5. Describe the environmental background and prepsychotic personality of the schizophrenic with special reference to the hypothesis of two distinct personality factors, $A$ and $H$, being involved in the development of the schizophrenic personality.
6. Briefly set down five theories of schizophrenia, the psychological, physiological, and sociological fields each being represented by at least one.
7. Relate the experimental findings on dysthymic psychoses to the clinical observations on general behavior.
8. List some of the actual experimental evidence on physiological and anatomical findings in regard to the dysthymic psychoses, and evaluate conclusions, especially where conflict exists.
9. Contrast manic-depressive depression and agitated involutional melancholia with respect to the observed syndromes and the theories of their origins.
10. Describe two organic psychoses in some detail as to etiology, prognosis, etc., and show what light they throw on the independence of factors in the normal personality.

## BIBLIOGRAPHY

1. ALFORD, L. B.: Epilepsy and Dementia Praecox Considered as Types of Abiotrophy, *J. nerv. ment. Dis.*, 68: 594–601, 1928.

2. ALSTROM, C. H.: Mortality in Mental Hospitals. *Acta. Psychiat. Kbh.*, Suppl. 24, 1942.

3. ANDRATSCHKE, B., and C. H. ROGERSON: Mild Depressive Psychosis, *Brit. Med. J.*, 1: 780–783, 1943.

4. ANGYAL, A., and N. BLACKMAN: Vestibular Reactivity in Schizophrenia, *Arch. Neurol. Psychiat.*, Chicago, 44: 611–620, 1940.

5. ANON: Wie Alt Werden die Unheilbaren Geisterskranken? Eine Erstmalige Statistische Untersuchung, *Arztebl.*, 8: 338–340, 1940.

6. BAIRD, P. C.: Biochemical Component of the Manic-depressive Psychosis, *J. nerv. ment. Dis.*, 99: 359–366, 1944.

7. BARRY, H., and W. A. BOUSFIELD: Incidence of Orphanhood among 1500 Psychotic Patients, *J. genet. Psychol.*, 50: 198–201, 1937.

8. BENDER, L.: Childhood Schizophrenia, Clinical Study of 100 Schizo Children, *Amer. J. Orthopsychiat.*, 17: 40–56, 1947.

9. BETZ, B.: Somatology of the Schizophrenic Patient, *Hum. Biol.*, 14: 192–234, 1942.

10. BIGELOW, G. H., and H. L. LOMBARD: *Cancer and Other Chronic Diseases in Massachusetts*, Houghton Mifflin Company, Boston, 1933.

11. BLUM, G. S., and S. ROSENZWEIG: The Incidence of Sibling and Parental Deaths in the Anamnesis of Female Schizophrenics, *J. gen. Psychol.*, 31: 3–13, 1944.

12. BOND, E. D., and F. J. BRACELAND: Prognosis in Mental Disease, *Amer. J. Psychiat.*, 94: 263–274, 1937.

13. BREW, M. H.: Precipitating Factors in Manic-depressive Psychosis, *Psychiat. Quar.*, 7: 401–410, 1933.

14. BUSCAINO, V. M.: Histoneuropathological and Encephalographical Researches on the Cerebrospinal Fluid in Dementia Praecox Cases, 1926–1928, *Riv. Patol. Nerv. Dev.*, 34: 1929.

15. CAMERON, D.: Studies in Depression, *J. ment. Sci.*, 82: 148–161, 1936.

16. CAMERON, D. E.: Some Relationships between Excitement, Depression, and Anxiety, *Amer. J. Psychiat.*, 102: 385–394, 1945.

17. CAMERON, N.: A Study of Thinking in Senile Deterioration and Schizophrenic Disorganization, *Amer. J. Psychol.*, 51: 650–664, 1938.

18. CAROTHERS, J. C.: A Study of Mental Derangement in Africans, *Psychiatry*, 11: 47–86, 1948.

19. CATTELL, R. B.: An Objective Test of Character Temperament: I, *J. gen. Psychol.*, 25: 39–73, 1941.

20. CATTELL, R. B.: An Objective Test of Character Temperament: II, *J. soc. Psychol.*, 19: 19–114, 1944.

21. CATTELL, R. B.: Fluctuation of Sentiments and Attitudes as a Measure of Integration and Temperament, *Amer. J. Psychol.*, 41: 195–216, 1943.

22. CLARK, R. A.: Cosmic Consciousness in Catatonic Schizophrenia, *Psychosomat. Rev.*, 33: 460–504, 1946.

23. CLECKLEY, H.: Antisocial Personalities, in Pennington, L. A., and I. A. Berg: *An Introduction to Clinical Psychology*, The Ronald Press Company, New York, 1948.

24. CURRAN, D., and W. P. MALLINSON: Depressive States in War, *Brit. Med. J.*, Part I, 305–309, 1941.

25. DANZIGER, L.: Some Theoretical Considerations of Dementia Praecox, *Dis. Nerv. Syst.*, 7: 351–361, 1946.

26. DESPERT, J. L.: Schizophrenia in Children, *Psychiat. Quart.*, 12: 366–371, 1938.

27. ESCALONA, S. K.: The Effect of Success and Failure upon the Level of Aspiration and Behavior in Manic-depressive Psychoses, *Univ. Ia. Stud. Child Welf.*, 16 (No. 3): 197–302, 1940.

28. EWEN, J. H.: The Psychological Estimation of the Effects of Certain Drives upon the Syntonic and Schizophrenic Psychoses with a Brief Inquiry into a Physiological Basis of Temperament, *J. ment. Sci.*, 77:.742–766, 1931.

29. EYSENCK, H. J., and P. M. YAP: Parotid Gland Secretion in Affective Mental Disorders, *J. ment. Sci.*, 90: 595–602, 1944.

30. FLUGEL, J. C.: *Man, Morals, and Society*, Gerald Duckworth & Co., Ltd., London, 1945.

31. FREUD, S.: *Mourning and Melancholia:* Chap. VIII, Vol. 3, *Collected Papers*, Hogarth Press, London, 1923.

32. GLUECK, B., and N. W. ACKERMANN: The Reactions and Behavior of Schizophrenic Patients Treated with Metrazal and Camphor, *J. nerv. ment. Dis.*, 90: 310–332, 1939.

33. HEMPHILL, R. E., and M. REISS: Investigation into the Significance of the Endocrines in Involutional Melancholia, *J. ment. Sci.*, 86: 1065–1077, 1940.

34. HOSKINS, R. G.: *The Biology of Schizophrenia*, W. W. Norton & Company, New York, 1946.

35. HOSKINS, R. G., and F. H. SLEEPER: Organic Functions in Schizophrenia, *Arch. Neurol. Psychiat.*, Chicago, 30: 123–140, 1933.

36. HUNT, J. McV.: An Instance of the Social Origin of Conflict Resulting in Psychosis, *Amer. J. Orthopsychiat.*, 8: 158–164, 1938.

37. HUNT, J. McV., and J. P. GUILFORD: Fluctuation of an Ambiguous Figure in Dementia Praecox and in Manic-depressive Patients, *J. abnorm. soc. Psychol.*, 27: 443–452, 1933.

38. KANNER, L.: Early Infantile Autism, *J. Ped.*, 25: 211–217, 1944.

39. KANT, O.: The Problem of Psychogenic Precipitation in Schizophrenia, *Psychiat. Quart.*, 16: 341–350, 1942.

40. KASANIN, J., and M. R. KAUFMAN: A Study of the Functional Psychoses in Childhood, *Amer. J. Psychiat.*, 9: 307–384, 1929.

41. KASANIN, J., and Z. A. ROSEN: Clinical Variables in Schizoid Personality, in Schizophrenia, *Stat. Stud. Boston Psycho. Hosp.*, Boston, 1925–1934.

42. KASANIN, J., and L. VEO: A Study of the School Adjustments of Children Who Later in Life Become Psychotic, in Schizophrenia, *Stat. Stud. Boston Psycho. Hosp.* 1925–1934.

43. KIRILLOV, I. S.: The Vegetative Syndrome in Psychic Depression, *Vop. sotsial. klin. Psikhonevrol.*, 3: 189–203, 1936.

44. KLEIN, M.: *Psychoanalysis of Children*, W. W. Norton & Company, New York, 1932.

45. KRETSCHMER, E.: *Korperban und Charakter*, Verlag Julius Springer, Berlin, 1929.

46. LANDIS, C., and J. D. PAGE: *Modern Society and Mental Disease*, Farrar and Rinehart, Inc., New York, 1938.

47. LEMKAN, P., C. TIETZE, and M. COOPER: A Survey of Statistical Studies on the Prevalence and Incidence of Mental Disorders in Sample Populations, *U.S. Public Hlth. Rep.*, 58: 19, 1943.

48. LEONTERA, M., R. PRATUSSEVICK, and E. KAGANOVA: The Peculiarities of the Work Process and Work Therapy in Psychoneurotic Children, *Nov. Psikhoneural. Det. Vozr.*, 8–46, 1935.

49. LEPEL, C. F.: Schizophrenie bei Ehemaligen Nusster Schulern, *Zsch. f. d. ges. Nur. u. Psychiat.*, 112: 575–604, 1928.

50. LORENZ, W. F.: Some Observations on Catatonia, *Psychiat. Quart.*, 95–102, 1934.

51. LOWENBACH, HANS, and M. H. GREENHILL: The Effect of Oral Administration of Lactic Acid upon the Clinical Course of Defensive States, *J. nerv. ment. Dis.*, 105: 343–358, 1947.

52. LUNDQUIST, G.: Prognosis and Course in Manic-depressive Psychosis: a Follow-up Study of 319 First Admissions, *Acta. Psychiat.*, *Kbh.*, Suppl. 35, 1945.

53. Martz, E. W.: Mortality among the Mentally Deficient, *Tramme Schl. Bull.*, 30: 185–197, 1934.

54. McNeil, H. and others: Parallel Psychological, Psychiatric and Physiological Findings in Schizophrenic Patients under Insulin Shock Treatment, *Amer. J. Psychiat.*, 98: 422–429, 1941.

55. Mischenko, M. M., and A. S. Poznanaski: Concerning the Relation between Physical Energy of Stimuli and the Nature of the Response in Schizophrenia, *Trud. Tsentral psikhonevral Inst.*, 10: 91–103, 1938.

56. Myers, H. J., and S. Von Koch: Reaction Depressions: a Study of 100 Consecutive Cases, *War Med.*, 8: 358–364, 1945.

57. Palmer, H. D., and S. H. Sherman: The Involutional Melancholia Process, *Arch. Neurol. Psychiat., Chicago*, 40: 762–788, 1938.

58. Panara, C.: Velocity and Rhythm in the Motor Reactions of Schizophrenics, *G. Psichiat. Neuropat*, (No. 3–4): 295–349, 1935.

59. Peters, G. F.: The Therapeutic Effect of Assisted Respiration in Established Cases of Dementia Praecox, *J. ment. Sci.*, 76: 662–667, 1930.

60. Polatin, P., and P. Hoch: Diagnostic Evaluation of Early Schizophrenia, *J. nerv. ment. Dis.*, 105: 221–230, 1947.

61. Preu, P. W.: Concept of Psychopathic Personality, in J. McV. Hunt, *Personality and the Behavior Disorders:* Vol. II, The Ronald Press Company, New York, 1944.

62. Rabin, A. J.: Differentiating Psychometic Patterns in Schizophrenia and Manic-depressive Psychosis, *J. abnorm. soc. Psychol.*, 37: 270–272, 1942.

63. Rickers-Ovsiankina, M.: Studies in the Personality Structure of Schizophrenic Individuals: II. Reaction to Interrupted Tasks, *J. gen. Psychol.*, 16: 179–196, 1937.

64. Rodnick, E. H.: The Response of Schizophrenic and Normal Subjects to Stimulation of the Autonomic Nervous System, *Psychol. Bull.*, 35: 646, 1938.

65. Schumacher, H. C.: Schizophrenia in Children, *Ohio St. Med. J.*. 42: 1248–1254, 1946.

66. Sherman, I. C.: Precipitating Factors in Manic-depressive and Schizophrenic Conditions, *Ill. Psychiat. J.*, 4: 20–24, 1944.

67. Smith, J. C.: About Dementia Praecox, *Hospitalstidende*, 77: 437–456, 1934.

68. Snessarer, P. E.: On Toxicity in Schizophrenia, *Sovetsk. psikhonevr.*, No. 5, 17–24, 1934.

69. Sokolskaya, S., F. I. Greenstein, and V. Moshinskaya: The Social Adjustment in Schizophrenia, *Oboz. psikhiat. nevr. i. refl. im. Bekhtereva*, 4: 208, 1929.

70. Spaer, E. Beitrag zur Kunst der Speziellen Psychotherapie bei Schizophrenie, *Allg. arzt Zsch. f. Psychotherap. u. psych, Hygiene*, 1: 148–152, 1928.

71. Stalker, H.: The Prognosis in Schizophrenia, *J. ment. Sci.*, 85: 1224–1240, 1939.

72. Strongin, E. G., and L. E. Hinsie: A Laboratory Method for Diagnosing Manic-depressive Depression, *Psychol. Bull.*, 39: 509, 1942.

73. Studman, L. G.: Studies in Experimental Psychiatry, No. 5, "W" and "F" Factors in Relation to Traits of Personality, *J. ment. Sci.*, 81: 107–137, 1935.

74. Sullivan, H. S.: Research in Schizophrenia, *Amer. J. Psychiat.*, 9: 553–567, 1929.

75. Titley, W. B.: Prepsychotic Personality of Patients with Involutional Melancholia, *Arch. Neurol. Psychiat., Chicago*, 36: 19–33, 1936.

76. White, W.: The Language of Schizophrenia, *Arch. Neurol. Psychiat., Chicago*, 16: 395, 1926.

77. Witmer, H. L., and students: The Childhood Personality and Parent-Child Relationships of Dementia Praecox and Manic-depressive Patients, *Smith Coll. Stud. soc. Work*, 4: 289–377, 1934.

78. WOLFBERG, L. R.: The Effect of Intercurrent Somatic Disease on Manic-depressive Reactions, *Psychiat. Quart.*, 9: 88–94, 1935.

79. WOODS, W. L.: Language Study in Schizophrenia, *J. nerv. ment. Dis.*, 87: 290–316, 1938.

80. YERBURY, E. C., and N. NEWELL: Factors in the Early Behavior of Psychotic Children as Related to Their Subsequent Mental Disorder, *Amer. J. ment. Dis.*, 47: 70–76, 1942.

81. ZIEGLER, L. H., and P. H. HEERSEMA: A Follow-up of 111 Non-hospitalized Depressed Patients after 14 Years, *Amer. J. Psychiat.*, 99: 813–818, 1943.

# CHAPTER 19

## LIFE STAGES IN PERSONALITY: I. CONCEPTION TO PUBERTY

1. Principles and Problems of Longitudinal Analysis
2. Natal and Prenatal Influences
3. The First Year of Life
4. Ages Two Through Four Years: Preschool or Nursery School
5. Ages Five Through Seven Years: Early Childhood
6. Ages Eight Through Fourteen Years: Childhood or Preadolescence
7. Review and Summary

### 1. PRINCIPLES AND PROBLEMS OF LONGITUDINAL ANALYSIS

**Contribution of Longitudinal Study to Total Organization of Knowledge.** Observed behavior is primarily organized and organizable with respect to only one real center of reference—namely the organism—the more-or-less-integrated personality in society. But knowledge about behavior can also be given special, restricted degrees of organization from other points of view, *e.g.*, with respect to the historical development of the organism, with respect to the social group of which the organism is a part, or with respect to physiological components.

Each of these approaches permits a considerable development of causal, explanatory systems, though they are never as complete as that which centers on the organism per se. The learning process of the student, however, requires that he consider personality from all these partial aspects before his mind is sufficiently furnished with vistas to provide the possibility of seeing personality as a whole. Accordingly, this book has already considered behavior from the viewpoints of hereditary determinations; of the influence of the family and society and other environmental patterns; of physiological interactions; and of the internal conflicts and learning processes that go on in the organism. The time has now come to consider personality in yet another vista: that offered by its longitudinal, developmental aspect, *i.e.*, as organized on a unity of a historical kind.

Of all special approaches to personality this comes nearest to providing a totally integrated view. It deals with, and requires as data, that which has been previously studied in connection with the adjustment process, the family and social environment, the physiological substrate, and, indeed, all previous approaches to personality. Consequently, it adds relatively little

555

in the way of new information, but strings the old facts on new threads of understanding, with the addition of factual connecting links at certain points. These two chapters concerned with development may be regarded, in short, as a weft which ties into place the warp of previous special causal threads. Although they involve, therefore, much repetition of contact with facts already known, these contacts have value as exercises in, and opportunities for, further proving and testing of the degree of understanding which has just been achieved.

It would be possible to section the longitudinal approach either by following the life development of particular aspects of personality, *e.g.*, abilities, social adjustment, speech, dynamic traits, or by considering the total personality (as far as possible) with respect to each of a number of life stages. Since the former would not be so very different from what has already been done in certain chapters, and since the express purpose of the present chapters is to maintain an over-all developmental view, the latter plan has seemed preferable, and we shall accordingly begin with earliest infancy and proceed, in suitable natural divisions of the life course, to old age.

**The Main Issues and Methods in Longitudinal Approaches.** Throughout this longitudinal study there are certain persistent, recurring problems of analysis and certain general principles that need to be kept in mind. First, there is the problem of distinguishing between learning and maturation. With existing methods and data this cannot always be achieved, but at least the student can guard against rashly interpreting some progressive change in behavior on the unchecked assumption that it is entirely due to one of them. Second, one can avoid confusing the different senses in which regression is used, for not all reversals of the general progression here studied are similar in definition and nature. Again, longitudinal study is constantly concerned with questions of how quickly a certain personality structure is acquired, how permanently it functions, and at what rate it may suffer extinction. This raises some very general problems of learning, dynamics, and rigidity, whose more abstract discussion is postponed to the last chapter. Similarly, the issue of ego structure, which runs as a central thread through developmental psychology and which is treated descriptively and causatively in these chapters, is postponed, in its more abstract analysis for the last chapter. Finally, it is necessary to keep constantly in mind that although one tends to study the life course of personality as if in relation to a stable background, the background is itself actually changing. The individual grows and changes, but so also do parents, siblings, society and its values—and even climate. Consequently, the true longitudinal study of personality requires allowance for a changing world as well as a changing personality, and when exact computations are possible they must use a calculus of relativity, embodying variables of the individual, his associated personalities, and the culture pattern, each in transition.

## 2. NATAL AND PRENATAL INFLUENCES

**The Greater Importance of Earlier Periods.** It is obvious that any particular set of divisions adopted in the continuous life course will be to some extent arbitrary. Some stages, such as the period from birth to puberty, are marked by definite physiological events, but most of those in common use, *e.g.*, the preschool period, "middle age," are fixed by cultural conditions that are often, historically, quite transient. It is not claimed that those adopted here have any greater validity than, say, the seven ages of man described by Shakespeare, but at least their choice has been guided both by physiological considerations and by appropriateness to our present culture pattern.

If the general proposition be true that the earlier periods of life are more powerful in their influence on personality and witness greater changes in it, psychology should study them more intensively, and it would be appropriate to cut the early divisions to shorter time periods, for closer study, than those later in life. Incidentally, this plan would fit in also with the impression of the life course gained through the stream of consciousness; for there is reason to believe that as the metabolic rate slows down the individual perceives time to pass more quickly, so that a short period in early life seems as long as a more extended period later on. Private, biological time does not keep step with public or mechanical time. In accordance with these considerations we shall, therefore, make the age divisions of study in general longer with later life, though unfortunately it has not always happened that the harvest of research findings is proportionately greater for the periods that require more intensive study.

**Influence in the Gestation Period.** The first important life period is that from conception to birth. In the chapter on heredity we distinguished clearly between hereditary and congenital qualities, defining the latter as including both hereditary characteristics and those acquired before birth, *in utero*. But in that chapter no more than a cursory reference was made to the nature of the influences and effects of embryonic life. Most systematic knowledge about the gestation period is of a physiological nature and is gathered by medical men or physiologists, but a few psychologists, notably Carmichael, Gesell and those mentioned below, have systematically studied the behavior and neural reactivities of the embryo.

In a broad sense it is obvious that physiological influences, at least, during this period can profoundly influence the resultant personality. This is shown most clearly where definite abnormalities are recognizable, as, for example, in Mongolian imbecility. As the student of general psychology knows, an appreciable proportion of individuals at the imbecile level of intelligence are of Mongolian type, born in families of good normal heredity, (but, fortunately, quite rarely) and characterized by striking physical features of a

Mongolian racial type as well as by mental characteristics of very low general intelligence, a comparatively good verbal ability, and a friendly, docile disposition. Mongolian imbeciles have been demonstrated to occur more frequently in older mothers and in mothers with many previous childbirths, but no more specific understanding of the causes of failure of normal embryonic development has yet been attained. In some other defective developments, *e.g.*, the defective sensory powers and general abilities resulting from venereal disease in the mother, the nature of the prenatal influences is more clearly understood.

**Effects within the Normal Range.** The question that remains largely unanswered is whether slighter systematic effects, not recognizable as definite abnormal syndromes, also arise from prenatal conditions. One of the most likely sources of such effects upon the development of the nervous system and the somatic basis of temperament is probably the endocrine condition of the mother during the gestation period. The separation of the foetal circulation from that of the mother or of a dizygotic twin does not prevent the sharing of most physiological influences. In cows, for example, the gestation of a male and female twin together results in the female being sterile (known as a "free-marten") as a result of the tissues being exposed to the male hormone generated by the twin. It is almost certain that the growth and the hormone balance of the embryo is affected by the hormone condition of the mother—particularly with respect to thyroid activity—though proof of this in terms of the ensuing personality and behavior characteristics is lacking.

A further proof of slight but significant prenatal influence is offered by the sufficiently confirmed finding that children conceived at certain seasons of the year tend to have slightly better intelligence than those beginning life in other seasons. As Fitt (25) has shown, this is only one aspect of generally higher vitality among those conceived in the fall months, for they also have a lesser frequency of illness, physical or mental, and greater life expectation. Attempts to explain this as a selection effect have so far been less convincing than explanations based on a seasonal biological rhythm; but the effect is so small that its attachment to a particular cause must still be considered uncertain.

Direct evidence on the development of the central nervous system, as shown by its reactivity, is steadily accumulating with respect to the first nine months of life. Although much of the nervous system, notably the cortex, is not myelinated during this period, so that the embryo is virtually decerebrate, many reflexes are functioning normally. The embryo reacts to sound, for example, with an embryonic startle reaction (shown by quickening of the heartbeat) for three or four months before birth. It also reacts by kicking and general foetal movement, to changes in the oxygen level of the blood. Most of the autonomic nervous system reactivity is present, with whatever capacity to form habits of reacting to stress that may entail. In general, however, the meager development of the central nervous system and the practical absence of definite external stimuli precludes any consideration of this period as one in which personality can form through habit formations. Whatever shaping of personality occurs in the embryonic period—and much may occur there—arises largely from the operation of the physiological condition of the mother upon the normal nervous maturation processes, upon the autonomic nervous system, and upon the somatic, largely endocrine, basis of temperament.

**The Effects of Birth.** Psychoanalysts, pursuing the origins of neurotic anxiety to ever deeper sources, claim that some role must be allowed to the trauma of birth itself. Rank (69), in particular, has argued that introspective evidence in adult neurotics provides evidence that. the fundamental orientation to life differs in those who have different degrees of shock from the birth experience. That personality should be affected by an experience of such duration is not intrinsically absurd. Physiologically the child passes from an experience of complete comfort and security, in which its temperature is maintained constant, its nutrition provided without feeding, etc., to one where it has to defend its temperature against cold and heat, to maintain oxygen balance by proper breathing, and to experience periodic stresses of hunger between feedings.

It is reasonable to expect that this sudden change might generate something in the nature of anxiety—a fear of functional disorganization (see below). And even if we do not accept as evidence of it the later introspections of clinical patients, we can see signs of it in autonomic disturbances and massive muscular tensions in the neonate himself. This traumatic experience of birth is exacerbated when the birth process itself is severe or when the child is not cherished and protected by the mother in the ensuing period.

The process of birth can also influence the child's personality in very tangible ways, apart from these effects on the general level of tension. That birth injuries to the head may produce some defects of general intelligence, but, more frequently, defects of motor coordination, or degrees of paralysis, has long been known. More recently it has been realized that a prolonged and difficult birth, subjecting the nervous system to severe oxygen shortages, may produce cerebral lesions, with permanent sequelae not very different from those of encephalitis.

Until recently no experimental or statistical evidence (apart from that on mental defect and motor defects) had become available to augment the purely clinical evidence that differences in the degree of birth trauma are associated with differences not only in abilities but also in personality and, particularly, in proneness to basic anxiety in later life. Wile and Davis (84) have now presented data (380 normal births compared with 120 difficult, instrumental births) which, while they are not sufficiently controlled (*e.g.*, as to matching of family and status, the conditions of rating, and the statistical significance of differences) are yet a real contribution beyond the clinical and psychoanalytic speculation which preceded them. As the following table from Wile and Davis (84) shows, there is a pattern of fewer conflicts and fears but more hyperactivity among the birth-injured. The lack of control of family size, etc. (birth-injured are more frequently only children and more intelligent), makes it necessary to discount some of these differences, but the hyperactivity is likely to be genuine.

RATING OF PERSONALITY DIFFICULTY

| | Percentage of normal birth children having these ratings | Percentage of difficult birth children having these ratings |
|---|---|---|
| Aggressive types of behavior (rages, tantrums, pugnacity)............. | 65 | 33.3 |
| General hyperactivity (restlessness, irritability, distractibility.......... | 25 | 50 |
| Submissive types of behavior (fears, unhappiness, phantasy life, no friends)........................ | 40 | 25 |
| Tics, nail-biting, food fads.......... | 70 | 33.3 |
| Peculation....................... | 12 | 6.7 |
| Infantile home relationships......... | 55 | 20 |
| School difficulties.................. | 45 | 22.3 |
| Intersibling conflicts............... | 30 | 15 |
| Physical ills...................... | 10 | 3.3 |

Shirley (74), moreover, has shown reliably on a sample of 200 children that a discernible behavior syndrome of somewhat greater general emotionality, poorer motor coordination (and, curiously enough, more sensitive feeling response to colors, sounds, and textures) exists in those prematurely born and subjected, therefore, to exaggeration of the usual demands at birth.

### 3. THE FIRST YEAR OF LIFE

**Maturation and the Growth of Abilities.** Through the researches of Gesell (28,29) and Buhler (12) and many others, particularly of those earlier workers who studied the growth of specific functions such as perception and language, psychology has much well-organized knowledge about the developmental course of motor and perceptual capacities and of abilities generally. But the information on the beginnings of personality is less systematic, and is in part a by-product of studies directed to discovering what innate equipment of emotional reactivity the child brings into the world with him.

Although the growth of motor, sensory, and perceptual abilities is well documented (7), factor-analytic or other approaches have not yet been employed to determine their structure. Attempts at "intelligence testing," from one through three years of age, in consequence have not been directed to measuring known relation-perceiving capacities and, as Bayley (7) points out with respect to the first year, and as the work of Wellman, Skeels, and Skodak (82) shows for the nursery-school period, the available tests give only a poor prediction of intelligence in later years.

Perhaps the outstanding fact about abilities in the first year or even later is, as the neat cotwin studies of Gesell and Thompson (30) show, that maturation proceeds so rapidly as to make learning relatively impotent. Gesell and Thompson show that both in motor and in verbal learning the untaught twin or the twin taught later quickly achieves the same level as the one taught. This is in accord with Dennis's observation that the Hopi child (16), despite being deprived of walking practice by being tied to the cradle board, walks with normal skill for its age at eighteen months. Wherever abilities are growing rapidly it is uneconomical to teach painfully at one moment what can be grasped much more quickly a little later—a fact overlooked by many enthusiastic teachers. And when the teaching happens to be in the same direction as maturation—as in the case of learning to walk—no trace of teaching experience remains later.

However, one should bear in mind that a difference (of degree) exists between training of specific skills and learning general adjustments to environment, and it is only on the former that any appreciable experimental evidence exists. It is quite possible, in view of what was said in the chapter on drives about optimum occasions for learning, that experience in the adjustment process, even where a maturation process is concerned, is indispensable.

Although relatively little is known about the structure of the infant's abilities and the dependence of acquisition of skills upon innate aptitudes, it seems quite unlikely such individual differences of ability as exist can have any influence on *emotional* development of personality comparable to that which occurs at the school age and later; for that influence occurs largely through an ego concept and social competition.

*Emotional Development.* Since within the first year the child usually can neither walk nor talk, his personality can manifest itself only in the manner of emotional expression, *e.g.*, the degree of excitability, ability to tolerate deferred satisfactions, frequency of temper-tantrums, etc. However, the student understands that in the study of each of these life periods we are concerned not only with describing personality as it develops at the time but also in discovering the influence of events in the period upon later personality growth. On either aspect experimental work is still scarce. Regarding emotional development, Watson, as is well known, claimed that the neonate experiences only anger, fear, and affection.  Bridges (11), by observation, claimed that there is at first only general pleasurable excitement and general "unpleasure" out of which more specific emotional reactions develop later (see Diagram 29, p. 188).  The experimental and biographical work of the Dennis's (17, 18) has done much to clear up the inaccuracies of earlier views and shows the neonate to be possessed of several distinct emotional reactions.  By six months or a year one can distinguish such primary drives as anger, fear, affection, hunger, sleep, curiosity, appeal, laughter, and perhaps, gregariousness,[1] and self-assertion (attention-getting).

**Possible Influences on Dynamic Structure.**  The possibilities of very diverse ergic conflict are thus present and one drive may be seen to suppress another, often in response to learned cues and as a habitual fashion.  But nothing in the nature of an ego formation controlling random drives for remoter ends of all drives can be seen in the first year.  One obstacle to such development seems to be that dynamic sets are too plastic, rigidity is low, extinction comes early, and memory is short.  Lindquist (57) studying eighty-five children of three to thirty-six months found that at six months children remembered mother or father only for a few days, and at twelve months only for three weeks.  This was by visual recognition: auditory recognition was poorer.  Using other criteria, earlier investigators have found somewhat shorter duration of recollections.

In view of the clinician's claim that emotional effects of having familiar or unfamiliar adults around can be perceived over much longer periods, e.g., a child's depression over the mother's absence may change when she returns after two months, it may be doubted whether these criteria of cognitive recognition exhaust the range of recognition experience.

Although experience is thus unlikely in the first year to have much effect —because of defective memory connections—on structural interrelationship of drives, clinical evidence suggests that it may powerfully affect the fixation form of individual drives as well as the manner of autonomic involvement in drives and the relative excitability of different drives.  Through the clinical indications from Freud of the importance of feeding experiences in the first few months of life, in causing passive oral and aggressive oral fixations, a certain amount of experiment has proceeded.  Hunt's experiments on rats (38), showing greater hoarding in adult life in those kept hungry in infancy, and Levy's (56) study of puppies, showing the persistence of sucking in those which obtained food with an insufficient amount of sucking activity, as well as Escalona's studies (21a) of feeding disturbances in

---

[1] Spitz (75) observing 251 children of zero to six months found the child at three or four months begins to smile, not at the human face alone, but with some regard for the expression on the face.  After six months it begins to show some dim awareness of its own group, smiling at familiar, friendly faces, but reacting with the beginnings of shyness to strangers.

children, point to the importance of departure from a hereditarily expected "normal" activity in emphasizing needed components or fixating unsatisfied components. Halverson (35) observed the feeding response of ten male children from six to forty-three weeks, from the breast and from nipples offering different degrees of difficulty. Strength of sucking and hand-muscle tension were found to vary together, declining through the feeding period. Hampered feeding caused greater and more oscillating muscle tension and restlessness. The general increase of excitement produced by frustration also caused penial tumescence.

**Affection Demand, Anxiety, and Disorganization.** The role of satisfaction and frustration in relation to the autonomic reactivity and general physiological harmony of the organism is stressed by Ribble (71), both with regard to feeding and to receiving warmth and physical contacts and caresses from the mother. A normal amount of activity and satisfaction of drives, it is argued from observation of a large number of infants, produces a favorable stimulation of bodily processes, such as breathing, circulation, and digestion. Only about 50 per cent of babies begin sucking spontaneously soon after birth, according to Ribble (71), and among those who do not are most of the unwanted babies and those receiving insufficient fondling from the mother.

Ribble and other psychiatric writers put stress on the child's "continual danger of functional disorganization" as the origin of primary anxiety. It is indeed important to remember that the infant *does* show difficulties of coordinating bodily processes and that the inefficiency of responding to heat and cold, digestion, etc., constitutes a real danger to life. Ribble makes a case, convincing at the clinical level of evidence, for frustration of infant drives tending to cause physiological disorganization, chronic tension, autonomic upset, and even fatal illness, of a kind long recognized in medical literature but not previously assigned to any cause other than "decline." In so far as crying is an indicator of anxiety we have surveys showing that crying in the first month is primarily to noxious stimuli such as pain and cold, to hunger, fatigue, and deprivation of exercise and movement. Its greatest frequency is between six and one half and ten months.

**Clinical and Psychoanalytic Evidence.** No repetition will be made here of the basic psychoanalytic views of the first year of life (Chapter 9), developed particularly by the writings of the Freuds (26,27) and Klein (49), except to remind the reader that (*a*) both deprivation and overindulgence of a need are considered to produce fixation; (*b*) that late weaning is supposed to produce a genial, outgoing, optimistic disposition and early weaning a grasping, greedy nature; (*c*) as the infant grows older some decline of urgency of the nutritional aspect of life permits attention to turn to elimination, where anal retentive experiences are said to be the roots of parsimony, pedantry, and irritability in later life, while emphasis on expulsive activities are connected with creative trends in personality, notably in painting and plastic arts.

If these associations between traits and infantile experience were proved it would still be necessary to explore the possible alternative explanation in terms of continuity of family atmospheres. A generous mother is more likely to continue feeding the infant herself. The infant, both by heredity and by later absorption of the family atmosphere that the mother has helped to create, is more likely to be generous and optimistic. Similarly, a pedantic, exacting family is likely to impose toilet habits early and insistently, causing anal-erotic fixations, and a correlation will thus exist between introspected anal-erotic experiences of infancy and pedantry of adult personality. Actually, as far as weaning is concerned, some three studies of a statistical kind have failed to show any relation between personality and either breast vs. bottle feeding, or length of breast feeding. Most primitive people, *e.g.*, the Hopi (16), wean their children very late and also feed them, not at regular intervals, but whenever the child shows signs of need. No anthropologist (prior to hearing this theory!) seems to have suggested that primitives are invariably generous and optimistic compared with civilized man.

· In spite of the dearth of scientifically objective evidence it is reasonable enough to expect that the happenings in the chief regions of consciousness of the dawning neonate mind, namely oral activities in connection with hunger, excretion in connection with visceral sensations, and the fondling and rocking in the mother's arms, would be of chief importance in shaping, in some fashion, the basic dispositional and energetic aspects of personality.

### 4. AGES TWO THROUGH FOUR YEARS: PRESCHOOL OR NURSERY SCHOOL

**The Effects of Mobility and Speech.** In the period now to be studied the child makes two great advances: first, he becomes mobile and capable of satisfying certain desires, approaching or withdrawing at will, and second, he gains command of language, with resulting possibilities of social and intellectual development. Precise data are available on speech development in almost all aspects (60). Whereas the child not quite a year old can communicate only by crying, smiles, and gestures, by eighteen months he is just obtaining some success with words and by four and a half years he uses language freely for social, emotional, and intellectual communication and self-expression, with a vocabulary of several thousand words.

The growth of verbal skill, more rapid here than in later age periods, is shown in the table below for mean length of sentence (graphically) and per cent of statements that are comprehensible. McCarthy found that this rise in language command comes a little earlier in upper-class than lower-class families, but whether through intelligence or opportunity is not known. Since learning language is, at the beginning, a trial-and-error process, with

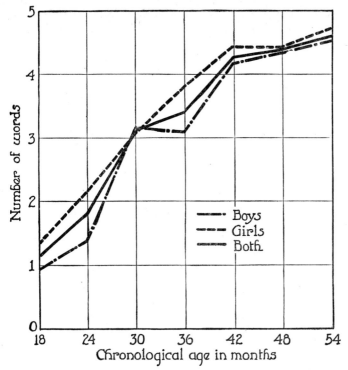

DIAGRAM 47. Mean length of response by chronological age and sex. (*By permission, from the studies of Dorothea McCarthy* (60).)

reinforcement of those sounds in the childish babble (or imitated sounds) that happen to make appropriate words, it is not surprising that the correlation is rather low between intelligence and age of initial speaking of words. Girls, however, tend both to start earlier and to maintain a higher level of verbal skill (throughout life in some slight degree) than boys, as the table above indicates.

MEAN PER CENT COMPREHENSIBLE RESPONSES BY CHRONOLOGICAL AGE AND SEX

|  | Chronological Age, Months | | | | | | |
|---|---|---|---|---|---|---|---|
|  | 18 | 24 | 30 | 36 | 42 | 48 | 54 |
| Boys | 14.0 | 49.0 | 93.0 | 88.0 | 95.5 | 99.3 | 99.6 |
| Girls | 38.0 | 78.0 | 86.0 | 99.3 | 99.8 | 99.8 | 100.0 |
| All | 26.0 | 67.0 | 89.0 | 93.0 | 97.2 | 99.6 | 98.8 |

From Barker, R. G., J. S., Kounin, and H. F., Wright, (6). (*By kind permission of authors and publisher.*)

Gesell's findings on skills generally indicate what he calls a "spiral of development." The child may manifest a new way of walking or word usage and then may either lose it for a while or show no improvement. Meanwhile developments in other behavior areas occur, and when the child "gets around" to this area again, another sharp increase of skill occurs. This saltatory progress is probably a reflection of the fact that the child has more new fronts of maturation than he can attend to. His interest dwells for a time in one region, say the development of speech sounds, and then, perhaps rewarded strongly by some act of early walking, his attention turns to mastery of ambulation, while for some weeks he is scarcely heard to babble or use what words he has. It might be expected that the age at which the child learns to walk skillfully and talk communicatively would have some appreciable influence on his personality development, for the sudden increase these skills produce in the capacity to satisfy desires, and the corresponding increase of need to apply inhibitions for the safety of the child and home property, results in a correspondingly sharp onset of emotional conflicts, and at a time when frustration tolerance is low. But no substantial evidence is available as to what happens at this point.

In general, differences in abilities still seem to play a small role, relative to other influences of personality development, at this period, compared with the later, school periods.

**Norms of Emotional Response and Personality Development.** A good deal of exact developmental information in the form of normative frequencies exists for various kinds of behavior in what is called in America the "pre-school period" and in Britain the "nursery-school period." The following diagrams from Macfarlane's study of 252 children (followed, in all, for fourteen years) concern mainly "problem" behavior.

One notices here the frequently observed (Buhler) peak in negativism and obstinacy at two and a half years, presumably occasioned by the first development of the ego, following the experiences of emotional conflict described above, and by the child's discovery that it has a will of its own. Further, we note a peak in fears, jealousy, and hypersensitiveness at four years, probably occasioned by the growing awareness of other children as individuals and the sense of insecurity that comes with awareness of a peer group intruding on the child-parent relation.

A more detailed study of growth trends has been made with respect to various particular areas, *e.g.*, to fears, by Jersild (45), and negativism by Benjamin (8). The latter observes that the trait of negativism manifests itself principally through overt resistance, feeding difficulties, and malicious mischief and is correlated with constipation, vomiting, disturbance of sleep, speech difficulties, breath-holding spells, nervous finger habits, enuresis, and encopresis. Seventy-four per cent of boys and ninety per cent of girls in a

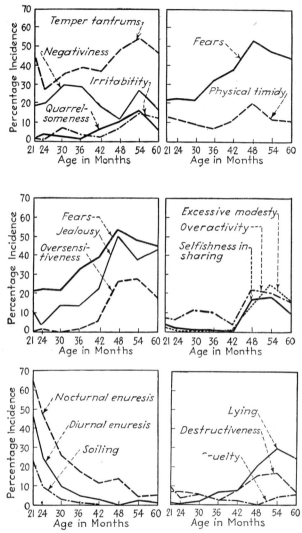

DIAGRAM 48. Age changes in incidence of problem behavior. (*By permission, from the researches of Jean W. Macfarlane (59).*)

large sample of "negativism" problem children were either only children or in two-sibling families. Between two and three years of age most negativism, in Benjamin's view, is due to anxiety and to lack of love and unwillingness to give responsibility on the part of the parents. A follow-up of forty-two cases for several years showed appreciable remnants of negativism in all but seven of those earlier referred for childish negativism. Sewall's study of the reaction of seventy children to the arrival of a younger brother shows that the negativistic syndrome is rather specific to this situation.  Fifty per cent showed definite negativism, 37 per cent by making bodily attacks on the child, and others by refusal to eat, general destructive behavior, and even by denial of the sibling's existence.  Evidently insecurity, as well as the newly discovered pleasures of "having a will of one's own," has a strong role in negativism.

As to children's early fears, Jersild (45) finds that in the first year fear is shown mainly to "noises and events previously associated with noise," also with falling and "sudden or unexpected movements, lights and flashes, persons or objects previously associated with pain, animals, and strange persons, objects, or situations" (page 335 (45)). . Between two and six years, as evidenced by actual experiments on 105 children by Holmes and observations on 153 children by parents, there is a decline in fear of falling, noise, and strange persons, while fear of animals rises and slowly declines.

These data are obviously concerned with purely situational fears.  Investigation of inner anxieties, "complexes," and special symbolic fears, determined as much by the child's inner conflicts as by the nature of the external object, is still not at a level where generally agreed statements can be made; for it rests on clinical evidence, biased by difference of "schools."

The data available from prolonged observations of infantile play, as made in parents' records, are best presented in summary form by diagrams, as below.

The growth of manifestations of behavior that can be called "curiosity," has been studied by Menaker (64) in 70, six- to twenty-four-month-old children.  At six to twelve months there was mainly exploratory, manipulatory activity of specific parts (highly colored or otherwise arresting): at twelve to fifteen months there was the dawn of fear of the unfamiliar, which conflicted with curiosity; at fifteen to eighteen months approach and confident curiosity was again predominant, and at eighteen to twenty-four months children began to show a need for social contact and speech in sharing the exploration of the object.

Fite (24) studied the attitude of nursery-school children to physical aggression.  Mainly they repeated the attitudes learned from parents, with comparatively little verbalization of their own experience of what consequences actually happened in aggressions among children.  There was little foresight as to consequences of aggression or nonaggression and surprisingly little relation between the child's actual behavior and the attitudes he had learned to express after the parents.

Brackett (9) made time-sampling studies of laughter and crying in 20 eighteen- to forty-eight-month children.  Four-fifths of both laughter and crying were associated with social contacts.  Girls laugh more with girls and

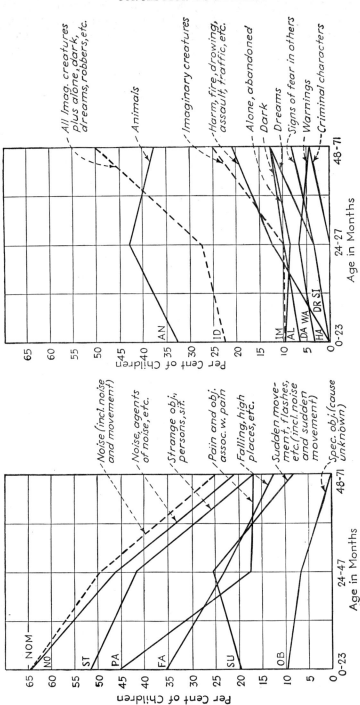

DIAGRAM 49. Percentage of children at biyearly age levels, showing one or more fears in response to various situations. Twenty-one day records on 31, 91, and 24 children at successive ages. (By permission, from the researches of A. T. Jersild (45).)

boys with boys.    More crying occurred on cold days.    The trends with age, etc., are best shown by correlations, as follows:

|                                | Laughing | Crying |
|--------------------------------|----------|--------|
| With chronological age         | 0.44     | −0.47  |
| With mental age                | 0.26     | −0.40  |
| With weight/age index          | 0.89     | −0.36  |
| With amount of language        | 0.60     | 0.00   |

Of all traits, other than general intelligence, that show trends during this period, probably the most rapid increase occurs in sociability, as estimated by contacts made with other children, and by the growth of exchanges rather than monologues in children's conversation.    The trend is variously witnessed by the researches of Barham and Sargent, Barker, Goodenough, and Murphy.    The first-named observe, incidentally, that sociability as an individually differentiating trait is very consistent between one and three years, whereas few other traits are.    Goodenough (31) found the correlation of age and social participation to be +0.71, while Berne noted that there is a correlation with mental age as well as actual age.    The growth of speech in connection with sociable activities has been documented by Jack.    He observed that at two years speech occurs with approximately equal frequency in all activity, in physical, manipulative, and imaginative play, and as often when playing alone as when playing with others, but by three and four years there is definitely more use of speech in group play and for social purposes.    More detailed studies of factors in the sociability and companionship of preschool children are available through Challman (13) and Hagman (34).

Regarding dominance-submission, the interpretation of existing results is difficult, for, under the confusing concept of "aggression," self-assertiveness on the one hand and pugnacity or anger in response to various frustrations on the other have been indiscriminately included.    Moreover, in estimating self-assertion or dominance itself, the necessity for a standard situation has been overlooked.    In a mixed group of nursery-school children, older children will show more dominance because they happen to be larger, but it is not clear that they would do so when placed with their exact coevals or with adults.    Jack's (42) results, however, suggest a slight increase in ascendant behavior throughout this period.    Leuba (55), putting children side by side in the experimental situation of completing peg boards, found at two years no rivalry reactions and, indeed, little social interaction of any kind.    At three and four years there was a variety of unpredictable rivalries and cooperations having in common only a slowing down of the performance; but by five years there was clear rivalry and an increase of output when together compared with that obtained when alone.

**Sources of Individual Differences in Early Personality Traits.** The relation of the above traits to sex, intelligence, family background, physical condition, etc., during this period is known only fragmentarily. Macfarlane (59) observes, for example, that poor physical condition tends to be associated with overdependence, negativism, eating difficulties, elimination problems, and nail-biting, in both groups studied, whereas no such associations were found for jealousy and temper-tantrums. Jealousy, at this period and later, is commonest in only children, in oldest children, and in those who manifest anxieties but are of "extravert" temperament. There is evidence of association of overactivity, lying, fears, and thumb-sucking with better than average physiological status. Macfarlane also finds in a general survey of her data that allergic reactions, hives, and eczema occur more with irritable and temper-tantrum cases.

The associations with intelligence found by Macfarlane were slighter than with physical or background factors, bearing out our generalization that abilities have less influence on personality in earlier than in later life. But undue dependence, speech difficulties, and continued enuresis were associated with low I.Q., while there was a slight tendency for stealing, lying, nail-biting, and attention-demanding behavior to go with higher I.Q. Probably the highest association is with fears, for Jersild (45) found a correlation of 0.53 between I.Q. and number of reported fears in two-to-three-year-olds, declining to zero by age five. The more intelligent child presumably perceives and foresees more possibilities of danger.

Relations with intelligence raise the question of the general structure of interrelationship of traits, *i.e.*, of correlation clusters and factors in the preschool child. As indicated in the first two or three chapters, we have been compelled to proceed on the assumption that the main personality factors found for adults and adolescence will be discernible also in children. No factor-analytic studies yet exist for this age, the studies of Koch (50) and Arrington (see (7), Chap. 3) being nearest. However, Macfarlane, using Tryon's cluster analysis (virtually factors) obtained at five years some four "factors" in problem traits, *viz:* (a) quarrelsomeness, mood swings, negativism, competitiveness; (b) withdrawn, "introverted," submissive, shy, somber, reserved, and underactive; (c) masturbation, unusual sex interest, and stammering; (d) diurnal and nocturnal enuresis and excessive modesty (modesty is noted to be more associated at this age with elimination than masturbation). The first factor is reminiscent of the C factor of general emotionality in adults, while the second seems an undifferentiated submissiveness, schizothymia, and desurgency. Macfarlane's observation that most severe behavior problems are found in children who are also jealous supports the C factor identification.

Through the two-to-four-year period sex differences of personality, barely demonstrable at two years, become clearly evident. Appel notes that the frequency of crying and screaming is the same for boys and girls at two, but thereafter the decline is more rapid for boys than girls. Boys also become more aggressive and hit out more frequently at objects and people whereas, as Jersild and Markey showed, girls already "handle" their social conflicts with more verbal activity and crying. The greater interest of boys in remoter objects and "action at a distance" and of girls in objects that come close to them is also striking. Jersild (45) found that in practically every experimental situation girls had a statistically significant excess of fear reactions. Ackerson found a higher frequency of daydreaming in girls at a somewhat later age, though the beginnings of greater imaginative withdrawal may be observed at this age also. Goodenough (31) found, in standard observation situations, that boys are more negativistic and distractible than girls. The drop from the peak of negativism and distractibility began earlier (eighteen months) in girls than boys (thirty months). Blatz and Bott found the same. Dawe (15) found in observations of nursery-school quarrels, most of which begin over possessions, that boys quarrel more than girls. Jealousy, however, is significantly more frequent, in the one-to-six-year period, in girls.

Family background influences have been discussed in a general way in Chapter 13 and only observations special to the period remain to be made here. Macfarlane (59) found negativism, temper-tantrums, attention-getting behavior, food finickiness, overdependence, and daytime enuresis more frequent in young children from unhappy or unadjusted marriages. Thumb-sucking and nocturnal enuresis were more frequent with favorable parental interrelations. Toward the end of the preschool period the items of the first group that showed most persistent relation to unfavorable family were negativism and temper. Lower economic status was also found to be associated with more problems, though only in the case of fears was the association as high as for strained family relations.

What organized "schooling" or special training can do in the nursery-school period has been much debated. It can obviously improve vocabulary and skills, as the work of Wellman, Skeels, and Skodak shows. It also hastens the process of socialization. Page (67) has shown that by exposing submissive children to experience of especial success it is possible, at the preschool level, to raise their dominance status in a group. Jack (42) has similarly shown that submissive four-year-olds can be brought to a statistically significant increase of ascendant behavior. McLaughlin (62), with older subjects, found that submissive behavior could be modified by training and change of social atmosphere, but not ascendant behavior. This links with further observations by McLaughlin and by Sears that dominant individuals tend to lack self-criticism and awareness of their assertiveness, and that when given insight they still prefer to be as they are, with or without social approval. The degree of extensity and permanence of this more ascendant behavior has not been investigated.

Perhaps this same trait of self-confidence and ascendance, rather than perseverance, is also involved in the experiments of Keister, who showed that children who give up easily on puzzles can be trained, by a graduated series of less overwhelming problems, to tackle problems of the original level of difficulty with more resource and persistence (48). But again it has not been demonstrated that there is any change in a broad personality trait, as distinct from a habit with a special artificial set of puzzles.

A review of probable general effects of early history on personality traits has been made by Wang (81). Thompson (77) has shown, with a sample of nineteen children, that, compared with children left much to their own devices, those given plentiful teacher attention, society, and guidance in a nursery school manifest more ascendance, social participation, and leadership. In general, however, the defective methodology of measuring traits (as distinct from specific narrow performances), the small numbers used, and the absence of follow-up studies to determine later effects on personality, leave us uncertain as to the role of particular factors in modifying personality at this time.

## 5. AGES FIVE THROUGH SEVEN YEARS: EARLY CHILDHOOD

**Theories Concerning the Early Problem Period.** There is much evidence indicating that the closing year of the period just studied is one of outstanding conflict and emotional instability—a miniature adolescence. A peak is reached at four years in jealousy, temper-tantrums, fears, attention-seeking, and probably also in lying, disturbing dreams (nocturnal), and phantasy. A closer inspection of the frustrations and fears involved has been presented by Dawe (15) and Felder (23); but one can see that in the main, since no internal or endocrine readjustments are salient, the maladjustments must arise from particular pressures in the environment.

Various theories as to the nature of this culture-pattern impact are possible. First, we may suppose that the whole of the first period of life is peculiarly fraught with dangers—of stress, because the discrepancy between the individual's equipment (native and acquired) and the complexity of the culture is at no time greater. By this theory the absence of symptoms in the preceding three years is simply due to the fact that the infant has insufficient ego development to manifest, by symptoms, the strains under which he lives. Besides, there is always a tendency for the results of strain to show themselves with some lag after the period of sustained conflict. Second, the more environmental theory may be tried that the parent alters his standards for, and attitudes toward, the child, in some inappropriate fashion, at about three years of age. One possibility would be that the characteristics of the baby stimulate parental, protective behavior, which postpone the parental impatience with the inconveniences of infantile behavior and which the parent may unconsciously drop as the child achieves "miniature adult" qualities of speech and mobility. (Support for this may be found in the fact that jealousy is commonest in oldest children who suffer more from such changes.) A second culture-pattern theory would be that some traditional standard in our culture pattern, *e.g.*, a school standard, presses too heavily on the child at this time. Action of this kind is not conspicuous and the theory of parental withdrawal of indulgence is also unlikely, for if true the arrival of a second child should be more closely connected with these disturbances than it is. Nevertheless, some undiscerned "rejection" of the child may well occur, because his more organized will power and greater mobility make him far more of a nuisance than formerly, occasioning the beginning of a refrain of "don't touch" or simply "don't." The possibilities of endangering his own safety, of damaging property, of carrying "dirt" everywhere, etc., are suddenly far greater than before (43). As Chapter 13 shows, there is definite evidence (5) of such a parental attitude change between three and nine years, and it is possible that most of this change occurs at the beginning of the period.

A fourth theory as to the "early problem period" is that the child, by his sociability, has moved partly from the protected parental world into a new world of peers, who are less skillful and considerate in regard to his problems. In this case there should be significant differences in trends between those who do and those who do not attend nursery school. There is insufficient evidence here. Lastly, we may ascribe the problem to the biological curve of intelligence maturation, which gives more growth in these four years than in any other, so that although the complexities of culture are not much more for the child of four than the child of two they are for the first time *perceived* in their complexity. If so, the above symptoms should show more relation to mental than chronological age. These theories await more data.

**Determination of Personality Traits beyond the Period in Question.** That the reactive "problem" behavior of the earlier period tends to determine personality trends in and beyond the present period is shown by the studies of Kathern McKinnon (61), Van Alstyne and Hattwick (80), and others. McKinnon noted, between three and eight years, consistent predominance of the traits noticed at the beginning, but with definite individual trends of change and with a general change of all children in the direction of greater conformity. (The earlier period, like adolescence, seems to be one of personality dispersion.) The second study, based on ratings from the nursery school through the elementary school, showed that the maladjusted at the end of the period were very largely those at the beginning, and less than 10 per cent of them developed undesirable traits (difficult to manage, temper outbursts, negativism) after four years of age.

Since the existence of such specific trend data on particular kinds of problem behavior may wrongly give the impression that that behavior is the most prevalent in the period, it is fortunate that in the periods now being studied the above curves can be seen in the perspective of surveys by Cummings (13), Laycock (see (31), Chap. 16), and others of the actual incidence of various kinds of problem behavior. Cummings studied 239 children in the two-to-seven-year age range, by rating and classroom observation, and found nervous restlessness and general or specific anxieties the most common symptoms. Compared with girls, boys showed more pugnacity (temper), assertiveness, negativism, cruelty, and lack of concentration. Anxiety symptoms occurred more in the overprotected, and stealing, lying, pugnacity, and cruelty in the neglected (*cf.* Chap. 13). The survey was repeated after six months and again after eighteen months. In all symptoms together there was no change of frequency with aging, but specific symptoms showed trends. In general, there was not much change after five years, but below five years there was more frequent clearing up of initial "problem" forms of behavior.

**Contrast of Early Childhood with the Ensuing Trends.** Although the *beginning* of the present period thus ends a critical phase for personality development (this is the period recognized by the psychoanalysts, *e.g.*, in Ernest Jones's writings, as "infancy,") it is with respect to the *end* of the period that a cardinal change in environment occurs. For, as Eng (21) points out, clinical observations suggest six or seven years of age as the age of psychological weaning from the parents. With that shift of loyalty to equals, in place of obedience to parents, begins the period of eight to thirteen, frequently called the most carefree (or, as in Chapter 9, the "little savage" stage) with greatest emotional stability, strengthening of the ego, extension of the number of persons the individual loves and is dependent upon, and general consolidation of personality.

By contrast with this later period, as Sisson shows, the present period does not show much cooperation in group play. Piaget considered the period of egocentricity as shown by language structure, to run through the seventh year. Naturally, like all of Piaget's periods, this is relatively indefinite, as Dennis has shown, and even the same child may advance and retreat irregularly with respect to a performance that is supposed to reach a plateau at a certain age. However, there is no doubt that the "period" of five through seven can be characterized as a comparatively solitary one, with a marked degree of imagination and phantasy. The difficulties of the earlier period—infancy—have been reacted to, first, with some negativism, then, as the ego becomes more formed, with temper-tantrums and self-assertion.

and now, as the cultural restrictions become more accepted, with some degree of compensation through phantasy. This growth of phantasy is also to be correlated with the growth of distinction between reality and phantasy— one of the achievements of the preceding period—which, by revealing the adamantive nature of reality, creates need for more phantasy. In any case, if one compares the world of the adult, with its stable, reciprocated relations to business, home, friends, intellectual and religious activities, and the possibilities of seeking recreation from stress occurring in one field by turning to another, it is evident that the young child's world has less varied and stable pressures and interests and thus fewer escapes, so that the safety valve of phantasy is essential.

**Phantasy and Play in Early Childhood.** Since this make-believe is characteristic of the period, it behooves us to study it more closely, along with the play of which it forms part. The general functions of make-believe and play have been reviewed in Chapter 15. It was there shown that it is by no means correct to regard all play as either compensatory or regressive, for it is also preparatory. But regression (Chaps. 7 and 9) should be looked at in the present context. No satisfactory experimental work on the amount of regression, or causes of regression, in this or any other growth period yet exists. The inquiry by Barker, Dembo, and Lewin (6) on five-year-olds, showed that play became less organized and constructive when children were returned to the same toys after an immediate experience of more attractive toys. Unfortunately, these results do not prove that this "regression" is due to "frustration," rather than boredom or distraction, since the experimental group was not divided in such a way that half of the subjects experienced the "frustration" at first contact and half at the last. The decline in "constructiveness" actually occurred on seeing "the same old toys."

Increases in *amount* of play activity almost certainly occur at times of cultural pressure and difficulty in adjustment, but how much of this represents regression (in either of the two senses defined in Chap. 9) and how much an attempt, by use of the repetition compulsion (in Freud's sense) to master a situation, literally or symbolically, is uncertain. The beginning of a real basis for rating the regressiveness of play exists in various careful surveys of normal changes of play with age. Beginning with children at two years of age Jack observed an increase through age four in group play (with talking), imaginative play (phantasy), and construction play, but a decrease in manipulative play and in wistfully watching the play of others. Banham Bridges (11) gives the following observationally obtained "norms" for assessing the more social aspects of play:

*At two years.* Solitary play, cling to parents, only fleeting interest in others
*At three years.* Play in pairs or small groups of three or four

*At 3½ years.* Play in small groups, share toys and possessions brought from home

*At four years.* Attempt to organize and command younger children

*At five years.* Really considerate of younger children. Organized games

Norms in phantasy are not yet available. Common observation indicates that before five years children enjoy fairy stories, whereas in the period now discussed there is a turning to stories that might be true and to movies of action, especially those involving phantastic self-assertion ("Superman"). An objective study by the psychogalvanometer of children's reactions to movies showed that below twelve years, and particularly in the region now being studied, the greatest mean deflections are to danger and conflict situations, whereas at sixteen they are to sex. This suggests that play is functioning more in its "preparatory" than "regressive" roles at this stage, for at five through seven the child is still not certain of his ability to cope with common dangers and is still given to withdrawing to the parents.

As Wolff (86) has pointed out, children's drawings can often be considered "graphic dreams" and a survey of drawings from this point of view might readily yield age norms of phantasy activity. Ackerman (1) presents data on the differences in play, observed in experimental situations, of well-adjusted, maladjusted, and delinquent children. There seems no demonstrable deficiency of constructive play in the maladjusted. (Creativity is, after all, often a consequence of internal conflict.) However, the experimenter observed that in the older, "adjusted" activities became more flexible, whereas the constructive and destructive play of the maladjusted remained, as they grew older, of a relatively rigid type. Lazar (51) has shown certain consistent differences in play at these ages according to intelligence level. Lower I.Q. children were less interested in reading and in things requiring a sense of humor. Bright children were significantly less interested in motor activities, religious and social activities.

An exhaustive survey of experimental studies of play has been presented by Hurlock (40). The more voluminous clinical contribution, scattered in numerous more or less complete case histories, argues that play is, first, a diagnostic aid, showing where the child's needs of self-expression lie, and, second, a therapeutic device, by which attitudes to parents, teachers, sibs, etc., can be lived out, and subjected to trial-and-error experimentation and corrected. Instances of symbolism in play and phantasy, *e.g.*, playing out the family situation in a doll's house, representing siblings by animals, indicating a desire for security by building walls, are as convincing as the more established action of symbolism in dreams. There seems little doubt, also, that play therapy not only discharges, harmlessly, pent-up aggressions and other desires, but, furthermore, gives the child an opportunity to experience

and evaluate the consequences of various alternative courses of action open
to him in real life, as it does for adults in "acting out" in sociodrama.

**Degree of Acceptance of Parental Restraints.**  If the prevalence of make-
believe play in the two-through-four and especially the five-through-seven
periods is related to the overwhelming complexity of the culture pattern
perceived beyond the area of parental shelter we might anticipate that
increased disciplinary restraint would yield an increase in phantasy.  For
after the preliminary "fling" around four, in which the child asserts his
newly found ego, there is a growing ability to accept and adopt the restraints
of parental authority, up to the age of seven or eight, in return for that
protection which the child still feels he needs.  Jack (43) found that five-
year-olds obey commands with less delay, less proneness to distraction (by
other toys, etc.), less substitute activity, and less forgetting than three-year-
olds.  The most and the least intelligent children were least ready in their
obedience.

Probably it is in this period, where parental discipline is most accepted
and is most capable of affecting conscious ideals, that it has the greatest
power for good or ill.  The problem of the optimum degree of restraint and
discipline is still being bandied about between "progressive" and "common
sense" educators, but with surprisingly little production of experimental
evidence.  Wright (88) and others have shown that more interchild aggression and more interchild moral discipline occurs when children are more
frustrated by restraints.  Greenacre (32), reviewing clinical, anthropological,
and experimental evidence for the period before this, concludes that at least
there is no evidence of intellectual impairment through even severe and prolonged restraint, though there is increase of sadistic and masochistic trends
and some regression to infantile eroticism.  The probability remains that,
up to eight years of age, an appreciable amount of restraint and authority is
welcomed by the child as evidence of parental interest and as a protection
against a larger and still unassimilable world.

### 6. AGES EIGHT THROUGH FOURTEEN YEARS: CHILDHOOD OR PREADOLESCENCE

**Comparative Stability of the Period.**  By eight the average child has
achieved an impressive array of skills and emotional adjustments.  In the
period from three to seven he has become socialized—*e.g.*, learned to share,
to take turns, to give and take, he has learned to manage his pugnacity and
other emotions to a degree where he is not in constant danger of being overcome by them, and he has a sense of appropriate rights and responsibilities
for the individual.  He has now mastered all ordinary, necessary manipulative skills, has an adequate command of language for most social purposes,
has insight into most standard human relations, and has adjusted himself to

other children, to the toleration of frustrations, to the regimentation of school life, and to the normal amount of obedience required by parents. So long as he is only required to be a child and not an adult, and so long as his parents are still in the background to be depended upon, his energies are no longer wholly absorbed in coping with new adjustments, and we witness the beginning of a comparatively carefree, adventurous, and easily adjusted phase of childhood, lasting to adolescence.

The child is, of course, by no means at the peak of his capacities; maturation and improvement continue in nearly all functions, *e.g.*, general mental capacity, reaction time, and muscular power. Regarding the last, Jones (46) found an approximately linear increase of dynamometer score from ten to fourteen years, and this steady linear progression is characteristic of the whole period.

**Trends in Interests.** Personality trends, from interest changes (including fears) to disposition, character, and emotional-control developments, have been tolerably charted, in terms of instruments available in the past twenty years, for this period. By and large it is a period of moderate and steady change. Interest trends have been assessed by memory tests (see charts in next chapter), free conversations (below), examination of collections, and statistical treatment of stated wishes. Witty and Lehman (85), using the last named methods, showed some very clear trends in the eight-to-seventeen-year period—for example, after nine there is a galloping decline in the percentage of boys who want to be cowboys! On 800 collections they found girls collecting more than twice as much as boys, of objects of aesthetic value, dolls and doll paraphernalia, household material, souvenirs, and objects of sentimental value. Boys collected more than twice as much as girls of objects associated with war and hunting, animal parts, insects, fishing material, games material, and miscellaneous junk. Boys did more finding and trading; girls exchanged by means of "gifts." The volume of material on interests being not yet anywhere arranged in form for condensed representation, the writer must refer the student to various original sources (51,63,68).

In perspective the most outstanding interest trends are an increase in social and "gang" activities, in leadership relations, and in action and adventure. An analysis of differences in these and reading interests according to intelligence and other differences has been made by Lazar (51). England's study of fears and worries in this period (20) show them to be relatively concrete, compared with the phantastic fears of infancy and the ideational fears of adolescence. His results show that still in this period that less intelligent children have fewer fears, and they also suggest fewer fears among delinquents, intelligence being held constant. Jersild (45) reports a widening variety of fears in the five-to-twelve-year range compared with the preschool period. Twenty per cent of them were concerned with imaginary creatures, bogeys, and the dark; 10 per cent with criminals; 20 per cent with corpses, death, remote dangerous animals, and with things of this character in stories, the rest not being readily classifiable. Imaginary and supernatural dangers declined from about 63 per cent at five years to 48 per cent at eleven and twelve years.

Children's annoyances and frustrations were studied by Zeligs (91), who found that twelve-year-old boys get most annoyed (in retrospect) about injustice, sarcasm, bullying, and people laughing when others get hurt, while girls have the highest aversion to having to witness pain or illness and to social relations that lower their personal status; but all of these are high for both sexes.

**Trends in Personality Traits.** Disposition and character changes are not so well mapped. In dominance-submissiveness some studies show a slight but definite increase of dominance throughout the period in question. Dennis and Dawe (15) found pugnacity, frequently connected with frustration of dominance at this age and inclined to show itself, in fighting, mostly between four and nine years in girls, and eight and fourteen years in boys (girls turn earlier to verbal substitution). Girls, even at this age, show less dominance and "extraversion" than boys, as any survey of delinquency statistics will show (less fighting and less stealing are noted for girls). On the Guilford-Martin questionnaire, applied toward the end of this period, the same differences are noted. Hewitt and Jenkins (36), analyzing the incidence of clinically noticeable "overinhibited" children, found a steady increase of frequency of the syndrome through this period and on through adolescence. It is uncertain whether this is an inhibition of dominance, *i.e.*, submissiveness, or the growth of the general character factors $C$ and $G$, with their inhibition of general emotionality and impulsiveness, but the latter seems more likely.

Messerschmidt demonstrated on a variety of suggestibility tests, that though there is a slight increase of suggestibility as the child settles down at six and seven, there is, through the present period, a steady decrease, perhaps connected with a lessening dependence on adult authority. In each of eight of the eleven years of age in which comparisons were made girls were found to be more suggestible than boys. The attitude to adult authority through this period seems to be increasingly that it is irksome, though there is rarely a full-scale revolt as in adolescence. Where children are in a position to complain there is ample evidence that they find adults too dominating and coercive, but in general the reaction against authority is more surreptitious or unconscious.

Individual differences in dominance, insofar as they are connected with this period, have been ascribed to awareness of low family status, undue parental restraint, and lack of opportunity for initiative in the home, number of social contacts and social approvals in the peer group, health, level of physique and athletic prowess, etc. McLaughlin (62) found the following characteristics associated with low dominance: physical defects, ridicule at home or from peers, and emotional, neurotic difficulties; while high dominance was particularly associated with early responsibility, many social contacts, prowess in athletics, and successful compensation for some defect.

**The Chief Influences on Personality in this Period.** In surveying systematically the environmental influences responsible for the personality trends just noted, it is necessary to consider primarily the home, the school, and the peer group. The slightly declining dependency in the attitude to the home, along with essential obedience and emotional involvement in it, and the normal tendency of parents to show less protective attitudes have already been discussed. The school is especially important because, through the child's greater involvement in the peer group, he is also more involved in the school than previously. Most observers note a good deal of transfer or of conflict between attitudes of the home and attitudes of the school, though the child frequently tries to separate the two concepts of himself involved. Anderson's study (2) shows definite transfers, at least with regard to bullying and withdrawal behavior, between the classroom and the sibling situation. However, it would be a mistake to suppose that the separation of the worlds of home and school is sheer loss from the standpoint of good adjustment. Each world provides, as if by adaptation to the limited frustration tolerance of the growing child, a brief holiday from the stresses of the other. And frequently, in clinical work, one can perceive ergic expressions in one of these areas which compensate for and redress the frustrations of the other.

Actually, the somewhat scrappy objective evidence that exists does not show any very powerful influence of the day school on personality. For example, Page shows that the degree of dominance is not much affected by relative success in schoolwork, perhaps because in the peer culture, school honors do not count much. School success is slightly correlated with emotional stability (though Hewitt and Jenkins (36) report a curious correlation between spelling ability and "unsocialized aggression"), but almost certainly because prior emotional stability favors good schoolwork.

However, Jasper (44) shows on an elation-depression scale that the academically less successful and the less intelligent children are more frequently depressed. Moreover, the whole of clinical experience on this matter, as summarized for example by Burt (see Chap. 16), indicates that academic failure in school can be a contributory factor in delinquency or maladjustment. Hilgard reviews studies, including the outstanding one by Sears, showing that successful children in school fix realistic aspiration levels whereas the duller are erratic, ranging from high, unrealistic views, clearly formed in phantasy, to despondent views below their real level of possible performance.   It has often been pointed out that competitive academic work can have distinctly disturbing effects on the self-regarding sentiment and general stability of the lowest section of the class.   Many studies have shown that at least academic success and failure are strongly associated with interests and liking for particular school subjects.   Thus, Nemoitus found correlations in high school ranging from $+0.64 \pm 0.04$ to $+0.49 \pm 0.04$ between liking a subject and success in it (66).

**The Influence of the Peer Group on the Verge of Adolescence.**   As mentioned above, an outstanding feature of the period is a growth of emotional involvement in peer society.   Before discussing this it is necessary to glance at the relations and relative development of boys and girls.   In physical development they are still very equal.   Jones (46) finds that boys are slightly superior in strength of grip and pull, but girls are actually superior in some measures, *e.g.*, thrusting strength.   At thirteen there is an inflection point, boys rising rapidly and girls barely altering in these measures.   In interests there is a difference in fears as indicated above, and as Murphy, Murphy, and Newcomb (65) show, girls tend to be more pacifistic and more acceptant of authority.   Zeligs (91) asked 160 twelve-year-olds about their wishes and interests, finding boys more interested in political and social questions, in personal development, and possessions and pleasures; and girls in family welfare.   Incidentally, he demonstrated the necessity for allowing for social trends, as mentioned elsewhere; for twelve-year-olds in 1940 showed more political, social, and family welfare interest than in 1935.   One of the prime causes of differences in boys and girls at this age is that boys are far more rapidly breaking away from parental attitudes.   Consequently, it is not surprising to find that in this sexual latent period, despite similarity of interests, coeducation, and comparative absence of any social pressure to separate the sexes, they still form like-sex groups more frequently than mixed. Tuddenham's (79) "friend choice" method shows that this pulling apart is perhaps more from the girl's side, for boys named girls as friends twice as frequently as girls named boys, while cliques or gang groups developed first among girls.

The social groups that now develop are typically strong in their demands on loyalties, exclusive in their attitudes to adults and others, fond of secrets, rigid in their mores and expectations, anti-individualistic, and of "horde structure" in regard to leadership.   Prior to eight years of age there has been little opportunity for leadership, since children are not sufficiently sociable or capable of organizing permanent groups; while at adolescence they become more individualistic and sometimes solitary through concern with inner conflicts.   Consequently, the present is the golden age of leadership, though not so definitely in girls' as in boys' groups.   This experience of leadership and followership probably causes divergence in dominance-submission scores and perhaps in surgency-desurgency (core of introversion).

If our interest tests were sufficiently analytical in terms of drives there can be little doubt that we should find in the average boy what is noticeable in clinical observation of the abnormal: that the major ergic swing in this period is toward sublimated homosexual expression. The mutual devotion of boys in this period is clearly the root of the sociability of the "gang." The gang is not held together by ideational and idealistic considerations, as is adolescent society; indeed, the moral sense is still shallow and expedient. It is held together rather by a rising tide of social interests, affections, and dependencies, arising out of sublimated homosexual feeling.

**The Self-sentiment and Its Molding Influences.** There can be little doubt that the self-concept during this period, while still substantially shaped by parent opinion, comes increasingly to be shaped by the group. Macfarlane (59) has traced some changes in the most "popular" character over the age range six to eleven years. At the beginning the most liked boy is quiet but a good sport and "ready to take chances." Being good at games becomes more important with age, and finally such qualities as being good looking, being a leader, and being friendly come to the fore. Among girls there is similarly a transition from being quiet, not quarrelsome, and a good sport to emphasis on good looks, friendliness, and neatness. Not being quarrelsome retains its position but a very marked downward trend occurs in being good at games and "taking chances." By a somewhat similar treatment of the actual reactions of children, but with analysis into a single "cluster," Tryon (see next chapter) showed that in adolescence popularity is associated with friendliness, enthusiasm, humor, being daring, and a leader. This seems a continuation of the trend through preadolescence.

A useful approach to determining the self-concepts and interests of children, by recording their spontaneous conversations, was followed by Zillig (92), on 80 boys and 386 girls of nine to twelve years. He found them predominantly characterized by a boastful and fantastic tone, by wishful thinking, and expression of personal and secret desires, mostly unchecked by modesty, ethical considerations, or practicability (all by comparison with adult standards). There was a certain ritual of listening, and recognized boasters were to some extent spurred on by the listeners. Girls exhibited wishes and self-concepts concerned with their good looks, possessions, the gifts and the invitations they received, being a favorite child, the social prominence of parents, and especially the father's wealth or attainments. Boys talked more about their physical strength and daring exploits, about war, bombing, and flying. The mother was not much mentioned by either sex and the siblings by only a few girls.

Other investigators surveying spontaneous and natural activities note in this period the interest in gangs and conspiracies; the atmosphere of phantasy; the predominance of egotism and exhibitionism; the lack of feeling, the capacity for cruelty (in boys); the simple, materialistic values; in which ethics consists of justice rather than mercy, and the virtues are the primitive ones of courage and endurance; the rigidity of rules and the narrow intellectual horizon, with lack of thoughtfulness or questioning. Toward the middle of the period they note the beginning of restlessness and wanderlust, the growth of sex curiosity and sometimes of sex play.

**The Chief Conflicts and Disturbing Influences.** Despite the general emotional stability of this period a readiness to develop new habits and to grow freely in new directions prevails. Moreover along with the good integration of drives there goes a certain splitting of personality between the home and the gang. This interesting phenomenon of the preadolescent "double life" is insufficiently investigated. Its presence in children of foreign parentage or of divergent social class is understandable and frequently noticed; but it also exists quite strongly where these are not found. For example, it is not at all uncommon, for young children particularly, to protest against their parents' appearing at school—once they are themselves adjusted to the school. Probably the degree of dependence on and submission to the parent is greater than the child likes to admit in the peer group—and this difficulty is likely to increase later, in the twelve-year-old peer group, where standards of independence and mischief become high. The absence of neurotic difficulties, however, suggests that the differing stimulus situations permit easy separation of the two "personalities," and that the real conflict on this and related matters arises only later in adolescence, when an attempt at general personality integration occurs.

There seems little doubt that though this period is one of comparative emotional stability and happiness, it is still subject to fierce aggressions, is replete with situations with great potentialities for humiliation and is bounded by very real fears. Yet it is as if the child is far less sensitive to them than he is later, in adolescence. He retains some anesthesia to emotional stresses that has been necessary to carry him through the greater strains of the earlier periods. Thompson and Kepler (78) found the ratio of pleasant to unpleasant memories from the daily round to be significantly higher for this period than for adolescence or later.

But even in the "little savage" period, with its forthright aggressions and fierce loyalties there is a discernible growth of social graces and kindnesses. Wright (89) put thirty-six eight-year-olds and thirty-six eleven-year-olds in the experimental situation of possessing toys in the presence of familiar and strange children without toys. He found the younger children more generous but the older ones more imbued with a sense of fair play, with regard to distributing among several children, as well as in relation to their own role. (The $r$ of "equity" ideology with age was $+0.42 \pm 0.08$.) With age there was also increasing regard for complicating aspects of the situation and special conditions. (The young children gave away more toys to strangers than to their friends, perhaps more in propitiation than to make them feel at home!) Wright noticed, incidentally, that the children who believed other people to be more generous than average were themselves more generous. Horton (37) notes, in accord with the theme of this passage, a marked growth of social skills during the eight-to-fourteen-year period, but observes also that there is a decline in truthfulness in favor of tact and diplomacy.

As shown in the next chapter, the endocrine harbingers of adolescence are already at work in the middle of the present period and, since puberty may come earlier to some than others, possibilities of maladjustment occur in the late preadolescent period. The California studies show a correlation of 0.50 between physiological measures and an index of height and weight, so that the early maturing boy can quickly move out of his group in size, strength, and appearance, causing some emotional stresses.

On an average, as Hughes's (39) study of a 1,000 boys shows, the first beginning of sex consciousness occurs at twelve and one-half years—a figure with which Kinsey's recent data agree—but a sufficiently active interest to constitute a real turning point does not occur until thirteen or fourteen years. The beginnings of psychological puberty are shown by various relatively sharp changes of interest. For example, Melbo (63) and Hurlock (40) show a comparatively sudden loss of interest in childhood play forms around fourteen years. Changes from this point onward are the subject of the next chapter.

## 7. REVIEW AND SUMMARY

The methodology underlying the results at present available in developmental psychology obviously leaves much to be desired. Even without actual improvements of method, the dovetailing of data and comparison of periods and influences would get much further if experimenters would agree on the definition of psychological variables to be measured, the variety of methods to be employed, and the age ranges to be considered in restricted studies.

Summaries at present have, therefore, to remain at the natural history level, embedding differing experimental approaches in a general matrix of clinical-type observation. Some laws can be established at this level, but nothing of a fine or exact nature. These criticisms may be illustrated by the simple example of the finding that intelligent children have more fears than unintelligent. Here we know that intelligent children have more interests of every kind than unintelligent. If precise curves or equations existed for the change in a known universe of interests with age and mental age, an allowance would be made to determine whether in fact *fearful* interests per se are proportionately greater for the more intelligent. Absence of standard data and defined concepts thus leaves a great many investigated issues still open to question and prevents any useful superstructure of integrating generalizations or extraction of basic principles.

Certain basic questions can frequently be raised, but in these circumstances can be answered only at the clinical level of certainty, and the answers remain at the level of certainty of the individual psychologist's own judgment as he surveys the uneven panorama of precise facts and casual observations. Among the unanswered questions is, first, the old one concerning the relative roles of innate maturation and cultural influence in various development curves. Second, one may ask how much truth there is in the oft-repeated assertion that a function must be exercised at the time it matures (or at the time it is intended to be used) in order to give it full development and avoid later problems of undischargeable or unintegrable functions. Again, we need exacter measurements on regression, to decide whether the level of regression is more dependent on the period of frustration or the magnitude of the frustration. One sees, in adult persons, regressions to homosexuality as of the twelve-year level, to parental dependence as of the eight-year level, to the rigidity of the six-year-old, to the defective socialization and egocentricity of the three-year-old, to the baby-speech difficulties of two years, or, as in some of the extreme cases illustrated by McDougall, to walking and crawling difficulties and infantile toilet habits. We still do not know whether the type of behavior marks the period at which developmental trauma occurred or whether it corresponds to the degree of severity of some much later, current difficulty.

Yet another interesting but unanswerable problem of the life course concerns whether the new learning at each phase of development proceeds by extinction or suppression of the preceding habits, attitudes, and sentiments. The operation of true repression and the conditions under which it does or does not become necessary are tolerably understood. But the extent to which normally inherent disposition rigidity causes older habits to persist beneath the surface and to require some degree of suppression is not understood. Presumably, in so far as the latter occurs it ties up energy, and the possibility arises that the slower learning of older people is not entirely due to organic change but also to the length of the learning road by which they are forced to approach their present habits. Such questions, properly the concern of developmental research, are obviously of prime importance for education and clinical psychology.

To the extent that a summary may itself be summarized the conclusions from this chapter are:

1. Both disposition and abilities can be influenced *in utero* by the physiological condition of the mother, though, except for slight seasonal influ-

ences, only extreme instances have been demonstrated. Apart from possible physiological injuries at birth there is clinical evidence of degrees of anxiety-creating birth trauma.

2. The newborn child has difficulties in maintaining even *physiological* integration and experiences diffuse tensions from purely internal states. Feeding or fondling deprivations militate against the decreasing of this tension and impede integration.

3. Though experiences of the first year can have little effect on ergic integration, the experiences in the realm of the child's greatest interest (feeding, fondling, excretion) can influence ergic fixations, which are claimed to affect later interests and the individual's general disposition.

4. Walking, talking, and self-awareness bring contact with increased stimulation and inhibition, with experience of conflict and willed action. These experiences produce between two and three years a variety of marked personality responses, notably a phase of negativism, which slowly subside thereafter.

5. The age of five has a maximum of instability and behavior problems, variously contributed by: cultural hurdles, the appearance of rival children, and systematic changes in parental attitudes.

6. Individual personality traits change more before five than after, in response to a number of factors which can be shown to be causally related to various traits. Normal and abnormal traits remain markedly constant from five to puberty.

7. Play and phantasy, having cathartic, regressive, and preparatory functions, are especially developed in middle childhood and change in systematic fashion with age.

8. At about seven or eight the child is to some extent weaned from parental dependence, acquires social interests, and becomes somewhat less suggestible to parental authority. He shows more dominant behavior and certain systematic trends in interests, fears, annoyances, etc.

9. Social interests become most evident in some sort of gang or play group, with marked horde characteristics. This grouping tends to separate boys and girls and gives marked scope for leader-follower relationships. The stereotype of the popular person in such a group changes with age, but in general favors "primitive" virtues.

10. Around ten or eleven the increasing vitality of the gang-and-school group begins to rival the ego-shaping power of the home. For some children there is the beginning of cleavage between home-approved and peer-approved personality, but most show transfer or easy alternation of attitudes from one to the other. The end of the period is complicated by adolescent interests appearing earlier in some individuals than others.

## QUESTIONS AND EXERCISES

1. Give some instances from human and animal gestation of modification of the organism's capacities for reaction while *in utero*.

2. Outline the psychoanalytic theories of oral and anal fixation and discuss the oral theories in relation to objective data on human and animal weaning.

3. Describe the development of perceptual and motor skills and of powers of emotional expression in the first year, with reference to maturation or learning and to the "spiral of development."

4. Indicate the general nature of the development curves from two to six years with respect severally to: length of sentence used in communication, curiosity, negativism, making social responses to other children, temper-tantrums, jealousy, and fears.

5. What seems to be the normal development of the trait of dominance and how are individual differences therein related to childhood experiences?

6. Describe the development of systematic personality differences between boys and girls between infancy and puberty and discuss their origin.

7. Set out four or more theories, alternative or commonly contributing, to account for the increase of "problem" behavior between four and six.

8. Describe the trends in play activities from one year to puberty, illustrate each of the three chief functions of play, and discuss the utility of play for the clinic.

9. Discuss the structure and activities of the preadolescent gang or clique and show the relation thereto of the personality pattern found most popular at various ages by the child's coevals.

10. Describe the development of personality and interests between eight and fourteen years of age and analyze the problems connected with transfer and conflict between home and school situations.

## BIBLIOGRAPHY

1. ACKERMAN, N. W.: Constructive and Destructive Tendencies in Children; an Experimental Study, *Amer. J. Orthopsychiat.*, 8: 265–285, 1938.

2. ANDERSON, H. H.: Domination and Social Integration in the Behavior of Kindergarten Children and Teachers, *Genet. Psychol. Monogr.*, 21: 287–385, 1939.

3. ANDERSON, J. E.: The Development of Social Behavior, *Amer. J. Sociol.*, 44: 839–857, 1939.

4. ARRINGTON, R. E.: Inter-relations in the Behavior of Young Children. *Child Develpm. Monogr.* (No. 8), 1932.

5. BALDWIN, A. L.: Differences in Parent Behavior Toward Three and Nine Year Old Children. *J. Person. Res.*, 15: 143–165, 1946.

6. BARKER, R. G., T. DEMBO, and K. LEWIN: Frustration and Regression: in Barker, R. G., J. S. Kounin, and H. F. Wright (editors), *Child Behavior and Development*, McGraw-Hill Book Company, Inc., New York, 1943.

7. BAYLEY, N.: Mental Growth During the First Three Years: in Barker, Kounin and Wright (editors), *Child Development and Behavior*, McGraw-Hill Book Company, Inc., New York, 1943.

8. BENAMIN, E.: The Period of Resistance in Early Childhood, its Significance for the Development of Problem Children, *Amer. J. Dis. Child*, 63: 1019–1079, 1942.

9. BRACKETT, C. W.: Laughing and Crying of Preschool Children, *Child Developm. Monogr.* (No. 14), 1934.

10. BRODBECK, A. J., and O. C. IRWIN: Speech Behaviour of Infants without Families, *Child Developm.* 17: 145–156, 1946.

11. BRIDGES, K. M. B.: *The Social and Emotional Development of the Pre-School Child*, Kegan Paul, Trench, Trubner & Co., London, 1931.

12. Buhler, C.: *The First Year of Life*, The John Day Company, New York, 1930.

13. Challman, R. C.: Factors Influencing Friendships among Pre-school Children, *Child Develpm.*, 3: 146–158, 1932.

13a. Cummings, J. D.: The Incidence of Emotional Symptoms in School Children: Part I, *Brit. J. educ. Psychol.*, 14: 151–161, 1944.

14. Cummings, J. D.: A Follow-up Study of Emotional Symptoms in School Children: Part II, *Brit. J. educ. Psychol.*, 16: 163–177, 1946.

15. Dawe, H. C.: An Analysis of Two Hundred Quarrels of Pre-school Children, *Child Develpm.*, 5: 139–157, 1934.

16. Dennis, W.: *The Hopi Child*, Appleton-Century-Crofts, Inc., New York, 1940.

17. Dennis, W.: The New Responses in Infants, *Child Develpm.*, 3: 362–363, 1932.

18. Dennis, W., and M. G. Dennis: Behavioral Development in the First Year, as Shown by Forty Biographies, *Psychol. Rec.*, 1: 349–361, 1939.

19. Dysinger, W. S., and C. A. Ruckmick: *The Emotional Responses of Children to the Motion Picture Situation*, The Macmillan Company, New York, 1933.

20. England, A. O.: Non-structural Approach to the Study of Children's Fears, *J. clin. Psychol.*, 2: 364–368, 1946.

21. Eng, H.: *Experimental Investigations into the Emotional Life of the Child Compared with that of the Adult*, Oxford University Press, New York, 1925.

21a. Escalona, S. K.: Disturbances of Feeding in Very Young Children. *Amer. J. Orthopsychiat*, 15: 76–80, 1945.

22. Fauquier, W.: The Attitudes of Aggressive and Submissive Boys towards Athletics, *Child Develpm.*, 11: 115–126, 1940.

23. Felder, J. G.: Some Factors Determining the Nature and Frequency of Anger and Fear Outbreaks in Pre-school Children, *J. juv. Res.*, 16: 278–290, 1932.

24. Fite, M. D.: Aggressive Behavior in Young Children and Children's Attitudes toward Aggression, *Genet. Psychol. Monogr.*, 22: 151–319, 1940.

25. Fitt, A. B.: Seasonal Influence on Functions and on the Limits of Development, Paper read before the 12th Int. Cong. of Psych., Edinburgh, 1948.

26. Freud, A., H. Hartmann, and E. Kris: The Psychoanalytic Study of the Child, *Psychoanal. Stud. Child.*, 1: 423, 1945.

27. Freud, S.: Three Contributions to the Theory of Sexuality; 1905 in *Basic Writings of S. Freud*, Modern Library, Inc., New York, 1938.

28. Gesell, A.: *Mental Growth of the Pre-School Child*, The Macmillan Company, New York, 1926.

29. Gesell, A., and H. Thompson: *Infant Behavior: Its Genesis and Growth*, McGraw-Hill Book Company, Inc., New York, 1934.

30. Gesell, A., and H. Thompson: Twins T and C from Infancy to Adolescence, *Genet. Psychol. Monogr.*, 24: 3–121, 1938.

31. Goodenough, F. L.: The Expression of the Emotions in Infancy, *Child Develpm.*, 2: 96–101, 1931.

32. Greenacre, P.: Infant Reactions to Restraint; Problems in the Fate of Infantile Aggression, *Amer. J. Orthopsychiat.*, 14: 204–218, 1944.

33. Guilford, J. P., and H. Martin: Age Differences and Sex Differences in Some Introvertive and Emotional Traits, *J. gen. Psychol.*, 31: 219–229, 1944.

34. Hagman, E. R.: The Companionship of Pre-school Children, *Univ. Ia. Stud. Child Welf.*, 7 (No. 4): 1–69, 1933.

35. Halverson, H. M.: Infant Feeding and Tensional Behavior, *J. genet. Psychol.*, 53: 365–430, 1938.

36. Hewitt, L. E., and R. L. Jenkins: *Fundamental Patterns of Maladjustment and the Dynamics of their Origin*, State of Illinois, Springfield, 1946.

37. HORTON, B. J.: The Truthfulness of Boys and Girls in Public and Private Schools, *J. abnorm. soc. Psychol.*, 31: 398–405, 1937.

38. HUNT, J. McV.: The Effect of Infantile Feeding Frustration upon Adult Hoarding in the Albino Rat, *J. abnorm. soc. Psychol.*, 36: 338–360, 1941.

39. HUGHES, W. L.: Sex Experiences of Boyhood, *J. Soc. Hygiene*, 12: 262–273, 1926.

40. HURLOCK, E. B.: Experimental Investigations of Children's Play, *Psychol. Bull.*, 31: 47–66, 1934.

41. ISAACS, S.: *Social Development in Young Children*, Harcourt, Brace & Company, Inc., New York, 1933.

42. JACK, L. M.: An Experimental Study of Ascendant Behavior in Pre-school Children, *Univ. Ia. Stud. Child Welf.*, 9: (No. 3) 17–65, 1934.

43. JACK, L. M.: Advice for the Measurement of Parent Attitudes and Practices, in Researches in Parent Education: I, *Univ. Ia. Stud. Child Welf.*, 6: (Part IV) 137–149, 1932.

44. JASPER, H. H.: The Measurement of Depression-Elation and Its Relation to a Measure of Extraversion-Introversion, *J. abnorm. soc. Psychol.*, 25: 307–318, 1930.

45. JERSILD, A. T.: Studies of Childrens' Fears, in Barker, R. G., J. S. Kounin, and H. F. Wright, (editors), *Child Behavior and Development*, McGraw-Hill Book Company, Inc., New York, 1943.

46. JONES, H. E.: Sex Differences in Physical Abilities, *Hum. Biol.*, 19: 12–25, 1947.

47. JONES, M. C., and B. S. BURKS: Development in Childhood, *Soc. Res. Child Develpm.*, 1: (No. 4) 1934.

48. KEISTER, M. E.: A Study of Children's Reactions to Failure and an Experimental Attempt to Modify Them, *Univ. Ia. Stud. Child Welf.* (No. 13), 1937.

49. KLEIN, M.: Psycho-analyses of Children, W. W. Norton & Company, New York, 1932.

50. KOCH, H. L.: Factor Analyses of Some Measures of the Behavior of Pre-school Children, *J. gen. Psychol.*, 27: 257–287, 1942.

51. LAZAR, M.: Reading Interests, Activities, and Opportunities of Bright, Average, and Dull Children, *Teach. Coll. Contr. Educ.* (No. 707), 1937.

52. LAING, A.: The Sense of Humour in Childhood and Adolescence, *Brit. J. educ. Psychol.*, 9: 201, 1939.

53. LEE, M. A. M.: A Study of Emotional Instability in Nursery School Children. *Child Develpm.*, 3: 142–148, 1932.

54. LEHMAN, H. C., and P. A. WITTY: A Study of Play in Relation to Intelligence, *J. appl. Psychol.*, 12: 369–398, 1928.

55. LEUBA, C.: An Experimental Study of Rivalry in Young Children, *J. comp. Psychol.*, 16: 367–378, 1933.

56. LEVY, D. M.: Experiments on the Sucking Reflex and Social Behavior in Dogs, *Amer. J. Orthopsychiat.*, 4: 203–224, 1934.

57. LINDQUIST, N.: Some Notes on the Development of Memory during the First Years of Life, *Acta paediatr., Stockh.*, 32: 592–598, 1945.

58. LORGE, I.: The Efficacy of Intensified Reward and Interpunishment, *J. exp. Psychol.*, 16: 177–207, 1933.

59. MACFARLANE, J. W.: Study of Personality Development, in Barker, R. G., J. S. Kounin, and H. F. Wright, (editors), *Child Behavior and Development*, McGraw-Hill Book Company, Inc., New York, 1943.

60. McCARTHY, D.: *Language Development of the Pre-school Child*, *Univ. Minn. Instit. Child. Welf. Monogr. No. 4*, University of Minnesota Press, Minneapolis, 1930.

61. McKINNON, K. M.: *Consistency and Change in Behavior Manifestations*, Columbia University Press, New York, 1942.

62. McLaughlin, M. A.: The Genesis and Constancy of Ascendance and Submission as Personality Traits, *Univ. Ia. Stud. Educ.*, 6: (No. 5) 95, 1931.
63. Melbo, I. R.: A Review of the Literature on Children's Interests, *Yearb. Calif. elem. School Prin. Ass.*, 12: 6–22.
64. Menaker, W.: Neugier im 1 und 2 Lebensjahr, *Z. Psychol.*, 137: 131–167, 1936.
65. Murphy, G., L. B. Murphy, and T. M. Newcomb: *Experimental Social Psychology*, Harper & Brothers, New York, 1937.
66. Nemoitus, B. O.: Relations between Interest and Achievement, *J. appl. Psychol.*, 16: 59–73, 1932.
67. Page, M. L.: The Modification of Ascendant Behavior in Pre-school Children, *Univ. Ia. Stud. Child Welf.*, 12: (No. 3) 1936.
68. Piaget, J.: *The Moral Development of the Child*, Harcourt, Brace and Company, Inc., New York, 1932.
69. Rank, O.: *The Trauma of Birth*, Harcourt, Brace and Company, Inc., New York, 1929.
70. Reynolds, M. M.: Negativism of Pre-school Children, *Teach. Coll. Contr. Educ.* (No. 288), 1928.
71. Ribble, M. A.: Infantile Experience in Relation to Personality, in J. McV. Hunt, (editor), *Personality and the Behavior Disorders*, The Ronald Press Company, New York, 1943.
72. Ross, B. M.: Some Traits Associated with Sibling Jealousy, *Smith Coll. Contrib. Soc. Stud.*, 1: 364–376, 1931.
73. Sanford, R. N., and others: Physique, Personality, and Scholarship, *Monogr. Soc. Res. Child Develpm.*, Vol. 8, No. 34, National Research Council, Washington, D.C., 1943.
74. Shirley, M.: A Behavior Syndrome Characterizing Prematurely Born Children. *Child Develpm.*, 10: 115–128, 1939.
75. Spitz, R. A.: The Smiling Response: a Contribution to the Ontogenesis of Social Relations, *Genet. Psychol. Monogr.*, 34: 57–125, 1946.
76. Stoddard, G. D., and B. L. Wellman: *Child Psychology*, The Macmillan Company, New York, 1934.
77. Thompson, G. G.: The Social and Emotional Development of Pre-school Children under Two Types of Educational Programs, *Psychol. Monogr.* 56: (No. 5) 1944.
78. Thompson, G. G., and M. O. Kepler: A Study of the Production of Pleasant and Unpleasant Items as Related to Adolescent Development, *J. educ. Psychol.*, 36: 535–542, 1945.
79. Tuddenham, R. D.: Belonging in a Group, *Educ. Leadership*, 1: 201–205, 1944.
80. Van Alstyne, D., and L. A. Hattwick: A Follow-up Study of the Behavior of Nursery School Children, *Child Develpm.*, 4: 1, 1934.
81. Wang, C. K. A.: Personality Traits and Early History, *Amer. J. Psychol.*, 44: 768–774, 1932.
82. Wellman, B. L., H. M. Skeels, and M. Skodak: Review of McNemar's Critical Examination of Iowa Studies, *Psychol. Bull.*, 37: 93–111, 1940.
83. Werner, H.: *The Comparative Psychology of Mental Development*, Harper & Brothers, New York, 1940.
84. Wile, I. S., and R. Davis: Relation of Birth to Behavior, *Amer. J. Orthopsychiat.*, 11: 320–335, 1941.
85. Witty, P. A., and H. C. Lehman: One More Study of Performance of Interest, *J. educ. Psychol.*, 22: 481–492, 1931.
86. Wolff, W.: *The Personality of the Pre-School Child*, Grune & Stratton, New York, 1946.
87. Woodrow, H., and F. Sowell: Children's Association Frequency Tables, *Psychol. Monogr.*, 22: 97, 1916.

88. WRIGHT, M. E.: The Influence of Frustration upon the Social Relations of Young Children, *Character & Pers.*, 12: 111–122, 1943.

89. WRIGHT, B. A.: Altruism in Children and the Perceived Conduct of Others, *J. abnorm. soc. Psychol.*, 37: 218–233, 1942.

90. WRIGHT, B. A.: The Development of the Ideology of Altruism and Fairness in Children, *Psychol. Bull.*, 39: 485–486, 1942.

91. ZELIGS, R.: Social Factors Annoying to Children, *J. appl. Psychol.*, 29: 75–82, 1945.

92. ZILLIG, M.: Prallereien unter Schulkindern. *Z. pädag. Psychol.*, 39: 241–220; 263–270, 1938.

93. ZUCKER, H.: The Emotional Attachment of Children to Their Parents as Related to Standards of Behavior and Delinquency, *J. Psychol.*, 15: 31–40, 1943.

# CHAPTER 20

LIFE STAGES IN PERSONALITY:
II. ADOLESCENCE, MATURITY, OLD AGE

## 1. GENERAL CONSIDERATIONS ON ADOLESCENCE

**Physical and Mental Growth Spurts.** Literature has always abounded in descriptions of the strivings and psychological problems of adolescence. Among the most sympathetic accounts one may mention *The Sorrows of Werther*, the more or less autobiographical work of Goethe, who insisted that adolescence is essentially a period of "Sturm und Drang." But the first adequately experimental, objective, and documented description of the period is found in the monumental work of G. Stanley Hall (22) which is still a valuable source book of data and contains theories still worthy of further experimental investigation.

Hall presents physical- and mental-growth curves, now known with greater accuracy through the work of H. E. Jones (28), Bayley (3), Henry (25), Shock (60), and others, which show that at about the age of thirteen or fourteen years the continuous course of physical and mental growth existing through childhood manifests a more or less abrupt change. Physically there is a spurt in growth, notably, in boys, of the muscular system, which develops more rapidly between sixteen and nineteen than at any other age. At the same time there is, along with the development of secondary sex characteristics (*e.g.*, distribution of hair, change in distribution of fat deposits), a change in the proportions of various bodily organs. A recent contribution to more exact understanding of these different time schedules and the resulting changes in somatotype has been made by Bayley and Tuddenham (3). With this change comes a greater liability to certain physical disorders, in contrast to the low rate of the preceding period of "mature," settled childhood (though in general still at lower rates than later life). Digestive disturbances, tuberculosis, chlorosis, cardiac troubles, and many others take a distinct upward turn, as if caused by the increased difficulties of achieving physiological harmony and efficiency during the reorganization of the physical organism.

Mentally the outstanding characteristics are an increase of emotional instability and a tendency to social awkwardness, along with the growth of sex interests and of wider social and altruistic feelings. The psychologists of Hall's time noted also a growth in general intellectual interests, a sensitization to poetry and love of nature, and the beginnings of genuine religious sentiments. The desire for self-expression and for real status in an adult calling is keenly felt. Many have noted that the capacity for artistic or literary expression that appears at this time often remains restricted to the adolescent period itself and the psychiatrist Möbius has expressed the observation more brutally by saying that "in most people after adolescence a certain degree of mental defect supervenes."

**Source of Increased Mental Conflict.** It was noted early that the emotional instability of adolescence is largely connected with a subjective sense of mental conflict, particularly connected with guilt over sex matters and with uncertainty over ego status. The principal sources of conflict arising specifically for the adolescent are (a) the task of gaining independence from the parents; (b) the task of gaining status in an occupation, preparing for that occupation, and achieving economic self-support; (c) achieving satisfactory sex expression by winning a mate; (d) achieving a stable, integrated personality and a satisfactory self-concept. It may be objected that the last has existed throughout childhood, but one must remember that in the adult world it is all to do again, because of the new desires and new standards that have to be integrated. Among the troublesome new standards are the specifically differentiated standards of "manliness" and "womanliness," for which the biological differentiation does not proceed to complete adequacy in all cases.

Among the constantly recurring debates on adolescence is that as to whether the onset of more acute conflict at this age is primarily due to biological changes within the organism or to especially difficult educational hurdles within the culture pattern. The answer is, as with heredity and environment, that both influences are at work and our problem reduces to giving the proper allowance to each. Anthropologists have, in general, stressed the especial difficulties created at this age by the culture pattern of Western industrial civilization and Christianity. It is pointed out, for example, that in Samoa (43), the Trobiand Islands, and other primitive cultures which either permit very early marriage or encourage premarital sexual intercourse, the "typical adolescent" tendency to mental conflicts, to seclusiveness, to exaggerated emotional expression, and to rebellion against the parents is not noticeable. Among the Arunta, the Andamanese, and other societies where a definite initiation ceremony, along with the adoption of a new name, makes a clear transition for the individual from childhood to adult life, the social clumsiness, shyness, and vacillating ego valuation, characteristic of the adolescent in Western culture, are not seen.

It has been pointed out earlier (Chapters 14 and 15) that the very complexity of our culture, from which the youth is guarded in childhood—only to experience the full, bewildering burden at adolescence—is itself, apart from any massive emotional frustrations, a provocation to revolt and to mental breakdown. Primitive cultures generally indicate the prescribed ways of behavior with very clear signposts, and even though to the intellectually curious Westerner those ways frequently appear illogical, they are simple enough to those who do not question them. The Kwoma adolescent (74), for example, achieves full adult rights as to marriage and property, but still pays the same ritual deference to specific relatives, namely, his parents and the paternal aunts and uncles, as when he was a child. By contrast, our own culture leaves a great deal unspecified in terms of any precise rule of behavior. It gives general directives—in fact, a host of abstract values and generalities on behavior, that are seldom explicitly taught—and leaves the individual to decide the line of action in any particular situation. This makes the adolescent uncertain of himself, increases the possibilities of social clumsiness, and adds to the stresses of entering the adult world.

Not enough is known about social psychology to determine whether it would be possible or desirable to lessen the strains of adolescence by changes in the culture pattern itself—notably by reductions in the amount of suppression and long-circuiting required in drives or even by reductions in social complexity. But at least we can say with some certainty that the greater part of the maladjustment of adolescence is due to the cultural demands. That this is so can be seen from the historical changes occurring in the adolescent behavior pattern with even the slight changes in culture pattern that have taken place during the last two generations. For example, Hall's studies reported frequently severe or paroxysmal guilt feelings with ensuing public or private religious conversions; but such prominence of religious conversion behavior is rare in present surveys of adolescents.

**Some Relationships of Biological and Cultural Readjustment Demands.** In general, as the following section will show, the greater part of the biological change in adolescence occurs in the first half, say, from thirteen to eighteen years of age, whereas the demands of adjustment to the culture pattern come a little later and extend well into the second half of adolescence, say, from eighteen to twenty-four years. For the genius who penetrates further into the culture pattern or the emotionally defective who can never stably assimilate it, some adolescent lability of the kind created by adjustment to culture may extend much beyond this age period. The phenomena of adolescence are likely to vary a good deal with the degree of coincidence of these two demands, and it may be that the apparently slightly less stressful nature of present-day, compared with late nineteenth-century, adolescence is due not only to more explicit and perhaps less suppressive sex teaching, but also to the prolongation of the educational period, which somewhat postpones the full stresses of adult responsibility so that they coincide less acutely with the biological adjustments.

## 2. EARLY ADOLESCENCE AND BIOLOGICAL READJUSTMENT

**Detailed Picture of Physical Changes.** With the assistance of the above general introduction it will now be possible to assimilate more detailed and recent findings, both as they extend the above framework and as they indicate new hypotheses and generalizations. The period from thirteen to eighteen years is most remarkable for its biological changes, though, as the previous chapter shows, the blood concentration of the sex hormones which in part induces these changes has already begun its upward course about three years before puberty.

Physical changes at puberty have recently been more accurately mapped by Jones (28,29), Shock (60), and others. As already indicated by Hall's study, static dynamometric strength is found to increase rapidly, both in boys and girls but especially boys, between eleven and fifteen years. Jones found that this increase was more closely correlated with measures of physiological maturation (which occurs in different individuals at different times) than with age alone. The changes in blood composition concern not only the hormone concentration, but also such indices of protein metabolism as the creatine-creatinine ratio (60). The decline in basal metabolic rate and pulse rate that has been going on through childhood continues, with a rather sharp dip in oxygen consumption at the menarche for girls. (Between eleven and eighteen years the fall is from 150 to 140 for boys and 140 to 114 for girls (60).) But the slight decline of blood pressure changes to a sharp upward curve for both systolic and diastolic pressures, more marked for boys and for diastolic pressure, before taking on that level which is maintained through early maturity.

Jones observes (28) that the various measures of physical and physiological adolescence are closely correlated, though they begin at different ages and proceed at diverse rates in different children. He also found that the puberal growth spurt occurred more strongly in the spring, so that, in girls for example, three-quarters of the total annual growth in height, skeletal maturation, and dynamometer pull took place through March, April, and May. The hormone changes in adolescence are a complex chorus of pituitary, adrenal, and gonadal contributions, the skeletal growth being stimulated by the early anterior pituitary action and arrested later by the full action of gonadal hormone. Although the average curve of hormone increase is a steady one, as shown by the following diagram from Sanford's study of

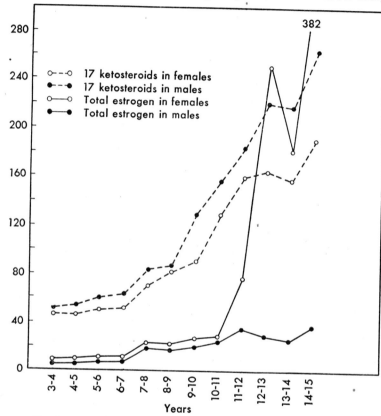

DIAGRAM 50. Increase of male and female sex hormone in the blood with age. (*From athanson, J. T., Towne, L., and Aub, J. C., in Physique, Personality and Scholarship. at. Res. Council, Washington, D.C., 1943. By kind permission of R. N. Sanford and the thors.*)

rty-five children, the individual curves of physiological and anatomical ange are relatively sudden.

The total picture is one of increasing physical capacity, but with some cline of the constant bodily activity level, especially in girls. Incidentally, e increase of pulse rate through a standard exercise situation declines in olescence (60).

**Psychological Reactions to Physical Changes.** The above changes are ch as to give the individual increased confidence with respect to his ability to cope with the physical world, with adults, and with children in his former status, but they may occasion embarrassments with respect to his peers. Indeed, self-consciousness, pleasant or unpleasant, over physique is a prominent feature of early adolescence. As Stolz (63) has shown in some detail by case studies, variations in bodily proportions and size, as well as variations from the conventionally accepted picture of secondary sex characteristics, are especially likely to become the focus of emotional disturbances at adolescence. Bayley and Tuddenham (3), measuring the emotional stability and adjustment of adolescents divided into four groups according to level of physical development, found the poorest adjustment in the two groups comprised by those very advanced in physique and those very underdeveloped, *i.e.*, those departing from the norm. Adlerian literature is full of instances of an inferiority pattern of behavior being precipitated at adolescence by some real or imagined blemish, and, as H. E. Jones shows (28), since physical strength and other physical advantages tend to correlate a good deal, the possibility of compensatory performance in this whole area is generally ruled out.

Psychological reactions to physical development at adolescence take place not only in regard to disadvantages or eccentricities, with the resulting changes in self-evaluation and in the extent of social participation, but also to other aspects of physique. Girls sometimes show guilt or embarrassment over secondary sex characteristics, hastening them into social and sexual roles for which they are not ready, while disgust and fear are not entirely unknown reactions to the onset of physical sex manifestations. Nevertheless, preoccupation with clinical material must not blind us to the fact that for the normal majority the increase of physical size and presence is an occasion for pride, increased confidence, and even narcism, while the secondary sex characteristics are exploited with pleasure.

### 3. EARLY ADOLESCENCE: ERGIC CHANGES

**Measured Changes of Interests.** The direct effects of the physiological changes at puberty, through changes in temperament and ergic balance (basic disposition), have already been described as an accession of sex interest, an increase in intellectual and emotional sensitivity, an increased self assertion and exhibitionism—but also increased sensitiveness of variation between assertion and submission, and an increase in that altruistic, responsible interest in society which probably springs from the parental, protective erg. These changes have not yet been adequately explored by measurement; but Stone and Barker (64) have shown with the Pressey and Sullivan interest tests that among girl adolescents of the same age the maturity pattern is significantly higher in those who have already menstruated, which may be initial evidence of an objective kind that this aspect of the growth of interests is more physiologically than socially determined.

The post-puberal girls scored higher on heterosexual activities and interests, on interests in physical appearance and adornment, and on worries over relatives, over themselves, and over conflicts in family life. They showed more daydreaming and a tendency to avoid physical exertion. Lund (42) found the number of girls asking to be excused from gymn (in a sample of 8,200 boys and girls) to increase 400 per cent between the seventh and the twelfth grades! Except with regard to athletic interests, the change for boys is not conspicuously different; for Sollenberger (59) found more interest in personal adornment, in the opposite sex, and (in a majority, but by no means in all) in strenuous and competitive sports. In physical activities of all kinds, however, boys also tend to show a decline, though less marked than for girls. Boys revealed more rapidly increased sex interest at least as shown directly in incidence of masturbation and erotic dreams.

These measures of adolescent change in interest stand in need of being repeated with more objective-test methods, with metric systems that permit comparisons of different fields, and with categories of universal application. The last of these improvements calls for analysis of the test measurements with respect to relative strengths of widely important sentiments, *e.g.*, to family, religion, sex object, career, and also into strengths of primary ergs. No such reliable analyses exist, but there are unanalyzed results available for methods more valid than self-report. The present writer used the method of exposing pictures and verbal material, recording the *amount remembered* with respect to each of fourteen categories of interests (see (5), Chap. 7). This checked well with the results of presenting book titles covering the same fields and asking children to choose which they would like to read. The data for 2,000 children, analyzed (on meaning, not on factor loadings of items) for sentiment objects is presented in the following diagrams. An analysis of the same data in terms of ergic strengths has been presented in Chapter 7, page 192.

It is interesting to observe that the rise in sex interests, as well as of other interests known to be strong in adolescence (*e.g.*, religion), begins before puberty and, in fact, coincides to a marked degree with the curves of hormone growth shown above.

**Clinical Views of Interest Changes.** What psychology lacks in the way of precise measurement studies on change of ergs and of ergic components as well as on temperamental dimensions during early adolescence, must at present be made up by less accurately demonstrable clinical observations. The outstanding clinical observation is that of the reactivation of the libido after the latent period which has prevailed since infancy, *i.e.*, of the first appearance of sex interest in the form of a drive. It is observed that this is accom-

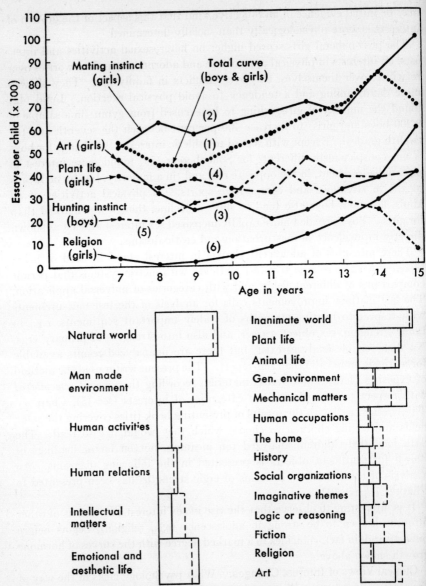

DIAGRAM 51. Curves and profiles of interest differences for sex and age. The uppe[r] diagram is an analysis of interests as shown in a large number of freely chosen essay sub[-]jects. The lower is based on the same and also on choices of books to read, among 2,00[0] boys and girls. (Latter shown by dotted line. See (8a).)

panied by more or less brief activities of the polymorphous perverse phases of sexual interest (Chap. 9). Thus, a transitory homosexual interest at puberty is not uncommon, while narcistic components and autoerotic interests are normally interwoven with adolescent life. How far these will become fixated and how they will be given expression within the structure of the personality depend both on infantile experiences and upon the impact of the adult cultural demands now and in later adolescence. The study of Landis and coworkers (38) on 153 normal and 142 psychotic women, concerning sex development in adolescence, presents reliable data here. They found, in accordance with our graphs obtained by other methods, that sexual interests, physical and intellectual, began to rise before puberty. Unusual experiences, such as overprotection or early insecurity in the family, or being subject to sex aggressions, were associated with abnormal adult attitudes to sex, deficient attachments to men, and poor adjustment in marriage. These occurrences were also more frequent in the background of the psychotic than the nonpsychotic. Emotional attachments to other women and masturbation were frequent and normal in the adolescent process. A great deal of the aesthetic, religious, and other dawning intellectual and cultural interests of adolescence are clearly seen in individual clinical cases to be sublimated attachments of this unchanneled, polymorphous sexual libido.

The observation commonly made in sex-hormone experiments with animals —that dominant and aggressive behavior is induced at the same time as sexual activity—is paralleled by observations at the clinical level. Aggressive and algolagnic (sadistic, masochistic) actions and phantasies reappear at the same time as the sexual interests, though, of course, a considerable degree of aggression has also existed from other roots through childhood. The greater self-assertion of the early adolescent, and his relative freedom from fears and worries (see below) is thus not wholly to be accounted for by his or her awareness of increased physical powers and capabilities, but constitutes the second of the principal changes in ergic strength and nature resulting directly from the somatic transformations. Some analysts, *e.g.*, Anna Freud, have extended this to the generalization that all id drives are augmented at puberty, but this is a matter of definition and experiment.

## 4. LATE ADOLESCENCE AND PERSONALITY CHANGE

**Measured Changes of Interest.** As indicated above, the emphasis in late adolescence is on cultural readjustment, to take on the status of adult responsibilities and opportunities expected by the culture, but the biological readjustment continues, while the beginnings of the cultural readjustment must in turn be traced to early adolescence. It is our purpose here to examine data on change in interests, stability, internal stresses, etc., leaving to the following section examination of the causes or associations of these changes in the external, social world.

The changes of interest recorded in late adolescence are less of a spontaneous outburst of sexual and sex-sublimated interests as in early adolescence and more a part of the shaping of old and new drives to fit the cultural role of the individual. In general, the fluidity occasioned by the biological irruption of new interests and values has subsided somewhat and a greater degree of stability is evident. Taylor (69), for example, using the Strong Interest Blank, found over four years of the mid-adolescent period, a test-retest reliability of 0.85, decreasing markedly with lapse of one, two, and three years, but showing significantly greater stability for intervals in later than in earlier adolescence. Indeed, as both Burt and Thorndike have reported in earlier studies among fourteen-year-old boys, some 50 per cent change their notion of the preferred career within one year.

Pressey, Janney, and Kuhlen (52) summarize their own and other studies covering interest change through late adolescence, as a decline, for both boys and girls, extending from ten through twenty years of age, in physical-activity interests (such as bicycling and roller skating), and a steady increase in interest in dancing and social affairs. James and Moore (27) studied 535 working-class adolescents (twelve to twenty-one years) by the objective approach of keeping diaries, though the evidence covers only leisure activities. They found that leisure increased somewhat with age (between schooling days and family responsibility) and particularly the amount of time devoted to talking, social activities, and dancing. Change of recreational forms occurred relatively abruptly, with the joining of clubs for older adolescents. They found that after mid-adolescence (sixteen to seventeen years) leisure activities were increasingly heterosexual and social, contrasting with the solitary reading and radio listening, or like-sex club or gang activities of early adolescence. There is no comparable data to show how much some of these trends are due to class or national culture pattern. An attempt to view late adolescent interests in terms of a number of primary foci has been made by Whiteside (73), but until interest and attitude measurement is more advanced the relative valencies of different objects is difficult to assess.

The view that religious interest in one form or another normally rises in adolescence has been questioned by Dimock (15), who obtained questionnaire-type data for 200 boys and found, indeed, a rise, but no adolescent spurt and no correspondence to physical-growth changes. He argued, therefore, that the results observed by others are socially rather than biologically conditioned and obtainable only in certain sociological climates. Obviously, the social material has to exist for the biological forces to operate.

**Problems and Conflicts.** Symonds's (68) study included problems as well as interests and found the adolescent men's interest primarily related to an urge toward success, whereas women (even at college) indicated greater passiveness, receptivity, and interest in people. Men were higher in the categories of health interest, money interest, and safety, with a more openly expressed interest in sex. Women scored higher in interests in personal attractiveness, personal philosophy, planning of the daily schedule, mental health, manners, personal qualities, and home and family relationships. The greater interest of the men in health and safety is strange unless we consider that for the more active, adventurous male the attainment of all else depends more upon the retention of intact personal powers.

Conrad and Jones found, as others have found with tests restricted to narrow fields, *e.g.*, vocational choice, very little systematic trend through adolescence in the matter of annoyances (though worries alter). They found, however, some marked adolescent sex differences, notably in girls' greater "annoyance at untidiness." The number of reported fears and worries, as the summary of Pressey (52) and the study of Cummings (see (14), Chap. 19) shows, declines rather rapidly in proceeding from infancy to childhood and, in spite of the inner tensions of adolescence, goes on declining somewhat through early adolescence. However, from mid-adolescence onwards, the increasing self-confidence occasioned by the physiological changes is met by the impact of adult responsibilities and worries, and, as far as the scrappy data can be interpreted, they point to an increase in things worried about, continuing at least into the latest adolescent ages.

**The Self-concept and Masculinity-Femininity Stereotypes.** Symonds's study bears also on the changing self-concept for boys and girls that occurs at adolescence. He found greater differences in interests and values than in problems and difficulties encountered; but his results show that both in interests and problems men differ from women more in late adolescence than at any other period of life. This finding of greatest disparity of masculine and feminine stereotypes in adolescence is in accord with the mean trend in Terman's indices of masculinity and femininity, which also show, however, that adolescents of both sexes are more masculine than at other ages and that the convergence in maturity is due to men becoming more "feminine" in interest pattern. C. M. Tryon (72), however, found that with respect to the peer culture, *i.e.*, the evaluations and standards of the adolescent club or gang, the change of prestige criteria patterns through adolescence makes greater demands on adjustment among girls than among boys. This may be because girls have been more family-dependent previously or because masculine standards tend to dominate the adolescent group. Tryon observes in this connection that tomboyish, dominant, hearty girls are accepted into boys' groups at this time much more readily than others, and that boys, to be successful with girls, must be admired by boys. Kitay (32) similarly found that girls at adolescence tend to shape their ego concepts and standards on the values of men, even if the latter are not favorable in terms of the preadolescent values taught to girls. (She notes, for example, the declining value given to "capricious" behavior.)

**Moral Values.** Among the most striking and important, but by no means the most investigated, aspect of adolescent change, especially as it affects the ego, is that concerned with moral values. Apparently, the *number* of actions considered wrong or sinful shows a decline from about the age of five on through adolescence. Buck's research (7) shows that children of twelve or thirteen consider about 50 per cent more things to be wrong, *e.g.*, borrowing, staying out late, smoking, flirting, than do college students of twenty or so. Perhaps this reflects partly an expansion of "rights" in adolescence, or the practice of parents of holding liberties in reserve until the child grows older. It seems unlikely, in view of the increase of suicide at adolescence, that this represents any decline in *strength* of superego activity; indeed, there is every indication clinically that the sense of guilt—when it does operate— takes on new depth at adolescence. Parenthetically, the psychologist must be prepared in making age comparisons in this generation to allow for a strong secular trend, for Pressey (52) has shown that in the ten years from 1923 to 1933 students of college age showed a drop of about one-fifth in the number and variety of things considered morally undesirable.

Although in this respect, *i.e.*, in degree of deference to outside moral authority, the adolescent may seem to show a stronger ego, the superego does not in fact lose any power; for it is now for the first time almost wholly internalized and, as psychoanalysts view dynamics, (16) it gains resources from the investment of the increased narcism of this period in the superego structure. The adolescent has a deeper and more sensitive pride in himself, a pride which makes infringements of an accepted moral code more difficult. It is in accordance with this more detached and exacting life of the superego that the aggressions of frustration are typically turned, via the superego, upon the self. This is witnessed by the sharp rise in suicide rate, by the melancholy spells of a characteristic adolescent nature, and by the phenomenon observed by Hall and others since, of adolescent asceticism shown by withdrawal, usually in mid-adolescence, from feminine contacts after a preliminary period of sex interest.

The difficulty in representing adolescent personality changes by precise transition curves resides in the fact that the numerous measurements that have accumulated are not yet subtle enough in conception, as shown by their frequent contradictoriness, and by the absence of the correlative socio logical data without which they cannot make sense. For example, the con clusions of various investigations are almost equally divided as to whether the adolescent becomes more introverted or more extraverted. This par ticular difficulty arises from using a confused and obsolete trait concept—

extraversion-introversion—instead of measurements of pure *source traits*. However, other contradictions in personality findings spring from more interesting causes and are to be explained either by trends being different in different culture patterns, periods, and classes, or by the fact that the most striking change in adolescence is a trend to greater standard deviation, rather than a trend in the mean itself, which presents the experimenter with pseudo trends in particular samples. Almost every variety of increased personality deviation arises in the adolescent's trial-and-error exploration of the new world of adjustments possible to him. Gruen (21), for example, has shown the tendency of maladjusted adolescents, on level-of-aspiration tests, to keep the level either abnormally high or abnormally low, with respect to actual powers.

**Discussion and Interpretation of Facts on Personality Trends.** On the whole, the outstanding trend is probably to increased emotional instability ($C$ factor), an increase in dominance ($E$ factor), and an increased interpersonal and intrapersonal variation in cyclothymia-schizothymia ($A,$) and surgency-desurgency ($F,$) factors. The difficulties and dismays of adolescents undoubtedly cause much surgency-desurgency oscillation, with descents to melancholy seclusiveness at one time and ascents to high-spirited sociability and playful fashions and fads at others. Some individuals may become even *more* absorbed in cyclothyme satisfactions in social group life, whereas perhaps most individuals shift towards schizoid adjustments with increased phantasy life, depending on the culture.

The increased instability, arising from greater problems of id frustration as well as from uncertainties over the form of the ego and self-regarding sentiment, is witnessed both by tests and by the sharp increase through early adolescence in crime rates, suicide, hysterical split personality, and neurotic traits (including psychosomatic disturbances). But, as Landis and Page point out (37), the popular view that insanity, especially schizophrenia, shows a high incidence (as distinct from a sharp acceleration) in this period is wrong, for first admissions between ten and nineteen are lower than any succeeding decade. The symptoms of mental conflict, however, both arise and subside much more slowly than their external causes, and it is probably correct, as Blanchard argues (5), to assume that a considerable number of later mental disorders have their origin in the stresses of adolescence.

Out of this period of conflict and experiment normally arises a new ego and a new superego. The ego has incorporated the new sexual and parental drives from the id and has developed skills for assertion, defense and social participation suitable for an adult. The superego has experienced some refashioning on admired characters and on friends of the peer culture, while in general linking itself with religion or some philosophy of life worked out in this period of intellectual activity. Although it is a period of difficulty and emotional instability, it is less subject to breakdown than later periods of the same kind, by reason of the adolescent's self-assertiveness, resilient optimism and youthful energy. Crook (12), for example, readministered a neurotic inventory to girls in adolescence, asking them, as they surveyed the matters to be rated, whether their personalities had improved or deteriorated during the year. Less than half thought their stability, etc., about the same: 5 per cent reported a decline, and 49 per cent considered their personalities had improved.

## 5. LATE ADOLESCENCE AND CULTURAL READJUSTMENT

**Adolescence and the Dynamics of "the Growing-up Gradient."** The end of adolescence involves for the normal person attaining a position of substantial acceptance of and adjustment to the culture pattern, its responsibilities, and its privileges. It is helpful to consider at least this last step in adolescent growth in the light of the concept of "the growing-up gradient" expounded in detail elsewhere (see (12), Chap. 14). Since growing up involves the acceptance of many irksome inhibitions, standards of attainment, and responsible duties, the rewards of growing up—its privileges— have to be so spaced by social conventions that they are adequate to make the individual go as far as is required and to face the difficulties at each step. This series of rewards, graded toward a goal, constitutes the growing-up gradient.

It requires little inspection to see that the rewards of the later growing up gradient are mainly ego satisfactions. The individual educates himself for a higher job not because he might starve if he did not (for generally he could find quite an agreeable casual employment) but because his prestige among friends and relatives and his self-assertive satisfactions require it. It may be true that the achievement of recognized adult status brings other, *e.g.* sexual, satisfactions too, but these are less important. Indeed, examination of Kinsey's data leaves some doubt as to whether, in modern American society, sex drive is being utilized at all in the interests of attainment of higher cultural performance by the individual. For, in the first place, sexual experience is allowed to be prevalent before the end of adolescence, second, it is greater in lower than in higher social-status groups, and third, as Kinsey clearly shows, the adolescents who rise from lower to higher status have a more sex-restrictive pattern than those who do not.[1] Clearly the last rungs

[1] Status may *appear* to the young as a symbol (cue) to wider satisfactions than purely ego rewards, but, as indicated, this is scarcely true. Thus Kinsey (see (26), Chap. 12)—"It is interesting to find that those males who do get into class 7 out of parental homes which rated 4 or 5, have class 7 patterns early in their teens. Indeed, the class 4 males who ultimately arrive at class 7 have the most restrained socio-sexual histories in this whole group, and depend upon masturbation more exclusively than the class 6 males who are derived from any other parental background. It is as though the bigger the move which the boy makes

of the ladder of growing up—those which lead to the higher standards of performance in the culture pattern—are scaled very little under the motivation of the sex drive and mainly through the dynamics of the self-sentiment and the satisfactions of the self-assertive and gregarious drives which principally operate therein.

The especial difficulty of the adolescent in satisfying his self-regard and building a stable self-concept as object of his self-sentiment is, as implied earlier, that he attempts to do so simultaneously with respect to four different worlds—his family, the adult world, his adolescent peers, and the fourth world of inner conditionings—the childhood superego—referred to in the past section.     The society of peers, the club, playgroup, or gang has been studied in Chapter 15.     It is typically a phenomenon of early adolescence and extends into late adolescence only in so far as the gang begins to lose its separation from adult society, except where there is especial need for regressive or antisocial activity.     Tryon (72) observes that girls start forming cliques a little earlier than boys (perhaps in accordance with earlier onset of physical changes) and that they begin organizing boys as "escorts" before the latter are really ready or interested.

**Conflicts in the Late Adolescent Self-sentiment.**     Studies of the "peer culture" of the normal healthy adolescent, such as that of M. C. Jones (30) and Tryon (72), reveal its strong tendency to dissociate itself defensively from adult culture by slang, catchwords, and the idiomatic speech of an in-group, by secrets and secret loyalties, by its provision of means for discharge of adolescent high spirits and tensions (ecstatic expressions, exaggeratedly noisy or dangerous activities) and by its tendency to build up hierarchies of personal valuation—even of moral valuation—different from those of adults.     In particular, it gives prestige to athletic prowess and a certain degree of revolt against the adult culture pattern.     Although the development of true individuality is a characteristic of late adolescence, with its inner conflicts, introspectiveness, and superego development, the effect of the early adolescent cliques, with their many characteristics of the gang and of late childhood, is to suppress individuality.     Anthropologists have compared the unwillingness to show individuality in these early adolescent groups to the solidarity of various primitive peoples.     The obliviousness of adolescent "smart sets" to the values of any group outside themselves is also similar to the absolute ethnocentrism of primitives.

---

between his parental class and the class toward which he aims, the more strict he is about lining up his sexual history with the pattern of the group into which he is going.   If this were done consciously, it would be more understandable; but considering that the boy in actuality knows very little about the sexual behaviour of the social group into which he is moving, it is all the more remarkable to find that these patterns are laid down at such an early age."

The adult culture pattern is, of course, represented partly by and through the parents, and the revolt against it, which occurs to some extent in all adolescents, is therefore expressed partly, and sometimes wholly, by hostility or negativism directed to the parents.

It is a promising psychological generalization that negativism occurs, as a persistent and pervasive trait, where the cultural pressure is greatest upon the individual. According to this theory it should occur in infancy, because the child is forced, almost inevitably, to take the greatest steps then; at adolescence, and perhaps again in old age. The negativism of adolescence has been discussed in connection with schizophrenia (Chapter 18) and has been studied in some detail by Bühler (8). It has frequently been suggested that the clumsiness of the adolescent is in part a motivated behavior aimed at breaking away from the values of politeness and tidiness approved in childhood by the parent, because it is realized that the world of manhood requires more than this complaisance. Similarly, to succeed as a woman, the girl needs other values besides those of childish goodness, and must, at least temporarily, repudiate the latter. Kitay (32) points out that the circulation of a questionnaire among 11 to-14-year-old children on the issue of how much their parents "understand" them brings a great majority of favorable replies, whereas from fifteen years onward favorable answers are much less frequent. Adolescents feel misunderstood and tend to stress that they belong to a different generation, with different standards.

Conflict with parents is often severe because the adolescent's attitude is ambivalent. Consciously he may love the parent but wish to gain independence. Unconsciously he may both hate the parent and fear to leave his protection. As usual, the pain of the inner conflict may be blamed upon the object of the hesitant, unresolved, ambivalent attitude. There is frequently reactivation of Oedipus attitudes, the hostility being directed to the father and the dependence to the mother. Some of the sharpest conflict is likely to be not directly with the parents but with the superego values which the parents have instilled in early life and which, as indicated above, constitute a fourth source of control and dynamic fashioning of the conscious ego concept. The striving of the thoughtful adolescent to achieve new moral values as well as the attempt to revolt against *any* moral values come into conflict primarily with these unconscious habits. The normal tendency to project the conflict outwards, into a revolt against the parents, is accentuated by the sensed historical connection of these values with the parents. Actually any new superego values acquired at this time are dynamically bound to take the general form, degree of severity, etc., of the unconscious values, but it may be necessary for the adolescent to put them in logical form opposed to those of the parents.

Naturally the individuals in whom this conflict is most pronounced will be those who have unsatisfactory family relations earlier. The stress of adolescence only brings out cleavages already present. Partridge (50) found adolescent maladjustment higher where there had been severe discipline and poor relations between the parents. Stott (65) found that serious criticisms of parents at adolescence correlated with low personality-adjustment scores. Watson found radical, antiauthority views, and Stott found low adjustment scores, in those more frequently punished and severely disciplined by parents, the scores being particularly low on self-reliance. Stott observed further that the correlation of maladjustment with criticism of parents was higher for boys than girls, and particularly when the criticism was of the mother. The pattern of maladjustment, adolescent conflict, severe parental discipline, and marked criticism of the parents indicated here has some resemblance to that to be expected from partial rejection of the child by the parents, followed by bad behavior, followed by excessive disciplinary attempts. Not only crime and schizophrenic disorders show a sharp rise in adolescence, but also, as Davis has shown in his survey of the ages of Russian revolutionaries, revolt against existing cultural authority. Nevertheless, in the average, normal adolescent, the transient hostilities to the parents stand embarrassingly against a background of stronger affection for them.

**Other Factors in Late Adolescent Conflict.** It must not be overlooked in this connection that the attitude of the parents and of society to the adolescent is also apt to be ambivalent. The parent may consider it his duty to guide and support his offspring into late adolescence, yet react with jealousy to the puberal sexual and dominance developments. The mother may be proud to see the child grown up yet wish to retain him in a dependent relation. On this side also the attitudes are complicated by Oedipus residues, the father being jealous of the son and the mother of the grown-up daughter. It has been pointed out by anthropologists that in many primitive societies the initiation rites at puberty are quite unnecessarily cruel, and psychoanalysts have suggested that this gives expression to the latent hostility and jealousy which adults are bound to feel for those who now crowd upon them as rivals. (The elaboration of examinations in our own time may be partly thus motivated!) Finally, we must take account of less common modes of unnecessary interference with the adolescent by his elders, such as the satisfaction of thwarted parental ambitions by the father's attempting to force the son into occupations which he did not have the opportunity or fortitude to break into himself.

Whatever the situation in these two worlds of the peer culture and the family, it is clear that the normally developing adolescent must in the end reject both, at least partially, in favor of fashioning his ego ideal upon, and achieving status in, the third or adult society. But the conflict may be considerable before this is achieved and the discrepancy between society and family may show itself in such ways as the rejection of parents in favor of teachers or admired literary characters as models. The important role of this particular conflict is shown by McBee's (44) demonstration that the children of foreign-born parents have a quite disproportionate frequency of adolescent personality difficulties. Obtaining independence of parents in graceful fashion is perhaps more difficult now than in some former times, due to the prolonged economic dependence and the resulting ambivalence of the parent and the possible damage to the self-regard and freedom of expression of the young adult. There is some suggestion that, for example, the payment of salaries to students as "working men," instead of leaving them dependent on parents, lessens the psychological strains of adolescence.

Davis (13) has recently surveyed such sociological factors in adolescent conflict and concludes that four are of outstanding importance: (*a*) the rate of social change, determining the distance between family values and adult society's values; (*b*) the relative complexity of social structure, affecting the weight of the "cultural burden" to be taken up by the adolescent; (*c*) the degree of integration of the culture (this, as we have seen in Chapter 15 is not an easy quantity to define, but there is no doubt that in our own time one of the greatest difficulties of the adolescent is the attempt to reconcile many different, and almost equally forceful, streams of teaching and propaganda—replacing the accepted religious framework of a century ago); (*d*) the amount of vertical mobility or "social percolation," which defines the extent to which the child is expected to "do better" than the parents, and compelled to change occupational level, up or down.

On this last point quantitative data exist showing for various occupational levels the discrepancy between the number desiring to enter and the number entering. Roughly, as might be expected, there is crowding toward the upper-status levels, the greatest discrepancy between jobs available and seekers of jobs being at the professional levels and at the unskilled workers' level, in opposite senses. There is less discrepancy for skilled workers than for office workers, the latter positions being preferred in spite of relatively poor pay. These choices, of course, were recorded at adolescence, in school, and before the subjects had experience of the arduousness of qualifying for some professions or of the nature of the work in some occupations, so that they represent discrepancies between opportunity and unrealistic rather than realistic, tried ambition.

### 6. MATURITY AND ITS PERSONALITY TRENDS

**The Trends in Constitutional Powers.** Although the period now to be examined, say from twenty-five to fifty or fifty-five years, is chronologically the longest, it is in most ways the least eventful in regard to personality change. As with adolescence, we shall find the issues best handled systematically by considering, on the one hand, the inner biological maturation and changes and, on the other, the typical environmental stimuli and modes of possible expression, finally reviewing the interaction of these. With the first category we must include all data on personality change *per se*, since at present there is no reliable means of separating the constitutional influences.

Generally speaking, there is a slight biological decline between twenty-five and fifty-five in most efficiencies, though resistance to diseases of some kinds may actually increase and some psychological potentialities may show a change that is barely perceptible, at least, for the first ten or twenty years of the period. Actually, owing to learning and experience the total efficiency increases, in all but physical capabilities, through most of this period, and it is understood that the above generalization applies to potentialities or constitutional powers.

The earliest downward trend occurs in basal metabolic rate, which has momentarily paused in its lifelong decline during early adolescence. There is strong evidence that autonomic reactivity also declines; for example, the magnitude of the psychogalvanic reflex falls from about sixteen years.

The special senses—vision and especially upper tonal hearing—suffer slight impairment from about eighteen years, whether judged by average trends or by the percentage of definite defects occurring in the population. As a survey of championship ages in sports will show, more complex physical powers, involving coordination and experience, reach their zenith somewhat later, from about twenty-five to twenty-nine years of age.[2] Surveys of such data are found in Wynn Jones (77) and Kuhlen (34, 35). As McFarland shows (45), the differences of output for groups of workers of different ages in industry are very slight and not easily interpretable, due to possible continuous selection. Creative ability in science and literature seems to reach its zenith, as Lehman (39) has shown, in the middle forties, and probably the best performances in business and politics occur even a little later.

On changes in defined and measurable personality source traits or factors there exist adequate data only with respect to general intelligence. The scores on intelligence tests administered in the usual way, with a time limit, change with age as shown in Diagram 52. •

However, as Lorge (41) has shown, if no time limit is imposed and *level* of performance apart from *speed* is measured, there is no decline—at least until extreme old age. Further, it has been shown by several studies that decline on speeded tests is less in verbal discrimination and in information and vocabulary than in perception of relationships in new material, *i.e.*, in

---

[2] Bühler records the following mean age of champions in the early twentieth century: sprint and long jump, twenty-three; long distance running, twenty-five; and tennis, twenty-eight. Wynn Jones (77) found champions in more strategic games somewhat older: golf, thirty-one, and cricket, thirty-four.

adaptability. The findings of Davies-Eysenck (14) have considerably clarified the scattered data on the ability functions that selectively decline with age. These facts, together with the finding that the *g* saturation of the same abilities is lower for adults than children (Garrett), and that brain injuries produce more decline in specialized abilities relative to general abilities, in adults, have suggested the theory of *fluid and crystallized general ability* (9).

According to this theory, general ability is of two kinds, fluid ability, which manifests itself in relation perception, in speeded performances, and in new

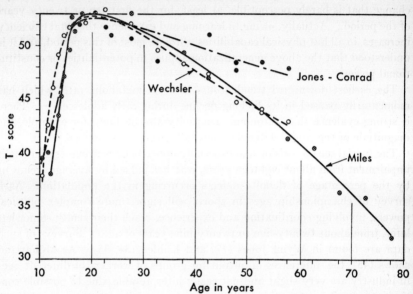

DIAGRAM 52. Changes of general mental capacity with age. The results of those major studies with timed tests have been combined via a standard *T*-score. (*From Jones, H. E. and O. J. Kaplan, Mental Disorders in Later Life, Stanford University, Stanford University Press, 1945, by permission of authors and publishers.*)

situations, and crystallized ability, which manifests itself only in relation perception in known material and in unspeeded performances. The correlation among abilities is produced by the fluid ability, which declines after about twenty-three, leaving the crystallized ability like a dead coral formation, maintaining, except where brain injury occurs, the levels of the original fluid ability. But through disuse, as well as injury, the crystallized abilities will lose their evenness of outline and their intercorrelations will therefore be reduced. The theory of fluid and crystallized ability thus serves as a general guide in understanding the areas in which the individual after adolescence will or will not encounter relative difficulty in comprehension, performance, and adjustment. Some of the unwillingness in later maturity to enter new fields may be due to appreciation of the fact that, through the lower level of fluid ability, the individual cannot think and perform with such credit to himself as in the accustomed fields where the crystallized abilities function.

The curve of rise and decline of fluid general intelligence, showing a slow decline from a brief plateau in the early twenties, is characteristic of many mental capacities, notably of manual dexterities, as Miles (46,47), has shown, and of ability to memorize, as Lorge's results indicate. The latter (41) and the results of Ruch (56) showed that new material can be memorized right on into extreme old age, though with a diminution to about 80 per cent of the youthful efficiency level at fifty years, and about 60 per cent at seventy years. This change in over-all learning ability apparently represents a decline in the dynamic strength of interests, so that if the older person can muster sufficient energy by depleting other fields of interest, he can learn as fast in some one specific field as a younger person.

These curves for intelligence, memory, etc., refer, of course, to basic powers: the *cumulative result* of learning *by* these powers reaches a plateau far later in life, as a man's capital might reach its maximum long after his salary has passed its peak. Consequently, where good performance is a matter of wide information, of wisdom and foresight born of experience, of shrewd tactics, and especially of truths of living less acquirable by explicit teaching than by trial-and-error learning, the older person has the advantage right up to senility or decease. Here we come to the shrewd view of the Privy Councillor, Francis Bacon, that "Young men are fitter to invent than to judge, fitter for execution than for council, and fitter for new projects than for settled business."

**Trends in General Personality Factors.** As to other source traits, such as emotional stability (*C* factor), cyclothyme-schizothyme tendencies (*A* factor), dominance (*E* factor), and surgency-desurgency (*F* factor), no systematic knowledge on life trends yet exists, though guesses can be made from a few scattered researches. Willoughby's studies on emotional maturity seem essentially to be concerned with *C* factor. He found by questionnaire methods that women scored lower than men and married women somewhat lower than women with careers, while both in men and women there was a definite rise in emotional stability after adolescence, continuing, with a plateau, to about fifty years. Thereafter there is a decline to old age, which is discussed and interpretted in the next section. As Kuhlen (34) points out, the incidence curve of neurotic symptoms clinically reported does not follow this form, but declines from about thirty-five. But this needs confirmation and correction for selection. If true, a probable interpretation is that older people either do not come for treatment or do not have insight into their neurosis. The continuous increase of psychosis incidence throughout life suggests the latter–if psychosis and neurosis have common elements.

Incidentally, this curve of improving emotional stability up to fifty corresponds with the curve of "freedom from accidents per mile driven" in auto driving, in spite of the slight decline in speed of mechanical reaction that must occur throughout this period. General observation and clinical consensus agrees with the above findings; for the man of thirty is better in general than the man of twenty and the man of forty better than the man of thirty in controlling emotional expression and probably with respect to giving way to self-pity, pride, fear, sex feelings, etc.

As Anderson points out (2), the mature individual has learned so many effective responses that the number of situations which provoke emotionality as an emergency or unstructured response has continually decreased. However, even apart from diminished provocation, the older person, in Anderson's studies, shows decreasing emotional response. Poets, such as Stevenson and Wordsworth, may hope for or claim as vivid an emotional reaction in age as in youth, but some poets, such as Matthew Arnold, and many scientists, such as Darwin, have commented on lessened emotionality and aesthetic responsiveness with age. In general, growing to maturity means an increase in the number of objects to which some emotional response is made, an increase in the variety of secondary, derived emotions, but a decrease in the frequency of violent emotions and some decrease, probably, in the intensity of all emotions.

Summarizing as to other temperamental and dynamic traits we may note that some questionnaire-type studies show an increase in "introversion" with age, but this may really indicate only the above-described trend to greater emotional control, though it might also imply schizothyme, or desurgent, or submissive trends. Findings mentioned above can also be summarized as a probable trend toward desurgency and perhaps as a trend to lower dominance in the latter part of maturity.

A longitudinal study, of a type somewhat rare in present psychological research, was made by Roberts and Fleming (53) to determine the nature of personality changes occurring from late adolescence through maturity. Twenty-five college women were studied by friends' ratings and questionnaires with respect to persistence of attitudes and traits in married life after college. On self-estimates, individuals thought they changed more than friends' ratings showed them to change. Traits (out of 55) with high persistence were: having creative ability and interests, accepting responsibility, having executive ability, being strongly self-assertive, being interested in people, being the life of the party, having few, but close, friends. Traits with low persistence were: apprehensiveness, having (or not having) a feeling of being welcome in a group, seeking help when needed, taking teasing from others, self-confidence and leadership, complacency, self-consciousness, loneliness, and happiness.

Changeability thus "measured" may be a changeability existing in all people or a tendency to change relative to others. Examination of the most and least changing trait-elements above suggests strongly that the source trait of surgency-desurgency is most subject to change with age and circumstances, and perhaps dominance-submission. In terms of field of interest Roberts and Fleming found highest persistence through maturity in interests in the opposite sex, recreational interests, personal appearance, and attitudes to parents, and most change in attitudes on religion, money, home and family, and health. The study needs more measurement and extension to wider samples before interpretation can be attempted.

**Trends in Dynamic Traits and Interest Investments.** Regarding dynamic adjustments and interests, tests such as the Strong Blank show, in the first place, remarkably little change of interest and attitude pattern between twenty-five and fifty. However, there are some trends well confirmed for the average man (52), notably a steady decline after twenty-five in liking for physical activities, such as playing tennis, car driving, and a decline in interest in large social groups, full-dress socials, smokers, etc., as well as in movies, competitive situations of various kinds, and activities involving continuous change. There is a corresponding increase in interest in reading and informative activities, in the home rather than activities outside the home, in observing nature and in gardening, in helping others with personal problems, in the association of intimate friends rather than crowds, and in philosophical matters.

Landis (38) interviewed 450 people over sixty-five concerning" the happiest period in their lives." Setting aside 7 per cent who could not decide, he found 18 per cent said childhood, 20 per cent, adolescence (fifteen to twenty-five years), 50 per cent, maturity (twenty-five to forty-five years), and 5 per cent, middle and old age. Those who preferred old age had had unhappy married life, terminated before old age. Two-thirds of single persons chose childhood and youth, but only one-third of those who had been married selected this earliest period as the happiest. If we assume that the average person is one who has largely solved the search for a mate and career by the end of adolescence (twenty-five years) the relative happiness and stability of this post-adolescent period is understandable; for the combination of comparatively steady biological powers and drives, with the existence of a relatively unchanging external situation giving the necessary satisfactions, is an ideal one for good adjustment. Consequently, for most people this is a period of happy absorption in careers and family life, with less time or provocation for maladjustments than at any other period.

However, the problems of the period must be given their proper weight. In the first place, we spoke of the *majority*, who solved the problems of adolescence. But at that parting of the ways there is a minority which fails to solve its problems, becoming shipwrecked in delinquency, increasing maladjustment, or psychosis, or which postpones solution, as in the genius, who often continues through a prolonged adolescent instability. The small group of those who are distinguished in literature, the arts, science, etc., as a glance at *Who's Who* will show, tends to late marriage. (Taking at random two diversely distinguished men of the nineteenth century—Tennyson and the Duke of Wellington—we notice that they married, for the first time, when about forty.) One must bear in mind too, that about 25 per cent of the population never marries at all. So that our generalizations about wife and work, above, remain to be supplemented in time by a study of the different maturity adjustments of some appreciable minorities.

Early maturity, as a period of life, means for most people some problems of adjustment to the discovery that adolescent dreams and aspirations, both with regard to career and to marriage, were partly unrealistic or are partly unrealized. The momentum of work and daily family cares seems to carry most people over these conflicts. Their nature has been discussed in the chapter on the family. At the latter end of maturity, when the needs of security have been somewhat assuaged and when some slight increase of leisure occurs, there is evidence of a tendency to a revival of romantic interests. This is shown, for example, in the Kinsey report, by a revival in men of extramarital interests. Hamilton and McGown (24) point out that the approach of the menopause in women often produces a wistful turning to romance. This may be the truth in the saying that, "In their first passion women love their lovers; in all the others they love love," except that it seems true to some extent of men also.

That the period of maturity results in a certain narrowing of interests and at length in a lack of spontaneity and a separation from unconscious needs, evident in some feeling of emptiness and dissatisfaction, has been discussed at length by Jung (31); but how prevalent this is and what its exact nature may be, is not known in terms of objective psychology. It may be that this is essentially a result of biological and other changes now to be discussed in connection with late maturity and old age.

### 7. LATE MATURITY AND OLD AGE

**The Trends in Constitutional Powers.** To describe the changes that are intrinsic to the organism in old age is at present difficult, for the average as we now know it may depart considerably from the normal or healthy. For example, we may wonder how normal are arteriosclerotic conditions or the senility of "senile psychosis"?

Certainly abilities decline, continuing the curves defined in the previous section. As Jones and Kaplan (29) point out, most investigators find the chief decline in tests which demand ingenuity in adjusting to novel situations, while performances demanding experience hold their ground. The decline in physical and sensory powers also continues with no sharp change and includes a decline in powers of preserving physiological equilibrium and harmony. Indeed, Shock (60) considers that the decline of homeostatic capacity is even more central in old age changes than the decline in, say, the capacity of the body to heal lesions. Lewis (40) studying twenty males of forty to eighty-nine years found that the decline of metabolic rate with age after fifty years of age was very little.

No precise data are available on personality traits, except general ability, but there is at least suggestive evidence in Willoughby's data of an increase, from about fifty years onwards, of emotional instability. This is surprising, for throughout maturity the growth of habits of duty and the development of social responsibility have been sufficient to stabilize many personalities which in adolescence were unstable. It is necessary to look, therefore, either for new stresses in the environmental situation, or for some special degenerative·changes in the organism. The fact that the curve of first admissions for psychoses shows a sharp upward trend after sixty (with the known role of physiological factors therein) suggests emphasis on some constitutional loss of adaptability (see Kuhlen (34)). The possibility that the incidence of arteriosclerosis and other degenerative disorders of old age may wholly account for this rise has been considered, but Robinson (54), studying psychotics over sixty years old, found that only about 30 per cent had pathological deterioration and that, in all, 70 per cent responded to psychotherapy. He claims that more frequently than deterioration one finds toxic delirious conditions and affective disorders, especially agitated melancholia. Involutional melancholia in women, however, has its maximum predominance somewhat earlier. Nevertheless, as pointed out in Chapter 18, the particular form of the psychosis is determined by the nature of the prepsychotic personality, and, as Rothschild (55) shows, cerebral damage rarely produces psychotic manifestations in individuals who are not psychologically handicapped beforehand.

Evidence from the field of delinquency is not complete and controlled, but at least it is clear that the decline of delinquency with age is not, in all groups, continued through the fifty-to-seventy-year period, and, as Pollak (51) shows, there is a high incidence of first offenders in this range. The incidence of suicide (see Kuhlen (34, 35) climbs steadily from infancy to late maturity—apart from a slight acceleration in adolescence—but after fifty there is deceleration in the curve for men, and an actual fall in the case of women. Gray (20) questions the whole argument for increased emotional instability. He points out that in 2,000 nonagenarians and centenarians examined at John Hopkins University emotional stability was noted to be "the predominant trait." However, it is probable that much *selection* goes on between sixty and seventy, and indeed throughout life, specifically with respect to emotional stability, and especially of freedom from fear and anger (for their somatic effects are so adverse), so that the survivors are actually a sample of individuals originally unduly high in stability. A possible conclusion from these sidelights is that whatever increase in emotional instability may occur, in the average person it is not much accompanied by superego conflict or by insight, and tends to delinquency and psychosis rather than neurosis.

**Trends in General Personality Traits and Interest Investments.** Literature ascribes many personality changes to the last period of life. Cicero speaks of the garrulity of age; Chandler (10*b*) tells us that Aristotle stressed the moderation of the aged ("They love as though they will someday hate and hate as though they will someday love.") Rupert Brooke says "The years had given them kindness," Matthew Arnold describes the absence of emotional feeling, and Shakespeare writes of age as "cold" or "crabbed." A modern anthropologist, Hooton, explains the last by saying, "Most animals (including man) get worse tempered as they grow older" (26). Undoubtedly there exist real dispositional trends not yet measured by psychologists, and if the central, increasing need in age is for rest, every outside stimulus is increasing a frustration. However, as Alexander has shown (1) with 716 subjects, the correlation between age and number of antipathies, at least from ten to fifty years, is somewhat negative; so the increasing considerateness brought by age and experience probably produces greater benevolence even though offset by impulsive irritability.

As to the opinions of modern psychiatrists we have summary of Cavan (10*a*) listing the following trends as frequent in later years:—

Worry over finances, attendant upon threatened retirement. (Aristotle said that the aged love money.)

Worry over health.

Feeling unwanted, isolated, lonely.

Feeling suspicious.

Narrowing of interests, leading to introspection, increased interest in bodily sensations and physical pleasures.

Loss of memory, especially for recent events and in the field of spontaneous recall.

Mental rigidity.

Overtalkativeness, especially of the past.

Hoarding, often of trivial things.

Loss of interest in activity and increased interest in quiescence.

Feeling of inadequacy, leading to feelings of insecurity and anxiety, feeling of guilt, irritability. (Of these, Aristotle noted only "querulousness" and lack of confidence in the future.)

Reduction of sexual activity but increased sexual interest, especially in the male; regression to earlier levels of expression.

Untidiness, uncleanliness.
Conservatism (one author dissents on the basis of opinion-poll material).
Inability to adjust to changed conditions.
Decreased social contacts and participation.

Beginning with experimental and statistical studies we find Pollak (51) studying first offenders in higher age brackets, revealing a relative increase in sex crimes, violations of narcotic and drug laws, and embezzlement. He notes in the personalities of the groups he studies tendencies to fatigability, stubbornness, narrowing of emotions, weakness of phantasy, and increasing egotism. Betzendahl considers the materialistic egotism of age to be necessary and self-protective, and points out that anxiety in the male and jealousy in the female become rather prominent at this time.

The trend of interests in old age in the main continues that seen through maturity. There is, in particular, an increase in philosophical and religious interests and a retrospective interest in evaluation of the individual's life and its goals. This last may also occur toward the end of the maturity period, with some redirection of remaining energies (see Jung). Strong points to a sharp increase in hobby interests, mainly absent throughout busy maturity, and shows that these interests decline only with enfeeblement. Morgan (49) analyzed the "comforts and worries" of age and found, among the former: family relationships, friends, material comforts, religion, own home, reverie, good health, work, and reading—in that declining order of frequency of reference. Worries, in diminishing order, were fear of dependence (financial worries included), concern for wife or family, poor health, inability to work, defective family relationships, and death. Anxiety, often expressed in somatic symptoms, is a fairly prevalent trait among aged people.

**Problems and Conflicts of Old Age.** Viewing the life situation of the aged, one perceives that loss of prestige and ego satisfactions is perhaps the most central cause of frustration and adaptation difficulties. Kuhlen (34) shows that the employability of the average person declines, in the opinion of employers, from about thirty years of age, and the difficulties of the individual over fifty in obtaining suitable employment are considerable. (Much of this attitude, incidentally, is unjustified, older workers having, for example, a much lower accident rate.) Morgan's study (49) of the attitudes of recipients of old-age assistance shows considerable ego wounding. Miles (48) argues that these situations are responsible for the gradual decline in self-confidence and the increase in feelings of inferiority and submissiveness, though these may also be an adjustment to real decline in powers. Dependence on relatives, arising from age, may bring not only ego losses, but also serious problems of personal adaptation at a time when adaptability is low, and it is not surprising that most old people are therefore found to prefer living near relatives but alone.

When retirement is voluntary, however, there is still a "let down" from loss of self-assertive satisfactions; for loss of position means, at least relatively, lack of remuneration and, in addition, lack of the deference connected with any position that concerns and serves other people. There are also psychological losses of a more obscure kind. In the first place, though the matter is insufficiently investigated, it is clear that the socially approved practice of seeking relief from maladjustments in work probably leaves, in the course of maturity, an accumulation of problems to be solved (insofar as they still exist) when work ceases. Second, our competitive civilization imposes a certain sense of guilt on idleness and relaxation; though relaxation may be the principal physical and nervous need of age. Parenthetically, this particular source of frustration might be expected to be more marked in men, for many women never cease to be housewives so long as there is a house. But in all, as Pressey (52) aptly says, there is a sense of "isolation from the swift traffic of life," a feeling that this "traffic" goes on regardless of his views and needs, and a pervading sense of loneliness. Though there are no adequately checked statistical analyses of the popular theory that retirement is often fatal to busy men, such analysis would throw additional light on the extent of the frustrations associated with this aspect of old age.

A second, but less situational, loss is that of sexual life, supervening comparatively suddenly in the case of women, at the end of maturity, and more slowly in the case of man. How far menopausal depressions are primarily due to sex loss is still uncertain. Many more superficial mechanisms can commonly be and commonly are indicated as causes, and the physical, endocrine disturbances are sufficient to reduce efficiency to the point where superego reproaches might ensue. As indicated in Chapter 18, however, involutional depressions tend to occur in "strait-laced" personalities who may either have a history of sexual opportunities turned down or who would experience guilt at that eleventh-hour revival of romantic interest which may commonly occur. Data on these questions are discussed by Hamilton (24).

The fact that involutional depressions are about three times as frequent in women as in man, and the observation that "man's love is of man's life a thing apart, 'tis women's whole existence," justifies an examination of the role of sex-loss readjustments in involutional melancholies, and may indicate a problem of readjustment important for all old people. In men, Stern and Menzer (62) point out that the depressions of age are not systemic but generally reactive, and that they are in fact often reactions to lost opportunities and failures occurring even decades earlier. The tendency of the old to live in youth, because of the greater dynamic investment of earlier memories, thus has its perils as well as its pleasures. Hamilton (24) claims that many changes of old age, *e.g.*, increase of psychosexual regressions, hostility, and conservatism, are situational and therefore reversible, rather than humoral and constitutional, and are due to frustrating social circumstances.

At the beginning of this chapter it was stressed that no study of the life course is sound which does not take into account the course of social change also. This is especially necessary in interpreting data on the long stretches of life span involved in maturity and old age. A survey in 1945 (see Kuhlen (34)) shows that about 40 per cent of the aged in the United States are dependent on public and private charity. The fraction of the population in this age range is likely to increase rapidly in the near future and social programs for the aged, based on the growing science of gerontology, will probably be brought into action. There are thus historically and economically new conditions to be considered which are likely appreciably to change the psychology of old age.

### 8. SUMMARY

1. Adolescence is a period making high demands on adjustments since biological and cultural changes practically coincide. The biological changes include a spurt in physical growth and the appearance of secondary sex characteristics, following endocrine changes. Directly, these produce a change in disposition, marked by increased sex interest, self-assertion, and parental (altruistic) feeling, as well as a general intellectual stimulation, while indirectly certain problems may be created by the aptness of the physical changes.

2. Culturally, adjustments are required to adult opportunities and responsibilities and to frustrations imposed by the unevenness with which these are accorded. The latter concern particularly the postponement of sexual opportunities, but also the restriction of ego needs through incompleteness of adult status. The main problems reside in achieving emotional independence of parents, achieving economic and occupational status, fitting the approved pattern of differentiated masculinity or femininity, finding a mate, and adjusting to adult cultural standards.

3. Personality changes observed in adolescence, apart from the biological, dispositional changes (with their more or less transitory, polymorphous-perverse sex interests), include increased interests in art, religion, and cultural matters generally, some decline in fears of authority and "things considered wrong," increased emotional instability, and probably a greater dispersion on most personality measurements.

4. The development of the ego, and of the self-regarding sentiment uniting ego and superego in the adolescent is to be understood in terms of his attempt to satisfy four worlds of appreciation: that of the parents; that of his adolescent peers; that of the adult culture pattern opening up before him in society, books, etc.; and that of internal residues of childhood, notably the childhood, unconscious superego. The two last normally predominate in the final adjustment.

5. The adolescent's attempts at adjustment are fully to be understood

only when considered in relation also to the adjustive reactions of the parents and of society. Parents commonly have ambivalent attitudes to the independence of children, while adult society generally finds it necessary to express unconscious jealousy by initiation difficulties, at least in primitive societies.

6. The period of maturity is actually one of slight, steady decline in most biologically based psychological powers, notably in sense acuity, speed of reaction, metabolic rate, performance on speeded intelligence tests, and power of learning. The change in abilities is most readily summarized by the theory of fluid and crystallized general ability.

7. Maturity is characterized by marked stability, as shown in Interest Tests, but by certain trends, *e.g.*, to more family, less social, more philosophical interests. There is an increase of emotional stability, and a decrease of leisure for most, though a minority follows a very different course.

8. Age continues the decline of biological powers, but in certain fields this is more than compensated for by the accumulation of information, social skills, and general wisdom. It is at present difficult to decide which are normal trends and which are due to prevalent chronic diseases of old age.

9. Cultural adjustment problems arise afresh in old age, due to loss of occupation and decreased social valuation, causing frustration of ego needs and a sense of insecurity. These are accompanied by some increase in emotional instability and a rise in the psychosis rate. Certain general trends in interests have been established.

10. The life course of personality is in general more profitably analyzed in terms of internal biological changes, on the one hand, and the changing demands and opportunities presented in each period by the culture pattern, on the other. Average personality trends are evident as a reconciliation of these two sets of conditions. Furthermore, it is necessary to allow, in all interpretations and predictions for the nonrecurring changes due to the progress of the culture pattern.

## QUESTIONS AND EXERCISES

1. Describe, with diagrams where possible, the known anatomical and physiological changes of adolescence, and indicate one or two curves of psychological measurements which show close correspondence with these.

2. Discuss the effects upon the form of adolescent psychological development of differences in culture patterns, as observed by anthropoligists.

3. Describe the development of masculine and feminine behavior patterns in adolescence, with reference also to their influence by the peer culture and to the differences in later life.

4. Outline the principal known changes in personality (especially of interests) in adolescence, with special reference to the interaction of cultural demands and biological capacities.

5. Discuss adolescent instability with reference to the changing ego concepts under the psychological pressures from four different sources.

6. Outline the principal changes of abilities and interest, as discovered by psychological measurement, during the period of maturity.

7. Describe the diverse sources of evidence on general ability measurement that contribute to the theory of fluid and crystallized ability, and examine the capacity of this theory to account for the behavior of abilities through maturity.

8. Discuss the probable reasons for the period of maturity being retrospectively regarded by most as the happiest life period, and indicate how far objective data appear to support this introspection.

9. Marshal the available evidence, from statistics of abnormality and normal test measurements, as to personality changes in old age and discuss their agreement and disagreement with popular, literary conceptions.

10. Discuss the extent to which personality characteristics of old age are due to the culture pattern and mention possible changes with the advance of gerontology.

## BIBLIOGRAPHY

1. ALEXANDER, C.: A Correlation between Age and Antipathy, *J. soc. Psychol.*, 23: 229–231, 1946.
2. ANDERSON, J. E.: Changes in Emotional Response with Age, Mooseheart Symposium on Feelings and Emotions, University of Chicago Press, Chicago, 1949. .
3. BAYLEY, N., and R. TUDDENHAM: Adolescent Changes in Body Build, *Yearb. nat. Soc. Stud. Educ.*, 43: 33–55, 1944.
4. BENEDICT, R.: Continuities and Discontinuities in Cultural Conditioning, *Psychiatry*, 1: 161–167, 1938.
5. BLANCHARD, P.: Adolescent Experience in Relation to Personality and Behaviour: Chapter 22 in J. McV. Hunt, *Personality and the Behaviour Disorders*, The Ronald Press Company, New York, 1944.
6. BRUMBAUGH, A. J., and L. C. SMITH: A Point Scale for Evaluating Personnel Work in Institutions of Higher Learning, *Relig. Educ.*, 1932: 230–235, 1932.
7. BUCK, W.: A Measurement of Changes of Attitudes and Interests of University Students over a Ten-year Period, *J. abnorm. soc. Psychol.*, 31: 12–19, 1936.
8. BÜHLER, C.: The Curve of Life as Studied in Biographies, *J. appl. Psychol.*, 19: 405–409, 1935.
8a. CATTELL, R. B.: The Measurement of Interest, *Character & Person.* 4: 1–23, 1936.
9. CATTELL, R. B.: The Measurement of Adult Intelligence, *Psychol. Bull.*, 3: 153–193, 1943.
10. CATTELL, R. B.: *Social Psychology* (in press).
10a. CAVAN, R. S.: An Index of Senility in *Social Adjustment in Old Age.*, Soc. Sci. Res. Council, New York, 1946.
10b. CHANDLER, A. R.: Aristotle on Aging, *J. of Geront.*, 3: 220, 223, 1948.
11. COWDRY, E. V.: *Problems of Aging*, Williams and Wilkins, Baltimore, 1942.
12. CROOK, M. N.: A Further Note on Self-judgments of Constancy in Neuroticism Scores, *J. soc. Psychol.*, 9: 485–487, 1938.
13. DAVIS, K.: The Sociology of Parent-Youth Conflict, *Amer. sociol. Rev.*, 5: 523–535, 1940.
14. DAVIES-EYSENCK, M.: An Exploratory Study of Mental Organization in Senility, *J. Neurol., Neurosurg., & Psychiat.*, 8: 15–21, 1945.
15. DIMOCK, H.: *Rediscovering the Adolescent*, Association Press, New York, 1938.
16. FREUD, A.: The Ego and Id at Puberty, in *The Ego and the Mechanisms of Defense*, Hogarth Press, London, 1937.

17. GARRETT, H. E.: A Developmental Theory of Intelligence, *Amer. Psych.*, 1: 372–378, 1946.

18. GARRISON, K. C.: *Psychology of Adolescence*, Prentice-Hall, Inc., New York, 1940.

19. GOODENOUGH, F. L.: *Developmental Psychology*, Appleton-Century-Crofts, Inc., New York, 1945.

20. GRAY, W. H.: The Mystery of Aging, *Harper's Mag.*, 182: 283–293, 1941.

21. GRUEN, E. W.: Level of Aspiration in Relation to Personality Factors in Adolescents, *Child Develpm.*, 16: 181–188, 1945.

22. HALL, G. S.: *Adolescence, Its Psychology and Its Relations to Physiology, Anthropology, Sociology, Sex, Crime, Religion, and Education*, Appleton-Century-Crofts, Inc., New York, 1904.

23. HAMILTON, G. V.: Changes in Personality and Psychosexual Phenomena with Age: Chap. 16 in E. V. Cowdry, *Problems of Aging*, 2nd ed., The Williams and Wilkins Company, Baltimore, 1942.

24. HAMILTON, G. V., and K. McGOWN: What Is Wrong with Marriage? Albert & Charles Boni, Inc., New York, 1929.

25. HENRY, N. B.: *Adolescence, Yearb. nat. Soc. Stud. Educ.*, 43, Part I, 1944.

26. HOOTON, E. A.: *Why Men Behave Like Apes and Vice Versa*, Oxford University Press, New York, 1940.

27. JAMES, H. E. O., and F. F. MOORE: Adolescent Leisure in a Working-class District, *Occup. Psychol.*, 14: 132–145, 1940.

28. JONES, H. E.: *Development in Adolescence*, Appleton-Century-Crofts, Inc., New York, 1943.

29. JONES, H. E., and O. J. KAPLAN: Psychological Aspects of Mental Disorders in Later Life, in O. J. Kaplan, (ed.) *Mental Disorders in Later Life*, Stanford University Press, Stanford University, Calif., 1945.

30. JONES, M. C.: A Functional Analysis of Colloquial Speech among Adolescents, *Amer. J. Psychol.*, 1: 252–253, 1946.

31. JUNG, C. G.: *The Integration of the Personality*, Farrar and Rinehart, Inc., New York, 1939.

32. KITAY, P. M.: A Comparison of the Sexes in Their Attitude and Beliefs about Women; a Study of Prestige Groups, *Sociometry*, 3: 399–407, 1940.

33. KUHLEN, R. G.: Age Differences in Personality during Adult Years, *Psychol. Bull.*, 42: 333–358, 1945.

34. KUHLEN, R. G.: Psychological Trends and Problems in Later Maturity, in Pennington and Berg, *Clinical Psychology*, The Ronald Press Company, New York, 1947.

35. KUHLEN, R. G., and B. J. LEE: Personality Characteristics and Social Acceptability in Adolescence, *J. educ. Psychol.*, 321–340, 1943.

36. LAING, A.: The Sense of Humor in Childhood and Adolescence, *Brit. J. educ. Psychol.*, 9: 201–210, 1939.

37. LANDIS, J. T.: What Is the Happiest Period of Life? *Sch. & Soc.*, 55: 643–645, 1942.

38. LANDIS, J. T., M. M. BOLLES, H. F. METZGER, M. W. PITTS, D. A. D'ESOPO, H. D. MOLOY, S. J. KLIEGMAN, and R. L. DICKINSON: *Sex in Development*, Paul B. Hoeber, Inc., New York, 1940.

39. LEHMAN, H. G.: The Creative Years in Science and Literature, *Sci. Mon.*, 43: 151–162, 1936.

40. LEWIS, M. H.: Changes with Age in the Basal Metabolic Rate in Adult Men, *Amer. J. Psysiol.*, 121: 502–516, 1938.

41. LORGE, I.: The Influence of the Test upon the Nature of Mental Decline as a Function of Age, *J. educ. Psychol.*, 32: 100–110, 1936.

42. Lund, F. H.: Adolescent Motivation: Sex Differences, *J. genet. Psychol.*, 64: 99–103, 1944.

43. Mead, M.: *Coming of Age in Samoa*, William Morrow and Co., New York, 1928.

44. McBee, M.: A Mental Hygiene Clinic in a High School, *Ment. Hyg.*, 19: 238–280, 1935.

45. McFarland, R. A.: The Older Worker in Industry, *Harv. Bus. Rev.*, 21: 505–520, 1943.

46. Miles, W. R.: Age and Human Society, in Murchison, C. (ed.): *Handbook of Social Psychology*, Clark University Press, Worcester, 1935.

47. Miles, W. R.: Measures of Certain Human Abilities throughout the Life Span, *Proc. nat. Acad. Sci.*, Washington, 17: 627–633, 1931.

48. Miles, W. R.: Psychological Aspects of Aging, Chapter 20 in E. V. Cowdry, *Problems of Aging*, Williams and Wilkins, Baltimore, 1939.

49. Morgan, C. M.: The Attitudes and Adjustments of Recipients of Old Age Assistance in Upstate and Metropolitan New York, *Arch. Psychol.*, N.Y., No. 214, 1937.

50. Partridge, E. DeA.: *Social Psychology of Adolescence*, Prentice-Hall, Inc., New York, 1939.

51. Pollak, O.: A Statistical Investigation of the Criminality of Old Age, *J. crim. Psychopath.*, 5: 745–767, 1944.

52. Pressey, S. L., J. E. Janney, and R. G. Kuhlen: *Life: a Psychological Survey*, Harper & Brothers, New York, 1939.

53. Roberts, K. E., and V. V. Fleming: Persistence and Change in Personality Patterns, *Soc. Res. Child Develpm., Monogr.*, 8 (No. 3), 1943.

54. Robinson, G. W., Jr.: Psychiatric Geriatrics: the Possibilities in the Treatment of Mental States of Old Age, *J. Amer. med. Assn.*, 116: 2139–2141, 1941.

55. Rothschild, D.: The Role of the Pre-morbid Personality in Arterio-sclerotic Psychoses, *Amer. J. Psychiat.*, 100: 501–505, 1944.

56. Ruch, F. L.: The Differentiative Effects of Age upon Human Learning, *J. gen. Psychol.*, 11: 261–286, 1934.

57. Shuttleworth, F. K.: The Adolescent Period: A Graphic and Pictorial Atlas, *Soc. Res. Child Develop., Monogr.*, 3 (No. 3), 1938.

58. Simmons, L. W.: *The Role of the Aged in Primitive Society*, Yale University Press, New Haven, 1945.

59. Sollenberger, R. T.: Some Relationships between Male Hormone in Maturing Boys and Their Expressed Interests and Attitudes, *J. Psychol.*, 9: 179–189, 1946.

60. Shock, N. W.: Physiological Changes in Adolescence, *Yearb. nat. Soc. Stud. Educ.*, 43: 56–79, 1944.

61. Shock, N. W.: Physiological Aspects of Mental Disorders in Later Life, in Kaplan, O. J. (ed.): *Mental Disorders in Later Life*, Stanford University Press, Stanford University, Calif., 1945.

62. Stern, K., and D. Menzer: The Mechanism of Reactivation in Depressions of the Old Age Group, *Psychiat. Quart.*, 20: 56–73, 1946.

63. Stolz, H. R., and L. M. Stolz: Adolescent Problems Related to Somatic Variations, *Yearb. nat. Soc. Stud. Educ.*, 43: 80–99, 1944.

64. Stone, C. P., and Barker, R. G.: The Attitudes and Interests of Pre-menarcheal and Post-menarcheal Girls, *J. genet. Psychol.*, 54, 27–71, 1939.

65. Stott, L. H.: Adolescents' Dislikes Regarding Parental Behavior and Their Significance, *J. genet. Psychol.*, 57: 393–414, 1940.

66. Sward, R.: Age and Mental Ability in Superior Men, *Amer. J. Psychol.*, 58: 443–479, 1945.

67. Symonds, P. M.: Changes in Problems and Interests with Increasing Age, *Psychol. Bull.*, 33: 789, 1936.

68. SYMONDS, P. M.: Changes in Sex Differences in Problems and Interests of Adolescence with Increasing Age, *J. genet. Psychol.*, 50: 83–89, 1937.
69. TAYLOR, K. VAN F.: The Reliability and Permanence of Vocational Interests of Adolescents, *J. Exp. Educ.*, 11: 81–87, 1942.
70. THORNDIKE, E. L., and others: *The Psychology of Wants, Interests, and Attitudes*, Appleton-Century-Crofts, Inc., New York, 1935.
71. TRYON, C. M.: Evaluations of Adolescent Personality by Adolescents, in (R. G. Barker, J. S. Kounin, H. F. Wright) *Child Behavior and Development*, McGraw-Hill Book Company, Inc., New York, 1943.
72. TRYON, C. M.: The Adolescent Peer Culture, *Yearb. nat. Soc. Stud. Educ.*, 43: 217–239, 1944.
73. WHITESIDE, S.: Some Life Foci of Women College Graduates, *Psychol. Bull.*, 33: 759–760, 1936.
74. WHITING, J. W. M.: *Becoming a Kwoma*, Yale University Press, New Haven, 1941.
75. WILES, J. S.: *The Challenge of Adolescence*, Greenberg: Publisher, Inc., New York, 1939.
76. WILLOUGHBY, R. R.: The Relationship to Emotionality of Age, Sex, and Conjugal Condition, *Amer. J. Sociol.*, 6: 920–931, 1938.
77. WYNN, JONES L.: Personality and Age, *Nature* (London), 136: 779–782, 1935.
78. ZACHRY, C. B.: *Emotion and Conduct in Adolescence*, Appleton-Century-Crofts, Inc., New York, 1940.

# CHAPTER 21

## PRINCIPLES OF PERSONALITY FORMATION

### 1. THE UNIVERSE OF PERSONALITY TRAITS

**Revision of Trait Concepts.** The variety of method and data in the many fields covered by the study of personality has compelled us, with due regard for scientific values, to develop in any given field only such general principles as are justified by the regularities in the data of that field. Except for certain principles of measurement, certain conceptions of the individual vis-à-vis society, and certain psychoanalytical generalizations from the wide survey of clinical observation in the early chapters, no attempt has been made until the present chapter to extract and assemble explicit principles and laws of a universal, or at least a widely integrative, nature.

At this point, however, the student should be prepared to systematize his understanding and particularly with respect to three crucial fields: (*a*) with regard to the nature and meaning of quantitative description of personality generally; (*b*) with regard to the laws of learning or growth of dynamic structure; and (*c*) with regard to the essential nature of personality and the self.

A complete presentation of the theory of quantitative approaches to personality, stopping short of epistemological questions, has recently been offered in the present writer's *The Description and Measurement of Personality*, to which the student who finds difficulties in the condensation made in this chapter section should refer. It is recognized there that personality has temperamental, ability, and dynamic aspects, and interrelated definitions of these three "modalities" are given. Briefly these are to the effect that dynamic traits are traits whose time or error measurements alter in response to changes in incentives, that abilities are those whose measurements (time or errors) change as environmental complexities change, and that temperament is indicated by measures which most constantly retain their value throughout change in complexity or incentive.

It is further stated there, as in the opening chapters of this book, that unitary patterns or "traits" are to be discovered by study of covariation, first at the level of correlation clusters or *surface traits* and, more analytically, by factor analysis (using $R$, $Q$ or $P$ technique or other possible modes shown in the *covariation chart*), leading to *source traits*,[1] common or unique. The student wishing to understand more fully the scientific implications and opportunities of factor analysis applied to observations on common variation is referred to a special introductory text (13a).

**Traits and Situational Indices Estimated for the Specification Equation.** The above conception of traits culminates in the principle, illustrated or implicit in earlier chapters, that any given performance or reaction can be expressed by the specification equation:

$$P_{ij} = S_{1j}T_{1i} + S_{2j}T_{2i} + \cdots + S_{Nj}T_{Ni} + S_jT_{ji}$$

where $P$ is the performance or reaction of the individual $i$ in the situation $j$, $S_{Nj}$ is the *situational index* for the source trait $T_N$ in the situation $j$, $T_{Ni}$ is the individual $i$'s degree of possession (in standard score) of the source trait $T_N$, $S_j$, $T_j$ are the index and the trait specific to this particular situation (whereas the other traits operate also in many other situations).

$P_j$ can be anything measurable along an acceptable continuum, *e.g.*, the number of items scored on a test, the intensity of a neurotic symptom, the frequency of a social act in time sampling, the strength of a libidinal fixation or an attitude. The $S$'s, as previously described, are situational indices which collectively define the "meaning" (or "valence" or "stimulus value") of the situation $j$ for the typical person (in the case of $R$-technique values) or for the particular individual (in the case of $P$-technique variables). Any single $S$ defines the emotional meaning (incentive value) or complexity (respectively for conditional (13a) dynamic and cognitive traits) of that situation

---

[1] It is also pointed out that factors will correspond to either *wholistic* or *conditional* source traits according to the number of modality conditions held constant in getting the data. Thus wholistic patterns are traits into which all modalities may simultaneously enter. For example, the manic factor has cognitive, temperamental, and dynamic elements. But conditional factors are more analytical and of only one modality. For example, most intelligence-test subtests are done under special conditions of (maximum) motivation, so that the resulting conditional factor is a purely cognitive one. But these refinements do not concern further problems discussed here. Suffice it that the use of the concept of *unitary trait as factor* requires an alertness to questions of population selection and to the definition of conditions of stimulation and measurement, etc., obtaining when the factor patterns are established.

for one particular source trait (see p. 68). The $T$'s represent the source traits (of single or mixed modality, according to manner of extraction, and of common or unique character, according to their origin in $R$ or $P$ technique) which give the dimensions of the individual's personality.

In reply to the question which may be raised at this point as to whether these dimensions do not "interact" instead of merely add up, it is sufficient here to point out that from the beginning the pioneers in factorial methods, *e.g.*, Spearman, Thurstone (50), Holzinger, Burt (5) have insisted that the *addition* of factors may turn out to be an approximation for some other functional relation, of a more complex kind, *e.g.*, multiplication; but no finding has yet called for a more complex formula. However, more theoretical aspects of this question will be discussed later in the present chapter.

**The Necessity for Appropriate Statistical Concepts.** The above suffices for a bare statement of the specification equation, its meaning and relation to later discussion of personality theory. Its use, however, requires attention to certain technical precisions of statement which must be set out quite briefly in these paragraphs, since some students will not wish to attend to them in greater detail at this point.

The $S$'s in the above equation are, of course, obtained from the original factor analysis. The $T$'s have to be estimated for each individual from a sum or weighted sum of the individual's scores in those variables which the factor analysis has shown to be highly loaded with each of the given source traits. Thus a person's endowment in $T_B$ (with $B$ factor defined as General Intelligence in Personality) is usually obtained by the unweighted addition of his scores in certain intelligence subtests, *e.g.*, analogies, classification, that have a loading of 0.8 or more in this factor.

In such computations it is necessary to make certain that appropriate concepts are used in various formulae. For example, both the $S$'s and the weights given to variables in estimating the $T$'s must be appropriate to the population and conditions of the attempted prediction. The fact that a given source trait is estimated by (slightly) different weights in different populations and that the situational indices will also vary somewhat with variations in the population range must not be taken to mean that these "traits" are insubstantial or unreal and merely mathematical conveniences. A trait is a system of relations between individuals and environment, and the particular "trait-elements" from which its pattern is composed, defined, and measured will vary with changing group heredity and forms of cultural expression.

The most glaring kind of error that could be made in this respect would be to confuse the loadings or situational indices for *common* traits with those for *unique* traits. As pointed out on various occasions above, the common trait pattern is found by studying common trends of covariation in populations of persons, by $R$, and sometimes $Q$, technique and represents an "average" of the pattern in all people. *Unique* traits, on the other hand, can be of two kinds, *intrinsic unique traits*, in which the individual shows some entirely new dimension not possessed by other people, *e.g.*, the ability visually to perceive radio-wave reflections, a theoretically conceivable extreme example, and *relative unique traits* in which the uniqueness consists only in the peculiarity of patterning of trait-elements known in all people.

One might expect that these (relative) unique patterns, *i.e.*, patterns of factor loadings, would scatter normally about the central values for the common trait pattern. The $P$-technique studies of unique traits now appearing (10,11) do indeed indicate individual trait patterns to be partly random modifications of the loading patterns obtained by $R$ technique; but also suggest that a few variables may systematically change their loading. For example, there is evidence that fluency of association participates little in the inter-individual differences due to $F$ factor, whereas the intra-individual differences—the day-to-day fluctuations—cause the individual to vary in fluency of association a good deal.

These considerations of the appropriateness of factor patterns and situational indices to the specification equation may be continued also to the consideration of units and scales. Individual and group specification equations deal with different universes of units. One must remember that measurement units in personality (and therefore in the whole of psychology) are broadly of three kinds: *interactive* units, and the *normative* and *ipsative* units derived from interactive units. Interactive units are raw scores— time, errors, repetitions, etc., in a defined physical situation. Normative scores, like I.Q.'s, percentiles, or standard scores, are interactive scores redefined and given meaning *with respect to a group*. Ipsative scores are given meaning *with respect to a population of occasions* for the individual, *e.g.*, above or below one's usual, or prepractice, or previous best score. Common traits are appropriately scored only in normative and unique traits only in ipsative form, except that both may be left in interactive units.

Finally one must take account of the modifications of conception and calculation to be heeded in stepping past racial and cultural boundaries. It can be surmised that certain source traits, *e.g.*, general ability, general emotionality, basic ergs, will preserve their form recognizably from culture to culture, with a sufficient number of common situations (*i.e.*, common loadings in situations) by which to recognize them. But others, *e.g.*, adolescent trait patterns, will be quite different. In the latter case individuals in one culture cannot be directly compared in the given trait with individuals in another, and indeed if an individual passes from one to the other the pattern of behavior will sooner or later change in him. If the same constitutional trait, *e.g.*, the temperament features associated with metabolic rate, actually exists in two groups (because they are at least genetically, racially similar samples) under quite different cultural conditions, its loadings in various acquired behaviors will be different in those groups. But, providing the trait can be cross-identified, it can be estimated—by differently weighted actual variables—equally for individuals in the two groups. Thus, general mental capacity may show itself differently in groups with different languages and habits, but it is theoretically possible to compare individuals in different cultures with respect to their endowment in this capacity.[2]

On the other hand as illustrated above, certain environmental-mold traits existing in one culture will not exist even in modified form in another, and comparison is impossible. Not the principles of personality, but only the dimensions in terms of which it is to be measured, will thus, as far as environmental-mold source traits are concerned, vary from culture to culture. An interesting theoretical problem, not to be pursued here, concerns whether these changes in loading or pattern for individual performances of persons in different culture groups can be calculated from the differences in syntality dimensions of the groups concerned.

However, although the constants of the specification equation are normally as much limited to the racio-cultural group as its monetary system or even its language, it would be possible, by factorizing a population from all cultures, to obtain supercultural patterns. Unfortunately the trait patterns found would lose some of the sharpness of the common traits found in one culture, just as the latter lose something by blurring the outlines of the individual unique traits.

**Specification Equation, Situational Index, and the Definition of Environment.** Our preoccupation with personality should not distract us entirely from the fact that the specification equation, being a relation between the individual and the environment, is just as capable of throwing light on the psychological meaning of the environment as on the structure of the individual. If two situations, $j$ and $k$, prove to have situational indices similar in sign and quantity for a given factor $T_N$, then they have the same psychological meaning. Thus if $T_N$ is the sex drive, they are both, whatever their *apparent* nature, possessed of sex appeal, and if $T_N$ is the escape drive they are both threatening situations. If the indices are similar for *all* source traits, then the total psychological meaning is similar.

Examination and ordering of empirically obtained situational indices thus present a means of systematically exploring and mapping the environment, including the culture pattern, independently of the "methods," limited by various preconceptions, by which we should otherwise set out to map the

[2] However, it is also possible that the only calculus that will ever permit expression of the give and take of the individual and society will be one in interactive units, rather than the normative units required by the above equations.

chief "presses" and interests of the culture pattern or environment. (Naturally this proceeds under the limitation that unless people *vary* in their
response to a situation its importance in regard to that response cannot be
picked up by correlation.)

Principally this approach offers rewards also to the psychometrist and the
philosopher, in that it permits us to group together all the situations that
operate on or provoke a particular source trait, and thus assists in finding
what will best measure it and what its essential nature is. For example,
the discovery of the situations highly loaded in the general-ability factor
permitted psychometrists to get the most saturated, valid tests and the
examination of the nature of the situations with high indices, in tests or life
situations, permitted the more philosophically minded to interpret the nature
of general ability as a generalized capacity to perceive relations.

## 2. DYNAMIC PRINCIPLES: *A*. THE SINGLE DRIVE

**The Necessity for More Explicit Formulation of Principles.** Of the three
modalities of personality traits—abilities, temperament characteristics, and
dynamic traits—that simultaneously enter into the determination of any
single act, most attention must be given to dynamic traits. This necessity
arises, as explained in Chapter 6, from their being more involved in personality changes and developments, as well as from the relative obscurity in
which the principles of dynamic-trait action are still enveloped.

The main problems that still call for more exact formulation of solutions,
in the realm of dynamic-trait action are: (*a*) analysis of the action of innate
drives (ergs); (*b*) formulation of principles governing "learning" or modification of single drives; (*c*) formulation of principles governing the general
interaction of dynamic traits with one another and with traits of other
modalities. All of these problems have occupied us in earlier chapters at a
factual level and in terms of local or implicit principles, but the time has
now come to attack them in terms of more general principles and to bring
both difficulties and solutions into explicit formulation. The present section
will confine itself to the first two of the above, covering the examination of
concepts used in connection with the single erg.

**Goal Tensions and Goal Gradient.** Since ergic action has been adequately
described and analyzed at a simple level in Chapter 7 no further reference
need be made here to details. The innateness consists in a readier learning
to attend to some stimuli or to perform certain actions than others: it also
resides in a preferred sequence of actions, shown by certain reactivities
requiring prior activities and, grossly, in the cycle toward a *goal*, after which
reactivity ceases. Physiologically, much of this behavior can, at least theoretically, be traced to greater readiness of certain conduction paths, due
either to innate structure or to innate reactivity to biochemical conditions.

The concepts of "goal tension" and "goal gradient" which have been loosely used up to this point now need closer examination. Experimental studies have so far based them on some single type of observation, *e.g.*, learning, in the generalization that learning occurs more rapidly as the situation occurs nearer to the goal (23). It would seem desirable instead to intercorrelate several characteristics of the organism's reactions, *e.g.*, strength of drive as measured by the obstruction method, amount of learning and retention, degree of pugnacity at frustration of action, length of deprivation, etc., to see whether a single goal-tension factor or more than

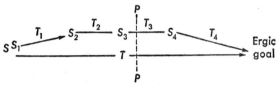

DIAGRAM 53. The relation of the major goal tension, $T$, to intermediate, stimulated goal tensions, $T_1$, $T_2$, $T_3$, and $T_4$.

one exist, and to determine how to estimate each. From more general evidence it seems likely that the strength of action at any point in the goal path (still with respect to the *innate* sequence only) is determined both by an over-all goal tension $T$ and *a series of tensions specific to particular subgoals*. The intermediate, means-end goals, $S_1$, $S_2$, $S_3$, etc., in the diagram are both stimuli and goals—goals dissolving the tension set up by the preceding subgoal and stimuli for tensions directed to a later subgoal. These subtensions may be illustrated, in their distinction from the main tension, by that "appetite" which arises from suitable presentation of specific foods and which is different from the general conditions of hunger tension.

At any point in the sequence represented by the cross section $PP$ at $T_3$, the strength of reaction or drive, $R$, would be represented as follows:

$$R = S \cdot T + S_3 \cdot T_3$$

Where $T$ is the strength of the internally predetermined tension and $S$ is the strength of the stimulus provocation. The functional relations may, of course, be more than simple multiplicative or simple summative ones. The above may be summarized as our first principle, as follows:

LAW 1. *The law of innate goal tension patterns: An innate drive may be analyzed into an over-all goal tension and a series of subgoals (means-end) tensions. Any tension is manifested and measured by attentiveness to a particular kind of stimulus and a tendency (variously measurable) to a particular kind of action. The main goal tension disappears as the main goal is reached, and the particular goal tension ceases as a particular intermediate goal is reached. The strength of action is a function of the total innate goal tensions (in their given appetitive state) and the strength of the stimulus situation.*

### 3. DYNAMIC PRINCIPLES: *B*. LEARNING WITH THE SINGLE MOTIVE

**The Varieties of Rigidity.** If we turn now to modification of the single drive—which may be considered the paradigm of most learning yet studied experimentally—proper theoretical caution requires that we ask why behavior does *not* change before we proceed to those examples in which it *does*. Except in the writings of Spearman (48), Dashiell (14), and a few others, the necessity for something equivalent to Newton's first law has been inadequately appreciated. A concept of disposition rigidity is required to account for the fact that an existing mode of action does not change, either spontaneously or even under changes of stimulus situation, and that a certain *resistance* to change occurs when dynamic rewards favor change, *i.e.*, the fully rewarded response is not immediately adopted.

This is manifested, for example, in the extinction of conditioned reflexes. Parenthetically, not all resistance to change is to be regarded as disposition rigidity, since once a trait becomes embedded in a general structure determining complex behavior, a dynamic gain from its alteration may be more than offset by a total dynamic loss from the rearrangement occasioned in the other traits. Thus a habit of punctually boarding a certain morning train may become intrinsically punishing by virtue of the company encountered, but an alteration of the trait is prevented by the other trait satisfactions (home and business demands) structurally tied up with it.

Much has been written on disposition rigidity or functional autonomy, but, apart from the successful delineation of $P$ factor or perseveration (12) no experimental work has defined the processes at work, and it is only recently that the existence of some four factors—of which $P$ is one—has been demonstrated in behavior of a "rigid" type (6). This work is too recent to give any final clarification of the field and the following analysis of rigidity must be considered tentative. Apparently, apart from the pseudorigidity of (*a*) structural dynamics (total-satisfaction situation) (*b*) low intelligence and (*c*) low motivation or fatigue (for motivation—specific or willed—and fatigue must be held constant before studying true rigidity (6)), we may recognize (*d*) a perhaps largely innate rigidity shown mainly in slowness of motor learning (12), (*e*) an acquired factor in rigidity, due to trauma, as seen in schizophrenia and neuroses, and perhaps associated with ergic regression, (*f*) factors in rigidity specific to particular areas (perceptual (6) or motor rigidity), or specific to dynamic traits of particular levels (innate contrasted with acquired, or early as contrasted with late dynamic traits), or specific to particular dynamic intensities (habits formed under strong as contrasted with weak motivation).

Despite these doubts concerning specific rigidities it is possible to formulate the role of rigidity in principle, as follows:

LAW 2. *The law of satisfaction in rigidity. Even when a dynamic gain exists from changing a trait, the change in behavior may be either resisted, i.e., may occur very slowly, or may not occur at all, due to factors of disposition rigidity.* This is manifested also in what might seem important enough for a separate principle, if it did not depend directly on the present, namely, *the tendency* of means to ends to become ultimate goals in themselves, as seen in sublimation and in phantasy. It also accounts for much retention, *e.g.,* symbols remaining as stimuli without reinforcement. It must be distinguished from pseudofunctional autonomy described on the opposite page, due to dynamically satisfying total structure, or to gains accruing to the need to avoid fatigue.

**The Need for Variability of Response.** Before any new habit can be formed, actions and perceptions different from those of the innate erg must arise as raw material for the new pattern. This faces us with the problem of the origin of random behavior in trial-and-error learning or of attention to the conditioning stimulus in conditioning. Now, in Chapter 8 where plasticity was analyzed, sufficient discussion has already been given to what is yet known about the phenomenon of "ergic dispersion" under deprivation. Under increasing deprivation there is increasing "excitement" defined, not introspectively but behaviorally, by various signs and variables not yet sufficiently investigated. Central among these signs is variation of response, perhaps produced by the fatiguing of the most natural ergic channels of perception and reactions or else by some sort of "overflow" when general energy mounts. This process is of sufficiently basic importance to require formulation as follows:

LAW 3. *Law of dispersion with excitement and deprivation. Continued stimulation of ergs, with deprivation of the goal, produces increasing variation in the stimuli to which attention is directed and increasing variation of response behavior (as well as introspectively, increased "excitement").*

It remains for more precise experimental studies to decide how much of this dispersion is due to various affiliated causes. One wonders whether it correlates more with duration of drive strength, or with magnitude of strength, occasioned either by increase of stimulation with time or by mounting of the goal tension, in appetitive drives, with time and deprivation.

Dispersion is accompanied, as cause rather than effect, by a *raised level of excitement,* which manifests itself also in restlessness and impulsiveness, *i.e., by a lowered threshold for drives other than the one deprived, and by increased fluency of association* (in memory and symbol material). That the *direction of dispersion* is toward ergic regressions, and, in the case of metanergic traits, toward historically early habits, is clear, (see Laws 8 and 16), but the available evidence suggests that it is by no means entirely in this direction. It may, for example, take the direction of motor outlets set up for other drives or dynamic traits, a fact utilized in conditioning.

**The Conditions of Positive Learning.** Formation of new dynamic traits, from among the new ways of behaving made possible by dispersion, has so far been formulated by psychologists largely under two concepts in the field of learning, namely, (*a*) the reflexological concept of "conditioning," and (*b*) the more or less dynamic concept of the "law of effect." The facts connected with these theories can perhaps be brought under a single formulation as discussed in Chapter 8. However, the extreme character of the conditioned reflex design from a naturalistic point of view, notably in its concentration on perceptual learning, in its narrow time relations and its concern with bodily "part reactions," has resulted in experiment too specialized to offer evidence permitting conclusions as to the fundamental nature of this common character.[3] The broad essentials of the common action in the two learning situations can, however, be expressed in a fourth principle as follows:

LAW 4. *Law of dynamic effect. When goal seeking behavior shows dispersion, the resulting attentions to new stimuli and accompanying behavioral responses become habitualized in proportion to the extent to which they shorten the distance to the goal.*

The notion of "goal distance" here, though conceivable to common sense, is by no means easy to formulate in exact operational terms. It has been roughly equated with "goal tension," under the belief that the successful response immediately reduces tension, but this is unsatisfactory unless there is proof that the main tension, $T$, declines continuously toward the goal. This is unsatisfactory because there is actually much evidence, *i.e.*, learning rates, observations on the degree of pugnacity, or appeal occasioned by frustration (such as the observation (44) that babies cry less at the removal of a bottle slightly emptied than one from which they have taken half or more), which suggests precisely the opposite, *i.e.*, that goal tension *increases* with approach (in time or distance) to the goal. Distance to the goal, as far as present knowledge goes, is therefore best defined in terms of the time and energy that remain to be expended until it is achieved. For one finds some instances, *e.g.*, rats in a maze, where the learned response shortens the time (the length of tension to be endured) to the goal, and others where the learned response actually increases the time but decreases the trouble and energy expended in reaching the goal.

The law of dynamic effect, it should be observed, does not define or limit the nature of the cognitive processes which have produced the behavior

---

[3] The student must be referred to the fuller discussion in Chapter 8 where we saw that to subsume the conditioning phenomena wholly under this law it is necessary to regard the reflex as a small drive, *needing* discharge, within a larger drive. Conditioning, by giving reaction to an *earlier* stimulus, shortens the distance to the goal.

leading to a shorter goal path. The connection may be made through physical trial-and-error behavior, through mental trial and error (imaginative anticipation), or through insight resulting from intelligent capacity to perceive essential relations. Once made, by processes no matter how irrelevant, the connection becomes habitual and preferred by reason of dynamic effect. Possibly further research may show that the new dynamic trait formation differs slightly in character according to the relative role of these processes in its formation, especially perhaps in regard to later unlearning; but essentially they embody the same *dynamic* principle.

Parenthetically, it should be pointed out that Law 4 can be also conceived as a "field" law, in that the fate of the relation of stimulus and response is determined by the position of the connection in a "goal distance" field.

## 4. DYNAMIC PRINCIPLES:
### C. CONFLICT AND LEARNING AMONG DYNAMIC TRAITS

**Solutions of Temporary and of Permanent Conflict.** Principles of learning or trait formation have so far been confined to those which can be expressed entirely in terms of a single dynamic trait or goal path—and, in the first law, to an *innate* goal. It is now appropriate to turn to the wider situation, more common in real life, in which the simultaneous stimulation of different drives occurs.

When two dynamic traits are simultaneously stimulated, hesitation or blocking may occur in expression, because the nature of the organism and the physical world is such that a single effective, organized motor expression cannot be found for both traits. Conflict, when (*a*) it occurs for the first time, or (*b*) the experience of expressing one drive does not produce obstacles to the *later* expression of the other, or (*c*) dissociation separates the associations, and blocks realization of the incompatible consequences of the two drives, we may call *immediate, temporary, or naive conflict,* to distinguish it from the permanent or interlocking conflict of the next principle. The outcome of such conflict may be briefly expressed as follows:

LAW 5. *The law of alternating expression in naive conflict. Except where a motor outlet can be found which leads to satisfaction of both of the stimulated dynamic traits, motor expression will be given to that which has the stronger combined stimulation and goal tension, but, when the goal tension of the dominant drive subsides, with satisfaction, the second drive may gain expression, thus setting up alternating expression.* This is seen in temporary "suppression" by the will as well as in "spontaneous recovery" of extinguished condition reflexes and in multiple personality. The immediate outcome of conflict of this kind may be expressed in terms of source-trait structure by

$$P = S_1T_1 + S_2T_2$$

in which it is understood that $S_1$ and $S_2$ are opposite in sign in this situation.

When the satisfaction of one dynamic trait leads to conditions which necessarily and permanently frustrate another, *e.g.*, a military act of cowardice conflicts with the soldier's self-respect, we may speak of "permanent" or *trait conflict*. Here the ideational associations and the conditions of the real world do not permit alternating or unrelated expression of the dynamic traits involved. As the observations discussed in connection with crossroads 3 and 4 (pp. 219 and 224) indicated, this can be formulated in a sixth principle, as follows:

LAW 6. *The law of suppressive mechanisms in permanent conflict. When trait conflict (permanent conflict) occurs, prevention of the expression of one dynamic trait takes place through the second trait commanding more attention for the stimuli which activate it, at the same time reducing the percepts or memories which activate the first drive.* It may be that this formulation of the mechanism in trait conflict will raise the objection that circularity of argument is involved, in that the activity of the drive is said to be a function of strength of stimulation, but now strength of the stimulus or percept is said apparently to be a function of goal tension. This apparent circularity may be otherwise expressed by saying that perhaps "attention" is only defined in the above by reference to the ensuing behavior, whereas we are trying to make it a *cause* of the ensuing behavior. Actually it is supposed in this law that stronger attention is defined by other things than the fact that stronger reaction ensues, though a "feedback" mechanism exists additionally. At the least it is defined by the introspective reports of greater conscious clarity of the given stimuli, as well as by the usual physiological associations. The statement then runs that experience of greater clarity of stimuli is followed by stronger action of the drive to which these stimuli apply.

This law therefore states essentially that the change in clarity of the cognitive appreciation of stimuli is a major link in the chain of events by which a stronger drive takes over motor expression from a weaker one. That a deprived drive, with high goal tension, is capable of directing attention to faint stimuli and even of creating hallucinations is common psychological knowledge. Law 6, however, does not deny the independence of $S$ and $T$ in $P = ST$, but only describes the way in which $T$ operates when the expression of one drive is denied, namely, by manipulation of the "cognitive pegs" on which dynamic structure hangs. $S$ is the external strength of the stimulus, which is independent of $T$; but $T$, among its other manifestations, can reduce or increase the *awareness* of $S$.

When conflict remains permanent, in the sense that alternating expression is not possible, permanent suppression must ensue, as described above. The greatest contribution of psychoanalysis has been to demonstrate that this tends to pass into the new condition of repression, which may now be introduced in a specific principle and separately defined (though no sharp line can be drawn between deep suppression and light repression); as follows:

LAW 7. *Law of the nature and conditions of repression in permanent conflict. The process of preventing access to perceptual or symbolic (memory) cognitive stimulation, as described in Law 6, may proceed further as a result of conflict with traits which are (a) massive and of wide range; (b) of dynamically strong tension, and (c) of certain ergic qualities, probably fear, self-abasement, and despair, rather than others. Through this denial of access to the cognitive apparatus, the dynamic trait, though still stimulated by its attached memories, becomes dissociated, or repressed—a condition which tends to be irreversible.*

**Deprivation, Frustration, and Blocking.** Any dynamic trait blocked in expression, either by continued deprivation, by suppression, or by repression, will, in accordance with Law 3, show increased dispersion of attempted modes of expression, and generate a raised level of excitement of the organism. But apart from these common consequences the results will be different. Excitement will have different qualities according to the ergs involved and it is a mistake to confuse, for example, excitement with anxiety. Thus Mowrer has correctly pointed out that in conflicts of ego and superego it is the superego rather than the id which sometimes gets repressed. But it is a mistake to say that repression of the superego generates anxiety (rather than excitement), for the specific fear motivation is against the id, not against the superego expression.

By definition, the student should be reminded, deprivation means a failure of the cues that lead to ultimate satisfaction to make an appearance. In some discussions on the subject this is confused with frustration, which may properly be defined as an outside intervention thwarting a course of action actually in progress. By blocking we mean a completely frustrating circumstance which frustrates also any of the adaptive responses usually made to frustration.

Blocking has necessarily been reached via the dynamic crossroads 2 and 3 (pp. 218 and 219), *i.e.*, the organism passes from deprivation to frustration and pugnacity and, failing such responses, to fear and despair. Thus fear and despair, together with the raised level of excitement, *constitute* the anxiety, which is commonly reactivated when the organism again encounters the original stimulus situation. Parenthetically, it is necessary to caution the student at this point against an error, which, in the writer's opinion, is rather prevalent among dynamic systematists. This is the assertion that anxiety is a normal, necessary, and invariable concomitant of unresolved conflict. Actually the addition of fear and despair, and even a history of anger, supervening on the primary deprivation sequel constituted by dispersion and excitement, depends, as we have seen, upon the conflict taking a particular, though not uncommon turn—into frustration and ultimate blocking.

Although the most numerous instances of internal conflict in man, as in animals, proceed only so far as the action described in Laws 5 and 6 above, those which have come in for most attention by *clinical* psychologists also involve the action of Law 7 and laws to be described below. Though *any* truly massive dynamic trait could cause suppression and ultimately repression of lesser traits, the chief known instance of such action occurs where a single massive dynamic structure arises, namely in the ego and self-sentiment in human beings.

Now the self-sentiment (see Section 8 below) includes the drive of fear for the safety of the physical and social self. Consequently *any* conflict with the self-sentiment is certain to bring in anxiety. Thus, although anxiety is not a necessary feature of mental conflict, it *is* a feature of all ego conflicts in human beings and rightly enters into the definition of the higher types of conflict which the next law describes. This law deals with the consequences of repression in what might be called the "neurotogenic principle."

LAW 8. *Law of consequences of blocking complete failure of expression. Complete failure of expression may occur through suppression, repression, or complete mutual interference through confusion of cognitive cues[4] or motor expressions. This results in an increased level of excitement-agitation (restless response to normally inadequate stimuli) and dispersion, as from deprivation; but also in some degree of reactivation of the drives, usually, but not necessarily, pugnacity and escape, leading to the suppression. (These appear, seemingly, in the reverse order of the history of their action, that is, fear before anger.) The general excitement, along with the specifically induced diffuse fear and irritability, tends to produce anxiety, with physiological disorganization and exhaustion.*

**The Second Generator of New Dynamic Structure.** Whether it is possible for the drive denied expression to discharge, in time, directly through the suppressing drives, as Freud (see (4, 5, 6), Chap. 8) claimed in his early observations of transformation of libido into anxiety, or whether the original chain of "conditioned" connections must always be followed remains for research to decide. However, it is certain that the increased plasticity (dispersion) of the suppressed dynamic trait, as well as that engendered by the counterpressure upon the suppressing trait, may lead to a solution through some new line of action which contributes to the eventual satisfaction of both. This application of the law of dynamic effect to the interaction of two interests can be expressed as follows:

LAW 9. *Law of combined expression. New dynamic structure arises not only by new linkages of cues and reactions in the goal path of a single desire, but also by responses emerging in conflict situations (from increased dispersion of both drives, either before or after suppression of one), which prove capable of simultaneously lessening the goal distance to two or more goals.*

This law, with those preceding, suffices to account for the rise of the entire

[4] As in the work of Pavlov (39), Gantt, Maier, and others already described in Chapter 17.

network of the dynamic lattice as described in Chapter 6, with its checking of individual desires by composite traits and its patterns of conscious and unconscious links.

## 5. DYNAMIC PRINCIPLES:
### *D.* THE MAINTENANCE OF LONG-CIRCUITED STRUCTURE

**Application of Above Laws to Attitude and Sentiment Formation.** The preceding nine laws will be found adequate to account for most observations in the earlier part of this book concerning the *formation* of traits. They appear, with the exception of the first, to apply equally to innate and acquired dynamic traits. They underlie and clarify, not only the clinical observations of the abnormal, but also the generalizations attempted in Chapters 8 and 9 concerning the growth of normal sentiment structure.

In regard to sentiment and attitude formation, for example, the generalization that a sentiment arises through satisfaction of a drive, following insightful or trial-and-error learning, occurring repeatedly in regard to a particular object, rests on Laws 3 and 4: the generalization of common satisfaction of two or more drives in a single sentiment is simply Law 9; and the third generalization on sentiment growth, namely, the growth of secondary sentiments as structures invoked to aid in reaching the goal of some existing sentiment, is again an example of Law 4. In practice, the application to the development of particular sentiments and attitudes may sometimes prove difficult, because of (*a*) unconscious connections, (*b*) the sublety of human rewards and punishments (contrasted with those presented to the rat in the Skinner box)—especially where self-assertive and social, symbolic and phantasy situations are concerned—and (*c*) the lack of research defining the essential characteristics of human ergic goals and stimulus situations. But the predictive power of the laws is at least as accurate as our present means of dynamic measurement in checking on predictions will justify!

**The Nature of Long-circuited Structure.** So far the dynamic laws deal almost entirely with processes in the rise of dynamic structures. The neglected aspects of personality dynamics which we must now encounter and deal with: (*a*) the maintenance of the dynamic structures whose formation has just been covered, and (*b*) with the rise of certain special, more complex structures within the general form of the dynamic lattice, notably of the integrating structure constituted by the ego itself. This section is devoted to the first issue—the conditions governing maintenance and retention of learned structures.

Our presentation at this point suffers because learning has been most systematically studied in the cognitive field, which, as stated earlier, has unduly restricted itself to experiments on learning under a single drive. Consequently the theory and laws yet available are not particularly appli-

cable to personality as a whole where learning occurs through complex interactions of drives. The present review of problems in retention has therefore
to depend on less rich arrays of data, mainly gathered in the personality
field itself, and its conclusions must accordingly be regarded as decidedly
more tentative, as our manner of statement indicates.

Considered in relation to general dynamics, as developed in Chapter 6,
the essence of learned activities is that they are "metanergic" or long-
circuited, *i.e.*, they approach ergic goals by more deflected and usually longer
paths than the original innate ones. Furthermore, the long-circuited path is
not always completed by outlets to the goal, for by disposition rigidity
(Law 2) the means to an end is sometimes accepted as a sufficiently satisfactory goal in itself. The more exact nature of long-circuiting (a process
which, it is necessary constantly to remind oneself, *invariably arises from
force of circumstance*, causing deprivation or frustration with respect to the
original goal path) now needs closer examination and definition.

Long-circuiting takes the form of (*a*) finding, by dispersion, a path alternative to the blocked or ineffective mode of response; or (*b*) adding an extra
step to an existing goal path (as when an animal trained to get food by
pressing a lever now has to walk on a plate before touching the lever);
(*c*) carrying out suppression of any responses, connected with other dynamic
traits, to the cues necessary in the new path to the main goal. For example,
an animal will learn to incorporate a slightly painful stimulus in a chain of
cues to food, suppressing the escape response it would normally make to pain.
Incidentally, such suppression of incidental paths is not peculiar to long-
circuited or learned traits, but it is more frequent there, because any departure from ergic behavior and cues is likely, in utilizing new cues, to trespass
into the region of cues natural to other ergs or dynamic traits. Thus the
long-circuited drive is more likely to encounter incidentally tempting and
punishing stimuli in its path.

After the initial learning, which necessarily means departing from the preferred ergic path, not all further learning is increased long-circuiting. Some
of it may be a return to shorter, less deflected or less conflict-ridden courses.
We should expect, therefore, that some generalizations will apply to learning
generally and others only to long-circuited behavior. However, before dealing with generalizations specific to long-circuited or learned behavior or both,
it is necessary to ask whether any generalizations about maintenance of
structure exist that need stating for both ergic and metanergic structures.
From previous discussions (Chapter 8) it is evident that disposition rigidity
affects both ergic and metanergic structures. We must therefore begin our
consideration with the already stated law of rigidity (Law 2), which states
that any mode of perceiving and responding offers intrinsic resistance to
change.

**The Strains and Losses of Long-circuiting.** This suffices to account for the stability of long-circuited structures. The next most important feature about them, from the standpoint of personality is that they create certain strains, even when they are well adjusted and integrated. These strains arise both from the maintenance of a "deflected" mode of perception and action, *i.e.*, one departing from the preferred innate patterns, and also through actual complication of new cues and discriminations relative to those in the innate cognitive activity. The laws that follow will tentatively assume that these sources may be distinct, pending research on their relationships.

LAW 10. *Law of deflection strain. Modes of learned perception and response can be arranged in a gradient according to their degree of dispersion from the innately easiest path. Greater dispersion arises in alternatives established with greater deprivation and excitement in the original deprivation or blocking underlying learning, and is maintained thereafter with a greater degree of "deflection strain." This is shown, perhaps, in a permanently higher excitement level, and greater irritability, anxiety, and fatigue. The deflection strain of any given goal path must include, in any total assessment of it, the deflections and suppressions of other goal drives that this path incidentally occasions.*

By deflection strain is meant specifically the strain associated with deflection, against the resistance of innate rigidity, from an innately preferred path. But long-circuiting involves other strains too, and though further research may separate these into a definite number of kinds, they perhaps have sufficient in common to be included for the time in a single law. They are mainly strains the toleration limit to which is set by certain given powers of the organism—intelligence, memory, capacity to inhibit.

For example, there is a well-known experiment in which a rat, after being trained to obtain food by pressing a lever, is further trained, by punishment, to delay three seconds after the lever (or signal) before taking the food. With most rats this is successful, but if the delay is increased to six seconds the learning breaks down: the rat either cowers in fear and despair or makes repeated attempts to take the food despite punishment. Here the deflection strain is entirely concerned with the time of maintaining a mental set and the limit is presumably set by the supply of neurones available for such activation.

These strains set by limits to cognitive powers and energy may be brought in a single law as follows:

LAW 11. *Law of cognitive-dynamic investment strain. Increase in the number of intermediate cues and subgoals in reaching a goal, as well as increase in the fineness of cognitive discriminations to be maintained, and increase of the length of time that intermediate, anticipatory mental sets (deferred action to cues) have to be maintained, occasion a strain of total cognitive-dynamic energy. This is probably specifically shown in decreased ability to learn new material, increased fatigability, increased vulnerability to trauma, and decreased incli-nation to react through the trait system concerned.*

This sort of strain may be cognate with that producing the syndrome of neurasthenia. It may also be the root of most preference for the old and familiar. The separation of the above two forms of strain involved in the retaining of learned reactions (metanergic structures) is in accordance with the theory that a special component of *innate* rigidity exists, distinct from metanergic rigidity or from low intelligence or defective memory. This rigidity is responsible for the deflection strain of Law 10. The present law defines a strain due to demands on intelligence and memory which is practi-cally identical with "effortfulness of task," as studied by Mowrer and Jones (37). Indeed, many psychological generalizations suppose that individuals differ in total capacity for long-circuited adjustments according to their possession of certain constitutional capacities. Usually (when intelligence is set aside) these generalizations reduce to capacity to tolerate deflection strain (as, for example, in the psychopath) and energy to maintain complex cognitive-dynamic sets.

It is probable that there should be included under Law 11 a further source of energy loss now to be defined. It occurs not only in learning more long-circuited behavior, but in any learning, *i.e.*, any change of one perception-response link for another. If maintenance of *any* habit requires a constant expenditure of interest energy, and if a habit, even when it progresses toward extinction, is never entirely lost, some energy must remain invested in *all* past learning. Consequently the facts require a further generalization:

LAW 11*a*. *Law of loss in previous investments. Some cognitive-dynamic investment strain occurs in proportion to the number of intermediate modes of response learned and unlearned on the way to the presently existing trait, regard-less of whether it is more complex or deflected than its predecessors.*

There are other factors to be taken into account in trait retention which, however, are as yet insufficiently clarified by experiment for formulation. For example, experiments on the goal-gradient hypothesis show that steps in a maze nearer to the goal are more quickly learned and strongly retained than those more remote. There are also experiments suggesting that traits learned at different ages have different retention qualities (see Lakey (26)). Again, traits acquired with different drive strengths remain different—for example, a conditioned response established on a conditioned response estab-lished on an innate reflex extinguishes differently from a first-order condi-tioned reflex. There are also experiments indicating that a trait acquired under one physiological condition, *e.g.*, drug condition (21), tends to dis-appear in another and reappear in the original condition. But these are too complex or specialized aspects of trait formation and retention for present formulation.

**Chief Bearing of Strain- and Energy-saving upon Learning.** One extremely important principle, dependent on the strains defined in Laws 10 and 11, remains, however, to be formulated, as follows:

LAW 12. *Law of short-circuiting. Learned traits tend to modify in the direction of behavior demanding less deflection strain and less cognitive-dynamic energy investment.*

This may sometimes operate in the direction of "historical regression" but is not to be confused with either ergic or personality integration regression. For the tendency to drop out intermediate goals and to simplify cognitive operation often operates in the direction of more efficient adaptation. Presumably, because of its origin, the tendency increases with any increase in rigidity or fatigue. It may be responsible for the pseudo rigidity already mentioned in connection with functional autonomy. Thus, although a particular activity no longer produces direct ergic reward it may be retained because dropping it in favor of a more adaptive, ergically rewarding habit would be too punishing from the standpoint of the need to avoid strain and anxiety operative in the present law. Closer examination of most instances of alleged functional autonomy usually shows, however, as discussed in Chapter 8, some remnant of the original satisfaction and reveals that the behavior, initiated by one ergic goal tension has secondarily come to satisfy others; so that the present explanation does not account for all.

## 6. THE CONTEMPLATED SELF: *A.* THE ACTUAL SELF

**The Three Chief Uses of the Term "Self."** The pursuit of dynamic generalizations cannot proceed further, as pointed out in the preceding section, until the rise of integrating structures—notably of the self-sentiment—within the dynamic lattice receives definition. For this rise requires some special laws, additional to the above, to account for it, while, in turn, the further dynamic generalizations require reference to such existing structures.

Let us now proceed, while keeping the clinical concepts of ego, superego, and self-sentiment at hand, to analyze more rigorously the whole concept of the psychological self, its varieties and their mutual articulation. Naturally we shall rule out from the outset any discussion of such peripheral concepts as the physical self, the "extended physical self" (29), the "larger self" (as when a man includes his family, city and nation), the "positional self" (38), the mere reputed self in the eyes of a particular group, the economic or legal self, and so on. The term has also been used in more discursive ways, *e.g.*, for the total personality, conscious and unconscious; or the "social stimulus value" (personality as it affects the social group); or specifically with respect to dominance behavior only, as when Sherif and Cantril (45) speak of any satisfaction of self-assertive drive as "ego-satisfaction"; or, as

Allport points out (1) as "the subjective organization of culture," or in other senses as presented in Allport's survey of the literature (1).

Neglecting such limited and specialized meanings we find the term "self" (and sometimes the term "ego"; though this is always used here in its strictly psychoanalytic sense) used in psychology essentially in three ways, (*a*) for the immediately felt, acting self, as when one says, "I feel happy," or "I am counting"; (*b*) for the *idea* of the self entertained by the individual, as when he says, "I am a poor mathematician," or "I am a popular person"; (*c*) for the organizing center of the personality or structural self, as inferred from behavior by an observing friend or psychologist.

Titchener and others have attempted to analyze the first—the self as a feeling—further into kinesthetic images or somesthesia, while McDougall has stressed its origin in a sense of conation, saying "the core of personal identity, the foundation of our belief in our own reality and continuity, is the experience of purposive striving" (33). The present writer has shown, by psychogalvanic records and introspective protocols, that it is indeed correct that the awareness of the self as distinct from the objective world is greatest in conation and least in distraction, quiescence, and emotional feeling (13).

By contrast the second sense is a purely ideational, conceptual thing, inferred from behavior. So also is the third. It is, to the psychological observer, an "intermediate variable." But unless we retreat into philosophical solipsism we must regard both as something more than ideas in the mind of an observer. They are concepts, as real as horsepower or the United States. They are both based on observations of behavior, but whereas the contemplated self is taken as it exists in one mind—the mind of the person who is contemplating himself—we refer in the other to the *structure itself* which several minds are contemplating, *i.e.*, in the above analogy we are talking about horsepower, not about the idea of horsepower in several minds. Incidentally, we do not *have* to depend on the individual's introspection to tell us what the contemplated self-idea is: we can infer it from his behavior.

This seeming hairsplitting in definition is necessary because the possibilities of misconceiving, psychologically and philosophically, what is intended are peculiarly great here. Before the self with which we are least concerned—the felt self—can be set aside, it is necessary to examine with similar analytic exactness the general relation of the three selves one to another. Principally we note that the directly experienced, felt self shows changes in conformity with the changing nature of the functioning of the structural self. When the flow of drives and the memories it carries alters, the individual "feels different." In dual personality he feels two strange selves; his awareness of himself is most acute in acts of will (2); in complete nervous exhaustion he has "feelings of unreality" and "depersonalization"; when schizophrenic dissolution of unified conation occurs the patients are frequently known to say, "I died," or, on recovery, "I lived in a dream"; and the unstable person, who commits some act he later regrets says, "I was not myself at the time."

With this side glance at the felt self (which, being entirely introspected, cannot be brought fully into systematic psychology) we may turn to the self-concept and the structural self.   Their functional relations are close and significant for personality development, notably in that a person's idea of himself is an important determiner of the structural, real self, while this actual self is, after all, the original, of which the contemplated self is supposed to be a portrait.

**The Contemplated Self Splits into Ideal and Real.**   The moment we examine, even casually, an individual's idea of himself, we find a duality—the self he would like to think himself to be and the self he has to admit himself to be, in his most realistic moments.   As the poet laureate Masefield expresses the matter:

> "And there were three men went down the road
> As down the road went he
> The man they saw, the man he was
> And the man he wanted to be."

The second and first of these are respectively the structural self and the social reputation or social stimulus value.   The third is part of the contemplated self: it is the second part discussed above, namely, the self he would like to think himself to be.   For it is obvious that though the individual has a more or less accurate idea of his actual self, *e.g.*, he does not attempt work for which he is by ability unfitted or choose companions for whom he is socially unfitted, yet he also has a conception of what he would like to become and perhaps may reasonably hope to become.   This aspired ideal self is determined in its moral aspects by the conscious superego, but other aspects are determined by ambition and wishful thinking.   Both the contemplated actual and the contemplated ideal self, incidentally, have many unconscious[5] roots.   For example, the individual's concept of the actual self may include the fact that he is afraid of cats, though he may not know why he is afraid of cats, and his concepts of the ideal self may include being a famous musician, though he may not know where he got the idea of being a famous musician.

**The Development of the Contemplated Actual Self.**   Before considering the dynamic interrelations among these two concepts and parts of ego structure let us take a naturalistic survey of the rise of the contemplated

[5] The word unconscious is used in at least a dozen senses in psychology as Miller (36) has systematically shown.   The principal uses in this book are three: (*a*) unconscious of ultimate goals of action, as in the Freudian "unconscious," (*b*) not in consciousness at the time but capable of being brought in, (*c*) not capable of being brought into consciousness.

selves, beginning in this section with the actual self. We need to study the extent to which it corresponds with reality, its growth with age, its responsiveness to reactions of the social and physical world, and its dependence on subjective emotional conditions. A rough, preliminary survey of this growth has already been made in Chapter 9, Section 2.

Gesell (17) observes that up to eighteen months of age, as reviewed in Chapter 19 and as indicated in Chapter 9 on the psychoanalytic view of infantile narcism and omnipotence, the child is self-engrossed, but not self-aware, since he does not very clearly recognize the "not self." At two years he begins to use self-reference words—mine, me, you, and I, in that order. The order indicates more interest in me than you and more interest in having "mine own way" than in me as an object. Goodenough notices that "I" is at first used more in free-play situations, dealing with parents, etc.

The predominance of "mine" may be further understood in terms of Banham Bridges's (4) observation that the chief sociability of two-year-olds consists in claiming the toys of others or interfering with others for personal ends. She argues, on poorer grounds however, that a more developed self is indicated by sympathetic responses to emotions of siblings or mother. For this could be a purely ergic response—the emotionally imitative element of the gregarious erg which McDougall called primitive passive sympathy. The same mechanism controls some kindly behavior, for it is conspicuous that the young child is kind to those to whom the group is kind and attacks those whom the group attacks. It is at least clear that at one year the child has perceived himself as a physically distinct organism, and at two years as a socially distinct person. In terms of basic dynamics and perceptions it is probably more correct to say, however, that the child separates the outer world from the self rather than the self from the outer world. His world to begin with is himself, and other children and objects are reluctantly separated out as not subject to infantile omnipotence.

The verbal behavior alone, however, at two years suffices to show the dim emergence of a self-concept (actual self) by the above terms and especially by the still more common use of "John likes," etc., in which the child calls himself as others call him (46). As indicated in the previous chapter, the rapid growth of negativism at this age, the habit of "ignoring," the growth of obstinacy and self-will (ego-assertion-for-its-own-sake) likewise indicate, among other things, the formation of the self.

At three years of age, according to Gesell's close observations, the idea of "persons" has become clear. The child's ego concept is shown among other things by his sense of dignity, as in the small boy who, when asked why he replied wrongly to the Binet test question, "Are you a little boy or a little girl?" replied, "She asked me a silly question so I gave her a silly answer." The existence of a more unified ego concept in three- and four-year-olds is also neatly shown by the beginnings of transfer of ascendance and submission relations from one social situation to another, as shown by Jack (see (42), Chap. 19).

The whole trend of development, viewed in the previous chapter, from two through five, from social unawareness to naive aggression and equally naive ergic sympathy, and finally to consideration and caution in dealing with others on the assumption that they have willful personalities like one's own, is evidence of change from a quite rudimentary to a quite realistic, if not detailed, self-concept. At five and six, says Gesell, "the child begins to see himself even in terms of individual qualities," established by comparisons. Speech, from the beginning is the special tool of self-concept formation, and by three years the child is beginning to speak, frequently, of individual differences (principally in physique) though he may reach five years before he can explicitly describe himself or before he is observed to make value judgments on his own behavior.

**The Form of the Matured "Actual-self" Concept.** Data on the *actual-self* concept in adults have been gathered in somewhat distorted form, through the preoccupation of experimenters with the "aspiration level" phraseology. Mostly, measures of the idea of the self have in consequence appeared in terms of relatively trivial skills and games. And even here the experimenters have not been able to demonstrate by "aspiration level" correlations that the experiments deal with a *general tendency* of the person to accurate or inaccurate, consistently too high or consistently too low self-estimates. However, some experimenters have been fortunate in hitting upon variables evidently organically tied in with a unified self concept and Gardner (16) has demonstrated some interesting reactivities of the self concept in adolescence in circumstances and associates.

Tschechtelen (53) found, by comparing childrens' self-estimates on personality and character qualities with those of their coevals and their teachers, that girls at all ages err on the side of overestimation of their adjustment and the attractiveness of their personalities, whereas boys underrate themselves, but less so as they get older. The experimenter suggests that this is wishful thinking on the part of the girls in response to a greater need (overcompensatory) for ego valuation. Rokeach (42) found that college women slightly overestimate (self compared with peer ratings) their physical beauty, but that this only reaches significant proportions in those rated below average. In general, however, maintenance of contact with reality compels the individual to judge himself by the standards he applies to others.

Individual differences in accuracy of the actual-self concept have also been established with respect to a variety of personality traits. The more intelligent are more accurate on all self-estimates but particularly on intelligence. In general, an individual is more accurate in estimating, both in himself and others, a trait in which he diverges from the mean. Introverts and those neglectful of society are poorer in accuracy. For example, Estes found philosophy and science students poorer than those in graphic arts.

Facts on the development of the actual-self concept can also be inferred from a variety of other experiments, such as the resilience of the aspiration level in response to success and failure (47), the relative tendency to recall successes and failures (43), and the tendency to intropunitive and extrapunitive responses to failure (41). In general the more mature (emotionally and in years) and the more dominant are better at remembering their failures (but not their incompleted tasks). Sanford suggests the likely reason that the more dominant consider themselves more likely to be able to return to the situation of failure and reverse the verdict.

### 7. THE CONTEMPLATED SELF:
#### B. THE IDEAL SELF AND SUPEREGO STRUCTURE

**The Ideal Self, the Reality Principle, and Moral "Unrealism."** The growth of the ideal self—the self that the individual wishes to be to satisfy his desires or his conscience, has been followed by an increasing number of empirical studies, but not to the point where more than a patchwork picture can be presented.

Havighurst, Robinson, and Dorr (19) analyzed the writings of an adequate sample of children on the theme, "The person I would like to be." From eight or nine onwards, as might be expected from the dynamics discussed in Chapter 19, they found the ideal person much less frequently chosen in the family circle. More and more the model became some glamorous person in the peer group, or even further afield, and ultimately an imaginary or composite person based both on literature (including the movies!) and real life.

It behooves us to examine a little more closely what is meant by the ideal self and whence it draws its power. It is the personality that the person *wishes* to be, and, during the years of growth it exercises considerable leverage on the person as he is. But after the period of growth the realistic person has little use for an impossible idealistic personality and the discrepancy narrows and persists only with respect to *moral* behavior. This means that the ideal personality becomes a personality that *ought* to be rather than one merely wished. The awkward question of dynamics that arises here concerns the reason for the discrepancy between real and ideal tending to persist when it is in fact painful and unrewarding. Obviously, in some cases this tension breaks down the reality principle, as in the psychotic who believes that he is the richest or most morally elevated person in the world, by allowing the concept of the actual self to approach the ideal self in defiance of realism. But in all people to some extent, and in the unadjusted and neurotic to a considerable extent (as Hendrick (20) points out), there is a self-indulgent vagueness about the extent to which the real self departs from the ideal self. In youth a considerable discrepancy can be tolerated, because of hope, but in normal maturation the two concepts converge into a single realistic self-concept. The ideal self is in any case a far less organized, less employed, less tested and realistic concept than that of the actual self and retains only a fragmentary existence, except, as indicated, in respect to moral standards. The indomitable character of the moral demands, persisting despite the severe punishment their existence brings to the total personality, can only be accounted for by (*a*) their frequent reinforcement by real social punishments, (*b*) their inaccessibility to learning, in so far as they exist embedded in the superego, and (*c*) the peculiar ineradicable character of frontal-lobe inhibitions, as shown, for example, in the high resistance of the obsessional-compulsive neuroses to psychotherapy. Moreover it is perhaps realistic to consider the ideal self in the moral realm as *close* to the real self in so far as its standards are, at least intermittently, actually attained.

The self-regarding sentiment as described by McDougall (34) included the ideal self and the actual self in an active process of mutual comparison and a reasonable degree of integration, as described for the adult in the above paragraph. Its description, however, paid little regard to the greater duality of actual and ideal self in childhood or the dissociated, unconscious nature of the superego, the relation of which to the ideal self must now be explored.

**The Relative Roles of Reasoning, Society, Parents, and Childhood Experience in Shaping the Ideal Moral Self.** That social pressure is responsible for part of the form of the ideal self is obvious and has been illustrated, for example, by the studies of the popular personality type in childhood and adolescent peer groups (Chapter 19). But it is incorrect to say, as Sherif does (45), "that social values constitute the major portion of the normal individual's ego." (Ego is used here apparently not in the structural and psychoanalytic sense used below, but as equivalent to ideal self.) For a considerable part of the ideal self is shaped, by reasoning and trial and error, to fit in with the emotional demands of the superego, operating from the unconscious source set up in childhood, and the form of which is determined by parental views and the traumatic experiences of childhood, not of adult society.[6] Of course, one might say that the parents are also "society," but this overlooks (*a*) the fact that they put their personal imprint on the general social values; (*b*) that they carry views one or two generations older than current social views; (*c*) that they are the carriers of unconscious values not

---

[6] It is interesting to compare this duality in origin of the self-ideal, as reached from psychological observation, with a linguistic duality in the Chinese concept of "face" as pointed out by Hu (22). "Face" or self-regard is represented by *lien* for the inner moral self-judgment and mine-tzü for social approval or prestige level.

explicitly expressed in such social institutions as the school etc.; (*d*) that childhood trauma can change the whole emphasis of the pattern of the superego as carried by the parents; and (*e*) that society's values operate directly on the self-ideal, whereas superego values operate at one remove, through the individual's attempt consciously to find self-ideals that are satisfying to his unconsciously rooted superego needs.

There is not space here to delve further into the superego modifications by infantile experiences, or the processes of shaping the later, conscious self-ideal in accordance with such factors as the degree of severity, the extent of narcistic investment, etc., in this basic superego; but these are considered at the clinical level of evidence in Flugel's penetrating study (15). Having shaped the self-ideal and, through that, the actual self, the superego remains largely to function through adult life as "conscience," as a nucleus of unconscious "thou shalts" and perhaps still more of "thou shalt nots," always retaining some degree of dissociation from the self-regarding sentiment.

Society, which is historically and perhaps in dynamic strength the *second* factor in the formation of the ideal self (and ultimately of the self-regarding sentiment which incorporates ideal and actual self), sets up on the one hand a more or less explicit pattern of the good citizen and, on the other, a more or less explicit reputation of each individual which determines the average reaction of society to him and through which he may learn in what way he departs from the ideal. Although something is known about the degree of precision, etc., of the approved patterns, little is systematically known about the social psychology of reputations and how they stimulate social groups and individuals. MacFarlane, Honzik, and Davis (32) studied by the "guess who" technique the agreement of teachers', children's, and individual's self-estimates of personality and found quite low correlations. It is of interest to our problem, however, that agreement was found better on uncomplimentary than on generally approved traits, suggesting that society's interest in personality and morals is largely aggressive in its ergic composition. With adults, however, the agreement of eight people with eight other people on the traits of a common acquaintance is amazingly high, as indicated by a correlation of 0.8 to 0.9 (8). There are indications, incidentally, that the correlation is lower among men than among women, suggesting a lesser role of society in shaping the male self-sentiment.

There seems little doubt (Chapter 9) that the manipulation of the ideal-self pattern by the group operates through shunning, attack, deference, or contempt, and various other attitudes which are merely cues for more material rewards. In the individual, consequently, most of the satisfactions and deprivations which shape the ideal self and encourage the actual self to follow it come through the gregarious erg (loneliness following nonconformity), through fear, through self-assertion and self-submission, and less directly, through the remaining drives. (Such expressions as "ego enhancement," "ego satisfaction," and "ego frustration," when only *the self-assertive component* of the total ego is intended are misleading, for the ego and the self-sentiment are more than the self-assertive erg.) These questions of motive will be taken up again in connection with ego structure. The possibility needs to be investigated that in early life some of these group rewards and punishments, particularly of gregariousness, set up reactions at an unconscious level, and certainly at some level of awareness intermediate between the true unconscious level of the superego and the conscious level of the self-ideal. For conscience often shows, clinically, accretions of later date than infancy and the home circle, but earlier than the "rational conscience."

A third and last (and frequently omitted!) source of the self-ideal is reality itself, *i.e.*, the facts of the natural and social world not actually incorporated in any social pressure. For there *are* values which the individual can perceive directly, without any social reinforcement, to be admirable and desirable, *e.g.*, skill, endurance, rationality, self-control. To some extent they can and do become acquired by the ego directly through random behavior with reward and punishment, but any normally intelligent perception of the physical and general environment leads to their incorporation among the consciously desired virtues of the ideal self before they become part of the actual self.

## 8. THE STRUCTURAL SELF AND THE EXTENT OF PERSONALITY INTEGRATION

**Unity of the Self Produced Both by Direct Learning and by Influence of the Ideal Self.** It is sometimes forgotten (at least in nonpsychoanalytic presentations) that a considerable degree of integration of the organism's purposes can occur without any pull from the contemplated self, simply as a result of the law of dynamic effect and of the law of combined expression producing a dynamic lattice appropriate to the opportunities and dangers of the situation. Thus animals behave in an integrated fashion, avoiding, for example, impulse satisfactions that might endanger them, within the limits of their learning capacity. The psychoanalytic ego "adjusted to the reality principle" is initially, and perhaps even ultimately, no more than this growth of sentiments and mutual suppressions produced by trial and error or insightful learning, and only gradually is increased unity given to the ego through the application of the contemplated actual and ideal self (the latter being, for the psychoanalyst, the superego).

**The Self as a Means to Ergic Ends.** As soon as the organism becomes able consciously to contemplate its own physical and social unitariness, however, a new degree of dynamic integration of the ego becomes possible. Here we approach the crux of the problem of the self-sentiment structure. Why should a sentiment about the self develop at all? Of what good is it, and what does it reward? And why should it achieve such a dominant role in the whole structure of sentiments?

First, at the level of perception of physical unity, the recognition that eye and limb and stomach employed in satisfaction of drive *A* are the same as those which will be required in drive *B*, or some other dynamic trait satisfaction, causes the excitation of any one drive to introduce associations referring to the satisfactions of the other. In the last resort, the very existence of the body, or its existence in some degree of intactness, is necessary for the satisfaction of most drives, so that the individual is restrained from damaging it under the impulse of one powerful drive because of the associations that arise through the demands of other drives. (A sophisticated instance of this is shown by the army officers who agree not to duel—since the erg of fear alone is not sufficient restraint—because they are needed to fight for their country.) This cross reference is the beginning of the self-sentiment.

Second, however, the self-sentiment acquires the strong interest in social reputation that we have seen operating in the contemplated self, because the continuation of the social self in good standing is almost as important for the maintenance of *all* ergic satisfactions as is the continued existence of the physical self. (There have been phases in history, *e.g.*, the French Revolution or the Russian Revolution, where loss of the social self is quickly followed by loss of the physical self; so we should not be surprised if personality dynamics makes the one almost as important as the other, and suicide a not uncommon consequence of severe loss of face.)

Thus the maintenance and cherishing of both the physical and sociomoral self are means to wider ergic ends, and the self-concept becomes a central object in the dynamic lattice, an instrument radiating to practically all ergic satisfactions. This may be expressed in an essential principle as follows:

LAW 13. *Law of integration by the contemplated self. Some integration (absence of mutual undoing) of behavior occurs through the normal formation of the dynamic lattice under laws already stated. Further integration occurs through the ability to contemplate the physical and social self, whereby the satisfaction of any desire becomes subsidiated in part to a sentiment for the welfare of the whole self. This sentiment becomes by such contributions the most powerful sentiment in the lattice, controlling all others in some degree.*

The structure described, which henceforth defines our use of the term self-sentiment or ego sentiment, stands as a symbol or referent on the path to all ergic satisfactions as shown in Diagram 54. It has to be "consulted" when any single drive or lesser sentiment is in course of seeking satisfaction. But although all ergic satisfactions occur through the self-sentiment it has long been evident, as indicated in Chapter 9, that some drives are much more involved than others. Psychoanalysis, for example, referred to the "ego instincts" and made them out to be narcistic libido, fear, and aggression. Primary narcism[7]—the sensuous satisfaction the infant perceives possible through his own body—is later reinforced by secondary narcism, which also invests the psychological and social self. Later, as Freud began to describe when speaking of the "ego instincts," there is added to this primary libidinal charge the escape drive—fear for the individual's safety and his

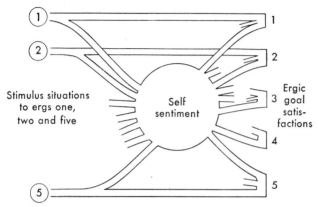

DIAGRAM 54. Reference of immediately possible direct ergic satisfactions to balance of satisfactions obtainable through the self-sentiment, showing the latter as an instrument for obtaining ergic goals.

capacity to continue satisfying his desires. In the small child, as we have seen, fear for the self, in the face of a world of uncertain possibilities, is a strong motive in suppressing and controlling other drives. The self at that period is also served by submissive and appeal drives. But even at two years of age the self-assertive drive is strongly evident, giving immediate satisfaction in controlling things, including other people and one's own impulses, in self-display and in competitive comparisons with others. This drive and the gregarious drive, their satisfaction responding to social approval and disapproval,[8] thereafter probably remain, with fear and self-submission, the ergs operating most powerfully within the self-sentiment.

[7] The role of primary narcism in giving the sense of selfhood can perhaps be best gauged indirectly from the phenomenon of falling in love, in which this narcism, in the psycho-analytic studies, is found to be turned outward upon the loved object. The lover then protests against the unreality of the distinction of everyday language between "you" and "I"—in short the self is coextensive with the narcistic investment.

[8] The effect of social approval and disapproval upon the self-assertive drive is perhaps nowhere more readily shown than with respect to clothes. The augmenting of self-confidence and self-satisfaction through being well dressed, as well as the contrary effects, has been studied empirically by Hurlock (24), though as Flugel (15) shows, the relationship is ultimately more complex.

As pointed out in Chapter 9, however, both self-assertive and self-abasive ergs obtain

Although the self-sentiment is the main focus within the dynamic lattice it does not normally, as clinical evidence of complexes and the superego show, succeed in integrating all dynamic traits in a system of conscious subsidiation chains. The facts we have studied in this connection can be thus formulated.

Law 14. *Law of persisting dissociations from the ego. As the self-sentiment forms it tends to dissociate from its structure those dynamic traits which cannot be made to fit in. This occurs principally in the very early years, with structures which have achieved some degree of autonomy before the ego is well formed, notably some polymorphous sex interests, and the superego. Later it occurs relatively more with responses of humiliation or fear which cannot be reconciled with predominant self-assertive and other drives in the ego. The dissociation is most complete with respect to the memory stimuli which provoke such responses. The reactions themselves are not necessarily suppressed but are even incorporated, with direct or symbolic expression, in the self and the ideal self.*

It remains now to formulate the relation discussed in the last two chapter sections between the actual and the ideal self.

Law 15. *Law of subsidiation and integration of the dual self-concepts in self-sentiment. The ideal self is a set of symbols carrying rewards to self-assertion, gregariousness, and other drives in the ego, as well as to the superego, and to which the ego is subsidiated. It is not necessarily as integrated and precisely known as the actual self, except in so far as the ready-made ideal taken over from society has already been tested for integration, and as the failures of the self are perceived to be failures to integrate and long-circuit. Normally the subsidiation of the actual to the ideal self tends to pass in time into a single self-sentiment, through abandoning of the symbols and behavior representing rewards which cannot be attained (or attained without too great a countervailing ergic*

---

satisfaction through the self-sentiment, though that of the latter has never been as clearly worked out as the former. It is satisfied presumably through admiration, reverence, and the subordination of the self to leadership and religious authority. Much of the amenability to superego pressure arises from the satisfaction in subordinating and even punishing the self; but, in spite of the illumination thrown here by Flugel (15*a*) the dynamics is still somewhat obscure.

Finally, in considering specific, modifying facts bearing on the above self-sentiment outline we must add a reminder, from Chapter 6, that neither the stimulus situations nor the goal satisfactions of the self-assertive erg are entirely social. In so far as the self is an instrument of mastery, over the physical world and the individual's drives as well as in merely social situations, it can directly satisfy and express the self-assertive erg. As an example of this nonsocial, immediate-mastery satisfaction we may quote a spontaneous introspection by an able writer, Jack London (28): "For forty minutes I stood there alone at the wheel, in my grasp the wildly careening schooner and the lives of twenty-two men . . . half drowned, with tons of water crushing me . . . With my own hands I had guided a hundred tons of wood and iron through a few million tons of wind and waves . . . My delight was in that I had done it, not in the fact that twenty-two men knew I had done it."

*deprivation*) or through the elevation of the actual self to the aspired performance *level. This latter rarely occurs with respect to the "absolute" demands of the unconscious superego, which for various reasons are not modified and remain disparate from the ego.*

In general it would seem that goodness of integration is rewarding, in an integrated society, in that it means more over-all satisfaction. In the first place the more *accurate* the self-concept, the more it corresponds to the individual's real powers and limitations, the less will the individual feel disappointment or encounter external conflict. Second, the more it is integrated with itself and with the demands of the superego, the more the individual will be rewarded and the less he will encounter internal conflict. However, if the superego itself makes exorbitant demands, out of keeping with the standards which society demands and rewards, the possibility of integration is reduced, for the rewards from integration are more than offset by the losses from deprivation.

**Implications of Self-sentiment Concept for Statistical-experimental Approaches.** If the above concept of the self-sentiment, its position and development, is correct, certain facts should appear in further research which have not yet been noted. In the first place, in clinical research there should be indications of the gradual emergence in the growing individual of a fourth structure—the self-sentiment—less obvious than id, ego, and superego, developing out of the ego and integrating it more and more with the superego, at least with its conscious manifestations.

Now it must be apparent that if the clinical approach is right in conceiving these distinct dynamic unities and in claiming that they show individual variability, *e.g.*, a strongly developed ego in some, an inadequate ego structure in others, they should reveal themselves as independent factors in factor analysis of dynamic variables. Moreover, measurements of these factors in experimental situations should behave as one would expect from their dynamic relationships.

Though such analyses are now being energetically pursued, it is too early to make confident and well-checked identifications of factors with ego structures. There is some ground for believing that the $G$ factor, usually described as Integrated Character, corresponds to the self-sentiment, but if so what is $C$, the factor of Emotionally Mature, Stable Character which also has loadings in conscientiousness and perseverance? This factor, elsewhere named as the obverse of neuroticism, probably has to do with freedom from dissociation and unconscious complexes, without regard to the soundness of the self-sentiment itself. The most likely factorial identification of the super ego is with factor $K$, which has marked emphasis on socialized and conscientious behavior, but the description of $G$ also gives it claims to this identification. Actually one would expect a change of the factor picture with age, two factors, corresponding to ego and superego, being manifest in children, and a third overlapping factor corresponding to the self-sentiment gradually becoming more prominent in adult life. Insufficient age samplings yet exist to throw light on this.

It is also possible that the third factor described above will emerge as a *second-order factor*. In the presentation of factor-analytic concepts in the earlier part of this book, and of the specification equation, the picture was not complicated by stressing the existence of some degree of *obliqueness* in factors, *i.e.*, of correlations among source traits. In short, the factors presented in the approximate propositions as independent and orthogonal are in fact always to some extent correlated. This is not surprising, for no part of a single personality would be expected to be entirely independent. However, when factors are correlated it is obvious that larger, *second-order* or superfactors can be extracted from among *them*.

Incidentally this shows still more clearly, as pointed out in discussing the specification equation above, that the source-trait theory of personality is no "atomic," "inorganic" breaking down of personality into noninteracting parts. By the specification equation itself it is clear that all traits interact in any single expression of personality. It is now further demonstrated that the source traits may act one upon another or be taken up in larger second-order factor patterns which represent wider over-all integrations in the individual or in the society in which his personality is embedded. (For example, in Chap. 14, a social-status second-order factor causing correlation of personality factors *B* and *C* has already been mentioned.) It is possible, therefore, that the self-sentiment is to be sought in a second-order factor.

**The Self-sentiment in Regression.** The laws of structure so far enumerated—13, 14, and 15 above, describe the conditions of formation of the main personality structures. But structure can deteriorate as well as develop, notably in the psychoses, and it remains to ask whether laws are required to account for this reversal, different from those already given. The psychological notion of regression has been much confused by the naive importation of value systems, *i.e.*, of "desirable" versus "undesirable" directions, or by defining regression with respect to operationally undefinable notions such as "degree of differentiation." By regression, as discussed in Chapters 7 and 9, we mean a return to a historically earlier form of behavior (by unlearning or reversal of maturation) which may or may not be less complex, or integrated, etc. If behavior becomes less integrated, or adjusted, or adapted (as defined in Chapter 9), or intelligent, it is better to say so and to use regression only for whatever return to earlier forms is also involved.

As seen in Chapter 9, regression can occur separately in two kinds of psychological response, (*a*) a regression of the total personality to earlier structural forms, and (*b*) a regression of ergs to earlier maturational forms.

he first process, which is an unlearning or extinction, producing, incidentally, a disintegration of adult personality structures, requires no new laws o account for it, being covered by the laws of learning and retention. It ccurs when the rewards for growing-up fail, (extinction of the new structures) or when the energy required to offset cognitive investment and deflecion strains fails. On the other hand, the phenomenon of ergic regression as not been mentioned, except incidentally in Law 3, as a probable direction f regression, and needs formulation.

LAW 16. *Of ergic and general regression. Personality regression to earlier orms of behavior is partly unlearning, explicable by laws of dynamic learning lready stated and sometimes also ergic regression, reversing the path of ergic 1aturation. Ergic regression is probably connected with (a) too intensively timulated expression at earlier stages, (b) traumatic deprivation at earlier tages, (c) frustration or deprivation, with a sequel of repression, at the conimporary stage* (see Klee (25) and Whiting and Mowrer (56) for experi1ental data on these last points).

## 9. PERSONALITY AND THE LARGER CONTEXT

**Personality Fluctuations with Changes in Social-stimulus Group.** Pereiving that greater integration and consistency is a constant trend in the levelopment of personality, we might be tempted to conclude that the goal f a fully self-integrated personality is at least theoretically possible, or that ersonalities could be measured by the extent to which they fall short of his aim. But the integration of the self is never to be conceived in this way: or the individual personality is a part of other systems, physical, historical, ocial, and ideational, which are also tending to their own integrations. A lisintegrated abnormal personality may be part of a beautifully integrated istorical movement. Let us now examine differences and fluctuations of ntegration more closely to see what light they throw on integration, and articularly on the need for wider principles of superpersonal integration.

Fluctuations of the self have been noticed most in relation to social groups, vhere it has been observed that a pluralism of groups produces a pluralism f selves. Our friend John is a pleasant domestic character when he is at reakfast and is called "Dad," a somewhat different character when we call im "Johnny" at the club, another character when he returns to the office nd is called "the sales manager," and still a different character to strangers 1e meets in a night club far from his home town. These oscillations have een studied in extreme forms in connection with the influence of the "mob," vhere it is observed that the individual sometimes becomes a totally differnt person, showing more frequently, according to Durkheim, transports of elflessness and altruism, and, according to Freud and McDougall, a loss of onscience and reversion to uncontrolled emotionality, due to rendering up he self-regarding sentiment to the horde leader or the crowd.

A review of the *experimental* studies of the influence of social situations o
personality or performance has been presented in Chapter 14, when the cor
cept of roles was discussed.    From these it seems likely that roles produc
only a relatively superficial change along the major parameters of personality

**Dissociation, Instability, and Hypnosis in Personality Fluctuation.**    Th
clinical studies of multiple personalities and fugue states, from those c
Morton Prince onward, deal mainly with hysteroid personalities, in whic
poor integration has combined with temperamental dissociative capacitie
(high $F$ factor) to produce temporary massive repressions of dynamic trait
not compatible with easy response to the existing stimulus situation.    Harri
man (18) has shown that changes of almost the same magnitude can be pro
duced in "normal" (but hypnotizable) subjects by suggestion, and believe
that the massive shifts of attitude take place in the typical multiple person
ality by unconscious self-suggestion.    That is to say, the dependence relatio
to a parent or parent substitute—an "approval" by the superego—is prob
ably necessary for such changes.

An experimental study of personality and attitude fluctuation amon
normal persons by the present writer shows (7) high fluctuation to be con
siderably correlated with (a) the $C$ factor of general emotionality and poo
personality integration, as estimated by ratings, and (b) cyclothyme temper
ament ($A$ factor).    This second finding calls attention to the attempts tha
have been made, *e.g.*, by McDougall (35), to account for the fluctuations c
excitement and depression in the manic-depressive as due to dissociatio
(through poor integration) of the self-assertive and self-submissive drive
within the self-sentiment.    But his hypothesis perhaps requires more corre
lation between $C$ and $A$ factors than has been found in existing factor studies

As far as evidence yet goes, therefore, fluctuation of personality arise
from many causes, as follows: (a) Fluctuation of id demands, through physio
logical, climatic and other changes, (b) poor integration of the self-sentimen
(low $C$ or $G$ factor), (c) the existence of relatively strong dynamic systems dis
sociated from the ego, as in the case of the weak ego of the neurotic (anothe
form of low $C$ factor), (d) constitutional tendencies, probably due to th
hysteroid, $F$, factor, to easy temporary neural dissociation and amnesi
(multiple personality; hypnosis), as well as to the $A$ factor, (e) prolonged an
powerful stimulation by the general environment of certain dynamic system
at the expense of others (effect of crowds, etc.).

**Theoretical Possibilities in Handling "Personality Change."**    The prob
lem which now arises in theory and measurement is as follows: Are we t
conceive that the personality has changed or to accept the frequent expla
nation of the victim of fluctuation that, "It is not I who have changed, bu
circumstances"?    In short, do we change the $T$'s or the $S$'s in the behavio
specification equation?

This raises a matter of fundamental theoretical importance in the attempt to formulate personality and its reactions. If personality changes so radically in relation to differences of milieu does this not undermine the whole conception of measuring personality in factorial terms? Naturally, the question cannot be completely answered until more complete source-trait calculations have been made for personalities which suffer apparently severe but consistent transformations with change of general social environment, etc. But the chief theoretical possibilities are (*a*) that such changes can be handled within the normal specification equation, the *S*'s being greatly altered correspondingly with the marked change of milieu. In this case no change of personality is admitted: one deals only with an extreme change of behavior from having the same personality under extreme conditions; (*b*) that the changes be handled by admitting a change in the *T*'s before the *S*'s operate upon them. This mean introducing a "second-degree situational index," something that operates upon the *T*'s singly or en bloc, so long as the individual is living in that particular world or milieu, so that the normal situational indices operate upon modified source traits. For example, if $-0.2$, $+0.6$ and $+0.4$ are the situational indices of the source trait of dominance, for a child at home, respectively for the situations of crying at punishment, quarreling with a brother, and speaking to a stranger, it may be that all should be raised 50 per cent for the child in the classroom situation. This would be achieved most readily by placing a second-degree situational index, $S^1$, equal to $3/2$, before the dominance source trait, for the child in the classroom situation, before applying the normal index for any special situation.

Thus if normally we have:

$$P = S_1 T_1 + S_2 T_2 + \text{etc.}$$

We should now have, in the change of personality in milieu $S^1$,

$$P_{s1} = S_1 (S_1{}^1 T_1) + S_2 (S_2{}^1 T_2) + \text{etc.}$$

Such treatment would involve statistical and mathematical complications that we have not ventured to raise here, but it may prove the truest and most economical method of handling not only the gross "personality changes" seen in abnormals but also the lesser fluctuations, in response to massive, over-all conditions, *e.g.*, a state of fever, a change of social group, an endocrine condition affecting the id, affecting normals. The two kinds of situational indices might be called specific conditioning situational indices, in the case of those which condition a change of personality, and simple situational indices when they apply to the normal personality.

Where the change in personality is one which affects everyone in much the same way—as is true when anyone adopts a standard social role, or comes

down with a fever or is in a state of extreme hunger—it would seem best t
deal with the modification of the specification equation by the addition of th
above conditioning indices, which change the personality so long as it remain
in that role.　But where the change is peculiar to an individual, as in a spli
personality or specific hypnotic state, it is obvious that *common* indices can
not apply.　It is as if the $T$'s themselves have then altered, and in a wa
peculiar to the individual.　Consequently it would then be necessary to pu
before each $T$ a constant $K$, peculiar to the individual and the $T$.

**Hierarchies of Partially Integrated Organizations.**　Viewing personalit
in such larger contexts one perceives the superficiality of the automaticall
repeated statement of some psychological texts that personality is one an
indivisible and that it is heretical to analyze out its parts.　The truth seem
to be that there are, on the one hand, tolerably integrated subsystems *withi*
personality and, on the other, larger unities *beyond* personality, *e.g.*, biologica
groups, cultural movements, of which the individual personality is only
part.　The first has just been illustrated; the second forces itself upon ou
mathematical notice at a very practical level in the finding that though th
*same* source traits (*i.e.*, factor patterns) may be found in individuals in differ
ent social groups the correlations *among* these traits may be very differen
as pointed out by Thurstone (50).　In short, the organization of parts withi
the individual is very much determined by their organization within societ

When the individual can sufficiently discount his primary narcism he per
ceives, as Wells has lucidly pointed out in *The Illusion of Personality* (54
that an astonishing amount of his private mental furniture is a public gif
and that the very structure of personality is largely the result of his positio
in a field of biological and social events.　All "wholes" are really "parts
of some presumed ultimate whole, the universe; and though personality ha
its degree of autonomy, it stands in a hierarchy of autonomies.　It is no
necessary to leave psychology for philosophy in order to realize that th
"integration" of personality can therefore only be given precise meaning i
regard to a larger set of purposes or trends than those of the individua
For the clinical psychologists occasionally see compactly "integrated" delin
quents—if "integration" is considered only with respect to the individua
personality and its goals—while individuals torn by conflicts have sometim
proved to be most integrated and effective in regard to the developments o
their era.

**The Limitations of Psychological Determinism.**　Whatever the degree o
theoretical determinism we are prepared to admit in regard to huma
behavior, it is certain that in practice, no matter how good our measurin
instruments and our understanding of the processes at work, the accurac
of our predictions is limited.　The limitation springs from the extent to whic
the number of factors at work transcends our memory capacity (machin

aided or otherwise), and from the extent to which the speed of our communications falls short of the speed of action of factors upon the psychological event in question.

This will be more obvious if we consider problems of social psychology, though it is quite as true, in principle, of personality study. Predictions are attempts to say from examination of one part of a system what is happening simultaneously at another, or from examination of a system at one time what will happen at some other time. Since the development of physics or the happenings of a world war are the products of the human mind it could theoretically be concluded that a psychologist with perfect understanding of psychology could deduce the course of these events. In fact, though he might know the principles of mental action thoroughly, the multiplicity of particular events and interactions would defy his grasp. Alternatively, if he had the means of keeping contact with all particulars, they would affect events at no slower speed than they could be communicated to him—even if his calculations took no time at all.

This is just as true of the happenings determining the behavior of a single individual as it is of a social event such as an election. Neither cross-sectional nor longitudinal study can supply us with sufficient data for a complete solution. We may very clearly apprehend the dynamic laws determining the outcome of mental conflict, yet be unable to tell, for lack of knowledge of what some trivial, last-minute stimulus really means to the individual, what he will decide to do next. Finally we must admit, additional to the limitations of range of fact and speed of communication, the possibility that some unknown "degree of freedom" will always remain in our calculation. As Whitehead (55) reminds us, the course of history is a continuous unfolding of never exactly repeated phenomena and the element of the unknown in the creative moment is of great philosophical importance in any theory of the universe.

These three limitations, however, need not hinder our carrying the scientific understanding and prediction of personality action far above the present level of accuracy, though our laws may always give only statistical statements of probability. They may be summarized in the following law:

LAW 17. *Law of superpersonal context and limitation of prediction. Integration cannot operate or be evaluated with respect to the individual organism and the self-concept alone. Personality is an element in larger biological and social patterns themselves to some extent integrated in historical trends. Prediction of personality responses is therefore limited by (a) the limits of the psychologist's ability to grasp all particular events, (b) the failure of his communications to exceed the speed of interaction of events, and (c) possibly by some inherent indeterminacy in psychological processes which the accuracy of our investigations has not yet been sufficient to reveal.*

## 10. SUMMARY

The principles of personality formation and operation have been incorporated, as far as dynamic traits are concerned, in seventeen laws as follows:

1. The Law of innate goal-tension patterns
2. The Law of satisfaction in rigidity
3. The Law of dispersion with excitement and deprivation
4. The Law of dynamic effect
5. The Law of alternating expression in naive conflict
6. The Law of suppressive mechanisms in permanent conflict
7. The Law of the nature of conditions of repression in permanent conflict
8. The Law of consequences of repression
9. The Law of combined expression
10. The Law of deflection strain
11. The Law of cognitive-dynamic investment strain
12. The Law of short-circuiting
13. The Law of integration by the contemplated self
14. The Law of persisting dissociations from the ego
15. The Law of subsidiation and integration of the dual self-concepts in the self-sentiment
16. The Law of ergic and general regression
17. The Law of superpersonal context and limitation of prediction

## QUESTIONS

1. Enumerate the varieties of experimentally observed covariation that can be used to determine trait unities; state whether the traits from each are common or unique, and whether normative, ipsative, or interactive units can be employed in their measurement.

2. State the law of satisfaction in rigidity and discuss its operation in functional autonomy, sublimation, and phantasy.

3. State the law of dispersion. Examine the extent to which it could be regarded as implied by the law of rigidity, of deflection strain, and of ergic regression. Review any experimental evidence known to you on the normal direction of dispersion.

4. Discuss the derivation of Law 6 (suppressive mechanisms) from clinical and other evidence concerning the course of conflict between major dynamic traits and minor dynamic traits.

5. Give six instances, three from human behavior and three from lower animals, of traits being formed through operation of the law of combined expression.

6. Distinguish, by definition illustrated by two or three examples, between deflection strain and cognitive-dynamic investment strain. Speculate, on available data, as to the differences in the consequences of each.

7. State the law of short-circuiting and give instances in which it contributes to integration and others in which it creates maladaptation or regression.

8. Define three basically distinct senses in which the term self is used, one behavioral, one introspective and ideational, and one introspective but nonideational. Discuss with illustrations the general relationships among them.

9. Recount available evidence on the growth of the actual self-concept and the ideal self-concept, with discussion of the sources of each.

10. Describe the ultimate view of personality structure at which we arrive, with reference to the principal dynamic dissociation barriers and the variation of integration from person to person. What experimental-statistical evidence can be brought to bear on the clinical view of this structure.

## BIBLIOGRAPHY

1. ALLPORT, G. W.: The Ego in Contemporary Psychology, *Psychol. Rev.*, 50: 457–478, 1943.
2. AVELING, F. A. P.: *Directing Mental Energy*, Nesbitt, London, 1927.
3. BERGMANN, G.: Psychoanalysis and Experimental Psychology, *Mind*, 52: 122–140, 1943.
4. BRIDGES, K. M. B.: *The Social and Emotional Development of the Preschool Child*, Kegan Paul, Trench, Trubner & Co., London, 1931.
5. BURT, C. L.: *Factors of the Mind*, University of London Press, Ltd., London, 1940.
6. CATTELL, R. B., L. G. TINER: The Varieties of Structural Rigidity, *J. Person. Res.*, 17: 321–342, 1949.
7. CATTELL, R. B.: Fluctuation of Attitudes and Sentiments As a Measure of Character Integration, *Amer. J. Psychol.*, 56: 195–216, 1943.
8. CATTELL, R. B.: The Primary Personality Factors in Women Compared with Those in Men, *Brit. J. Psychol.*, 1: 114–130, 1948.
9. CATTELL, R. B.: An Ergic Theory of Attitude Measurement, *Educ. and Psych. Meas.*, 7: 221–246, 1947.
10. CATTELL, R. B., and L. B. LUBORSKY: P-technique Demonstrated As a New Clinical Method for Determining Symptom Structures, *J. gen. Psychol.*, 42: 3–24, 1950.
11. CATTELL, R. B., A. K. S. CATTELL, and R. H. RHYMER: P-technique Demonstrated in Determining Psychophysiological Source Traits in a Normal Individual, *Psychometrika*, 12: 267–288, 1947.
12. CATTELL, R. B.: *General Psychology*, Sci-Art Publishers, Cambridge, 1941.
13. CATTELL, R. B.: The Subjective Character of Cognition, *Brit. J. Psychol. Monogr.*, *Suppl.* No. 14, 1930.
13a. CATTELL, R. B.: *Factor Analysis in the Human Sciences*, Harper and Brothers, New York, 1950.
14. DASHIELL, J. F.: Experimental Studies of the Influence of Social Situations on the Behaviour of Individual Adults, in Murchison, C. (ed.), *Handbook of Social Psychology*, Clark University Press, Worcester, Mass., 1935.
15. FLUGEL, J. C.: *Psychology of Clothes*, Hogarth Press, London, 1930.
15a. FLUGEL, J. C.: *Men, Morals and Society*, Duckworth, London, 1944.
16. GARDNER, J. W.: The Relation of Certain Personality Variables to Level of Aspiration, *J. Psychol.*, 9: 191–200, 1940.
17. GESELL, A.: *The Psychology of Early Growth*, The Macmillan Company, New York, 1938.
18. HARRIMAN, P. L.: A New Approach to Multiple Personalities, *Amer. J. Orthopsychiat.*, 13: 638–644, 1943.
19. HAVIGHURST, R. J., M. Z. ROBINSON, and M. DORR: The Development of the Ideal Self in Childhood and Adolescence, *J. educ. Res.*, 40: 241–257, 1946.
20. HENDRICK, I.: Ego Development and Certain Character Problems, *Psychoanl. Quart.*, 3: 320–346, 1936.
21. HILGARD, E. R., and D. C. MARQUIS: *Conditioning and Learning*, New York, 1940.
22. HU, H. C.: The Chinese Concepts of "Face," *Amer. Anthrop.*, 46, 45–64: 1944.
23. HULL, C. L.: *Principles of Behavior*, Appleton-Century-Crofts, Inc., New York, 1943.

24. HURLOCK, E. B.: Motivation in Fashion, *Arch. Psychol.*, New York, 17 (No. 111): 1929
25. KLEE, J. B.: The Relation of Frustration and Motivation to the Production of Abnormal Fixations in the Rat, *Psychol. Monogr.*, 56 (No. 4): 1944.
26. LAKEY, M. F. L.: Retroactive Inhibition as a Function of Age, Intelligence, and the Duration of the Interpolated Activity, *Cath. Univ. Amer. educ. Res. Monogr.*, 10 (No. 2) 1937.
27. LANTZ, B.: Some Dynamic Aspects of Success and Failure, *Psychol. Monogr.*, 59 (No. 1): 1945.
28. LONDON, J.: *The Cruise of the Smart*, The Macmillan Company, New York, 1928.
29. LUNDHOLM, H.: Reflections upon the Nature of the Psychological Self, *Psychol. Rev.*, 47: 110–126, 1940.
30. MASSERMAN, J. H.: *Principles of Dynamic Psychiatry*, W. B. Saunders Company, Philadelphia, 1946.
31. MASSERMAN, J. H., and P. W. SEEVER: Dominance, Neurosis and Aggression; an Experimental Study, *Psychosom. Med.*, 6: 7–16, 1944.
32. MACFARLANE, J. W., M. P. HONZIK, and M. H. DAVIS: Reputation Differences among Young Children. *J. educ. Psychol.*, 28: 161–175, 1937.
33. McDOUGALL, W.: *An Outline of Psychology*, Charles Scribner's Sons, New York, 1923.
34. McDOUGALL, W.: *The Energies of Man*, Methuen & Co., Ltd., London, 1932.
35. McDOUGALL, W.: *An Outline of Abnormal Psychology*, Charles Scribner's Sons, New York, 1926.
36. MILLER, J. C.: *Unconsciousness*, John Wiley & Sons, Inc., New York, 1942.
37. MOWRER, O. H., and H. M. JONES: Extinction and Behaviour Variability as Functions of Effortfulness of Task, *J. exp. Psychol.*, 33: 369–386, 1943.
38. MURPHY, G.: *Personality*, Harper & Brothers, New York, 1947.
39. PAVLOV, J.: *Conditioned Reflexes*, Oxford University Press, New York, 1927.
40. REICH, T.: *Listening with the Third Ear*, Farrar & Rinehart, Inc., New York, 1947.
41. ROSENSWEIG, S.: An Outline of Frustration Theory, in *Personality and the Behaviour Disorders*, The Ronald Press Company, New York, 1944.
42. ROKEACH, M.: Studies in Beauty: II. Some Determiners of the Perception of Beauty in Women, *J. soc. Psychol.*, 22: 155–169, 1945.
43. SANFORD, R. N.: Age as a Factor in the Recall of Interrupted Tasks, *Psychol. Rev.*, 53: 234–240, 1946.
44. SEARS, R. R., and P. S. SEARS: Minor Studies in Aggression: V. Strength of Frustration Reaction as a Function of Strength of Drives, *J. Psychol.*, 9: 297–300, 1940.
45. SHERIF, M., and H. CANTRIL: *The Psychology of Ego-Involvements*, John Wiley & Sons, Inc., New York, 1947.
46. SKINN, M. W.: Notes on the Development of a Child, *Univ. Cal. Pub. Educ.*, 1: 1898; 2: 1907.
47. SNEDDEN, P. S.: Effects of Success and Failure on Level of Aspiration, *Psychol. Bull.*, 33: 790, 1936.
48. SPEARMAN, C.: *The Principles of Cognition and the Nature of Intelligence*, The Macmillan Company, New York, 1924.
49. SPENCE, K. W.: The Nature of Theory Construction in Contemporary Psychology, *Psychol. Rev.*, 51: 47–68, 1944.
50. THURSTONE, L. L.: *The Vectors of the Mind*, University of Chicago Press, Chicago, new ed., 1944.
51. TIMMONS, W. M.: Personality Changes from Acting in a Play, *J. soc. Psychol.*, 21: 247–255, 1945.
52. TOLMAN, E. C.: *Purposive Behavior in Animals and Men*, Appleton-Century-Crofts, Inc., New York, 1932.

53. TSCHECHTELIN, S. M. A.: Self-appraisal of Children, *J. educ. Res.*, 39: 25–32, 1945.

54. WELLS, H. G.: The Illusion of Personality, *Nature* (London), 153: 395–397; 1944.

55. WHITEHEAD, A. N.: *Religion in the Making,* The Macmillan Company, New York, 1926.

56. WHITING, J. M., and O. H. MOWRER: Habit-progression and Regression, *J. comp. Psychol.*, 36: 229–253, 1943.

57. ZANDER, A. F.: A Study of Experimental Frustration, *Psychol. Monogr.*, 56 (No. 3): 1944.

58. ZENER, K. E.: Significance of Behavior Accompanying Conditioned Salivary Secretion for Theories of the Conditioned Reflex, *Amer. J. Psychol.*, 50: 384–483, 1937.

# NAME INDEX

Shirley, M., 560, 591
Shock, N. W., 309, 327, 593, 596, 617, 625
Shuey, A. M., 149
Shulz, I. T., 329
Shurrager, P. S., 326
Shuttleworth, F. K., 117, 625
Simmons, L. W., 625
Sisson, E. D., 575
Skaglund, C. R., 326
Skeels, H. M., 561, 572, 591
Skinn, M. W., 666
Skinner, B. F., 212, 234, 328, 329
Skodak, M., 561, 572, 591
Slaght, W. E., 407
Slater, E., 149, 487, 517
Slater, P., 484
Slawson, J., 461
Sleeper, F. H., 527, 552
Sletto, R. F., 397, 409, 417, 448
Smalley, J. P., 370
Smith, G. B., 484
Smith, H. C., 149, 408
Smith, J. C., 553
Smith, L. C., 623
Smith, M., 411, 490, 503, 515
Smith, Whately, 307
Snedden, P. S., 666
Snessarer, P. E., 553
Snyder, B. J., 463, 484
Snyder, W. U., 463, 484
Sollenberger, R. T., 286, 299, 625
Sololskaya, S., 532, 553
Solomon, A. P., 327, 511, 515
Solomon, J., 516
Sontag, L. W., 137, 143, 148
Sorensen, M. T., 144, 149
Sorokin, P., 452
Sorokin, R. A., 386, 417
Sowell, F., 591
Spaer, E., 533, 553
Spearman, C., 4, 59, 91, 101, 117, 474, 629, 634, 666
Speer, G. S., 462, 484
Spence, K. W., 666
Spencer, S., 297
Spengler, J., 391, 396
Spiegel, J. P., 318, 487, 488, 498, 502, 510
Spitz, R. A., 237, 269, 562, 591
Spragg, S. D., S., 329
Srole, L., 417

Stagner, R., 364, 385, 408–410, 417, 453, 491
Stalker, H., 531, 532, 553
Steinach, E., 286, 299
Steinetz, K., 299
Stephan, J. M., 308, 328
Stephenson, W., 30, 91, 117
Stern, C., 150
Stern, K., 620, 625
Stevenson, Robert Louis, 614
Stewart, D. N., 512, 517
Stewart, G. M., 490, 515
Stockard, C. R., 141, 150, 491, 493, 517
Stoddard, G. D., 591
Stogdill, R. M., 357, 358, 379, 385
Stolz, H. R., 598, 625
Stolz, L. M., 598, 625
Stone, C. P., 285, 299, 479, 598, 625
Stott, L. H., 365, 385, 421, 453, 609, 625
Stouffer, S. A., 378, 385
Stowell, M., 354, 358, 384
Strecker, E. A., 329
Strong, E. K., 117, 419, 439, 453, 619
Strongin, E. G., 541, 553
Studman, L. G., 117, 553
Stumpfle, H., 130
Sullenger, T. E., 407, 465, 484
Sullivan, H. S., 530, 555
Super, D. E., 409, 432, 453
Sward, R., 625
Symonds, P. M., 48, 56, 73, 178, 269, 356, 358–361, 365, 385, 602, 603, 625, 626

### T

Taylor, J. G., 77, 117
Taylor, K. van F., 602, 626
Tennyson, Alfred, 239, 544, 616
Terman, L. M., 4, 100, 117, 340–342, 354, 358, 365, 476, 477, 485, 490, 603
Thomas, M., 354, 360
Thompson, G. G., 573, 584, 591
Thompson, H., 142, 143, 148, 150, 561, 589
Thomson, G. H., 27, 44, 284, 299, 463
Thoreau, H. W., 301
Thorndike, E. L., 4, 46, 141, 150, 178, 192, 206, 212, 217, 234, 409, 417, 422, 424, 432, 453, 602, 626
Thorndike, Robert L., 407, 421, 453, 510, 517

# SUBJECT INDEX

## A

Abilities, definition of, 35
  in relation to orectic traits, 98
Abnormality, definition of, 454
  dimensions and limits of, 455
Acetylcholine, 310
Adaptation, 261
Adjustment, definition of, 262
  process of, *in toto*, 257
Adlerian modifications of theory, 257
Adolescent conflicts, 594
Adolescent growth, 596
Adrenal gland, 282, 285
Aim inhibition of ergs, 168
Alcohol and personality, 317
Allergy, 510
Ambivalence among siblings, 382
Amentia, 14
Anaemia and personality, 301
Anxiety, development of, 220
  genesis of, 222
  nature of, 223
  physiological relations of, 288
Anxiety hysteria, 17, 256, 498, 500
Anxiety neurosis, 3, 17
  incidence of, 498
Arthritis and personality, 302
Association tests, objective of, 90
Asthma, 510
Attitude and sentiment formation, 641
Attitudes, definition of, 84
  direction of, 85
  dynamic specification of, 174
  ergic theory of measurement of, 84, 172
  as related to interest, 84
  as syllogistically related, 88
  vector representation of, 84
Autonomic nervous system, 277
  patterns of action of, 279–281

## B

Behavior-rating conditions, 49
Biochemistry and personality, 308

Birth difficulty and trauma, 559
Blood pressure, 281
  excessive, 303, 511
Body-mind relation, 270
Brain metabolism, 546

## C

Calcium concentration, 310
Cerebral cortex, 272
  frontal lobes of, 275
  injury to, 274
Cerebrotonia, 39, 135
Character, 89
Child-to-parent attitudes, 348
  changes of, with age, 365
  as related to sex, 363
Cholinesterase, 312
City character and personality, 424
Cognitive-dynamic investment strain, 643
Color-form sorting test, 93
Combined expression or confluence law, 640
Common traits, 32
Complexes, nature of, 226
Compulsion neurosis (*see* Obsessional compulsive neurosis)
Conflict, 215
  alternating expression law of, 637
  law of suppression of, 638
  and learning, 637
Conflicts, of adolescence, 594
  of childhood, 584
  of late adolescence, 602, 608
  of maturity, 613
  of old age, 618
Confluence, 215
  long-circuiting, 216
Congenital traits, definition of, 119
Constitutional traits, definition of, 119
Conversion hysteria, 3, 18, 38, 255
  factors in, 499
  incidence of, 498
Correlation cluster, 11
Correlation coefficients spatially represented, 23